Principles of Developmental

Authored or coauthored by John Money

Hermaphroditism: Inquiry into the Nature of a Human Paradox, 1952
The Psychologic Study of Man, 1957
A Standardized Road-Map Test of Direction Sense, 1965
Sex Errors of the Body and Related Syndromes, 1968/1994
Man and Woman, Boy and Girl, 1972/1996
Sexual Signatures, 1975
Love and Love Sickness, 1980
The Destroying Angel, 1985
Lovemaps, 1986
Venuses Penuses: Sexology, Sexosophy, and Exigency Theory, 1986
Gay, Straight, and In-Between, 1988
Vandalized Lovemaps, 1989
Biographies of Gender and Hermaphroditism, 1991
The Breathless Orgasm, 1991
The Kaspar Hauser Syndrome of "Psychosocial Dwarfism", 1992
The Adam Principle: Genes, Genitals, Hormones, and Gender, 1993
The Armed Robbery Orgasm, 1993
Reinterpreting the Unspeakable, 1994
Gendermaps, 1995

Edited or coedited by John Money

Reading Disability: Progress and Research Needs in Dyslexia, 1962
Sex Research: New Developments, 1965
The Disabled Reader: Education of the Dyslexic Child, 1966
Transsexualism and Sex Reassignment, 1969
Contemporary Sexual Behavior: Critical Issues in the 1970s, 1973
Developmental Human Behavior Genetics, 1975
Handbook of Sexology, Volumes 1-7, 1977-1990
Traumatic Abuse and Neglect of Children at Home, 1980
Handbook of Human Sexuality, 1980
Handbook of Forensic Sexology, 1994

Principles of Developmental Sexology

JOHN MONEY

CONTINUUM • NEW YORK

1999
The Continuum Publishing Company
370 Lexington Avenue
New York, NY 10017

Printed in the United States of America

Library of Congress Cataloging-in-Publication Data

Money, John, 1921–
Principles of developmental sexology / John Money.
p. cm.
Includes bibliographical references and index.
ISBN 0-8264-1026-X (alk. paper)
1. Sexology. 2. Psychosexual development. 3. Children—Sexual behavior. 4. Youth—Sexual behavior. I. Title.
HQ21.M733 1997
306. 7—dc21 96-40050
CIP

To my sister Joyce
Elizabeth Hopkins
and her family

Acknowledgments

The National Institute of Child Health and Human Development, Department of Health and Human Services, United States Public Health Service has supported the author in psychohormonal research for 40 years, currently under Grant number R25 HD-00325-40.

Sally A. Hopkins and William P. Wang worked industriously on this manuscript. Thanks!

Thanks are due to D.S. Borgaonkar, Medical Center of Delaware, for providing photographs of the XX and XY chromosomal karyotypes; to Stuart Swezey of Amok Books and Jeffrey Leal for computer assistance with Appendix I; to L.C. Miccio-Fonseca, Ph.D., for providing data for the cases in Chapter 17 and in Appendix II. Data for the case in Chapter 16 were abridged from *Sexuality and Disability*, 9:297–309, 1991; and data for Appendix I were adapted from the *Journal of Psychology and Human Sexuality*, 1(1):113–28, 1988. In Chapter 14, material on aphrodisiology is adapted from Money et al., in *Handbook of Sexology, Vol. VI: The Pharmacology and Endocrinology of Sexual Function* (J.M.A. Sitsen, ed., J. Money and H. Musaph, series eds.). Amsterdam, Elsevier, 1988.

Contents

Preface

This book fills a void in today's library of sexology and lives up to its title by being the first of its kind. Lacking a precedent, it required at the outset that a system of developmental categories and stages be devised. In the table of contents, categories are superordinate, and stages of development subordinate, though the two partially correlate. Some categories of development come into full flower earlier, and some later than others.

The *Principles of Developmental Sexology* is a book that is transdisciplinary. Its data are animal and human, prenatal and postnatal, genetic and ideological, prepubertal and postpubertal, hormonal and social, experimental and clinical, romantic and lustful, masculine and feminine, normal and abnormal, legal and criminal, healthy and sick, transcultural and culture-bound, contemporary and historical, technical and humanistic. By not neglecting data from any of these sources, developmental sexology avoids becoming one-sided and partisan. Thus, it does not ride on the presently popular bandwagon of social constructionism and, conversely, it does not ride on the bandwagon of the so-called biomedical model. Its ideology is the ideology of all empirical science, namely an ever vigilant search for new data that might require theoretical revisions and reformulations.

Ideological flexibility is built into the *Principles of Developmental Sexology* by its avoidance of the lexicon of cause and effect, even to the point of avoidance of the word, because. Causal explanations are replaced by sequential (temporal) explanations which eventually may earn the right to have causality attributed to them. To avoid the slick and superficial use of causal explanation, the *Principles of Developmental Sexology* does not use motivation in any of its guises, for example, instinct, drive, choice, preference, or wish, as an explanation of anything, for such an explanation, far from genuinely explaining, simply restates or paraphrases what it presumes to explain.

As with motivation, so also ideation and imagery as experienced cognitively in fantasies, reveries, dreams, and daydreams do not have causality attributed to them in this book. Rather, they are manifestations or rehearsals of what may be transformed into practice. Far from being neglected, ideation and imagery are given a position of special preeminence. They are what separates human from animal sexology, since animals cannot report their ideas and images, and there is, as yet, no technology for reading them directly from the brain, except in science fiction.

One genre in which this book does not belong is that of crusader's handbook. Sexology has always attracted reformers, strong on rhetoric and weak on empirical evidence. Although there's a place for both, reformist ideology is more effective if it is supported by empirical data. Of course, empirical data do not have to be orthodox, as this book demonstrates. It is, indeed, a highly unorthodox book. Some people would say that it is iconoclastic and disputatious, which will be all to the good if it generates more research and funding, more teaching and more training in developmental sexology.

Introduction

As the twentieth century becomes merged into the twenty-first, sexology is a science the development of which compares with that of celestial science (mathematics and astronomy) in the age of Galileo (1564-1642).

One parallel is the threat posed by both sciences to ideological orthodoxy. Galilean science adhered to the heliocentric astronomical principle of Copernicus, namely that the earth and the other planets revolve around the sun, and not vice versa. Galileo himself was brought before the Inquisition and charged with heresy, for which he spent the final seven years of his life under virtual house arrest. Although sexological science does not have an exact parallel of the heliocentric principle, its very existence is a threat to orthodox sexual ideologues for whom sexologists are modern day heretics. The penalty for heresy is lack or cancellation of research funding and salary support, academic censorship, and employment discrimination.

A second parallel between Galilean and sexological science is that, although each accumulated significant new hypotheses and data, both fell short of formulating a grand theoretical synthesis. After Galileo, it remained for Isaac Newton (1642-1727) to surmount the barriers of orthodoxy and to formulate the grand synthesis of the laws of gravity and motion, together with the principles of differential calculus, as part of his quest for the divine in the plan of the universe. Thus he laid the essential foundations from which all of modern physics, mathematics, and astronomy has benefited and evolved.

Today's sexology has too many competing ideologies that are ephemeral, and in some cases banal. The dimensions of sexology's grand theoretical synthesis cannot yet be envisaged in the newly arrived era of computer simulations, brain imaging, and sequencing of the genetic code.

A third parallel between Galilean and sexological science pertains to enforced interrogation without the informed consent of the subject. In the Galilean era of the Inquisition, officers of the criminal justice system alone were authorized to conduct interrogations and, under the threat or actuality of torture, to force a suspected heretic into self-incrimination and a false confession. This coercive monopoly still holds. For sexology it means that only officials designated by the criminal justice system may conduct a sex-history interrogation without the subject's informed consent, with a view to obtaining a forced confession, either true or false. Within the court system, a sex history obtained in this way becomes property in the public domain, and may be published in the media without the subject's informed consent. Outside of the criminal justice system, sex histories are subject to informed consent. All sex survey data are, therefore, biased by both the volunteer and the refusal rate. Minors are by law not competent to give informed consent to a sex-history interview, which makes random probability sampling of minors impossible, and severely curtails all developmental sexological investigations.

A fourth parallel between Galilean science and sexology is that both astronomy and human sexology are dependent on experiments of nature, so-called, rather than on contrived laboratory experiments in which variables are able to be held constant or controlled. In human clinical sexology, the constraints on contrived experiments are ethical, whereas in animal sexology contrived experiments are less ethically constrained. One outgrowth of this disparity is that animal experimental sexology has raced ahead of human clinical sexology. However, there is so much species specificity that data on developmental sexology are not automatically, and without confirmatory evidence, transferable from the subhuman to the human species. Moreover, human and animal sexologists have kept aloof from one another, to the detriment of both.

Animal sexologists have called their specialty reproductive biology and sexual behavior. Thus they have avoided the stigma attached to the terms, sexology and sexologist. Human sexologists began to rehabilitate the neglected term, sexology, in the late 1970s. Otherwise they use the noun, sexuality, adjectivally and awkwardly, as in the expression, human sexuality research and education. Eroticism is for the most part neglected.

A fifth parallel between Galilean science and sexology is the prolonged period during which both existed without the systematic paraphernalia of scholarship. Today, sexology has commenced to fill the void with glossaries and dictionaries (Money, 1988a; Francoeur et al., 1995); encyclopedias (Money and Musaph, 1977; Bullough and Bullough, 1994; Perez and Rubio, 1995; Francoeur, 1997); abstracts of publications (Cornog and Perper, 1996; Frayser and Whitby, 1995); textbooks (Katchadourian and Lunde, 1972; Kolodny et al., 1979; Rosen and Rosen, 1981; Masters et al., 1982; Luria et al., 1987; Langfeldt, 1993); and writings about sexology's own history (Bullough, 1994). By contrast, full service, on-line electronic data bases specifically for sexology do not yet exist.

No historian of sexology has yet taken on the task of writing a history of the transformations of the developmental principle in sexology. Yet, the proposition that sexology must inevitably be a developmental science has always been indisputable, if for no other reason than that human beings develop and are transformed sexologically at puberty from juvenility through adolescence into adulthood. Juvenile infatuation and sexuality were attested to in biographies, confessions, and other literary writings from the eighteenth century, if not earlier, and onward (Moll, 1912).

Jean Jacques Rousseau (1712-1778) backhandedly acknowledged juvenile love and lust by naively advising, in *Emile*, that parents and educators delay juvenile sexual awakening for as long as possible. Under the influence of Simon André Tissot (1728-1797) and his theory of degeneracy caused by loss of the most precious essence of vitality, namely semen, juvenile sexuality became equated, from the eighteenth century until the twentieth, with masturbation (see ch.1). The consequences of masturbation were declared to be as morbid as those of promiscuity with prostitutes who transmitted syphilis, gonorrhea, and other sexual contagions.

Moral revulsion against masturbation was so maniacally intense in the nineteenth century that it put empirical and observational research on the sexology of childhood on hold. With its early-life data base missing, developmental sexology also went on hold where it remained until the end of the nineteenth century. Its revival began with case history data obtained retrospectively as for example by Krafft-Ebing (1840-1902) in his 1886 publication, *Psychopathia Sexualis,* and Havelock Ellis (1859-1939) in his six volume *Studies in the Psychology of Sex* (1920), begun in 1896 and published serially.

Sigmund Freud (1856-1939) had a part to play in the revival of developmentalism in sexology when in 1905 he postulated the oral, anal, phallic, and genital stages of infantile sexuality (see ch.3) in his *Three Essays on Sexual Theory* (1905). The scientific legitimacy of these stages has been much disputed. There has been no dispute, however, that the *Three Essays* endorsed sexological developmentalism, and lowered the recognized age of when sexological development begins from the juvenile to the infantile period of life.

Freud was not himself a sexologist but a psychiatrist who formulated a sexual theory to explain the symptoms of psychopathological development and, eventually, of nonpsychopathological development also. The first developmental sexologist who was an empiricist rather than a theoretician was Freud's contemporary, Albert Moll (1862-1939). He wrote *The Sexual Life of the Child* (1909), which was translated from German into English and published in New York in 1912. In this book, Moll established the principle that the sex life of adulthood develops from the sex life of childhood, which includes juvenile love affairs and masturbation. He obtained data partly from direct observation of children and of castrates, and mostly from the retrospective recall of adults, some of whom were clinical patients, and others not. The developmental history is applied to the explanation of sexually abnormal as well as normal behavior.

Moll wrote about sexual development without mentioning hormones. He had a good alibi: the term, hormone, had been coined only in 1904 by Bayliss and Starling (see Money, 1983a), when they had discovered secretin, a gut hormone governing the release of pancreatic juice and bile. The concept of internal secretions from specialized glands was already in circulation, but it was not until the 1920s that the sex hormones were extracted and purified from the ovaries and testes and, in the 1930s synthesized and marketed. Moll could define puberty only on the criteria of the maturational changes of the so-called secondary sexual characteristics, and of behavior.

Childhood in Moll's scheme of development extended into teenage and corresponded to today's age of being legally a minor more than to what are today's juvenile years. His subdivisions of developmental age were as follows:

> If we regard the beginning of the fifteenth year as the termination of childhood, we may divide childhood into two equal periods, the first extending from birth to the completion of the seventh year, the second from the beginning of the eighth to the end of the fourteenth year. I shall in this work designate these two periods as the *first* and the *second period of childhood* respectively. In the first period of childhood, the first year of life may be further distinguished as the *period of infancy*. The first and second periods of childhood comprise childhood in the narrower sense of the term. The years that immediately follow the beginning of the fifteenth year I shall denote as the *period of youth*. Inasmuch as the symptoms of this latter come to differ from those of childhood proper, not abruptly, but gradually, the first years, at least, of youth will often come under our consideration, and I shall speak of this period of life as the *third period of childhood*. Although childhood in the narrower sense comprises the first and second periods only, childhood in the wider sense includes also the third period.

Based on its Latin etymology, puberty may mean either the age of getting pubic hair, or of attaining procreative capacity and becoming an adult. Moll wrote that he resolved the confusion of usage in his day as follows:

> In this work I shall mean by *puberty* the period of life between the completion of sexual development and the extinction of the sexual life. The period during which the state of puberty is being attained will be spoken of as the *period of puberal development*, and I shall therefore speak of the *beginning* and the *end* of the puberal development.

The term, adolescence, does not appear in Moll's book. It is defined in *The Shorter Oxford English Dictionary* as:

> **adolescence:** the process or condition of growing from childhood to manhood or womanhood; the period of growing up.

For the differentiation of puberty and adolescence, one turns to a contemporary textbook of pediatric and adolescent endocrinology (Kappy et al., 1994), where Kelch and Beitins in chapter 5 offer the following:

> The terms adolescence and puberty, are often used interchangeably but this imprecise practice blurs some important distinctions. From a biological perspective, puberty is the stage of physical maturation in which an individual becomes physiologically capable of sexual reproduction. In contrast, adolescence refers to the entire period of physical and psychological development which extends from the end of childhood to adulthood.
>
> Then follow many pages of texts, graphs, and illustrations of the morphological, and hormonal, and procreative changes that mark the transition from childhood through puberty and adolescence to adulthood.

The sexological development of childhood and adolescence, being largely a taboo subject, has long lacked a textbook, though it has recently gained a handbook (Perry, 1990). This lack may be attributable to a nonexistent demand from nonexistent university and college courses as well as to a paucity of primary childhood data. Maybe it also reflects the absence of an established classifactory principle for a table of contents that combines the principle of the chronology and the principle of the logical categories of development.

The organization of this present book essays the combination of these two principles, the chronological and the logical. The term *Principles* in the title indicates that as new primary data are generated, there will be a classifactory slot in which to accommodate them.

A multivolume, interdisciplinary encyclopedia of sexology would undoubtedly have separate volumes on male and female reproductive anatomy and physiology, the genetics of sex, and pregnancy and childbearing. In this present book there are no obligatory chapters on these specialty sciences, per se, as information about them is already widely available.

There are also no obligatory chapters in this book on currently contentious ideological issues such as abortion, child abuse, family values, teenaged contraception and pregnancy, battered wives, genital mutilation, gay and lesbian rights, pornography, and so on. The role of scientists, sexologists included, is to to produce empirical data, not to engage in adversarial polemics and sermonizing. The ideology of sexology is the ideology of all the sciences, namely belief in the principles of the scientific method for the advancement of knowledge.

Although experimental animal data are not excluded, the book is about sexological development that is specifically human, beginning with conception, and extending to young adulthood, but not through mid-life and the older years. The book addresses young people themselves, instead of talking about them or talking down to them. It may be read alone, for which reason a glossary is provided, or as a textbook in a class with a mentor or teacher. It is written to provide information that is historical and transcultural as well as from the clinic and the laboratory, without finger-wagging and tongue-clucking, but with as much nonjudgmentalism as possible. Young people can direct its contents toward the formation of their own system of moral values. By being explicit about sexological development, instead of prudish or prurient, some of the contents of the book will be offensive to some critics. Fortunately, in a democracy of knowledge, critics do not have the power of the Inquisition at their disposal as in Galileo's day, although some of them do have the power to stall the progress of scientific inquiry.

1

Sexual Ideology

Nature/Nurture
Semen Mythology
Masturbation Mythology
Antisexual Crusaders
Sexual Taboo

Nature/Nurture

Sexuoeroticism is the singular noun for sexuality and eroticism. In the individual human being, sexuoeroticism is developmentally culture bound, not culture free. Like language and intelligence, it must manifest itself in action before it can be evaluated. Linguistic ability cannot be measured or predicted before words are spoken or, later, written. Intelligence, language, and sexuoeroticism—all three bear the imprimatur of the cultural surroundings in which they function. They do not exist in a void as pure essences of molecular, biological, social, occult, or any other type. They can not be isolated, extracted, and quantified in purified form. As they come into existence, they are behaviorally and cognitively shaped by the very habitat that they themselves will behaviorally and cognitively shape.

To question how much of sexuoeroticism is nature and how much nurture is pointless. Nature and nurture work together, hand in glove. They do so at critical periods of development. The outcome of their collaboration may become fixated and immutable and, yes, thenceforth as biologically indwelling as if it had been there from the beginning.

There is no universal form of human nature which can be tested for pristine, culture free sexuoeroticism. Invariably, therefore, the sexologist must pay attention to the sexuoerotic ideology—the traditions, customs, and stereotypes—of the culture in which each individual's own personal biography of sexuoeroticism unfolds from infancy onward. The sexuoerotic ideology of a culture constitutes that culture's sexosophy—its collective sexuoerotic philosophy and values.

In addition to its sexosophy, every culture has also some practical and empirical knowledge of sex which, no matter how meager, constitutes its sexology. Thus, in all societies, people know that males and females have different sex organs, and that genital union is an essential prerequisite to getting pregnant—outmoded claims to the contrary are pseudoscientific. All societies know also that juveniles cannot create a pregnancy and that the age of first menstruation precedes the age of first pregnancy in girls. Herding and farming societies, if not all others, know that males without testicles do not breed. All peoples have some knowledge of midwifery as a specialty of people who assist in childbirth. Men everywhere know subjectively about their own male orgasm. Some women do not experience orgasm.

Semen Mythology

SEXOLOGY IS SCIENCE. Like all sciences, it is transmitted and shared worldwide, whereas sexosophy being ideological is regionalized. Sexology is a recent science, not much more than a century old. By contrast, the origin of the sexosophy still in use in our own society today dates back in all likelihood to a stone age mythology of the significance of the semen (La Barre, 1984). According to the mythology, loss of semen depletes the body of its most vital essence, the spirit of life itself.

In ancient Ayurvedic Indian medicinal texts, *sukra* is the Sanskrit name of this vital spirit (Money et al., 1992). Depletion of *sukra* is still regarded in contemporary Ayurveda as a cause of debility and death, a belief handed down over the course of many, many generations. In the Hellenistic era more than two millennia ago, the mythology of saving the *sukra* became contaminated by an additional biological error. Being white, the seminal fluid was said to originate in the white marrow of the spinal cord which, in turn, originated in the white matter of the brain. Warnings of the harmfulness of draining away brain fluids by masturbation persisted into the twentieth century in sex education books for boys (Stall, 1909; Hall, 1913; Jefferis and Nichols, 1919).

The counterpart of semen depletion is semen conservation, achieved ideally through total continence or, failing that, by having as few ejaculations as possible. Procreation was accommodated by the theory of the reciprocal exchange of the vital essence between the two copulating partners. In ancient Chinese medicine, the exchange was between the feminine *yin* and the masculine *yang*. This exchange was alleged to be more favorable to women than men insofar as women, lacking semen, consumed more of the *yang* essence of the male than men obtained of the *yin* essence of the female, as a replenishment. Thus was semen conservation theory adapted to endorse the social and philosophical stereotype of men being endangered by women, as well as being superior to them. Ayurvedic semen depletion theory led to exactly the same conclusion of women's intrinsic inferiority to men insofar as they had no semen to be depleted.

Probably of equal antiquity, the polar opposite of semen conservation theory is semen transfusion (or semen endowment) theory (see chap. 10). The custom of semen transfusion is geographically traceable in a great crescent of Melanesian cultures stretching from northwest Sumatra through the south coast of Papua New Guinea to Fiji (Herdt, 1984). Until the final quarter of the twentieth century, the custom of semen transfusion was preserved intact for contemporary study among the isolated Sambia tribesmen of the Eastern Highlands of Papua New Guinea (Herdt, 1981, 1987). Its underlying mythology is that semen is a nonexpendable tribal resource that must be invested within the tribe by being donated from one generation of males to the next. For a prepubertal Sambia boy to be fertile as a man, it was necessary for him to consume a supply of semen sufficient to last him for a lifetime. Without it, he would fail to develop pubertally and to mature through adolescence not only into manhood, but into fierce, man-killing warriorhood. Therefore, at age seven or eight, he was sequestered from the influence of women and infants and put to live in the central men's house, under the tutelage and supervision of men responsible for his progressive initiation into warriorhood. The first initiation ceremony included sucking the flute, symbolizing sucking the penis. Just as he had needed woman's milk in infancy, now in prepuberty he needed man's milk. It was supplied from the penises of older postpubertal adolescents, still too young for marriage. When he became able to ejaculate his own man's milk, it was his duty to feed it to younger, immature companions during the subsequent premarital years of his initiation as a warrior. After marriage, tribally arranged at around the age of nineteen or twenty, he graduated to using his semen exclusively in intercourse with his wife.

In both the conservation and the transfusion mythologies, the supply of semen is assumed to be limited. In the Sambia tradition semen is a tribal essence, to be passed on from one generation of warriors to the next. In our own semen conservation tradition, semen is a personal essence, and it is the responsibility of each male to conserve his own.

The stone age doctrine of semen conservation was made to order for mystical religious doctrines in which the spirit or the soul was supernatural and superior to the physical being of the flesh, the former being pure and of the deity, and the latter impure, and of the devil. The preliterate roots of this duality may be traced to Aryan religious doctrine that took root in India and Persia and subsequently influenced the development of philosophical doctrine in Greece (see chap. 10). In Athens of the classical period the superiority of the spiritual was elevated above the physical by the followers of Gnosticism, but it was not until later, especially in the era of the early Christian fathers, that denial of the flesh became the doctrinal way to achieve spiritual superiority. This doctrine evolved in the ferment of sectarian philosophizing that heralded and then accompanied the dawn of Christendom. It was prominent in the Gnostic and Neoplatonic schools, from which much was absorbed into the teachings of St. Paul and of the early Christian fathers. From the beginning of the second century A.D., Christian theologians endorsed Gnostic and Neoplatonic doctrine of asceticism which entailed renunciation of the flesh, and abjuration of its concupiscent desires and appetites. Semen, the Church declared, should be discharged, if at all, only for the purpose of procreation, and never for pleasure. There was no exemption even for involuntary nocturnal semen depletion in wet dreams. Semen conservation became merged with not only chastity and abstinence, but also the unmarried state of celibacy as the ecclesiastical ideal for the clergy. This ideal continues to influence today's secular sexosophy. Of course not everyone adheres to the ideal, and there are some who repudiate it.

Semen conservation theory made its way through the twentieth century and into the twenty-first by way of its medical revival and transformation in the eighteenth century. The revival began with an anonymous tract with a long-winded title: *Onania, or the Heinous Sin of Self-Pollution and All its Frightful Consequences, in Both Sexes, Considered with Spiritual and Physical Advice to Those Who Have Already Injur'd Themselves by this Abominable Practice* (Anon., Undated). It was first published in London, not later than 1717, and went through multiple reprintings and translations (Hare, 1962). Its author may have been a Dr. Becker (or Bekker) who may have been of Dutch origin and who, from the sermonizing style of his writing, was probably a preacher.

Masturbation Mythology

IN 1717, THE TERM masturbation was not in general usage. It does not appear in the Bible, nor is the practice of masturbation referred to in the Bible by another name. According to Weston La Barre (1984), the campaign mounted against masturbation in *Onania* began:

> ". . . with the blatant misrepresentation of the Biblical story of Onan. . . . Scholars are agreed that the 'sin of Onan' was not his spilling seed upon the ground as such, but in so doing evidencing his refusal to 'raise up seed' for his deceased brother with his widow, that is, shirking the traditional brotherly obligation of the levirate."

Biblical misrepresentation notwithstanding, onanism entered the language as a socially acceptable term for the practice otherwise known as masturbation.

In 1717 the dawn of modern scientific logic and methodology was still on its way. It was, therefore, sufficient that *Onania*'s exclusive proof of its dire prophesies of doom and death from self-abuse be put forth in the form of testimonials of salvation from sexual depravity and sin. At least there was a possibility of salvation from onanistic sexual sin. By contrast, from the fourteenth century to the eighteenth, uncounted thousands of women, had been burned at the stake as witches for falsely confessing, under torture, to having sexually sinned with the devil or one of his demons, especially while asleep and dreaming. In comparison with antecedent demon possession theory, the revival of semen depletion and conservation theory as an explanation of illness and suffering seemed to be scientific in the new eighteenth-century Age of Enlightenment. It certainly seemed that way to the Swiss physician, Simon André Tissot, who medicalized *Onania* in his book, *A Treatise on the Diseases Produced by Onanism*. The first edition, 1758, was in Latin, and was subsequently translated into French and English, and published in many editions. The first American translation was published in New York in 1832.

Tissot's book was immensely influential. It incorporated up-to-date medical knowledge and principles in support of the doctrine of semen depletion and conservation. In addition, it gave physicians a plausible explanation of the cause of disease to fill the void left by the demise of causation by demon possession. Moreover, it had the dubious merit of being an irrefutable explanation insofar as the physician could always blame treatment failure on failure of compliancy, for example, on failure to pray devoutly enough, or on failure to follow strictly a bland diet free from rich sauces and spices including salt, an alleged cause of salaciousness.

Tissot's treatise was influential in another way: it correctly recognized the symptoms of the "social disease," namely, the combined symptoms of gonorrhea (the clap) and syphilis (the pox) which, until after the discovery of germ theory in 1870, were lumped together as one disease. Likewise, Tissot's treatise recognized the symptoms of congenital syphilis in the babies of prostitutes suffering from the social disease while pregnant. Although he did not spell out his purpose explicitly, Tissot was fumbling in the scientific dark, looking for the cause and prevention of the epidemic of syphilis still, in the eighteenth century, ravaging Europe. Though there are voices of dissent as to whether Christopher Columbus's sailors returned from the New World carrying the syphilis spirochete to the port of Naples, it is agreed that the new epidemic began there, in Naples, at the end of the fifteenth century (Bullough, 1976). From Naples, French troops in Italy spread the epidemic northwards through Europe.

Tissot linked the symptoms of the social disease to an excessive loss of semen attributable to the social vice of promiscuity. Then he made a colossal intellectual error of profound, long term consequence. Reasoning by analogy, he jumped to the conclusion that loss of semen attributable to the secret vice of masturbation or self-pollution (including wet dreams), could produce the same symptoms as those produced by the social vice. Thus was the way prepared for an increasing crescendo of antimasturbation furor that swept through the nineteenth century and, spilling over into the twentieth, still has not entirely dissipated.

Antisexual Crusaders

EARLY IN THE nineteenth century, one of the American standard bearers of semen conservation theory was the Reverend Sylvester Graham (1794-1851), now remembered for graham crackers made from wholewheat flour. Vegetarian health foods, fresh air, physical fitness, and abstinence were prominent in his cure for manifold ills, including those that he attributed to semen depletion. In 1834 he published *A Lecture to Young Men*, an influential warning of the dangers of sex destined to influence a large following of crusaders against sex and vice for the remainder of the century.

One of Graham's staunchest followers was John Harvey Kellogg, M.D. (1852-1943) whose name is now virtually an eponym for corn flakes and other breakfast cereals. As an adolescent youth, Kellogg worked in the printing and publishing house of the newly established Seventh Day Adventist Church in Battle Creek, Michigan. There he encountered Graham's writings. He became a convert and remained so throughout his medical training and until his death at age 91. He believed that eating meat, in other words being carnivorous, induced the arousal of carnal passion and desire. As superintendent of the Adventists' Battle Creek Sanitarium, for which post the Church had financed his medical training, his hobby was to devise recipes for a nut and cereal menu, minus meat. His greatest technical success, perfected in 1906, was to convert wet Indian corn mash into crisp corn flakes—the secret being to soak the grains for several hours before flattening them.

Kellogg was so literal in his semen-conservation fervor that his marriage remained unconsummated. Instead he conducted an experiment in "race betterment" by either adopting or fostering 42 children. His sexual life was restricted, so that, instead of penovaginal intercourse with his wife, an enema administered every morning by a medical attendant served as a substitute—a sexual anomaly or paraphilia known as klismaphilia. While on his honeymoon in 1879 he spent his time writing *Plain Facts for Old and Young*, a treatise on the unsubstantiated dangers of semen loss. This book was subsequently enlarged to become a practical home doctoring and nursing book, in which capacity it was sold in all English-speaking countries around the Pacific rim, including India. It's practical obstetrical and other medical advice made it very popular and lent credence to the falsity of its antisexual fanaticism.

Masturbation was the target of Kellogg's fanaticism at its most absurd. For boys who masturbated, in refractory cases he recommended punishment as extreme as circumcision without anesthetic, or suturing the foreskin with silver wire ostensibly to prevent erection. The corresponding treatment for girls was to apply pure carbolic acid to the clitoris. To parents Kellogg pruriently recommended that "if the suspected one becomes very quickly quiet after retiring . . . the bedclothes should be quickly thrown off under some pretence. If, in the case of a boy, the penis is found in a state of erection, with the hands near the genitals, he may certainly be treated as a masturbator without any error. . . . If the same course is pursued with girls . . . the clitoris will be found congested, with the other genital organs, which will also be moist from increased secretion."

For those who failed to catch masturbators in the act, Kellogg listed 39 signs and symptoms so universal in childhood that none could escape. The list has been borrowed by today's victimologists as signs of sexual child abuse. Thus does Kellogg's antisexual absurdity linger on.

Anthony Comstock (1844-1914), Kellogg's contemporary, conducted his own exterminator crusade against vice which he defined as gambling, contraception, obscenity, and female nudity. In 1873 he personally lobbied the U.S. Congress into legislating against vice in what have become known today as the Comstock Laws. He also had Congress appoint him as the first U.S. postal inspector with power to censor and seize outgoing and incoming U.S. mail, a power still possessed by his successors and actively pursued for the prosecution of pornography, particularly in the campaign against pedophilia.

Antisexual crusaders of the nineteenth century were hard pressed to fit females into semen conservation theory, since females have no equivalent of the male's semen depletion. One solution was to equate any white vaginal discharge, including leukorrhea, with semen. A more favored alternative, however, was to equate femininity with a level of vital spirit so low, and so much used up by pregnancy or menstrual flow, that females were rendered too fragile for vigorous brain work, physical exercise, or sexual activity. Idealized Victorian femininity was tepidly asexual. One of a wife's marital duties was to tame the sexual beast in her husband's loins, so as to prevent the profligate waste of his semen (Mahood and Wenberg, 1980). The widely quoted epitome of the Victorian woman was written in 1857 by the British surgeon, William Acton (1813-1875) and repeated in all five subsequent editions of his book, *The Functions and Disorders of the Reproductive Organs in Youth, in Adult Age, and in Advanced Life*:

> I have taken pains to obtain and compare abundant evidence on this subject, and the result of my inquiries I may briefly epitomize as follows: I should say that the majority of women, happily for them [and for society, says the 5th edition] are not very much troubled with sexual feeling of any kind. What men are habitually, women are only exceptionally. I admit, of course, the existence of sexual excitement, terminating even in nymphomania, a form of insanity that those accustomed to visit lunatic asylums must be fully conversant with; but, with these sad exceptions, there can be no doubt that sexual feeling in the female is, in the majority of cases, in abeyance, and that it requires positive and considerable excitement to be roused at all; and even if roused, which in many instances it never can be, is very moderate compared with that of the male. Many men, and particularly young men, form their ideas of women's feelings from what they notice early in life among loose, or at least low and vulgar women. There is always a certain

> number of females who, though not ostensibly prostitutes, make a kind of trade of a pretty face. They are fond of admiration; they like to attract attention of those immediately around them. Any susceptible boy is easily led to believe, whether he is altogether overcome by the siren or not, that she, and hence all women, must have at least as strong passions as himself. Such women, however, give a very false idea of the condition of sexual feeling in general. Association with the loose women of London streets, in casinos and other immoral haunts, who, if they have not sexual feeling, counterfeit it so well that the novice does not suspect but that it is genuine, all seem to corroborate such an impression. Married men, medical men, or married women themselves, would, if appealed to, tell a different tale, and vindicate female nature from the vile aspersions cast on it by the abandoned conduct and ungoverned lust of a few of its worst examples. There are many females who never feel any excitement whatever. Others, again, immediately after each period, do become, to a limited degree, capable of experiencing it; but this capacity is only temporary, and will cease entirely until the next menstrual period. The best mothers, wives, and managers of households know little or nothing of sexual indulgences. Love of home, of children, of domestic duties, are the only passions they feel. As a general rule, a modest woman seldom desires any sexual gratification for herself. She submits to her husband, but only to please him; and but for the desire of maternity, would far rather be relieved from his attention [pp. 473-474].

Acton's juxtaposition of the two types of females and their male partners leaves no doubt as to the cultural dualism of Victorian semen-saving sexosophy. It is a sexosophy that has not only lingered on but has also been reinforced since the identification, in the early 1980s, of HIV/AIDS which conflates sex with death. Sexosophical dualism becomes culturally bound to sexuoeroticism in contemporary childhood and adolescent development. Its dualistic incompatibilities confront young people. They will continue to do so until a fully effective method of the prevention and control of HIV is discovered.

Sexual Taboo

THE DANGER OF semen loss became a cornerstone of the more generalized sexual taboo that has followed the great religions, especially in Christendom and Islam, in their spread widely across the earth. The sexual taboo profoundly influences the sexuoerotic development of each new generation that it touches.

In addition to sex, the world's major taboos apply to eating, talking, eliminating, and dying. More specifically, the eating taboo applies to breast-feeding, to dietary restrictions, and to conditions under which food may and may not be prepared—not by menstruating women, for example. The talking taboo applies to restrictions on vocabulary and forms of address, on the gender of the listener, on topics of address, and on whom one may address directly, with eye to eye contact instead of out of sight and through an intermediary. The elimination taboo applies to restrictions on where and under what circumstances and in whose presence one may urinate, defecate, menstruate or give birth and dispose of the products thereof. The dying taboo applies to restrictions on talking about impending death, on precipitating death, on funerary rites, and respect for the spirits and burial places of the deceased.

A shared characteristic of all taboos is that they apply to something that usually happens to, or is done by the human organism in the course of its development and daily living. Whatever that something is, it must be responsive to prohibition and regulation. Thus, it is not feasible to have a taboo on breathing or blood flow. Nor is it feasible to have a taboo on all eating, but only on selective food intake and fasting. Sex is an ideal candidate for a taboo, as total renunciation does not, like total renunciation of food, water, or air, inevitably become a form of suicide. Moreover, there are various partial renunciations that may be met, with greater or lesser success, in conformity with the prohibitions and demands of the taboo.

To achieve maximum efficacy, a taboo must be introduced early in childhood, with conformity required consistently. Assimilating a taboo is a form of behavior modification according to the principles of reward for conformity and punishment for nonconformity. Imposition of the sexual taboo begins early in babyhood with disapproval if the baby touches the genital area or, later in infancy, displays the genitals in public. For the most part, taboo training is negative—punishment for nonconformity. Punishment may be particularly brutal and abusive if, in late infancy or the juvenile years children are caught breaking the taboo by using "dirty" words or engaging in games of sexual rehearsal play. Thus do sexuality and eroticism not have an auspicious beginning in infancy and childhood.

The sexual taboo does not exist in primate species other than the human. The origin of the taboo in the evolution of our species is undated. It could be extremely ancient. One possible scenario is that stone age ruler priests were also psychologists who invented taboo as a form of behavior modification that gave them power and authority over their followers. Once a taboo has been inculcated in childhood, even the threat of reprisal for breaking it in adulthood brings rapid conformity. Fundamentalist televangelists and new right politicians still today rely on the sexual taboo to gain followers from whom they raise large sums of money by pressing the panic button of, say, pornography videos that defy the taboo on explicit sex.

The societal significance of the sexual taboo is that it enhances the power of those who wield power over those who do not, unless and until the have-nots rise up and rebel. Adolescent rebellion against the sexual taboo is one way of retaliating against authority and asserting autonomy. So great is the power of the sexual taboo that it can wreak havoc on sexuoeroticism at two polar pathological extremes, either by repudiating it, or by criminalizing it.

2

The Search for Man's Animal Nature

Animation

So deep has been the divide between the carnal and the spiritual in the culture of Christendom, and over much of the rest of the world, also, that it is wise to ponder the diversity of animal nature according to nature's procreative designs for different species. Even the division of a species into male and female is not such an eternal verity as people assume it to be. Even the concept of animal nature itself needs a second look. If we human beings speak of animal nature, which animal do we have in mind?

For Aristotle (384-322 B.C.) animal spirit had no reference to wild animals or beasts, but to human rationality. It was one of three spirits or vapors that kept the soul in communication with the body. The other two were vital spirit and natural spirit, corresponding to the sensitive and vegetative functions, respectively. Aristotle's ideas were expanded by the Roman physician, Galen (A.D. 130-200). Galen taught that natural spirit was produced in the liver and refined into vital spirit in the heart. From the heart vital spirit ascended to the ventricles of the brain which refined it into animal or animating spirit. Animal spirit provided the soul with sense, memory, and intellect. Vital spirit from the heart provided the soul with emotions. In everyday speech we still use such expressions as heartfelt thanks, and loving someone with all my heart, and the shape of a heart is a symbol of love.

In classical Latin *animalis* meant the vital breath of life, the mind or the soul. By medieval times it had gained a different meaning, beastly. Bestial or brutish is the meaning given to animal nature, today, especially in its sexual sense.

The animals or beasts that the people of the middle ages knew most about were those that they had domesticated and farmed, as had their ancestors for millennia before them. When they heard or spoke of man's animal nature, therefore, the animals of the pasture and the barnyard would be their models. These few models have biased our religious, legal, and moral sexual ideology until today. They adversely restrict our scientific vision.

Male, Female, Hermaphrodite

VIEWED FROM THE barnyard, the ubiquitous feature of animal sexuality is that like human sexuality, it is diecious. In other words, each species is divided so that the male reproductive organs are housed in one individual and the female in another. The principle of the barnyard is that without the two sexes, reproduction would not exist. Nonetheless, this principle, although it haunts our own conception of ourselves sexually, is not an eternal verity. Nature is not as fixated on male/female duality as we are wont to think. In the realm of bacteria and other microscopic creatures there are monecious species galore. They reproduce asexually, by subdividing. Some plants, like dandelions, are monecious. Although they produce seeds, they reproduce asexually, also, by cloning. Other plants, including some trees, are capable of both asexual reproduction by budding or growing new shoots from their roots, and sexual reproduction by flowering and producing fertilized seeds.

Having separate male and female individuals is not an absolute prerequisite of sexual reproduction, for the male and female sex organs may coexist in the same individual plant or animal. Such an individual then qualifies as a hermaphrodite. Earthworms are hermaphrodites, and so are garden slugs and garden snails (Halliday, 1980, p. 113). When two such individuals mate, the male organ of each supplies sperm to the female organ of the other, reciprocally.

Being hermaphroditic innately is not the only way of possessing both eggs and sperms. The two sexes may begin separately and then be fused into one, which is what happens in the case of species of angler fish that live in the black depths of the ocean. The angler fish derives its name from the long cord-like appendage attached to its snout like a fishing line that dangles a fleshy lump of bait with which to lure prey. Although the angler fish begins its life as either a male or a female, it does not remain that way. The young male, upon encountering a young female locks onto her with his sucker-like lips and becomes attached. He is transformed into a permanently nourished appendage of the female. Except for the testicles, his organs atrophy, but hers, including her ovaries, remain whole and intact. Supplied with her own ovaries, and now possessing attached testicles, she becomes a de facto hermaphrodite, able to release eggs and sperms into the ocean concurrently.

Oysters are another example of a marine organism that can release both eggs and sperms, although not concurrently but serially or sequentially on different occasions. Oysters in the Chesapeake Bay of Maryland begin life as males and spawn as males, releasing into the water sperms that encounter and unite with eggs released by spawning females. With age, the male oyster changes to female and releases eggs (Otto, 1979). These oysters are serial, not simultaneous hermaphrodites.

Although not permanently anchored like the oyster, the transparent sea butterfly of the Maine coast (*National Wildlife*, 29[2]:18, 1991) is also a mollusk and also a serial hermaphrodite, but with a different timetable. These creatures join together in pairs, exchange sperm that then unite with the recipient's eggs which in turn are released into the ocean.

Sex Changing Fish

IN VERTEBRATE OR bony fish, the counterpart of serial hermaphroditism in mollusks is a form of sex transformation (Chan, 1977; Shapiro, 1987) that involves not only the gonads but also the body shape and color. It may be likened somewhat to transexualism in human beings. Some species of wrasse (family Labridae) are among those that undergo this type of hermaphroditic transformation. Wrasses are plentiful in coastal waters of the world. In the course of a lifetime, some wrasses change sex from female to male. They breed initially as female, and then as male, changed by arginine vasotocin (AVT).

One species of female-to-male changing wrasse is the cleaner fish, *Labroides dimidiatus* (Robertson, 1972; Warner et al., 1975). These small fish of the Australian Great Barrier Reef live in harem groups of ten or a dozen. The largest cleaner fish is the one and only male. All those of lesser size are females. The group subsists by keeping clean the mouth and gills of much larger fish such as their giant wrasse relative, the blue grouper. If the lone male cleaner fish dies or is taken away, its absence stimulates a physiological sex transformation of the largest remaining member of the group from breeding female to breeding male. It grows testicles to replace the ovaries that degenerate.

The breeding system of the cleaner fish is said to be polygynous, meaning many females per one male. By contrast, the breeding system is quite different in the bluehead wrasse (*Thalassoma bifasciatum*), another sex-changing species of Labridae. This species inhabits coral reefs of the western Atlantic. Both males and females hatch from the eggs of this species. The sperms are provided by only the older and larger males. Some of these males have a history of having begun life as a small fertile male, and some as a small fertile female. The latter, after having grown large enough, undergoes a sex transformation so as to become a breeding male (Warner et al., 1975). On a daily basis, the large breeding males of the species congregate or lek (see below) on a coral patch at the outer edge of the reef. There they await inspection by visiting breeding females each of which is attracted to and breeds with only the larger and brighter colored of the male breeders. The lesser males bide their time, quietly.

The transformation from female-to-male may be accompanied by a transformation of color, as in species related to the wrasses, the tropical parrot fish (family Scaridae). In one species of parrot fish, the female is red, and the male blue (*National Wildlife*, 21[3]:26-27, 1983). Not only color, but shape also may be transformed, as exemplified in the transformation of the rotund yellow female Fijian bass into the elongated, so-called purple-blot male (*International Wildlife*, 24[4]:48-49, 1994).

Sex transformation is not exclusively from female to male. In the case of the clownfish (*Amphiprion percula*) that inhabit the Indian and Pacific Oceans, the transformation is from male to female (*National Wildlife*, 21[3]:28, 1983). Clownfish are known also as anemone fish, in recognition of the fact that they live symbiotically with a sea anemone into the tentacles of which they attract other fish as food for the anemone. They themselves are immune to the anemone's poison that kills other fish. Clownfish are said to be monogamous, meaning that they live and breed in pairs. The female is larger and older than the male. Should she die first, the male transforms into a female and finds a smaller, younger male as a breeding partner (*National Wildlife*, 24[2]:17, 1986).

The orange-colored goby (*Tirimma okinawae*) that is found along Japan's shores is sex versatile. It is able to switch from female to male if it is the largest of an all female group, or from male to female if it is not the largest member of the community in which it lives (*National Geographic*, 186:xix, November 1994).

Parthenogenesis

PARTHENOGENESIS IS also known as virgin birth. The most celebrated human case is, ostensibly, that of the Virgin Mary. A parthenogen (or parthenogenone) is an organism produced not from the union of an egg and a sperm, but from the development of an egg into an embryo without the collaboration of a sperm.

Parthenogenesis is a form of cloning. It is not uncommon in primitive forms of life, like blue-green algae, and even insects, whereas it is extremely rare in animals with backbones. One species in which it has been rather thoroughly studied is a type of whiptail lizard, *Cnemidophorus uniparens*, found in the southwestern United States (Crews and Fitzgerald, 1980). Other parthenogenic whiptails live in the Australian desert (Moritz, 1983).

Parthenogenic whiptails are related to diecious species of whiptails, i.e., species in which there are both males and females. These parthenogenic lizards resemble females more than males of the two-sexed species insofar as they lay eggs from which young ones hatch. They differ from diecious females and males by having three copies of every chromosome instead of the usual two in the nucleus of all their cells—which is to say that they are chromosomally triploid instead of diploid. The genetic redundancy of the third set of chromosomes is presumably related to the spermless self-fertility of the parthenogenic egg.

Although parthenogenic whiptail lizards are able to breed without sperms, they nonetheless participate in copulatory behavior with one another in pairs, as if they were female and male. The lizard that is at the preovulatory stage mimics the female role. The other lizard is one that is at the postovulatory stage. It mimics the male role. This exercise stimulates the hormone-regulating regions of the brain which in turn speeds up the rate of ovulation and increases the number of clutches of eggs that will be laid annually (Crews, 1987; 1989).

From the point of view of sexological theory, the significance of the whiptail example is the reversibility of each roll. This reversibility demonstrates that the program or schema for female-typical and male-typical mating behavior are both stored in each individual's brain. This may very well apply not only to whiptail lizards' brains but to the evolutionarily earliest regions of mammalian brains, also, including yours and mine! In human beings male and female schemas are represented in the evolutionarily early limbic brain or paleocortex, as well as the evolutionarily more recent neocortex. One schema typically dominates the other. We say that either the male or the female schema is mine, and the other is thine. However, there is a bisexual penumbra of thine in all of us (see chaps. 6, 15).

Male Pregnancy

THE SEA HORSE (genus: hippocampus), of which there are many species, is neither sex-changing nor parthenogenic, but has a unique system of reproduction. Males and females pairbond, monogamously. As a courtship gesture, the male shows the female his empty brooding pouch. The female then gives the male her ova, anywhere from ten to several hundred, dependent on the adult size of the species. She deposits them in her mate's brooding pouch. There they unite with the male's sperms. The male is then pregnant and he carries the responsibility of gestation. The young are born alive after three weeks. whereupon the male becomes pregnant again, and repeatedly does so for all six months of the breeding season (Vincent and Grall, 1994).

What the sea horse achieves unaided is experimentally possible in mammals. The technology is in place. Except for ethical prohibitions it could conceivably be applied to a normal human male (Tiresi, 1994), in which case it would resemble an ectopic pregnancy in a hysterectomized normal human female. There is such a case on record in which a normal female infant was delivered by Caesarian section (Jackson et al., 1980). With a donor's egg, there have also been cases of successful pregnancy in chromosomal (46,XY) human male hermaphrodites (Frydman et al., 1988; Sauer et al., 1989) who were born with a partial uterus, and lived all their lives assigned as females. Male-to-female transexuals would be eager applicants to become pregnant, but the risks and complications of male pregnancy by in vitro fertilization make it unlikely to become a routine procedure at least for the foreseeable future.

Mating Bond: Exclusive and Otherwise

THE PEJORATIVE VIEW of sex in the barnyard defines man's animal nature as being sexually indiscriminate, promiscuous, opportunistic, unchaste, transitory, and unfaithful. Furthermore, males are characterized as being sexually more brutish than females, and indifferent to the responsibilities of paternity. Even within the barnyard, however, there are avian species whose mating patterns must be discounted or overlooked in order to maintain this pejorative view of man's animal nature. Geese and doves belong to barnyard species that should not be overlooked. Unlike barnyard mammals, these barnyard birds become monogamously mated and parentally long-term pairbonded, as do a great many other avian species in the wild.

Greylag geese have special claim to fame as they have been exhaustively studied by the ethologist, Konrad Lorenz (1952), and his colleagues. Newly hatched greylag goslings become bonded to members of their species by becoming bonded or imprinted first to their mothers. If in a contrived experiment the mother goose is replaced by a moving, squat-shaped substitute, the goslings become imprinted to the substitute. By squatting and waddling, Lorenz himself contrived to become their human mother substitute, and the goslings became his brood. Later, at the first mating season, they neglected their own species and attempted to bond instead with a human partner.

When a goose and a gander become pairbonded, they reunite as a nesting couple each year. A great many other species in the wild do the same. Kittiwakes, birds of the ocean, are an example. Males and females look alike. They nest in colonies, bring food to one another, and share parenting of the young.

Emperor penguins provide another example of pairbondedness that continues season after season (Peterson, 1979). After the male and female penguin have left the ocean and met and mated at the same place in the rookery where they brooded in the preceding year, the female lays only one egg. The male positions the egg on the insulated pads of his webbed feet, below a warm covering of his feathers. The female spends the next four and a half weeks in the ocean fishing and gaining a surplus of body fat, while the male stays on the ice, not moving even to eat, incubating the egg in the twenty-four hour darkness of the Antarctic midwinter. When the female returns to complete the nine-week incubation period, he returns to the ocean and regains lost weight. After the young one hatches, the parents alternate the duties of keeping it warm and fishing for its food.

In the contemporary new genomic age of DNA matching (metaphorically known as DNA fingerprinting) it is possible to prove whether or not a female bird's nesting partner and egg-fertilizing partner are one and the same male. Among pairbonded species in which the female lays a clutch of eggs, DNA matching has shown that there may be more than one genetic male parent (Ridley, 1994). Such species exemplify the principle that pairbondedness of parentalism in hatching and caring for the young, on the one hand, is separate from the pairbondedness of monogamous copulation, on the other hand. This avian system allows for either member of a pair to have a transient copulatory liaison without jealousy or attack from a rival, while allowing also for parental care of all the young of the species, irrespective of the paternal origin of their DNA.

An important contingency in the avian parental system in which genetic paternity is separable from social paternity is that male and female social parenting are indistinguishable. In mammals by contrast, only the female is equipped to nourish the young with milk. Paternity in barnyard mammals is limited to fertilization without long term attachment to either the partner or the offspring. More than anything else, this lack of paternal attachment has been responsible historically for the ostensible elevation of man's spiritual nature, and the corresponding denigration of man's animal nature which is equated with that of the animals of the barnyard.

In some mammalian species beyond the barnyard, however, attachment is characteristic of breeding partners toward one another and toward the young, on at least a seasonal basis, or longer. The members of these species commonly congregate in troops or families and become troopbonded. Wolves are such a species, and so are most species of primate, including our own.

The tenacity of primate pairbonding may correlate with level of position in the dominance hierarchy. It may then become jealously possessive (Kano, 1992). Alternatively it may be an agreeable and mutual consortship, as when a mating male and female chimpanzee go off together away from other members of the troop for one to several days (Tutin, 1979), as if for a short honeymoon. In human beings, pairbondedness has long been known as being in love, or being love-smitten, and more recently as being limerent (Tennov, 1979; see chap. 8). The high level of limerence lasts usually from two to five years, and it may be serially repeated successively with different partners. Limerence is a feature of man's animal nature despite its transcendent poetic and spiritual reputation. Birds of the barnyard display the prototype of limerent pairbonding, but for its prototype in mammals one must search beyond the barnyard in the zoo and in the wild.

Inbreeding and Outbreeding: Incest

IF WHILE IT lasts a pairbonded relationship with a stranger guarantees the exclusion of any other relationship, then that guarantee covers also, by definition, the exclusion of another and maybe incestuous relationship. Pairbonding amongst birds, since it does not exclude a transitory outside relationship, does not exclude at least the fortuitous possibility of incest, but it does reduce the likelihood of its occurrence.

Although less widespread than in birds, long-term male and female pairbonding is a characteristic of some mammalian species. Mammalian pairbonding between strangers may be so close that it greatly reduces, if not prevents the possibility of incest, according to data from a small American rodent, the prairie vole *(Microtus orchrogaster)*. The social organization of this animal is the family of two parents and their offspring (Getz and Carter, 1980; Getz et al., 1981; Insel and Carter, 1995). Virgin females remain reproductively dormant postpubertally so long as the males they smell and otherwise encounter are family members only. If approached by a familiar male, the virgin reacts with a threatening gesture. To become reproductively active, a virgin female prairie vole must engage in vomeronasal genital sniffing and grooming with a male stranger. Direct contact with the odor, or pheromone, from a male stranger's genital organs releases the hormone, oxytocin, which facilitates pairbonding (Carter et al., 1992). It also brings the female into estrus (heat) within two days, allows the closed vagina to open, and makes copulation anatomically possible. The couple remain pairbonded throughout life.

Among primates, the erotic power of smell is less a factor in the lives of Old World than New World monkeys, in particular Amazonian marmosets and tamarins of the callitrichid species. Among tamarins, the dominant female monopolizes the two or three males of a troop, and she alone breeds (Abrahamson, 1985). Menstrual cycling in young, mature females of the troop is suppressed until they disperse from their natal family and are exposed to the smell of strangers instead of to that of family members alone (Pusey, 1990). The young are usually born in pairs. Adult males bond with the infants of the troop, carrying them and feeding them (Abrahamson, 1985).

The converse of the erotic magnetism of the stranger, as exemplified by the prairie vole, and the marmoset and tamarin, is the erotic anhedonia, inertia, or indifference between troop mates who are too closely familiar. Named after the nineteenth-century sociologist as the Westermark effect, this phenomenon as applied to human beings has been called upon to explain outbreeding or exogamy, and the avoidance of inbreeding or incest. Joseph Shepher (1971) showed that kibbutz children in Israel raised from infancy in the same children's house, even though genetically unrelated, were romantically inert toward one another in the friendships of adolescence. They married outsiders with whom they had not grown up in infancy.

The Westermark effect is known to apply not only to the human species, but also to various other primate species that live in troops and that have been intensively studied in the wild or without being caged in isolation. Under free-ranging conditions, either the males or, less usually, females may leave the home troop as adolescents or at the latest as young adults (Anderson and Bielert, 1990; Pusey, 1990; Taub, 1990, de Waal, 1990). They may join another troop, become the cofounder of a new troop, or in the case of males lead a solitary or males-only group existence for a while. Among colobus monkeys *(Colobus badius)*, hamydryas baboons *(Papio hamadryas)*, and chimpanzees *(Pan troglodytes)*, females rarely linger with the home troop after reaching adolescence. Their dispersal ensures that they do not breed incestuously with a male whom presumably they do not recognize as father, or maybe brother. Males who do not disperse from the troop recognize their siblings who, like themselves, are closely bonded to the same mother. Toward their sisters and mother they are sexually indifferent. They are not indifferent, however, to other females of the troop.

Human beings have a self-congratulatory disposition to elevate the incest taboo to a spiritual position of high moral worthiness. If one looks beyond the limited sexology of the barnyard species, however, it becomes evident that outbreeding and incest avoidance are, in fact, a component of man's animal nature, shared especially with other primates.

Male Rivalry, Display, Lekking

Male Rivalry. The barnyard model of man's animal nature has for the human male been caricatured as a minotaur, bovine above the shoulders and human below, with huge genitalia (Berkeley and Tiffenbach, 1983). This caricature is heavily biased toward the aggressive behavior of mating rivalry exhibited by bulls and other barnyard males that fight for priority of access to females of the herd in heat. The counterpart of this bias is the comparative docility of barnyard males castrated as juveniles. Male competitive fighting over mating rights is a widespread phenomenon among herding mammals.

Male competitive fighting is characteristic also of some sea mammals, for example elephant seals (Halliday, 1980) and sea lions (*National Wildlife*, 20:30-31, 1982). They fight to possess females and form a harem. At a breeding site each bull, in the role of beachmaster, rules over his own territory and its female occupants.

As compared with herding mammals, among troopbonding primates male competitive fighting is more sporadic, and is related to dominance rivalry and challenge to an individual's established authority within the power hierarchy of the troop.

Male Display. According to popular social tradition, the counterpart of male sexual rivalry is female sexual display. In some mammalian species, however, and in many avian species, sexual display characterizes the male. In these species, male aggressive rivalry is supplanted by courtship competition in which males do not fight over a mate, or mates, but put themselves on display so as to solicit the attention of one or more females in search of a mate. In the case of birds, it may be the vocal display of singing that is the mating attractant, as it is for the male canary or zebra finch (Taylor, 1992).

Alternatively, the display may be of the plumage. A familiar example is the peacock whose extravagance is matched by various birds of paradise in Papua New Guinea, for example the blue bird of paradise and Count Raggi's bird of paradise (*Smithsonian*, 13[11]:94, 97, 1983).

A remarkable avian alternative to self-display is the display of an outdoor courtship arena or bower elaborately constructed by the male of various species of bowerbird native to Australia and New Guinea. Making his presence known vocally, the male waits at his little theater ready to solicit a visiting female by putting on a courtship show during which he presents her with items from his bower collection. Lawes' six wired bird of paradise is a New Guinea bird of paradise which is also a bower builder. Visiting females sit on a twig watching the male's performance which is staged daily, until the male succeeds in attracting a mate (*Smithsonian*, 13[11]:94, 1983).

The yellow-fronted gardener bowerbird *(Amblyornis flavifrons)*, also from New Guinea, is a bowerbird that constructs a mossy circular arena around a center pole (e.g. the stalk of a dwarf tree fern) which the bird decorates with projecting twigs. He decorates the arena also with three mounds of fruit colored blue, yellow, and green, respectively. As a female watches from the foliage of the center pole, the male displays blue fruit against the gold of his puffed out chest feathers (Diamond, 1982).

Three other species of bowerbird are indigenous to Australia, namely, the spotted bowerbird, *Chlamydera maculata* (Halliday, 1980); the great bowerbird (*International Wildlife*, 2[Sept/Oct]:2, 1981); and the satin bowerbird, *Ptilonorhynchus violaceus* (Rathbun, 1993). The arenas of the males of these three species are constructed with sheaves of straw and sticks and decorated with brightly colored flowers, feathers, or found objects such as a red toothbrush.

Lekking. Avian male courtship display is, according to species, both solo and in groups. A group display is called a lek, and the place a lekking ground (from the Swedish, *leka*, to play) (Hoglund and Alatalo, 1995). The cock of the rock (the "rock" refers to the females' nesting site) is an avian lekking species, native to Surinam on the north central Atlantic coast of South

America. Many males assemble on the same tree, where females visit them and pick a mate (*National Geographic*, 164:830-39, 1983).

The male sage grouse of Utah and other western American states is also a lekking bird (Halliday, 1980, p. 44-5). Several males visit the same lekking ground annually. With chests inflated and tails fanned (*National Wildlife*, 27:50-51, June/July, 1989), they advertise their presence with long-distance booming sounds. Females that visit the lek converge on the star performers who do most of the breeding, without competitive rivalry or attack from those who are left out.

Lekking, although not entirely absent among mammalian species, is rare. It occurs, for example, in the kob antelope (*Kobus kob*) of Uganda and the African savannah. Females do not fight with one another for access to a star stud at a lekking ground, nor do males fight with males (Schuster, 1976). By contrast, in other species of hoofed mammals, the females congregate as a herd, and males may maim and kill one another in competition to be master of the herd. Elk (*National Wildlife*, 19:3, Oct/Nov, 1981) and red deer (*National Geographic*, 170:556-57, 1986) are examples. The females of these species do not compete with one another for access to the stag, but wait their turn for mating when in heat.

Pheromones, Female Aggression, Dominance and Attachment

Pheromones. The sexual signal with which to attract a mate may be neither visual nor auditory, but odoriferous. An odoriferous attractant is a pheromone. Many insects are experts at pheromonal mating, so much so that pheromonal extracts are used to attract and entrap males in programs of insect control.

In mammals, both males and females may secrete pheromones either in the urine or, especially in males, as a concentrate from hormonally regulated special glands variously located at either end of the body. The hormone is testosterone. In four-legged pheromonal species, male pheromone is sprayed or spread as a boundary marker where it serves also to signal females of the availability of a male nearby. The corresponding signal from the female to the male is a pheromone secreted from the vagina only at the ovulatory period of being in heat. The scent of the pheromone released into the air is picked up by extremely sensitive receptors with which the male is equipped. In mammals, these receptors bypass ordinary smelling. They are located in the highly specialized vomeronasal organ of odor detection, within the nasal cavity (Wright, 1994).

When a bitch is in heat, male dogs in the neighborhood are pheromonally attracted to her. As the males mill around competitively, the bitch engages in a proceptive teasing ritual. Finally, it is her prerogative to elect a copulatory partner. The two become penovaginally locked together by the swelling of his penile bulb. His rivals disperse without further ado.

In the mammalian phylum, pheromones are less significant as sexual attractants in primates than in subprimates. In primates, including human beings, visual attractants are more significant. Where the nose leaves off, the eyes take over. Comparatively, the eyes are more important for male than female sexual arousal, whereas for female sexual arousal the cutaneous senses are more important. If vomeronasal attraction exists in the human species, then the intriguing possibility arises that it may bypass conscious awareness.

Female Aggression. Lack of female aggression in mating is widespread across species, although not universal. Among some insect species, including crickets and praying mantises, as well as some spiders, females have achieved notoriety of sorts by turning their heads and devouring the head and thorax of the copulating male partner (Caras, 1974; Halliday, 1980).

Among mammals, the spotted hyena (*Crocuta crocuta*) is a carnivorous, troopbonding species that has been rather well studied in free ranging captivity in California and in the wild in Kenya (Yalcinkaya et al., 1993; Stevens, 1993). The female spotted hyenas of a clan are remarkable for outperforming all the males of the clan in dominance and aggression in any context, including mating. The female spotted hyena is larger, heavier, and stronger than the male, and a more ferocious killer. She is born with a clitoris which is fused on the underside along the midline in the manner of a male penis (Stevens, 1993; Smale and Holekamp, 1993). Urination is through the opening at the tip of this organ. The same opening serves double duty as the orifice through which sperm are received from the male, and through which the young, twins or triplets, are delivered. At birth, the teeth of the young are fully erupted, and females are already larger than males. Newborn siblings attack one another viciously and fight to the death. In most neonatal brother and sister attacks, the brother succumbs and the sister survives.

By contrast with the female of the three other species of hyena, as well as with the female of mammalian species in general, the hormonal history of the female spotted hyena is atypical. Her unusual body morphology and her fierce aggressiveness have been traced to an extremely high level, from intrauterine life onwards, of androstenedione (secreted by the ovaries) and its derivative, testosterone, which is typically much higher in males than in females of other mammalian species.

Dominance and Attachment. Among primates, there are no known species that resemble the spotted hyena with respect to competitive dominance and aggression of the female. Likewise, there are no known primate species that closely resemble the kob antelope with respect to nonaggressive lekking of the male; or, conversely, no species that closely resemble the elk and red deer (or the elephant seal or sea lion) with respect to aggressive male fighting to be the sole master of a female herd or harem. The human ruler of a harem does not personally fight a rival for possession of a particular woman. His power over others is military, economic, and political, as the ruler of a tribe or state.

Primates that troopbond are capable also of forming personal attachments or pairbonds, which in human beings means being love smitten.

Primate mating on the basis of personal attachment coexists with mating by right of one's position of power in the primate dominance hierarchy. This coexistence applies to females as well as males, except that a female's position is subordinate to that of her consort, and that a male is always at the top of the hierarchy. Each may become aggressive in response to the intrusion of a same sex mating rival. A mother's high rank in the dominance hierarchy confers a competitive advantage on her sons.

Courtship

IN THE HISTORY of barnyard and animal husbandry, the mating practices of animals have been conceptually reduced to the lowest common factor of fertilization. Species variations in the preliminaries of courtship, which is the first or proceptive phase of mating (Beach, 1976), have been overlooked as more or less trivial and unimportant. In many instances, however, the proceptive behavioral ritual, sometimes called the mating dance, is an essential prerequisite of the second, that is the acceptive or receptive phase of penial-vaginal union. Without genital union, fertilization fails to occur, and so also does the third or conceptive phase of pregnancy.

The barnyard model in which sexuality is reduced to genital union and reproduction falsely represents animal nature in and out of the barnyard. It also gives an incorrect and contrived representation of man's animal nature that paves the way for all nonprocreative sexual practices to be classified as unnatural. Although the list is not yet thorough and exhaustive, several nonprocreative practices have been observed in the mating repertoire of various species in the wild as well as in captivity. By the laws of logic, therefore, since they happen in nature, they are natural. Regardless of their prevalence or frequency, they cannot logically be defined as unnaturally deviant or perverted, even though they may be ideologically unacceptable according to the sexosophical principles of a religious or moral doctrine.

Masturbation, Anal and Oral Sex, Positioning

Masturbation. The evidence has not been systematically quantified, but it leaves no doubt that animals of both subprimate and primate species in the wild as well as in captivity stimulate their own genitals. Self-licking of the penis, or rubbing it against furniture or people's legs, is a common complaint brought to veterinarians by dog owners. A trained male dolphin once gained masturbatory renown amongst onlookers by performing his self-devised act of rubbing his erect penis against the guy ropes of his aquarium.

Although stimulus deprived monkeys and apes in captivity that stimulate themselves by masturbating may do so as a relief from boredom, those that are free ranging also masturbate, either alone or in the presence of conspecifics. Male monkeys are able to masturbate either orally (self-fellatio) or manually, and they may eat the ejaculate. Solo manual masturbation by male rhesus monkeys (*Macaca mulatta*) and Japanese macaques (*Macaca fuscata*) is documented in the photographic collection of the Wisconsin Regional Primate Research Center.

Female monkeys are more likely to masturbate by squatting and rubbing the vulva against something than by manual or oral self-stimulation. A human-reared female chimp once was observed to open a Playgirl magazine and squat-rub over the centerfold of a nude male. She also gave overtly sexual invitations to male visitors, although not to the males of the household in which she was reared (Temerlin, 1975).

Anal Sex. When two animals mount, especially when a male mounts a female, it is difficult to observe and prove whether anal penetration has or has not occurred. Penetration has, however, been proved in the case of rams segregated in an all male flock. A veterinarian in New Zealand (D.F.L. Money, personal communication) once traced a mysterious epidemic of sterility in valuable stud rams to microorganisms (*Brucella ovis*) transmitted from one to the other by anal penetration (see also below, under Homosexuality).

Oral Sex. As compared with anal penetration, oral-genital sex is readily observable. Investigative licking, poking, and smelling of the vulva presented to the male by the female in heat is, in many species, preliminary to penovaginal penetration. Although it may be prototypical of cunnilingus, this type of genital investigation is not the same as mouth-genital sex performed by the male on the female as a method of sexual foreplay. Cunnilingus is also a genuine form of foreplay in the repertory of primates, however, witness the example of the orangutan (*Pongo pygmaeus*) as photographed by Ron Nadler (personal communication) at the Yerkes Regional Primate Research Center in Atlanta, Georgia.

Whether or not fellatio is in the repertory of adult primate heterosexual foreplay remains to be ascertained. There is no doubt, however, that it is in the repertory of male-male juvenile sexual rehearsal play, as observed and photographed by Frans de Waal (personal communication) in the bonobo (*Pan paniscus*) formerly known as the pygmy chimpanzee.

Positioning. The dorsoventral or "doggie" position of rear-end presenting and mounting is anatomically dictated in four-legged species. It is also anatomically the most convenient position for the majority of monkeys and apes. In some species the ventroventral (face-to-face) or so-called missionary position may also be used, and has been photographically documented by Nadler and de Waal in two species, namely the gorilla (*Gorilla gorilla*) and the bonobo. For the gorilla the rear mount prevails, whereas it is the other way round for the bonobo. As compared with other apes, the bonobo vaginal opening is well positioned for face-to-face mounting. De Waal (1989) reported 80 percent of bonobo copulations he observed to be in this position. Bonobo copulation is not restricted as it is in other subhuman primates to the ovulatory phase of the female's menstrual cycle. It may occur during at least 75 percent of the cycle.

Cross-species Attachment

IT IS POSSIBLE for two animals of different species to become attached to one another in both a comradely and a sexual way, and for the attachment to be so pervasive as to preclude conspecific mating. Pet owners know that a history of having been reared together favors the development of cross-species bonding.

Subhuman primates reared in captivity are able to form a long-lasting sexual attachment, either heterosexual or homosexual, to a particular human keeper, an attachment so explicit that it may be an embarrassment (Temerlin, 1975). De Waal (1989, p. 198) recorded an incident with a bonobo. He wrote: "A new zookeeper, unfamiliar with sexual encounters of the bonobo kind, once accepted a kiss from Kevin [an adolescent male]. Was he taken aback when he felt Kevin's tongue in his mouth! The habit of French kissing is one of the striking differences between [the bonobo's] impassioned eroticism and the somewhat boring, functional sex of the common chimpanzee. . . . Bonobos perform every conceivable variation." French kissing has been observed between juvenile bonobos, including two young males (de Waal, 1990, p. 386).

Homosexuality

IN THE WILD, follow-up observations and proof of a long-term, pairbonded relationship that is isosexual (meaning between members of the same sex) are less readily achieved in mammalian than in avian species. Isosexual means the same as homosexual, but without implying a fixated orientation and with no moral or legal implications. Isosexual is the antonym of contrasexual.

Isosexual pairbonding does occur in birds. It may be interpreted as a phenomenon of nesting and parentalism rather than of genital sexuality. Each of the pair may be female, for example, in western gulls, or male, for example, in nesting swans (personal communication, J. D. Weinrich).

From Tiritiri Matangi Island in New Zealand there is a unique story of two pairbonded male takahes, members of a species of flightless bird once considered to be extinct. Rescued onto a sanctuary island, these two males were the only representatives of their species there. They became broody and began nesting. Provided with an egg from another sanctuary island, they hatched it and together fed and raised the young bird (Money, 1994a).

Male-male mounting, as in the case of anal sex between rams (see above) constitutes a male-male isosexual act. Male-male mounting has been observed to occur also in rams that have lived socially sex-segregated since infancy (D'Occhio and Ford, 1988). In their first mating season, these rams neglected ewes in estrus and mounted one another instead. During the next mating season, they were able to engage with ewes as well as rams, thus demonstrating bisexual capability. Male-male mounting with anal penetration has also been observed in ram lambs raised segregated from ewe lambs under farm conditions in India (Mathur and Joshi, 1994; Mathur et al., 1994). When mature at a year of age they were indifferent to mating with ewes in heat, but not with their male flock mates.

At a sheep experimental station in Idaho, in a population of 94 sexually inexperienced rams aged one to two years, Perkins and colleagues observed two rams that were mounted repeatedly by other male pen mates. Eight others (referred to as male-oriented or homosexual) were never observed mounting ewes. Two of the eight homosexual males mounted each other exclusively. Under controlled test conditions, various hormonal responses of homosexually and heterosexually oriented males were compared with one another and with those of ewes. There were no significant hormonal differences, except that the prevalence of estrogen receptors in the amygdala of homosexual rams' brains was lower than in heterosexual rams' brains, and similar to that in heterosexual ewes' brains. The origins of these brain differences and of the rams' homosexual behavior remain to be elucidated (Perkins and Fitzgerald, 1992; Perkins et al., 1995).

Like rams, stallions are sociosexually susceptible to developmental variations of rearing (Tischner, 1982). Free roaming stallions ordinarily mate with mares and do not attempt to mount males; but those reared in stalls in a stable will attempt to mount other stallions as well as mares. They also attempt to mount dummies, and when alone try to masturbate (Tischner, 1982).

Bisexually or monosexually, sheep and horses pair only transiently as copulatory partners, whereas among various primate species individuals may establish more lasting, even though not exclusive sexual attachments. Such attachments as well as more casual ones in primates are predominantly between male and female. However, male-male and female-female sexual interaction also occurs and in several primate species has been recorded on film.

Two male langur monkeys photographed together in a male-male sexual mounting position belonged to an all male group the members of which had left the natal troop, but had not yet joined or founded a troop with female members (Hrdy, 1977).

Among Japanese macaques, male-male sexual interaction is on record at the library of the Wisconsin Regional Primate Research Center. Two adult males may assume the face-to-face position as well as the rear-mount position; and juvenile males in pairs may practice the regular rear mount.

In the bonobo, male-male interaction not only occurs, but also has dual significance, one being erotic, and the other peace-making. At all ages, a male bonobo's genitalia function dually as gestural organs of dispute prevention and friendly reconciliation, and also as sensory organs of erotosexuality together with the possibility of procreation in adulthood. Each function may occur independently of the other, or the first may lead into the second.

Two bonobo males may end a dispute by engaging in a species typical method of genital appeasement or reconciliation. In the context of tension reduction, a pair of male bonobos were photographed in the wild by Takayoshi Kano (1990) one mounting the other from behind. Another maneuver is for the subordinate male, who may be adolescent, to indicate surrender by lying on his back. His penis emerges erect from its sheath, and the dominant male, who may be an older adult, performs a genital massage, though not to the point of ejaculation. There is also no ejaculation and no penetration, if the dominant male mounts the other from behind (or vice versa). If two reconciling males embrace face to face with thrusting and mutual penis rubbing, there is also no ejaculation (de Waal, 1989, p. 201; Kano, 1990). Regardless of the type of activity, the role of the dominant male is to provide a guarantee of safety to the subordinate male (Kano, 1992, p. 181).

Genital gestures of amicability and recreation in bonobos are not exclusively male-male. They may also be female-female, or male-female. In the wild as well as in captivity, female bonobos engage in intensive sexual contacts, as when one leads another away for an episode of mutual genital rubbing. After leading the other away, the one squats over the other, face to face, and positions herself for genitogenital rubbing, in which the two clitorides are juxtaposed.

Macaque monkeys of two species, rhesus and stumptail, may also engage in what may be characterized as subhuman primate lesbianism. For example, two rhesus females engage in the preliminary seeking phase followed by the simulated male mount which eventually culminates in the orgasmic clutching phase (Akers and Conaway, 1979). Orgasm is signaled when the bottom partner turns her head right and toward her partner and extends the right arm to clutch the abdominal-genital region of the partner.

In what is believed to be the first scientifically documented occurrence of orgasm in a nonhuman species, two stumptailed macaque females engaged in a lesbian interaction (Goldfoot et al., 1980). They began with the phase of genital inspection and continued with mounting and thrusting to orgasm. As orgasm occured the female on top shaped her lips as if to hoot, and her partner underneath turned her head so that the lips of the two partners could meet. Physiological measurements, including measurement of uterine contractions, confirmed the gestural and vocal evidence of orgasm.

Juvenile Sexual Rehearsal Play

THE BARNYARD CONCEPTION of sex as an instinct carries with it the implication that at the appropriate time the instinct will manifest itself in much the same way as a preprogrammed robot begins its performance when its battery is switched on. There is no place in this barnyard conception for the idea that early rehearsal or practice may be prerequisite to successful performance later. However, when it has been looked for, juvenile sexual rehearsal play has been observed in the young of diverse animal species. It is a necessary aspect of healthy sexual development of the young of mammals in general, not only of the higher primates.

Among primate troops in the wild, sexually immature infants and juveniles have several years in which there are opportunities to watch older troop members copulating. Documentary evidence is on record for the gorilla (Nadler, 1982), the stumptail macaque (Wisconsin Regional Primate Research Center), and the bonobo (de Waal, 1989; Kano, 1990).

Bonobo infants and juveniles may actually accompany their mothers in sexual activity. Thus, with a daughter clinging to her, a mother lies flat on her back, and invites an adult female friend to back onto her genital swelling to perform mutual genitogenital (GG) rubbing (de Waal, 1989, p. 202).

According to Kano (1992, p. 196), from the age of six months onward, when a juvenile male bonobo in the wild "encounters his mother or other adults engaging in [male-female] copulation or [female-female] GG rubbing, he immediately runs and clings to either one's stomach or back and screams. Then, when the adults conclude their activity, they embrace the juvenile and practice similar behaviors with him. There are juveniles that cannot wait to thrust; they cling to the male's hips during copulation. They also insert their penis into the top female in the midst of GG rubbing."

Juvenile sexual rehearsal play in primates is not restricted to either observation of, or participation in the sexual activities of older members of the species. Among primates in the wild, the young have virtually unrestricted opportunity to engage in age-mate sexual rehearsal play. In Zaire's Wamba Forest, for example, the image of two juvenile bonobos, male and female, was caught by a cameraman as they practiced sexual intercourse in the ventroventral (missionary) position prevalent in their species (*National Geographic*, 181:51, March 1992).

Anderson and Bielert (1990) wrote of young baboons that "both sexes present themselves in the sexually inviting postures typical of adult females to other baboons rather indiscriminately, regardless of age or sex; and [infants and juveniles of] both sexes mount and are mounted by other infants and juveniles (p. 179). . . . Juvenile and infant males mount females of all ages but rarely if ever achieve intromission . . . [whereas infant and] juvenile females are mounted [only] by infant and juvenile males who do not achieve intromission" (p. 191). Among juvenile male bonobos, a pair may engage in fellatio (de Waal, personal communication).

In the laboratory, the rhesus monkey is the species in which the deprivation as well as the manifestation of juvenile sexual rehearsal play has been extensively investigated (reviewed in Goldfoot, 1977; Money, 1986a) and photographically documented. Early in the first year of life rhesus infants interpolate sexual mounting and presenting with chasing and fighting in their play acrobatics. Only with practice do they achieve correct positional orientation and male-female reciprocity with adult style footclasp mounting. As beginners they mount males or females. They mount sideways, or at the head end, alone or in jumbled groups; with and without attempted footclasping. With a head mount, a male may attempt to receive fellatio.

Monkeys deprived of sexual rehearsal play by being raised in social isolation are permanently sexually impaired and fail to breed. Even a half hour of peer group play daily may prevent permanent impairment, but only for one-third of the group, and at the cost of retarded sexuobehavioral development and a lowered birth rate in adulthood.

In Frans de Waal's (1990) investigation of bonobos, a seven-year-old adolescent male bonobo was observed being mounted face to face by a two-year-old infant female. She pressed her vulva against his penis while he made rapid pelvic thrusts without intromission. Another two-year-old infant male presented to an adult male for a ventrodorsal mount, without intromission.

It is clear from the foregoing survey that barnyard models of juvenile sexual rehearsal play are singularly lacking. Beyond the barnyard the zoo does better, but the distortions of life in confinement require that zoo models be augmented with models from life in the wild. Primate models in the wild or in free-ranging captivity provide more humanly relevant information than do subprimate models. Lack of knowledge about primate sexology during centuries past has left the human species spectacularly ignorant and in error, today, regarding the place and significance of juvenile sexual rehearsal play in man's own animal nature. Human juveniles do, however, engage in sexual rehearsal play (see Money, 1986b, p. 523).

Even among the primates there is no exact model of human developmental sexology. In primate and in subprimate species as well, we find some of those sexological aspects of ourselves that we have, in our sexual ideology—our sexosophy—despised as beastly, and some that we have admired as saintly. It comes as a surprise to discover that the beasts variously share with us many of those aspects of our sexuality that, in our conceit, we have claimed to be spiritually transcendent over animal nature.

Although, our animal nature is our own, there is much that human beings must learn from the study of other species. What we learn from them, however, are metaphors and hypotheses of what to investigate in ourselves. There is no fixed line of evolutionary descent along which to trace the evolution of man's animal nature. Even among our closest evolutionary relatives, the primates, there is extraordinary sexological diversity rather than a systematic evolutionary progression. There are no sexological facts or principles in animal nature that can be borrowed from other species and applied blindly, by faith, to ourselves. The great sexological challenge of man's animal nature is not what it is or is not, but its extraordinary epistemological power in shaping and misshaping our conceptions of ourselves.

3

Phylogenesis/Ontogenesis

Social Constructionism/Essentialism
Phylisms
Autogenitalism
Grooming
Freudian Psychosexual Stages
Neonatal Circumcision

Social Constructionism/Essentialism

The concept of man's animal nature is more or less tied to the concept of instinct, in this instance the sexual instinct. In popular usage, to do something instinctively means to do it reflexively and without logical thought, by intuition rather than reason, as if in obedience to a preordained program. As an academic term in psychology, the sexual instinct is defined more diffusely as a generic drive or disposition that powers the various manifestations of sexual behavior. The drive itself is mostly postulated as being biological and in overly simplistic thinking as hormonal, although it is also postulated that hormonal effects are subject to conditioning, training, and voluntary control.

In social science and psychology, explanations according to learning theory (which includes conditioning and training) on the one hand, and biological theory, on the other, are separated as if on either side of an unbridged chasm. The in-vogue term for the learning side is social constructionism, and for the biological side, essentialism. In the ultimate analysis, the separation of the two is indefensible, for learning and remembering take place simultaneously in the mind and in the brain and nervous system where they metamorphose into biology.

One way to construct a bridge over the chasm between biology and learning is to postulate that sexological development has its origins in both phylogenetics and ontogenetics. Phylogenetic development belongs to us simply by reason of our being members of the human species, whereas ontogenetic development is specific to the person. Phylogenetic development relies on both biological and social input, and so also does ontogenetic development. Thus the two together provide a way to circumvent being entrapped in the mind/body, social-constructionist/essentialist dilemma.

Phylogenetic and ontogenetic determinants do not carry their own labels. It is possible to get some help in getting phylogenetic determinants disentangled from those that are ontogenetic by looking for parallels between human sexuoerotic behavior and that of other higher primates, and by looking for transcultural regularities in cultures that are otherwise dissimilar—for example, regularities associated with puberty, menses, and menopause all three of which are transculturally universal phenomena. Transcultural data on juvenile and adolescent sexology are presently too few in number and too often haphazard rather than systematic in coverage. Ethnographers have been as much affected by their own cultural prudery as have other scientists. Nonetheless, existing studies do provide a nucleus for the future expansion of transcultural comparisons.

Phylogenetic determinants are characterized as being innate or inborn. In the ultimate analysis, what they determine is a chain of developmental events the onset of which is preordained in a part of the individual genome that is shared by all members of the species. In that sense, phylogenetic determinants are inherited, but not all innate or inborn characteristics are inherited. There is an internal environment of the womb which differs from one womb to another, and from one pregnancy to another. Even within an embryo or fetus one may speak of an environment, for each colony of developing cells provides an environmental molecular chemistry for its neighbors.

The genomic code, in addition to carrying instructions for the phylogenetic determinants that make all human beings similar to a certain degree, provides also for ontogenetic instructions that make each of us individually to some degree unique, just as everyone has a unique face, but a face that is also recognizably human. It is a developmental marvel that the genome is able to differentiate the two programs of instruction with a relative sparsity of errors.

Innate means only that something has been inborn, that is present or preordained before birth, not necessarily that it is evident at birth. Its actual appearance may be of delayed onset. It may also be subject to the delay of a developmental latency period, as in the case of the age of the onset of puberty, for example.

Something that is innate is not necessarily immutable or irreversible. Even something attributable to a specific gene may be subject to modification by genetic engineering, by gene therapy, or by the use of medications in utero. The converse also applies: something may be irreversible even if it is brought on not by a specific gene, but by something in the intrauterine environment, for example, a toxic substance transmitted by the mother to the fetus through the placenta and umbilical cord.

Translated into the language of heredity and environment, the foregoing exemplifies once again the futility of the nature/nurture dispute. The way to circumvent this dispute is to adapt the imprinting paradigm first formulated by the European school of animal ethology (see chap. 2). According to this paradigm nature and nurture meet and reciprocally match at a critical period of development. Nature is represented by an innate recognition mechanism (or schema), and nurture by a preordained environmental releasing stimulus. The textbook example is that of a newly hatched gosling or duckling that will follow a squat-shaped moving object, the releasing stimulus, which is normally the mother, even though that stimulus is a waddling human being. The outcome is that the hatchling becomes imprinted to the moving object either immutably or for a very long time, to the exclusion of its own kind, even at the first mating season. The imprint becomes fixed in the brain. It becomes part of the biology of the brain, where there is a biology of learning and remembering.

The two-term nature/nurture paradigm thus becomes one with three factors: nature/critical-period/nurture in which nature and nurture collaborate at a critical developmental period to produce a long-term effect. It is of scientific interest to know the when of this collaboration, how it is processed in the brain, and where it is stored in memory. It is of greater pragmatic interest to know how permanent and immutable is its effect, and how readily it may or may not be modified.

Phylisms

AN INNATE RECOGNITION mechanism belongs among the elemental bits and pieces of the mental and motor "animation" of living creatures that are phylogenetically coded into them as members of their species. These elemental bits and pieces do not need to be learned, in the ordinary sense of learning, although they may need to be practiced to be perfected—just as upright locomotion needs to be practiced, one step at a time, with support, before walking without support becomes perfected. Some of these elemental bits and pieces have been traditionally named reflexes, and some as fixed action patterns. The generic name proposed for all of them is phylism (Money, 1983b; 1990), of which the formal definition is as follows (see also chap. 16).

> **phylism:** (from Greek *phylon,* Latin *phylum,* tribe or race). A unit or building block of an organism's conjoint mind-body existence and experience which all members of a species possess by reason of their phylogenetic heritage as a member of that species.

Many phylisms have everyday vernacular names, such as breathing, coughing, sneezing, hiccupping, drinking, swallowing, biting, chewing, pissing, shitting, fucking, laughing, crying, walking, grasping, holding, sweating, touching, hurting, tasting, smelling, hearing, and seeing. The complete list has not been counted.

One or more phylisms may be incorporated into a larger and more comprehensive pattern of behavior. Conversely, a phylism may be subdivided into progressively smaller units which is what usually happens as a phylism becomes increasingly subject to scientific experimentation and analysis. For example, the phylism of penile and clitoral tumescence (erection) may become merged into a pattern of masturbation or of sexual intercourse. Conversely, it may be subdivided into smaller phylisms of the cellular chemistries that regulate the genital blood flow and the neurochemistries of the brain and spinal cord's innervation of tumescence, which includes the release of nitric oxide (NO), a neurotransmitter substance in the form of a gas (Nelson et al., 1995).

Phylisms that have significance for sexological function are distributed among each of the three phases of sexuoeroticism. Phase one is proceptive. It includes all the species specific maneuvers of courtship or the "mating dance" that lead up to coital union. Human proception includes attracting and being attractive, and becoming love-smitten or limerent. It includes also preparatory copulatory foreplay.

Phase two is acceptive (or receptive), in which two partners accept or receive each other in genital union or in some other maneuver of reciprocal acceptance. Typically the two partners are male and female (heterosexual) but they may be both of the same sex (isosexual); or there may be three or more partners.

Phase three is conceptive. It is contingent on reciprocal fertility at the time of intercourse, and on whether contraception was used or not. Contrary to accepted teaching, maximum fertility is immediately prior to, not after ovulation (Wilcox et al., 1995). Conception progresses into pregnancy, and pregnancy to parenthood which has its own array of phylisms.

Autogenitalism

AMONG THE SEXOLOGICAL phylisms, erection is the one that has been documented at the youngest age. Using the ultrasound technique of visualization, erections were recorded pictorially in utero at the fetal age of seven months (Calderone, 1983; Sherer et al., 1990; Shirozu et al., 1995). In another inutero case, at twenty-eight weeks of gestation, an ultrasound sonogram revealed ostensible masturbatory movements that were followed for fifteen minutes as the fetal penis was held in the grasp of the fetal hand (Meizner, 1987). Erection and masturbation in utero are a preparatory rehearsal and a guarantee, so to speak, that the genitals will be functional in later life. Whether the female genitalia go through a corresponding rehearsal is a question which ultrasound imaging has not yet been able to answer.

In newborn boys, erections occur periodically, awake and asleep, and pass unnoticed unless the baby is being diapered or bathed or, in a warm enough environment, wearing no clothing. From earliest life onward through old age, sleep erections go under the name of NPT (nocturnal penile tumescence). NPT occurs particularly although not exclusively in association with REM (rapid eye movement) sleep, in three or more episodes per night, for a total of up to three hours in the juvenile and adolescent years, and one hour from young adulthood onward. After puberty, an episode may spontaneously culminate in ejaculation. Dreaming is frequently reported by those awakened from REM sleep (Karacan, 1966; Karacan et al., 1975).

REM sleep is not specific to males. It occurs in females also. The female counterpart of NPT in the male is increased vaginal blood flow (VBF). In a sleep study of two females (Cohen and Shapiro, 1970), change in VBF was found to be associated with periods of non-REM sleep as well as with periods of REM sleep, thus paralleling NPT in the male. The sleeping VBF changes were similar to those found to accompany fantasy-induced sexuoerotic arousal while awake. The technology for measuring vaginal lubrication, awake or asleep, has not been perfected. The measurement of clitoral tumescence is also subject to technical difficulty, as the organ is too small for the fitting of a ring shaped measuring gauge. This difficulty can be overcome in some patients with congenital adrenocortical clitoromegaly, as occurs in the syndrome of congenital adrenal hyperplasia (CAH). Two patients with this syndrome did manifest nocturnal clitoridean tumescence (Karacan et al., 1970). It is not feasible to generalize from the CAH clitoris to that of the normal sized organ, as the CAH clitoris has a much larger volume of the erectile spongy tissue of the corpora cavernosa.

In male babies, erections may occur briefly in association with urination, defecation, crying, coughing, or stretching (Karacan, 1966). In infant girls, genital arousal, being inconspicuous as compared with boys, has escaped documentation.

Mothers who breast feed a baby may experience erotic sensations possibly culminating in orgasm. The baby also may manifest genital arousal. For example, at a children's July 4th pool party, an unweaned infant aged between three and four, had already had a hamburger and hot dog lunch when he came naked from the pool for "dessert" at the breast. As he sucked the milk, his penis maintained a prolonged erection of which he and his mother were apparently oblivious while she continued to be engaged in conversation with adults.

The prevalence and the age relatedness of the connection between eating and genital arousal in the human species remains unascertained. A phyletic food-genital connection is not, however, unique to our own species. In another primate, the bonobo (see chap. 2), this connection is species typical. It is manifested when a male's penis protrudes, erected, from its sheath as he puts food into his mouth while lying on his back. A female requests and obtains food from him by backing onto his penis with her vagina. In this way strife over food is avoided. Among bonobos, the genitalia are organs of not only eroticism and breeding, but also of conciliation and conflict resolution (Kano, 1992; de Waal, 1989).

Grooming

THE ONE WORD that covers all types of skin contact is grooming. It includes holding, cuddling, caressing, kissing, rocking, patting, rubbing, massaging, fondling, and in early infancy, breast feeding. The outcome of grooming deprivation is failure to thrive. Prematurely born babies who are kept alive in an incubator and given an adequate amount of grooming flourish and are ready to go home a week or more earlier than those who are grooming deprived. Groomed babies averaged 47 percent greater weight gain daily, were more active and alert, and scored higher developmental ratings on the Brazelton Scale (Field et al., 1986; Schanberg and Field, 1987). These human data agree with those previously discovered in experiments with newborn rats (Schanberg and Kuhn, 1985) that had been deprived of maternal licking (tongue grooming). One highly specific outcome of this deprivation was a depletion in the level of growth hormone circulating in the bloodstream. Growth hormone is one of the many hormones secreted by the pituitary gland which is situated adjacent to the hypothalamic region of the brain, deeply behind the bridge of the nose (Odell and Moyer, 1971). The low level of growth hormone was found to be associated with a low level of the enzyme, ornithine decarboxylase (ODC) in the tissue of the brain, liver, heart and kidneys. ODC acts as a powerful catalyst in the regulation of cell growth.

The molecular chemistry of grooming in human infants has not yet been ascertained. The behavioral sequelae of grooming, by contrast, are readily recognizable. The baby gurgles and coos, wiggles its arms and legs, and makes a smiley face. More prevalently in baby girls perhaps than in baby boys, the hands briefly find the thighs and the genital area, from which one may infer that the precursor of the erotic feeling of touch is already present. Whether or not it should be classified as an erotic precursor, grooming is certainly of major significance in establishing mother-baby pairbonding. For most of the history of our species pairbondship of the infant with the mother has taken precedence over pairbondship with the father for the obvious reason that the female supplies breast milk and the male does not, although in modern times, with the invention of bottled formula feeding, the difference is no longer so absolute.

Older infants who lack a sufficiency of human grooming improvise an impersonal substitute in the form of a cuddly, fluffy toy, which is carried around and taken to bed as an aid to going sleep. Another substitute is a fuzzy piece of security blanket, so called, pressed against the lips and nose while thumbsucking—also as an aid to going to sleep. Later in infancy and childhood, an animal pet may take on the role of grooming companion.

For the infant, pairbondship with either parent is the developmental prototype of what in later years will metamorphose into pairbondship with a lover. In the lover-lover pairbondship, the various activities of grooming remain the same as in parent-infant pairbondship. The rehearsal in infancy of what will become the practice of maturity is common in nature. One sees it, for example, in the hunting rehearsal play of kittens.

Ideally, parent–child pairbondship entails reciprocal and consistent trustworthiness and reliability. When this ideal is met, the way is paved for its transfer to the subsequent development of a lover–lover pairbondship. By contrast, when trust is betrayed, as it is in abusive parental neglect and violence, which includes abusive punishment, then the way is paved, quite possibly irretrievably, for subsequent pathology in the lover-lover pairbondship (Money, 1992, chap. 21). It may also pathologize the pairbondship of parent and child in the next generation.

Freudian Psychosexual Stages

FREUD COMPLETELY MISSED the proverbial bus with respect to neonatal and infantile grooming, and the psychosexual significance of the cutaneous surface of the entire body. Instead he began his psychosexual schema with the oral cavity, and followed it with the anal orifice, and after that the genital, from which were derived the oral, anal, and genital (or phallic) stages of infantile psychosexual development.

These three stages are Freud's psychosexual counterpart of the Darwinian evolutionary stages of sexual reproduction as formulated by Ernst Haeckel in his gastraea (from Greek, *gaster*, stomach) theory. Marine sponges were Haeckel's research specialty. From them he hypothesized stages in the evolution of sex. In the evolutionary beginning, the primitive organism is asexual and, like an egg in a shell, completely skin covered. It procreates by dividing itself into two cells. The first stage of sexual evolution is characterized by an invagination forming a mouth at one end connected to a blind stomach cavity. In the next stage a second opening or cloaca forms at the distal end, connecting with the stomach. Finally, the male and female sex organs differentiate at the position of the cloaca.

According to a popularized version of gastraea theory at the end of the nineteenth century (Sulloway, 1979), sexual reproduction in vertebrates evolved, by analogy with marine sponges, in three stages. Stage one was ingesting and subdividing. Then came cloacal exchange of germ cells, as in today's birds, and some reptiles. Finally came genital differentiation and the intake of germ cells from and through the genitalia, as in mammals.

According to Haeckel's "biogenetic law" that ontogeny recapitulates phylogeny, the three stages in the phylogenetic evolution of sex are recapitulated in the ontogenetic development of sex in the mammalian embryo. Freud transposed the biogenetic law of recapitulation from embryology to the ontogeny of psychosexual development in infancy and early childhood. He named the three stages of psychosexual development as oral, anal, and genital, respectively. They became a cornerstone of his explanation of the development of psychopathology and of nonpathological development also.

The Freudian explanation of psychopathology was secular. It filled the gap left by the decay of the religious explanation in terms of demon possession. It had immense appeal in an increasingly secularized century until it was given a backseat, which it still occupies, by so-called biological explanations.

Freud's psychosexual stages are not sacrosanct, as they were once wont to be, but are as unsubstantiated as the biogenic law from which they are descended. The oral stage may be reformulated as belonging to the haptic, grooming stage. The anal stage may be reformulated as belonging to the maturation of the phylisms of sphincter control. The genital stage may be reformulated as belonging to the differentiation of gender identity/role. All three stages are subject to developmental overlap. All three are subject to their own hedonic developmental satisfaction, and to pathological interference and obstruction which induces developmental sexological pathology.

Neonatal Circumcision

ONE OF THE MOST brutal contraventions of hedonic grooming in infantile development is neonatal circumcision. Prior to the second half of the nineteenth century, circumcision of boys was not routinely practiced in gentile Europe. The British began circumcising their newborn sons on the basis of the false and untested premise that it would prevent masturbation later in life. The British example, although not adopted in continental Europe, spread to many of the Commonwealth countries and to the United States where it was avidly pursued until, in the twentieth century, the prevalence of neonatal circumcision was close to 100 percent. Nowadays, with a burgeoning anticircumcision movement, the prevalence has fallen to 59.5 percent nationwide, and 35.5 percent in the western states (NOCIRC, 1995).

Although there is no health justification for infantile circumcision (Wallerstein, 1980) now that the antimasturbation rationalization has been discredited, various equally unsubstantiated justifications have surfaced—for example, that the uncircumcised penis exposes the vagina to an increased risk of cancer and of HIV infection; and that an uncircumcised boy will be cosmetically traumatized by looking different than his circumcised friends or his father. The principle of cultural lag gives a more likely explanation of the persistence of neonatal circumcision, and so also does its profitability. Foreskins are used, cost free, for the culture of healthy human cells in tissue culture in research laboratories. In Britain, prevalence of neonatal circumcision fell to nearly zero when it was exempted from reimbursement under the national health scheme.

In conformity with the fallacy that babies do not feel pain, their foreskins are usually surgically removed without anaesthetic. They are, however, traumatized by the procedure, as is evident by their screaming, followed by breath holding, and then a torpor-like state. The surgery itself, like all surgery, is potentially hazardous. The wound is subject to life threatening infection (Cleary and Kohl, 1979) and possible death. Clumsiness and human error may lead to permanent mutilation of the penis, including stricture of the urethral meatus, and iatrogenic hypospadias. Some cases are recorded of removing the foreskin with an overheated electrocautery which cooked the entire structure of the penis so that it dried up and, like an umbilical cord, dropped off.

In tribal and ethnic societies around the world (Gregersen, 1994), circumcision may be performed not on infants but on older boys between the age of seven and prepuberty. Among the aboriginal Australians of the Northern Territory, in coastal Arnhem Land, circumcision is a prepubertal initiation rite of late childhood, and a ceremonial test of masculine bravery. Circumcision precedes the Koran by more than three thousand years, at least. Although it is not mentioned in the Koran, it is performed up to the late prepubertal age on the boys of Islam, and likewise on non-Islamic boys in regions south of the Sahara and in the northeast of Africa. It is in these same Islamic and non-Islamic regions, and in at least one tribe of Amazonian Peru (H. Money, personal communication), that girls also undergo some form of mutilatory genital modification (Lightfoot-Klein, 1989), including infibulation (see chap. 13).

The female procedure is known somewhat euphemistically as female circumcision. The least mutilatory form, known as *sunna*, entails removal of the hood of the clitoris. In modified *sunna*, the clitoris itself is excised along with its hood and the labia majora, and the wound is closed. Pharaonic circumcision is the most severely mutilatory. It entails the total excision of the clitoris, the clitoral hood and labia minora, and the labia majora. The wound is infibulated, that is to say closed so as to heal with only one small opening for urination and menstruation. Subsequently, to permit sexual intercourse, and again in childbirth, the hole will need to be cut larger. The risk of morbidity is high.

Emigration from Islamic and African regions has introduced female circumcision to Europe and America where, increasingly it is made illegal. It has been declared illegal also in some of the home countries. Elsewhere, indigenous feminist organizations demand that it be outlawed, but with limited success as uncircumcised girls are considered unmarriageable. Wealthier families resort to a professionally trained surgeon so as to minimize the risk of morbidity.

The sequelae of circumcision may be insidiously long lasting. From Toronto, Koren and associates (Taddio et al., 1995) reported that neonatally circumcised male babies showed a greater response to pain when vaccinated at age four or six months than did intact baby boys. In another neonatal study, Richards et al. (1976) compared circumcised American and uncircumcised British baby boys. Their data showed that alleged behavioral differences in American boy and girl babies were actually not male/female differences but differences that could be attributed to circumcision alone.

The origin of circumcision of both the male and female genitalia is unknown. The earliest pictorial representation is of the circumcision of two male youths, painted in 2040 B.C. on the wall of the underground tomb of an Egyptian nobleman at Sakhara, near the Great Pyramid of Giza. The actual origin of the practice could date back to the stone age. Its original significance is lost in the mists of history. Possibly it was a substitute for sacrifice of the whole person. Historically, its prevalence was most extensive among peoples of Semitic origin or influence. Today circumcision of either boys or girls is medically and scientifically indefensible, unnecessary and traumatically unbeneficial.

4

Male/Female Dimorphism

Digametic/Apogametic

We human beings are mammals and, like all mammals, we are as a species digametic (from Greek, *di*, twice; + *gamos*, marriage, *gamete*, wife, or *gametes*, husband; + *-ic*), meaning that we originate from two different gametes, one each supplied by the male and female, respectively. Apogametic (from Greek, *apo-*, off, from; + *gametic)* means originating from a single spore, or gamete. Many mosses, ferns, fungi, and microscopic forms of life are apogametic. So also are the parthenogenic lizards of chapter 2.

Not only do we human beings originate digametically from two different gametes, but also we are diecious (from Greek, *dis*, twice; + *oikos*, house) meaning that, like all mammals, we house the gametes in two different structures. The male houses sperms and the female, ova (eggs). Provided no error intervenes, the die is already cast as to which house it will be from the moment of conception when the two gametes, egg and sperm, find each other and fuse into a zygote.

When the sperm and the ovum fuse to form the zygote, they each transport half of the genomic code which carries the blueprint that will program the zygote to develop progressively into an embryo and then a fetus which is either male or female. In the blueprint for female development, there is one X chromosome from the ovum and a second X chromosome from the sperm (figure 1). In the blueprint for male development, the X chromosome from the ovum is matched not by a second X but a smaller Y chromosome (figure 2). If there is a genomic error in the blueprint, as in some cases there is, then the progress of development may not be consistently all female, or all male,

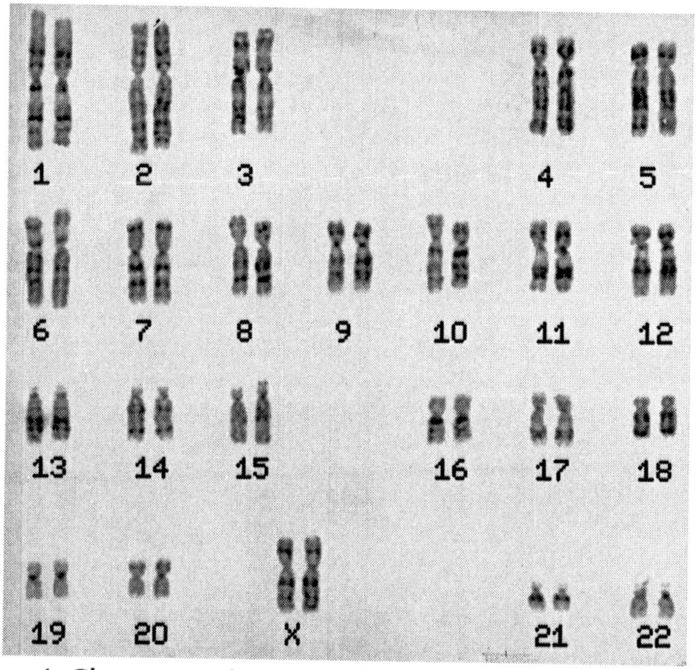

Figure 1. *Chromosome karyotype of a typical female, showing two X chromosomes and no Y (courtesy of D. S. Borgaonkar)*

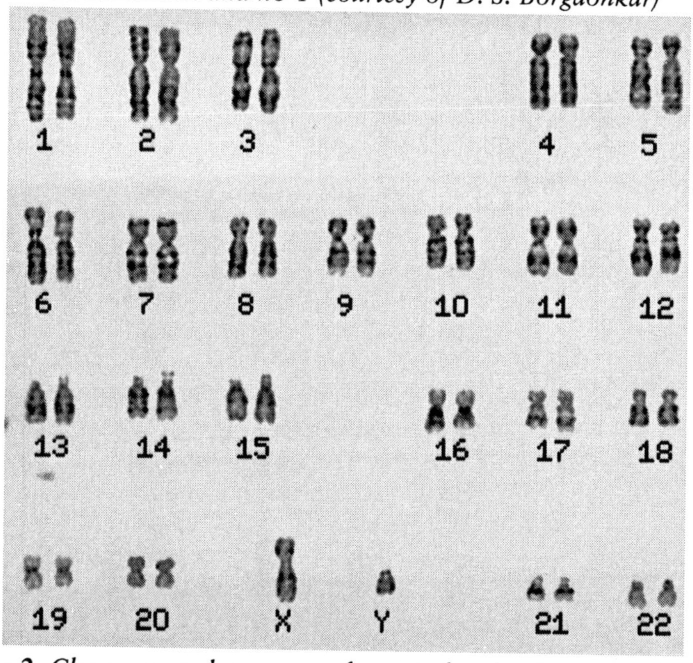

Figure 2. *Chromosome karyotope of a typical male, showing only one X chromosome and a Y (courtesy of D. S. Borgaonkar)*

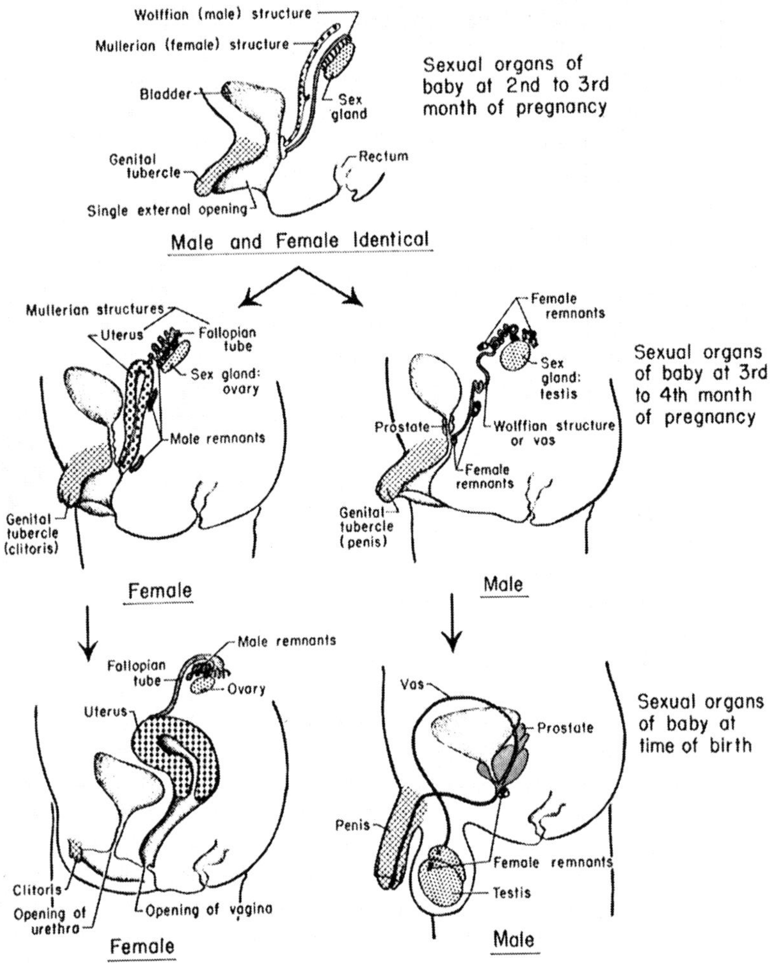

Figure 3. *Bipotentiality and differentiation of the female and male internal genitalia*

respectively. Instead, either male or female development may be incomplete, with something omitted; or development may inconsistently mix male and female (Money, 1994b), which is what happens in cases of birth defect of the sex organs, namely intersexuality or hermaphroditism.

Errors of male/female differentiation that are not coded into the genomic blueprint may be grafted onto it from nongenomic sources such as, for example, toxins transmitted from the mother in the nourishment that reaches the fetus through the blood vessels of the umbilical cord.

In the development of the embryo, switching from male to female differentiation, or from female to male, is not as outlandish as it may seem to be, for the sex organs in their earliest beginnings are bipotential. In other words, they are

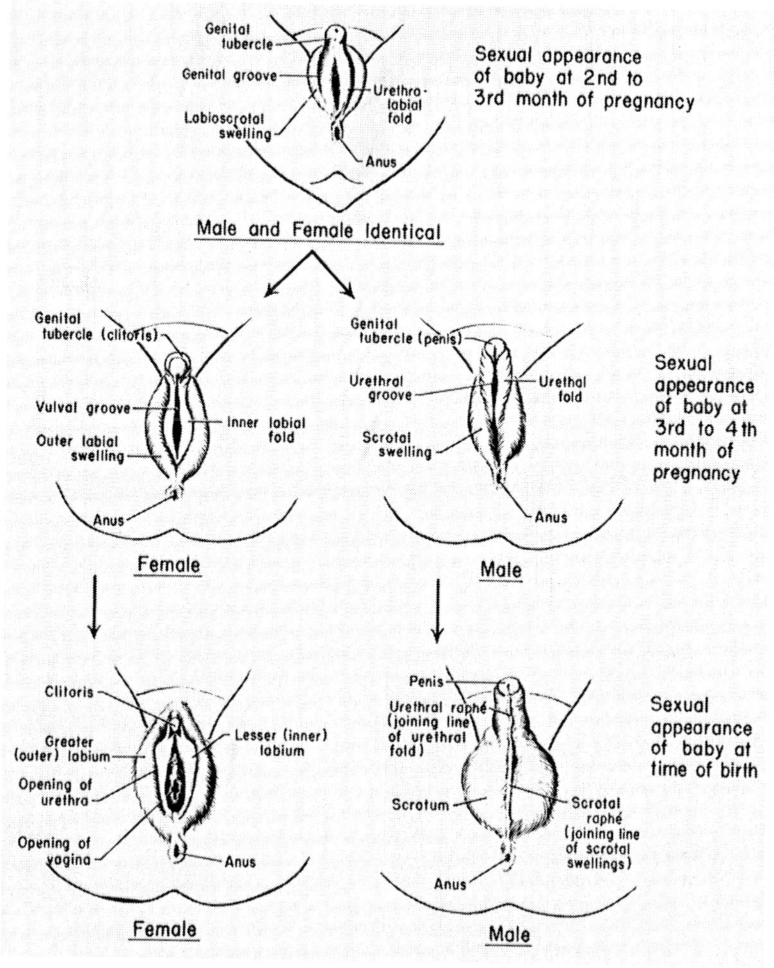

Figure 4 *Bipotentiality and differentiation of the female and male external genitalia*

capable of becoming either feminine or masculine (figures 3, 4). Internally, if the tiny bilateral müllerian ducts fuse and grow, they form the uterus and fallopian tubes, and the pair of wolffian ducts wither away. By contrast, if under the influence of müllerian inhibiting hormone (MIH) from the embryonic testicles, the müllerian ducts wither away, the wolffian ducts respond to testicular androgen and form the internal tubes, the vasa deferentia, that on each side connect the testicle with the penis through which sperms will eventually pass.

Androgen from the fetal testicles directs the penial/clitoral organ to become a penis, not a clitoris. Likewise it directs skin tissue on the left and right to join along the midline in the male so as to form the foreskin, the covering of the shaft of the penis, and the bag of the scrotum. Otherwise, the left and right halves stay separated to form the hood of the clitoris, the labia minora, and the labia majora. Incomplete separation of left and right down the midline creates the same appearance as does incomplete fusion. An incompletely fused, small penis looks the same as a partially fused and enlarged clitoris.

Developmentally, a basic principle of the prenatal male/female differentiation is that the female blueprint takes precedence over the male blueprint. This is the Eve principle. An error in a male blueprint is typically an error of omission and demasculinization. Developmental demasculinization is, in part, the equivalent of feminization. Masculinization is contingent on something being added to what would otherwise be feminizing. This is the Adam principle. An error in a female blueprint is typically an error of inclusion of something masculinizing, and not of defeminization.

An indisputable example of the Eve principle is the type of hermaphroditism known as the androgen insensitivity syndrome (AIS). An AIS baby is born with female external genital anatomy and two internal testes, and has an XY chromosomal pattern. Developmentally, the explanation is that, on the basis of a genomic error, all the cells of the body are resistant to the masculinizing effect of testosterone, the male hormone made by the fetal testes (figure 5).

An indisputable example of the Adam principle is the type of hermaphroditism known as congenital adrenal hyperplasia (CAH). A CAH baby who has the XX chromosomal pattern is born with external genitalia that are masculinized even to the extent of having become a penis and empty scrotum. Developmentally, the explanation is that, on the basis of a genomic error, the adrenocortical glands are programmed to secrete not their proper hormone, cortisol, but a closely related form of masculinizing hormone. This begins at the fetal stage when the precursors of the external genital structures are being differentiated. So, under the influence of adrenocortical androgen, they do not feminize, but masculinize instead (figure 6).

Adam/Eve Principle and Brain

WE ARE A DIECIOUS species not only in the pelvis but also in the sexual brain. For some people, the principle of a male/female brain difference is virtually a sacrilege, so deeply ingrained is the separation of the spiritual and mental from the physical and organic in their way of thinking. For them, brain based biological determinism is incompatible with freedom of choice and moral responsibility. Except for the male and female roles in the actuality of procreation, such people reject the maxim that biology is destiny with respect to male/female differences.

Dissent notwithstanding, it is impossible to eradicate the evidence of brain science that there are male/female brain differences. It is still a very young science. Its experimental research is predominantly with animals, it being ethically forbidden to impose contrived experiments on human beings. Human

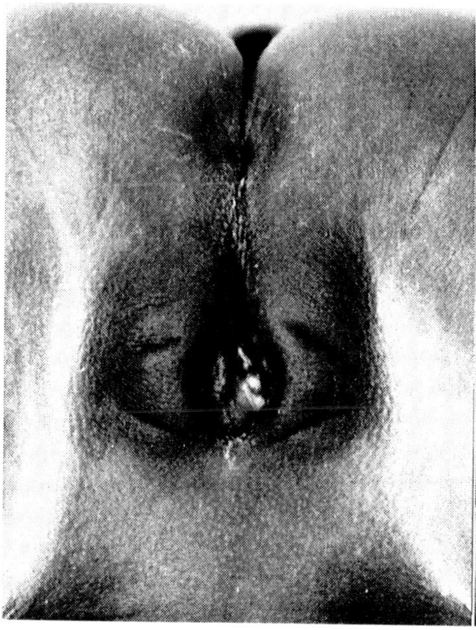

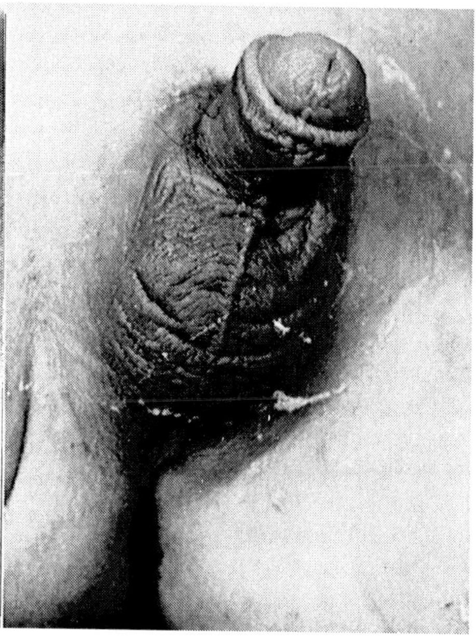

Figure 5. *The Eve principle as represented in the external sex organs in a case of 46, XY androgen insensitivity syndrome (AIS).*

Figure 6. *The Adam principle as represented in the external sex organs in a case of 46, XX congenital adrenal hyperplasia (CAH).*

data come from observations of so-called experiments of nature, namely sexual syndromes such as hermaphroditism.

Animal data point to the hypothalamus as a region of major significance for male/female difference in the regulation of mating and breeding. The anterior hypothalamus regulates the performance of mating, and the posterior hypothalamus the hormones of breeding. The pituitary is adjacent to the posterior hypothalamus the cells of which secrete releaser hormones (RH) that in turn instruct the pituitary to release its tropic hormones. The pituitary's sex tropic hormones are follicle stimulating hormone (FSH) and luteinizing hormone (LH). In females, the cycle of FSH and LH regulates the ovarian cycle of the female hormones, estrogen and progesterone, which together regulate the cycle of ovulation with, in subprimate mammals, the cycle of being in heat, and in primates the cycle of the menses. In males, FSH and LH are not cyclic but constant. They regulate the production of male hormone, testosterone, in the Leydig cells of the testes, and of sperms in the spermatic tubules of the testes. The hormones from the ovaries and the testicles close the loop between the hypothalamus, the pituitary gland, and themselves by having a feedback effect on the hypothalamus.

Neuroanatomical discoveries of human male/female differences in the dimensions and connections of nerve-cell clusters of brain nuclei are of recent vintage (reviewed in Allen et al., 1989; Hopkin, 1995; Nottebohm and

Arnold, 1976; Zhou et al, 1995). Whether or not these structural differences correlate functionally with behavioral and/or mental male/female differences is for the most part conjectural. Conjecture yields to actuality in the case of the anterior hypothalamus, a bilateral structure, where Gorski and colleagues (1978; 1980) discovered the sexually dimorphic nucleus (SDN) of the preoptic area (POA). The SDN/POA is larger in males than in females. Animal data indicate that the size difference correlates with male/female difference in the preliminary courtship, or proceptive phase of genital union and its culmination in male mounting and thrusting and female presentation or lordosis.

Animal experimental data show that the SDN/POA male/female size difference originates prenatally, or in some species, in neonatal infancy. It does so according to the dictates of the Adam principle, namely, that male differentiation requires something added, in this case the male hormone, testosterone. Testosterone is taken up by brain cells where it achieves its masculinizing effect by being converted by an aromatizing enzyme into estradiol. The same hormone may serve to prevent SDN/POA cell shrinkage postpubertally.

In the human species, in male babies between the ages of two weeks and three months, there is a high tide of the androgen, testosterone, in the bloodstream that reaches the level of puberty before it recedes to near zero for the remainder of childhood (Migeon and Forest, 1983). It is possible that some of this testosterone hormone is absorbed into brain cells where, aromatized in the usual way to estradiol, it has a masculinizing effect. Baby girls, who escape this masculinizing effect, may have a higher level of the neurotransmitter, serotonin, in the hypothalamus, as compared with boys in the newborn period. A high level of serotonin, in the case of newborn rats, has been found to correlate with behavioral feminization and demasculinization of mating and other behavior in adulthood (Wilson et al., 1986; 1991; Farabollini et al., 1988).

The idea that masculinizing hormones administered prenatally or neonatally might bring about a permanent female-to-male masculinization not only of the genitalia but also, by way of the brain, of subsequent mating behavior is not new. It dates back to 1912 in Vienna when Eugen Steinach (1940, pp. 239-40) first published his data on "sex reversal" in guinea pigs. William Young and colleagues (Phoenix et al., 1959; Young et al., 1964) updated these experiments and formulated the principle (herein named the Adam principle) that masculinizing hormones have an organizational influence on the sexual pathways and regions of the fetal and neonatal brain, whereas subsequently, at puberty, they have an activational influence on the functioning of these pathways and regions.

The sum total of the animal experimental and human clinical evidence of the Adam principle, to date, points to the conclusion that neuroanatomical cell clusters destined to become either male or female are initially bipotential. Whether they remain bipotential or differentiate as masculine or feminine is predominantly hormone dependent. Differentiation characteristically takes place only once in the course of development. In species that have been studied in the

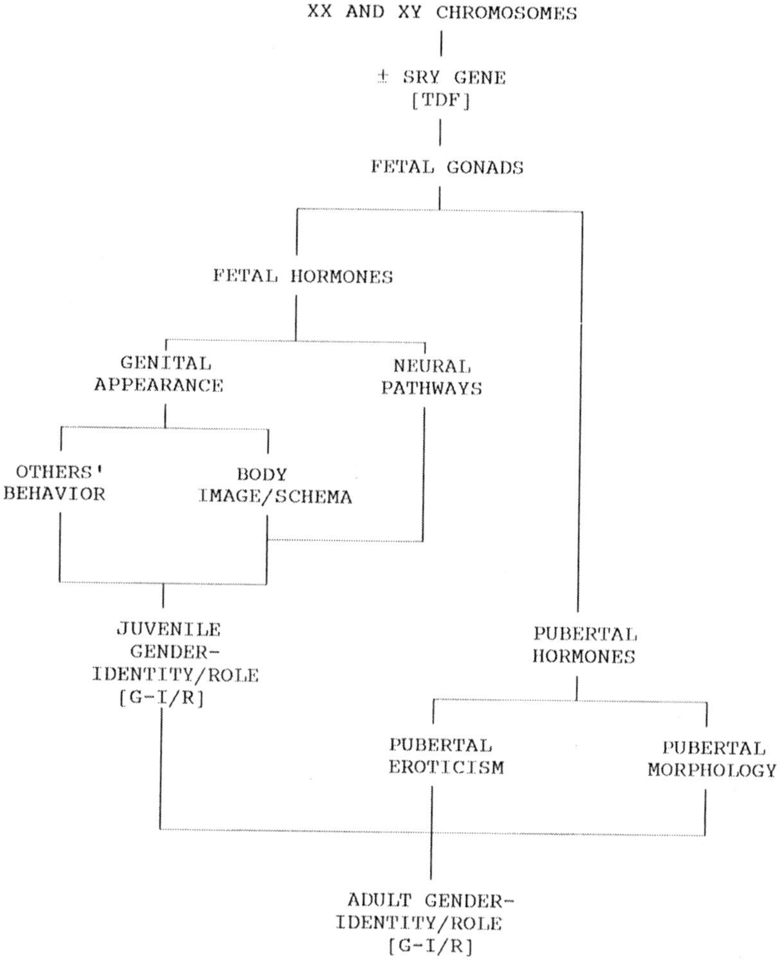

Legend:
SRY=SEX-DETERMINING REGION Y CHROMOSOME
TDF=TESTIS DETERMINING FACTOR

Figure 7. *The multiple and sequential, prenatal and postnatal determinants of masculine versus feminine differentiation from chromosomes to G-I/R*

laboratory, there is typically a sensitive or critical period of prenatal or neonatal life when differentiation takes place, and the outcome is essentially irreversible.

In subprimate laboratory species, once the critical period has been passed, prenatal male/female differentiation of the brain is closer to being finalized than is the case in primates. Correspondingly, the prevalence of masculinity or femininity subsequently in the behavior of courtship and genital union (meeting and mating) is stereotyped, rather as if the animal were a hormonally coded robot—but not totally! Even in subprimates—sheep for example (see chap. 2)—it is possible for social intervention in the juvenile months of life to alter the prenatal hormonal coding instead of reinforcing it. In primates the power of social intervention over prior hormonal coding is even greater than in subprimates, so much so that hormonal coding can be characterized as laying down an unfinished predisposition toward the polarity of masculine or feminine. The outcome of this predisposition will be contingent on what happens socially to reinforce or contravene it. In other words, postnatal social coding of masculine, feminine, or mixed (mediated via the sensorium), is prerequisite to the completion of what was begun prenatally.

In the development of masculinity/femininity in human beings the sequential input of prenatal hormonal and postnatal sensorial coding is graphically illustrated, from conception to maturity, in figure 7. It is particularly well demonstrated in the case of the two hermaphroditic "experiments of nature" already mentioned: AIS (androgen insensitivity syndrome) and CAH (congenital adrenal hyperplasia).

Experiment of Nature: Eve Principle

THE ANDROGEN INSENSITIVITY syndrome (AIS) is a paradigm of what happens when the Adam principle fails developmentally and the Eve principle takes over from prenatal life onward. The syndrome occurs in family pedigrees. An AIS proband may have affected relatives in three or more generations; namely AIS sisters, AIS maternal aunts, and maternal sisters' AIS daughters. In affected pedigrees, a mother carries the gene for the condition on only one of her pair of X chromosomes. Thus the syndrome is X-linked which means that it is able to develop only if a fused egg and sperm contain a paternal Y chromosome and an affected maternal X chromosome. The normal XY genotype is male. In the AIS genotype, development as a male is vetoed by a gene on the single X syndrome that blocks the cellular use of androgen, the masculinizing hormone. Androgen is not needed in embryonic development until after the testicles are formed and ready to make it. They make also the müllerian inhibiting hormone (MIH) that suppress the growth of the müllerian ducts into a uterus and two fallopian tubes. Thereupon, masculinization comes to a halt, so that the remainder of AIS sexual differentiation is phenotypically female. The external genitalia are female, except that the vaginal cavity is a blind pouch since the cervix and uterus are unformed. Presumably, although it remains to be experimentally demonstrated, brain cells also resist androgenization and so are phenotypically feminized. At birth the baby has all the appearance of a daughter, and so is declared a girl. In some AIS pedigrees there is a shortage of sons, their place being taken by AIS, XY chromosomal daughters. The AIS incidence estimate is one in up to 64,000 XY births.

In the AIS baby, whereas the chromosomal sex, the gonadal sex, and the sex of the internal reproductive anatomy are all three masculinely concordant, they are discordant with the prenatal hormonal sex, the sex of the external reproductive anatomy, and the declared sex from birth onward which are, all three, femininely concordant not only among themselves but also with the sex of rearing and, except for absence of a uterus and menses, with the hormonal sex of puberty. The explanation for pubertal hormonal feminization is that, in the testes, progesterone is converted into testosterone, a portion of which is converted into estrogen. AIS cells are indifferent to testosterone, but not to estrogen of which there is sufficient to induce a feminizing puberty, except for absent or sparse axillary and pubic hair which is androgen dependent.

Except for being deprived of childbearing and, in some cases of being in need of vaginal dilation or surgical vaginoplasty, the romantic and sexuoerotic life, as well as a daily life of AIS womanhood does not systematically differ from that of women picked at random (see chap. 15). The pervasiveness of AIS femininity is concordant with the developmental sexological history. It is presumed that, from fetal life onward, the cells of AIS hypothalamic and related nuclei are androgen resistant and, therefore, are not hormonally masculinized. Thus the AIS baby has a predisposition toward subsequent developmental femininity. This predisposition is reinforced when the baby is declared, named, and registered as a girl, and routinely reared as a girl with no questions asked for as long as fifteen years until failure of the menses leads to a diagnosis of AIS. A diagnosis may be precipitated sooner, if AIS is known in the family pedigree, or if lumps in the labia prove to be testes unable to descend. After adolescent femininization is completed, removal of the intrabdominal or intralabial AIS testes may be recommended as a prophylactic against testicular cancer.

The sequence of concordances that together are responsible for the feminine destiny of an AIS zygote begins prenatally with the feminizing (nonmasculinizing) hormonal sex, which, in turn, is responsible for the feminizing of the external genital morphology and the sex dimorphic regions of the hypothalamus. The postnatal continuation of concordances begins, in conformity with the female external genital morphology, with the announced or assigned sex as female which, in turn, is responsible for the feminizing sex of rearing which, in turn, is confirmed by the morphological and secondary sexual indices of puberty. The one discordance is the sex of the internal reproductive anatomy which precludes fertility, though not parenthood.

The importance of not breaking the continuity of the foregoing concordances is made evident in those very rare instances in which an AIS baby is announced, or as an infant reannounced as a boy on the basis of the erroneous assumption that chromosomal and gonadal sex are the ultimate criteria on which to base the sex of assignment and rearing. Multistaged surgical attempts at phalloplasty notwithstanding, such a child ends up with an external genital morphology that disconfirms his sex of rearing as a boy, as does also his pubertal development with feminine breasts, body shape, voice, and absence of masculine hirsutism. It was such a developmental history that destined one AIS patient to quit his existential failure as a man by committing suicide. He wrote that he was incapable of following the example of his AIS cousin who had undergone reassignment from male to female and who had recommended, in vain, that he do the same (Money, 1991a, chap. 2).

Experiment of Nature: Adam Principle

THE SYNDROME OF congenital adrenal hyperplasia (CAH) is a paradigm of what happens when the Eve principle is superseded by the Adam principle in the course of development from prenatal life onward.

CAH masculinization of an XX conceptus is able to occur only if both parents carry the mutant CYP 21 gene (also known as the 21-hydroxylase gene) which is responsible for the CAH syndrome, when it is located on the p or short arm of not both, but only one of each parent's pair of chromosome 6. Such parents are said to be heterozygous or "hidden" carriers of the mutant CYP 21 gene. They do not themselves have any CAH symptoms. When they reproduce, however, there is a one in four chance that the sperm and the egg that fuse to become a conceptus each will carry a number 6 chromosome on which is located the mutant 21-hydroxylase gene. Then the offspring will be said to be homozygous for the mutant gene, and to have the CAH syndrome. The estimated incidence of homozygosity varies regionally in accordance with the statistics of inbreeding. In an isolated inbred community of Yupik Eskimos in Alaska, the CAH incidence was 1 per 282 live births, half chromosomally XX (female) and half XY (male). In the French overseas department of Reunion, the incidence of CAH was 1:2,141 live births. International statistics indicate an estimated overall incidence of 1:15,000 live births (Pang et al., 1988).

The normal 21-hydroxylase gene carries the code for the production of the enzyme, 21-hydroxylase, which instructs the adrenocortical glands to release their proper hormone, cortisol. The mutant 21-hydroxylase gene instructs the adrenocortical glands to release a precursor hormone, androsterone, which can be converted into the masculinizing hormones, testosterone, and dihydrotestosterone, by intracellular enzymes in various parts of the body, notably in the liver, adipose tissue, skin and gonads.

Adrenocortical androgens are the hormones responsible, from fetal life onward, for switching XX/CAH development from that of Eve to that of Adam. The switch is thrown at about the eighth week of gestation which is when the external genitals begin to differentiate from their bipotential stage into male or female. Prior to that, in the absence of the Adam principle, the ovaries have differentiated and müllerian ducts have proliferated into the fallopian tubes, uterus, cervix, and cervical part of the vagina. Then masculinizing takes over. What would otherwise be a clitoris becomes a clitoridean phallus, or even an anatomical penis with its urethra formed by the fusion of what would have been the labia minora. The fusion of what would have been the labia majora forms an empty scrotum. The vaginal opening is internal, near the neck of the bladder. This is the most extreme degree of XX/CAH masculinization. Lesser degrees are more prevalent. In them the phallus looks like an enlarged clitoris above the urinary orifice, with partial fusion of the labia majora. The vaginal opening is internal and not visible from the outside.

Regardless of the degree of masculinization of the external genitalia, from their appearance alone it is not possible at birth to establish the XX/CAH diagnosis. A differential diagnostic workup is indicated if the genitals look malformed, and/or in the event of an acute adrenal crisis secondary to a deficiency of aldosterone, the adrenocortical salt-regulating hormone. The mortality rate is high in CAH babies whose adrenocortical hormonal error is not corrected by cortisol replacement therapy. In untreated survivors, adrenocortical masculinization continues postnatally. It accelerates morphological growth and induces a very early onset of puberty, as early as the second year of life. The pubertal changes are androgenic and masculinizing, not feminizing.

The play and activities of XX/CAH infants and young children are characterized by indifference to dolls and maternal rehearsal play, and vigorous kinetic energy expenditure that in girls is called tomboyism. The romantic and sexuoerotic life as well as the daily life of XX/CAH adolescents and adults is contingent in part on their prenatal history of androgenization, in part on their personal history of sex assignment and rearing, and in part on their clinical history of the efficacy of surgical and hormonal case management.

Cortisol was a newly synthesized and not yet marketed hormone when, in January, 1950, it was discovered to be effective in suppressing the masculinizing hormone of CAH. Prior to 1950, there were some adolescent and adult XX/CAH untreated survivors who were extremely virilized whether living as women or men. More such virilized women than men maintained contact with hospital clinics.

CAH babies diagnosed since 1950 have been treated with cortisol to prevent a salt-losing crisis and to suppress continuing postnatal masculinization. Upon diagnosis the prevailing pediatric policy, neonatally, is to announce or reannounce the baby's sex of assignment as female, and to regulate the hormonal therapy and perform genital reconstructive surgery in conformity with the rearing as a girl. The rationale for this practice is that it preserves the prenatal female concordance between chromosomal sex, gonadal sex, and the sex of the internal reproductive organs, and promises the possibility of reproductive fertility. With the help of hormonal (cortisol) replacement therapy to suppress adrenocortical androgen and release ovarian hormones, puberty is concordantly female, and likewise the hormones of pregnancy, should the woman plan to have a baby.

Although treatment with cortisol suppresses further masculinization, it does not reverse that which has already taken place. Thus, to the extent that masculinization of hypothalamic and related brain nuclei may have taken place in prenatal and neonatal life, it is not reversible.

The romantic and sexuoerotic life in XX/CAH adolescents raised as girls is slow to manifest itself in teenage. After the delay, it is revealed as heterosexually oriented in imagery and practice in about 50% of cases. Among the remaining 50%, it is bisexually oriented in imagery, if not in practice, in two thirds of the cases, and in the other third the orientation is exclusively lesbian (Money et al., 1984; Dittman et al., 1992). These percentages are not fixed, as even in their twenties some subjects are quite reticent in self-disclosure. These data are similar to those from XX/CAH women who, prior to 1950, had reached adulthood heavily masculinized (Ehrhardt et al., 1968), though in that earlier era of no treatment self-disclosure as exclusively lesbian was nil.

A followup on the fertility of eighty adult XX/CAH women from the same clinic as those studied by Money and colleagues was reported by Mulaikal et al. (1987). The full sample was subdivided into 40 with simple virilizing CAH uncomplicated by salt loss, and 40 with salt loss.

> Among the 40 women with the simple virilizing form, 7 (17.5%) had an inadequate introitus (only 2% in normal women), 12 (30%) reported no sexual activity (about 5% in the general population), and 50% never married (10% in American women). Among the 40 women with the salt-losing form, 21 (52%) had an inadequate introitus, 18 (45%) reported no sexual activity, 13 (33%) had abnormal menses, and 35 (87.5%) never married.
>
> Considering the 40 subjects (25 with simple virilization and 15 with salt loss) who had an adequate introitus and any reported heterosexual activity, the fertility rate was 60% in the simple virilizing form and 7% in the salt-losing form (Migeon and Donohoue, 1994, pp. 785-86).

XX/CAH cases with clitoral hypertrophy or a fully formed clitoridean penis and male sex assignment, rearing, and clinical management are few. The number of published cases is still fewer. However, there are enough data to show that the romantic and sexual life of XX/CAH men is not inhibited or delayed. They are heterosexually oriented toward normal women who respond to them as to normal men (see chap. 15). They are lacking in bisexual or homosexual orientation (Money, 1970a; Money and Ehrhardt, 1994, chap. 8; Money and Daléry, 1976). Devoid of testes, XX/CAH men are infertile.

In two cases in which the genitalia and the sex of assignment were ambiguous, there was a sex reassignment at age twelve, one from boy to girl, the other from girl to boy. In the latter case, the boy was heterosexually oriented but subsequently a loner without a partner. In the former case, the girl was subsequently bisexually active for a time, and eventually lesbian only (Money, 1991a, chap. 9), until she died in the HIV/AIDS epidemic.

In the history of XX/CAH manhood, the prenatal developmental stages of the phenotype change from being concordantly female to being concordantly male after masculinizing adrenocortical hormones take control. They masculinize the external genitalia and, presumably, the hypothalamic and related brain nuclei. The postnatal stages of differentiation continue to be concordantly male when the sex of assignment, the sex of rearing, and the clinical management also are male. Concordance continues with a masculine boyhood socially, and a masculine erotosexual orientation in adolescence and adulthood.

By contrast, in the history of XX/CAH womanhood, the masculinizing adrenocortical hormone of fetal life breaks the concordance of the feminization that preceded it and that will be resumed if the sex of assignment and rearing are female, and if the clinical case management is efficaciously feminizing. These feminizing concordances are at odds with the hormonally induced prenatal masculinization of the external genitalia, and the presumed masculinization of the hypothalamic and related brain nuclei. They may also be deemed discordant with a juvenile history of tomboyism, though arguably so, and likewise with a history of lesbian or bisexual orientation, and a history of not marrying or not having a male sexual partner. The low rate of fertility is also not concordant with standard feminization.

In the XX/CAH babies born with a penis, greater developmental concordance is achieved when the sex of assignment is male rather than female. Male assignment is concordant with the masculinization that began with fetal hormonal sex and will continue with a male sex of rearing and clinical management as a male. Masculine developmental concordance is compromised when, instead of a fully differentiated penis and empty scrotum, there is a malformed clitoridean phallus too small to be adequately reconstructed as a fully functional penis.

Despite the lesser degree of concordance when the XX/CAH sex of assignment is female and discordant with the fetal hormonal history of masculinization, it is possible for assignment and rearing as a girl, together with concordant case management, to be concordant in adulthood with an exclusively heterosexual orientation. Thus, it appears that in some individuals sensorial and social coding as female overrides the masculinizing prenatal hormonal coding and prevents it from being autonomous as a determinant of sexuoerotic orientation. If hormonal and social coding are concordantly masculine, however, then masculine sexuoerotic development follows suit without obstacle.

This principle of concordance applies not only to the XX/CAH syndrome, but to the androgen insensitivity syndrome also—to the Adam principle and the Eve principle equally. This is the principle of brain coding. It specifies that insofar as the prenatal or neonatal brain is coded as masculine or feminine, its coding is mediated by early input from steroidal sex hormones. Primordial feminization is hormonally converted to masculinization. Postnatal coding is mediated by sensory brain input generated by the masculine or feminine dichotomies of the social environment. Concordance between prenatal and postnatal input, though not always attainable in cases of hermaphroditism, is the ideal.

It is possible to envisage comparative experiment-of-nature data on demasculinizing the XX/CAH brain by diagnosing and treating CAH in utero, before fetal masculinization takes place. An early version of such an intervention has already been attempted (Migeon and Donohoue, 1994, p. 782). There is no corresponding intervention for the androgen insensitivity syndrome.

The Adam principle and the Eve principle apply to the development of ordinary males and females, respectively, from fetal life onward. It is from atypical syndromes, however, that their functions are highlighted and more readily appreciated.

5

Genital Discovery

Self-Discovery

Information between the brain and the neural periphery travels both ways, back and forth. The brain is where information is coded, coordinated, and stored. Some coding is phylogenetic, by which is meant that it is species determined and not in need of being learned by experience or practice. Urination and defecation in early infancy are examples. By contrast, a large part of ontogenetic coding does need to be learned and requires personal experience and practice. For example, in later infancy, after sphincter control has matured, the personal hygiene and the where and when of urination and defecation are learned in conformity with family and community customs.

Discovery and naming of limbs and organs of the body, although it has no fixed onset, generally begins in the second year of life. Discovery of the genitalia is multipartite. It comprises cutaneous proprioceptive sensory imagery that the genitalia themselves generate; haptic (tactual) perceptual imagery from the genitals and from the hand that fondles them or the thighs that squeeze them; and visual imagery of the hands and the genitalia when they are not covered. From these sources, the mind and the brain in synchrony (the mindbrain) incorporate the genitalia into the body image.

The extent of the experience and practice that goes into the incorporation of the genitals into the body image is culturally contingent on the extent to which the sexual ideology of a society, or of a particular family or community, prescribes or proscribes infantile nudity for boys, or girls, or both. In a society that uses diapers, infants have limited opportunity to touch and see their own genitalia, to observe those of others, or to be themselves observed. Opportunities are restricted to times of diapering and of bathing. If there are siblings, they may share the bathtub, or neighbors may share a tradition of infantile nudity at the poolside, or on the beach.

Unswaddled and freed from the constraints of clothing, babies kick and thrust with sounds of glee. Their hands reach up to touch the face, or down to touch the toes or thighs. Either spontaneously or in response to the cutaneous stimulation of being washed or diaper changed, the fingers may rub, stretch, or squeeze in the crotch area—hedonically, according to the accompanying smiling and cooing of contentment. The fingers do not linger long, and there is no evidence of the concentration on and paroxysmal ending of masturbation as ordinarily defined (Kleeman, 1975). Colloquially it is referred to not as masturbation but as scratching an itch or fiddling with oneself.

Fiddling with oneself is sufficiently casual and transient as to not be troublesome in public. It does not require treatment. It is sufficiently prevalent that it is rated as statistically normal, with only a minority of infants never doing it, and at the other extreme a minority unable to quit doing it recurrently and fixatedly, even in public. The statistical norm is based on numbers and percentages, and differs from the ideological norm that, no matter how capricious and arbitrary, is based on the authority of those who possess the power of enforcement. A persistent fixation on genital stimulation that is uncontrollably recurrent in public is beyond not only the ideological norm but the statistical norm also.

An early infantile history of a persistent, uncontrollable fixation on genital stimulation is rare. In later infancy it is rare also, though it may be self-originated as compensation for a history of insufficient infantile grooming, poor pairbondedness, sensory deprivation, excessive social isolation, social neglect, and surreptitious child abuse. It is encountered in children who have been institutionalized for mental retardation and who receive insufficient personalized attention. It is encountered also in children whose parent-child pairbonding has been severely ruptured. The mother may be pathologically depressed or in some other way rendered incapable of adequately nurturing her infant child.

As a social problem, episodic, nonfixated genital stimulation by rhythmic rubbing, rocking, thigh squeezing while lying on, say, a cushion, may be reported by preschool and kindergarten teachers. It may occur in children, mostly girls, without a history of deprivation and neglect. In the case of a four year old girl, Routh and Schroeder (1981) used a reward system to change the location of this type of absent-minded genital self-stimulation from the living room, while watching television, to the privacy of the bedroom. It appeared to involve, if not orgasmic culmination, then hedonic arousal. The practice may be self-originated and, like thumb-sucking or sucking a comforter, eventually self-limiting. It may also begin as an extension of cutaneous grooming that incorporates genital grooming with hedonic arousal. Genital grooming is said to have been formerly practiced by nursemaids as effective in calming crying and distress, and getting children to go to sleep—a practice that would today be legally defined as sexual molestation or abuse.

In the very literal sense, nonmanual genital self-stimulation by pressing or rubbing in infancy or early childhood is not masturbation, insofar as the hands are not involved. Etymologically, masturbation is derived from Latin, *manus*, hand, and *stuprare*, to defile. Genital stimulation by thigh pressing, squeezing, or rubbing against an external surface like a mattress, pillow, or post, without using manual manipulation ought to have a name of its own, like compressive genitalism.

Genital Paroxysm of Infancy

COMPRESSIVE GENITALISM may be manifested in a hitherto unnamed syndrome, namely genital paroxysm of infancy (Money, 1996). Under the title of "Masturbation in infants," Bakwin (1952) reported three female cases (one with a mildly affected younger sister) less than one year of age. He equated his observations with those which G.F. Still, a British pediatrician, had reported in his textbook of the *Common Disorders and Diseases of Childhood* (1915).

In Still's era, masturbation was still widely considered a sexological pathology as it had been in 1909 when Albert Moll published in German his volume on *The Sexual Life of the Child*. Case 15 was that of a girl who stimulated her sexual organs "by means of rubbing movements of the crossed thighs." Her mother had noticed rocking movements associated with a fixed stare which aroused her suspicion that sexual orgasm had occurred. The girl was followed until age nine. Mechanical methods of intervention met with no success. By age eighteen there were no residual symptoms and the girl was academically a diligent scholar.

In 1973 Bakwin published a followup of his cases under the title of "Erotic feelings in infants and young children." He summarized his observations:

> Masturbation was accomplished by friction of the thighs, rubbing the body against an object, or by manipulation. This was accompanied by grunting and flushing and progressed to what appeared to be an orgasm, followed by general relaxation, pallor, sweating, and sometimes deep sleep.

By categorizing his patients' strange behavior as masturbation, Bakwin was able to disqualify it as pathology in need of treatment. In two cases it went into spontaneous remission before age five, and in one of these two cases the girl was followed until she became a medical student.

Bakwin's type of so-called masturbation has been considered in the differential diagnosis of epilepsy in several papers published since 1975 (Livingston et al., 1975; Bradley, 1985; Fleisher and Morrison, 1990; Mendelsohn et al., 1992; Wulff et al., 1992).

Livingston et al. (1975) published a report on "Masturbation simulating epilepsy" in which the mother of a seven year old girl described a history of spells since age 3 years 4 months as follows:

> During the rocking movements, the hands are kept tightly between her thighs. She lies on her abdomen, stiffens her legs, and rocks. After a few minutes, her eyes would stare and she would sweat. Sometimes she would be drowsy after the spell. When we see her during a spell, she continues to rock. We are able to communicate with her, but she prefers not to be disturbed by us.

When the symptoms first appeared, the girl had undergone an extensive diagnostic workup with a discharge diagnosis of seizure disorder of undetermined cause. By age seven, she had not responded to anticonvulsant medication. A second diagnostic workup resulted in a revised diagnosis of masturbation. However, Livingston et al. did point out that the same set of symptoms, namely, recurrent attacks of staring, stiffness, and rocking movements with onset between birth and age two (they may have added in girls), may be attributed to either masturbation or epilepsy. There was no followup on the outcome of their case.

The phenomenology described by Bakwin and by Livingston et al. applies transculturally to cases reported from Denmark and Israel. Wulff et al. (1992) reported two Danish cases, summarized as follows:

> Two infants, one girl, 5 months old, and one boy, 6 months old, presented with rhythmic and sustained motor activities of a stereotyped nature accompanied by moaning and grunting, facial flushing and altered awareness. The episodes occurred frequently and were initially believed to be epileptic. Normal electroencephalograms during the fits, lack of response to antiepileptic medication given to one child and careful reviewing of videotape recordings, enabled us eventually to diagnose the 'seizure-like' episodes as masturbatory activity.

Mendelsohn et al. (1992) reported in Hebrew the case of an Israeli girl with a mentally retarded cousin who had "infantile spasms." Their English language summary follows.

> We describe a 7-month-old girl referred for evaluation of a convulsive disorder. The tentative diagnosis of epilepsy was based on what were apparently paroxysmal events which occurred many times during a day. A cousin had suffered from infantile spasms and is mentally retarded. The episodic "attacks" in our patient consisted of sudden rhythmic body movements, crossing of thighs, altered awareness, glassy stare and profuse sweating. While the attacks subsided spontaneously, they could easily be aborted by changing the infant to a sitting position or by picking it up and holding it, when it would revert to completely normal behavior. A detailed history and personal observation of the "attacks" made it clear that they were really physical manifestations of masturbation. The diagnosis of epilepsy was therefore discarded. Awareness of masturbation in infants is

> essential for establishing the correct diagnosis, and spares infants and families many superfluous investigations and the anxiety associated with a diagnosis of convulsive disorder in children.

Fleisher and Morrison (1990) extend the differential diagnosis to include abdominal pain. They present five cases and include photographic illustrations of the bizarre posturings that are quite atypical of ordinary masturbation. One case in particular illustrates the iatrogenic damage that can be the sequel to misdiagnosis. The five cases share twelve features in common, as follows:

> (1) All were girls younger than 3 years of age. (2) The events began after 2 months of age. (3) The posturing was stereotyped and involved tightening of the thighs or mechanical pressure applied to the suprapubic or pubic area, or both. (4) The episodes were accompanied by intermittent quiet grunting, irregular breathing, facial flushing, and diaphoresis. (5) The episodes lasted for less than a minute to several hours. (6) There was no alteration of consciousness. (7) Physical examination findings were negative except for surgical scars or minor irritations of the perineal region in three patients. (8) There was no evidence of sexual abuse. (9) The episodes invariably caused parental alarm. (10) The behavior was mistakenly attributed to abdominal pain or seizures by parents and physicians. (11) Physicians who had not previously recognized children with this behavior often ordered unnecessary diagnostic tests and thus exacerbated parental concern about the episodes. (12) The events disappeared in time without medication or surgical treatment.

Diverse in their origins and dates, the foregoing reports are clearly about the same syndrome first recognized by Still, Moll, and Bakwin. Its etiology continues to be a mystery, and so does its absence in boys. Its female specificity justifies a hypothetical conjecture that it may be hormone related—perhaps in some way to the postnatal withdrawal of maternal hormones. Its prevalence remains unknown. It may have contributed to sexological misconceptions about masturbation and orgasm in infancy, up to the age of five.

Quite apart from genital paroxysm of infancy, nonmanual masturbation in girls raises an unanswered question, namely whether the ultimate outcome of prepubertal masturbation is orgasmic enhancement in adulthood. It is possible that orgasm, like many other skills, should be practiced to become perfect, and that in girls, if not boys, the earlier the beginning, the higher the ultimate achievement. In most boys, after they have reached the age of ejaculation, orgasm is readily achieved, whereas there is no corresponding milestone in girls' development.

In boys before puberty a nonejaculatory experience resembling a dry-run orgasm in men is an ostensible though arguable possibility (Kinsey et al., 1948, pp. 175-77). Convincing data are lacking. Direct observation and measurement are not legally permitted. Data on very young male infants are too few to be trustworthy, although it has been claimed that something which to an observer looks orgasmic may occur (Kinsey et al., 1948, pp. 177-78). Anecdotal information from boys who have been the partner of an older male pedophile, and from the pedophile also, suggests the proposition that there may be some kind of climactic build up, but that it is not the same as in the first ejaculatory orgasm. This proposition gains further support from males born without testicles or with defective testicles and who do not receive hormone replacement therapy with testosterone until well beyond the normal age of puberty. If they have experienced a climactic feeling before the hormone kicks in, it differs from the feeling of orgasm after the hormone has kicked in and produces ejaculatory fluid (Money, 1961a).

Show Me

In a tribal village where infants and young children have ample opportunity to see one another naked, they know, without prurience or prudery, the basic anatomical difference between boys and girls at a very early age. By contrast, in prudish Western households, there are boys and girls, especially those without siblings, who may not see the genitalia of a naked person in life or in a picture until the third or fourth year of life when they and their agemates play "show me" games. By showing and seeing, they get confirmation of their own genital sex, and of its difference from that of the other sex. Their discovery is legitimized when they display their genitalia to older people, as if for approval. A little girl does it coyly, lifting her skirt and pirouetting like a ballerina. A little boy shows off his penis, standing up to pee. Genital pride is too important as a precursor of sexual health in adulthood to be subverted by humiliation and punishment in the early years. The alternative is for parents, teachers, and other responsible adults to have been prepared in advance to give a beginner's lesson in the sociology of sex, namely, the difference between public and private sexual behavior and vocabulary. The dividing line is arbitrary, to be sure, but failure to obey the social code brings opprobrium and more trouble than it's worth.

Genital pride begins with knowledge of the visible difference in the appearance of the genitalia, and continues with age-graded and honest knowledge of the irreducibility of their procreative role as masculine or feminine, respectively. Boys and girls both need to know that beyond the visible exterior of the female vulva lies the clitoris, the vagina (baby canal) and the uterus (baby nest) in which the baby egg grows into a baby. They both need to know also the role of the penis in pumping sperms (only one winner!) into the vagina to rendezvous with the egg.

Secure in their knowledge of what is irreducible in masculinity and femininity, boys and girls are freed from enslavement to the arbitrary conventions and stereotypes of what is masculine and what is feminine. Authentic, age-graded knowledge of sexual intercourse, with no beating about the bush, gives them also the promise of freedom from sexual dysfunctions and disorders in adolescence and adulthood.

One of the pillars of the structure of psychoanalysis is the doctrine of penis envy in the psychosexual development of infant females. As a universal phenomenon applicable to all girls, this theory is no longer adhered to as widely as it once was, through lack of substantiating evidence. As a sporadically occurring phenomenon, penis envy may better be formulated as an outcome of not having sufficient knowledge of the anatomy within the folds of the external vulva to generate the pride of pregnancy power.

Pregnancy envy, the counterpart of penis envy, occurs sporadically in the psychosexual development of young boys. Although transient and not of morbid significance in the majority of cases, it may in some boys be a sign of discordance between the natal sex and the development of a feminal identity. With the persistence of a feminized identity, breast envy may also appear. Breast envy may also occur in growing girls as they compare themselves with older girls and women.

An accurate image of male and female genitalia is particularly significant for children with a history of birth defect of the sex organs. Such defects include undescended testicle(s), micropenis, atresia of the vagina, hypospadias of the penis (with an opening too far back on the underside of the shaft of the penis), epispadias (in either sex, failure of the bladder and the urethra to fuse in the midline), and the genital ambiguity of the various hermaphroditic syndromes. Surgical intervention is required in many, if not all such cases. Surgery is also needed to repair serious neonatal circumcision accidents of which the most severe is complete ablation of the penis by an overheated cauterizing appliance.

Even in early infancy, children may become terror stricken by the sights and smells of a hospital. When older they may misconstrue a former or upcoming genital surgical procedure as a form of genital mutilation. To correct this misconception, they might be guided to inspect a living baby, a three dimensional model, or medical photographs. All three are helpful. In many instances the final stage of genital reconstruction is delayed until after the pubertal increase in size and development of genitalia. Children who have been taken into confidence and understand the rationale of the delay are better able to cope than those who have not.

As they advance in age, children with any kind of genital defect are susceptible to worry, long before puberty, about future coital competency and fertility. Their worry is compounded by the unapproachability of their parents, doctors, or counselors whose obligation it is to open these topics to discussion (Money, 1994b).

Intergenerational Modesty and Revived Seduction Theory

AT THE AGE OF comprehending the genital difference between boys and girls, children are also comparing the differences between themselves and adults. Sons and daughters both know that fathers have voices that are deeper than those of mothers or children, and that fathers either shave or grow a beard or moustache. They are fascinated with watching their fathers shave and their mothers put on makeup, and they sometimes play act at doing the same. In households that are not too prudish, they take notice of breasts and body hair, and wonder why they do not have the same. In families where the father is the only male, small daughters may be fascinated by watching him urinate while standing. They may try to catch hold of the flow with a hand, or the mouth. They may explore the possibility of standing to urinate themselves, which boys do more successfully and proudly.

In most families, the issue of parental nudity means specifically whether or not children will be excluded when parents are dressing and undressing, or while they are under the shower or in the bathtub. The issue does not, of course, arise in societies or communities in which nudity or partial nudity is ideologically acceptable. Today, for example, topless bathing is acceptable for women as well as men and children at some beaches and poolsides. At nudist resorts, total nudity is not an offense against decency, nor is even the skimpiest bikini as beach wear in the West. By contrast, in fundamentalist Islam, the woman's face as well as her body must be covered.

In the psychotherapy professions, there have long been those who, under the influence of psychoanalytic orthodoxy, have disapproved of intergenerational nudity. Although lacking empirical substantiation, their reasoning is that parental nudity feeds into the developing child's oedipal fantasies of seduction—of the boy by his mother, and girl by her father. In orthodox psychoanalytic oedipal theory, seduction is not a parental practice in the literal sense, but is constructed in the child's fantasy and projected onto the parent. In the development of psychoanalytic theory, Freud formulated the oedipal, fantasy version of seduction to replace his earlier literal version, now known as the seduction theory.

The literal version grew out of Freud's collaboration with Joseph Breuer which culminated in the publication of *Studies in Hysteria* (Breuer and Freud, 1895). The next year, in *The Etiology of Hysteria*, Freud (1896) expounded his new theory of the origin of hysteria, attributing it to "infantile sexual scenes" and "sexual intercourse" in childhood. Among the words he used to characterize the sexual scenes, namely, rape, abuse, seduction, attack, assault, aggression, and trauma, seduction gave the new theory its name.

In the mid-eighteen-nineties, Freud was in the throes of a very active period of theory building. By 1897, he had replaced the literal version of seduction theory by the oedipal, fantasy version (Sulloway, 1979, pp. 204-7). Seduction theory, by failing to account for the etiology of neurosis in the absence of childhood sexual seduction, was too constrictive. It could not be universalized, and Freud was searching for a grand, universal theory of psychosexual development. This he realized in his formulation of the universal oedipus complex and its universal fantasy of parental seduction. Literal seduction theory was thrown off center stage where it languished for the best part of a century before it was revived.

Slowly at first, the revival of seduction theory geared up after child abuse, renamed the battered child syndrome, was rediscovered following a century of neglect (Kempe et al., 1980; Williams, 1980; Money, 1991c). It gained momentum with the publication by Jeffrey Masson (1984) of *The Assault on Truth: Freud's Suppression of the Seduction Theory.*

The revival of seduction theory coincided with the rise of victimology, a new specialty for the treatment of posttraumatic stress disorder (PTSD). Among its clientele, victimology included not only victims of physical disaster and war, but also victims of child battering, wife battering, sexual child abuse, and rape. An actual history of sexually abusive victimization in childhood was not invariably recalled and reported, however. In such instances the revival of seduction theory was a godsend, for it postulated that the magnitude of traumatic stress in child sexual abuse might promote a complete repression or dissociation of all memories of what had happened.

Thus the function of therapy would be to retrieve those ostensibly repressed memories and validate them. There is no technique, however, for validating whether the retrieved memories are of fantasies of sexual seduction and abuse, or of an actual history of sexual seduction and abuse. Hence the dangerous possibility of relentlessly questioning and indoctrinating young children to confabulate tales of sexual abuse, including Satanic cult practices, that never took place. Hence also the possibility of having adults in mid life retrieve fictional or added-to memories of events that ostensibly took place in childhood, even as early as at the age of six months (Prendergast, 1995).

In victimology, sexual child abuse is defined overinclusively. Thus to have allowed one's nudity to be seen by one's own child may be conflated into a complaint of sexual seduction and reported to the child sexual abuse authorities—which is what might easily happen in a vindictive divorce and custody battle. If the complaint is pursued by the authorities, it is conceivable that it could be further conflated into an accusation of coercive sexual child abuse.

Whereas such an outcome is, admittedly, not very likely on the basis of family nudity alone, the very possibility creates a Catch-22 dilemma for a parent, especially a father, of being damned if he is excessively prudish, and damned if he isn't. Either way, it's a no win situation for the child, too. The dilemma is worse in the case of a complaint or accusation of cutaneous contact with the child, as in grooming.

Sleeping Arrangements

In addition to being a grooming species by day, human beings are a nesting species by night. There is creature comfort in huddling and cuddling. The safety of the parental bed reassures young children awakened by sickness or night terrors. In overcrowded households, siblings share their sleeping places. Lovers and spouses fall asleep together. Parents have their own bedroom where they sleep together, dress and undress, and where they might uncover their nakedness.

Most children reach adulthood and parenthood without overlap between the pairbonding phylisms for bonding with a child and bonding with a lover or sexual partner. In adulthood, the possibility of their being sexuoerotically aroused by a minor does not exist. They can take a scared or fretful child into the parental bed without anyone needing to be concerned about seduction or erotic fondling. The contemporary revival of seduction theory and its misuse do, however, make parents vulnerable to a false accusation of child sexual abuse, should someone be vengeful enough to confabulate a complaint.

In accordance with the long established sexosophy of our culture, fathers more than mothers are vulnerable to false accusations of parent-child sexual abuse. Thus suspicion is attached to a father, but not a mother whose juvenile child, son or daughter, sleeps with the parent in the same bed.

Occasional bed sharing with either parent need not arouse concern. By contrast, when one parent regularly shares a bed or a room with a son or daughter, as a maneuver to escape from the other parent, then there may be concern, namely, not about the actual sleeping arrangement but about the dispute between the parents responsible for it. The child gets caught in the crossfire as each parent vies for his/her allegiance. This also is a typical Catch-22. The child is damned if he does give allegiance to one parent alone, and excludes the other, and vice versa.

The sexually healthy child has versatility in being able to sleep with both parents, together or singly, as well as to sleep alone, or with siblings or agemates. The pragmatics of sleeping arrangements are dictated as much by economics as by modesty. Transculturally, they vary widely. The world is not a victimologists' global village haunted by American middle class victimology theory.

Discovering Intercourse

ONE CONCERN ABOUT having young children share the parental bedroom is the possibility that they will wake up when the parents are having sexual intercourse. So they share the parental bedroom, if at all, only until old enough to be awake and pay attention to what the parents do in the dark. When families live in overcrowded tenements and rooms, parents may keep sexual intercourse hidden from children by doing it infrequently, noiselessly, and rapidly when the children are ostensibly asleep. The woman is deprived of orgasm. This is what happens in much of overpopulated Asia, and elsewhere.

In bedrooms with doors and locks, as in our own society, parents are able to maintain visual privacy, but not necessarily auditory privacy, so their opportunities for the abandon of unconstrained sexual intercourse are limited. Precautions notwithstanding, it is always possible that a young child will inadvertently walk in on the parents, or if not them, then someone else, in the midst of intercourse. Orthodox psychoanalytic theory makes much of the trauma of an encounter with copulation, the so-called primal scene. The trauma lies not in what children witness, however, as in its being the source of yet another Catch-22: they're damned if they're not told the truth and then tell their friends what they saw, and damned if they are told the truth but dare not break the sexual taboo by sharing their newfound knowledge at school or with best friends. The situation is messy for the parents also. If the child talks to his friends, the parents could end up being reported to the child sexual abuse authorities for indecent behavior involving a minor.

Observing intercourse is one of the multiple occasions that arise in the course of a child's sexual learning when he/she must come to grips with an age-appropriate explanation of the difference between the sexological and sexosophical significance of the same event. Years ago, a well-informed graduate student couple told me of how they dealt with just such a situation involving their six year old son. They referred to what he already knew about making a baby, and said that intercourse was a kind of game for grown-ups, and that it was always played in private. Therefore he should not walk into their room unannounced. In return, they would not interrupt his privacy by entering his room without knocking. Also, sexual intercourse was private family knowledge. To avoid gossip, ridicule, and the meanness of other kids, he should not talk about it in public.

The same balancing of sexological and sexosophical knowledge is appropriate if a child's encounter with intercourse is not live, but in magazines or on videos or late night television programs, or on the Internet. All children need to learn how to live simultaneously in the real world as it exists, and in the ideological version of the world as it might be. That's where enlightened adult guidance comes in handy, but few adults are trained in sexual enlightenment.

Sphincter Control

As already mentioned in chapter 3, the psychoanalytic doctrine of three stages of psychosexual development, namely, oral, anal, and genital, represent Freud's transposition of Haeckel's biogenetic maxim that "ontogeny recapitulates phylogeny," from its embryological to its psychosexual application. In the absence of a postulated anal stage of psychosexual development, the recapitulation hypothesis would not hold up. Substantive evidence, however, as compared with inferential evidence of a specifically anal phase of psychosexual development is lacking. Rather, it is a phase of sphincter development and function popularly known as the stage of toilet training.

Training is a misnomer. The sphincter muscles that control urination and defecation are not trained. They mature at their own rate, usually around the age of two, or later. What is learned is the duration of the interval of urgency between the first warning of the impending loss of sphincter control, and where to go to urinate and defecate. The human species has a phylism for what in other mammalian species, like the familiar cat and dog, or even the rabbit, is known as being housebroken. In other words, children, do not need to be trained to go to a special place of elimination, but they do need to learn what and where those places are. Field animals, like the cow and horse, that cannot be housebroken lack the necessary phylism.

Children experience the hedonic joy of achievement when they pass a developmental milestone. Gaining toilet control is thus a hedonic experience. It fits together with investigating the appearance of urine and feces, one's own and other people's, and with being curious about the orifices from which they come. At the same time there is the achievement of learning the associated vocabulary. This is one of the earliest occasions when children encounter parallel sets of nouns and verbs for the same things, one polite and one impolite. Playfully, they use the impolite words and test the limits of where they may and may not be used. They are also words that can be used as weapons of retaliation, rebellion, revenge, and insult.

Anatomical proximity of the organs of elimination and procreation allows for overlap between sex and elimination. Excessive disgust imparted to the process of elimination may generalize to disgust with the sexual organs and be a handicap in later years. Similarly, excessive zeal in attempting toilet training at too young an age may have negative long-term consequences that affect not only bowel and urinary functions, but sexuoerotic function also.

The conjunction of bowel and sexual function is apparent in the case of excessive zeal and frequency in administering enemas to young children. The volume of the enema fluid may itself stimulate the genital nerves and genital responses, reinforcing cutaneous stimulation of the genital area. The delayed, long-term outcome may be the condition named klismaphilia (Greek, *klusma*, enema + *philos*, loving, dear) in which sexual arousal and orgasm are contingent on being given an enema by one's partner, or on the replay from memory of the imagery of a recent such experience.

Another possible outcome of traumatization associated with the functions of elimination early in life is the condition of being erotically fixated on excrement and/or urine. Coprophilia (Greek, *kopros*, dung, + *-philia*) signifies that sexual arousal and orgasm are contingent on the actuality or memory imagery of being smeared with feces and/or eating them—and correspondingly with urine and urophilia (Greek, *ouron*, urine, + *-philia*).

6

Gendermap Coding

Characteristics of the Gendermap

The gendermap, a template or matrix for masculine and feminine, exists synchronously in the mind and the brain (the mindbrain). Synchronicity of two explanatory theories of gendermaps, one neural and one mental, analogously resembles wave theory and particle theory that in physics are used to explain the same phenomenon. The mind-and-brain explanations of gendermaps, although eventually they should coalesce, do not yet do so.

One's gendermap is defined as a personal developmental representation, schema, or template that exists synchronously in the brain and in the mind, depicting whatever is coded as one's masculinity, femininity, or androgyny. It incorporates whatever is so coded vocationally, educationally, recreationally, sartorially, and legally, as well as in matters of etiquette, personal grooming, body language, and vocal intonation. It invariably incorporates also one's sexuoeroticism as heterosexual, bisexual, or homosexual in orientation, either with or without malfunction or pathology.

At the outset of its development in prenatal life (see chap. 4), the gendermap is bipotential or androgynous. Although it may retain bipotentiality to a greater or lesser degree, and express itself in adulthood as a bisexual gendermap, it is more likely to differentiate from bipotential to monopotential. In adulthood a gendermap is said to be, if not bisexual, then monosexual. If concordant with the natal sex of the external genitalia, a monosexual gendermap is heterosexually oriented, whereas, if discordant, its orientation is homosexual or, to use the less depreciatory term, isosexual.

Isosexual (or homosexual) signifies that, on the criterion of the body morphology and of the external genital anatomy, two partners have the same natal sex, regardless of their chromosomal or gonadal sex. Conversely, heterosexual signifies that they have disparate natal sex. Being heterosexual and engaging in a homosexual act, either once or many times, may be rated as having a history of bisexual performance, which is not the same as being homosexual with a monosexual G-I/R (gender-identity role) that is homosexually oriented. Correspondingly, the same applies to a monosexual homosexual's heterosexual acts.

The earliest phase of gendermap coding from bipotential toward monopotential takes place before birth under the control of steroidal sex hormones that govern the presence or absence of masculinized clusters of brain cells and their connections (see chap. 4). The fetus makes its own steroidal hormones. It also receives hormones from the mother and from the placenta released into the fetal circulation by way of the umbilical cord. Nonsteroidal substances, including some medications and toxins that reach the baby from the mother may also be masculinizing or feminizing, possibly with a delayed action effect on the gendermap.

When a baby is born, the personal precursor form of the gendermap is, like a plant with seedling leaves in place, in the mindbrain and ready to discriminate and assimilate input from a new source, namely the personal sensorial social environment. At each new stage of development, the contours of masculine and feminine already in place in the gendermap exercise a discriminative function as to what will be absorbed, replaced, or analogously with apoptosis (developmentally programmed cell death), discarded at the next stage of sensorial input. The existing configuration of the gendermap determines and puts limits on what it will become. The paradigm that applies here is of development that takes place at a critical period, whereupon it becomes fixated, with no possibility of backtracking. Gendermaps eventually become fixated and strongly resistant to change by known methods of intervention.

Gendermaps, like brainmaps in general, are bipolar. Foodmaps, for example, designate what is included and excluded as edible or inedible, respectively. Age maps designate how a younger person addresses an elder, and vice versa. Similarly, gendermaps designate the polarities of masculine and feminine or, to be more accurate, the polarities of masculine versus nonmasculine, and feminine versus nonfeminine. The criteria of masculine and feminine are in part phyletically universal and in part historically and culturally relativistic or arbitrary.

To conform to the requirements of a masculine gendermap, one must also disconform to the requirements of a feminine gendermap, and vice versa. These two conditions can be met if one experiences at first hand that which is designated as masculine and which as feminine in the family and community. One of the pair then becomes self-designated as mine, and the other nonself-designated as thine (see chaps. 2,15). Without having both mine and thine designated in their gendermaps, males and females in their reciprocal interaction from childhood onward would have no predictability, each of the other.

The designation of what is mine includes personal subjective experiences, and so is more entire than the designation of what is thine. To illustrate: a male is able to claim a more entire knowledge of the experience of male orgasm than a female is able to do, and vice versa. Men and women, even those engaged in sexological research, may assume that the subjective experience of orgasm in males and females is identical, but there are no substantiating data. In the gendermaps of all individuals there are assumptions about the gendermaps of the other sex that are, in variable degree, erroneous and irreconcilable. Inside of the eggshell of our own solipsism, we cannot enter the solipsistic eggshell of another.

Gendermap Transpositions

FROM INFANCY ONWARD, the gendermap may develop consistently to be a facsimile of a societally defined macho stereotype of masculinity or baby-doll stereotype of femininity. Mine and thine are then likely to be clearly demarcated with little or no crossover, even if crossover were the only means of avoiding death at, say, the hands of terrorists.

Characteristics of the male stereotype of two generations ago are exemplified in the cumulative development of a stereotyped gendermap, from birth through college age, in the case of Subject #2283 of the Fels Research Institute's longitudinal study (Kagan and Moss, 1962, pp. 161-63). At age three, the boy had been described as follows.

> In the nursery school Sy was extremely energetic. Even when he was pushing small cars around the floor he seemed to be putting the greatest possible force into it. He talked loudly and accompanied his car and train play with plenty of imitations of engine noises and whistles. Outside he ran around furiously some of the time and played fearlessly on the apparatus. He also played construction games in the sandpile. In the house, he built garages, roads, and usually used blocks in connection with cars and trains.

In day camp, at age seven and a half, he was said to have "combined the aggressiveness, dominance, and competitive gross motor activity that characterize traditional male-role behavior . . . [namely, of being] athletic, competitive, and fearless."

He began dating at age twelve, and going steady and engaging in erotic activity at age sixteen. About his sexual history, he said:

> In my sophomore year I went on a rampage, I guess—I mean, I went out every weekend. For a while, different girls, then I would take out one girl for three or four weeks and then another girl, usually for a semester, once a week or sometimes twice a week if I was dating two girls at the same time.

Before he graduated, although he continued multiple dating, he said he might be in love with a girl he had known for several years, but he was ambivalent about getting engaged.

By contrast with Subject #2283, #2373 consistently developed a nonmacho male gendermap (Kagan and Moss, 1962, pp. 163-65). His nursery school summary at age three described him as:

> a pale, bleached out looking child with blond hair, light blue eyes, very little color in his face, tall, thin and stooping. He lacks compactness and sturdiness of muscle or body build . . . gangling, and did not have good control over his body. . . . Whenever he was stimulated, he overreacted. His body tensed, his face showed some strain, and there were many excess movements.

At age six it was noted that:

> He was picked on a good deal, and much of his behavior invited teasing. When someone turned on him, he became helpless, cried, ran to an adult, or sat with a mute grin.

At age eleven he was described as one who is a loner and daydreamer, fearful of aggression, interested in reading, and avoidant of being on the playground with other boys.

The followup when he was in college, at age twenty, noted that he was:

> tall, thin, and very tense . . . unsure about a career because of excessive doubts over his intellectual ability. He reported much tension and anxiety with girls and a strong reluctance to initiate erotic activity with them. He was afraid that a girl would reject him if he were to become sexually aggressive, and he usually waited for her to initiate any romance. He had never petted with a girl or experienced sexual intercourse.

Although there were girls as well as boys in the Fels study, Kagan and Moss do not give examples of developmental consistency in conforming and nonconforming to the feminine stereotype of the era.

The two schemas, mine and thine, in the gendermap allow for two possibilities other than complete demarcation between them. One possibility is overlap or blending. The outcome of blending masculine and feminine is, in variable degree, androgynine. An androgynine gendermap, if it includes genitopelvic eroticism, is also a bisexual one. Otherwise an androgynine gendermap may be either heterosexual or homosexual in genitopelvic erotic expression.

The second possibility is crossover of the two schemas, from masculine to feminine, or from feminine to masculine, instead of blending. The thine becomes mine. This is the phenomenon that is formally diagnosed in prepuberty as the gender identity disorder of childhood which, in a boy is a fixation on becoming a girl, and in a girl is a fixation on becoming a boy. In the boy, the syndrome is colloquially known as the sissy boy syndrome (Green, 1987). The corresponding term for the girl, the tomboy girl syndrome, is not used, as tomboyism in girls is predominantly considered to be within the normal limits of femininity. The most prevalent long term, postpubertal outcome of the syndrome in boys is a homosexual gendermap without psychopathology (Money and Russo, 1979; 1981; Green, 1987). Green's outcome statistics are based on 44 of the 66 subjects; 22 were lost to followup. When interviewed in adolescence or young adulthood, 33 of the 44 were homosexual or bisexual. One was transexual, none was transvestitic, and the remainder were heterosexual. For the adolescents without interpersonal sexual experience, the ratings were made on imagery and ideation only, whereas for older subjects with actual experience with a partner, that was also included. The most prevalent long term, postpubertal outcome in girls still awaits documentation. According to clinical statistics, the incidence of complete crossover in the prepubertal gendermap of girls is less prevalent than in boys, although that imbalance may be an artifact of sampling.

Identification/Complementation

IF A SONOGRAM, amniocentesis or other sex determination test is done so that the sex of a fetus is known, then the differential treatment of male and female may begin immediately. It is nowhere more evident than in overpopulated areas, as in India and China, where political and economic pressure to reduce a population explosion impinges on family pressure to have a male heir. If abortion is a viable option, the male bias may then be manifested in an elective abortion if the fetus is female.

In the case of a live birth, the gendermap of the parents and other representatives of the social environment preordain that they will provide sensorial input that is different for boys than for girls. Thus there is a two-way feedback loop: a baby has a precursor gendermap with some degree of prenatal tilt toward receiving either masculinizing or feminizing sensorial social input, which having been received strengthens the tilt, which in turn strengthens the next round of masculinizing or feminizing sensorial social input, and so on.

When a baby's sex remains unknown prior to delivery, the most awaited news from the birth attendant is the announcement of whether it is a girl or a boy. Thereupon, without being explicitly aware of it, everyone follows the pink protocol for a girl, and the blue protocol for a boy. They are sure that they are responding to cues given by the baby and that they are not projecting their own pink and blue codifications onto the baby. If, however, the baby is videotaped in unisex yellow clothing, and if experimental subjects are deprived of definitive male/female cues and told that the videotape is of a boy, then they will give descriptions and ratings that conform to the social stereotype of a boy. Conversely, if other subjects are told that the same videotape is of a girl, then they will give responses that stereotype the baby as a girl. The stimuli are the same, but the meaning attributed to them is filtered through the stereotypes in the observers' own gendermaps (Money and Evers, unpublished).

When, instead of watching a videotape, experimental subjects interact with a live baby in yellow unisex clothing, then their own behavior differs in accordance with whether they have been told that the baby is a boy, or a girl, or if its sex has not been declared. Golombok and Fivush (1994) review several of these so-called Baby X studies.

Such studies do not lead to the one-sided conclusion that, beginning as neutral, gendermaps become masculine or feminine solely as a function of social shaping. Instead, they confirm that gendermap formation is a two-way process that combines outgoing stimuli from the baby with incoming stimuli from the social environment, and registers the outcome in the mindbrain. Masculine/feminine characteristics that are culturally arbitrary are developmentally malleable, whereas those that are phyletic and irreducible are culturally accommodated. They are the basis on which, historically, the culture has been formed. One of the characteristics of a gendermap is that it conflates its malleable and its unmalleable components together.

During the second year of life, development of the gendermap gains from a coalition with the development of the native language. Language divides the universe of people into mommies and daddies, grandmothers and grandfathers, aunts and uncles,brothers and sisters, boys and girls, men and women, he and she, him and her, his and hers. In life or in pictures and stories there are cows and bulls, horses and mares, nanny goats and billy goats, hens and roosters, ducks and drakes, lions and lionesses, and so on. Except for a few that are androgynous, proper names too are sex coded. They code one's very identity as masculine or feminine. Unlike one's clothed and concealed genitals, one's name and one's pronouns are a public declaration of one's sex, more constant and more permanent than one's clothing style, haircut, or other insignia of being a boy or girl.

The pronouns he and she designate oneself as being in the same category as, respectively, all others who are he or all others who are she. That designation provides the linguistic basis for identification that is not epicene or androgynous, but is isosexual—identification that is with one or more members of one's own sex.

Identification with a member of no species other than the human species is prerequisite to becoming entirely human. Since all human beings are pronouned either he or she, identification is either masculine or feminine, even if the two become mixed. The special significance of the mother as an identification model is phyletic: irrespective of whether it is a boy or a girl, the baby's neonatal survival is contingent on the pairbondship of the baby with the lactating mother or with a surrogate mother. The father-infant pairbondship, or its substitute, lacks the phyletic feature of lactation. That it exists phyletically, however, is attested to by its ubiquity in societies with cultures that range from virtual stone age to industrial age (Eibl-Eibesfeldt, 1983, 1993).

The models with whom infants identify are not their parents exclusively. As children advance in age, other identification models may be members of the family, the community, and the peer group. The entertainment industry also supplies identification models, especially those actors and cartoon characters who enter children's lives regularly from the television screen.

The opposite of identification is nonidentification, but its reciprocal is complementation. Thus, what the little girl assimilates from identification with her mother or other female as the identification model, she puts into practice with her father or other male as the complementation model. Correspondingly, the little boy's identification models are male, and his complementation models are female. The principles of identification and complementation are contingent each upon the other. One cannot exist without the other. The two principles together account for an equilibrium in what would otherwise be a lopsidedness in the relationship between son and mother and daughter and father, as coded in the gendermap.

In the annals of child development, the principle of complementation has been overlooked almost completely. Instead, small experiments have been devised to test whether, in a contrived situation, infant sons and daughters interact differently with mother and father; and vice versa, and whether mother and father with an infant son or daughter interact differently with the boy and the girl. Mirabile dictu, of course there are differences, even if only in the use of pronouns and nouns, like "be a good girl," or "brave boys don't cry." Regarding other criteria, for example, whether mothers talk to daughters more than sons, or whether boys tolerate separation from their mothers more than girls do, the data indicate that similarities outweigh differences in the way that parents interact with their sons and daughters, especially in the earliest months of life (Moss, 1967; Goldberg and Lewis, 1969).

At this early age, the complementation role of the infant is toward the parent as caregiver, primarily, and except for breast feeding, as a female or male secondarily. From the second year of life onward, however, the infant begins to manifest the differentiation of male and female in its own roles of complementation and identification vis à vis not only the parents, but also their relatives and friends who engage the child's attention with playful approval. Sometime after the second birthday the two roles of identification and complementation become manifested in what may be called the flirtatious stage of infancy.

Flirtatiousness of Infancy

LIKE OTHER STAGES of gendermap development, the flirtatious phase of infancy has no fixed duration. It begins naively and continues with age to become more sophisticated and grown up. Boys and girls both take their cues from the adult world. A girl performs and, with winning ways, charms the man who is the recipient of her attention by throwing his way a newly learned compliment, singing to him a line of a top-ten love-song, or coyly pirouetting for him in a new skirt or other piece of clothing, and so on. A boy, by contrast, is more matter of fact and directive. He takes advantage of an opportunity to play the role of a lady's guide or junior escort.

Initially, for boys as well as girls, the flirtatious playways of infancy and early childhood are directed not at an agemate but at a grown-up, often a visiting relative or family friend who finds time to pay attention to the young one, and who fills the role of romantic complementation model. This person's approbation of the child's flirtatious role endorses the child's developing self-concept of gender constancy. Male/female reciprocality between the small child and the large adult anticipates gender constancy as male or female in subsequent juvenile and adolescent development. Achievement of gender constancy is a major milestone of gendermap development.

The prognostic value of infantile flirtatiousness has clinical significance in the case of children with a diagnosis of intersexuality (hermaphroditism) whose chromosomal and gonadal sex is discordant with the sex of assignment and rearing. The boyishness or girlishness of their early rehearsals of flirtatiousness prognosticates the subsequent masculinity or femininity, respectively, of the sexuoerotic component of their gendermaps and whether its orientation is toward someone of the same or other sex of assignment and rearing (Money, 1991a, chap. 7).

In the case of young children with transposed or partially transposed gendermaps, namely sissy boys and tomboyish girls, there is a void where there should be data collected on site regarding the sex of the parent or other adult who is the recipient of infantile flirtatiousness. The retrospectively recalled biographies of some gay men in psychotherapy (Silverstein, 1981) include early memories of gay sexuoerotic fantasies, but they are dated not from the years of infantile flirtatiousness but from the prepubertal juvenile years of sexual rehearsal play.

The formulation of infantile flirtatiousness as playful rehearsal and as an endorsement of gender constancy is a nonviolent version of what Freud formulated as the patricidal fantasy of the oedipus complex. In the nonviolent version, flirtatiousness may become an overtly stated intention to marry the older person, if he/she will wait long enough. In true oedipal style, this declaration may in rare cases be directed explicitly, and not metaphorically at a parent, if the parent occupies a complementation role. Although not common, it is not unheard of that a boy or girl will express explicitly an intention to marry, or to engage genitally with a parent. The very explicitness of such a statement might come under suspicion as a sign of sexological pathology not only in the child, but also within the household, though not invariably so.

The principle of infantile flirtatiousness as playful rehearsal applies to both boys and girls, whereas the Freudian oedipus complex is poorly applicable to the psychosexual development of girls. The principle of flirtatiousness has an added advantage in that it does not connect psychosexual development with homicide or castration, as does its Freudian counterpart. Theories can be mischief making. To what extent, if any, a century's worth of oedipal theory may have made mischief between today's parents and children remains to be ascertained.

Among those who become complementation models for the gendermaps of growing children, the great majority have no difficulty in dealing with infantile flirtatiousness, per se, and in not conflating it with genitosexual arousal. The converse holds true for infantophiles, who are erotically aroused by very young infants, and by pedophiles, who are erotically aroused by older juveniles up to the age of puberty. For infantophiles and pedophiles the parent-child and lover-lover bonds become fused (see chap. 16). Such fusion is so intensely outlawed in the contemporary sexosophy of our society that it is an exercise in futility to argue the phylogenetic pros and cons of any form of intergenerational cutaneous contact that may possibly be characterized as sexuoerotic. Even in the absence of force and coercion, the sanctions against infantophilia and pedophilia are so severe that they create a traumatizing Catch-22 that is potentially more injurious than nonviolent cutaneous contact per se. For protection against the secondary trauma of this Catch-22, it is necessary for children to be deprived of any affectionate cutaneous contact with someone older, including a parent or grandparent, lest it be socially misconstrued as pedophilic or infantophilic. If paraphilic violence or cruelty is involved, then the issue becomes one of sadism, not simply of age discrepancy.

Wisdom gets lost in the new sexual abuse prevention dogma of "good touch and bad touch." Children do become the victims of cutaneous deprivation (Krivacska, 1990). Even grandparents are known to have become afraid to cuddle or hug their own grandchildren for fear of accusation of sexual abuse. Nursery school and kindergarten teachers disobey the phylism that directs them to hold and comfort a distraught and crying child, lest they too be subject to false accusations of fondling and child sexual abuse.

Infantile flirtatiousness involves not only older complementation models, but also, by the fourth or fifth year, agemates. This is the age of kindergarten boyfriend/girlfriend romances, some shorter lived than others, and some recalled well into adulthood. Some children of this age and older fabricate elaborate fantasies of romance and marriage. Some of them also stage wedding games.

This is the age also of continued interest in bodies, in taboo functions of elimination, and in the forbidden words of elimination and sex (see chap. 5). It is the age of show me: "You show me yours and I'll show you mine." It is the age of comparing one's own body with that of agemates—of worrying about an undescended testis or a protruding clitoris, for example; of wondering why some boys have foreskins and others don't; and of questioning why big people have sexual hair and small people are bare. It is the age of play-acting gender differentiated career roles, which may include the exploration of boy/girl differences in hospital, doctor and nurse play, doing genital examinations and taking rectal temperatures.

Genital/Gender Constancy

ONCE HE, ALWAYS HE. Once she, always she. This is the principle of gender constancy which, for a young child, is not to be taken for granted as self-evident. Gender constancy is a particular example of the more general cognitional principle of object constancy, a principle that requires considerable epistemological sophistication in recognizing similarities in the midst of multiple differences, and in predicting their stability over time. For example, the principle of object constancy requires that a child recognize that a chair is a chair despite its many stylistic and structural transformations, its change from being intact to broken, and its rotational orientation from right to left, front to back, and bottom side up to down.

The principle of object constancy is contradicted by its opposite, the principle of mutability. According to the mutability principle, an object changes its name and significance according to its positional orientation or some other adventitious factor like its place in a sequence. In learning to read, for example, a b rotated becomes a d or p, and the sequence of letters, as in dog and god, changes their meaning. Meaning may change also according to the syntactical positioning of words in sentences.

Recognition of the principle of constancy and continuity from babyhood to adulthood is illustrated in an anecdote regarding a boy nearly three years old. He had not seen a foal before, and had no name for the first one he saw. He called it instead a calf horse. Logically, his concept was correct, even though he lacked the correct term.

He might have extended his concept to include the human species and correctly predicted that children who grow up to be men always have a penis. He may, however, have been incorrect in predicting that children who grow up to be women are those who have not a penis but pubic hair (Conn, 1940). This would be a reasonable conclusion if the boy had never observed or inspected an adult male or juvenile female naked, but had fleetingly glimpsed his mother naked in the bathroom.

In our own society, children may be deprived not only of the developmental evidence of the lifetime constancy of the genitalia as male or female, but also of the universality of their difference from the outset. Thus there is logic to the infantile proposition that a boy can turn into a girl by having the penis wither up and drop off; or conversely that just as a girl can grow breasts, so also may she turn into a boy by sprouting a penis. Some children have such conceptions when young, but easily correct them when properly informed (Conn, 1940). By contrast, children whose gender-identity/role develops to be discordant with their natal sex may maintain these propositions quite insistently. They may pray to God to make a change of genitalia come true (Green and Money, 1960). One's external sex organs as insignia of male or female are, for them, wrongly conceptualized as being in the same category as one's haircut, name, clothing style, or play interests. It may be that such a misconception is formulated by a young child with an advanced capability in conceptual reasoning, but a grossly-deficient and defective data base from which to make alternative formulations. The error regarding genital inconstancy may prove intransigent. In that case, the outcome may be a transposition of gendermap coding of which the most prevalent is from heterosexual to some degree of homosexual (Money and Russo, 1979; 1981; Green, 1987).

Where Babies Come From

MALE/FEMALE CONSTANCY in the development of the gendermap is reinforced by first hand acquaintance with pregnancy as a specific attribute of femininity. When a new baby is expected in the household, even two-year-old members of the household may be cognitively well enough developed to comprehend that the baby grows in the mother's belly, if they are given the information heuristically, in three dimensions, by being allowed to see the mother's pregnant belly, to pat it, and perhaps to feel the baby kicking.

In the mentality of two year olds, three dimensional reality does not translate well into verbal or flat-surface, graphic representations. To explain delivery, even a static anatomical model is not realistic. In the counterculture movement of the sixties and seventies, some children were witness to a home delivery, but the logistics of that arrangement, and the possibility of obstetrical complications, forbid its becoming widespread. Young children must, therefore, make do with the explanation that the baby is born through a birth opening (not the anus and not the navel) in the crotch. With advancing age, this explanation can be expanded and illustrated with pictures, preferably a videotape, of an actual birth.

It requires more than knowing about a mommy's pregnancy to ensure that becoming pregnant will be built into a girl's, but not a boy's gendermap expectancies. If a baby grows in the mother's belly, then by the logic of childhood it could get there by way of what the mother eats. If so, then a father should be able to have a baby, too. The mother's pregnancy does not, by itself alone, guarantee to a two-year-old that a daddy is not able to carry a baby. The missing piece of information is about impregnation, which is exclusively a masculine gendermap expectancy, just as pregnancy is feminine.

It required eons of human evolution on earth before, in 1677 Anton van Leeuwenhoeck, with his newly invented microscope, reported having seen male spermatozoa for the first time ever. Small wonder, therefore, that it is difficult for young children, let alone very young children, to conceptualize sperms, eggs, and fertilization as precursors of pregnancy.

The role of the male in coital union as a precursor of pregnancy is easier for children to grasp. Coital union, like pregnancy, is three dimensional. Dependent on the degree of prudery, it can be demonstrated diagramatically (for older children) or on videotape, or in real life performance. The latter may carry potentially severe penalties for indecency and for contributing to the corruption of a minor. This is one place where science and sexosophy collide in the developed world. In developing countries, where privacy is less secure, children do encounter sexual intercourse at an early age.

Polite and user-friendly vernacular vocabulary is a prerequisite to frankness in providing sex education regarding sexual intercourse. The penis gets stiff so as to fit into the vaginal canal, the sperms are spurted out and embark on a swimming race, three hundred million of them and only one winner. The prize is to join with the egg, of which there is normally only one. Together they start growing into a baby.

More and more scientific details can be added with advancing age, with accompanying photomicrographic video movies—surely one of the wonders of biology! There is always a question of why people do it so often. The answer is that sexual intercourse is synchronous with ecstatic joy, at least for those who gendermaps are in good shape.

One of the items of sex education that is commonly overlooked in the early juvenile years pertains to the paraphernalia of menstrual hygiene used by adult and adolescent female members of the household. Sooner or later children become aware of brand names on packages of tampons or sanitary pads brought home from the drug store or supermarket, and eventually they become curious about their significance. The blood-stained used products, should they come across them, may well arouse not only curiosity, but also anxiety and fantasies of fear and danger regarding their bloody significance.

Children also discover birth control devices used by their parents or other adults in the household and need an explanation of their use and significance. Fathers are not very thorough in keeping condoms hidden from their sons and daughters, and likewise erotic magazines and videos if they have them. Kept in the dark about such items, children may confabulate dangerous and morbid explanations that developmentally distort their own gendermaps. They and their parents and teachers still lack consensus on a user-friendly vocabulary for the unexpurgated explanation of such matters.

Gendermap Rehearsal Play

VARIOUS SUBHUMAN primate species provide animal models for juvenile sexual rehearsal play (see chap. 2) with agemates. Initially the play is with male or female partners indiscriminately, and the positioning is inept. Eventually the roles get sorted out so that males predominantly mount females, and females predominantly present to males who mount them. Thus does heterosexual mating get consolidated in the gendermap.

In rhesus monkeys, study of the outcome of isolation rearing and deprivation of sexual rehearsal play with agemates has demonstrated severely deficient adult mating performance, zero or reduced birthrate, and failure of mother infant bonding (Goldfoot, 1977).

In human children, infantile flirtatiousness merges into the era of juvenile sexual rehearsal play sometime between the ages of five to seven or eight. The variable age of onset reflects, in part, what the culture tolerates or encourages in the play rehearsals of its children. In its earliest manifestations, juvenile sexual rehearsal play will be contingent on what the child already knows or has experienced. Hence playing the roles of doctor, nurse, and patient getting a rectal temperature taking and receiving a genital examination may expand to include genital play that is more explicitly sexuoerotic.

Among preschool children who are already aware of sexual intercourse, the game of playing house, or mothers and fathers, may be inclusive of nightime activities and going to bed. What the parents do in bed may then be enacted, with the game becoming more explicitly genital and erotic. Aboriginal Australian girls in Arnhem Land played a version of this game in groups forbidden to boys. One girl would play the male role by applying a smooth twig to the vulva of another as a penis substitute (Money, unpublished data).

Between ages two and five, girls or boys who have been informed about a mother's pregnancy and can see or palpate her enlarged belly may themselves play at being pregnant by stuffing paper or cloth under their own dress or shirt. The girl is more likely than the boy to win approbation. By age five, if she has also learned about birth, or has older cousins, sisters, or friends to teach her, she may with agemates and a doll play act the obstetrics of delivery. Although the game could expand into genitoerotic play, it is more likely not to. It is a game of maternal, not copulatory rehearsal.

From the ages of five through seven or eight, and from then through the prepubertal juvenile years, the extent to which a boy or girl gets involved in heterosexual or homosexual rehearsal play is contingent on opportunity and on the availability of like-minded partners which, in turn, is contingent, at least in part, on the mores of the tribe or community. In part it is contingent also on personal sexuoerotic history and individuality. Some prepubertal children are indifferent to sexual rehearsal play. Others are ardent practitioners. The difference may reflect what the family and community forbid, encourage, or tolerate.

The extent to which prepubertal boys and girls get involved in heterosexual versus homosexual rehearsal play is contingent also on whether girls and boys are segregated educationally and/or institutionally. Whereas at school their reputations would be at risk if they were seen together, boys and girls at home and on vacation may mix easily.

After age eight and until puberty, agemate rehearsal of sexual intercourse is not, as it may be in younger years, an adjunct to another game, but an exercise in its own right. No one has collected verifiable statistics on its prevalence, nor on the prevalence of preliminary erotic foreplay, the prevalence of penovaginal intromission as compared with interfemoral thrusting, or the occurrence of orgasm versus a climactic release resembling orgasm (see chap. 5). Statistics are equally lacking on homosexual and heterosexual rehearsal play and practices between agemates. Anecdotally, it is known that two girls together may engage in nongenital and genital massage with pronounced hedonic feeling, and possibly in mutual digital masturbation, and vulva-to-vulva rubbing. Two boys may engage in interfemoral thrusting, penoanal intromission, fellatio, and mutual manual masturbation.

Ethnographic Variations

FOR RELIGIOUS, MORAL, and legal reasons, it is not possible to plan comparative outcome studies of the gendermaps of groups of children deprived and not deprived of juvenile sexual rehearsal play. The missing data might have been supplied from comparative ethnographic studies of tribal societies that have and have not deprived their children of sexual rehearsal play, but ethnographic sexology has a history of having been neglected and deficient in developmental childhood detail. From the data that do exist (see Currier, 1981, chap. 2; Herdt, 1981; 1984; 1987; Money et al., 1970; Money and Ehrhardt, 1994, chap. 7) one may at least infer that children who are not deprived of sexual rehearsal play are not adversely affected by engaging in it, and that the formation of the sexuoerotic component of their gendermaps is positively benefited.

One way in which a society institutionalizes sexual rehearsal play is by having a children's dormitory or sleeping compound set apart from the main village. Schlegel and Barry (1991) name as examples the tribal Ifugao and Bontoc in the mountain provinces of the Phillipines, and the Muria, a Gond-speaking, pre-Hindu people of the hill country of eastern south central India. The Muria were studied by Elwin (1947; 1968; 1989) who from the 1920s onward spent time living among them. Muria villages traditionally had a children's dormitory compound, named the ghotul.

Each ghotul operated as a sort of children's cooperative requiring adherence to rules of membership administered by the membership itself. Each member had age-assigned duties and obligations. Nonconformity was penalized by the threat or shame of public exposure, or by a prescribed endurance test while listening to a song or a chant of wrongdoing.

The threat that ghotul brothers and sisters would boycott the offender's eventual wedding had much power as, without their ceremonial dance and song, a wedding could not proceed. This threat might be used to discourage a too exclusive relationship between a boy and a girl whose totemic clan membership precluded their marriage to one another.

Full initiation into the membership of the ghotul was formally recognized by the bestowing of a traditional ghotul name which replaced the home name and could not be used outside the fraternity of the ghotul. Ghotul names signified both rank and type of work to be carried out within the ghotul. As they grew older, the names of small children would be upgraded from lower to higher rank until, eventually they took over the training and discipline of the juniors. Leaving home for the ghotul was rather like going away to boarding school and being supervised by prefects, but with adults on the periphery only.

Children were usually ready to join the ghotul between ages six and eight, though they may have visited there much earlier. Initially they would eat at home and go to the ghotul only for the early evening activities. They then went home to sleep.

> When children first begin to attend the ghotul regularly, they are left alone for a week or so. Then the elder boys ask them if they are going to be regular in their attendance and why they did not come before. The children usually reply that their parents kept them away. Then the Sirdar says to a boy, "Now that you have begun to come to the ghotul, you must come every day. You must bring one bit of wood every day. You must first salute

> me and then all the other chelik and you must do what they tell you to do." To a girl he says, "You must obey the Belosa and Dulosa, and clean the ghotul every day" (Elwin, 1987, pp. 358-59). [Sirdar is the name of a head boy, and Belosa and Dulosa of head girls. Chelik are boys.]

After the early evening activities—chatting, story telling, singing, planning upcoming events, dancing, and dozing—the ghotul was ready to settle down for the night.

> By about 10 o'clock, the girls collect around the girl leader, who allots to each her sleeping partner. Every girl then goes up to a boy, often but not necessarily this partner, to comb his long hair and massage his back and arms. This, of course brings them into close contact with one another, and the boys often call out sexy remarks about themselves or others. When the massages are finished, it is bedtime. Girls visiting from another ghotul are now expected to leave. (If any visiting girl is discovered by her own ghotul boys to have remained the night, they get very angry and she is punished with a heavy fine.) The younger children go to sleep in a row. The adolescents pair off, two on a mat. . . . Those who intend to have intercourse may retire to a small hut in the compound. Soon all is quiet. Everyone arises before dawn, for they should be at home and working when their parents arise.
>
> While girls are expected to have intercourse at least some of the time, forcing the girl is extremely offensive and can result in a heavy fine. In some ghotuls, couples are paired off and expected to remain faithful to one another, although it is unlikely that one's "ghotul husband" or "ghotul wife" will be one's eventual spouse. In others, there is a rule against sleeping together too often, which the boy and girl leader enforce. Even in this sexually charged atmosphere, there are strong rules of propriety and sanctions against speech or actions in bad taste.
>
> There are several snakes in this adolescent paradise. One, of course, is pregnancy. The Muria have various beliefs about conception, that it is likely immediately after the girl's menses or that it is unlikely if one changes partners frequently, and they take steps to avoid it. The young people in the ghotul practice coitus interruptus when they fear the possibility of a pregnancy, and abortions are performed. Probably most often, though, the couple get married, or she is married to her betrothed, who is expected to accept the child as his own.
>
> Jealousy is another problem. Younger boys are jealous of the older ones, and the "drab-looking older girls" of eighteen or so may be jealous of the "young and beautiful" ones in their early teens. Ghotul members resent it when others are assigned to sleep with their preferred partners and are known to have temper tantrums (Schlegel and Barry, 1991, p. 108-109).

Elwin provided additional information about the sexual instruction of the young within the ghotul. He wrote as follows (p. 437):

> The ghotul leaders do not interfere unduly with the young children, but they see that they receive proper sexual training and instruction. "As a young bullock is broken to the plough, so a young boy is taught." The evidence for this sort of statement is best presented in actual "documents." Here is one from [the village of] Kapsi.

> A big girl teachs a little boy by letting him fondle her breasts and hug her. Then she opens and spreads her legs and makes the little boy lie on her breasts. She shows him how to open her clothes and insert the little penis with his hand. The first time the boy doesn't know what to do and juice comes out too soon. But the next day she says, "You only pressed me last night, nothing was done properly. I had no pleasure." The boy replies, "Today I'm really ready; now I know what to do."

Elwin further records that it was not considered proper for an older, mature boy to have "full congress" with a young girl before she had passed the menarche (p. 437). He noted also that the kiss as a means of sensory excitement was little used, and that he had not heard of fellatio being practiced (p. 432).

The ghotul institutionalized juvenile heterosexual rehearsal play. By contrast, in a totally different culture, that of the Batak people of Lake Toba in Sumatra, juvenile homosexual rehearsal play was institutionalized. The location was the big bachelors' house at the center of the village. At around the age of seven or eight, the same age that Muria children entered the ghotul, Batak boys would leave the family dwelling to spend the night among males only in the big house. According to the account, based on his own experience, given in 1969 by an American Ph.D. student from Lake Toba (Money and Ehrhardt, 1994, p. 130), the juvenile and adolescent males took part in sexual play, chiefly with one sitting astride the other and manually masturbating the two penises together. Sexual contact with girls was strictly forbidden until age nineteen, the tribal marriage age. Then with the help of a boy's best friend as a go-between, his family would negotiate with the family of the girl on whom he had set his sights. Once he was married, homosexual rehearsal ended and husbandhood and fatherhood began (see also chap. 1, 10).

Children who grow up in a culture that, like our own, has a taboo on juvenile sexual rehearsal play, heterosexual or otherwise, are caught on the horns of a dilemma which is yet another example of a heterosexual Catch-22. On the one hand, they are threatened with the prohibitions and penalties of breaking the taboo if they engage in juvenile sexual rehearsal play with agemates. On the other hand, if they do not engage in sexual rehearsal play with agemates, they incur the harm of a gendermap developmentally impaired by lacking experience with the definitive feature of gendermap coding, namely the reciprocality of male and female in their procreative roles. It is this reciprocality that, sooner or later, is rehearsed in juvenile sexual rehearsal play.

Like the adults responsible for their welfare, our children cannot be effectively insulated from the Catch-22 of the taboo on heterosexual gendermap rehearsal play. The three options for dealing with the Catch-22 are obeying the taboo, defying the taboo, or navigating between these two extremes. Navigation requires being secretive and deceptive about the occurrence of sexual rehearsal play, so as not to be self-incriminating. Parents, sex education teachers, and sex researchers are entrapped in the same no-win situation as are the juveniles. They live in the same Catch-22 world as the children do. However, they have the advantage of age in being able to describe and explain the Catch-22 world, so that the children under their care will be better able to deal with its duality. Dealing with this duality becomes especially urgent with the advent of puberty, and even more so while presently in the late 1990s an effective method for the prevention and cure of HIV/AIDS, the lethal epidemic, is awaited.

7

Lovemap Coding

Lovemap/Gendermap

The coding of the lovemap incorporates one province of the gendermap, namely the province that is specifically sexuoerotic. Gendermap coding introduces the dualistic principles of masculine and feminine into the lovemap, and also their possible overlap for which the preferred term is androgynine. The source of masculine and feminine lies in phylogeny, but their realization is subject to ontogenetic overlay, some of which is historically, societally, and arbitrarily determined.

In the lovemap, masculine and feminine are each coded as being sexuoerotically either heterosexual or homosexual. Androgynine is coded as being to some degree bisexual, though not necessarily 50:50. The lovemap codes for sexuoerotic arousal and performance both quantitatively and qualitatively. Absent or too little is hypophilic or hyposexual. Too much is hyperphilic or hypersexual. Too kinky or bizarre is paraphilic (see chap. 16). Parasexual is not a currently used term. Paraphilias may be societally either tolerated or condemned, and in some instances criminalized, dependent on the society's sexosophy.

The potential for hypophilia and hyperphilia is phylogenetic, but its actuality is ontogenetic. In extreme form neither is common, though there are no absolute criteria as to what is extreme. The source of paraphilia lies in phylogeny, but only in the sense that a phylism not usually associated with sexuoeroticism becomes ontogenetically coopted in the service of sexuoeroticism. The ontogenetic factor in hypo-, hyper-, and para- philia may be secondary to either neural or hormonal pathology, or secondary to experiential learning and developmental trauma.

Before the term l*ovemap* was coined and first published (Money, 1981; 1995) it was preceded by the term *loveblot.* Metaphorically and by analogy with a Rorschach inkblot, a loveblot is a person onto whom one's love is projected. Something about the loveblot matches one's idealized version of the perfect lover and the perfect sexual relationship. Before 1981, there was no name for the entity that the loveblot matches. Without a name, it could not be talked about. Hence the coinage of the noun, lovemap, a word that sounds indigenously English and that has proved to be virtually self-defining. The formal definition of a lovemap is as follows.

> lovemap: a developmental representation synchronously existent in the mind and the brain (the mindbrain) depicting the idealized lover, the idealized love and sexual affair, and the idealized solo or partnered program of sexuoerotic activity projected in private imagery and ideation or in observable performance.

The most extremely stripped down version of a lovemap would be coded to specify nothing more than attraction of a female to any male, and of a male to any female, indiscriminately, and for genital union. This would be the minimum to ensure, as in animal husbandry, the conjunction of ovum and sperm as expeditiously as possible. There would be no playing around, no superfluous enjoyment, and no alternatives like solo masturbation or same-sex coupling.

Since medieval times, this stripped down version of the lovemap has been embodied in ecclesiastical dogma as God's Natural Law that sexual intercourse is exclusively for procreation. To be stripped down even further to the bare bones of digametic procreation, the lovemap would be coded not for genital union of man and woman, but for union of the two gametes, egg and sperm. That union could be accomplished by artificial insemination of the woman's ovum with a sperm in the ejaculate collected from the man and inserted into her vagina with a syringe. Alternatively, the ovum-sperm union might be manipulated in vitro, that is in a glass Petri dish. Then the united product, the zygote, would be inserted into the woman's womb.

The lovemap is never entirely stripped of its diecious bias toward either masculine or feminine which could hardly be otherwise insofar as the primordial evolutionary criterion of male and female mammals is diecious procreation. The diecious component of the actual, unstripped down version of the lovemap is masculine, feminine, or androgynine, and its sexuoerotic expression is developmentally heterosexual, homosexual, or bisexual.

The unstripped down version of the human lovemap is complex and individualistic. Like one's face, it may be individually unique, while at the same time sharing its major features with those of other people, and also resembling some people more closely than others.

In the human species, the dependency of lovemap coding on the conditions of the infantile and juvenile social and sensorial environment is greater than among subhuman primates. This human dependency is sufficiently great that environmental perturbations are able to mold lovemap coding even to the extent of producing a lovemap that excludes the possibility of procreation as, for example, in a lovemap programmed for serial lust murder, or one programmed for autoerotic death by self-asphyxiation.

Lovemap Precursor Coding

LOVEMAP CODING HAS its earliest beginnings in hedonic cutaneous grooming of the newborn period. Deprivation of cutaneous grooming neonatally, and in subsequent stages of development as well, leaves the lovemap permanently impaired with respect to pairbonding.

Hedonic cutaneous grooming has no age of termination, but the methods of how it is done undergo change with age. Hedonic grooming is an integral part of the discovery of the two types of genital self-stimulation, the compressive and the digital—the so-called masturbation of infancy.

During the age of attending preschool, hedonic cutaneous grooming may appear as rhythmic pelvic thrusting, for example, when at mid-morning nap time, children have the opportunity to lie in close proximity side by side. Aboriginal infants of Arnhem Land had a corresponding opportunity when, according to ancient custom, they went to sleep at night in the open air around a campfire, before the adults had finished cooking their own meal. A year or so later, by age five, they might be observed, again before going to sleep beside the campfire, in a more explicit copulatory position. It was acceptable to the adults to see that they knew how to do it (Money et al., 1970).

Hedonic cutaneous grooming may be part of the investigations and comparisons of the preschool "show me" years. It is transposed into masturbation in the early-pubertal and pubertal years (see chap. 5). It is prominent in the courtship of adolescence and adulthood, and in sexuoerotic foreplay. Nongenital hedonic grooming survives the progressive diminution in advanced age of genitally focused hedonic responsiveness.

René Spitz, the psychoanalyst well known for his studies of maternally neglected and stimulus deprived infants reared in an institution for foundlings, reported that the infants whom he observed were too apathetic to engage in genital self-stimulation. This failure correlated with a dire outcome in subsequent psychosexual and personality development. Other infants whom Spitz observed as controls began genital self-stimulation at around one year of age (Spitz, 1970).

During the flirtatious period of late infancy and early childhood, hedonic cutaneous grooming becomes manifest as hugging, cuddling, kissing, and caressing, without being explicitly genitoerotic. It belongs with the joy of being the favorite of say, a family friend or relative, especially an adoring and indulgent grandparent whose role permits that the duty of disciplinary training belongs not to the grandparent but to the grandchild's parents. Flirtatious playfulness is likely to be misconstrued by pedophilic adults as having genitoerotic significance instead of being a nongenital gendermap rehearsal (see chap. 6).

Pairs of preschool and kindergarten boys and girls from between ages three to four and upwards establish, on again, off again, special attachments (see chap. 8). Together the couple engage in grooming activities like hugging and kissing that bear the trademark of courtship rehearsal. The following incident illustrates such a boy-girl attachment, and also demonstrates its vulnerability to well-meaning adult mishandling. School had finished for the day and the children were in the cloakroom putting on their snow suits. The teacher spotted Tommy and Carla in a heavy kissing embrace. She was shocked. For her, kissing in public was obscene, according to the moral standards of her upbringing in India. She separated the two children and admonished them. They disregarded her admonition, and resumed their kissing. Again they were separated. This second time, Tommy admonished his teacher, saying: "We can kiss if we want to, and you can't stop us." That left the teacher bewildered. No one had instructed her on how not to damage two developing lovemaps of two inner city, American black children. Their lesson in transcultural sexology was of the unfathomable arbitrariness of the rules governing kissing and endearment and, as they would soon learn, of many other sexual expressions as well. All children, sooner or later, encounter arbitrary and inconsistent sexual rules, with little or no explanation of how to accommodate them in the lovemap.

There are no prevalence statistics on hedonic genital self-stimulation in boys or girls of any age, and no statistics on the age of transition to behavior that qualifies as full-fledged masturbation. Nor are there systematic statistics on factors that may or may not be responsible for the transition. Although genital masturbation may have a prepubertal onset, it is unlikely, or at least arguable, that a full-fledged orgasm can actually occur before hormonal puberty has taken hold. In boys, the marker event is semenarche, the first ejaculation of semen (see chap. 5). There is no corresponding marker for the evidence of the onset of full-fledged orgasm in girls.

Masturbation to climax cannot be classified as a manifestation of sexual rehearsal belonging specifically to the pubertal and adolescent period. Orgastic masturbation occurs in people of all ages, married or unmarried, whether or not they practice sexual intercourse also (Michael et al., 1994; Laumann et al., 1994).

The fantasies that accompany masturbation qualify as rehearsals in a different sense regardless of age, insofar as, like erotic dreams, they depict in ideation and imagery the lovemap's stratagems and tactics before they are carried out in actual performance.

Latency Is Not Latency

THE TRANSITION FROM infantile to juvenile coding of the lovemap is not abrupt but progressive. The salient developmental feature of the prejuvenile lovemap is the coding of its gendermap component as masculine, feminine, or androgynine. The salient developmental feature of the juvenile lovemap is the narrative or dramatic coding of its ideation and imagery as either orthodox or unorthodox. Neither the prejuvenile nor the juvenile coding of the lovemap is exempt from developmental hazards, such as abusive parental neglect, deprivation, humiliation, admonition, and brutality.

The transition from early juvenile to juvenile lovemap coding takes place typically around the age of eight. Eight is a pivotal age in lovemap development, if one judges by the frequency with which it emerges in reports of childhood sexological development (Langfeldt, 1981a, pp. 67-68), and in clinical biographies of paraphilias (Money, unpublished data).

Linguistically, eight is the age of comprehending double meanings in jokes, puns, riddles, and conundrums. The existence of the second meaning defies the one-word/one-meaning principle of linguistic constancy, and so introduces a moment of surprise. The surprise of the second meaning may be that it is sexual, and has found a tricky way of outwitting the strictures of the sexual taboo. Its very utterance recognizes the taboo and at the same time triumphs over it. A lovemap also may be developmentally subject to the same principle of coding the prohibitions of the sexual taboo while at the same time coding a stratagem to circumvent it.

Another milestone of development of possible significance to lovemap formation pertains to dreams. According to the research of Foulkes (1983, p. 357) it was between the ages of seven and nine "that fairly substantial and credible self-participation characterized children's dream accounts . . . a larger sense of purposefulness guides the integration of disparate image sequences into a coherent narrative." The coherent narrative may be projected into a dream that is romantic and/or erotic, or into a masturbation fantasy. It may or may not be pathological.

By age seven or eight, the brain is able to create the phenomenon of a phantom limb in a juvenile amputee, which it is not able to do prior to age five or six (Tomkins, 1992, p. 248). The phantom phenomenon is a mindbrain phenomenon that belongs to both the mental body image and the neural network of the body schema. Representations of the body image, especially those that are kinesthetic and tactual appear in orgastic dreams (wet dreams) and in masturbation and coital fantasies. Although explicitly erotic representations of the body image in dreams and fantasies are predominantly a pubertal and postpubertal phenomenon, their rudiments in the coding of the lovemap are of an earlier vintage. Absolute musical pitch is gained only before ages 8–10.

The prepubertal years of the juvenile period subsequent to age eight belong, according to orthodox oedipal doctrine, to the period of psychosexual latency. In actuality, however, latency does not exist (Finkelhor, 1981, pp.

135-36). The prepubertal juvenile years are active, not latent years of lovemap formation in ideation, imagery, and rehearsal play. In culture areas where the sexual taboo prevails, in the juvenile years children either obey the taboo and do not disclose the evidence of their lovemap formation, or as dissidents, flaunt it, even at the risk of getting into serious trouble as sexual delinquents.

During this same period of juvenile development, boys hang together in male bonding groups, and girls in pairs or small groups of best friends. In each instance, they consolidate their gendermaps as, respectively, masculine and feminine, according to societal stereotypes. When the stereotypes call for heterosexual rehearsal play, they get together.

Boys and girls may get together in same-sex tryouts as well. Boys, for example, may engage in competitive masturbation to see who can "come," or who can "come" first. Same sex tryouts, for either boys or girls, may be premonitory of a homosexual or bisexual lovemap in adolescence and adulthood. Otherwise they prove to be transitory and age limited. It is not possible to make secure predictions about the long term outcome. As a general rule, however, juveniles who are already gender transposed and likely to develop as an adult with a gay lovemap are disinclined to be members of same-sex juvenile bonding groups. The majority of the members of boys only, or girls only, groups will develop an adult heterosexual lovemap. Being a loner, instead of being a member of a sex segregated group, also is not a definitive prognosticator of a homosexual lovemap in adolescence and adulthood.

In the later prepubertal years, the societal incidence of sexual rehearsal play is extremely variable. It is in the very nature of a taboo's origins that the taboo is partly obeyable. So, even within the same city, there are some communities in which children obey the sexual taboo meticulously and some in which they do the reverse. Tribal or community mores and childhood traditions exert their influence on not only the prevalence, but also the procedures of rehearsal play, whether they are consensual or coerced, for example. Thus is the lovemap coded in a positive or negative way, far in advance of the arrival of the hormones of puberty.

Hormonal Puberty and Lovemaps

THE LOVEMAP DOES not explode into existence like a giant fireworks display fueled by the arrival of the gonadal hormones of puberty, namely progestin, androgen, and estrogen. Indeed, these pubertal hormones themselves do not have a sudden arrival. On the contrary, the onset of the gonadal puberty is rather insidious. It has a subliminal precursor period of about two years during which the blood level of dehydroepiandrosterone (DHEA), a sex steroidal hormone secreted by the adrenocortical glands, increases. This increase begins typically between the ages of seven and nine, earlier in girls than in boys. Girls mature about two years ahead of boys (Kelch and Beitins, 1994, pp. 205-6).

The visible and palpable signs of the onset of puberty, namely pubic hair, breast budding, testicular and penile enlargement, the height spurt, menarche and semenarche, are preceded by a silent and invisible change in the pulsatility of hormone release from hypothalamic brain cells. These gonadotropin releasing hormones (GnRH) induce the release of FSH (follicle stimulating hormone) and LH (luteinizing hormone) from the nearby pituitary gland, situated deep behind the bridge of the nose. FSH and LH circulate in the bloodstream and prompt the testicles to secrete testosterone, the primary masculinizing hormone in boys, and the ovaries to secrete estrogen and progesterone, which regulate the menstrual cycle and also pregnancy in girls.

When the hormones of procreation were isolated and first synthesized in the 1920s and 1930s, they were named for what they were at the time known to regulate in tests performed on laboratory animals. Androgen (from Greek, *andros*, male) was known to regulate masculinization of the male. Secreted mostly from the testicles, it was also called testosterone (from Latin, *testis* + Greek, *steros*, solid + Latin, *-ol* from *oleum*, oil). Estrogen (from Latin, *oestrus*, gadfly; from Greek, *oistros*, everything that drives one mad or creates strong desire) from the ovarian follicle was known to regulate the breeding period of estrus or heat in mammals. Progesterone (Greek, *pro-*, before + Latin, *gestare*, to bear + *-sterone*) from the postovulatory, luteal phase of the follicle of the ovary was known to regulate pregnancy and gestation. Estrogen and progesterone together, in sequence, regulate also the menstrual cycle, so they became known as female hormones.

It was an easy next step in reasoning to make the assumption that male hormone regulates everything masculine, and female hormone everything feminine. Hormonal regulation of pubertal body changes, the so-called secondary sexual characteristics, has proved to be indisputable. Regulation of masculine and feminine pubertal mental and social characteristics, by contrast, has proved to be entirely more complicated. These are characteristics that belong to the gendermap and the lovemap. Hormones are, at most, only peripheral to their regulation which, to be complete, needs more knowledge than presently exists. Homosexuality, gay or lesbian, is a good example.

In the 1940s, after the sex hormones had been commercially synthesized and marketed, there was a flurry of attempted use of testosterone to change male homosexuals into heterosexuals. Neither estrogen nor progesterone was used to attempt to change female homosexuals. Apart from the fact that each of these hormones disrupts the menstrual cycle (which is the rationale for their use in the contraceptive Pill), there is a long biomedical tradition of inattention to women. In any case, women were not the losers, for the attempt to change male homosexuality hormonally with testosterone was a failure. It had either a negligible effect, or intensified the subjective sense of sexual drive, but only if the blood level of testosterone had been deficient prior to treatments.

In conjunction with treating gay men with testosterone, attempts were made also to measure sex hormone levels in their blood and urine, to test the hypothesis of an excess of estrogenic, feminizing hormone. The findings were, at best, equivocal or contradictory, but the methods of measurement in the 1940s were crude as compared with the minute precision made possible by the method of radioimmunoassay, discovered in 1955 (Yalow, 1978) for which Rosalyn Yalow received a Nobel prize in 1977. In the 1960s, there began another, more sophisticated flurry of searching for a homosexual/heterosexual hormonal difference in adulthood (Money, 1988a, pp. 110-14). Like its predecessor, this flurry has also led to a dead end (Gooren, 1995b).

The role of sex hormones in regulating the lovemap as homosexual, heterosexual, or bisexual, although negative at puberty and subsequently, may be positive in prenatal and neonatal life, at which time sex hormones shape the precursors of the gendermap as masculine, feminine, or androgynine. Much more remains to be discovered about the possible role of peptide hormones, neuromodulators, and neurotransmitters that may influence the lovemap in the brain and at the peripheral sex organs. The most newly discovered neurotransmitter is responsible for penile erection. It is nitric oxide and is unique in being the first gas molecule known to have the property of a neurotransmitter (Snyder, 1992; Burnett et al., 1992). The second is carbon monoxide (CO).

Testosterone Effects

APOTHEGMATICALLY, THE overall role of pubertal sex hormones is not to fabricate the lovemap but to activate it from a less to a more productive state, and to enhance, intensify, and expand its output. The prepubertal coding of the lovemap activated by pubertal hormones varies according to the lovemap's history of conformity to societal orthodoxy, which is shared by others, and to its history of being singly pieced together and idiosyncratic, eccentric, or bizarre. Some lovemaps have a personal history of having been metaphorically mutilated so severely that they present problems of serious morbidity when activated by pubertal hormones. In others the pubertal transition is smooth.

Personal idiosyncrasies coexist in the lovemap with transcultural similarities. One transcultural similarity is that the lovemaps of boys are coded for ejaculation which is contingent on the presence of testosterone. With few exceptions, orgasm and ejaculation are paired. They occur spontaneously in sleep, as dreamless nocturnal emissions or as visually illustrated wet dreams, provided their spontaneous occurrence while asleep has not been preempted by masturbation while awake, or by frequent coitus initiated in the prepubertal era of juvenile sexual rehearsal play. In nineteenth-century sex manuals, wet dreams were diagnosed as nocturnal pollutions, pathologized as spermatorrhea, and subjected to harsh, costly, and unnecessary treatment (Graham, 1834/1974; Kellogg, 1888/1974).

Girls do not as a general rule have an acute and uninvited introduction to orgasm in their sleep as boys do, and they do not have a seminiferous ejaculate. However, some women, looking back, recall having had, at around the time of first menses, romantic dreams that had a climactic erotic build up. It is not known whether or not this type of dream occurs in girls who have a particularly sensitive G-spot, the Grafenberg spot or region on the anterior wall of the vagina, from pressure on which orgasm can be intensified. Nor is it known whether such girls are among those who experience the so-called female ejaculation of fluid through the urethra, secreted from the periurethral glands of Skene (the female prostate), at the time of orgasm (see chap. 13).

It is possible for a pubertal boy to have an ejaculation in his sleep and to know about its occurrence only from the evidence of a semen stain on the bed sheets or his pajamas after he wakes. Otherwise the orgasmic feeling of ejaculation in the wet dream is proprioceptive and genitally focused, as when awake. The ideation and imagery of the wet dream, by contrast, is predominantly visual rather than of the other senses. It is also predominantly sexuoerotic and explicitly genital rather than sensuoromantic and cutaneously diffused. The ideation and imagery of the boy's masturbation fantasy is like that of the wet dream. Masturbation survey figures vary, as do all survey figures, but concur in the conclusion that virtually 100 percent of pubertal and adolescent boys have masturbated, some with religious guilt and self-loathing, and all without physical harm to the body.

The girl's masturbation fantasy, if she masturbates, has sensuoromantic and cutaneously diffused ideation and imagery. The lover-lover content of her sleep dreams and daydreams is similar. The girl's lovemap imagery is of being swept away by a passionate lover. The corresponding imagery in the boy's lovemap is of being assertive and the lover who passionately sweeps away.

These male/female differences in the imagery and ideation of the lovemap appear, widely dispersed, in the novels, poems, dramas, and songs of many peoples around the world, though they have not yet been subject to a worldwide ethnographic survey. They are good candidates for being phyletic rather than idiosyncratic in origin.

Testosterone is the primary hormonal activator of the lovemap in boys at puberty. It is the primary libido hormone in males. In pubertal girls and women also it may be the primary libido hormone (Money, 1961b; Everitt and Herbert, 1969; 1970; Sherwin and Gelfand, 1987; Bancroft et al., 1991). In both males and females, testosterone might exert its activating influence by being taken up by brain cells that, within their own nuclei, convert (aromatize) it into estradiol, a form of estrogen, before using it. This conversion has been confirmed in prenatal life when selected sex centers in the brain are masculinized.

The function of the small amounts of estrogen and progesterone normally present in males remains to be ascertained, and to be reconciled with their role in males as antiandrogens, if given in large enough doses. In an earlier era of forensic sexology, estrogen treatment was used as a substitute for surgical castration of criminal sex offending or paraphilic men many of whom have had a prepubertal history of severe lovemap mutilation. In addition to having an antiandrogenic effect on the male lovemap, estrogen promotes the growth of breasts which is unacceptable to males, unless they happen to be male-to-female transexuals whose body image includes having a large bust.

The alternative to using estrogen for sex offenders is to used a synthetic steroidal substitute for progesterone, of which there are two, medroxyprogesterone acetate (MPA) trade named Depo-Provera (Money, 1970b; 1987b), and cyproterone acetate, trade named Androcur (see chap. 17). Goserelin acetate (Zoladex), a GnRH analogue, is a newer alternative (Reid, 1997).

In the contemporary popular media, it is fashionable to attribute male, although not female aggression to "testosterone poisoning." Studies purporting to attribute human male aggression and sexual violence to blood levels of testosterone have not been statistically convincing. From subhuman primate studies, however, there is an indication that with defeat and loss of status in the masculine power hierarchy there is a fall in testosterone level, whereas in victory the level of testosterone rises (Sapolsky, 1991). In human sports competition, not only the victors but also their fans in the stadium have a triumphal elevation of testosterone, whereas the fans of the losers do not (Holden, 1995).

Athletes who inject anabolic steroids, in other words testosterone or testosterone derivatives, get a build up of muscle tissue, muscle strength, and endurance, but not a guaranteed increase in overall violence. Many rapes are violent, but raptophiles are not noteworthy for having an excess of testosterone in the bloodstream.

In the clinic, boys with CAH, the congenital adrenogenital hyperplasia syndrome, who are not under cortisol treatment have extremely high levels of circulating androgen and advanced growth in height and strength. Their pubertal development is precocious, beginning in infancy or early childhood. They are gentle, however, rather than aggressive or violent (Money and Alexander, 1969).

The most promising new work on the origins of violence rules out an elevated testosterone effect entirely and implicates in its place a genetically engineered deletion of neuronal nitric oxide synthase (nNOS) which deprives the brain of NO, one of its two known gaseous neurotransmitters, the other being CO (carbon monoxide) as already mentioned (Nelson et al., 1995). Male mice with the genetic "knockout" or deletion become marauding killers and predatory copulators, persistently mounting females not in estrus. Females with the deletion do not undergo an increase in belligerence, except perhaps in the context of protecting the newborn.

Estrogen/Progesterone Effects

IN FEMALES AS in males, the coding of the lovemap is well on its way prior to the initial signs of the onset of puberty as indicated by breast budding which may begin as early as age eight or as late as age twelve or more. Pubic and axillary hair usually appear after breast budding. The average age of first menstruation (menarche) is around twelve and a half, although it may be as early as age nine or late as age fifteen without being rated as pathological. Initially, menstrual periods are likely to be irregular and frequently without ovulation and, hence, infertile. This so called adolescent infertility has no counterpart in boys, although there are no data on how long it takes after the first appearance of sperms, the semenarche (or spermarche), at the average age of 13-15 years for the sperm count to become high enough to guarantee fertility (Kappy et al., 1994, p. 209).

There are no systematic data regarding a correspondence between the ages of onset of puberty in females and of erotosexual dreams, fantasies, and reveries. So also, there are no satisfactory data on concordancy between the hormonal fluctations of the menstrual cycle and fluctuations in erotosexual ideation, imagery, and practice in adolescence and beyond. Investigative attempts to uncover concordancies have been, overall, inconclusive or inconsistent, for which the explanation may lie in the hypothesis that estrogen and progesterone, either singly or together, do not regulate sexuoeroticism in the human female, but only the cycle of ovulation and fertility, and the copulatory secretions of the vagina.

In four-legged mammals, the cycle of ovulation and fertility is regulated by the periodic or seasonal fluctation of the levels of estrogen and progesterone secreted by the ovaries into the bloodstream. The ovulatory period is accompanied by maximum receptivity toward the male in sexual intercourse. Subhuman female primates, although less robotic than subprimate mammals, copulate more during the ovulatory period than at other times during the menstrual cycle. As compared with the copulation of other primates, human female copulation is not cyclically enchained to the cyclic fluctuations of estrogen and progesterone in inducing the ovulatory peak of the menstrual cycle. Moreover, suppressing the cycle by ingesting estrogen and progesterone in the birth-control Pill, to prevent ovulation, has no systematically predictable effect on the copulatory schedule or on the timing of sexuoerotic attraction and arousal (Alexander and Sherwin, 1993; Cullberg, 1972).

In evolutionary sexology, there is a principle by which to explain this human lack of copulatory periodicity, namely, the principle of upright locomotion. Locomotion on all fours allows the male of subprimate species more easily to smell and taste the genital pheromones produced by the female in heat, and to respond by reciprocating in copulation. In the human upright position, the ovulatory smell of the genitalia is less accessible. The alternative evolutionary strategy for ensuring copulation and pregnancy has been to desynchronize copulation and estrus and have the female and the male accept one another genitally throughout the female's hormonal cycle. A corollary of the strategy is that sexuoerotic turn-on is through the eyes and cutaneous senses instead of the nose. In evolutionary primatology, emancipation of the nose from breeding was contingent on emancipation and ideation of the human lovemap, which in turn was prerequisite to the emancipation and diversification of the mindbrain for human intelligence and the syntactical symbolization of language and logic (see chap. 17).

Today, human sexuoerotic attractivity and arousability (proceptivity, also named courtship, as well as copulatory acceptivity are no longer contingent on the estrogen/progesterone cycle. Hormonally, then, on what is our species survival contingent? The most likely hypothesis (Money, 1961) is that conception and gestation are estrogen/progesterone dependent, whereas the phase of proceptivity that is consummated in copulation is contingent on a low level of testosterone from the ovaries and adrenocortical glands in females, and on a higher level from the testes in males. There is a sporadic experimental support for this hypothesis in both subhuman primate data (Baum et al., 1977) and in human clinical studies Udry and Morris, 1968; Persky et al., 1978; Morris et al., 1989; Sherwin, 1988; and Alexander and Sherwin, 1993.

Most likely, the role for testosterone in female and male sexuoeroticism is the same, namely, that a minimum amount of the hormone, less for females than males, is necessary, but that there is no quantitative correlation between the level of testosterone and the level of sexuoeroticism. Other variables indubitably play a contributing role. They well may be mediated not by steroidal hormones, but peptide hormones, opioids, catecholamines, serotonin, nitric oxide, and other sexoactive brain chemicals yet to be discovered (Baum, 1992).

Hormonal cyclicity may have an indirect effect on female sexuoeroticism by way of the spasmodic, colicky, uterine cramps that herald the onset of the period in some females, especially in young adolescents when the period is anovulatory. Possibly accompanied by nausea, headaches, and other symptoms attributable to an acute excess of hormone-like prostaglandins, this is the condition named dysmenorrhea (Kelch and Beitins, 1994). It may respond to antiprostaglandin treatment.

Dysmenorrhea may be preceded by the mental and physical instabilities of the poorly-defined premenstrual syndrome (PMS). PMS exists also without dysmenorrhea. At its least extreme, PMS is debilitating with edemetous fluid retention, fatigue, anxiety, irritability, and reduced concentration (Foster, 1996). At its greatest extreme, PMS is grossly incapacitating (Frank, 1931).

One of the most serious variants of PMS is the so-called periodic psychosis of puberty. This illness is marked by the alternation of periods of total lucidity and periods of what in the vernacular is called stark, raving madness, with delusions, combativeness, and destructiveness requiring constraints. The condition is made worse by treatment with estrogen, but under treatment with progestin (e.g., Depo-Provera) it can be kept in remission (Berlin et al., 1982).

The use of testosterone as a sexual "upper" for females is contrindicated except, possibly, in miniscule doses. The hormone too easily induces irreversible beard and body-hair growth and permanent masculine deepening of the voice.

Precocious Puberty

IN BOYS, THE beginning visible signs of the onset of puberty are pubic hair and testicular enlargement. It is considered within normal limits if pubic hair begins to grow at any age between 10 and 15, and is completed between the ages of 14½ and 18. The corresponding intervals for testicular enlargement are from ages 10 to 13½ and 14½ to 18. The intervals for penis enlargement are from ages 11 to 14½ in onset, and 13½ to 17, when full grown. The growth spurt in height is within normal limits if it begins between 10½ to 16 years and ends between 13 to 17½ years, with 14 as the average age for the peak rate of growth (from Marshall and Tanner, 1970, in Kelch and Beitens, 1994).

In girls, the beginning visible signs of the onset of puberty are pubic hair and breast budding. It is considered within normal limits if both first appear between ages 8 and 14, and are completed within 3 years. For onset of menarche, the normal limits are between ages 10 and 16½. The duration of the female growth spurt in height is typically from ages 11 to 14 (range 9½ to 14½ years) with the peak rate of growth at 12 (from Marshall and Tanner, 1969, in Kelch and Beitens, 1994).

Though the age range that is within average for the onset of puberty is broad, the extremes are even broader, stretching from the first year of life through to age 19 or 20. At the far extremes, the cases are of heuristic value in throwing light on the disjunction between chronological age and the age of the lovemap.

Ovarian hormonal cyclicity with corresponding menstrual cyclicity may have its onset during the neonatal period, with other signs of puberty, also precocious, appearing subsequently. Typically, however, it is at a later age, up to age eight, that the signs of precocious hormonal puberty first appear. Ovarian fertility may be achieved by age five. In a much quoted celebrity case from Peru, early in the twentieth century, an Indian girl was six years old when she delivered a baby—a possible world record.

The incidence of precocious puberty in girls may be sporadic or multiple within the family pedigree. It may occur without other associated pathology, in which case it is said to be idiopathic. It may also be said to be not peripheral in origin, but central, which signifies that the biological clock of puberty in the brain's hypothalamus or elsewhere has begun accelerating its pulsatile secretion of the gonadotropic releasing hormone (GnRH) too soon. Abolition of the pulsatility by providing a continuous, nonpulsatile supply of GnRH, puts pubertal precocity on hold. An alternative form of treatment is with the synthetic progestinic hormone, MPA (medroxyprogesterone acetate) which puts the ovarian secretion of estrogen on hold and thus arrests continued pubertal development. Neither form of treatment is able to arrest the progress of the pubertal growth spurt which, by occurring too soon, accelerates bone maturation and reduces what would otherwise be full height.

Precocious puberty in boys, as in girls, may be of central origin. In boys, however, the biological clock of puberty is less likely to be wrongly set than to be defective and disrupted by neuroanatomical brain pathology. One such pathology is a hamartoma, a benign, tumor-like nodule of the hypothalamus. Besides interfering with the biological clock of puberty in the hypothalamus, a hamartoma may interfere with the phylism of laughter. The outcome is gelastic epilepsy, a laughing or chuckling spell occurring spontaneously in the absence of humorous stimulus (Money and Hosta, 1967). The ideational content and imagery accompanying the spell, usually diffuse, are not necessarily lovemap related.

In addition to having its source originating in the biological clock of the hypothalamus, precocious puberty in either boys or girls may originate not in the brain, but elsewhere in a hormone producing tumor of one of the endocrine glands or some other internal organ.

It is not, however, a tumor that is the most typical peripheral source of precocious puberty but, in boys, the glandular malfunction of congenital adrenocortical hyperplasia (CAH). CAH originates in boys as well as girls (see chap. 4) in a defect in the genome that requires two parents, both of whom are hidden (heterozygous) carriers of the defect, before it can appear in the offspring. The defect disrupts the hormone secretion of the adrenocortical glands so that they fail to produce cortisol and produce androgen instead. They begin to do so in prenatal life and, in the event of lack of treatment (with replacement cortisol) continue to do so postnatally, in which case precocious pubertal virilization becomes evident by as early as eighteen months of age.

Girls as well as boys with CAH (see chap. 4), if left untreated postnatally, undergo not feminization, but progressive precocious pubertal virilization.

In rare cases, precocious feminizing puberty may be triggered exogenously, in boys or girls who ingest a mother's birth control Pills. Although highly conjectural, it is also possible that exposure in food, to industrial or agricultural chemicals that masquerade as female hormones may lower the age of pubertal onset in girls and induce feminizing or demasculinizing puberty in boys (see also chap. 13).

In precocious puberty, the factor that all cases share in common, irrespective of etiology and diagnosis, is the presence, too early, of the pubertal sex hormones. They all have a pubertal hormonal or physique age that is discordant with the chronological age by being accelerated ahead of it. The lovemap age lies somewhere between the two, neither young and naive enough to match the chronological age, nor old and sophisticated enough to match the physique age. The sexuoerotic imagery and ideation of the lovemap of a six year old boy who is at the fourteen-year-old stage of puberty, for example, does not include representations of penovaginal intromission unless he has been given explicit knowledge of sexual intercourse, or has encountered it directly (Money and Hampson, 1955). The chances of direct involvement are restricted by his social age which leads him to babyish friendships with other children of the same pubertal age as himself. Thus the sexuoerotic representations of his lovemap, in his masturbation fantasies and wet dreams, are derived from infantile feeding at the breast, and from close body contact, hugging and kissing, which can be seen in public and on the television screen.

The six year old girl with precocious puberty, even though she may know about sexual intercourse, has a lovemap that, in its idealism and imagery is less genitally and orgastically focused than the boy's, and more romantically and sensuously focused. It may include having a boyfriendship, perhaps with a boy at school, but one that remains undeclared.

The earlier the onset and the more advanced the degree of precocious pubertal maturation, the more troublesome are the reactions of parents and other caretakers to the child's nudity likely to be. A father may exempt himself from attending to the bathing and hygiene of a three year old daughter with well developed breasts, or of a son of the same age with a fully virilized penis, but someone, usually the mother, must take the responsibility. For her it may not be easy to know how to react to a three year old boy in the bathtub with an erect penis as large as his father's, and hands touching her in a cutaneously amorous way. There are no preestablished rules to go by.

When first encountering the mismatch between a pubertally precocious child's physique age and social age, strangers are prone to follow the principle of enslavement to the eyes, and to jump to the conclusion that what they see is an adolescent who is mentally retarded or psychiatrically peculiar. Neighborhood people spread the scare that the precocious child will molest their children, or will attract child molesters to the area.

In actual fact, pubertally precocious children, with supportive help such as being accelerated educationally so as to bring the lovemap age into closer approximation with the pubertal age, adapt to the mores of the family and community. The rapidity with which the lovemap age accelerates to match the pubertal age is contingent on local conditions with respect to the prevalence and age range of juvenile sexual rehearsal play among the children with whom they might associate. In some localities, children with a history of pubertal precocity begin a sex life early, with early pregnancy. In others they go on prolonged hold, until they have finished high school, and marry still later. Either way, the social coding of the lovemap is evident, irrespective of its precocious hormonal coding.

Pubertal Failure and Delay

AT THE FARTHEST extreme from pubertal precocity, pubertal onset may be delayed for a lifetime, in which case delay becomes permanent failure. Contrived permanent failure of puberty in juvenile males as a consequence of gelding was discovered in the course of the prerecorded history of animal domestication and farming. Castration was applied also to human beings. Young boys were castrated to serve as slaves, harem attendants, and as bureaucrats or priests without the distraction of having offspring and descendents to inherit their wealth. Until as recently as the eighteenth century, prepubertal choir boys were castrated to preserve their soprano voices for cathedral choirs and female opera roles. Today, in the era of endocrinology, testosterone replacement therapy will largely counteract the effects of prepubertal castration. Postcastration infertility is, however, irreversible.

Testosterone is used for the treatment not only of prepubertal castration, but also for pubertal failure secondary to primary anorchia in which the testicles are absent at birth or shrivel and disappear soon thereafter. Their disappearance is attributable most likely to a self-immunizing phenomenon. The onset of puberty in response to testosterone is predictably reliable and satisfactory when pubertal failure is secondary to missing or inert testicles.

When the testicles are intact, and the defect is in the hypothalamic pituitary axis which regulates testicular function, then the failure of puberty is attributed to hypogonadotropic hypogonadism. In that case, the reliability of testosterone treatment in initiating the onset and advancement of puberty is questionably satisfactory. The standard replacement dosage of testosterone may prove to be insufficient in some cases of hypopituitary dwarfism in which there is a deficiency not only of pituitary growth hormone but also of other pituitary stimulating hormones, in particular the gonadotropins, LH and FSH (Money and Clopper, 1974; Clopper et al., 1983).

The standard dosage of replacement testosterone may need to be doubled in cases of deficient pubertal masculinization associated with Klinefelter syndrome which originates genetically from a supernumerary X chromosome. The chromosome count is 47,XXY instead of 46,XY. From neonatal chromosomal screening, the incidence of the syndrome has been estimated to be 1:1000 male live births. Various physical and mental anomalies are sporadically associated with the syndrome in addition to the defining symptoms of failure of spermatogenesis and insufficient pubertal virilization. The gendermap is in most cases masculinized, whereas the lovemap is likely to be hypophilic, with a tendency toward sexuoerotic inertia.

One of the syndromes of hypogonadotropic hypogonadism is named after the early geneticist in psychiatry, Franz Kallmann. He recognized that some men with pubertal insufficiency had also an insufficiency or complete lack of the sense of smell (Kallmann et al., 1944). Small genitalia are characteristic of Kallmann syndrome. Other congenital defects occur sporadically, affecting particularly the nervous system and mental functioning. Its incidence has been estimated at between 1 in 10,000 to 1 in 60,000 births, with a large preponderance of males over females, and with possible multiple occurrence in a family pedigree.

Bick et al. (1992) published data implicating a gene, KALIG-1 (Kallmann syndrome interval gene 1) on the Xp22.3 region of the distal end of the short arm of the X chromosome in patients with Kallmann's syndrome. They offered an explanation for the coexistence of defective puberty and defective smell sense, namely that the KALIG-1 gene is, in early embryonic life, involved in directing the migration of cells from a site in the precursor of the forebrain to two separate destinations. One destination is the hypothalamus where their ultimate destiny is to regulate pubertal maturation. The other destination is the brain's olfactory bulb, where their ultimate destiny, is inter alia, to regulate the functioning of the sense of smell. Failure of a defective KALIG-1 to direct this two-pronged migration of cells to their correct destination would account for the pubertal and olfactory deficiencies of Kallmann syndrome. One may speculate that a defective KALIG-1 gene might also be held indirectly responsible for a lovemap deficiency in Kallmann syndrome, namely a deficiency in pairbondship and falling in love (Bobrow et al., 1971; Money and Sollod, 1978).

Delayed onset and chronic insufficiency of pubertal development are more prevalent in boys than girls. The ovaries are surgically more inaccessible to castration than are the testicles in boys, which historically accounts in part for the lesser frequency of female than male castration.

Congenital absence of the ovaries is one of the defining characteristics of Turner syndrome of which the incidence is 1:5000 female live births (Migeon et al., 1994). The syndrome originates in one missing or defective sex chromosome, the remaining one being an X, and the full count, 45,X instead of 46,XX. Multiple physical and mental anomalies are sporadically distributed among the Turner population. The two consistent anomalies are short stature and agenesis of the ovaries. At the appropriate age, administration of estrogen, or estrogen plus progesterone, in the same dosage as in the Pill, induces the onset of puberty. Cyclically administered, the hormones induce cyclic menstruation, as the uterus is present and is, in fact, capable of pregnancy if provided with a fertilized, donated ovum. The gendermap of girls with Turner syndrome develops almost invariably to confirm to the traditional female stereotype, and is strongly maternal. The lovemap age may be retarded in development as a sequel to social infantilization secondary to short stature and procrastination in initiating hormonal treatment for the onset of puberty.

Concordance and discordance between statural age, chronological age, and lovemap age is evident in a comparison of two syndromes, Turner and Swyer. Both syndromes are marked by congenital absence of the ovaries and by having only one X chromosome. The chromosome count in Swyer syndrome of complete gonadal agenesis differs from the 45,X of Turner syndrome, and is 46,XY. In both syndromes the prepubertal body morphology is female and capable of a feminizing puberty when feminizing hormonal treatment is given. In both the uterus is present and, with appropriate hormonal treatment, capable of menstruation and pregnancy by in vitro fertilization of a donated egg. In both syndromes the gendermap is typically feminine and the lovemap heterosexual. The difference is that in Swyer syndrome, in which height is average or higher, there is no history of social infantilization and no retardation in the maturation of the lovemap secondary to short stature.

Delayed puberty converges with precocious puberty in revealing the overall principle that the lovemap age is not an automatically determined correlate of the pubertal hormonal age, nor of the chronological age, but is a compromise somewhere between the two, mediated by the social age.

Regardless of origin, all varieties of pubertal delay illustrate the principle that the developmental age of the lovemap is contingent on the matching or mismatching of the birthday age and the pubertal or physique age. When the physique age is too far behind the chronological age, hormonal intervention to elevate the pubertal age is indicated, so as to allow the lovemap age not to lag too far below the chronological age.

For boys, the chronological age at which being pubertally a late bloomer becomes too late is between 15 and 16, if there are no signs whatsoever of the onset of puberty. In girls the age is between 13½ and 14½. If at these ages a specific etiological diagnosis cannot be established, the delay may be characterized as "constitutional delay of growth and adolescence," and perhaps identified as familial, and left untreated. In some cases, the individual may eventually go into puberty, maybe as late as age 19 or 20; but that is too late to have been left in lovemap limbo, socially too sophisticated to mix with those of regular prepubertal age, and in physique too immature to be acceptable among those of one's own chronological age.

Some of the cases left undiagnosed, except as constitutional delay, and not treated, eventually may be recognized as cases of the Kaspar Hauser syndrome of psychosocial dwarfism (Money, 1992). This is a syndrome in which the pituitary gland shuts off and fails to make growth hormone. It has remarkable heuristic significance, for all growth, physical, social, and mental, goes on hold while an affected child is subject to grossly abusive deprivation, neglect, and violence. The treatment is intervention and rescue from abuse, whereupon growth hormone secretion resumes, and catchup growth begins. The longer the period of abuse, the less the degree of catchup growth. Thus the lovemap may never mature completely, but remain permanently juvenile to some degree. This is what happened to a boy who was not rescued until age sixteen, at which time his physique age and mental age were at around the eight year level, with no signs of the onset of puberty (Money, 1977; Money et al., 1985). After rescue, the onset of catchup growth in stature was at the spectacular rate of 10 cm (4 in) in 10 months. The first signs of the onset of puberty were at age 17 years 8 months, but behavioral adolescence was procrastinated.

Less extreme cases of the Kaspar Hauser syndrome, perhaps of later onset, may present as cases of a short stature and pubertal delay in boys at age fifteen or older (Lewis et al., 1977). In these cases the abusive psychosocial factor is difficult to uncover as the parents and child are locked into a three-way, imposturing collusion, resembling Munchausen's syndrome by proxy (Money and Werlwas, 1976; Money et al., 1985; Schreier and Libow, 1993).

In contemporary statistics, the age of the onset of puberty is 4 to 5 years earlier than it used to be in the middle of the nineteenth century. It has gone down at a rate as rapid as four months each decade. This is a secular change, which means a change occurring in the course of one century or more. During the same period, adult height increased by 4 to 5 inches, on average. Both changes presently have stabilized (Zacharias et al., 1970). Many speculations have been advanced to explain them, but none has been satisfactory (Tanner, 1962; Wyshak and Frisch, 1982).

The secular change in the age of puberty has implications for lovemap development insofar as the official sexual morality of puberty and adolescence has not changed to be concordant with the lowered age of the onset of puberty. Our ancestors of three and four generations ago matured sexually between middle and late teenage and their lovemaps followed suit: they were married and breeding very soon thereafter. The average life expectancy was short, as brief as 35 at the time of the American Revolution (Christhilf, 1976) and 40 by 1900, as compared with between 75 and 85 by 2000—for women longer than for men. It was necessary to breed young. Today, with a much reduced age of puberty, the officially idealized age of marriage and first parenthood is, paradoxically, not younger than it used to be, but older. At the same time, in a large segment of society, the age of the onset of premarital or nonmarital intercourse and first parenthood has unofficially lowered, for both fathers and mothers, so as to be concordant with the lower age of puberty. Society is gravely at odds with itself about the age of first parenthood. Teenaged pregnancy and unwed motherhood are hyperbolized as a new epidemic. The disease is named children having children.

Syndromes of pubertal delay or failure that are contingent on pituitary gonadotropic failure, and/or failure of the releasing hormone of the hypothalamus are less prevalent in girls than boys. This is so whether pituitary growth hormone is also deficient, with consequent statural dwarfism of the hypopituitary type. An adequate explanation of this male/female difference has not yet been found. In girls, pituitary dysfunction is more often related to dysfunctional ovulatory and menstrual cycling than to pubertal maturation. Thus the lovemap age may be relatively unaffected.

8

Limerence

Limerence Defined

Grief, religious ecstasy (equated by some with being converted or born again), and being love smitten are a trio of human experiences that resemble one another in being potentially sudden in onset, overwhelming in intensity, slow in fading, systemically mental and somatic in manifestation, and long-term in influence. The English language lacked a noun singular for the state of being love smitten, or having fallen in love, until Dorothy Tennov (1979) coined the term, limerence, to fill the void. It is formally defined as follows:

> **limerence** (adjective, **limerent**): the personal experience of having fallen in love and of being irrationally and fixatedly love stricken or love smitten, irrespective of the degree to which one's love is requited or unrequited.

Limerence requited is known metaphorically as walking on air, being on cloud nine, or having stars in your eyes, as well as being love stricken or love smitten. In mythology, Cupid with his arrows is the symbolic agent of limerence. He takes aim at his targets capriciously.

Limerence requited is euphoriant. It fills reveries and dreams with ideation and imagery of the beloved, diminishes the appetite, and relieves fatigue. It makes compromises and sacrifices on behalf of the beloved, and extravagantly bestows gifts. Even to the point of elopement, it overcomes obstacles to close body contact that eventually culminates in genital union with the beloved.

A sure way to intensify requited limerence, for example in adolescence, is for parents or others to try to break it up. The prospect of reunion after even a brief period apart from the beloved is frought with anticipatory symptoms resembling those of stage fright, namely, butterflies in the stomach, labored breathing, trembling hands and knees, stammering, palpitations, dry mouth, goose bumps, and clammy hands. Limerence for the beloved consumes all twenty-four hours of the day. There is no place for a rival.

Sudden limerence, or love at first sight, may be triggered even across the crowded room of operatic fame by the appearance of a stranger. The trigger is the close match between the visual image of the stranger and the visual image of the perfect lover in the lovemap of the beholder. When love flashes simultaneously back and forth between the eyes of both the beholder and the beheld, it is attributed poetically to that old black magic.

When limerence is recognized in juveniles and is approved of as being cute, it is called puppy love. When it is recognized in adolescents whose pair-bonding flouts family or community mores, it is called infatuation, a term which is also applied to disparage adulterous and other socially condemned limerence. In preadolescence, limerence mixed with hero worship is called a crush. When concordant with social mores and age specifications, limerence is known variously as being in love, falling in love, having a love affair (or if less approved, an affair).

Limerence is a phylism, phylogenetically coded into the human mindbrain. It is a species phenomenon that does not need to be learned. Although the circumstances of its manifestation are subject to ontogenetic molding and personalization, its phylismic autonomy leads to the popular dicta that true love is blind, and that lovesickness is an affliction brought on by love unrequited. The greater the degree of reciprocal mismatch of two lovemaps, the greater the likelihood that limerence, if it strikes at all, will be one sided and unrequited. Then it will be a source of anguish and grief, even to the point of murder or suicide.

Rehearsal of Limerence

BY REASON OF neighborhood proximity or by congregating in preschool, or day care play groups, some children have an early opportunity to socialize with age-matched boys and girls from households different than their own. Then, from around the third birthday onward, the phenomenon of best friends begins to emerge (see chap. 7). Two best friends may be a boy and a girl. Adults observe that they seek each other out, are attentive to one another, and spend more time together than with any other playmate. The parents will hear comments like he/she's my best friend. If they ask why, the range of responses conceptually available to the child is still too narrow to include a causal explanation like, "Because she's pretty," even though adults would confirm her as the prettiest in the class, and him as the most handsome.

Retrospectively recounting the memories of his kindergarten love affair, at age forty-one a man expressed himself as follows (Gilmartin, 1987, pp. 274-75):

> In my kindergarten class, there were these two twin sisters, Rita and Ruth. They were fraternal twins. They looked entirely different. And before Thanksgiving I found myself looking all the time over at Ruth who was the really pretty one. By Christmastime it got to be really intense. When I went to bed at night I would think so intensely about her before I fell asleep that I would feel really warm and wispy and goosebumpy all over. Part of my body would go moist, and I would dream that she was sleeping there beside me. You have to understand that I was just five years old at this time. . . . But I can remember Ruth as clearly as I can remember the things I did at work today. After all these years I've never forgotten her.

This man's mother had no comprehension of her son's secret kindergarten passion for Ruth. She discouraged it, saying that the twins were Jewish and he was Catholic. Other mothers are more positive, even playing the role of coaching a daughter in guiles and wiles of wooing a boyfriend, and a son in the attentiveness and compliments that outclass a rival in winning a girlfriend.

A kindergarten love affair lasts for weeks, perhaps months, until the class disbands at the end of the year, or until it takes in new members and a competitor appears.

By the age of eight, boys and girls will often be able to name an agemate as a girlfriend or boyfriend, even though she or he may not know it yet. As coyness fades with age, the evidence of being boyfriend and girlfriend may be some special attentiveness like his carrying her books home from school, sending love notes, or communicating through an intermediary.

Some socially condoned party games of the upper and middle class legitimize kissing as preadolescent boyfriend/girlfriend play—spin the bottle, for example, in which the prize is to receive or give a kiss. The age of the party game kiss merges into the age of going steady. This has a variable beginning, ranging between 11 to 12 and 13 to 14, earlier in girls than in boys, and more prevalent after than before puberty. As adolescence progresses, limerent rehearsal gives way, fully fledged, to limerent performance.

Dependent on neighborhood mores and personal opportunity, additional evidence of limerence in preadolescent rehearsal might include explicit genitosexual rehearsal play. Like adults, children do not readily disclose self-incriminating evidence, so that no systematic statistics exist on the prevalence or frequency of the occurrence of genitosexual rehearsal play in minors. Evidence is based on the casual statistics of school teachers and child healthcare officers (Baugh, 1977; Langfeldt, 1981b).

A crush is less condemned as a form of limerent rehearsal if it is devoid of genital contact. As young as age eight, or older, a boy or girl can have a crush on, say, an admired school teacher, pastor, recreation leader, or favorite relative.

There is a definite sexuoerotic attraction in a crush—the female's prettiness and the male's handsomeness. Otherwise it is not a crush, but hero worship. Sexuoerotic attraction increases with the advancement of puberty, and may become intense. In adolescence it may become infatuating, in which case age discrepancy is a hazard if infatuation leads to erotic involvement. To the chagrin of many a teacher, mentor, or priest, an age discordant affair with a minor, male or female, is subject to prosecution as child sexual abuse, even retrospectively, after a dormant period of as many as thirty years or more.

A crush is pretty much ensured of being one sided when the idol of infatuation is an entertainment star or sports hero publicly shared at a distance in a live performance, before a swooning and squealing youthful audience. Pinup portraits and posters must then substitute for the live performer, in absentia. The predominant erotic imagery of a male to a pinup picture is to possess the pinup figure and to have sex together, whereas the imagery of the female is more likely to transform the pinup figure into her own lover with whom to have sex, or at least a romantic adventure. The pronouns change for gay or lesbian versus heterosexual attraction, but the male/female difference does not.

Puppy Love

THE LIMERENT REHEARSALS of childhood are typically transitory, with more than one partner in sequence. Beginning as early as age eight, however, juvenile limerence may begin and, not coming to an early end, burn with a flame that is maintained through adolescence into adulthood. When it begins, such a durable bonding is likely to bring forth ridicule and teasing from age mates. Adults discount it by calling it puppy love. If puppy love is discovered to involve juvenile genitoerotic rehearsals, severely abusive punishment is likely to ensue.

A narrative of a juvenile puppy love affair that became transformed into the limerence of undying love in adolescence and adulthood was audiotaped and transcribed twenty-odd years ago. It was one section in a series of interviews with a young black father who, leaving his wife at home with three other young children, had taken military leave to bring his infant son from out of state for a surgical admission. The boy had been born with hermaphroditically ambiguous sex organs. After neonatal indecision for some time as to whether the sex of assignment should be as a girl or boy, the baby was brought up as a boy. Now at age four, he was admitted for surgical masculinization of the genital birth defect (hypospadias).

Discussion of future management and guidance led to talk about children's sex play. The father had no hang up with the topic. He commented on a mother who had beat her son when she found him playing sex with a girl, saying:

> I guess she thought she was right, but I don't. A boy's got to find out sooner or later. Why beat him because he's trying it young? I tried it. I didn't know what the hell I was doing, but I tried it. I was five or six I guess; I really can't remember.

With this lead in, he went on with the following narrative about himself:

> As a matter of fact I fell in love with my cousin, first cousin, at age eight years old. I remember that. I'll never forget that. It was the first time I'd seen her. She was a red-head, and she was bright. She was good-looking. She had freckles on her face. She came to visit us for a week or ten days. We had a small house then, and all the cousins had to sleep with us. So Cathy, that's her name, she would sleep with me, but at the other end of the bed, head to toe. We were both the same age. And the way she would sleep, she would always push down in the bed, and my foot would be up between her legs. And it was very warm there! I would be wiggling my toes between her legs. She wouldn't be doin' nothin', but she would take her feet and start wiggling them between my legs.
>
> Then we would just continue on. I don't know if we thought of ourselves having an affair or sexual intercourse or anything. I don't recall whether I felt for her vagina or not, but I know we did something. I mean we got on top of each other. And she had her panties off, and I had my underwear off.
>
> The whole time she was there, we would wait until everybody would go to sleep, and then we'd get together and get out of bed, quietly, not waking my little brother and the other girls, onto the floor. Or go in the kitchen, or outside and sit on the back porch.
>
> You know, right now, she and I are just like this (demonstrating)—tight. We're real close. . . . She used to write to me till after she found out I was married. She didn't like the idea of me getting married, because she always said I thought you were going to wait for me, and all this. And I would say something like, well, you know, they wouldn't let us get married [being cousins], no way. And she would say something like, we'll just wait till we get old enough to where we wouldn't need anybody's consent but our own.

In comparing his feelings for Cathy and for his wife, he said:

> Well, I really couldn't say, because I've never really compared them. I love my wife, quite naturally, and I don't know what you'd call it between Cathy and me. When I found out that we were related, I thought it would be incest, between first cousins. I think I tried to change my feelings for her. I'm not saying that I did it. I can't explain the feelings that I feel toward her. I doubt if she could explain her feelings toward me either. I guess the reason why we don't write each other is because we've told each other we wouldn't contact any more, unless we accidentally run up on each other. But it seems as if she's been trying to sort of keep up with me. When I joined the service, she found out, and six months later she joined the service. Same branch. But where she's stationed I don't know. She doesn't know where I'm stationed, because I didn't tell even my family, in case she'd find out. . . .
>
> After I was married and back from California, she came to visit home. She called on the phone, and she was talking to my wife first, and my wife told me to pick up the phone. She and I were talking, and my wife was eavesdropping on the other end. And she was talking to me as if I was her long lost love. . . . We drove out to my mother's house, where she was staying. Before I stopped the car, she was embracing me not like relatives, but as if we were really lovers. And my wife didn't like this!

> I don't know [whether Cathy and I had been in love at age eight]. I guess you could say love. It might be; it might not. If it was love, well, I guess you could say yes. People say it's puppy-love but I don't know if it was puppy-love. It wouldn't be going on. Every time we see each other now it wouldn't continue as puppy-love. . . . I think it was the same thing [my feelings for Cathy at age eight and in teenage]. It feels the same thing. I often dream about her, and I did then too. I would always talk about her, and occasionally I do now. Not to my wife, of course, but around my mother or dad, or my sisters and brothers. So I don't see any difference in it. [Once in adulthood] we were trying to figure out [about having sex together again], whether we should continue and do it or not. We didn't know, so we just messed around, and then we got up (Money, 1980).

Not only can limerence begin as young as at age eight with puppy love, but also at any age up to the seventies and beyond. If with age the sexuoerotic functioning of the genitalia has fallen below par, then cutaneous grooming, close cuddling, and hugging will assume prominence over coital penetration as an expression of limerence.

Limerence may occur only once in a lifetime, or its occurrence may be multiplicative, with a wide range of individual variation in frequency, upwards from zero. Following the loss of a partner, new limerence may be an early sign of recovery from grief and mourning.

The age of first limerence most typically is postpubertal, though neither physique age nor chronological age give an exact prediction of when limerence will be first manifested in adolescence or young adulthood.

Puberty and Limerence

NARRATIVE, POETRY, and dramatic literature and movies are saturated with depictions of love and lovesickness, but science has barely begun to accept them as worthy topics of scientific attention. Even rudimentary statistical data on the mean and standard deviation of the age of first being in love, that is of being limerent, have not yet been collected. Casual observational data, however, point to puberty and beyond as being the time of the first experience of limerence, but with very wide individual differences in age.

Some juveniles arrive at the threshold of puberty, scheduled as it were, to fall in love without delay, whereas others are scheduled for late blooming. This range of schedules applies to children with precocious onset of puberty (see chap. 7) as well as to those whose puberty is at the early limit of normal in onset. In the absence of an adequate scientific explanation for the difference in schedule, people jump to simplistic conclusions about raging hormones, innate shyness, societal repression, moral restraint, and so forth.

The relationship of sex hormones to limerence is not on a dose response curve of more hormone, more limerence; but on the basis of enough hormone suffices and adding more has no additional effect. Limerent late bloomers typically have no pubertal hormonal deficiency. However, some late bloomers do have a history of delay in the onset of hormonal puberty.

Even when they have received hormonal treatment and have become pubertal, some of these late comers to puberty may continue to be late in blooming limerently. This is notably so in the case of delayed puberty attributed to hypogonadotropic hypogonadism (see chap. 7), as in cases of Kallmann's syndrome, for example, in which the delay of puberty originates not in hormones, per se, but in failure of the brain to regulate its own hypothalamic, pulsatile secretion of releasing hormones (RL) that stimulate the pituitary gland and the onset of puberty.

In such cases it is possible that hypothalamic malfunction is not restricted to the biological clock responsible for the scheduling of pituitary hormones, but that there is an additional malfunction in or adjacent to the hypothalamus, namely a malfunction of the biological clock responsible for the pairbondship of limerence. There are, in fact, some instances of hypogonadotropic hypogonadism in which, after testosterone replacement treatment, there appears to be a permanent failure of limerence. The affected individuals are able to establish a companionable relationship, but they do not fall in love (Clopper et al., 1976). They also do not experience concupiscent lust to a strong degree.

It is in only a minority of cases of late blooming limerence that there is a diagnosable endocrine condition to which the lateness of limerent pairbonding might be attributed. Among those undiagnosable cases there are some that constitute a syndrome, not as yet formally named, of sexuoerotic inertia and apathy that continues until the occurrence of the first experience of limerence. In the case of a male scientist in training, apathy and inertia included a self-reported history of no recall of orgasm or ejaculation with or without erotic dreaming during puberty and adolescence, and no recall of ever having had an ejaculation by masturbation. During the adolescent years there was no dating, and no experience of coitus or other sexuoerotic activity. He was in his early twenties when limerence struck suddenly. Though he and his girlfriend delayed having first intercourse penovaginally, it was with her that he had his first orgasm and ejaculation. Orgasmically liberated, he was thereupon able to masturbate, and did so when away from his girlfriend. He dramatized his demands on her limerence, however, by testing it in grotesque and illogical ways that destroyed the relationship.

Another case is that of a male, also a scientist, successful, and in mid-career. As an adolescent, he recalled, he had not masturbated, nor had an interest in dating. He followed the path of conformity in marriage and parenthood, but his sex life with his wife became increasingly dowdy and apathetic until the frequency of sexual intercourse fell off to three or four times a year. Then he experienced limerence for the first time when he was on a temporary job assignment far from home. There, on a tropical resort island, it was feasible to investigate just what he might have been missing by having had no other sex partner than his wife. Under the influence of limerence toward an island girlfriend, he had orgasms the ecstasy of which he had never before experienced.

Apathy and inertia rapidly vanished from his sex life whether with his new partner, or subsequently when alone and masturbating, after returning home. With a view to sharing his new discovery, he told his wife what had happened. Her reply was that she too had taken a new lover during his absence and, having discovered what she had been missing through all the years with her husband, was ready to request a trial separation.

Diuturnity of Limerence

THERE IS NO FLAG and no stopwatch with which to mark the beginning and end of limerence. At its most dramatic and overwhelming, limerence begins suddenly with love at first sight, even though the person sighted is a stranger. Limerence may also declare itself, possibly quite unexpectedly, after a preliminary period of knowing one another. A prolonged period of preliminary buildup is also possible but less likely, limerence being, by analogy, more like spontaneous combustion than the flame slowly kindled from hot embers.

The signs of mutual attraction between two people, upon first encounter, are the same whether they culminate in enduring limerence or a more transient romance. They are expressed both vocally and in body language, and are remarkably constant transculturally (see chap. 13). Observable signs are accompanied by changes in the functioning of the autonomic nervous system and, in the brain, of the limbic system or paleocortex in the region of the amygdala and nearby temporal lobe. After the initial limerent encounter, and over a prolonged period of time, additional changes relate to being preoccupied in anticipation of the next meeting: eating less, sleeping less, concentrating with less focus, having fantasies, daydreams, and dreams about the beloved, and being euphoric in mood (Money, 1986c). For some, limerence also means writing love poems, singing love songs, or being otherwise expressive in the arts. Limerence is profoundly intolerant of interference, and jealously possessive, even to the point of alienating the partner or endangering oneself or others, especially a suspected rival.

All of the foregoing manifestations and characteristics of limerence are the same irrespective of whether the attraction is homosexually or heterosexually oriented.

Phyletically, limerence has its own agenda which is to bring a couple together in genital union, not simply in a casual liaison, but in a pairbonded one that endures over time. Though the timetable is variable, it begins with a phase that leads up to sexual intercourse from which a pregnancy ensues. Then follows nine months of gestation, during which time the intense initial ardor of limerence may begin to change toward the more steady glow that typifies young parenthood. Though different from the excited initial state of limerence, this more steady state is, in its own way, equally satisfactory for that proportion of couples who stay together. For others, the steady state loses its glow, and their pairbondedness, if it continues, becomes one of utility or convenience, devoid of limerence—which is also the way that some couples begin. Either or both of the partners then becomes a potential target of attack for a fresh cycle of limerence with a new partner. The length of a cycle, though not fixed, is typically from two to three years. Helen Fisher (1992, p. 154), wrote that from an evolutionary point of view:

> Human pairbonds originally evolved to last only long enough to raise a single dependent child through infancy, the first four years, unless a second infant was conceived.

Fisher recast the seven year itch of the popular adage into a four year one. The precise timing is less significant, however, than the fact that popular wisdom recognizes that a mismatch between two lovemaps leads eventually to a day of reckoning. On that day, the realization dawns that the mismatch will remain forever uncorrected. One possible solution is to conceive a new baby on whom will fall, in vain, the responsibility of cementing the marriage together. Another solution is a new cycle of limerence—a new love affair.

Some couples bypass the steady glow state of limerence. For them the bright flames of initial limerence burn on. They do not tire of making concessions, each in favor of the other. Every adventure in bed is as exciting as all those that have preceded it. Although devoted to one another, they do not short-change their children; but they do delight in the day when, having fulfilled their parental duties, they are romantically alone again. The first to die leaves the other irrevocably bereft. No new partner can ever completely replicate the lost one and fill the limerent void.

It is from couples with so strong a degree of limerent pairbondedness that one deduces the principle that limerent falling in love is a developmental milestone. It is the milestone that marks the accommodation of one's own lovemap, as need be, to match that of the other. In some cases it appears as a wholly healthy, bilateral accommodation, whereas in others it has the appearance of a wholly unhealthy, bilateral collusional pathology.

Limerence and Childbearing

THE JOINT ADVENTURE of pregnancy may serve to intensify the strength of the limerent pairbond. In the extreme case, the man may experience a mimicry of some of the symptoms of pregnancy, a phenomenon known in anthropology as the couvade. By contrast, there are some men for whom pregnancy and the prospect of delivery are traumatizing so that they take leave of absence as the date approaches. For some women, the hormonal changes of pregnancy are blissful, whereas for others being pregnant is the equivalent of being seriously ill.

Labor and delivery bring about additional hormonal changes in the mother, notably in oxytocin and vasopressin, two neuropeptide hormones secreted by the hypothalamus, and prolactin, secreted by the pituitary gland. Oxytocin is responsible for the uterine contractions of labor and the milk-ejection of nursing, the milk supply itself being under the control of prolactin. From studies of small mammals, most notably the prairie vole, there is evidence that oxytocin and vasopressin play a significant role in establishing the pairbondships of sexual partners and of parents and offspring (Insel and Carter, 1995). It is still only a hypothesis, but a viable one, that the same hormones play a role in human lover-lover and parent-baby pairbonding.

Whatever the ultimate hormonal explanation, it is clear that a mother-infant pairbond is phyletically ordained and nutritionally necessary for survival, even though, nowadays, it may be circumvented by nutrient formulas and baby foods. To accommodate the mother-infant bonding, the pairbonding of the two parents must open up and become a three-way bonding, the process being repeated with each subsequent birth.

The transition from two-way to three-way bonding is not without hazard. Postpartum changes in the progesterone/estrogen ratio in some women precipitate a postpartum depression. Then the baby suffers the hazard of neglect, abuse, and possible death. Conversely, in mothers who become fixatedly possessive of the baby to the exclusion of its father, it is the bond between the two parents that is at stake. Some fathers, however, have a disability for father-infant bonding and become unyieldingly possessive of the mother and jealous of her attention to the baby. Otherwise, in general, the greater the interaction between father and baby, the stronger the bond between them. This is the principle that underlies enthusiasm for natural childbirth, with prenatal training and preparation for the father to be present with the mother at the delivery.

Some babies (see chap. 6) are, from birth, more or less talented than others in playing their part in displaying the body language of pairbonding. Those with a diagnosis of infantile autism are extremely lacking in this talent, and do not pairbond with either parent. On the other side of this coin is the baby whose two parents are defective parent-infant pairbonders. They not only neglect the baby, but may also subject it to physical abuse and abandonment, or they may contrive its death.

9

Maladies of Limerence

Love Shyness
Lovesickness
Stalking
Cyclic Limerence
Imposturous Limerence
Paraphilic Limerence

Love Shyness

Being love shy (Gilmartin, 1987) does not signify lacking or being deficient in limerence. Rather, it signifies being so handicapped by shyness and social ineptitude as to be unable to translate the ideation and imagery of limerence present in one's lovemap into actual limerent performance. Thus, an intellectually achieving graduate student, a man in his twenties, may be so profoundly socially inept and love shy that the very anticipation of inviting a fellow woman student to join him over a cup of coffee, or to go to a movie, renders him immobilized and tongue-tied. Moreover, should an invitation be female initiated, it is possible that the love shy male will be overcome with embarrassment and panic, so as to be unable to accept. Each failure makes the future look worse.

Recognizing in one another a facsimile of their own love shyness, five male undergraduate students some years ago called themselves informally the Inept Club. Their agenda was to disqualify for membership by going steady and getting married. They shared social activities together. At the end of one semester, two of them made an itinerary that would take them through Nevada where prostitution is legal, and where they could make a stop at the famed Chicken Ranch. They were too old, they agreed, never to have been laid and, by taking this plunge, they might become more confident in dating. Their first experience of sexual intercourse did not, however, have this spill-over effect. It took longer than ten years, but eventually all the members of the Inept Club were claimed in marriage.

Females as well as males may have the same experience of social ineptitude and love shyness. In females it tends to be discounted by other people, and held to be appropriate to society's stereotypes of femininity, namely modesty and reticence. The good woman, according to the stereotype, waits to be invited. It is the harlot who zeros in on a man and claims him as her prize.

Limerent pairbondship in human beings, the bonding between lover and lover, resembles parent-child pairbondship insofar as in both the bonding is between two people. Troopbondship, the other type of human bonding is among more than two. Both types are phylogenetically ordained and belong to us as members of our species. Both are subject to possible maldevelopment and malfunction. In love shyness, the primary malfunction is in troopbondship, from which failure to pairbond is a spin-off, manifested as love shyness.

A particular example of how complete the disjunction can be between limerent pairbondship and social troopbondship belongs to the long-term followup of a case of a girl with the rare combination of a diagnosis of 45,X Turner syndrome and a history of severe autistic thought disorder since infancy. The case was written up as follows (Money, 1983b):

> In the histories of autistic children, one may obtain evidence to the effect that, as newborns, they seemed to be aloof and self-isolating, instead of strongly mother-bonded. But it is in the impairment of troopbonding that autistic children are most extensively handicapped, so much so, that one may postulate failure to troopbond as pathognomonic of the syndrome of autism. Impairment of the phylism of troopbonding is the primary pathology of autism.
>
> On the basis of the hypothesis that impairment of the troopbonding phylism may be highly specific, it follows that much in the symptomatology of autism that is otherwise puzzling becomes less so. For a child deficient in troopbonding, people become irrelevant and neglected, except as moving objects in space—comparable, by analogy, to unseen color in the vision of the colorblind, or to neglected injury in the apperception of the congenitally painblind (pain-agnosic).
>
> Without troopbonding, linguistic communication with members of the troop becomes irrelevant and neglected. The phylism for language is not itself directly impaired, however. Private linguistic, numerical and related symbols may be used elaborately—even hypertrophically—in feats of mnemonic, intellectual, and calculational virtuosity. This was formerly known as the phenomenon of the idiot savant, and now is known simply as savantism.
>
> Such hypertrophy and virtuosity may be precocious, as in the extraordinary case of Nadia (Selfe, 1977). At the age of three and a half, this autistic girl repetitiously sketched carousel horses and riders, modeled from pictures, with the graphic skill of an accomplished art school senior.
>
> The drawings of Nadia, and analogous feats of other autistic children, suggest the hypothesis that the process responsible for impairment of the troopbonding phylism in autism may also be responsible for, or associated with

either hypertrophy and/or precocious maturation of other phylisms. The phylism of repetition, for example, may fall into this category, and be responsible for monotonous repetition of mannerisms, vocalisms, and rituals.

The phylism for object-constancy may be similarly affected, and be responsible for obsessional orderliness of time and place. The phylism for rotational motion and giddiness, if affected, would be responsible for the spinning that is characteristic of some autistic children. The phylism for rocking motion is probably not specifically related to autism, but rather to isolation and neglect which triggers rocking in divers contexts. Likewise headbanging which, paradoxically, hurts only initially, and then induces euphoria, perhaps by releasing analgesic and euphoriant endorphin from the brain's own opiate system.

It is no more possible for an ordinary person to inhabit the experiential universe of an autistic person than to inhabit an egg inside its solipsistic shell—and the same holds true in reverse. The autistic and nonautistic are forever mismatched, and so become potential adversaries in a no-win, no-lose, power struggle. Feuding may revolve around the phylism of limerent (lover-lover) pairbonding.

The phylism for limerent pairbonding, unlike that for troopbonding, is not impaired in autism. Nonetheless, since socializing is usually a precursor to meeting and pairbonding with a lover and sexual partner, expression of the phylism for limerent pairbonding becomes impeded. In consequence, the matching of an autistic with a nonautistic partner has a high probability of being a mismatch—of being reciprocally discordant instead of concordant. The love affair is one-sided and unrequited.

The feuding and misunderstanding that may ensue are exemplified in the biography of the above-mentioned girl with a diagnostic history of both autism and 45,X Turner syndrome, and with a history of treatment for both. By age sixteen, she was hormonally adolescent, puberty having been induced by treatment with estrogen, as is necessitated in Turner's syndrome, owing to congenital absence of ovaries.

From the family's point of view, their adolescent daughter was jealous of her younger brother, aged thirteen, angry and spiteful toward him, and yet also devoted to him. She was irrationally dictatorial about what color of socks he could or could not wear, about washing his socks for him, and about requiring him never to walk around the house with bare feet, always to wear long pants even for summer sports, and never to expose bare skin on his legs above his socks.

From the girl's point of view, her brother and her family were negative. She could not explain herself. She had fits of despaired rage and destructiveness. Only after months of frequent therapy was she able to give words to her own point of view: After showing his bare feet and bare legs, she asked, what would it be next? Eventually she was able to speak about a very explicit fantasy of having sex with her brother, which was stated in the past tense of delusion as actual history. The more mean she was to her brother, the more desperate she became at being unable to control herself, which led only to more anger and destructiveness. She wanted romance and marriage, like her sisters, but had no strategy except to wait for it to happen. Dating was absolutely prohibited by her parents. Her conversations were handicapped by residual autistic verbalisms,

> but by far the greater handicap was her ineptitude in social reciprocality. She was not only shy, but eccentrically idiosyncratic and socially inept, as well.
>
> Shyness and social ineptitude, without a prior history of autism, may represent an attenuated manifestation of the same phylismic deficit of troopbonding that, in more intense degree, produces autism. To illustrate this hypothesis, I am able to draw on a comparison between a girl and her maternal grandmother's sister. Each of these two people, the autistic girl and her great aunt, had a history of having required extensive psychiatric help, including hospitalization. The child's diagnosis was autism of the most severe degree. Her great aunt, had, at one time in younger life, been given a diagnosis of schizophrenia, from which she subsequently became wholly rehabilitated as both a reticently shy person and an internationally esteemed genius among creative artists. She compared her own shyness with that of her grandniece in the following anecdote. She was on one occasion visiting the child's parents, when company arrived. She gravitated away from the roomful of people into an empty hallway, still visible through an open door, but with a rapid avenue of escape available. There in the hallway, she found that the child also had gravitated away from the people, and was hidden from their view. She recognized that, quite independently, each of them had had the same reaction. It was a reaction of social phobia with which she had been familiar all her life—hovering in a doorway, or near a stairway, ready to slip away and be alone, should the presence of people become too jeopardizing. She recognized that, whatever the unknown entity that made the company of people, especially strangers, jeopardizing to her, her grandniece had a stronger, and more incapacitating degree of it than she did, herself.

Love shy men and women may have an attenuated form of whatever it is that underlies the extreme deficit of troopbonding in autism. The analogy extends to savantism, for the intellectual achievement of some, though not all of the love shy is hypertrophic, as is reflected in their being nicknamed nerds. With luck, they may be rescued from aloofness by a partner with a lovemap that is reciprocally as audacious as their own is shy. The no-holds-barred sexuoerotic exuberance of their masturbation fantasies is then freed for live performance, and they are not inhibited as lovers. Their emancipation is dependent on the new found partner, however. If the partner should leave, they are beset by an immoderately severe attack of lovesickness, and are vulnerable to major somatic and mental symptoms.

Lovesickness

UNREQUITED LOVE IS a synonym for unrequited limerence. It leaves a person vulnerable to an attack of lovesickness. Lovesickness may be transitory or prolonged, and major or minor in degree. It may be brought on by a person's anticipatory uncertainty about getting or not getting a reciprocal response to his/her limerence. Lovesickness may be brought on also by unequal proportions of limerence, for example, 100:70 instead of 100:100. The most unequal match is 100:0, total rejection.

The formal definition of lovesickness (Money, 1986) is as follows.

> **lovesickness**: the personal experience and manifest expression of agony when the partner with whom one has fallen in love is a total mismatch whose response is indifference, or a partial mismatch whose reciprocity is incomplete, deficient, anomalous, or otherwise unsatisfactory.

The bodily signs of unrequited limerence resemble those of stagefright (see chap. 8), but they are more intense and more persistent. Loss of appetite and insomnia add to the overall debilitation. Distractibility multiplies, and concentration gives way to intrusive and obsessional rumination, and to the rehearsal of scenarios of unrequited limerence being converted to limerence requited. Concessions and alibis are concocted to justify the beloved's indifference, while waiting in vain for token evidence that a change of heart may be on the way.

When the token fails to materialize, the lovesick person cannot take the advice of friends and colleagues to seek out a new partner, for limerence at its height precludes the possibility of being limerent toward more than one person at a time. When the break is final, a possible although by no means universal ending is a spontaneous transfer of thought and activity to an all consuming preoccupation with work that temporarily excludes being limerent.

Conversely, the all consuming preoccupation with unrequited limerence persists, at the expense of scholastic achievement or job performance. In the case of a college student, he/she can't get out of bed on time, can't keep on schedule for class instruction, can't concentrate on studying, can't finish assignments, and can't halt failing grades, but mopes around alone, too often unable to socialize, and falls into tears if trying to account for what has gone wrong.

Among college and university students, lovesickness of this incapacitating type is a good candidate for the syndrome that most frequently escapes diagnosis. It has no officially recognized name, and is not listed in textbooks or diagnostic manuals. Without a diagnosis, it has no recognized prognosis or form of treatment. It is subject to misdiagnosis, for example, as depression.

For many students afflicted with incapacitating lovesickness, the first therapeutic relief lies in the discovery, familiar in many different diagnoses, that the malady has a name and is not personally blameworthy. Although no specific treatment exists, in the majority of instances lovesickness goes eventually into spontaneous remission. In the interim, the nonjudgmental support of friends and healthcare professionals is called for, and maybe an absolute necessity as a constraint against suicide or homicide, or both.

Lovesickness is most prevalent in the years of unattached adolescence and young adulthood, prior to the establishment of long term pairbondedness. Although the ratio of its prevalence in men and women is not known, it is possible that males are more susceptible than females. Male lovesickness contradicts the widespread notion that men's sexuality is unlike women's in being animalistically physical, exclusively, and lacking in romantic attraction, love and limerence.

Lovesickness may take the form of a bizarre and obsessional fixation known in the clinical sexological literature as Clérambault-Kandinsky syndrome (CKS) (Jordan and Howe, 1980), and also known as erotomania (see chap. 14). It is characteristic of this syndrome that limerence is foredoomed to be unrequited since it is directed toward a person who, relative to one's own status, is inaccessibly high in the social order, for example, an entertainment star, sports idol, politician, priest, teacher, physician, aristocrat, billionaire, and so forth.

A well-known case of CKS is that of John Hinkley whose hapless inamorata, the film star, Jodie Foster, was unresponsive to his importuning in writing and by phone. She had recently been acclaimed for her role as a teenaged prostitute in the film, *Taxi Driver*, directed by Martin Scorsese. She played her character so convincingly as to make her continued limerent eligibility seem feasible to Hinkley. But she was not eligible. Her rebuffs increased the desperation of his limerence unrequited until the only way of commandeering her attention was by a suicidal assassination attempt on the life of someone as prominent as the President of the United States of America. Ronald Reagan was the President, and the date was March 6, 1981, in the morning. Hinkley's farewell note was addressed to Jodie Foster and was dated 1:00 A.M., March 6, 1981. It read: "Goodbye! I love you six trillion times. Don't you like me just a little bit? (You must admit I'm different.) It would make all of this worthwhile. John Hinkley" (*Johns Hopkins Magazine*, 35[1]:44-45, February 1983). Hinkley had been undergoing psychiatric treatment, but the diagnosis had been of schizophrenia, not CKS.

Intense one-sided, unrequited CKS happens not only at a distance but also face to face, as in a teacher-student, therapist-client, or doctor-patient relationship. The only safe way to handle such a CKS relationship is to keep out of it, right from the beginning. Don't shit where you eat is the saying that engraves this advice in a student's memory. In other words, as a professional, provide only the professional services contracted for, and don't switch to the sexual services of a love affair. The legal and professional penalties are too great a risk. CKS is capable of contriving mischief so deviously that its target person is legally always well advised to consult with a colleague, and possibly with an attorney, instead of reacting alone. The CKS person is falsely convinced, to the point of delusion, that the target of his/her one-sided limerence is actually limerent in return, but dares not reveal it until a later date, even years ahead. When that date passes, delusion may become a full-blown psychotic breakdown with a manic depressive cyclicity. When on a manic high, the CKS patient is limerently optimistic, but homicidally and suicidally despaired when on a depressive low.

In medical practice, the intimate tactual contact of the pelvic or the genitourinary examination may be an incitement not only to limerence, but also to sexuoerotic arousal and attraction, either homosexual or heterosexual. For males, there's no hiding the evidence of an erect penis which, for some adolescent males may be an embarrassment, and for others an inducement to make a sexual advance. It is not part of the health education of either patients or doctors to have been prepared for such a sexological exigency. The young and inexperienced medical student needs a formula of how to proceed, namely, to have available a hand towel that can be placed over the genitalia with a comment that the genital reflexes are all in normal working order. This comment opens the door to a more detailed sexological history, should it be needed.

Stalking

AS THE UNREQUITING target of limerence, you become part of the mental furnishings of the limerent person's mind. There you may stay forever, trapped and unable to engineer your own escape. A person owns his/her own mental furnishings which means that, entrapped there you wield inordinate influence, simply by depicting the image of love unrequited. As your three dimensional self, you may be subject to reprisals for not being a reciprocating lover. You may be subject also to blackmail, and to being stalked until, failing to reciprocate on demand, you are issued a death threat. If the death threat materializes in homicide, then the stalker's suicide may follow.

The melodramatic madness of the stalking version of CKS justifies the syndrome's alternative name, erotomania, for it may intensify, like a tropical depression intensifying into a hurricane, into a monomaniacal psychosis. Characteristically, it is a self-sabotaging mania, mindless of consequences.

In 1992, a case of maniacal stalking that received national attention was that of Sol Wachtler, chief judge of the New York State Court of Appeals (Wolff, 1992; Henican, 1992). His marriage of forty-one years ran concurrently with a limerent affair that began at a family reunion. The limerent couple were distant step-relatives. He was a handsome and wealthy young lawyer and husband in his early thirties, and she a future New York socialite of great wealth and beauty, still only fourteen. Their limerent affair, prudently and discreetly shielded from gossip, survived his one and her three marriages until, after her third divorce she took a new paramour and broke up with Judge Wachtler.

The normally circumspect judge, respected for his intellect and judgment, was precipitated into a frenzy of limerence unrequited. In a series of anonymous cards, letters, phone calls, and even posing as a private investigator, he made bizarre demands and threats of blackmail, ostensibly to bring about a restitution of limerence, but actually to destroy it totally, and his career to boot. Echoing the onset of his limerence when it was requited by the lady when she was a fourteen year old, he wrote to her own fourteen year old daughter, with a condom enclosed, making unseemly sexual suggestions. By the time he had threatened to kidnap this girl for a ransom, the FBI were already at work on the case. FBI agents traced threatening phone calls to Judge Wachtler's mobile car phone and to pay phones. Sounding frantic, in one threat from a payphone he said:

> You're gonna get a letter from me and you better listen to every word of it and do what it tells you to do or you're gonna be in serious deep trouble and you're not gonna see your daughter again, you hear me? I'm a sick and desperate man and you'll be hearing from me (Wolff, 1992).

The judge's final undoing was to make phone calls, heedless of FBI wire-tapping, demanding payoff (in absurdly small amounts) to prevent further threats of kidnapping and blackmail. Finally he set the time and place for a pickup. FBI agents trailed him, of course. Instead of adhering to his own instructions, he apparently became distracted, or perhaps disoriented and in a trance-like state. He left Manhattan and headed back to his home on Long Island. After he drove past Exit 33 on the expressway, the agents sounded their sirens and swooped in—a posse of eighty or so strong, to catch a single, unarmed, lovesick judge. Presumably no one in the FBI knew about Clérambault-Kandinsky syndrome.

Cyclic Limerence

THE STALKER CANNOT let go of the illusion of the power of love to conquer all, even the one on whom it is fixated in vain. The clinical reverse of stalking is having a reiterative dependency on the elated high of multiple new love affairs. The fixation is on repeatedly going through the cycle of a broken heart, a period of debilitating misery, and a return of elation generated in a new love affair.

This cyclic fixation does not have a proper clinical name of its own to match the street term, love junky. This term not only names but also trivializes and jocularizes the condition. Far from being trivial, however, it can seriously undermine and destroy the afflicted person's career, especially the career of someone prominent in public life. Quite apart from the possibility of provoking reprisal from a jealous rival, the prominent person's new love affair may be politically too sensitive to be officially overlooked, as in the case of a former senior diplomat. He confided that the level of his work efficiency increased and was contingent on the elation of being high on a love affair.

This dependency thwarted good sense and good judgment. He could not explain it to himself. It had, however, ever since small boyhood, been dangerous for him to have faith in the long-term continuance of a major relationship. He was six when he suffered the trauma of arriving home from school to be the first person to discover his father lying dead from a heart attack while mowing the lawn.

Biographically, despite its importance, such an event does not have explanatory value sufficient to encompass in full the origin of a fixation on cyclic limerence. A more comprehensive explanation is needed.

Contributing to that explanation, Liebowitz (1982; Liebowitz and Klein, 1979) came up with a brain-chemistry hypothesis based on the resemblance between people who are high on amphetamines and those who are high on limerence. According to the hypothesis, a limerent high might be mediated by a heightened brain level of the neurotransmitter substance, phenylethylamine (PEA), which resembles amphetamine in chemical structure. Chocolate is a natural source of PEA. Chocolate is also a self-medication of love junkies when they are limerently deprived. The media has gained much mileage out of this chocolate connection, and of the significance of boxes of chocolate as Saint Valentine's Day gifts. But the PEA hypothesis remains still in the realm of science fiction.

Imposturous Limerence

THE LIMERENT IMPOSTOR, if a man, is named after the literary character, Don Juan, or the Italian autobiographer, Casanova. There is no corresponding eponym for the female limerent impostor. She is likely to be characterized in the vernacular as a siren, or more pejoratively as a nymphomaniac. In the psychiatric vocabulary, nymphomania in the female is the counterpart of satyriasis (see chap. 14) in the male, both of which are terms for ostensible insatiability of the sexual appetite.

Irrespective of the name by which they are known, imposturously limerent people are not simply hypersexual in terms of the multiplicity of their sexual acts and sexual partners. Their defining characteristic is that, though they are able to embark upon what appears to be a limerent relationship, something from within intervenes to prohibit its continuance. Each failure propels them to begin anew. In the vernacular, they become compulsive cruisers, finding and failing, finding and failing, over and over again, and being not able to explain their compulsion to themselves. Unlike cyclic limerents, imposturous limerents do not fall into the depths of depressive despair, but remain buoyantly afloat, leaving broken hearts behind them as they move from one affair to another.

In some instances, limerent imposturing is a seductive bait that gives access to additional imposturing. For example, by imposturing as a lover and as a financial advisor to a lonely, elderly widow, an impostor may embezzle all of her wealth. Correspondingly, a young woman may imposture her way into marriage with a mentally declining nonagenarian and within a year or two become heir to his millions.

Don Juans and their female counterparts have, in the popular imagination become symbols of envious lechery. They are not, however, symbols of sexuoerotic fulfillment. On the contrary, they are symbols of an insatiable quest for a holy grail that cannot be found except in the concealed recesses of the quester's mind. A compulsive Don Juan may, for example, be on an unfulfillable quest for a replica of the girlfriend of his childhood puppy love who was killed in an explosion from which he himself escaped. Each unsuccessful quest terminates with a vow never to repeat it. But the power of the compulsion to repeat prevails, and the vow is broken, no matter how dire the consequences.

Imposturing occurs irrespective of orientation as homosexual, heterosexual, or bisexual. Among religious and highly achieving youths there are some with a three-way imposture of sexing, thieving, and lying which may be regarded as a syndrome. The sexing is covertly gay, the thieving kleptophilic and not for gain, and the lying confabulatory and patently fantastic (pseudologia fantastica).

Paraphilic Limerence

PARAPHILIA IS THE biomedical term for what in the law and in psychoanalysis still goes under the name of sexual perversion. On the street, paraphilia is called kinky or bizarre sex. In adolescence, a paraphilia presents itself as a mental rehearsal in the form of a dream or fantasy waiting to be put into practice. Its imagery and ideation are sexually exciting and at the same time disturbing for the young person to whom the paraphilia presents itself.

With respect to limerence, the special feature of a paraphilia is that it is a formula for keeping limerence sacred and free from profane and concupiscent lust. In the course of growing up, many children are exposed to the idea, if not actually trained in the belief that sexual lust and the sex organs are sinful and of Satan, whereas affectionate love is spiritual and of God. Lust is below the belt and between the groins. Love is above the belt and between the ears. Lust is condemned and punished. Love is endorsed and rewarded. A paraphilia upholds this partition of love and lust. Spiritual love is for one kind of partner, and concupiscent lust for another, and the two cannot be combined for one partner alone. For example, a paraphilic serial rapist does not assault his wife or girlfriend for whom he has love and affection, but a deficiency or absence of concupiscence and carnal desire, whereas for the women he assaults, he has no love, only carnal concupiscence.

The partitioning of two incompatibles is a compromise that preserves each of them, but at a price. The alternative would be for one of the two to become atrophic. Concupiscent atrophy is apparently what happens in the development of many girls, whereas the development of love and limerence remains intact. In adolescence and adulthood such girls have a phobia for genital touch and vaginal penetration. Sexual intercourse for them lacks pleasure and must be tolerated if not for the sake of the partner, for the sake of becoming pregnant.

Phyletically, it is not feasible for concupiscent lust to become atrophic in boys insofar as the procreation of the species is dependent upon erectile arousal of the penis and the ejaculation of sperms. Paraphilic partitioning of love and lust preserves lust from extinction, even though love and limerence may become partially split off or wholly atrophic as well. In its own devious and roundabout way, a paraphilia represents a triumph over the potential tragedy of losing the function of lust altogether (see also chap. 16).

10

Traditions of Pairbonding

Transculturalism and Limerence

Before the 1980s, cultural anthropologists circumvented romantic love as being perhaps too ineffable and perhaps tainted with lasciviousness to be seriously studied in tribal peoples. Marriage customs were more readily documented and less controversial. In our own culture, psychologists too have with few exceptions veered away from romantic love and attraction. Pundits complain that science leaves nothing sacred or mysterious, and that love belongs to poets and philosophers. For adolescents awakening to the ascendancy of a first love affair, the primary sources of guidance are the media: comics, movies, television, videos, novels, popular songs, rap, and the Internet. This is true in cultures as widely separated as Europe, North America, Latin America, Islam, India, China, Japan, and Australia.

Limerence is phyletic and is distributed transculturally throughout our species, not just to selected groups. From puberty through adolescence and beyond, it confronts young people everywhere. Their response is not transculturally identical. On the contrary, it is transculturally variable, for different cultures have different sexosophies of limerence—different stipulations as to the role of limerence in the social order. In particular, each regional and local culture, large or small, stipulates its own sexosophy regarding its conventions of limerent bonding, with respect to procreative and marital bonding.

In our own culture, there has long been an uneasy alliance between marriage as a family dynastic arrangement and marriage as an individual limerent arrangement. Marriages arranged by families are contracts for the union of wealth, title, property, and power, as well as for the provision of heirs. Whether or not they include limerent love is coincidental. By contrast, limerent marriages are arranged exclusively by the two individuals concerned and are family contracts only coincidentally. The limerent intensity of mutual attraction varies. It may prove to be evanescent. With ulterior motive and intent to gain, and on the basis of the verbalism, "I love you," attraction also may be impostured.

In today's love matches, there are vestiges of the dynastic arrangement, insofar as in many families there is pressure on the offspring to marry within the faith or ethnic and economic group, and to bring the prospective spouse home for family approval. The prospective groom asks his prospective bride's father for her hand in marriage and it is the father who, at the wedding ceremony, gives his daughter away.

The millions of young people whose love lives are in one way or another affected by today's Euro-American marital system are unaware that the system is actually a compromise between two equally ancient systems. One is the betrothal system of ancient vintage predating recorded history in tribal Europe. The other is the dynastic system of historic early civilizations of the Middle East that followed Imperial Rome into northern Europe.

Betrothal System

THE DEFINING CHARACTERISTIC of the betrothal system is pregnancy after betrothal and before marriage. Proof of the capability of family formation is a prime consideration in a rural community in which the unit of subsistence is the family. In Europe, the betrothal system has remained virtually intact in Iceland, and in somewhat more attenuated form also in sub-Arctic Scandinavia. In Denmark it is called "night courting," (Hertoft, 1977). The literal translation of its Finnish name is "taking your night legs for a walk."

In Finland, and elsewhere in northern Scandinavia, it is still possible to find a "girls' house" among the buildings of nineteenth-century farms. From the ceiling of the first floor storage area a trap door could be lowered to provide access to the girls' sleeping loft on the second floor. It was only after the spring thaw, when the season was warm enough, that the girls of the farm took up occupancy. In winter they and everyone else slept around the hearth of the great fireplace in the farmhouse kitchen, so as to keep from being frozen to death.

On Saturday evenings in spring, roving bands of local youths would go from farm to farm, serenading the occupants of the girls' houses. If the boys were welcome, the girls in a loft would lower a rope ladder from the window of the loft, and the boys would climb up. By the nineteenth century, and perhaps earlier, they would bring vodka for a party.

Should it become evident that a boy and girl were sweet on one another, their friends would eventually arrange for them to be alone after party time on Saturday nights. The customary protocol dictated that initially he would sleep fully clothed, above the bed covers, then partly undressed, between the covers, and finally together with his beloved under the covers. The two would then advise their families of their betrothal which would be publicly celebrated with a grand party. Not until after a baby was born would the couple be considered married. The obligation of a church marriage did not become established legally until as recently as the eighteenth century in Sweden (Hertoft, 1977).

Remnants of the betrothal system can still be traced through the mountainous rural regions of eastern Europe to the Alps. From Britain, Scotland, and Holland it migrated to the New England colonies where, in the eighteenth century, it was known as "bundling" (Stiles, 1871). Bundling was practiced more by the lower than the higher social classes. It was practiced by lovers or would be lovers. Thus it institutionalized limerent attraction as the basis of pregnancy and marriage subsequently endorsed by family, church, and community.

Dynastic System

THE DYNASTIC MARITAL system is the one favored especially by the rich and powerful, as the bride and bridegroom bring in a new increment of family power and wealth. In the absence of written records, its origin may be assumed to be a concomitant of the invention of fortress cities and monuments together with hierarchically distributed and inherited title, authority, property, concubinage, and enslaved manpower. Alliances by marriage have succeeded where feuding or force might have failed in the consolidation of political, economic, or military power. They posit the authority, usually patriarchal, of the ruler or parent to enforce the compliance of the bride or bridegroom to be.

From wherever dynastic marriage first appeared, it gained currency across a vast portion of the planet in the most ancient civilizations. It was carried across Europe by Imperial Rome, but made its initial entry into Europe through ancient Greece.

In Athenian democracy, although there was no titled nobility, there was a social hierarchy and a privileged elite for whom arranged marriage favored the maintenance of privilege. For Athenians of this class, marriages were dynastic arrangements contracted primarily for the convenience of procreation. The Athenian resolution of the discrepancy between dynastic and betrothal marriage was effected by disregarding betrothal marriage and substituting in its place limerent love relationships that were ideally between not men and women but between youths and their older male mentors who had themselves graduated from being youthful lovers. It was an ideal for the education of the upper class, recorded for posterity by Plato in two of his books, *Symposium* and *Phaedrus*, written two and a half millennia ago (Jowett, 1892).

In *Phaedrus* there is a passage that describes the experience of limerent love:

> [He] who has been the spectator of many glories in the other world, is amazed when he sees any one having a god-like face or form, which is the expression or imitation of divine beauty; and at first a shudder runs through him, and some "misgiving" of a former world steals over him; then looking upon the face of his beloved as of a god he reverences him, and if he were not afraid of being thought a downright madman, he would sacrifice to his beloved as to the image of a god; then as he gazes on him there is a sort of reaction, and the shudder naturally passes into an unusual heat and perspiration, as he receives the effluence of beauty through the eyes.

Apostrophizing the soul as she, Plato continues:

> . . . the soul is oppressed at the strangeness of her condition, and is in a great strait and excitement, and in her madness can neither sleep by night nor abide in her place by day. And wherever she thinks that she will behold the beautiful one, thither in her desire she runs. And when she has seen him, and drunk rivers of desire, her constraint is loosened, and she is refreshed, and has no more pangs and pains; and this is the sweetest of all pleasures at the time, and is the reason why the soul of the lover never forsakes his beautiful one, whom he esteems above all; he has forgotten his mother and brethren and companions, and he thinks nothing of the neglect and loss of his property; and as to the rules and proprieties of life, on which he formerly prided himself, he now despises them, and is ready to sleep and serve, wherever he is allowed, as near as he can to his beautiful one who is not only the object of his worship, but the only physician who can heal him in his extreme agony. And this state, my dear imaginary youth, is by men called love.

In the *Symposium*, Plato has Aristophanes relate the myth that explains the three variations of limerent love. It is the myth of the children of the moon (androgynous), the sun (males), and the earth (females). In their primeval form, all three sexes

> were round, with back and sides forming a circle: and they had four hands and four feet, one head with two faces, looking opposite ways, set on a round neck and precisely alike; also four ears, two privy members, and the remainder to correspond. . . . They made an attack upon the gods and the gods could not suffer their insolence to be unrestrained. At last after a good deal of reflection, Zeus discovered a way. . . . I will cut them in two, he said, and they will be diminished in strength and increased in numbers; this will have the advantage of making them more profitable to us.

To save the split halves from the frenzy of trying in vain to reunite, Zeus turned their parts of generation to face one another. Thereafter, they joined together again only as lovers. Aristophanes continued his story, saying:

> Men who are a section of that double nature which was once called androgynes are lovers of women. . . . The women who are a section of the female do not care for men, but have female attachments. . . . They who

> are a section of the male follow the male, and while they are young, being slices of the original man, they hang about men and embrace them, and they are themselves the best of boys and youth, because they have the most manly nature.

Plato's idealization of ephebiatric love (love of adolescent youth) was also an idealization of bisexuality. It did not exclude man-woman relationships but rather maintained the segregation of boys from girls during the adolescent years of exclusively male education until they were ready to become the head of an Athenian household. In later centuries, this system became unofficially and in part resumed in sex segregated monastic institutions, and later still, before females became eligible for higher learning, in boys' boarding schools. To some extent, the system has persisted also in military schools, barracks, and prisons.

Although Imperial Rome absorbed much of Greek culture, and although it was no stranger to ephebophilic and pedophilic sexual practices, it did not institutionalize academic ephebophilia as the Greeks had done. Military Rome was more given to dynastic power than democratic Athens had been. Family arranged marriages for the enhancement of dynastic power became the social norm. Limerent love might be consummated, but with concubines or slaves, not in formal marriage unless coincidentally. Women were subservient to men, and children to the caprices of their fathers.

The arranged marriage survived the collapse of the Roman Empire and thrived in Europe under the rise of feudalism and the spread of Christianity in the Middle Ages. According to Christian doctrine, the betrothal system was sinful, for it promoted sexual intercourse prior to the sacrament of marriage. It also condoned the pleasure of sexual intercourse which the Church condemned except as a carnal necessity to be reserved for procreation exclusively. Early Christian theologians, borrowing from Neoplatonism and the pre-Christian Greek gnostic doctrine of the opposition of the spirit and the flesh (Lawrence, 1989; see also chap. 1), had adopted a severely ascetic theology regarding the carnal delights of limerent love as being of the flesh and the devil. Pure and sinless spiritual love was the ideal. Women who got carried away with erotic enjoyment and orgasm were cast in the role of harlots. Later in the Middle Ages they would be accused of being witches and heretics and burned at the stake.

Being phyletically ordained, limerent love could not, of course, be eradicated from individual lives. Saint Augustine (354-430), the great Christian theologian and philosopher, wrote of his own experience with it in his *Confessions*, calling it concupiscence, the lustful passion that arouses the flesh. A Roman by parentage, Augustine was born near Hippo in the northeast corner of present day Algeria and educated there and in nearby Carthage, now Tunis. His mother, Saint Monica, was a Christian by upbringing. His father became Christian later in life.

As a student in Carthage, Augustine and his girlfriend, quaintly called a concubine, began what he later called "a bargain struck for lust." For fifteen years they lived together. When he was twenty, they had a son. Two years later the three migrated to Rome, to be followed by his widowed mother, and thence on to a post in Milan. As a teacher of rhetoric, Augustine struggled with the rival doctrines of Neoplatonic Manicheanism and Christianity.

Favoring an arranged marriage over a long term love affair, Saint Monica found a suitable bridal family, with a daughter soon to be of marriageable age. Compliantly, Augustine sent his son's mother back to Hippo where she joined a religious community. His son's sad fate was to die by age seventeen. Of the forced breakup, Augustine later wrote, "This was a blow which crushed my heart to bleeding, because I loved her dearly." Beset by the weakness of the flesh, he prayed, "Give me chastity, but no not yet." While waiting for his bride-to-be to become of age, he took a second concubine. His agony of yearning ended abruptly when, in the garden with Olympius, a student, he underwent a mystical experience of religious conversion and gave up "lust and wantonness" forever. After returning to his home town in North Africa he lived unmarried with companions until called to the Christian priesthood, eventually to become Bishop of Hippo (Wright 1981; Gaden, 1981; Harris and Levey, 1975; see also Money, 1985).

Troubadours: Romantic Love

SAINT AUGUSTINE'S PERSONAL life symbolizes the victory of the dynastic system of marriage by family arrangement over the betrothal system of marriage by mutual attraction and limerence. Confronted by the combined power of the feudal state and the Christian church in shoring up marriage for dynastic union, betrothal marriage for concupiscence was doomed. Concupiscence for one's own wife was as great a sin as concupiscence for another man's wife, according to Vincent of Beauvais in his *Speculum Doctrinale*, a manual of moral doctrine much adhered to in the Middle Ages. It declared that:

> A man who loves his wife very much is an adulterer. Any love for someone else's wife, or too much love for one's own, is shameful. The upright man should love his wife with his judgment, not his affections (Boswell, 1980, p. 164).

Moral doctrine, despite its penalties and penances, is no match for the power of a phyletically inbuilt response like limerent attraction. Limerence, although banished from medieval marriage, could not be banished from medieval lives. It survived by shedding its connection with procreation and being transformed into a new social convention, under the name of courtly love or romantic love. The agents of the transformation were the troubadours, roving bands of street musicians and entertainers, also known as jongleurs. Their historical record begins in Provence, in the southeast corner of France, in the eleventh century, and coincides with the rise of Catharism, a Manichean religion, also known as the Albigensian heresy. It was brutally persecuted and exterminated by Rome in the Inquisition of the thirteenth century.

Troubadour political poems were popular as also were their songs of war, nature, and especially love. They were sung not in the Latin of church chants, but in the Provençal vernacular. Their influence may be compared with that of rock-n-roll musicians and rap poets of our own era. It spread widely across France, into Italy, and northward to the minnesingers (love singers) of Germany. The troubadour songs and writings that have been preserved for posterity are those composed by members of the aristocracy.

The recurrent theme of the troubadour love song is the hopeless agony of love that cannot ever be consummated. The marriage of the fair lady, for whom the lovelorn knight is ready to die, has already been arranged or has taken place. The lovesick knight begs for any token of her love, a tender touch, or an undying glance. One troubadour song laments: "Never was archer able to draw more straight than she who shot into my heart the sweet death of which I wish to die, unless she restore my joy with a glance of love." Ostensibly the knight's affection is wholly honorable, and his love spiritual, but the weakness of the flesh is quite transparently ready to surrender at the slightest encouragement, regardless of consequences.

In Italy, Dante (1265-1321) was heir to the troubadour tradition. He denatured carnal desire and spiritually idealized it extravagantly in the poetical history of his mystical love for Beatrice. When they first saw one another, each was nine years old. His love for her remained permanently unrequitable. She died at the age of twenty-five.

Love forever unattainable culminating in murder, suicide, or both, became a melodramatic staple of Italian and European grand opera, and remains so to this very day. The apical expression of the troubadour plaint of limerence unrequitable, however, awaited Shakespeare's *Romeo and Juliet* in 1594. This drama infused the troubadour formula of romantic love permanently into the English language. There it still exercises compelling power through the arts and entertainments on young people from adolescence and early adulthood onward.

Aphoristically the modern legacy of the troubadours is summed up as marrying for love versus marrying for money. Love and the checkbook are the sources of family feuding over the suitability of a potential bride or bridegroom. They are also, in the final analysis, the two great categories of marital feuding and breakup.

Slavery's Legacy

In America, there was neither marriage by betrothal nor by arrangement for black slaves, American slaves had no legal rights, including the right to the legality of marriage and parenthood. Thus, by definition, it was impossible for the baby of a black slave mother to be illegitimate, and equally impossible to be legitimate.

As prepubertal juveniles, slave boys and girls knew from the evidence around them that they would encounter no impediment to early breeding. On the contrary, a slave girl upon attaining menstrual maturity would be encouraged, if not forced, to produce new slave babies. She would not know in advance, however, whether her baby would be fathered by a lover or by enforced copulation with a slave selected for breeding, or by a white youth or man from the plantation house. It was not expected that the same male would father all of a woman's children, but rather that there would be serial fatherhood. It was acceptable for a black female to be a white man's concubine, insofar as the colored babies could be classified as slaves, maybe as house slaves, with a semi-privileged position. By contrast, there was no place in the plantation mansion for the colored babies of a white woman. Her black lover was automatically classified as a rapist and most likely lynched.

Although it is not to be spoken of lightly in polite company, there is an aftermath of miscegenation still today. Among the offspring of many black families, there is a hierarchy of prestige and privilege based on lightness of skin color. Genealogically, light skin signifies that black female slaves had white men's babies. Whereas white men do not today have a position of prestige in the lovemaps of black women, by contrast white women do have a position of prestige in the lovemaps of some black men. To have a white girlfriend is a mark of male achievement that was absolutely unattainable in the era of lynching.

Following delivery, the young black mother was put back to work as soon as possible. Those responsible for baby care were the yard slaves, the elderly and infirm. Living quarters were provided at the discretion of the plantation manager who also supplied food and clothing. A mother and her child's father might be separated by distance and different ownership, or, if the father was white, as a consequence of miscegenation. She might lose her children if the family was put up for auction and sold separately.

Some slave owners, especially those with only a few household slaves, were more humane than others. Nonetheless, the main outline of the breeding system under slavery was evident to all, namely, pregnancy early in teenage whether within a limerent love affair or by arrangement of the master; separation of the father from his children and their mother; childrearing by the grandparental generation of yard slaves; and food, clothing, and shelter at the discretion of the master.

The significance of this system is not only historical but also contemporary, for by the process of cultural lag, it has persisted in both rural and urban traditional, ungentrified black culture. The main difference is that subsistence food, clothing, and shelter is now the responsibility of the welfare check, not the plantation manager. The family in this system is three generational. It is anchored by the grandparents, particularly the maternal grandmother. The proper age for marriage and the responsibility of household formation is in midlife as grandparents, not as young parents.

The three-generational family has a significant, not surplus role for grandparents, and it recognizes the sexual and procreative energy of youth. Its flaw, in contemporary America, is that it is not supported within the nation's economic, legal, and tax system, and is out of synchrony with the two generational, nuclear family of the white majority, middle class population.

The black cultural heritage of the three-generational family is under political and moral attack by the majority who have declared war on unwed motherhood and have classified teenaged pregnancy as an epidemic, even up to age nineteen,. As the twentieth century ends the attack escalates, with no end in sight. In other nations and at other times, young parenthood has been encouraged with family payments and incentives. There is, in fact, much to be argued in favor of early instead of late childbearing. Adolescent parenthood clears the way for females to plan a second career, but only if the necessary economics of young parenthood are accommodated within the national cultural pattern, which is not the case in the United States today (Money, 1994).

Black gentrification is the process whereby blacks assimilate white culture and leave black culture behind. Acculturation is not, however, a one way street. Black culture also becomes assimilated by whites—in the case of black music, not by whites only, but by people everywhere, worldwide. Thus the three-generational family of early unwed parenthood and late household formation and marriage has become increasingly assimilated into white culture, particularly at the lower economic level. At the upper economic and educational level, unwed motherhood is also a feminist political statement. The change toward being unwed is evident, in addition, among young college age adults who live together for an extended period before becoming parents and marrying. In the age of HIV/AIDS, this may with solo masturbation prove to be the most secure protection against the deadly infection.

Under the banner of family values, the white middle class, majority culture of the two parent, two generational nuclear family is in mortal combat with the minority culture of the three generational family which is the legacy of slavery. Especially if they are black, young women are economically punished for being unmarried mothers. Law enforcement, notably under the strategy of the war on drugs, disproportionately imprisons the jobless fathers of their children.

Cultural traditions are not wiped out by self-righteous justification, legalism, and moralism. Cultural traditions disappear only when the people who carry them are wiped out by disease, war, or genocide. Let us not await that extreme! Teenaged pregnancy in the tradition of the three generational family is not an accident, not a crime, and not a sin. It has its own honor, its own morality, and its own cultural history, the cultural history of a minority, and it deserves its own respect.

Dying for Love

IT IS POSSIBLE that the two partners in a limerent love affair are approved of by their families as a suitable match for an arranged marriage, but such a coincidence cannot be counted upon. Another possibility, in a polygamous society is that, after an arranged marriage, a subsequent marriage may be a love match. Where polygamy is illegal, the love match would be with a kept mistress or concubine whose existence might be either overtly or covertly acknowledged.

Yet another way in which the arranged match and the love match are concurrent is if they are pitted against one another in the expectation of provoking a feud. This was an ancient aboriginal system of population control, remnants of which survived until as late as the 1960s and beyond, among the Yolngu of Elcho Island, Arnhem Land, on the southern shore of the Arafura Sea, in Australia's Northern Territory, an aboriginal reserve (Money et al., 1970).

The settlement of Galiwinku on Elcho Island owes its location to the availability of fresh artesian bore water during the annual drought that follows the monsoon. It is one of a string of denominational and/or governmental settlements that functioned in the aftermath of World War II to provide tribal aboriginals with the option of an introduction to membership in contemporary Australian culture. The alternative was threatened extinction from the perils of living in small stone-age troops on "walkabout" in the bush.

At Galiwinku, contact with the outside world was from the airstrip or the jetty, or by walking. The mission aircraft made monthly deliveries of food and medical supplies needed by people whose leaders had not yet brought them in from the bush. The coastal supply ship docked three or four times a year bringing gasoline for the farm machinery, bulk foods, school, clinic, and building supplies, and goods for the general store.

Small plane service from Darwin, 300 miles (500 km) to the west was twice a week. Darwin was the nearest place from which to obtain any type of alcohol containing beverage. Alcohol was totally prohibited in Galiwinku.

The cash economy was poorly developed at Galiwinku, service in some cases being in exchange for goods. The industries were fruit and vegetable farming; wood carving, bark painting, and basketry; fish exporting (until stopped by an outbreak of typhus); and housing development. Housing was in two camps. Upper camp housing was mission built and sturdy. Lower camp houses were temporary shacks. Some families used their houses for storage, and lived outdoors, sleeping around the campfire. Educational, obstetrical, and medical services were free. Membership in the church (Methodist) was optional.

There were approximately nineteen different variants of language or dialect spoken by the thousand or so people living on or near Galiwinku. The speakers of each variant belonged to the same totemic clan and were classified as kinsmen. Eligibility for marriage was determined by complicated totemic rules of social permissions and avoidances which applied in particular to those eligible to be "promise" partners in marriage. Promise partners belonged to different linguistic and totemic clan groups. Children learned two languages, the father's and the mother's. English was becoming the lingua franca. In addition, a Yolgnu lingua franca was being forged from the different dialects.

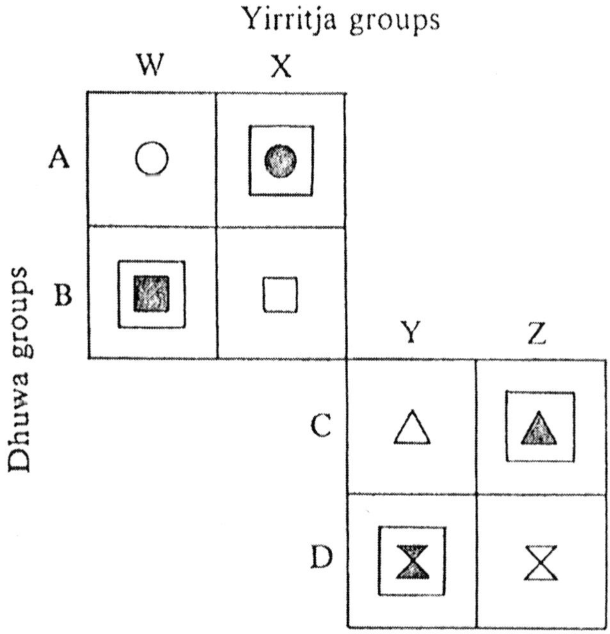

Figure 8. *Groups permitted to intermarry can be schematized in a dual 2 X 2 table. Solid symbols enclosed in squares indicate second choice; open symbols, first choice*

After a boy went through the initiation ceremony of circumcision, the dhapi, in late prepuberty, the relationship between him and a female eligible to become his future mother-in-law was one of respectful avoidance. The two must not address each other directly, but only when looking away from each other, through an intermediary.

The avoidance rule did not apply to women who, by reason of a boy's totemic classification, were ineligible to become his mother-in-law. The avoidance rule did, however, apply to their daughters. The boy's own sisters were in this category. So also were the daughters of his mother's sister who, by reason of sisterhood polygamy, might be his half-sisters as well as his first cousins. To prevent breaking the avoidance rules, males and females of all ages mixed not together, but in sex segregated groups.

The eligibility of a female to be a male's mother-in-law was decided in theory, and according to the genealogy of totemic clan relationships, even before either of them was conceived. Mathematically, one could classify the relationships in the same way that a biologist schematizes an experimental breeding design in a dual 2 x 2 table (figure 8). Instead of having strains of mice, one has "strains" of Yolngu: four of them classified as Dhuwa type and four of them as Yirritja type. The mating is fixed, so that each Dhuwa strain is matched with its own special Yirritja strain. However, one alternative matching is permitted as a second choice. Thus if all a man's available partners have been used up, then one, and only one, second choice "strain" is permitted. If all his available partners in that alternative strain have been used up, then the hapless man should resign himself to spending his life single, unless in the future an eligible widow might become available. There is no corresponding problem for a woman, since she can go to a man who already has one wife or more.

Actually, this dual 2 x 2 system is said to be a fairly modern borrowing from the Arunda people of the central desert of Australia. The older system which it purports to replace, though not completely, is even more restrictive, for it simply dictates that a male shall have his mother's brother's wife for a mother-in-law. All of her daughters (his first cousins), no matter how many, will be his wives. If his mother had only one brother, whereas he himself has three or four brothers younger than himself, then that would be his good luck and his brothers' misfortune. He would get all the cousins as wives and, unless he would lend a wife to a junior brother, the junior would remain wifeless. Responsibility for paternity if the wife on loan became pregnant was not an issue insofar as, granted the antecedent necessity of copulation, the actual occurrence of conception was held to be the responsibility of benevolent spirits.

The promise system did not prevent boys and girls in teenage from falling in love with partners to whom they were not promised. The promise system and love-affair system existed side by side in irreconcilable juxtaposition. Officially, a girl went obediently to her promise man when her mother told her to, even if he were twice her age or older. Equally officially she illicitly flirted, making bold and open sexual suggestions to a youth to whom she was attracted. The young man, too, followed the same formula of bold but illicit sexual invitation, culminating in a secret rendezvous and sexual intercourse in the bush, probably after dark.

One example of the risky challenge of the love affair was that of a young man who would wear a dress with stuffed breasts as a camouflage so that at nightfall he could accompany a group of girls along the beach below the village and then sneak off illicitly into the shadows with his girlfriend.

In another example, the risky challenge of the love affair became evident in the murmuring sounds of awe that rippled across the water from the shore to a motor launch loading in preparation for a trip to an outer island. A young woman was wading out from the shore, carrying a bucket of food for her lover on the boat. Their love affair had already been rumored. Flaunting it in public, so that her promise man could no longer ignore it, was an act of desperation in defiance of the incorrectness of their totemic relationship. It was also a challenge to her lover to take her across the sea, where they would elope into walkabout in the bush.

An illicit love affair generated for both the boy and the girl the tension and excitement of gambling, lest their identities be revealed. For the boy, it was a case of walking knowingly into a trap, and for the girl of knowing that she had knowingly led him there. In former times the pair might take off by foot or canoe to a far distant camp, in the hope of escaping the offended promise man until he had cooled off and was willing to take a material compensation. But the greater likelihood was that the offended promise man would respond with having no option: only the death of the intruding lover would be sufficient revenge. Once marked for murder, a young man had no foolproof means of escape from the treachery that would almost certainly get him, in the long run. His death would then need to be avenged by the death of the one who killed him. Only violation of sacred places compared with "woman trouble" as a provocation for vengeance feuding.

Falling in love thus was a highly dangerous business. It occupied a central position, quite literally, in the world order of things, in the balance of life and death, regeneration and extinction. Love led to violence. Violence got rid of male lovers. Lust and aggression both having been taken care of by death, the shortage of men could then be offset by polygamy—and a self-perpetuating system was in existence. Such a system was self-limiting with regard to population growth: one man can repeatedly impregnate several wives, but he cannot guarantee the survival of all their progeny—and the progeny of monsoonal Australia has always been remarkably low, like that of neighboring, head-hunting New Guinea, as compared with the millions in nearby Indonesian islands whose fisherman have visited Arnhem Land for centuries.

Falling in love as a means, albeit indirect, of regulating population growth is in all likelihood a uniquely aboriginal Australian cultural institution. To offset excessive sexual deprivation of some tribal members, there was also the institution of the kunapipi festival, a weeklong celebration of chanting and dancing the tribal mythology. Sexual constraints were relaxed at the kunapipi.

Serial Bisexualism

BEING CONCURRENTLY bisexual means being a person who engages in explicit sexual activity with at least two people, one male and one female, together or severally, during a particular period of time. It is possible to engage in sexual acts with both male and female once, or even several times, and thus to be bisexual by history, without changing from being predominantly heterosexual or homosexual in orientation. In the person with a predominantly bisexual orientation, the ratio of hetero-to-homo sexual orientation may be 50:50, but the ratio may be disproportionate, 60:40, for example, or 25:75.

Being serially bisexual means being a person who engages in explicit sexual activity exclusively with a male or males and with a female or females at two different periods of time. Being serially bisexual is compatible with being predominantly heterosexual or homosexual, or with alternating more than once.

Serial bisexuality is known to occur selectively, among, for example, some boys who are institutionally sex segregated at puberty in residential schools, or at a later age in prison or in the military. They engage in homosexual acts, but their predominant orientation is ultimately heterosexualism in the majority of cases.

Serial bisexuality is not elective but a cultural imperative for all boys of the Sambia people in Papua New Guinea (see chap. 1). Isolated in the remote mountain vastness of the Eastern Highlands and maintaining their stone age way of life as warriors, the Sambia were not discovered and pacified by the Australian government until the late 1950s onward. In 1968 their tribal warfare was finally eliminated. Six years later the anthropologist Gilbert Herdt (1981, 1984, 1987) began living in Nilangu, one of a dozen Sambia villages or hamlets with a total population of 930 in the valley of the Sambia River. There he stayed for two years. He learned the language and recorded the customs. Subsequently he returned several times.

Herdt was permitted to be a participant observer in the triennial initiation cycle, the twenty-third one of the twentieth century. The traditional brutality of the hazing and breaking-in of young boys was unadulterated by modernism. It forcibly instilled their obedience to the brutalities of warriorhood, even though the traditional culmination of initiation in an actual war raid, outlawed by the Australian administration, would no longer take place.

Initiation took place in six stages, each lasting approximately three years. Novices might be as young as seven or eight or as old as ten years. The first two stages were prepubertal, the third began after puberty the onset of which might be as late as fourteen or fifteen. By stage four, a boy's kinfolk would have found a suitable bride. Sex segregation being total, he would not have seen her, and would not do so until after her first menstruation, possibly in the late teens. He would then live with her and be considered a married man, but would not reach the sixth and final stage of manhood until he became a father. He would have arrived at this final stage of exclusive heterosexuality by way of a prior prepubertal and adolescent stage of exclusive homosexuality. Until he went to live with his wife, he was in adolescence strictly forbidden even to see a female, including his own mother and sisters. Contact with or the smell of their body fluids, he was warned, would sicken him and he would die.

For the Sambia youth, marriage was an arrangement of the tribal elders over which he had absolutely no say-so. Likewise, he had been given absolutely no option regarding the tribal arrangement of the homosexual phase of his career which began with the symbolic, stage one initiation ceremony of sucking the flute. This ceremony was preceded by three arduous days of exhaustion from sleep deprivation, restricted food and water intake, being beaten and thrashed, bled from a sharp cane thrust into the nostrils, stung all over with stinging nettles, and harangued by the elders—all without knowing in advance what would happen next. At the secret ceremony of sucking the bamboo flute, the youths and older men revealed their secret knowledge of the necessity to drink men's milk, semen, as they themselves had done to become men. The boys would need to do the same, and to do so as often as possible. Then, led by a shaman, the boys dressed as novice warriors, were paraded around the decorated dance ground and led into the men's new culthouse. There they would sleep for the remaining four nights of initiation, joined by adolescent and unmarried bachelors. Although there was erotic talk and frantic sexual horseplay inside the culthouse, men's milk was sucked from the older males' penises outside in the dark, in private.

Subsequently, back in the home village the two age groups would live together in the men's large clubhouse, guarding their secret relations from the women and children of the village. They engaged only in oral sex, not manual masturbation and not anal sex. Once mature enough to ejaculate, a boy graduated to stage three of initiation, which required him to give his semen to the younger boys. To take more semen himself was forbidden. The homosexual arrangement continued until the fourth stage of initiation, the age of marriage. At the beginning of marriage, the husband gave his man's milk to his wife initially only by mouth. Vaginal coitus came later. Contacts with boys progressively diminished and with rare exceptions, perhaps during periods of menstrual or postpartum abstinence, ceased.

Having matured sufficiently to be able to ejaculate and donate semen to prepubertal boys, adolescents would (Herdt, 1987, p. 162):

> . . . go through a phase of intense sexual activity, a period of vigorous homoerotic activity and contacts, having one relationship after another with boys. Their sexual behavior is primarily promiscuous, for the initiates are concerned mostly with taking in semen, while the bachelors mainly desire sexual release through domination of younger boys. Occasionally a youth and a boy will pair off for a few days or even weeks. But these infatuations seldom last long, both parties fearing that others will stigmatize them as "unmanly."

What Herdt characterized as infatuation might be construed as a transient, age-limited, limerent love affair. Some boys were more sought after as fellators than were others. One atypical boy who was extremely enthusiastic as a juvenile fellator avoided being fellated after he became an adolescent. As an adult he had a permanent fixation not on being fellated, but on fellating boys, including prepubertal boys, which other villagers considered highly bizarre. His whole life was bizarre from the time that his father had repudiated him instead of taking his pregnant mother as a second wife. Consequently he had no paternal relatives and no recognized sponsor for his initiation. He was an outcast (Herdt, 1981, pp. 166-67; Stoller, 1985, pp. 116-17). By contrast, another boy who evaded being a fellator before puberty, also evaded getting fellated in adolescence. In adulthood he was more closely bonded with his wife than were other Sambian men, apparently in a love relationship (Stoller, 1985, p. 132).

Despite the future warrior's long sequestration from girls and women, and the terror inculcated in him of the danger of being contaminated by female secretions and odors, in adolescence he began to become heterosexually interested. Herdt (1987) wrote:

> Teenage boys also begin having daydreams about sexual encounters with women. This is very private talk: they share these daydreams only with their most intimate male friends as they fear being shamed or punished. These conscious thoughts are also reflected in their night dreams. At this point adolescents report that their wet dreams shift from homosexual to heterosexual images. In a sense, these are the youths' first heterosexual experiences, so they react with anxiety when they awaken from a wet dream, fearing a spirit woman (the flute spirit) may have stolen some of their semen. These fears pass soon enough, however, to be replaced by more powerful concerns about interacting with and marrying real women.

An excerpt from one of Herdt's interviews (quoted in Herdt and Stoller, 1990, pp. 117-18) illustrates the adolescent transition to heterosexual ideation and imagery. The informant is nineteen-year-old Moondi. The girl picked for him is seventeen, but he must wait until she has her first menses, and is not supposed to look at her. He says:

> She really hides it when she wants to look at my face. I haven't seen her face very well, so I only can think of parts of it. I sometimes sit down and think: the nose of my woman is like this; it goes down and curves up a little bit. And I think, "Oh that's really nice." And I think, "At night we would sleep together and do it, what all the *nupos* (married initiates) do. . . . They screw in the mouth. . . . Sometimes I think, "Suppose we constructed a house, a square house, the same kind as this one, with several rooms and one bed. We'd sleep in it, and when I wanted to, I could shoot [semen] in her mouth. Because we would sleep in the same bed, I'd feel even more excitement. And she'd feel excitement from being with me.

Moondi confirmed that whenever he thought about his girl his penis would get hard. In his daydream, he would ask her:

> "Can we do it?". . . And she says . . . "Oh, that's all right; we can do it." And I feel real excited; I really like sleeping with her. . . . I ask her softly. . . . I'm just asking her softly, that's all. I just want to ask her softly. It's just the two of us, I shouldn't have to really make big noises . . . in asking her. I just talk quietly. She's not far away. We're close together.

About daydreaming of boys, Moondi said:

> That belonged to before, when I was a new bachelor; then I used to imagine the boys. . . . I don't have sex much with the initiates any more. Before, yes. When we were down at Yellow Valley I used to do it lots of times with that boy . . . who was sweet on me. . . . But now? Not at all. I don't do it with boys now.

Moondi's lovemap was quite evidently preparing him for a limerent heterosexual relationship without any evidence as to whether or not it would be reciprocated by the girl. There is no corresponding report of an interview with her. Given the Sambia's strict segregation of men's and women's talk and affairs, an interview with her would, with virtual certainty, have required a woman interviewer. That lack accounts for the sparsity of information about Sambian girls and women, and their actual situation regarding the secrets of the men's house, and their own erotic and sexual secrets.

Whereas in marriage the range of partners was restricted to one alone, in adolescence Moondi had several potential partners among the novitiates, one of whom became his favorite. Their relationship was perhaps in part hero worship, and in part protolimerent. But it would last only so long as the boy remained prepubertal, after which he would no longer need to take men's milk, but to give it. Thus a long term homosexual affair was excluded by the cultural protocol. Sambian culture prescribed male homosexuality as a preparation for heterosexuality, but only after homosexual initiation into a fierce, all male sect of warriors, free from the distractions of limerent heterosexual love and love sickness. Limerence, if it occurred at all among fully qualified warriors who were not yet married, would be either limerence for the bride to be, or else would be adulterous, since mature women were either married or assigned to be married. Adultery would provoke a war raid against the intrusive offender's village.

Ten Constants of Pairbonding

TRANSCULTURALLY, SYSTEMS of pairbonding are not static. Although they are subject to change, they are not infinitely changeable, however. The extent to which they are flexible is under the constraints of ten transculturally constant criteria which are as follows:

Age: Each system specifies whether sexual partners will be age-matched or not. If not, then tolerance limits of age disparity are specified. A child bride in one system is, in another system, regarded as a victim of child sexual abuse.

Physique: Conformity with the age specification may apply only at selected stages of physical maturation. Juvenile sexual partnering with agemates, positively endorsed as sexual rehearsal play in one system, is prohibited and abusively punished in another. Geriatric partnering is ridiculed in one system, and necessary to survival in another.

Gender: Specifications as to when or where to pair with a member of the same sex, the other sex, or both, or neither, vary as to whom, within a system, they apply. In homosexual pairing, what one society prescribes as imperative in adolescence, another prohibits and punishes as sin, sickness, or offense. Teenaged pairing with ensuing pregnancy also is judged antithetically as either ideal or reprehensible, depending on how great a premium there is on young grandparenthood.

Kinship: Within a social system, kinship may be bestowed either genealogically, or on the basis of totemic descent. Either way, the sexual pairing of two individuals may be enforced if they have the correct kinship relationship, and denied if they don't. The enforced marriage of first cousins in one system, in another is prohibited as incest.

Caste or Class: The specification of within-clan pairing in marriage is, by extension, analogous to the specification of marriage to a person of the same caste, class, religion, race, or language group. A partnership that is stigmatized or penalized as miscegenation in one system may be tolerated or even romanticized in another.

Number: A system specifies how many sexual partnerships it permits or condones. If more than one partnership is tolerated, then the when, where, and with whom of the multiple partnerships is specified. What is punished as adultery in one system is institutionalized as errancy under the double standard in another. Monogamy in one society is replaced by polygamy or concubinage in another. Prostitution is outlawed in one society, and legalized in another.

Overlap: Multiple partnerships are either concurrent or sequential. Legal polygamy under one system is a crime under another system which may, nonetheless, permit serial divorce and remarriage. Concurrent partnerships may exist in isolation from one another or, conversely, may coexist in communal sharing of more than two partners together in group sex.

Span: Either single or multiple partnerships may be transient or long-lasting. A system that specifies monogamous pairing for life may either persecute nonconformists, or tolerate them—especially transient ones.

Privacy: The extent of the specification of privacy in a sexual pairing is total when it forbids any proceptive flirtation whatsoever in public. It is partial when certain proceptive interactions are restricted in public. Both kissing and genital eroticism, for example, may be specified as indecent or illegal in public. Alternatively, if kissing is tolerated, and eroticism below the belt is not, then the latter is prosecuted as obscene and pornographic. Indeed, pornography can be defined as that which is depicted when a system's privacy specification regarding sexual pairing is disregarded. Even behind closed doors, the privacy rule may restrict a couple, if the rule applies to sounds of sexual intercourse, as well as its sights.

Accessories: The specifications applied to the where and when of sexual pairing may be detailed and intrusive—and likewise the specifications of what to do sexually with the organs and limbs of the body, either plain, or decorated with tattoo, scarification, mutilation, or ornamental accessories. A wedding band is an accessory that signals a change in what is permitted. Sexual toys may or may not be acceptable as erotic accessories, and the same applies to animals. It is, however, another accessory, namely, the contraceptive device in its various forms, that incites divisive controversy as to whether it should or should not be used in a copulatory relationship. Lack of contraception followed by abortion also incites controversy.

For practicing sexologists, the foregoing ten constants are applicable sociologically to the comparative analysis of different or changing cultural, moral, religious, or legal systems of sexuality. In the clinic, they are applicable to the diagnostic analysis of couple mismatching, and the formulation of therapeutic strategy.

11

Reformation and Counterreformation

Illegitimate Grandparents
Germ Theory
Rubber
Going Steady
Penicillin
The Pill
Age Distribution
Sex Ratio
Counterreformation
Sickness
HIV/AIDS

Illegitimate Grandparents

Adolescence brings to the forefront two exigencies of existence. One is to become ecologically viable with respect to food, shelter, and clothing. The other is to become procreative. Progress toward the one is not necessarily in synchrony with the other. Transculturally, it is common for procreative maturation to precede ecological adulthood. In other words, adolescents can create a pregnancy before they are educationally and vocationally sufficiently autonomous to support a family economically, without some form of subsidy. This discrepancy is particularly prevalent in our own automated and computerized industrial society, where we have run out of formulas for keeping adolescents in training and off the job market for as long as possible, and for providing universal employment in adulthood. Likewise, we have run out of formulas to prevent premature grandparenthood.

In vain do we whistle in the wind and call for adolescent abstinence, even from masturbation. We suppress explicit instruction on the use of contraception in adolescence, and we ban abortion. When a baby is born to an unmarried adolescent, the girl's parenthood is classified as illegitimate. More accurately, however, it is grandparenthood that should be classified as illegitimate. The baby's grandparents are the ones who must absorb most of the responsibility for its rearing, if the parents have not yet themselves conformed to society's expectation of economic independence preparatory to parenthood.

Illegitimate grandparenthood is fraught with ambivalence. On the one hand it is stressful, especially in the absence of family wealth. On the other hand it is sentimentally and affectionally highly rewarding. Teenagers know of this ambivalence in the society in which they live. At the same time they know it is not to be talked about openly, even if they are privately planning to become parents, or tempting fate to make the decision for them by having sexual intercourse without contraception.

For adolescents, not only is there a societal veto on talking across the generation gap about their sexuoerotic practices, but also there is no colloquial vocabulary with which to bridge the generation gap. A bridge would open the way to greater intimacy of two-way personal disclosure between parents and children, or teachers and students, than adults have been prepared to deal with. There are questions about their own sex lives that adults might be too embarrassed to answer, or that, in some cases, require answers that would be legally self-incriminating. It is easier to leave many questions unasked, or unanswered. In many instances, adolescents must get whatever education they can from their peers and from the media. Their role models, too, come often from the same sources.

Between the generations, privacy rules. Sex therapists specialize, by and large, in treating the problems of adults, not of adolescents. No matter how severe their problems of sexual dysfunction or of sexual psychopathology, most adolescents incubate these problems in private, with the exception of those who come to the attention of the law as sex offenders.

The decade of the 1990s is a decade of social and governmental antisexualism. The counterreformation that geared up in the 1980s in reaction to the sexual reformation of the 1960s and '70s stirs up moralizing passions. An impartial history of what has happened is needed, beginning with germ theory.

Germ Theory

THE SEXOSOPHY OF the Victorian era, like much else in the zeitgeist of that era, is noteworthy for its Janus-faced blend of negation and permission. In obedience to the sperm depletion theory of Tissot (see chap. 1), Victorian sexual morality was intensely restrictive, whereas the private lives of the wealthy and aristocratic were libertarian, if not licentious. At the same time, medical sexology was unobtrusively putting down roots and paving the way for sexual emancipation to expand and include a larger proportion of the population.

The formulation of germ theory in the 1870s, following the experimental discoveries of Pasteur and Koch, marks a watershed between the old and the new in sexological medicine (Woodward, 1989). Before germ theory, it was plausible for the adherents of semen conservation theory to attribute many symptoms of illness to excessive depletion of semen in promiscuity and masturbation. After germ theory, these symptoms were attributable to a history of infection, particularly of syphilis and/or gonorrhea. The doctrine that sexual sinfulness alone could cause illness was no longer tenable.

Rubber

EUROPEANS FIRST MADE their acquaintance with rubber in the form of balls used in games played by pre-Columbian Americans. They were fashioned from the resinous latex sap of the tropical *hevea* tree. Charles de la Condamine, leader of a 1731 French expedition to the Amazon, wrote of this resin:

> They cover molds of earth in the shape of bottles with this material and when it is dry they smash the mold, take the pieces of earth out through the bottle neck, and have an unbreakable bottle which is useful for all kinds of liquids (Trumbull and Newton, 1958, p. 605).

Who in 1731 would have thought that, a couple of centuries later, this Amazonian technology would be industrially adapted to cover the shape not of a bottle but of a penis? The invention of the latex condom (by conjecture, named perhaps for de la Condamine) was not a planned antecedent of the sexual revolution of the twentieth century, but a fortuitous spin-off of the new industrial technology of rubber.

The condom story begins as early as 1839 with Charles Goodyear's experimentation with the vulcanization of the sap of the rubber tree, a process that he patented in the U.S. in 1844. Hancock, in England, modified the process and obtained his patent first, in 1843. Crepe rubber was eventually applied to the manufacture of contraceptive devices for women and men. Hearsay has it that the rubber condom was introduced to the general public in Philadelphia at the U.S. centennial World Exhibition (Himes, 1963, p. 201).

The popularity of condoms was limited by their coarseness, until improved technology in the 1920s allowed them to be made directly from liquid latex. The new product was not only extremely thin and strong, but also mass produced and inexpensive. Legally, however, it could be marketed only under the ruse of being for protection against disease, not for contraception. Condoms were widely distributed in newly invented vending machines placed in men's toilets, gas stations, taverns, and tobacconist shops. Gynecologists, fearful of legal consequences, mostly refused to fit women with rubber diaphragms on the basis that they encouraged women to be immoral without the penalty of pregnancy.

In the early twentieth century, the technology of the automobile became allied with rubber technology. Together with the rubber condom, the automobile also contributed to the dawn of the sexual revolution in the era in which courting changed to going steady. Young people who had access to an automobile were provided with backseat privacy for heavy petting and "making out" up to, or including orgasm, with or without penovaginal intromission.

From the 1930s onward, for the benefit of long-distance travelers, a new industry began to spread along highways, namely, the roadside motel. Motels provided more comfort, privacy, and anonymity than the backseat of a car for young couples who adhered to the standards of the new morality of sexual emancipation.

By the time the liquid latex condom was on the market in the 1930s, the women's movement of the late nineteenth and early twentieth century had succeeded in gaining the franchise for women in many countries. Europe and America had undergone the disruptions of World War I (1914-18), and had embarked on a prolonged celebration of peace in the extravaganza of the jazz age, until the collapse of the stock market in 1929, followed by the Great Depression and the outbreak of World War II in Europe in 1939.

Going Steady

THE JAZZ AGE brought with it a new degree of sexual emancipation, initially for young adults among the educated and wealthy from whom it filtered down to the less privileged social classes. The old and conservative rules of courtship were that, very soon after a young couple began "keeping company," their families and friends would expect a formal notice of engagement. After an interval of about a year, possibly less, the wedding would be announced (Cate and Lloyd, 1992).

Under the new, emancipated rules of going steady, young women would flirt with and date several boyfriends for variable periods of time, before committing themselves to marriage. Petting and heavy petting might be engaged in, possibly culminating in orgasm. Penovaginal coition, with or without contraception, remained problematic, however, as young men, especially those of college age, would boast of their conquests, whereupon a girl would become branded as a slut and an easy lay. That label could be somewhat avoided if a couple had announced their intention to marry, and if she remained faithful to him. He did not necessarily have to remain faithful to her.

Whereas dissemination of knowledge about contraception in the United States was officially prohibited well into the twentieth century by the so-called Comstock laws against obscenity, publicity of arrests related to birth control was not. For example, news coverage of Margaret Sanger's arrest in 1917 for operating a family planning clinic in the Brownsville district of Brooklyn, New York, informed millions of the existence of contraception for women overburdened with poverty and too many pregnancies, and for all other women too (Kennedy, 1970). Information spread also by word of mouth from contraceptive users. Progressively, the plausibility of separating sexual intercourse from pregnancy and sexually transmitted disease became disseminated not only throughout the adult population, but also down the age scale to adolescents in high school. Among them, too, contraception led progressively to the obsolescence of the old system of courtship and engagement, and replaced it with the new system of going steady.

Students of high school age might let it be known that they were going steady by an exchange of class rings. Wrongly sized for the finger, they would be worn as a pendant. At college age, a girl might wear her steady boyfriend's fraternity pin or his letterman's sweater or varsity jacket. Quite apart from such tokens, a couple going steady would be known to their friends who would gossip about a breach of fidelity. For some couples, fidelity would merge into marriage and long-term monogamy. For others, going steady would be time-limited for a few weeks or months, or until the end of the school year, with no stigma attached to separation, or to going steady with different partners, sequentially. The majority expected that eventually they would marry. Some would save their virginity for marriage. That meant not having penovaginal penetration. It did not necessarily exclude heavy petting manually or orally to orgasm, especially orgasm for the man rather than the woman. Irrespective of orgasm, however, going steady represented more of a change for young and adolescent women than men, insofar as it wedged open the door to a sequence of partners before becoming bonded long term and embarking on parenthood. Sexuoerotic variety of partners had formerly been the prerogative of males.

Going steady in combination with the consistent use of condoms diminished not only the chance of becoming a parent, but also of contracting a sexual infection in the era before antibiotics.

Penicillin

IF THE TWENTIETH century history of the serendipities of science on planet Earth should ever be mythologized by marooned Argonauts of an earth colony lost far out in the galaxy, then the penicillin story would qualify as a truly great myth. Its serendipity begins in 1928 with a bacterium, staphylococcus, growing in tissue culture fluid in a glass Petri dish, on a laboratory bench by an open window. Mysteriously, an expanding circle appears on the surface of the culture, within which all the cells die off. Sir Alexander Fleming examines the die-off microscopically and finds an invasion of cells of a species of mold from the genus *Penicillium*. The killer spores have drifted down from a mold colony in the laboratory on the floor above, and through the open window. Fleming realizes that there must be an active substance in the *Penicillium* mold that could be used to kill disease producing bacteria that invade human beings. And there the matter lies for eleven more years, until 1939, by which time World War II begins and wounded soldiers are dying from bacterial infections. The secret substance that would cure them is still locked away in Fleming's mold.

In 1939, biologists working on antibiotics in the laboratory of Sir Howard Florey begin trying to identify the secret antibacterial substance produced by *Penicillium*, and to purify it. In 1941 they reach success, and penicillin is born. It proves to be safe for human use, and to be effective in the treatment of a variety of pathology producing microorganisms.

So much for history as myth. The wartime demand for penicillin was immense. It's manufacture as a laboratory procedure was, by 1941, transformed into industrial mass production, with the *Penicillium* mold grown in vast fermentation vats. Penicillin proved to be only the first of a great many antibiotics derived from molds and fungi, or synthesized in the laboratory. Early in its history, penicillin proved to be very effective against the bacteria of syphilis and gonorrhea, and it remains so, although various other antibiotics are satisfactory substitutes.

In the late 1940s, after the conclusion of World War II, penicillin became no longer a rare commodity, but a mass marketed pharmaceutical product, readily available for the treatment of syphilis and gonorrhea. It was also used prophylactically, although that practice was advised against lest it lead to the development of bacterial resistance. Either way, in the 1950s it had an immense, though silent influence as a serendipitous herald of the sexual revolution about to be precipitated among those who would come of age in the '60s, as well as those who came of age ahead of them. The catalyst that finally set the revolution rolling, however, was the contraceptive Pill.

The Pill

THERE WOULD HAVE been no Pill except for the great burst of sex hormone research that led up to it. In the 1920s, steroidal hormones from the ovaries and testicles, and peptide hormones from the pituitary gland were extracted from animal tissue, and their role in the regulation of reproduction began to be elucidated. In the 1930s, their chemical structure was deciphered, thus paving the way for their synthesis in the laboratory and their mass production at an affordable price. First, however, there had to be a plentiful supply of raw materials. It was in the discovery of steroidal raw materials that fortuity played a part. Their discovery, like the discovery of penicillin, is the stuff from which myths are made (Djerassi, 1984; McGarry, 1987; Bullough, 1994).

The story begins in the laboratory of Russell Marker who, in 1935, quit working at the Rockefeller Institute in New York City to become eventually a professor of chemistry at Pennsylvania State University where he could pursue his own interest in steroidal chemistry, particularly of saponins and sapogenins, and specifically diosgenin. Sapogenins are steroidal substances found in plants of the genus Dioscorea. When shaken with water they make a soapy froth. In Latin, *sapo* means soap. Diosgenin is named for Dioscoredes of Anazarbos, a botanist, pharmacist, and encyclopedist of materia medica who, in the first century A.D., described a herbal drink made of sapogenin, said to prevent conception.

Diosgenin is biochemically a steroid, as are also the sex hormones, progesterone, which is a precursor of testosterone, which is a precursor of estrogen. By 1940, Russell Marker had already used diosgenin as a raw material from which to synthesize progesterone in small amounts. He needed a plant with a much greater yield of diosgenin. In 1943, after screening 400 plant species, he found one in the jungles of Veracruz, Mexico. It was a tropical yam known locally as the black headed yam (*cabeza de negra*). The yield of diosgenin from the root of the barbasco vine was even greater.

Marker was more at home in the laboratory than in business. His discoveries reduced the cost of progesterone from several dollars to a few cents a gram, but he did not exploit it commercially to his own advantage. Nor did he pursue the laboratory development or clinical applications of the hormones he had produced. In fact, in 1949 he quit steroid chemistry altogether and retired. Other scientists expanded the research he had begun and met its challenges, of which the most significant was the challenge to produce an orally active steroidal contraceptive pill with no unpleasant or undesirable side effects. The substance that fulfilled these conditions was an analogue of progesterone, 19-norprogestin. It was synthesized and announced by Carl Djerassi in 1952. According to Vern Bullough's account (1994, p. 193):

> The impetus for an oral contraceptive based on Djerassi's discovery came from a coffee table meeting of Margaret Sanger and Gregory Pincus in Abraham Stone's New York apartment in 1950. Stone and his wife, Hannah, had founded one of the first fertility clinics in the United States, if not the world . . . Pincus was codirector of the Worcester Foundation for Experimental Biology. Sanger, a continual crusader for better contraceptives, ended up urging Pincus to investigate the possibilities of steroids for contraceptive use. Sanger, however, did more than urge. She also had a source of money willing to support such research. The money came from Katharine Dexter McCormick [heiress to the International Harvester fortune, and an MIT graduate].

Pincus and his research team conducted clinical trials of what would become the Pill in collaboration with the Family Planning Association of Puerto Rico, with additional trials in the United States and Haiti. Their product was trade named Enovid. It was cleared by the U.S. Food and Drug Administration and put on the market in 1960.

The popularity of the Pill, marketed under various trade names, spread rapidly. As a contraceptive it was more dependable than other methods. To borrow from computer jargon, it was also user friendly. It gave women personal control over their own fecundity. It was taken, like a medicine, by mouth, instead of having to be put in the vagina. Also, it was taken as a daily routine, without having to be coordinated with advance planning for sexual intercourse on a specific occasion. The hiatus between swallowing the pill and having sexual intercourse offered protection from pregnancy for those who, although intending to abstain from penovaginal intercourse, succumbed in a moment of high passion to the weakness of the flesh. For most people, however, the Pill was a pragmatic and rational technique of sexual emancipation.

The latex condom, the automobile, penicillin, and the Pill are four examples of technological innovation, either invented or borrowed, that fortuitously change the mores and the morals of how people relate to one another. The other type of fortuity is demographic, namely, changes in population size and density, or in the age and sex distribution of the population.

Age Distribution

IN THE TWENTIETH century, the planet Earth began to show foreboding signs of being overpopulated by the human race, relative to its resources. People were breeding too prolifically. Infant deaths in the first year of life became fewer wherever modern medicine and public health penetrated. Those who survived their first birthday lived longer into old age. Whereas in the eighteenth century the estimated life expectancy of those who survived their first birthday was around thirty-five years, by 1900 it had increased to forty years (see chap. 7). Today, in developed countries, males may expect to live until between seventy and eighty, and women even longer.

Another factor that contributed to the population explosion could be traced in record-keeping countries over the last two hundred years, namely, the lowering of the age of the onset of puberty from midteenage and upward, to early teenage or preteenage and upward. The younger the age of puberty, the younger the probable age of first intercourse. In all likelihood, except for the use of contraceptives, the younger the age of first intercourse, then the younger the age of first pregnancy and of increasing the population explosion.

In addition to the phenomenon of the population explosion, there was also at the conclusion of World War II a shift in the age distribution of the population. During the war, people had held back on having babies, but when the war was over they made up for lost time and produced the baby boom. Postwar babies born from 1945 onward became the first of a generation of teenagers to come of age just in time to swell the ranks of the sexual revolution of the '60s and '70s. If they used contraception, they had protection against pregnancy, and if they resorted to antibiotics, protection against disease. In an overpopulated world, they had no obligation to be early breeders. Procreative and recreational sex were two different entities in the sexual revolution.

The sexual revolution signified sexual liberation in an era of political liberation movements: liberation from colonial oppressors; black liberation; women's liberation; and gay and lesbian liberation. Liberation movements that were politically focused were not closely allied with the sexual revolution. Very briefly in the late fifties and early sixties, sexual liberation was included on the agenda of women's liberation. It soon yielded to equal rights politically, legally, and vocationally. Men became not the allies of women's sexual liberation, but in some quarters its targets.

For many people sexual liberation was only one segment of a larger protest against what many baby boomers considered to be moral bankruptcy of their elders. They protested also against the war in Vietnam. Thousands left the country to avoid the draft. In 1970, when Nixon was president, National Guardsmen gunned down four white student anti-war protestors at Kent State University, and two black students were killed at Jackson State. Thousands gave voice to protest in the philosophies of rock and roll lyrics and music that their elders abhorred. They enshrined their own pantheon of hippy poets, singers, artists, and writers, and adopted their own hippy form of dress and adornment. Men wore long hair. Discharged from Harvard, two psychologists, Timothy Leary, and for a brief period, Richard Alpert, became their gurus and guides to the New Age mysteries of mind-changing psychedelic seeds, fungi, herbs, and synthesized drugs like the newly discovered LSD. Entranced, New Age adolescents and young adults found unity with the cosmos. By living in self-providing communes, they found unity with their fellow beings. With multiple sexual partners, they found unity in being sexually emancipated. They were the flower people; founders of the counterculture. Their slogans were "tune in, turn on, and drop out," and "make love not war." Some used contraception. Some had babies with midwife assisted home deliveries. Some resorted to abortions, the right to which was protected constitutionally as reproductive autonomy in the 1973 Supreme Court ruling of *Roe vs. Wade.* In unanticipated thousands, New Age people converged from all over the nation at Woodstock, N.Y., in 1969, for the Summer Rock Music Festival, which marked the unplanned zenith of the countercultural revolution.

When the children of the Woodstock generation of the countercultural revolution reached adolescence, they defined the identity of their own generation, in part by rebelling against what their parents stood for. When they themselves became parents, many drifted away from the impracticalities of the counterculture and back into the American mainstream to exploit it. Some outwitted their elders at their own game, on Wall Street, for example, and as crusaders against drugs, equal rights, abortion, and sex. No longer activists in the countercultural revolution, the Woodstock generation as it grew older became indifferent to the antisexualism of the sexual counterrevolution that had begun as early as the '70s to get into gear under the auspices of the archconservatives of the political and religious New Right.

Sex Ratio

OF ALL THE babies that are conceived, for every hundred born as females, a hundred and four or more are born as males. The ratio at the time of conception may be as disproportionate as 100:140. More males than females perish prenatally. Additionally, the death rate for males exceeds that for females, postnatally, and continues to do so until the male:female ratio becomes even in the fifth decade of life. After that, the longevity of males being briefer than that of females, there is progressively an excess of older women.

In societies that value sons over daughters, boys may disproportionately outnumber girls as a consequence of female infanticide, wherever that practice is condoned. Modern obstetrical technology, namely amniocentesis and chorionic villus sampling, has rendered infanticide obsolete insofar as sex determination of the fetus is possible early in the pregnancy. In India and China today, early abortion as a method of controlling the rate of population expansion is performed selectively on female fetuses among families that favor a son (see chap. 6). It has already been calculated that the generation about to come of age in China will be one in which women as potential brides will be in short supply for the excess of marriageable men. How Chinese society will respond to this male to female disproportion remains open to speculation. Having more than one husband (polyandry) or a husband and a male escort are possibilities.

Disproportionate availability of either males or females as sexual partners in a society or a segment of society has not been the subject of serious demographic scholarship. Thus there are unanswered questions as to how different societies have dealt with a major kill-off of young men in war, or with mass emigration of males in search of work. The surplus of women maybe absorbed into institutionalized abstinence or, conversely, institutionalized adultery, concubinage, polygamy or, as a substitute for the polygamous private harem, the promiscuous public harem or whorehouse. Single parenthood, like widowhood, is also a possibility. Another possibility, when boys are in short supply, is to follow the high school example of girls dancing with girls, when boys are in short supply, and maybe attempting a lesbian affair, a practice which in some feminist quarters is a political statement of liberation from the evils of patriarchy.

An up-to-date solution of the male:female imbalance is to use the Internet to search for a partner at some location where the imbalance is reversed. Some towns or work locations have an excess of eligible men and others of eligible women. What appears to be an excess of eligible men may in some cities, however, turn out to be an excess of men who are ineligible except as homosexual partners. At some urban social gatherings, some eligible young women have found that the most well groomed and good looking young males avoid flirting, except with other men.

Disproportionate representation of eligible young men or women in society, whether temporary or long term, strains society's institutions of idealized sexual propriety. The strain that it puts on those in the role of matchmaker also is considerable, but less than the strain experienced by the young person in a society, like our own, that puts the primary responsibility on the individual of "waiting for the right one to come along" to make the perfect romantic match. Although a disproportionate male:female ratio was not a major factor in the sexual revolution, in the event that it did occur, the sexual liberation of the counterculture provided, as solutions, cohabitation, extended family sharing, partner sharing, or swinging. Unobtrusively, cohabitation preceding marriage has survived the strictures of the counterreformation. As a possible safeguard against HIV/AIDS, it no longer brings social ostracism and disgrace. In some families, however, parents of teenagers are still pretty iffy about having cohabitating offspring sleeping in the family home or eating at family dinner parties.

Counterreformation

ALTHOUGH IT BECAME dubbed the sexual revolution, the sexosophical change of the 1960s and '70s was more a reformation than a revolution and, as is historically typical of all reformations, it was overtaken by and still overlaps with a counterreformation. Socially and politically, the sexual counterreformation is part of a revival of fundamentalist religious doctrine which carries a strong heritage of nineteenth century antisexualism.

Boys and girls coming of age today encounter the ideological positions of the sexual reformation and counterreformation as being adversarial and irreconcilable—or, at least, as being unreconciled by many in the generation of their parents and grandparents. They encounter also a counterreformatory ideology that, in some political and geographical localities, successfully deprives them of an unexpurgated sex education and of open access to a full range of up-to-date sexological knowledge in the library, on radio or television, or on the Internet (see chap. 5). In many instances they must rely on the transmission of folk sexology and gossip among themselves, errors and all.

Folk sexology includes some topics that are forbidden in the academic curriculum. Nonetheless, they are topics in the public domain in the news and entertainment media, although only if they are dealt with euphemistically, or condemned as horrors of moral turpitude, without too much explicit detail. Thus it is not possible to advise boys and girls at puberty on the wisdom of masturbation, showing explicit live illustrations of male and female masturbation on videotapes. The same applies to education regarding pornography, homosexuality and bisexuality, oral and anal sex, incest, sex offending, and the publicized transgressions of priests, teachers, politicians, and other well known persons. For the most part, parents and educators themselves are sexologically illiterate as mentors of the young regarding these topics.

In folk sexology, there is no teenaged issue for which the counterreformatory logic is more garbled than teenaged pregnancy. In the media and in professional literature teenaged pregnancy is given the status of epidemic disease, which is very inauspicious for the self-esteem of a young mother, and eventually of her child. Preteen education on contraceptive methods for the prevention and timing of pregnancy is illogically strongly taboo. So also is explicit video instruction on how to use or apply contraceptives. For minors who need access to contraceptive devices, their availability is rarely without embarrassment or hindrance. Logic is further twisted once pregnancy has occurred. Counter-reformatory policy is against abortion and in favor of picketing abortion clinics. The final twist is the political illogic in the proposal to deprive the baby of maternal care by forcing the young single mother to find employment, even in high unemployment areas, and to deprive any additional siblings of subsistence by withholding welfare payments. Victims of this chain of illogic are not only teenaged, but also predominantly black.

Sickness

REVOLUTIONS, LIKE NEW medications, are subject to unforeseen side effects. In the beginning of the sex-revolutionary decades of the 1960s and 1970s, the carnival exuberance of multiple and frequent changes of partner, and of partying in group sex clubs, was not compatible with actuarial computations regarding the epidemiologic transmission of infection by way of sexual contact. Although the age-old venereal infections were still around, people gambled and took their chances. Syphilis and gonorrhea could be cured with antibiotics, and other venereal symptoms were regarded as minor. The possibility of a new microorganism, or of the resurgence of an old one was not of major concern.

Prior to the sexual revolution, the paradigm for the health dangers of promiscuity had for centuries been prostitution, namely that a diversity of infection is pooled in a small concentrated population of women by a dispersed and much larger population of men, some of whom become newly infected and carry the infection elsewhere to another partner. The sexual revolution changed the paradigm so that a large and dispersed population of women as well as men would form couples transiently and serially. Over time, each woman had many different male partners, and vice versa. This was the system that, by the late 1970s, permitted the spread of an epidemic, of the long known type 2 (genital) herpes virus. Some cases were benign; but, even in the severe cases, the frequency of symptom recurrence would eventually subside. Also, by 1983 the ointment, acyclovir, was on the market and was effective in ameliorating recurrent attacks.

The sexual revolution brought another change of the paradigm for promiscuity, namely a revival of the ancient bacchanalian or dionysian type of festival as an orgiastic sex party. As typified by Plato's Retreat in New York City, these gatherings became established for heterosexuals (admitted in couples only) in the early 1970s. For gay men they had begun earlier in bathhouses that had originally served as saunas for north European immigrants. Gay bathhouses became heavily patronized in New York, and San Francisco, as well as Los Angeles and in other cities. Patrons were not required to bring a partner, as in an all male establishment there were multiple potential partners.

For some patrons oral-anal stimulation (rimming) was a major erotic turn-on. Performed on a series of partners, this practice was a guaranteed method of transmitting the highly contagious hepatitis-B virus, a major killer, especially of children in the Third World. In the 1970s, the virus spread like wildfire among patrons of gay bathhouses in major cities. It lost its epidemiological threat when a vaccine had, with the cooperation of gay volunteers, been discovered and made available commercially by 1982 (Kaugman, 1982).

With the hepatitis-B virus subject to control by vaccine, there still remained the gay male health problem of gastrointestinal parasites and amoebic dysentery transmitted by oral-anal contact. Those conditions were treatable.

The apparent end of the health problems connected to the sexual revolution was, however, a mirage. The symptoms of a case of a new undiagnosable, untreatable, and lethal disease had been recorded in Denmark, and traced back to equatorial Zaire, where the patient, a physician, had practiced before she died in 1977 (Shilts, 1987, p. 7). This case remained unknown to American physicians who, in 1980 began to see patients with rare symptoms of what would eventually prove to be this same lethal disease. Five patients in Los Angeles had the same rare lung infection with *Pneumocystis carinii*. Six in New York had Kaposi's sarcoma, a rare form of skin cancer. All eleven patients had various other rare and unexplainable symptoms, some of which were typical of a case of a severely impaired immune system. All eleven had a history of being gay young men who were gay bathhouse patrons. The two sets of cases were first brought to medical attention in the *Morbidity and Mortality Weekly Report* of the Centers for Disease Control (CDC) in 1981, Gottlieb and Weisman's Los Angeles cases on June 5th and the New York cases of Friedman-Kien and Laubenstein on July 3rd (Shilts, 1987).

The new disease underwent name changes until July 27, 1982, when it was officially named AIDS (Acquired Immune Deficiency Syndrome). The discovery that it was a viral disease was announced in April 1984, but the official name of the virus, HIV (Human Immunodeficiency Virus) was not settled until two years later. By then it was already obvious to epidemiologists that an epidemic of sexual doom was already on its way to encircling the globe.

HIV/AIDS

EPIDEMIOLOGICAL SLEUTHING traced the HIV/AIDS epicenter to equatorial Africa, and there the trail ended. To this day, there exists no sufficient explanation as to where or how the virus originated, or when the first case of AIDS appeared. With the knowledge of hindsight, it is evident that, by the 1970s, some European men and women, residents of central Africa, had symptoms of AIDS and had died after they were flown home to be treated in vain.

During this same period, French speaking Haitians had resided and worked in recently decolonialized French speaking equatorial Africa. It is possible that some of them may have carried the virus back to Haiti. In Haiti, as in central Africa, the virus infected both men and women, its major route of infection being presumably through sexual contact with a plurality of partners.

From Haiti there was a direct connection with the wealthy New York gay community via the gay summer resort on Fire Island at Cherry Grove. Several gay landlords who rented rooms and apartments to gay clients at Cherry Grove in the summer had rental properties for the same clientele during the winter months in Haiti. One of the attractions of Haiti was the availability of Haitian men who were not gay but sufficiently bisexual to play, for pay, a masculine copulatory role in performing anal intercourse on, or receiving oral sex from gay American vacationists. Not all of the vacationists were New Yorkers, so that the virus was able to travel directly to other U.S. cities, also. In addition, contact between members of the gay communities of New York, Los Angeles, San Francisco, and other U.S., Canadian, and Mexican cities was frequent enough to ensure the virus an opportunity to spread to and from several centers.

The virus was, of course, quite lacking in discrimination as to whether it was being transmitted by a male or female, heterosexual or homosexual host. It simply took advantage of the transmission system available in Haiti, namely from heterosexual Haitian men to either women or gay American men. Gay men became the shock troops of its spread into the United States. This fortuitous circumstance led to the initial error of naming the illness produced by the virus the gay plague. Fundamentalist televangelists preached that it was God's vengeance on gay males for not being heterosexual.

The very name, gay plague, gave heterosexual people a false sense of security. As evidence of heterosexual transmission rolled in they found alibis: heterosexuals are infected only if they got transfusions of HIV contaminated blood, or if they are needle-sharing, intravenous (IV) drug users or the girlfriend or wife of a user; of if they live in Africa or Asia where prostitution is widespread and where men and women often can't obtain treatment for genital lesions through which the HIV/AIDS virus can find easy entry into the bloodstream.

Today, seventeen years after the first cases of full-blown AIDS were recognized in the U.S., heterosexual young people as they come of age still do not comprehend that the world counts the magnitude of HIV infection in the multimillions, and of AIDS in the millions of females as well as males. Nor do they realize that HIV/AIDS does not respect their heterosexuality. They are wrapped in the adolescent cloak of invincibility, sure that, no matter whom else the virus gets, it will not get them. They are the first generation to come of age in the era of HIV/AIDS and to bear the brunt of denial which their elders are reinforcing with denial of their own. Especially those of the middle or upper class are led by survey researchers into denying the presence of the virus in their heterosexual midst (Michael et al., 1994), the rapidity of its spread, and the certainty that it always kills those whom it infects, irrespective of the brevity or longevity of the incubation time.

Until a foolproof method is found of preventing infection or of killing or immobilizing the HIV/AIDS virus, young people coming of age in the present era, unlike those of any previous era, are confronted with the equation that sexual love plus the virus equals death. They need the nitty gritty of unexpurgated sex education so as not to depend on the capriciousness of the laws of chance to stay alive (see chap. 12).

12

Adolescent Sexual Practicalities

Conflicting Ideologies
Abstinence
Masturbation
Safe and Unsafe Sex
Mutual Precautions
The Virus Can't Get Me
Age of First Parenthood
Compatibility
Mismatched Lovemaps

Conflicting Ideologies

Long before arriving at the threshold of puberty and adolescence, children have since infancy been absorbing the folk ways and folk knowledge of sex, some of it adapted from ancient sexosophical teachings and some from modern scientific sexology (see chap. 1). Information from the two sources does not come neatly and separately packaged, but intertwined.

As early as between the ages of three and four, children pick up clues that words which name parts and functions of the body between the legs are less fit for polite company than words which name parts and functions of the face and the limbs (see chap. 5). Children who go to nursery school or who belong to a community play group also pick up clues that some words for the lower parts are naughty, and not to be uttered in the hearing of most adults. So, under the protective cover of silly laughter, they use the naughty words to ascertain with whom and when their use is either tolerated or chastised. Developmentally, this is an example of the way that children become attuned to the existence of two universes of sexual discourse and practice, the one tabooed and morally dirty, and the other polite and morally clean.

Sex did not become dirty until the twentieth century according to the Oxford English Dictionary. It quotes a 1912 letter of Rupert Brooke: "I shall repeat poetry to you; you will repeat dirty stories to me." The respectability of dirt as a synonym for soil or earth dates from the seventeenth century, and is derived from Old Norse and Middle English *drit*, excrement.

The use of dirty sexual words and practices is chastized and punished in childhood. Thus, as already mentioned in chapter 5, dirty words become weapons of defiance, retaliation, and insult. Sexual swearing or cursing is so effective in evoking wrath, that it is one of the strongest weapons children have when, in combat or dispute, they are unfairly matched in size, strength, and authority.

Enraged defiance of the sexual taboo is one way of circumventing its prohibitions. Humorous defiance is socially more tolerable. It has a venerable history in bawdy songs and ballads, narratives, novels, limericks, and dirty jokes. Sexual humor is also visual, especially in cartoons, in three dimensional trick toys, and on the burlesque stage. Part of the code for breaking the sexual taboo humorously used to be, formerly more than today, that it not be broken in mixed company, or with juveniles in attendance. Females as well as males complied with the rule of sex segregation, but juvenile boys and adolescents rebelled against exclusion from sexual humor. They circulated their own sexual humor, obtained undercover. It became a source of information otherwise excluded from their sex education. That put girls at a disadvantage, the disadvantage of inequality.

Humor is an antidote to the apprehension that the sexual taboo is able to generate. In the fine arts, the taboo is circumvented by metaphor and symbolization, with varying degrees of explicitness in which the sex organs and the sexual act are symbolized.

There is no hard and fast dividing line between sexual symbolization and photorealism in the fine arts. The threat of crossing it, however, mobilizes the sexual taboo police to the rescue of juveniles and adolescents. One of the tenets of the taboo is that youth must be protected from exposure to explicit depictions of sex in any medium. This tenet is based on the erroneous principle that sex is contagious. Minors, it is wrongly said, imitate whatever they become acquainted with, particularly if it has the allure of being prohibited. The sexual taboo expressly dictates that explicit knowledge of lovemaking, eroticism, and sexual intercourse be withheld from the curriculum of sexual learning. What is left is the reproductive physiology of eggs, sperms, and menstrual periods presented in a moralistic sexosophical context for which the current buzz word is no longer family life, as it used to be, but family values.

Contrary to the sexual taboo doctrine, the older juvenile years prior to puberty are an auspicious time in which to acquire an unexpurgated body of sexuoerotic knowledge in preparation for the exigencies of adolescence.

Having been well informed ahead of time, adolescents are able to have faith in the integrity and honesty of parents, teachers, and other older people. Before puberty, they are also spared the possible embarrassment after puberty of becoming genitally aroused by the precipitous release of formerly censored information.

Intelligent sexual learning, which happens also to be a democratic birth right, requires the availability of all sexual data, sexosophic and sexologic, suitably age-graded for comprehension. Without the necessary knowledge, children are unable to navigate their way around the two worlds of sex, in the one conforming to the orthodoxy and respectability of the doctrine of taboo, and in the other conforming to the doctrine of sexological science and health. Each world has its own vocabulary, manners, and etiquette, and the occasions of its own appropriateness. Keeping the two distinct is essential at times for the children whose sexual upbringing is liberated at home, but taboo-ridden at school. For all of us there is a formal sexual vocabulary and an informal one—one for a television interview, and one for the locker room or therapy hour, for example.

Well informed young people, as they arrive at the threshold of adolescence, ideally with continuing tutorial guidance, can then gain experience in formulating their own personal sexosophy, and in weighing the pros and cons of conflicting ideologies for themselves—whether or not to come out gay to one's family, for example. Then, as junior citizens, they are enabled to become as sexually responsible as their elders lay claim to having been in adolescence.

Abstinence

THE IDEOLOGY OF adolescent abstinence has undergone a revival in governmental, educational, and religious campaigns in response to the HIV/AIDS epidemic and to the so-called epidemic of teenaged pregnancy. The same slogan is applied to sex as to drugs: Just say no. It has been singularly ineffectual.

Just as some adolescents abstain from food, namely those with anorexia nervosa, until they fast themselves to death, so also there are some who abstain from sex. In both instances, however, something is wrong mentally and in the central nervous system. In sexual abstinence, there may be a genetic anomaly that affects, among other things, the hormonal system. This is sometimes the case in girls with Turner syndrome, who have one X chromosome missing (45,X instead of 46,XX); and in boys with Klinefelter syndrome, who have an extra X chromosome (47,XXY instead of 46,XY). Boys and girls with defective hormonal functioning of the pituitary gland also are disposed toward adolescent abstinence and failure to fall in love, even when given replacement hormonal therapy. In males without other identifiable defect, the mental fixation on adolescent abstinence may occur in the form of the Skoptic syndrome of self-castration, so as to become a eunuch who renounces sex (see appendix 1).

For ordinary healthy adolescents, self-enforced abstinence from sex is as difficult as self-enforced abstinence from food or water, or from defecation or urination. Self-enforced sexual abstinence partially corrects itself in erotic dreaming while sleeping which includes in boys emission of semen. It may also find a substitute outlet in masturbation and the erotic imagery of masturbation fantasies. Adolescent abstinence campaigns are, however too prudish to mention masturbation, let alone to recommend it as an approved alternative.

In the celibate priesthood, being celibate means being unmarried, not necessarily being abstinent. Clergy receive no training in sexual abstinence, including abstinence from masturbation. Among young Roman Catholic clergy, failure to maintain abstinence is prevalent (Sipe, 1990).

Masturbation

IN THE PRESENT HIV/AIDS era, one of the early tasks of adolescence is to separate the sexological from the sexosophical ideologies of masturbation. For a while in the 1960s and '70s, it seemed as though the old masturbation demons of semen depletion theory (see chap. 1) might have been permanently silenced. It was common knowledge that masturbation wrought no harm and that if not everyone, then a great many people, especially males, masturbated. Nonetheless, it remained self-incriminating to admit doing it. Until after World War II, the Boy Scouts' Manual and other advice books cautiously warned that, even in the absence of physical harm, masturbation weakened the moral fiber and the strength of character. It might be overlooked in youth, but its persistence into adulthood is still likely to be deplored as a sign of psychosexual immaturity, to be outgrown.

Television talk show hosts today capitalize on many erstwhile forbidden sexual topics, but no guest comes forward to recommend being a masturbator, nor to describe his/her masturbatory technique, including the rare gymnastic feat of self-fellation. Magazines that publish readers' personal accounts of masturbation are generally regarded as indecent or pornographic, as are demonstrations of masturbation on videotape. Didactic films produced by Gorm Wagner, M.D., in the 1970s at the Institute of Medical Physiology, University of Copenhagen, Denmark, demonstrated the sequence of the physiological responses of the female and the male to sexual stimulation. The filming was made with each actor alone in the Physiological Laboratory. The sexual stimulation was by means of digital masturbation, culminating in orgasm. These films were banned not only from the sex education curriculum in high schools and colleges, but also in some instances from medical schools, despite their being incontrovertibily clinical and scientific.

An excellent no-nonsense book and video demonstration of male masturbation, with an accompanying video and book on how to put on a condom, were authored by Hingsburger (1995, 1996), initially for the sex education of the mentally handicapped.

Although masturbation is recommended as a sex-therapy exercise for the treatment of anorgasmia, especially in women, how-to videos and books (Dodson, 1996) are few and not readily available. Masturbation as treatment has also been used with sex offenders. Ostensibly, although not convincingly, masturbation to orgasm reinforces a positive response in a sex offender to conventional pictures of sexual intercourse viewed while masturbating.

Most people have very little masturbatory virtuosity. The technique with which they began persists—the same finger positioning, same dryness or lubrication, same use of sex toys, same visual or narrative aids and fantasies, same pressing or rubbing, same duration, and so on.

The virtuosos of masturbation each have their own specialty. A live-show performer in Copenhagen in the early 1970s was publicized as being able to masturbate to the music of Ravel's *Bolero*, not getting a full erection until the final bars, and then ejaculating. Three times a night he lived up to his billing!

Not in public, but strictly in private, the virtuosity of another performer, a teenager, lay in his devising a no-hands "vagina trainer." In this way he literally circumvented the strictures of his religious indoctrination against the sin of manual masturbation. He formed his trainer by pushing an overstuffed armchair against the mattress of his bed. Then, sliding himself across both pieces of furniture, he could insert his penis between them, and thrust up and down to achieve orgasm (Early, 1975).

In India a Brahmin boy devised a similar no-hands method of masturbating. He lived at home where there was no privacy. He slept on a cot bed with criss-crossed webbing in the place of a mattress. Lying on his stomach, he could force a gap between the warp and woof of the webbing through which to push his uncircumcised penis and then silently slide it up and down, in and out of its foreskin, until it ejaculated.

Lack of masturbation privacy necessitated an entirely different solution among teenaged offenders remanded to a juvenile-hall, dormitory style of living in San Diego. They circumvented the stigma attached to manual masturbation by having a shared girlfriend known by tradition as Fi-Fi. A Fi-Fi was constructed from a rubber glove purloined from the kitchen and lubricated with cooking grease.

A more mundane substitute for Fi-Fi is the ubiquitous pillow in the place of hands and, for girls perhaps more than boys, the pulsating high pressure jet from a shower nozzle.

By the 1990s, some young college people were resurrecting the old masturbation demons (Money, 1993b, 1995). Might masturbation have a delayed effect, they asked, like leaving one impotent, anorgasmic, or infertile by mid-life? The answer is no. People who begin masturbation as juveniles may continue doing it through mid-life and beyond until old age. Data from the recent national survey of *Sex in America* (Michael et al., 1994) revealed that:

> Among Americans aged eighteen to fifty nine, about sixty percent of the men and forty percent of the women said that they had masturbated in the past year. About one man in four and one woman in ten reported that they

> masturbate at least once a week. And these are not all adolescents, they are adults, most of whom have regular partners for sexual intercourse . . . masturbation is like using erotica and having frequent thoughts of sex—not only an outlet, so much as a component of a sexually active lifestyle (pp. 158-59).

In December of 1994 the Surgeon General of the United States, Jocelyn Elders, M.D., made a comment during an AIDS meeting at the U.N., endorsing masturbation as a positive protection at any age, but especially for the young, against HIV/AIDS infection. Her boss, Bill Clinton, President of the United States, promptly fired her from her job. In the true tradition of American Gothic, he thereby sounded the death knell of uncounted thousands who will be killed by the HIV/AIDS virus.

Jocelyn Elders, a pediatrician well experienced in the ways of childhood and adolescence, was correct. It would have been more appropriate as well as politically brave to have put her in charge of a masturbation olympics that, by awarding medals to the winners, would put masturbation on the public agenda as a highly acceptable and morally proper thing to do.

The old sexosophy of masturbation as a cause of deterioration and illness has been proved wrong by the newer scientific sexology. Masturbation does not injure ordinary people of any age. Those few whom it might seem to injure are those who already have some other very serious disease affecting the function of the brain. For the vast majority of males and females, the frequency of masturbation is self-limiting.

Reversing today's prudery, society might well headline a public health policy of overtly endorsing and promoting masturbation as a safe-sex practice. At the outset masturbation would under such a policy be morally approved and promoted. For the present, and in preparation for the coming era of electronic "virtual reality," explicit erotic videos of the highest cinematic quality and verisimilitude would be broadcast, as adjuncts to good masturbation, on an exclusive sexological cable channel or Web-site on the Internet. The programming would include accurate news and information segments. It would give precise and exact sexual education, and answers to personal and youthful sexological concerns—concerns about falling in love and lovesickness, for example, and about growing up gay; or about having bizarre (paraphilic) erotosexual fantasies, thoughts and dreams (Money, 1986a, 1988a); or unjustified concerns about wasting one's oats by sowing them too wildly and too often and having none left for mid-life and later.

Until the day when a method of killing or containing the virus is finally discovered, solo masturbation is the only form of safe sex that absolutely guarantees total protection against infection with HIV/AIDS. The enormity of this statement has not yet permeated the minds of the general public. If it had, fewer people would be acting as if they have a privileged immunity against the virus. HIV/AIDS, they assume, is for media stars like Magic Johnson of basketball's dream team and Greg Louganis, Olympic gold medalist, and for homosexuals and drug needle users and their consorts (Johnson, 1992; Louganis, 1995). The epidemiological fact is, however, that among the 1996 cohort of college males the incidence of HIV positive is 1:200 (Gorman, 1996) and that pediatric AIDS is already a major challenge to child survival in Africa (Moy, 1995).

Young people should then no longer be ashamed to be discovered masturbating. They should wear a masturbation badge of courage in the fight against the lethal disease that has completely changed the code for growing up sexual.

Safe and Unsafe Sex

THE HUMAN IMMUNODEFICIENCY virus (HIV) lives in human white blood cells where it makes billions of copies of itself. They overwhelm the body's immune system and thus provide an opportunity for killer diseases to take hold. From the day of infection until the day of death may be as brief as one or two years, or as long as fourteen or fifteen years. The white blood cells in which HIV lives themselves exist in body fluids. They are highly concentrated in lymph, blood, and semen. A sure-fire way to become infected oneself is to have HIV infected blood or semen get into one's own body. Infected blood can enter through a blood transfusion, or from an injected needle stick, a cut or sore on the skin, or a raw place in the mouth, anus, vagina, or urethra.

In the early days of the HIV/AIDS epidemic when gay males were predominantly affected, it was speculated (incorrectly it is now recognized) that the vagina might have its own protection against the virus, whereas the rectum did not. Eventually, it was speculated that in the case of oral sex performed by males or females, the mouth also might have a degree of protection against HIV infected semen. There is no absolute confirmatory evidence, however. Now that the epidemic has spread to heterosexual women, as it did long ago in equatorial Africa, it is quite clear that the vagina does not offer protection enough, and that the virus can spread from vaginal fluid to men, as well as from semen to women, in routine heterosexual intercourse. The evidence is particularly evident and alarming in Thailand and in India where the epidemic is presently spreading like wildfire through the heterosexual population.

Saliva is one of the body fluids that can be exchanged in oral-genital or oral-anal sex, and in deep tongue kissing. For lack of definitive evidence, it is impossible to give a guarantee that saliva from either oral-genital sex or deep kissing are irrefutably HIV safe. Some people take comfort in the fact that the total count of white blood cells in saliva is low.

Another controversial body fluid is breast milk. It also may carry the virus, which may be transmitted to a baby. Logistically it is difficult to prove whether or not the HIV-infected mother did or did not harbor the virus while pregnant. If she did, the virus may have infected the baby prenatally, or during the delivery.

For those who plan on staying alive until the HIV/AIDS epidemic is brought under control, the body fluids story offers little solace with respect to close body-to-body intimacy with a sexual partner. That is why there is wisdom in advising those newly thrust into sexual high gear by the hormones of puberty to begin their sex lives with masturbation and masturbation fantasies, supplemented, maybe, with erotic narratives, pictures, and videos. Such a beginning allows time for exploring the terrain of one's lovemap. It is a time of adolescent rehearsal, prior to embarking on a safe-sex partnership with a partner who also is HIV/AIDS aware and masturbation emancipated.

Ideally, the two partners will live in a family and community as enlightened or as educable as they themselves are, so that they need not be handicapped by secrecy and fear of discovery. Initially, and progressively they will agree to hugging, clinging, cuddling, stroking, skin licking, body to body pressing, and massage. They may graduate to watching one another, directly or in a mirror, display their skills in self-masturbation, talking sexy to each other and possibly looking at a high quality, explicit erotic videotape together.

Eventually the day will come when they graduate to mutual masturbation. If the skin of all four hands is perfectly intact, with no scratches or tears where a virus may lodge, a couple may forego the added safety of wearing latex gloves of the type worn by dentists and physicians—but it is better to be safe.

With either solo or mutual masturbation, both may achieve an orgasm so satisfactorily that they can continue with the same activity for weeks or months before getting involved in penovaginal penetration, always with protection. Penetration can be either oral, vaginal, or anal, and it can be done with either the penis, the tongue, fingers, or the hand. Any variety of unprotected penetration involves the possibility of exchange of a body fluid: saliva, vaginal lubrication, menstrual blood, anal mucus, urethral lubrication, semen, or blood from torn tissue, a pin prick, or a bleeding gum.

Lip kissing without tonguing is probably safe, although it has not been incontrovertibly proved to be so. It would be tempting fate to lip kiss with a person who is already HIV positive. Unless tested, a person could be HIV positive without knowing it. Also, the test may come back seronegative for the first few weeks after infection before conversion to seropositive.

Mutual Precautions

HEAVY PETTING IN the era before HIV/AIDS adhered to the code of remaining technically a virgin by stopping short of penovaginal penetration, while at the same time allowing the boy to reach the climax of ejaculation by a "hand job" or a "blow job" (fellatio or oral sex). Whether or not the partner also achieved a climax was often wrongly a matter of indifference.

In the present era of HIV/AIDS, for maximum safety against infection, unprotected oral sex is not recommended. In other words, don't use the unprotected mouth to lick or suck a penis (fellatio, popularly known as giving head, or a blowjob), or to lick and suck a clitoris and vulva (cunnilingus, popularly known as eating out). Protection consists of putting a condom on the penis or a barrier sheet of latex or an equivalent material over the clitoris and vulva. A second use for the barrier sheet is as a protection in oral-anal sex, popularly known as rimming.

Latex barrier sheets first became known as dental dams, after the use for which they were initially manufactured. They are not user friendly, and not readily obtainable. As a substitute, a condom sliced open lengthwise is more agreeable for its thinness, but not its area or feel. Another substitute, improvised from what is easily available, is a large piece of plastic cling wrap (Saran wrap, for example), but not the sort manufactured with vent holes in it for use in microwave cooking. Where there's a will, there's a way! But the fact remains that there's no incontrovertibly proven way to have safe oral sex.

Nor is there any incontrovertibly proven way to have totally risk-free, safe penetrative sex with a penis in a vagina or in an anus. However, without any shadow of a doubt, it is safer to have a penis covered with a condom instead of bare and exposed. If used simultaneously with a male condom, the female condom (see chap. 13) offers additional protection to the couple in penovaginal intercourse. There is no corresponding anal condom. The female condom has a short history, a small market, and is not easily available. It is also considerably more expensive than the male condom.

By contrast, male condoms are easy to buy in drugstores and some supermarkets and vending machines. They are not expensive. By law in some states they are available free in drugstores for those who, regardless of age, have a Medicaid card. They are also given away in some clinics, and in some bars, although free distribution is not made widely known to teenagers who have begun their sex lives and who lack spending money. Free distribution of male condoms in schools, churches, and clubs, together with explicit lessons and sermons on lowering the rate of HIV/AIDS infection, would contribute significantly to preventing death from HIV/AIDS.

In the U.S. 450 million male condoms of different sizes, color, shape of tip, thinness, lubrication and strength are sold each year. (The U.S. Census Bureau estimates that as of early 1996 there were approximately 264 million people of all ages in the U.S.) It is not possible to test every condom for weak places, microscopic holes, or other flaws. So the manufacturer tests a few from each batch either by filling them with water to see if they leak, or inflating them with air until they burst (*Consumer Reports*, 1995). That gives a degree of quality assurance, but it does not guarantee that the condom you and your partner use will offer defect-free, one hundred percent protection. Used as a contraceptive, condoms have been rated as only 94 percent effective if worn correctly every time without exceptions. Otherwise they are only 82 percent effective (*Consumer Reports*, 1995). No matter how conscientiously condoms are used, they fail to guarantee total protection against pregnancy. Thus they cannot guarantee total protection against the HIV virus in either vaginal or receptive anal intercourse, if the partner is infected. Once the virus enters your body, it cannot presently be gotten rid of. It stays with you until it kills you any time from months upward to a dozen years later (Herek and Greene, 1995).

In case the condom breaks or leaks, some brands of condom are coated with slippery, non-greasy substance containing a small amount of nonoxynol-9, a chemical that is used with condoms to kill sperm. In the test tube, nonoxynol-9 inactivates various microbes, including HIV. There is, however, no test of whether it does the same in the human body, and if so, what the quantity should be. The amount of nonoxynol-9 inside a condom can be augmented by using a sexual lubricant fortified with nonoxynol-9 on the outside of the condom-covered penis, and also put inside the vagina or anus with an applicator syringe.

The latex rubber condom becomes useless if it comes in contact with petroleum-based grease or oil, both of which corrode and weaken rubber, and allow it to rip.

Some people, male or female, need to practice at unrolling a condom on a penis, making sure to begin so that it unrolls with the correct side out, and for its full length, to the base of the penis. Then it won't easily slip off. The procedure is easier if the penis is firmly erect and not partially soft. The partner may assist, and incorporate the wearing of a condom into the total sexual adventure.

One of the curiosities of sexology is allergy to latex. Once in a blue moon, a male or female is discovered to have an allergic inflammatory itching or burning of the genitals as a reaction to the latex from which condoms are made (Sotos, 1989). He/she is allergic to surgical gloves also. This allergy puts the burden of responsibility on those rare individuals who have it to devise alternative safeguards, like masturbation or total fidelity, against HIV/AIDS infection, and to use an alternative method of contraception.

Another allergic curiosity in sexology is allergy to a chemical or drug present in the man's semen in even the most minute amount. In one case the culprit proved to be dicloxacillin, a form of penicillin which the man was taking. In the woman, it produced swelling and a painful rash every time she and her partner had sexual intercourse (Sotos, 1989).

The total adventure of sexual intercourse may include also playing with sex toys, in particular a dildo and a vibrator. Both of these devices allow direct, gentle stimulation of sensitive erotic places, not only genital places, without exchange of fluids. For those so inclined, male or female, an anal dildo or butt plug enhances deep internal erotic sensation through the rectal wall, focused in the male in the prostate gland, and in the female in the G spot (see chap. 13). For some people, the larger the dildo in the rectum or the vagina, the greater the intensity of erotic ecstasy; and for some the ultimate ecstasy is to be penetrated by the partner's entire hand and forearm, popularly known as fisting, a rather dangerous practice, prudently avoided.

Dildo and vibrator attachments require washing with soap or detergent after use, and, should like fingers not be transfered from anus to vagina, or vice versa, without washing. HIV does not survive in cold water, nor on dry surfaces. In finishing up a session of sexual encounter, it is always a good idea to wash the genital and perineal areas, the face, and the hands, if not the entire body.

Before the era of HIV/AIDS, self-protection for those who embarked on a sex life in early youth meant using contraception as a protection against premature pregnancy, and protection against sexually transmitted diseases (STD). Though these diseases could have serious and dangerous complications, they did not, like HIV/AIDS, kill everyone whom they infected. So, to reiterate yet once again the now familiar message: Never before in history have young people been confronted, as they are today, with the equation that sex + virus = death. AIDS death is a wretched death, horrible with terminal suffering, and no one escapes. A single exposure to the deadly virus is sufficient to become infected (see chap. 11).

The Virus Can't Get Me

DENIAL MAKES US immortal in our innermost selves, and so we gamble with fate, like a gambler at Las Vegas, Nevada, instead of insuring against it, like a life insurant at Hartford, Connecticut. At the onset of the HIV/AIDS epidemic, the most typical response of individuals, governments, and the media was to deny the power of the epidemic to get everyone. It would get only people at risk, it was said: homosexuals, Haitians, hemophiliacs and other recipients of contaminated blood products, and drug addicts who shared intravenous injection needles. Third world governments declared their people to be immune to an epidemic from the West. As recently as 1994, the authors of the survey, *Sex in America* (Michael et al., 1994), already referred to in chapter 11, reassured middle class Americans and their children that, insofar as people date and marry within their own social class, the epidemic would pass them by. Even as they wrote, the virus was proving them wrong (Carey and Kalichman, 1995). It had already established a foothold in the middle class and its college generation. It will continue its stealthy spread. To deny that is to live in the false security of a fools' paradise.

In fools' paradise, there are some who play HIV Russian roulette. They practice unsafe sex with different partners, get infected with the virus, and then transmit infection to others, until death intervenes.

Instead of practicing unsafe sex consistently, some people do it only sporadically. They resolve either to avoid having unsafe sex, or to avoid having sex altogether. Then a high wave of passion carries them away. When it is too late to turn back, the only protection is that, by the laws of chance, neither partner will be infected with the virus and able to infect the other. If both are already infected, the risks of reexposure remain to be ascertained.

Each one of us knows our own health and sexual history with enough detail, usually, to know whether there has or has not been a chance of HIV/AIDS infection. To be certain, however, it is necessary to get a blood test specific for the virus. Likewise, one's partner or proposed partner should be tested also. If both tests come back negative, it is necessary to retest again in six months, as the virus may take as long as six months to incubate and show up as positive in the test result.

After two young, pairbonded lovers have confirmed that each one is HIV/AIDS negative, each may take a vow of fidelity and a vow never to take any action that might bring the virus into the relationship. You will know about yourself, and whether you took any risk or not, but no one else will know that with the same certainty you do. Each of two partners never know whether the other is telling everything. People are notorious for not telling everything about their sex lives, especially things that are self-incriminating, like infidelity. One's working assumption might as well be that no one can be trusted to disclose everything about sex. That creates a quandary for partners in an extended sexual relationship when they are ready to pass from the stage of mutual masturbation and skin contact to unprotected activities that might entail the exchange of body fluids. Obviously, it creates a quandary with respect to pregnancy which necessitates an unprotected discharge of semen.

Some couples are so caught up in a reciprocally limerent relationship that from adolescence or young adulthood onward fidelity to one another is their only option. Their trust in one another has been tested over many years. For young adolescent lovers, however, trust has not undergone the test of time. It is an act of fragile faith born of the exuberence of being in love. It may prove to be justified, and it may not. To be assuredly safe, it is wisest to continue with safe sex practices until it is time to have a pregnancy. That, of course, necessitates the agreement of two people, which is by no means always easy, especially if one dominates the other.

Age of First Parenthood

WHEN USED TO entrap semen and deter the transmission of HIV/AIDS from one partner to another, the male condom serves also as a contraceptive device. The female condom should give the same double service, though confirmatory data are needed. A lubricant containing nonoxynol-9 with germicidal properties that possibly deter the HIV/AIDS virus, has a partial contraceptive property as well. No other contraceptive, for instance the Pill, the IUD, or the diaphragm, protects against HIV/AIDS, only against a premature or supernumerary pregnancy.

The youngest age of fertility is a statistic that belongs to sexology, the science, whereas the ideal age of first pregnancy belongs to sexosophy, the ideology. Like the ideal number of offspring, the ideal age of first pregnancy has a history of variability, and it still varies transculturally. Its variability is related to the life expectancy in a particular community, to the community's population density, and to the economics of its production and distribution of wealth.

The briefer the life expectancy, the greater the likelihood that social policy will favor pregnancy early in adolescence so that young parents will have time to replenish the population before they die at a young age. At the time of the American Revolution when the average life expectancy was around thirty-five years, the age of consent to sexual intercourse was as low as twelve, and marriage and first pregnancy in the mid-teen years was socially approved and encouraged.

Early pregnancy meets with social approval also when there is a need for more population to fill a shortage of low cost manpower. Tribes and nations preparing for war and conquest of territory need a population increase to take the place of battle casualties, or to become citizens who colonize and secure newly acquired lands. Slave owners in the Old South needed an increase in the slave population to expand productivity on the plantations and to meet the demand for slaves as a commodity for sale at auction. Thus plantation policy was to endorse, if not enforce adolescent breeding as a human equivalent of animal husbandry.

Nations and regions within them that are too densely populated to be self-supporting put constraints on breeding too young and too frequently. A contemporary example is the People's Republic of China where it is politically correct for a couple to have no more than one child. Nonconformists may be subject to enforced abortion or sterilization.

In the United States and other industrialized countries, the progressive increase in automation and computerization has been met by a progressive decrease in the demand for low cost manual labor and in the availability of unskilled jobs. The demand for military personnel has also decreased with the cessation of the Cold War. Concurrently, there has been an increase in unemployment, underemployment, and poverty especially among ethnic minorities. At the same time there has been a rising level of wealthy and middle class taxpayer revolt against support for the indigent. One particularly self-righteous attack is against teenaged pregnancy, labeled as an epidemic. This means that a whole generation of babies will grow up, like an epidemic of American germs, as an epidemic of American citizens to be eradicated by being governmentally deprived of adequate healthcare, nutrition, housing, and education. They are surplus people not for having had teenaged parents or unwed mothers, but for being poor and mostly black.

Governmental policy about mid-adolescent pregnancy could reverse abruptly in the upcoming years if no HIV/AIDS treatment is found to contain the spread of the epidemic—which already affects as many as 40 percent to 50 percent of pregnant mothers in parts of central Africa (Moy, 1995). The rationale for the reversal would be that the younger the parents, the fewer the opportunities to have become infected with the virus, and the greater the likelihood that the baby will be born uninfected and, therefore, not destined for early death. In the worst scenario, the very survival of society might depend on early pregnancy.

Quite apart from HIV/AIDS, early pregnancy in the mid to late adolescent years, has points in its favor, provided the mother is healthy, receives capable prenatal health care, and is not subject to economic deprivation (see chap. 10). Consider for example the case of the woman with two careers, one domestic, and the other in business, academia, industry, or one of the professions. If she is in medicine say, her progress from medical school through internship, residency, and specialty training does not allow for a pregnancy break without paying a penalty. She loses her place in the competitive career hierarchy.

So she postpones pregnancy until older than thirty, which is too old to be the ideal age for first pregnancy. The pregnancy is successfully delivered, but she needs an extended leave of absence for early motherhood. Early fatherhood leave might be a good compromise, but his career would be penalized if he interrupted it. They both ask themselves the question: Might it not have been more feasible to have started a family when they were young, in high school, and had more career and schedule flexibility, and more time for parenting? Provided they could rely on financial support which would come from their own parents to them as parents, and then from them as parents to their own children when they become parents, and so on, the answer in many if not all cases would be yes. Then they would spend the second half of their lives, now that the life expectancy is until the seventies or beyond, advancing in their extradomestic careers without distraction.

In sexological development, the duration of the period between puberty and first parenthood is governed by two sets of factors. One set is personally unique. The other set is societal. A society of total sexual abstinence, as in a monastic order or convent, fails to procreate itself. So also does a society of eunuchs or castrates, such as the Christian Skoptics, now extinct; and in India the cult of the hijras. Societal factors, economic factors especially, govern the reproductive lives of all the members of a society, even without their recognizing what is happening.

In the final analysis, however, the social governance of the age of first pregnancy is contingent on the age of the onset and duration of fertility: ovulation in the female and spermatogenesis in the male. For a female to become pregnant it is not essential that she reach a sexual climax or orgasm. By contrast for a male to contribute his part in creating a pregnancy, it is virtually imperative that he have an orgasmic ejaculation of semen containing not just thousands of live sperms, but up to as many as 300,000,000 of them per ejaculate.

Compatibility

BEING BEST FRIENDS carries the childhood promise of compatibility forever, but the promise cannot be relied upon as a prophesy. The incandescence that lights up the beginning of a crush, an infatuation, or a love affair in adolescence also is supposedly prophetic of compatibility forever, but again the prophesy cannot be relied upon. Compatibility is not a fixed quantity that can be measured once and for all. Rather, like blood pressure, it is liable to fluctuation, deterioration, or improvement in the course of time. In some couples compatibility, like good wine, ages well, and in mutual harmony. In others it ages poorly and breaks down in mutual discord to become incompatibility.

In couple sexology, there are five possible systems of compatibility, as follows:

- Long-term partner compatibility is irrelevant. The contract is for short-term, transient-compatibility, maybe for pay, or maybe for a one night stand or weekend of sportive sex without pay, with no strings attached, and with or without protection against pregnancy and sexually transmitted diseases (STD).
- Partner compatibility is time-limited and contraception is avoided. If already pregnant, the female's agenda might be to feign the identity of the father. Otherwise her contract might be to become a single-parent or a lesbian mother, unencumbered by problems of long term compatibility with a male. Conversely, the male's contract may be to become a gay male father (Morgen, 1995) or a single parent unencumbered by the problems of long term compatibility with the baby's mother. Freedom from STD is a prerequisite.
- The duration of partner compatibility is fortuitous. By engaging in sportive sex without contraception, and without STD protection, a couple plays the roulette wheel of pregnancy and STD. If pregnancy ensues, then parenthood dictates the challenge of long-term compatibility in child care, which may or may not be met. This system produces a glut of father-absent households, and of babies and parents with HIV/AIDS.
- Long-term compatibility is societally coerced. Premarital chastity and postmarital fidelity are strictly enforced on females, less so on males. Marriages are arranged by the elders. There is no period of courtship in which to put compatibility to the test. In India and elsewhere, this is the traditional scenario. In instances of incompatibility, it is the female's obligation to concede. Nonetheless, many couples prove to be highly compatible over the long term. The man is more likely than the woman to become a carrier of STD or HIV/AIDS.
- Long-term compatibility is serially segmented. Each segment is pretested during a period of courtship, and its onset is dictated by being in love. Subjectively defined, being in love may signify the experience of being limerent, infatuated, or love smitten, or it may be only a self-feigning verbal formula. Although the promise of compatibility may be long term, it may be poorly matched in scope. The degree of matching being close enough, however, then one or each of the partners concedes the incompatibility, but with the proviso that eventually, love will conquer all. Time goes by. Love does not conquer all. Instead their compatibility ages poorly and incompatibility multiplies. Then love smites again, and the partner newly smitten must obey the formula and begin the scenario all over again with someone new. The formula for the other partner is to retain a lawyer and sue for divorce and alimony.

This latter is the system of serial marriage which is now pretty much a fixture of life and family values in America and elsewhere. American marriages that end in divorce are estimated at fifty percent or more, to which should be added an unknown percentage of nonmarital cohabitations that break up, and a still greater percentage of broken love affairs.

The woes of a broken heart are dealt with in romantic novels for teenagers, but not in sex education texts. A broken heart may drive some people to suicide. But the maximum penalty of the failure of compatibility is paid for not by the two teenagers or adults but by their offspring. Children cannot break the parent-child pairbond by divorce like parents and lovers can break theirs.

America does not yet admit to itself that the nineteenth century, sentimental ideal of the rose-trellised, picket fenced, nuclear family, held together by the mutual long-term compatibility of the parents, is no longer the only accurate representation and model for its juveniles and adolescents to prepare for. It is equally accurate for them to prepare themselves for a personal history of time-limited compatibility with two or more partners in sequence.That will ameliorate the anguish of self-blaming failure for loss of compatibility. It will also make it easier for the children of divorce to claim dual custody and their right to keep both parents. It will not provide safely against the possible transmission of STD, however.

Mutual compatibility, like mutual communication, is all too often held up as being in itself a positive and therapeutic ideal to be striven for. The fact of the matter is, however, that compatibility and communication reside on both sides of the ideological fence of good and bad, dependent on which criterion one applies (see chap. 8). Terrorists communicate compatibly with one another. So do counterterrorists and double agents.

In sexology, sexual compatibility, although appearing to be admirable, may be pathological and contingent on insidious collusion. This was the case in a family in which the father would brutally discipline one or the other of his two sons at the instigation of his wife, as a prelude to marital sexual intercourse. As is typical in such cases, neither parent was able to put two and two together so as to recognize their collusion explicitly and perhaps bring it to an end. The case was brought to attention by a young man, a school worker. He himself had an early childhood history of, while asleep, a sexual encounter with a teenage male somnophile, his baby sitter. He was seen periodically in long-term follow-up. He told the story of what he had ascertained about the two boys, Marshall and Clive, and their parents, Maureen and Victor, a police officer. His report was as follows (Money and Werlwas, 1982):

> I observed Marshall's inability to sit down, and decided to investigate. I found a number of bruises and welts on his behind, lower legs, and his back. He said that his mother got angry at his father, so his father had beaten him up and then left him alone with his younger brother, Clive, to watch a late-night movie. The father and mother then went to bed. Later, Clive opened up and said they got hit three or four times a week, but only when his father was home at night, not when he did the midnight shift.

I made a home visit and became friendly with the parents. It was obvious they had social problems. They had no friends. So I began doing things—volley ball, shopping—with them; and Victor opened up to me. He talked alot about his experiences as a Green Beret in Vietnam. I talked about the problems of children. I had better rapport with him than her. She was still threatened by my presence. He was not. I realized it when he said something about having sexual problems with her and that she didn't enjoy having sex with him anymore. He said, "It seems as though the only time I ever have sex with her is after I spank the kids." He was a very active male sexually, and seemed to want and get sex often. He was up front with me about how easily he got women.

The first instance I actually observed was on one of the weekends I stayed over. Marshall wanted to go to a dance for junior teens at the church. His father said no. I urged him to give in and let the boy go with his friends. The mother was listening, angry at something. I went outside to warn the child, "When your father says come home by eleven, you come home by eleven, and don't be a jerk, if you don't want to get a beating."

So the child did not come home on time, and in addition he left his coat at the dance. The father beat the kid pretty badly, and then was rewarded by his wife later on that night with sex. I heard them doing it, rattling the bed.

On another occasion, an incident happened with Clive. His mother found a cigarette butt in the bathroom. The next thing, I heard her calling Victor upstairs, and it amazed me how he seemed to know what she meant, just by the way she called him. So he picked up his police belt which he had used earlier in the day in a beating. They had sex again that night. Earlier in the day he had been told, no sex. So when she found the cigarette butt, he capitalized on it. Next morning, he and I took the boys away camping. He and I were in the front of the van, and I said, "You must have had a good fuck last night, you almost knocked the walls down." He said, "Sure did." In the seven days we were away, he never once took a strap to the boys.

He hit the girl, the youngest, only once that I know of. His wife went crazy, and threw glasses at him in the kitchen, because he had hit the girl. If anyone would hit the girl, she would do it, she said, not him.

Maureen had been an abused child. She had been made a ward of the state at age ten. She lived with her parents and four sisters, but all decisions about punishments or denials were made by a probation officer. At seventeen she married Victor and left home. Then her youngest sister was abused.

Maureen's story about the boys' beatings was that she realized Victor was very cruel to the children and she didn't know how to stop it. She thought that if she gave him sex, he would be less cruel to the children, but she really didn't enjoy having sex with him. But the way it actually went was that he got sex only when he did beat the kids. He told me some things about Vietnam, about torturing and killing people, whole families, to get confessions about the Viet Cong and about sexually exploiting early teenage girls.

Mutual lovemap compatibility in this case was not the conventional type of sadistic male and masochistic female. Rather, the husband was a sadist by proxy, and the wife a masochist by proxy. As proxies, the two boys were beaten by their father on their mother's behalf. Simultaneously, they took the punishment that should have been bestowed upon those who had once abused their mother as a child. Their sister was fiercely protected.

In a sexodynamic of this sort two questions arise: Did the parents somewhat mysteriously recognize a portent of their peculiar compatibility when they first met? Or did one of the pair lead or follow the other into collusional sexopathological compatibility after they first met? With human beings there is no ethical way to contrive an experiment that would provide an answer. The most that one may say is that, in some couples, their compatibility evolves, and stays strong for a lifetime, even if it is sexopathological. In other couples, compatibility of the two lovemaps fails to evolve and eventually disintegrates.

Mismatched Lovemaps

When two people have mismatched lovemaps, that does not augur well for their copulatory relationship. They may be able to go through the motions of copulation, but in a dull and perfunctory, unlively sort of way. A videocamera can capture the motions of copulation, but it has no power to capture the two independent copulatory fantasies being played privately on each partner's mental videotape. Each partner's copulation fantasy has either no role at all for the actual partner, or else a reciprocally unmatching one. "I know I'm not in his/her head," she/he says. "I feel left out." Or: "Kim's off some place else without me and doesn't need me." The principle of lovemap mismatching quite frequently surfaces as homosexual/heterosexual incompatibility or partial incompatibility.

There is a difference between engaging in a heterosexual act and having a heterosexual lovemap, or engaging in a homosexual act and having a homosexual lovemap. The skyscraper test illustrates the difference. The test can be worded for men or women, gay or straight. For a straight male, the test is worded thus: You are at the top of the tallest skyscraper. A crazed sex terrorist with a hand gun entraps you at the edge of the parapet and says, "Ok, suck my dick or you go over." If you obeyed, would you be a homosexual, or would you have engaged in a homosexual act, simply to have saved your life? The answer is that, in your sexological record you would have to declare the performance of one homosexual act, but not the possession of a homosexual lovemap. The ultimate criterion of having a homosexual lovemap is that the experience of limerence, that is of falling in love or being love smitten can happen only when the partner and the self have the same body morphology. For a heterosexual lovemap, the two body morphologies are contrasexual, one male and one female. Body morphology is the key, as is definitively evident in those cases of hermaphroditism in which the body sex is discordant with other criteria of sex, e.g., the chromosomal or gonadal sex (see chap. 4).

It is possible to have a heterosexual lovemap and to engage in not one, but multiple homosexual acts or, conversely to have a homosexual lovemap and engage in multiple heterosexual acts. Segregation of males and females, as in boarding schools, prisons, or military installations, increases the prevalence of homosexual acts without changing the heterosexual orientation of the lovemaps. Under conditions of heterosexual deprivation, in homosexual acts between two males or two females, the two roles may be interchangeable, or one may be more assertive than the other. Especially in prison the assertive role may be also a brutal one.

From the years of prepuberty through early adolescence, homosexual acts between sex segregated boys are predominantly more genitally focused than are those between girls. Among sex segregated girls, homosexual acts are more focused on cutaneous grooming, without necessarily being genital.

Under conditions of sex segregation, irrespective of age, there are some individuals whose lovemaps are so fixately heterosexual that genital and erotosexual arousal by someone of the same sex is an utter impossibility. Even after many years of heterosexual deprivation while sex segregated, as in prison, such an individual cannot be aroused to erection and orgasm by another male prisoner, even one who is a preoperative male-to-female transexual and seductively feminine. Lacking a female partner who is congruent in detail with the specifications of his lovemap, he must rely exclusively on heterosexual ideation and imagery in a masturbation fantasy or wet dream that is congruent with his lovemap (Keyes and Money, 1993).

The disparity between the homosexual act and the homosexual lovemap has a counterpart in the disparity between engaging in various paraphilic (kinky or unorthodox) sexuoerotic acts and being the person who possesses a paraphilic lovemap. For example, engaging in a test trial of sadistic or masochistic practices does not convert the lovemap into a fixated sadomasochistic one. Similarly with other atypical sexuoerotic practices, like cross dressing (transvestism). Cross dressing once, or more than once, doesn't convert the lovemap into a fixated transvestophilic one.

The same principle applies to paraphilic pornography. Witnessing or reading pornography that is sadomasochistic, pedophilic, transvestophilic, or of any other paraphilic category, does not convert one's lovemap to that category. On the contrary, paraphilic pornography appeals to those whose lovemaps already contain the same category of paraphilia. This principle applies to all ages, juvenile, adolescent, and adult. Pornography is not socially contagious. It does not, willy nilly, recruit people to the practice it portrays. Thus, homosexual pornography does not recruit heterosexual youth into being homosexual. Nor, by the same token, does heterosexual pornography convert homosexual youth into being heterosexual.

A mismatched lovemap dilemma becomes a Catch-22 dilemma when there is no formula for compromise or coexistence. In the absence of a truce, the outcome of a Catch-22 dilemma is, in the ultimate analysis, reducible to the principles of the familiar triad: freezing, feuding, or fleeing. They apply to young and old alike, and they apply to the Catch-22 dilemmas of incompatible and mismatching lovemaps (see chap. 16).

The principle of freezing signifies being frozen into the status quo of incompatibility. Each partner is covertly locked into a collusional role of mutual martyrdom, one usually appearing the more tragic and the other the more heroic of the two. Both collect grievances and seek allies to confirm their respective victimhood. The stress and strain of martyrdom shows up insidiously, as in diminished work achievement and in susceptibility to bouts of acute illness, loss of well being, chronic invalidism, and sexological dysfunctionalism. The heroic martyr of the pair assumes the financial responsibilities of living, including, in some cases, support of the other partner's invalidism and alcoholic or other drug dependency. The subtlety of collusion is such that the heroic and tragic roles of martyrdom are potentially exchangeable between the two partners, and sometimes are exchanged.

The principle of feuding in response to the dilemma of lovemap mismatching and incompatibility signifies an escalation of dispute and violence, with neither party clearly victorious, and neither conceding defeat. If one party is more reliant on brute force, then the other must rely more on surreptitious and circuitous methods of attack. Feuding has the contradictory outcome of alienating the partner and, in the worst scenario, culminates in homicide and/or suicide. Nonetheless, the cycle of victimization and reconciliation may be recurrent on the basis of the ironical proposition that the human organism is able, by way of the opponent-process principle (see chap. 16), to become addicted to abuse.

The principle of fleeing in response to the dilemma of lovemap mismatching and incompatibility signifies submission to defeat and dissolution of the relationship. It does not necessarily signify an end to feuding, which may be continued at a distance, legally, with the assistance of a paid attorney. It may also be particularly vicious, as in alimony and child custody battles, and in false accusations of incestuous child sexual abuse. Some cases end in stalking, murder and/or suicide, some in reconciliation, and some in a relatively amicable settlement.

In the mores and in the curriculum of sex education for American teenagers, incompatibility and the breakup of a relationship, receives little or no attention at all. Breakups are more likely to be regarded as failures than as opportunities for a new beginning. How then does a couple avoid entrapment into a mismatch of incompatible lovemaps?

One precaution is to not take the ideation and imagery of each other's lovemaps for granted, but to disclose and discuss their dimensions and details to the maximum extent feasible, with a view to discovering and predicting their lovemap compatibility. That is easier said than done. Lovemaps often contain embarrassing material, some of its censorable, and some of it potentially self-incriminating. Once disclosed, it becomes subject to to gossip and misuse. It is safer to donate a pint of blood than a paragraph of private information. The blood gets used up, whereas information can circulate in perpetuity. That is the ultimate sexological Catch-22 of the generation making the counterreformational transition into the twenty-first century.

13

Orgasmology

Orgasmic Cycle
Proceptive Phase
Acceptive Phase
Conceptive Phase

Orgasmic Cycle

Orgasmology (Money, 1992) is the science of the orgasmic cycle, that is the cycle of what leads up to and away from the sexual climax or peak of orgasm in males and females.

A subdivision of the sexual response cycle into four phases was formulated and first published by Albert Moll in 1908 in the original German edition of his book, translated into English as *The Sexual Life of the Child* (1912). Moll wrote as follows:

> In woman, as in man, the curve of voluptuousness exhibits four phases: an ascending limb, the equable voluptuous sensation, the acme, and the rapid decline. There are, however, in this respect, certain differences between man and woman . . . Whereas in the male the curve of voluptuousness both rises and falls with extreme abruptness, in the female both the onset and the decline of voluptuous sensation are slower and more gradual. There is an additional difference between man and woman. In woman very often voluptuous pleasure is entirely lacking; certainly such absence is far commoner in women than in men—a condition of affairs which must on no account be confused with *absence of the sexual impulse*. Even when the sexual impulse is perfectly normal, the entire voluptuous curve with its acme may be wanting. In such cases, the after-sense of complete satisfaction, which occurs more especially when ejaculation has been associated with an extremity of voluptuous pleasure, is commonly also lacking.

In 1966, the sexual response cycle was again subdivided into four phases, this time by Masters and Johnson. In *Human Sexual Response* they wrote:

> A more concise picture of physiologic reaction to sexual stimuli may be presented by dividing the human male's and female's cycles of sexual response into four separate phases. Progressively, the four phases are: the excitement phase; the plateau phase, the orgasmic phase; and the resolution phase. This arbitrary four-part division of the sexual response cycle provides an effective framework for detailed description of physiologic variants in sexual reaction, some of which are frequently so transient in character as to appear in only one phase of the total orgasmic cycle (p. 4).

The graphic representation of the male sexual response depicts one orgasmic peak, with the possibility of a second one after a refractory or rest period if the penis does not get completely flaccid. By contrast, the graphic representation of the female sexual reponse depicts three types of response. One depicts a rapid build up to, and drop off from a single orgasmic peak. The second depicts multiple orgasmic peaks ascending from the plateau level in quick succession, and then descending to the resolution phase. The third depicts a repetitive ripple of small orgasms at the plateau phase, with no high peaks.

In the sexological laboratory, Masters and Johnson broke new ground in recording, measuring, and photographing the physiological and anatomical concomitants of the sexual response cycle, including those occuring within the cavity of the vagina. They were interested in the stimulus and response of all the organs of the body in the sexual response cycle. The stimuli of arousal and excitement were in their research predominantly cutaneous. The role of the other senses and of erotic fantasy in the preliminaries of the excitement phase were too complicated to deal with.

Under the terms of their research contract, the subjects who participated in the Masters and Johnson research on the sexual response cycle signed a protocol ahead of time. That ensured that they knew what to expect and would find it compatible with being stimulated to orgasm either alone, by masturbating, or in pairs by copulating with a partner. The partner would be, if not one's own regular partner with whom one was already compatible, then a compatible professional surrogate. In other words, even in the Masters and Johnson therapy, before the four phases of the response cycle can begin, there is an extra, preparatory or introductory phase.

Proceptive Phase

TRADITIONALLY, THIS introductory phase was one of the functions of courtship. Even in communities where the rule of premarital chastity was rigidly enforced, an indulgence might be granted to an engaged couple to be unchaste prior to the wedding so that they could test their sexual compatibility. Old parish registers show a high proportion of postmarital births from a premarital pregnancy. The criterion of indulgence has been changed by today's youth to a declaration of love, not of intent to marry. If the boy declares that he is in love, then the girl consents to have intercourse, provided she too declares that she is in love. The possible transience of being in love is not taken into account in this formula. However, being in love ostensibly implies a long term commitment.

Before 1976, animal sexologists sometimes used the concept of the courtship ritual, especially in birds, and also the concept of the mating dance. Then, Frank Beach (1976) provided a specific term, proceptivity, for the introductory phase of animal mating behavior (see also chap. 2). The title of his paper is, "Sexual attractivity, proceptivity, and receptivity in female mammals." The proceptive phase is a generic name for the behavioral courtship ritual or mating dance, that two animals, male and female, must perform after they are in a sexually attractive state, seasonally, hormonally, or otherwise, without which actual coitus cannot be consummated.

The example of the urban dog is easy to observe. Under the governance of sex hormones secreted by the ovaries, the bitch periodically ovulates and comes into heat. Her vagina manufactures an odoriferous substance, a pheromone, the smell of which is left where she urinates for the male to smell. On his own urinary strolls, the male marks many posts, sniffing all of them for the female's pheromone, or for that of a male rival. His acute sense of smell also allows him to smell her pheromonal attractiveness from a considerable distance. With singleness of purpose and oblivious to traffic or other danger, he trots with tail aloft and snout forward, until he converges, along with rivals, on the estrual female. The males mill around panting, trying to get closer, to smell the female's genitals, and to get a chance at mounting her. She plays a game of tease, face to face with a male, crouching on her forelegs, with rump held high, and then running away a few yards until a male catches up, and the ritual is repeated again and again. Eventually she teases one dog more than the others, and gives him the go-ahead to mount her. The rivals hang around for a while and then disperse, as the pair remain locked until the swollen bulb of the male's penis detumesces and he can pull out.

In the human species, when an olfactory stimulus is attractive it is called a perfume, and when it is not, a smell or a stink. As compared with dogs and males of other four-legged species, human males resemble other primate males in being less dependent on smell than vision for specifying what is sexually attractive. Transculturally, there is no absolute standard of human sexual attractivity, but a great many local and ethnic standards.

In our own culture, with a cosmetic history going back as far as ancient Egypt, women use color to accentuate the eyes and the mouth as organs that attract male attention. Fashion changes that variously accentuate parts of the body by decorating, covering, exposing, or amplifying them also attract male attention. Women are not inattentive to the visual attractivity of males, but for them the greater attractivity of the male is contrectative—that is to say his attractivity lies in the prospect of his approaching to hold, touch, and fondle them, and to sweep them away by the power of his stimulation of their cutaneous and haptic senses. It is not, today, politically correct to accept such a difference between men and women. However, regardless of the origin of the difference, it is one that a great many males and females can attest to.

In addition to transcultural differences in the specification of the sexual attractivity of males and females, there are enormous individual differences. These differences are coded in each individual's lovemap (see chap. 7).

The proceptive phase in the human species is expressed gesturally, in body language, and vocally in sounds and words (see also chap. 8). Proception is not culture bound but is transculturally similar (Eibl-Eibesfeldt, 1972; Perper, 1985). It begins with establishing eye contact and holding the gaze, while at the same time perhaps becoming flushed or blushing. Then one of the pair tests the other by demurely drooping the eyelids and averting the gaze so as to see, upon returning the gaze shyly with a squint, smile, or flutter of the eyelashes, whether the other person has continued to look. This maneuver may be repeated as a prelude to moving closer together. The opening gambit in conversation may be banal, but it is the vocal animation, not the content that counts. The flow of speech becomes accelerated, more breathy, and louder. Banality is outweighed by the vocal enthusiasm of simply being heard. Laughter, even if the humor is contrived, invites the couple to rotate so that, facing one another, they can share it and bring themselves closer and closer. The tongue emerges, wetting the lips. Clothing is casually adjusted or shed, fortuitously revealing a little more bare skin at least around the wrists, ankles, or neck. Arms and legs change positions, and gesturing brings them, as if inadvertently, in contact with the other person, sending a shiver running up and down his or her spine. If there is no recoil, then there is closer touching, patting, or holding, and the two people before they know what they are doing begin mirroring each other's gestures, and synchronizing their bodily movements as if in preliminary rehearsal for copulatory synchrony. Meanwhile, in addition to the observable cues of body language and vocal communication, there are the autonomic nervous system signs of increased heart and breathing rate, dry throat, goose bumps, sweatiness, and maybe butterflies in the stomach, and genital arousal. If the female vulva is not vasocongested and wet from vaginal lubrication, and if the male penis is not erect from vasocongestion and damp from urethral glandular ooze, then these signs of genital arousal will appear in the ensuing segment of the proceptive phase.

This ensuing segment of the proceptive phase is generally referred to as foreplay. It may begin with undressing one another, though some people are very shy about full nudity. Others like to have lights on and to watch what they do in a mirror. Foreplay involves cuddling, hugging, kissing, rubbing, stroking, licking, tonguing, chewing, and sucking various parts of the body that are erotically responsive, including the mouth, nipples, anus, toes (shrimping), and genitals. The various organs and places vary in degree of erotic sensitivity from one person to another. Some people have an unexpectedly intense erotic pressure spot, for example in the soft tissue, left or right, below the ribs, or on the inner surface of the thighs. Some people, men or women, can't tolerate sucking, nibbling, or biting on their nipples, whereas others are driven crazy by such stimulation and may then explode into orgasm from it. For women, the response to having the clitoris sucked is equally divergent. Some people detest light scratching and massage of the skin, whereas others can't get enough of it; and the same with pinching or love-biting so as to leave a bruise-like mark, for example, a hickey on the side of the neck.

People who are sexually versatile are able to cut the period of foreplay short when they are pressed for time, and to prolong it for an hour or longer when they are free. Others are less versatile in speeding up or delaying the onset of orgasm.

The beginning segment of the proceptive phase is phyletically geared to attracting a new partner. If repeated over and over, unmodified, by two people whose mutual attraction is already established, it would appear contrived and lacking spontaneity. Loss of spontaneity also typifies an established relationship if all of the beginning segment of proceptivity falls into a state of neglect. The element of spontaneity and vivacity may disappear, in addition, from the second segment of proceptivity, that of foreplay. There are no intermissions, no special requests, no laughter, joking, or chatting, and no sexy jubilation—just a solemn monotony. Both partners are equally losers. Having sex becomes a service not too far removed from being equivalent to giving or receiving donor insemination.

Acceptive Phase

IN EXPERIMENTAL ANIMAL sexology it has long been a convention to speak of the female in heat as being receptive—ready to receive the male. There is no corresponding term for the male. It is not said that the male receives the female, but that he does something to her. He mounts her. The dictionary is at fault. It does not have a respectable, everyday term that can be used reciprocally for what the female does to the male, and the male does to the female when they copulate. To avoid the sexist implications of receptivity, especially as applied to human beings, in the 1970s I switched to the terms acceptivity and acceptive phase (Money, 1980).

The acceptive phase is the generic name for what the male and the female do sexually together when the two bodies accept one another, genitally, usually though not invariably in penovaginal (or vaginopenial) intromission culminating in the climax of orgasm. In the sexology of subprimate mammalian species, the transition from the proceptive to the acceptive phase is equated with the penis being received in the vagina into which the semen is ejaculated. In primate species, particularly the human species, the transition from proceptive to acceptive, instead of being abrupt is, among those who are sexually well qualified, a merging of advanced foreplay into the acceptive behavior that will progress toward orgasm, or to the actual achievement of orgasm. Penovaginal intromission is the most prevalent acceptive behavior that culminates in orgasm. The alternatives are orgasm from oral-genital stimulation, anogenital stimulation, or manual-genital stimulation. An alternative for a few people, male as well as female, is to reach orgasm from strong nipple stimulation; and for even fewer from erotic imagination, with the partner in absentia.

Alternatives to penovaginal union may be used as playful options, as ways to maintain a claim of being technically a virgin, as alternatives to penovaginal discomfort associated with, say, pregnancy, and as forms of gay male and lesbian acceptivity. A vibrator to augment and intensify erotic sensation is another playful alternative. So also is a dildo, used as a substitute for a penis or as a duplicate penis. Other sex toys, such as cockrings or straps, nipple clips and butt plugs enhance erotic sensation for some people, but are a turn-off for others. The same applies to genital and nipple rings and bars which, like earrings and nose rings, require piercing the flesh where they will be worn.

The acceptive phase is the phase of copulatory gymnastics. The placement of the human genital anatomy makes six positions feasible for most people. They are the face to face with the man on top, the so called missionary position; the knees-to-shoulder position, with the woman lying on her back; the horse-rider position, with the man on his back and the woman riding on his erect penis; the rear entry or doggie position with the man standing facing her back and the woman on her feet leaning forward over the bed, or with her legs drawn up, kneeling on the bed; the spoon position with the couple lying side by side with his front to her back; and the scissors position, a variant of the spoon in which he has his uppermost leg and groin between her legs. Another possibility is for the couple to be facing one another, him sitting on the floor with legs extended, and her approaching his penis, on her knees between his legs. This position, traditional among Australian Aborigines of Arnhem Land (Money et al., 1970) allows the two people to watch for intruders in all directions.

As well as being customary, copulatory positioning may be mandated by traditional authority. Thus the missionary position was carried to native peoples by missionaries whose religion mandated it as divinely ordained to symbolize the authority of the husband and the subordination of the wife. Conversely, the doggie position was condemned as being ordained by the devil to reduce human beings to the status of beasts.

There is no respectable vernacular verb that can be used in everyday speech to signify equality of what men do to women and women do to men in the copulatory part of the acceptive phase.

There is an old verb of Welsh origin, to quim, that applies to what the woman does to the man and another of Anglo-Saxon origin, to swive, that applies to what the man does to the woman (Money, 1982). The only verb of ancient lineage that applies reciprocally to what men and women do to each other is the verb to fuck, commonly printed as f___, which yields the phonetic verb, to eff, the noun, eff, and the participle, effing (Sheidlower, 1995). Fuck itself has not yet become sufficiently gentrified for respectable academic usage (Money, 1988a). While working on the earlier chapters of this book, from the noun orgasm I formed the verb, to orgasmocate, as a respectable substitute for fuck. For everyday, down-home speech, however, it does not sound vernacular enough. Maybe also it challenges the long held stereotype that the female who risks being the equal of the male in copulatory initiative risks also being likened to a harlot.

If the sexological climate in society is one of moral prudery, especially if domestic overcrowding deprives a husband and wife of visual and auditory privacy, sexually, then sexual intercourse gets reduced to a rapid and silent act of male insemination. The woman is a semen receptacle. Her orgasm is of no consequence. This was the coital role of respectable women in many sex and marriage manuals of the Victorian era and early twentieth century. In the 1920s, marriage manuals became more liberated, and the man was recommended not only to give his wife an orgasm, but to time it it be simultaneous with his own (Van der Velde, 1926).

Today's sex manuals recognize no special virtue in having orgasms either simultaneously or consecutively. The best advice is to have both, on different occasions. There is a great enhancement of the intensification of the build up to orgasm if both are accelerating at the same rate, reciprocally. If one partner is faking, or if both are, the enhancement is lacking, so much so that it can be easily detected even in a video. It is common for a man to be completely fulfilled only if he and his partner have reached the same height of ecstasy, and likewise for a woman.

If the woman comes to orgasm first and is able to have multiple orgasms, as some women are able to do, then, if the man's climax can be delayed, that is obviously advantageous to both. If he recognizes that he is approaching the moment of orgasmic inevitability, then he may intensify the woman's orgasmic inevitability by pausing and positioning so as to be able to stimulate her clitoris and surrounding area, manually, while maintaining intravaginal thrusting. If he comes before she does, then he can continue digitally stimulating her or he can explode her orgasm by means of oral-genital stimulation, which some women find more orgasmic than penovaginal thrusting. Another possibility is that either of them may apply a vibrator to the most responsive places in her genital area. Correspondingly, if he is too slow in coming to a climax, and time is running short, she can perform manually or orally on his penis and scrotum, with or without the augmentation of a vibrator. For gay or lesbian couples, the same principles apply.

Orgasmic versatility means that both of two partners are able to keep in synchrony regardless of whether they have five minutes before getting up on a working day, or an entire weekend evening of playing around.

In the sexological literature there has been no history of argument as to whether the male has only one type of orgasm or more, depending on the organ from which the orgasm is triggered. By contrast, there has been a century's worth of argument, begun by Freud, as to whether in the female there is a difference between clitoral and vaginal orgasm. Basically the argument is ideological, as the orgasm from the vagina was considered womanly, and from the clitoris, masculine. Masters and Johnson (1966) settled the argument: anatomically and physiologically both are indistinguishable.

That, however, does not finalize the argument with respect to subjective report. Both men and women report that orgasms on different occasions may be different, and that some are better than others. Mental imagery and ideation are powerfully influential. In addition there is the dimension of deep pressure sensation and the sense of fullness which is unknown to men unless they experience anal penetration, and which is known to women from vaginal penetration.

Data are sparse, but it would appear that multiorgasmic women are multiorgasmic episodically, in the course of a specific copulatory encounter, rather than on the basis of a regular daily quota. Women who are multiorgasmic may have a protracted series of orgasms, with an interval of only a few moments between them at the height of orgasmic excitement, before they become orgasmically exhausted. For them, each orgasm is a full bloom.

It is dubious that a male may be multiorgasmic in the same way as a female. However some males may stop just short of having an ejaculatory orgasm, and repeat the sequence several times before coming.

Some women discover that they can accelerate the onset of orgasm and intensify its strength by stimulation of a zone which they can palpate an inch or so within the vagina, anteriorly. Named for Ernest Grafenberg, a gynecologist refugee in New York from Hitler's Germany, it is known as the Grafenberg spot (Grafenberg, 1950), or more popularly as the G spot (Ladas and Whipple, 1982). It had first been described in the seventeenth century by Regnier de Graaf, the Dutch gynecologist who also discovered the ovary's Graafian follicle (Sevely and Bennett, 1978).

Anatomically, the G spot is not part of the vagina but of the urethra. It corresponds to the male prostate gland, and is made up of the periurethral glands of Skene. It is individually variable in size. It can be stimulated by thrusts of the penis, or digitally. When stimulated, it swells and contains fluid which may escape through the urethra.

In some, though not all females, the muscular spasms of orgasm are accompanied by spurts of fluid through the urethra. Formerly this fluid was considered to be urine escaping. After Grafenberg's rediscovery of the G spot, however, it was said to come from the Skene's glands of the G spot, and was called female ejaculation. Chemical tests have not yet provided an absolutely conclusive verdict (Zaviacic and Whipple, 1993).

The G spot in the female and the prostate gland in the male both are supplied with erotically sensitive nerve fibers. Though there are many exceptions, some men are able to get intense sexual stimulation from pressure on the prostate gland, especially as orgasm approaches. The pressure may be either from the partner's finger, or a small sized dildo or, when two males are together from a penis (covered with a condom as a protection against HIV/AIDS).

Some women have also obtained intense stimulation from having one penis in the vagina and another one, or a butt plug in the anus. The gymnastics are a bit complicated but it is possible for a woman with two male partners to have both penises in the vagina, or one in the vagina and one in the anus. One man lies on his back, the woman sits on his erect penis, and the second man mounts her from behind.

The amount of movement and vocalization that accompanies the climax of orgasm varies individually from quite still and quiet to thrashing around and groaning, crying out, and breathing heavily. The extreme of orgasmic release may include multiple vocalizations, together with muscular twitchings and convulsive spasms of the arms and legs that, for a minute or longer, resemble an epileptic seizure; but this is probably a rare extreme. People's sexual privacy guarantees the virtual impossibility of obtaining accurate frequency statistics from direct observation of a large, random sample of subjects. Direct observation of a small sample of three men and three women was, however, undertaken by Mosovich and Tallaferro (1954). They observed three types of masturbatory orgasmic reaction. Two subjects showed no evidence of bodily tension except a slight contraction of the jaws. Three subjects evidenced less rigidity, deep breathing, staring eyes, and a crescendo of spasmodic twitchings. One subject became pale, perspired, and collapsed into complete relaxation and light sleep.

Orgasm is able to survive loss of genital tissue even in considerable quantities. The penis, for example, may be amputated in a case of penile cancer, or it may be accidently severed in a mutilating accident. Provided the nerve fibers to the stump are intact, then it will be possible for orgasm to be triggered from the stump. In the case of a boy whose penis and right testicle were severed in a motorbike accident, a plastic surgical expert in microsurgery was able to connect the nerve fibers, veins, and arteries of the stump with those of a replacement graft taken from the top of one foot (Horton et al., 1981; McManus, 1982). When the surgical wound had healed, the grafted replacement part of the penis was not numb, but had sensation and feeling.

Transculturally, the most prevalent mutilation of the penis is circumcision performed either in infancy or as a prepubertal ritual (see chap. 3). In the United States, the practice of newborn circumcision is either a religious ritual, or a secular ritual derived from a fallacious nineteenth century belief that circumcision would prevent masturbation (Wallerstein, 1980). Males circumcised in infancy are not devoid of orgasm, but there is no way of comparing their own orgasm with that of the uncircumcised male. Before-and-after data from males circumcised in adulthood indicate that those who formerly ejaculated too quickly evaluated the outcome positively, whereas those who formerly relied on skin-stretch elasticity did not (Money and Davison, 1983). The cosmetics of having a foreskin are very important to some circumcised males (Bigelow, 1992).

Genital mutilation in girls (see chap. 3), so-called female circumcision, is a secular ritual prevalent in Nilotic, Sahelian, and northeastern Africa. It is performed without anesthetic. In the Sunna form, the clitoris or only its hood is removed. In the Pharaonic form, the entire vulva is removed, including the labia majora, and the wound is infibulated, leaving only a small hole for the escape of urine and menstrual blood. The hole is too small for sexual intercourse without being cut larger. Lightfoot-Klein (1989, 1991) interviewed Pharaonically circumcised women of whom some reported orgasmic climax, and some did not.

Some women with a history of hermaphroditic birth defect of the sex organs have in infancy undergone surgery to correct the defect. In some cases the correction entailed resection of a grossly enlarged clitoris. In adulthood some of the women reported an orgasmic climax, but others did not (Money, 1961b, p.1395).

In males, erection of the penis is not an absolute prerequisite of orgasm. Loss of erection may be reversible or, as a sequel to penile injury or deterioration, ireversible. Although penetration may be impossible, ejaculation may be achieved manually, or orally, or with the aid of a vibrator. When the penis remains limp, the quality of orgasmic feeling is different than with a hard erection.

The climax of orgasm on every coital occasion is not an absolute prerequisite of sexual enjoyment. This is more prevalently so in advanced age than in youth, more often in women than in men, and more frequently in some life situations than others. Male sexual physiology is such that there are very few males who have never had an orgasm. By contrast, the same cannot be said of women. Therapeutic orgasmic training helps some women who can find and afford training sessions. Probably, however, intervention would be more often effective if made available at an early stage of adolescent maturation rather than long after anorgasmia has become apparent, and has had time to become immutable. Like training for sports, or music, the younger one begins, the better, and the greater the degree of brain cell involvement.

Anorgasmia in women is easily neglected, as it is not necessary for the female to have an orgasm to conceive, whereas the man's ejaculatory orgasm is prerequisite to his impregnation of her. The comparison is made very obvious in cases of spinal cord injury (paraplegia) which leaves the lower body totally paralyzed and numb. Even though deficient in genital feeling (Dekoker, 1996) and movement of the legs, the paraplegic woman is able to be inseminated, to conceive, and to carry a pregnancy to delivery by Caesarian section. The paraplegic man, however, cannot ejaculate except with the aid of an electric vibrator (electroejaculator) rectally inserted so as to stimulate the prostate gland to release its sperm laden fluid into the upper urethra, whence it drains down the tube of the penis into a condom collector, ready for artificial insemination of the partner.

Conceptive Phase

CONCEPTION AND pregnancy do not invariably follow every act of sexual intercourse. For conception to occur, the male ejaculate must contain no fewer than 40 million mobile sperms and preferably 200 or 300 million. The female must be at the ovulatory stage of her menstrual cycle, when an ovum (egg) is released from the ovary, which occurs midway between the end of one menstrual cycle and the beginning of the next (Simpson, 1995; Wilcox et al., 1995). The few days of menstrual bleeding and immediately thereafter are the so-called safe or infertile period when intercourse does not produce pregnancy—but it is not easily calculated, it restricts one's sexual calendar, and above all is not safe enough to be reliable.

In males there is no period of infertility as there is in the female. The only way for the male to practice unassisted contraception is to not ejaculate in the vagina. In penovaginal intercourse, that means pulling out before he comes. This withdrawal method is not safe enough to be relied upon. Even before he ejaculates, there may be some sperms in the urethral fluid, and after ejaculation there certainly will be some, maybe enough for conception if the penis reenters the vagina.

In some adolescent females, after the onset of menstruation, the onset of fertility may be delayed over the course of the next several menstrual months. For adolescents whose sex life has already begun it may create a false and unreliable sense of security. Fertility begins unpredictably.

A prevalent assumption in the adult generation of sex educators today is that adolescent pregnancies are unplanned and unwanted, and could be reduced by more widespread knowledge of methods of contraception, and availability of contraceptive devices. That is not necessarily so (see chap. 12). Nonetheless it is correct to characterize society as Janus-faced in preaching against adolescent pregnancy, while at the same time preaching against adolescent contraceptive knowledge and availability. Yet there are some adolescents who want to make sure that sexual intercourse is not infallibly followed by conception and pregnancy. For them there is contraception. The rationale that lies behind all the methods of family planning and birth control is that the timing and frequency of pregnancy be planned in advance.

The contraceptive method most easy for people, female as well as male, to find and pay for is the male condom, a barrier method. Today's smart female carries her own supply of male condoms, stored at room temperature and no older than the marked expiration date. So also, the smart male does the same. That helps to ensure that there will always be no chance of an unplanned pregnancy. The condom deteriorates if overexposed to heat, as in the glove compartment of an automobile, or in a back pocket wallet. For a backup, a condom should be used with a birth control jelly squirted through an applicator tube into the vagina beforehand, and again afterwards, especially if the condom has torn, or slipped off. The jelly must always be one that is water soluble, and never one that contains oil or grease, both of which eat at the rubber and weaken it (see chap. 12). It's a good idea for the female as well as the male to have practiced unrolling a condom on a live penis and not an artificial substitute, so as to ensure being able to unroll it all the way to the pubic hair at the base of the penis. Although a spermatozoon is invisible except under the microscope, it is thousands of times larger than a virus. A virus can get through a minuscule defect in the rubber of a condom which a sperm cannot penetrate. Thus a condom guarantees more protection against pregnancy than it does against the AIDS virus.

The newest of the female barrier methods of contraception is the female latex condom (see chap. 12). There has not yet been time for it to have achieved widespread popular acceptance. Nor has there been time to collect statistics as to its efficacy as a contraceptive or as a barrier to the transmission of HIV/AIDS. It is the only device that a female can wear to reduce, if not prevent the chance of HIV/AIDS infection.

With a history of success over a century or longer, the diaphragm is a barrier inserted into the vagina and placed like a cap over the cervix to prevent the passage of sperms from the far end of the vagina into the uterus and the two fallopian tubes in one of which they may find an ovum, freshly released from the ovary, searching for them. Diaphragms are manufactured in sizes to fit the different sizes of cervix, which requires that the measurement and placement must be made by a gynecologist. The diaphragm is smeared with contraceptive jelly and put in place in anticipation of sexual intercourse, minutes or hours ahead, and may be left in place for a few hours before removal.

Like the diaphragm, the intrauterine device (IUD) needs to be fitted by a gynecologist but, unlike the diaphragm it may be safely left in place for upwards of ten years. It then requires a gynecologist to remove it. The IUD acts by inhibiting fertilization of the egg and or its implantation on the wall of the uterus. Several shapes and varieties of IUD were popularized in the 1970s and subjected to revision and redesign for greater efficacy. Treiman et al. (1996) in *Population Reports* recommend the IUD as one of the most safe, efficacious, and convenient forms of contraception marketed worldwide. Some are made of pliable plastic. One type carries a year's supply of a slow release progestinic hormone to augment its contraceptive efficacy. The efficacy of others is augmented by copper embedded in the plastic. The copper-type is the longest lasting (up to ten years).

Like the IUD, the hormonal contraceptive Pill dispenses with planning each coital event in advance, but it must be taken regularly on schedule, with no omissions. First available in 1960, early versions of the Pill needed dosage adjustments to get rid of undesirable side effects. Today's version contains a minimal amount of an estrogenic hormone combined with a progestinic one, and is considered safe from side effects as well as highly efficacious as a contraceptive. Hormonal contraception can also be used, under medical supervision, with a dosage appropriately adjusted, as a so-called morning-after pill. (AASECT, 1996b).

In addition to being in pill form, progestinic steroidal hormones for use as contraceptives may be obtained as long-acting intramuscular injections, good for three months, and as even longer-acting subcutaneous implants, good for three years or longer.

RU-486, also known as mifepristone, is an antiprogestinic substance that may be used mostly in the very early stage of conception and pregnancy as an abortifacient or "contragestive" that allows resumption of the menstrual cycle (Baulieu, 1989). For the first seven to nine weeks of pregnancy, RU-486 is combined with prostaglandin E1 (misoprostol), which induces uterine contractions. It may be used contraceptively during the immediate period after unprotected intercourse, as a so-called morning-after pill (see above) under medical supervision (Baulieu, 1989).

There is an ongoing search for a long-acting hormonal method of contraception for males, so far unsuccessful. The hormones that suppress male fertility also have negative side effects. They may inhibit erection and ejaculation, and diminish the frequency of sexual arousal and activity.

For teenagers who are not financially independent of their families and not legally of age, all the female methods of contraception present a dilemma: they are expensive and they necessitate the services of a physician who may demand parental consent. Some teenagers and their parents are able to work out an agreement about the age of starting a sex life, the usage of contraception, and protection against HIV/AIDS. Others are not. So some teenagers embark on a sex life and leave it up to fate to decide on pregnancy. When the evidence of pregnancy is upon them, fate again is left to decide what will happen, at which time there may be no entirely satisfactory solution.

One possible solution is to resort to abortion which is never as personally satisfactory as contraception would have been in the first place. Certainly there are situations and considerations, for some people and under some circumstances, when abortion is indisputably the only reasonable way. Also, there are some national policies in which abortion officially outweighs contraception to curtail overpopulation. Nonetheless, logic dictates that, ideally, contraception outweighs abortion in personal and social policy.

All methods of contraception to control the rate of fertility are subject to error, some more than others, no matter how tiny the percentage. The greatest guarantee of infertility, except for male or female gonadectomy (castration), is female tubal ligation and male vasectomy. Many millions of men and women, worldwide, whose family size has been completed, have elected this surgical method of infertility. Unlike gonadectomy, it does not rob the body of its sex hormones.

Tubal ligation and vasectomy may be acceptable to young people who are carriers of dread genetic diseases that may be passed on to their offspring, if they plan on having a sex life without pregnancies. Some young people who are so disabled as to be unable to carry a pregnancy or to care for offspring may also elect to have a sex life only after tubal ligation or vasectomy. Otherwise, these surgical procedures for fertility control in very young people are mostly ill advised as a substitute for nonsurgical methods of fertility regulation which are readily reversible. There is no guarantee of the reversibility of tubal ligation or vasectomy, but it is not impossible.

Castration to eliminate testosterone from the testicles is used in the treatment of some forms of cancer. Also with more than a tinge of vindictiveness, castration is from time to time advocated as a method of treatment for sex offenders. However, postcastration sterility does not prevent continued sex offending, and the loss of testicular testosterone does not invariably do so. Moreover, the missing sex hormone is easy to replace by intramuscular injections or pills.

Temporary or reversible sterility in adolescent and young adult males and females may be a concomitant of extreme starvation, as in famine or concentration camp victims; and also in cases of extreme fasting for cosmetic effect in young fashion models and ballet dancers; and in patients with a diagnosis of anorexia nervosa, the syndrome of asexual virginal purity, sometimes known in females as the Virgin Mary syndrome. Females in these categories fail to ovulate and menstruate. So also do those who devote inordinate amounts of time and energy to gymnastic and athletic sports training. Subfertility occurs also in fasting males, and in males in sports training. It becomes more severe in those who also ingest an anabolic steroid, testosterone or one of its derivatives, which augment muscular strength at the cost of suppressing spermatogenesis in the testicles as well as their normal secretion of testosterone. Nonathletic males with a history of chronic fatigue, overwork, and sleep deprivation may also be reversibly infertile. In young females there are some unexplained cases of failure to conceive that do not respond to any type of therapy other than counseling therapy with an empathic therapist, usually male.

Subfertility in males is a possible long-term effect of environment chemical pollutants that enter the food chain and masquerade as hormones when ingested by animals and people (see chap. 7). They are named endocrine disrupters. These chemical suspects include phthalates, used in plastics, paints, and inks, and alkyl phenols, which are the products of microbial breakdown of paints, detergents, cosmetics, and herbicides (Lutz, 1996; Colburn et al., 1996). Dispute about causality notwithstanding, the sperm count in males has been declining in the past twenty years by an estimated 2 percent a year. Now, in the mid-1990s, it is an estimated 30 percent lower than thirty years ago (Lutz, 1996; AASECT, 1996b).

Persistent infertility has multiple sources that include genetic defects, gonadal defects, sexual birth defects, hormonal deficiencies, anatomical anomalies or injuries, and infections, as well as side effects of chemical, pollutants, illicit drugs, medication, radiation, or surgery. These various conditions produce infertility in three ways: when sperms from the testicles and ova (eggs) from the ovaries are missing, insufficient, or defective; when the egg fails to meet up with and take in a fertilizing sperm; or when the egg-sperm combination (the zygote) dies or fails to implant itself into the wall of the uterus where it can form a placenta and grow into a baby.

In some cases of birth defect or injury, those with congenital absence of the testicles, ovaries, or uterus, for example, infertility can be predicted from childhood onward. If step by step sexological counseling is provided for the parents and for the developing child, with information on how to achieve eventual parenthood, then that information becomes incorporated into juvenile rehearsal fantasies. Sudden disclosure of the information, delayed until adolescence, produces traumatizing shock waves, and a sense of having been betrayed by truth withheld in childhood. Well informed, an infertile adolescent or young adult can enter into a romantic relationship that need not break up through lack of agreement on a plan for parenting or, conversely, a plan for childless careers.

Infertility attributable to spermatic deficiency or defect can be circumvented by resorting to a fertility clinic that operates a sperm bank from which a female receives a donor insemination from an anonymous donor at the time of her ovulation. Conversely, when infertility is attributable to failure of the ovary to produce ova, then a male's sperm may be used to combine with a donor ovum. This procedure is known as an in vitro fertilization (IVF). After the fertilized cell (the sperm plus egg combination) has begun to multiply, it is transferred from its glass Petri dish into the female's uterus. This procedure is far more complicated and expensive than donor insemination. IVF is used also with a female's own ovum if infertility is attributed to failure of egg and sperm to meet and combine.

Infertility attributable to a female's failure to ovulate may also, in some cases, be pharmacologically treated (for example with clomiphene citrate) to stimulate the ovary to ovulate. More than one egg may be released, producing multiple births.

A different type of hormonal treatment, namely with the adrenocortical hormone, cortisol, is available for fertility failure in females with the newly identified late onset version of CAH (the syndrome of congenital adrenal hyperplasia, of which the prenatal form is presented in chapters 4 and 15). Affected females have irregular menstrual cycles, or none at all. In variable degree they manifest bodily signs of hormonal masculinization induced by androgen erroneously secreted by the adrenocortical glands. The ovaries become polycystic which is also a diagnostic characteristic of the Stein-Leventhal syndrome of infertility and partial androgenization of the body. Infertility attributable to a birth defect of the uterus may yield to surgical correction with the possibility of pregnancy if there is at least one ovulating ovary. Otherwise IVF may be resorted to (Frydman et al., 1988; Sauer et al., 1989). In the case of complete congenital or postsurgical absence of the uterus a sense of feminine integrity may be upheld if the person is told about the actual occurrence of extrauterine pregnancy including one case (Jackson et al.,1980) of pregnancy after hysterectomy and the delivery of a normal daughter by Caesarian section. It is gynecological science fiction as of now, but a uterine transplant is technologically feasible at some future date. No one should be denied hope, even the hope that science fiction will become reality.

Adopting, fostering, or step-parenting (marrying an "instant family") is the age old method of surmounting childlessness. It may be the first option, the only option, or by those whose lives have been too disrupted by a series of failed attempts at assisted pregnancy, the option of last resort.

When in the ordinary course of events conception does occur, since it does not immediately declare itself, the schedule of sexual intercourse will not immediately change. As the pregnancy advances, some men will find the bodily contours of pregnancy erotically exciting. Whether or not the intercourse timetable changes during pregnancy varies according to the couple, and especially according to the female's health and well being. If a miscarriage threatens, then the contractions of orgasm may precipitate loss of the fetus. If all goes well, the size of the abdomen in the third trimester may render the missionary position uncomfortable, as compared with an alternative coital position, or with some other erotic activity.

Some women have found orgasms during pregnancy to be exceptionally powerful (Pranzarone, 1991). It has been claimed anecdotally that, in natural childbirth with the husband as coach, his manual massage of the wife's clitoral zone and mons veneris may combine with labor contractions so as to diminish pain and intensify erotic sensation, which is even more explosively intensified with the expulsion of the baby. The proportion of women who can claim such an experience is unknown. In support of the claim, it is experimentally established in rats, and in women also, that intravaginal stimulation increases pain blindness (pain agnosia) and improves pain tolerance (Komisaruk, 1991).

Back home with a new baby, a couple's coital schedule will be partly dictated by the speed of the woman's vaginal recovery (especially if she had the surgery of episiotomy to enlarge the vaginal exit), and partly by the baby's sleeping, waking, and feeding schedule, as well as their own work and sleep schedules. This is a period when, rather than becoming irritably out of synchrony with one another, the parents can combine sexual intercourse on some occasions with solo masturbation on others. This is also a period when unilateral attention to the baby and erotic neglect of the partner are hazards to be attended to.

One of the possible hazards for the mother of a new baby is a loss of superior well being that accompanies uncomplicated pregnancy in some women, and that is a bonus of the high level of the pregnancy hormone, progesterone. After delivery, as the level of progesterone falls, unexplained postpartum depression may intervene. In rare cases a full blown postpartum psychotic depression develops, with episodes of hallucinosis. Responding to the voices of hallucination, the mother may kill the baby. Postpartum psychosis responds to antidepressant medication.

14

Copulatory Concerns

Terminology

The prefix *hypo-* means not enough, *hyper-* means too much, and *para-* means altered. In sexual medicine, each prefix may be followed by either *-sexual*, or *-philia* (from the Greek term for love). Logically there should be hyposexual, hypersexual, and parasexual disorders, or else hypophilic, hyperphilic, and paraphilic disorders. In sexological usage, however, paraphilia is the scientific substitute for what the law calls perversion, and parasexual means nonsexual reproduction. Hyposexual and hypersexual are both used quantitatively, and hypophilic and hyperphilic have a qualitative significance as well as being quantitative.

Masters and Johnson published their second book under the title, *Human Sexual Inadequacy* (1970). The inadequacies it deals with are, in men, premature ejaculation, ejaculatory incompetence, impotence, and dyspareunia (coital pain). In women the inadequacies are orgasmic dysfunction, vaginismus (muscle spasm), and dyspareunia. All of these inadequacies represent, to some degree, an insufficiency or loss of coital function at some stage of the sexual response cycle. Thus they are various manifestations of hypophilia.

Hypophilias

IN PREMATURE EJACULATION and vaginismus (also known as vaginism) the muscular contractions appropriate to bringing the sexual response cycle to a close appear much too soon. In the male, the penis ejaculates before it enters the vagina or immediately thereafter. In the female, the vaginal entrance closes so powerfully that the penis cannot enter it.

In impotence, vasodilation of the spongy tissue of the penis fails to keep the penis sufficiently hard to enter the vagina. The corresponding phenomenon in the female is failure of the vaginal wall to secrete droplets of lubrication, so that it remains too dry to admit the penis comfortably. Both failures may be situationally transient, or chronic and long-lasting.

In dyspareunia, vaginal entry and thrusting produces severely painful discomfort in the genitalia of either the male or the female so that continuing with penovaginal intercourse becomes unbearable. In the penis, pain may begin simultaneously with ejaculation and persist as a burning sensation in the urethra. Dyspareunia affects the vagina more frequently than the penis. The exception is Peyronie's disease, in which, without a prior history of trauma or injury, scar tissue forms in the penis (and possibly in the ball of the thumb also) and creates a persistent penile curvature that does not respond to and may be made worse by surgery.

Rarely, pain occurs in either men or women as a postcoital, migrainous headache attack of sudden onset coterminous with the onset of orgasm. It may be responsive to medication. Migraine headache is vascular in origin. Another vascular response to orgasm is rupture of the minute capillaries of the retina, diagnostically known as valsava retinopathy (Friberg et al., 1995). It is experienced as sudden and temporary spottiness, blurring, or loss of vision in one eye. This reaction is so rare as to be almost nonexistent. It is more likely to be induced by forceful breathing during nonsexual physical exercise.

Anorgasmia means failure to reach the climax of orgasm and applies to both the male and the female. In males it is known also as ejaculatory incompetence and signifies that, in the absence of the subjective feeling or orgasm, the spasmodic muscular contractions necessary to pump or squirt out the seminiferous fluid are also absent. It is possible, however, that fluid, chiefly from the prostate gland, may seep out without either the feeling of ejaculation or the contractions of ejaculation. Another possibility is that, although the feeling of orgasm does occur, no ejaculatory fluid leaves the penis. This is the dry-run orgasm, so-called, a sporadic side effect of some antihypertensive and antidepressant medications. Alternatively, it is a sign of retrograde ejaculation, in which the fluid of ejaculation goes backward into the bladder from the urethra instead of forward through the penis, usually as a sequel to urethral surgery, as in prostatectomy.

In females, anorgasmia has also been called hypogyneismus (Musaph, 1977). Formerly it was referred to as frigidity, but that term has been dropped as being too pejorative. Anorgasmia is reported more frequently in females than males. It may be secondary to painful vaginal pathology. It may also be situationally specific, occurring with one partner and not another; or it may have a long term history of never having had an orgasm either autoerotically or with a partner. Although anorgasmia may be a symptom of vaginal penetration phobia, it is not necessarily a symptom of generalized sexuoerotic anhedonia or aversion. With advancing age and experience, female anorgasmia may go into spontaneous remission. Even if it does not remit, anorgasmia is not totally incompatible with enjoyment of sexual intercourse.

Although not universally so, each of these foregoing hypophilias may be attributed to some type of so-called organic etiology. In other words it may occur as a sequel to a congenital condition, or as a sequel to a precipitating disease, infection, injury, thrombosis, or drug toxicity, or as a side effect of cardiovascular or psychiatric medication. The latter include in particular antidepressants, like the much popularized fluoxetine (Prozac), that belong in the category of selective serotonin reuptake inhibitors (SSRI) (Riley, 1995; Demyttenaere and Vanderschueren, 1995).

A hypophilia, if untreated, may be persistent or short-lived. Nonetheless, it is probable that the disorder will respond to ameliorative pharmalogic treatment, alone or together with sexological counseling, even if it cannot be completely cured or reversed.

There is no adequate antonym of organic to apply to the etiology of a hypophilic disorder. The most usual term is psychogenic. Psychogenic usually means that the disorder does not fit any other diagnosis and so, by exclusion is put in the diagnostic trash can. Maybe the symptom will go into remission either spontaneously or in response to a regimen of talking and behavioral counseling. This regimen goes by the name of couple sex therapy.

In cases in which hypophilia responds to couple sex therapy, or to individual therapy, it is not uncommon to find an early chronically negative or acutely traumatizing sexological history that defined sex as an unspeakable monster in the person's life. With the advent of adolescence, the only escape from the monster was to defy it by having sex or getting married. Alas! The escape gets foiled. The partner gets cast in the role of being an ally of the monster, and the relationship of the couple becomes one of adversarial feuding. The sex organs become secret weapons, deviously undercutting one another by not functioning properly. The penis refutes the vagina. The vagina refutes the penis. They fail one another. The logical connection between this sexual failure and the prior history of the sexual monster becomes totally dissociated—that is, deconnected and unrecognized.

Nonetheless, the couple may remain locked into one another in what amounts to an unrecognized collusion of reciprocal lovemap pathology. There are ways of coaxing the collusion into being recognized. For example, to tell a couple together that, "if he as a premature ejaculator is coming too soon, then that means she is not coming soon enough," is to invite an angry denial from him. The responsibility, he says, must be all his. Sexual intercourse, however, is a dual interaction and so is its failure. Once that becomes recognized, the pathology will have a chance of becoming unraveled.

The interactive input of the man and the woman in premature ejaculation is illustrated in a case the sexological history of which begins with the wife's early puberty at age six. As a child she had been a victim of her mother's anxious admonitions against boys and pregnancy, and of her mother's railing against her father for his drinking and his irresponsibilities and neglect of his family. As a young college graduate and school teacher the daughter married a fellow teacher. Part of his premarital attraction was his being, like herself, sexually undemanding. Their attempts at marital intercourse were bungled, hers by vaginal penetration phobia, his by premature ejaculation. Giving a "sportscaster technique" account, she described how she would lie in bed turned away from him, aware that he was stimulating his penis to erection. Moving into the spoon position, he would attempt penetration from the rear, and would come before getting his penis into her nonaccommodating vagina. Then, with a disparaging tone of voice, she would turn and say, "Oh, Michael, you did it again."

They agreed to set up separate apartments, but to continue seeing one another, though only for romantic dating and dining. There was no sexual intercourse. Love was split off from lust—dissociated. When the time came for his annual military reservist camp, she agreed to drive him to the airport. As he prepared to depart, a mystifying thing happened to her. He was upstairs in the shower. She spied his wallet and cigarettes on the table. It was as if a little devil got into her, she surmised. She would make him miss the plane by seducing him into having sex such as he had never had before. The chance came for her little plot to hatch when he called for her to bring up his cigarettes. Against his protest of being short of time, she collapsed him onto the bed, fondling and sucking his penis as she had never done before. After she got his penis into her vagina, she worked on it vigorously for half an hour before he came. The little devil had unleashed the whore in her, she said. That whore must have been there all the while, dissociated and imprisoned. So also the husband's sustained responsiveness must have been present and dissociated. After he returned from camp, the little devil got loose only once again, and then disappeared, apparently forever.

Eventually they went their separate ways. She found a new boyfriend, a workaholic with two jobs. At night he took inventory in a warehouse where she would visit, entertaining herself reading until 2 A.M., by which time they were too fatigued to bother with sexual intercourse. On weekends, when they had more time, it turned out that he, also, was a premature ejaculator.

Sexuoerotic Anhedonia

ANOTHER HYPOPHILIC outcome of sexual feuding is observable as the syndrome of sexual inertia or apathy, which translates subjectively into a lack of sexual drive or desire. The more comprehensive term is sexuoerotic anhedonia, meaning lack of pleasure. There may not be some accompanying degree of erotic anesthesia or numbness of the genitalia.

To know about seeing, one who is blind must once have had at least some sight, so as to make the comparison. So also with feeling sexual drive or desire: to know about it, one must have had some intimation of it so as to have a standard of comparison; and never to have had it means not to know what one is missing. Irreversible and absolute lack of sexual drive or desire is rare and, if not always, then frequently associated with some other rare diagnostic condition.

Persistent anhedonic loss or diminution of sexuoerotic desire once present, in both sexes may be a side effect of hypertensive and SSRI psychiatric medications, already mentioned for their suppressant effect on erection and orgasm. In some individuals SSRIs have a paradoxical effect of genital arousal, possibly accompanied by yawning and spontaneous orgasm (AASECT, 1996b). Yawning has been recognized as a sexual signal in at least one species of ape.

Anhedonic lack of drive or desire may signify a sexual aversion, formerly subsumed under the now politically incorrect term, frigidity. The aversion may be to a person, perhaps an erstwhile partner whose very touch becomes repulsive and unbearable. Alternatively, the aversion may be phobic: in the female, a specific vaginal penetration phobia, and, in the male, a specific penile insertion phobia which, in folklore, is the phobia of the toothed vagina. The prevalence of the female phobia exceeds that of the male. In both instances, phobia does not interfere with sexual attraction and solicitation in the proceptive phase, nor with foreplay above the waist.

In the female with vaginal penetration phobia, the male's attempt at penetration releases panic so intolerable that the female equates the attempt with rape, and the male is falsely accused of rape. The male may also respond to female penetration phobia with situationally induced premature ejaculation (the formula is, "Let's get it over with quickly"); or with loss of erection (the formula is, "Let's give up trying"). Each of these two male reactions may be situationally induced also as a side effect of the phobia of the toothed vagina. The corresponding female reaction is anorgasmia.

As a secondary reaction, penetration and insertion phobias generate recrimination and a fresh cycle of feuding with the sex organs. The cycle may possibly be broken with the intervention of couple sex therapy. Otherwise it may lead to a breakup of the partnership, although not necessarily so. If a male brings to a partnership his own lovemap imprinted with impotency, and a female hers imprinted with vaginal penetration phobia, the two of them may be able to adapt to a sex life that sidesteps sexual intercourse, except for conception. They then may obtain the special assistance of artificial insemination of the wife with semen from the husband. This is an example of compromise and of the unspelled-out sexual collusion that governs some people's lives.

To strive to become sexually inert, rid of all subjective feeling of sexual urge, drive or desire, is incomprehensible to the general population of adolescent males. In a male with the Skoptic syndrome, however, adolescence brings with it an all-abiding and obsessional fixation on becoming a eunuch (See Appendix I). The fixation is so intense that it leads some to succeed in self-castration. They use, for example, an animal castration kit. In females there is no exact counterpart of self-castration, so the fixation is on persuading a surgeon of the absolute and unyielding necessity of removal of the uterus and ovaries.

Skoptic derives from the Russian word for castrated ram. It was applied to a Christian sect that existed in Russia and Romania for two centuries until the early twentieth century. Interpreting Scripture (Matthew 19:12) literally, the Skoptics became religious eunuchs by castration of the testicles alone, or with amputation of the penis also. For women, the substitute for castration was removal of the nipples by burning.

Nipple removal guarantees no milk for a newborn baby, but it does not impede either the acceptive or the conceptive sexual phases (see chap. 13). Castration alone alters the frequency of acceptive sexuality, but it guarantees only sterility. Even without a penis, proceptive sexuality may not be totally abolished, even though lessened.

In appendix 1 there is a personal account of experience with the Skoptic syndrome up to the point where the syndrome appeared to have gone into remission.

Sex Therapy

IN ADDITION TO sexological counseling, possibly with demonstration videos, treatment for hypophilias entails graduated exercises in foreplay, termed sensate focus, that lead up to penovaginal intromission. Sometimes together and sometimes alone, the couple share a single therapist or a male and female pair of therapists, with whom they discuss their progress, a few with the use of home videos of their progress in treatment.

For the treatment of impotence, in the 1960s surgical attention began to be directed toward flexible strips of plastic implanted into the shaft of the penis. Alternatively, elongated plastic balloons were implanted in the penis and inflated from a container of fluid implanted in the lower abdominal cavity and operated by a squeeze bulb implanted in the scrotum. The rate of long term surgical complications dampened enthusiasm for both forms of surgical technology, especially after 1983 following the new pharmacologic discovery of inducing erection on demand by direct injection into the corpora cavernosa of the shaft of the penis (Sitsen, 1988; Peles and Panter, 1996). The most effective injectable substance in current use is prostaglandin E1 (PGE1), a hormonelike chemical widely distributed in the human body. PGE1 works by regulating the opening and closing of the smooth muscle that regulates blood flow through the microscopically small blood vessels of the spongy, erection inflatable tissue of the corpora cavernosa. PGE1 may be used for a trial period regardless of the etiology of impotence. In cases of situational or transient impotence, once improvement has occurred, the medication may be discontinued.

Sex therapy for premature ejaculation combines couple counseling with a special stop-and-go squeeze technique. In a pause period, the fingers of either partner periodically apply pressure tightly to the head of the penis to discourage ejaculation.

Supplemental pharmacologic help for premature ejaculation (Segraves, 1995) is newly available in the form of drugs, commonly used for the treatment of depression, that are selective serotonin reuptake inhibitors (SSRI). The most popularly known SSRI is Prozac (fluoxetine), already mentioned. Prozac floods the brain with one of its own neurochemicals, serotonin, by blocking its cellular uptake and reuse. The flood of serotonin is presumed to slow down the nerve impulses responsible for the build up to sexual climax in both males and females. Hence its value for the treatment of premature ejaculation in males.

In addition to couple counseling, sex therapy for vaginismus may introduce a couple to gentle dilation of the vagina with plastic dilators graduated from very thin to penis-sized. If it can be tolerated, a finger might also be inserted—or any other smooth and suitably sized and noninjurious dilating object.

Sex therapy for hypophilias, although not denied premaritally to adolescents, provided they can afford it, is not made easily accessible for them. In professional journals as well as the media, writings on sex therapy are pitched at an older audience, as if to assume that adolescents ought not to have discovered whether they have any copulatory concerns, or not. Nonetheless, sexological histories taken in adolescence or later reveal that hypophilias are, in fact, encountered at young ages, and often have their origins at a still younger age, in childhood. The longer they remain unattended to, the more tenacious they become.

Hyperphilias

HOW MUCH IS too much? Or not enough? How often is too often? Or not often enough? In surveys of hyperphilia and hypophilia, even husbands and wives disagree not only in their ratings of their own mutual sexual intercourse, but also on their estimate of the average or normal frequency.

Statistically, average implies a bell curve distribution with two extremes and a bulge in the middle. The bulge comprises the cluster of the middle fifty or sixty percent of the population. They are the statistically normal. Those at either extreme of the cluster are the statistically abnormal.

The ideological norm is different. It is not statistically determined, nor based on what people actually do, but on what they are told they ought to do. Applied to sexual intercourse, it signifies obedience to an ideal standard enforced by some authority that has the power to make rules and command conformity. Thus sexual intercourse only once a year would be ideologically too often for a member of a monastic religious order who has taken a vow of chastity; whereas, according to the statistical norm for his neighbors in the surrounding community it would be not often enough.

Males are individually variable as to the length of the refractory period between one orgasm and the next, the range being from minutes to hours to days. For most males, early adolescence is the age of maximum frequency of orgasms, which may be as many as five or more per twenty-four-hour day. It is not unheard of for a man in his twenties or thirties to have three orgasms daily, but one or fewer is more likely, as few in some cases as one a month. With advancing age, orgasmic frequency drops off, but it may continue at the rate of two or three orgasms daily. This was the frequency of masturbatory orgasms in a widower in his seventies, until a year or so before he died, at age seventy five, of congestive heart failure. Throughout his adult life, he had had a rating of hypersexual, with upwards of five or sex orgasms daily, more by manual self-masturbation and homosexual anal penetration of himself than by coitus, out of consideration for his wife.

Among either women or men there is no effectively reliable way to increase the orgasm frequency rate. It certainly cannot be done by voluntary effort or training. The neurochemistry of the brain-genital connection responsible for hyperorgasmia, and for hypoorgasmia too, has not yet revealed its secrets to sexological science. The data are lacking for women as well as men.

Although orgasmic frequency rates are individually variable for females as they are for males, there are some male-female differences (see chap. 13). More girls than boys go through a protracted period between puberty and the first orgasm induced either autoerotically, or with a partner. The period of female anorgasmia may continue well into young adulthood, and may survive multiple conception and motherhood. There are on record cases of women who experienced an orgasm for the first time postmenopausally, in their seventies or eighties.

After a female's first experience of orgasm, the calendrical frequency of orgasm varies with age as it does also in males, and also with general health and well being. Orgasmic frequency may also fluctuate with the menstrual cycle, though not with predictable consistency.

Women who live in close proximity, as in a student dormitory, tend toward menstrual synchrony, all being concurrently in season, so to speak, under the influence of pheromonal cyclicity (McClintock, 1971). Whether they simultaneously tend also toward synchrony in orgasmic frequency is too multivariately determined to have been ascertained.

For some and perhaps many women, the key factor in orgasmic frequency is not contingent on autoeroticism, but on the nearness and availability of a pair-bonded partner. In the absence of a partner, as from separation or bereavement, women more than men are likely to enter into a transient period of what might be called sexual dormancy. At the height of grief, overall eroticism becomes inert for such women, and men too. Its return is a sign of recovery from mourning.

On the criterion of the length of the refractory period between one orgasm and the next during a particular sexuoerotic encounter women far exceed men in being multiorgasmic. The range of individual differences is wide. At one extreme, a female may be not even uniorgasmic from penovaginal penetration, although multiorgasmic from oral-clitoral or oral-digital stimulation, or from vulval clitoral stimulation with a vibrator. At the other extreme, a female may be multiorgasmic virtually nonstop from the moment of intromission, indefinitely, each orgasm reaching the highest peak, until not another orgasm is left and the vagina constricts, exhausted.

Different from these two extremes is the female whose multiple climaxes build up to become progressively more intense until the final big climax explodes and a period of rest or sleep ensues. This type of multiorgasmia is most likely to be the closest analogue of what male multiple orgasm is claimed to be by those who make the claim. Anyone who claims that my orgasm is the same, better, or worse than yours is in the same position as one who claims that I can taste orange juice the same, better, or worse than you can, and I defy you to prove otherwise.

For both men and women the frequency of sexual intercourse is regulated in part by the familiarity of routine, as when a working married couple with young children settle into a monotonous routine of intercourse once, or maybe twice a week, except on special festive occasions or vacations. In the era before HIV/AIDS, a small minority of the population broke the monotony of routine by the excitement of the so-called Coolidge effect (Wilson, 1982), namely by changing partners in swingers' clubs or at group sex parties. The novelty of a new partner can be as exciting for the female as for the male; witness the illicit thrill and risk of cheating and adultery in women as well as men.

Males, however, would appear to be more adaptable than females to the novelty of what has been known in sexual slang since the 1950s as the sportfuck (for which there is no polite equivalent), or its analogue, the mercyfuck (Sheidlower, 1995). Females, by contrast are more likely to give up on the sportfuck scene that shows no future promise of one-on-one limerence. Nonetheless, some women find themselves well-suited to what in the contemporary vocabulary is called polyamory. The arrangement in polyamory is one in which erotosexual relationships rotate among members of a closed, exclusive, small group either frequently at sex parties, or over a longer interval. The longer the interval, the greater the likelihood that the relationship has become limerent, and exclusive. Women quit the polyamorous scene more readily than their men do.

In adolescence, although some boys as well as girls begin their sex lives as a limerent partner, girls do not have the same long tradition as boys do of beginning their sex lives with nonlimerent sportfucking. For adolescent boys in Latino culture, for example, the tradition still continues whereby a boy is introduced to heterosexual intercourse by an uncle, older brother, or friend who takes him to a house of prostitution to be initiated. Sportive sex continues with multiple partners who are not chaperoned as virgins. Traditionally, their brides are supposed to have remained virgins.

Among boys who grow up to discover themselves gay or bisexual in adolescence, some begin their sex lives as a limerent lover, whereas other engage in sex with other males sportively. Some take up a youthful career as commercial sex workers, hustlers, or call boys, and engage in sportive sex with many male customers, for pay.

In the case of girls who in adolescence discover that they are lesbian or bisexual, there is also the duality between limerent versus sportive sex with female partners, although the ratio between the two is probably less in favor of sportive sex than it is in gay boys. Also, when lesbian or bisexual girls engage in commercial sportive sex, the customers are predominantly if not exclusively male; and limerent sex is with only one lesbian lover in a continuing, noncommercial relationship.

Once but no longer called lagnesis and lagnosis, respectively, nymphomania and satyriasis are popular names for hypersexuality. Nymphomania is defined in the Oxford English Dictionary (OED) as excessive or uncontrollable sexual desire in a female. The corresponding male term is satyromania, also known as satyriasis. Each is a term of reproach, and is demeaning. They imply not only multiple partners and high frequency of casual sexual encounters, but also demandingness up to the point of exploitation.

Don Juan was a legendary Spanish nobleman known far and wide for his seductions. His name has become an eponym for a man with a reputation for womanizing. To be known as a Don Juan is more respectable and enviable than to be known as a satyr. In Greek mythology a satyr is half man, and half horned goat with a split penis. A man with satyromania evokes the disreputable image of a horny old goat.

In nymphomania and satyromania, the defining characteristic is not the frequency of having sex, but the fixated compulsion on having to have sex with a stranger every time, and to be tortured by the incapacity to establish a long term limerent relationship with only one partner. Both conditions are more accurately called a paraphilia (see chaps. 9, 16). The paraphilic fixation is on having to have a stranger as a sexual partner, every time, no matter what.

Some women have been known to be snidely dismissed by healthcare practitioners as nymphomanic when in fact they have a rare form of orgasmic epilepsy of the temporal lobe type. It brings on a very distressing feeling of sexual urgency in highly inappropriate situations, and cannot be relieved by any type of genital stimulation. The attack lasts for half an hour or longer, and then fades. Attacks can be brought under control by treatment with antiepileptic medication. It would not be surprising if orgasmic epilepsy exists in males also, without being recognized. Its frequency in adolescence and young adulthood remains unascertained.

Anecdotally one hears from time to time of a case of multiple orgasms triggered, without cutaneous contact, by sexuoerotic ideation and imagery as the only stimuli. As in orgasmic epilepsy, these orgasms are not subject to voluntary control. Their possible relationship to epilepsy has not been systematically investigated. Rarely they may be a side effect of treatment with Prozac (Demyttenaere and Vanderschueren, 1995).

Erotomania is the old name for a syndrome of hyperphilia now known eponymically as the Clérambault-Kandinsky syndrome (CKS) (see chap. 9). Erotomania is defined in the OED as excessive or morbid sexual desire. In CKS, he morbidity lies in the fact that desire is fixated on attracting the romantic and proceptive attention of a person who is socially unattainable. This person may, like a stage or movie star have been encountered only remotely or, like one's doctor, boss, or estranged lover or spouse, face to face. The person with CKS becomes unilaterally more and more love stricken. With each failure to garner a response of love requited, lovesickness intensifies, and the stratagems to gain a response become increasingly delusional. They include stalking and suicidal or homicidal threats. The recipient of CKS attention is well advised to obtain protective psychiatric and legal advice on how to proceed, for the CKS patient, as is typical in paranoia, lacks the insight to do so. The syndrome may slowly burn itself out, or it may progress to full blown bipolar disorder.

A more limited hypersexual manifestation is priapism, a condition of persistent and prolonged erection which fails to detumesce (Money and Hirsch, 1965). Although an etiology may not always be ascertained, priapism has been attributed to brain and spinal cord lesions, leukemia, and red blood cell clumping in sickle cell disease. It may also be a transient side effect of the injection of vasoactive drugs (for example, papaverine hydrochloride and prostaglandin E1), directly into the corpora cavernosa of the penis, for the treatment of impotence (Granata et al., 1995). The longer the persistence of priapism, the greater the increase in anhedonia and pain, and the greater the damage to erectile tissue and permanent flaccidity of the penis. Loss of erection, however, is not accompanied by loss of ejaculation and orgasm.

Jealousy

PROFOUND SEXUAL jealousy is a hyperphilic syndrome. Like CKS, it is a manifestation of limerence gone awry. In the male, a man with a youthful history of sportive sex, as a male prerogative, or even with a history of only lusting after sportive sex, typically sees the sexuality of other men through the sportive sex focus of his own personal lenses. In other words, he sees every woman, his girlfriend or wife included, as succumbing to being seduced or coerced by another sexually sportive male as successful in making conquests as he expects himself to be. Having been reared according to the tradition of the double standard, however, he expects and demands that his woman's sexuality never to be sportive but chaste, or feigned to be chaste, and faithful to him exclusively.

He becomes suspicious that his woman will, simply by being too close to another man, be paying him too much attention. Establishing eye contact arouses the same suspicion. In a rage of jealousy, he is likely to challenge the other male as well as his own female, and possibly to make a preemptive strike against either or both of them. In the event of his maiming or murdering another male and/or his own female upon discovering them in the act of intercourse (in flagrante delicto), in some jurisdictions, using the crime of passion defense, he may be acquitted.

Possessive male sexual jealousy has recently surfaced in evolutionary sexology, reworded as parental investment. The male's strategy, according to parental investment theory, is to ensure the perpetuation of his genes by possessing and inseminating the maximum number of females and by dominating rival males. The female's strategy, by contrast, is to ensure the perpetuation of her genes by maximizing the number of her ova fertilized by genetically superior semen, and also maximizing parental care of the offspring so that they live to be reproductively mature. Replacing the vocabulary of sexual jealousy with that of sexual investment explains neither jealousy nor investment. It simply translates the same phenomena of mating rivalry from one set of words to another.

Neither rivalry nor jealousy apply to the mating of all species (see chap. 2). For instance, mating rivalry is phyletically irrelevant in monecious species which, by definition, do not have male and female sexes. It is also phyletically irrelevant in diecious species in which males and females pairbond not competitively, but in lasting monogamous unions.

In primate species, sexual jealousy has more to do with troopbonding and with rivalry for powerful alliances in the leadership hierarchy of the troop than it does simply with pairbonding and mating rivalry. Rivalry for power affects female as well as male alliances. So also does sexual jealousy.

Pathological sexual possessiveness belongs to females as well as males. It may be strongly violent, up to the point of being homicidal, when two females of similar strength and power confront one another in competition for the same male. Otherwise, with a discrepancy in size and brute strength, as is typical between male and female, the female's power lies in making alliances and in being devious. In one case, a wife took revenge on her allegedly unfaithful man, by pouring gasoline on him while he was asleep, and setting him on fire (see chap. 16). Similarly, small children in a power struggle with a parent are obliged to resort to devious tactics. With matches as their most powerful weapon, a child may set fire to, say the parent's clothing closet.

Pathologically possessive jealousy is not exclusively sexual. In the context of parenthood, it may overtake a single mother who is left in lonely isolation when her daughter, an only child, marries and goes to live in proximity to the husband's widowed mother. Suddenly, as if hit by a thunderbolt, the girl's mother is hit by pathological jealousy of the new mother-in-law, who quite unexpectedly becomes the equivalent of a kidnapper. The girl's mother cannot explain what has happened to her; it is completely alien to her and out of character.

Sexually jealous rage attacks are self-defeating. They nullify the relationship which the enraged one is defending. All too often they end in assault, murder, and suicide. Among primates, human and subhuman, the neural mechanism for the transformation of protectiveness into jealous rage has not yet been scientifically deciphered. Nor has the mechanism for its reversal.

Reconciliation Sex

LIKE THE SPORTIVE and limerent fuck, there is also the reunion and the reconciliation fuck. Both of these qualify as hyperphilic on account of their erotic intensity and the power of their orgasm.

During a longish period of separation and abstinence, two lovers have ardently anticipated their first reunion in sexual intercourse. When it does occur, each one lets go and transports the other to higher and higher slopes of sexual ecstasy, and their orgasms are of fantastic excellence. For most people this course of events would seem to be understandable and not in need of any special explanation. The greater the hunger, the better the taste of the food!

The reconciliation fuck, by contrast, defies common sense explanation. It has been known to occur only once, for example, when a couple is breaking up, acrimoniously, after twenty years or more of marriage and a grown family. To divide their belongings, they agree to his returning to their home, now sold, to collect his possessions. Though their sex life has always been source of contention, and puritanically devoid of passion, on this last night, unexpectedly, they fall together onto the bed and cut loose in the most passionately roisterous performance of their lives, ending with sublime orgasms. Sexual passion must always have been there, but in a state of dissociation, unable to get out from under the weight of passionless sex, except for its one-time mutual release.

Even more perplexing and in need of understanding is the repetitive cycle of abuse and reconciliation sex. One partner administers verbal and violent abuse and the other accommodates to it by covertly provoking more of it. The interval before reconciliation sex may be brief or prolonged. The couple may separate and then reunite. It looks as though the overtly victimized partner, male or female, always returns for more abuse; but no one explains or asks about the power of the reconciliation orgasm as the magnet. Abuse itself is a magnet, too, for it is possible to become addicted to abuse and to get high from it (Money et al., 1985). A likely explanation is that abuse releases endorphin, one of the brain's indigenous opiates in response to pain. Endorphin, in turn, induces the high and, indirectly, the return for a repetition of the cycle, regardless of the youth or age of the partners.

Aphrodisiology

SINCE VERY ANCIENT times, aphrodisiacs have been in demand predominantly by men. For older men, an aphrodisiac would be an elixir of youth to rejuvenate the sexual power of adolescence. For lovesick men, it would be a love potion that could be given to activate an indifferent or rejecting partner into a positive responding one. For hypophilic men, an aphrodisiac would be a concoction to sustain erection and increase the duration of sexual performance. Regardless of age, from youth onward, an aphrodisiac would be any substance to hedonically amplify and enhance erotic experience. Rejuvenation, activation, sustentation, and amplification: these are the four different demands made of an aphrodisiac.

Among today's adolescent and young adult males and females, hedonic amplification is the most prevalently required function of an aphrodisiac. This requirement is met as a sporadic side effect of various drugs formerly made popular in the counterculture and listed in what follows (Money et al., 1988).

Alcohol: In low dosage, and in the absence of a progressively increasing tolerance, alcohol may be a disinhibitor, especially for those who are inhibited during the proceptive phase of an erotic encounter, and especially in a social context conducive to a halo effect. Drinking is the standard method of intake, though a few also have alcohol as an enema, with approximately the same effect. There is no special effect of either age or male/female status.

In large dosage, the aphroditic effect of alcohol is lost, and replaced by the sexuoerotic and genital incompetence of gross intoxication. In advanced and chronic alcoholic toxicosis, there may be persistent impairment of sexuoerotic interest and function.

Amphetamine: The aphroditic reputation of amphetamine (speed) and its derivatives may relate at least in part to its effect in prolonging wakefulness, rather than to its other central or peripheral nervous system excitatory effects. However, because they also induce the sympathetic nervous system to release norepinephrine, amphetamines may also stimulate genital function directly, amplifying genital sensation. When injected intravenously, amphetamine produces an additional and temporary generalized rush effect. However, reports of amphetamine's aphroditic effects are inconsistent, both proceptively and acceptively, ranging from negative through neutral to positive on all three of the sexuoerotic criteria, namely, activation, sustentation, and amplification.

The risk of chronic, high-dose usage is an intoxication psychosis similar to schizophrenia and with it the possible release of, inter alia, paraphilic pathology.

There is no consistent evidence of a halo effect, and no evidence of an age effect. In men, the drug's suppressant sexuoerotic potential may be more prevalent than it is in women, notably with respect to inducing impotence at the acceptive phase.

Some compounds sold illicitly on the street are amphetamine derivatives or analogs that have a reputation as aphrodisiacs more potent than ordinary amphetamine. MDA (3,4-methylenedioxyamphetamine) is one of them. So are MDMA (3,4-methylenedioxymetamphetamine), also known as Ecstasy, and DOM (2,5-dimethoxy-4-methylamphetamine), also known as STP (Serenity/Tranquility/Peace). On the street, the availability of these and other illicit drugs depends on their manufacture in underground laboratories, which is not conducive to systematic research on their aphroditic and other mental effects.

Amyl nitrite: This is an inhalant, popularly known as a popper. It causes a generalized dilation of the venules. It is inhaled as an aphrodisiac because of its vasodilative effect on the genitalia. It produces a rush or magnification of genital erotic sensation. Properly timed, this magnification culminates in orgasm. The effect of inhalation is short lived, and is followed by a decrease in blood pressure. In women, this decrease is compatible with resumption of buildup toward another orgasm, whereas in men, if it coincides with or induces detumescence, there is a prolongation of the refractory period.

Provided an optimum amount is inhaled, amyl nitrite's aphroditic effect is not dosage related, nor subject to a tolerance or age effect. An overdose may cause fainting due to reduced cerebral blood flow. There is a halo effect, insofar as it may be inhaled by, for example, nightclub or disco patrons for the heightened bodily sensation, not necessarily aphroditic, which it engenders. As an aphrodisiac it is specific to the acceptive rather than the proceptive phase, and particularly to the orgasmic peak of the acceptive phase.

Cannabis: In both the medicinal and religious practice of India and the Orient, the psychotropic attributes of the flowering tops of the hemp plant (*Cannabis sativa*) have been on record for centuries, and have been known and unrecorded for perhaps millennia. The most important psychoactive principle is delta-9-tetrahydrocannabinol. It is obtained either as resin (hashish) from the flowering tops of the plant, or in dried leaves. The leafy product of the seedhead is known as marijuana (Hispanic), ganja (India), kif (North Africa), and as pot, grass, or weed (U.S. argot). Either form may be smoked, ingested, or made into a drink (bhang in India). The history of the use of cannabis as an aphrodisiac is not known. Its effectiveness as an aphrodisiac is secondary to its effectiveness as a euphoriant and amplifier of subjectively recognized feelings engendered haptically, through the skin and the sense of touch, and perhaps proprioceptively as well. There may be a concomitant prolongation of perception of the passage of time which, therefore, allows the aphroditic effect to be experienced as prolonged.

The haptic aphroditic effect of cannabis appears to be dosage related up to the point of optimum dosage, beyond which it is supplanted by relaxation and sleepiness. There is no evidence of a tolerance effect. The onset of the effect is more rapid when the route of administration is by smoking rather than by ingestion. There is a halo effect, insofar as the amplification of skin feelings favors those who are already in a sexuoerotic situation with an available partner, and those whose sexuoerotic inhibition is not so extreme as to be aversely resistant to disinhibition. There is no phase effect, the proceptive and acceptive phases being equally enhanced. So far as is known, there is no age or male/female effect. Overall, the aphroditic effect of cannabis applies to amplification rather than sustentation or activation.

The aphroditic amplification effect of cannabis is a property shared, inter alia, by the synthetic substance, PCP (phencyclidine or 1,1-phenylcyclohexylpiperidine hydrochloride), known popularly as angel dust. It is cheap and easy to manufacture in the drug underground. It may be sprayed onto a herb, like parsley, and smoked, and so may be used to fortify low-grade marijuana. In high dosage, it is a dissociative anesthetic. With prolonged, high dosage use it may precipitate acute psychosis and, especially if impurely synthesized, may be lethal.

Cocaine: The effect of the active principle in the leaves of the coca plant, from which is extracted a crystalline alkaloid, cocaine, has a history of having been known for its several different properties. The Incas considered it a beneficence of the Sun God. Their Spanish conquerors were so impressed by the stamina of Indians who chewed coca leaves, and their endurance of the hardships and deprivations of forced labor, that they defined coca as nutritious and invigorating. Freud, as an early medical investigator of the effect of the crystalline extract, defined it as exhilarating, euphoric, and as an antidote to fatigue. Shortly thereafter, Koller discovered the drug's local anesthetic effect. The history of the recognition of the drug's euphoriant aphroditic effect is not known. However, this effect was widely appreciated in the drug culture of the 1960s and 1970s, the hippie era.

As an aphrodisiac, cocaine's effect is dosage and tolerance related. It is more effective in low, infrequent dosage. In high and frequent dosage, it may be antiaphroditic. Some users consider it more effective if absorbed through the mucosa of the genitalia than by inhaling, swallowing, or intravenous injection. There is a halo effect insofar as it amplifies or enhances genital/erotic responsiveness already underway rather than activates or initiates it. Amplification may apply during either the proceptive or the acceptive phase. Cocaine may prolong or sustain the proceptive phase, possibly at the expense of suppressing orgasm, less so in women, probably, than in men. There is no known evidence of a specific age effect.

Heroin: Among opiates, heroin has only a tenuous claim to being an aphrodisiac insofar as it produces a euphoric rush effect when injected intravenously which, for some users, surpasses genital orgasm. Infrequent users may claim to amplify genital orgasmic feeling by correctly timing the intake of a low dose of heroin, or heroin mixed with cocaine. However, with frequent, high-dosage usage, opiate tolerance rapidly increases and produces a reaction of erotic apathy and inertia. This antiaphroditic effect is unrelated to method of intake, age, male/female status, or halo effect. Paradoxically, especially among those with a prior history of premature ejaculation, vaginismus, or painful copulation, heroin's antiaphroditic effect may be perceived as a beneficial prolongation of the phases of proception and acception, and postponement of orgasm. The same applies to other opiates, including methadone, an alternative drug that is legally prescribed for heroin addicts.

Psychedelics: Psychedelic is a term of recent vintage formed from the Greek, *psyche* (mind) and *delos* (manifest, visible). The botanical psychedelics are psilocybin from a Mexian mushroom (*Psilocybe mexicana*) and mescaline from the peyote cactus (*Lophophora williamsii* also called *Anhalonium lewinii*) used by Native Americans of the Southwest from pre-Spanish times to the present in religious ceremonies. The modern era of synthetic psychedelic hallucinogens was ushered in by the synthesis and accidental ingestion of LSD (D-lysergic acid diethylamide) by Albert Hoffmann in 1943.

In the drug culture of thc '60s, psychedelics became the fountainhead of cosmic consciousness—the union of the individual with the all of the universe, in an intensification of meaning and expansion of understanding, as a sequel to infinitely prolonged and amplified sensory perception.

The psychedelic expansion of consciousness may or may not include aphroditic consciousness. The determining factor is almost certainly dosage related: the greater the dosage, the greater the amplification of cosmic union effect, and the lesser the amplification of aphroditic union effect. On the lesser dosage, the aphroditic effect is subject to the halo effect of prior sexuoerotic readiness, either alone or with a partner. There is no known tolerance effect, and no known effect related to route of drug intake, age or male/female status. The proceptive phase may be prolonged, or the refractory period may be shortened with multiple repetitions of the acceptive phase and orgasm in both men and women. However, none of these effects can be predicted. They are sporadic and unpredictable not only for different individuals, but also for the same individual on different occasions, even when drug purity and amount are, so far as can be ascertained, held constant.

Methaqualone: Initially marketed officially as a sedative and hypnotic, methaqualone (known on the street as ludes, an abbreviation of its trade name Quaalude) soon became popular in the counterculture of the '60s, where it became valued for, inter alia, its property as an aphrodisiac. There was insufficient time for its aphroditic status to be investigated empirically before it was declared illegal. According to evidence retrievable from those who used it, methaqualone's aphroditic properties simulated those of cannabis, the amplification of cutaneous sensuousness being perhaps more intense.

15

Body Image and Gender

Image, Schema, and Morphology
Morphology: The Turn-on Test
Female/Male: Feminoid/Masculinoid
Gynemimesis/Andromimesis
Ardhanari: Dual Body Image
Cosmetic Intervention

Image, Schema, and Morphology

The body image is a representation simultaneously in the mind and in the brain that depicts one's body and its parts and functions. The body schema, also a representation in the mind and brain, is more or less restricted to those parts and functions of the body which have been located in the brain, either experimentally or in the course of brain surgery. A distinction either made or implied is that the body schema is neurologically represented in the brain, whereas the body image is psychologically represented in the mind. However, in actuality the two coexist in the mindbrain (or the brainmind).

For the great majority of people, the adolescent maturation of the body image and the body schema is concordant with the adolescent maturation of the gender identity and role (G-I/R), and both are concordant with the hormonally regulated sexual changes of the body at puberty, which are themselves concordant with the natal sex announced at birth.

Although a minority, some people are betrayed by the hormonal changes of the body at puberty: these changes are discordant with the body image and with the G-I/R. Females are betrayed when their bodies produce an excess of virilizing hormones so that puberty brings them a deepened voice, an excess of facial and body hair (hirsutism), a masculine body morphology and lack of menstruation. One syndrome in which this dilemma occurs is untreated or improperly treated CAH (congenital adrenal hyperplasia; see chap. 4). There is a late onset version of CAH which may commence in time to prevent the menarche or to suppress menstrual periodicity. The ovaries then become polycystic. Another syndrome of polycystic ovaries and hormonal masculinization is the Stein-Leventhal syndrome (see chap. 13).

Males are betrayed when an oversensitivity to the female hormone normally produced in the male body allows the growth of glandular mammary tissue so that the breasts may enlarge to equal in size those of an adolescent female (gynecomastia).

It is virtually unheard of that pubertal virilization of the female body is accompanied by virilization of the body image and the G-I/R. Correspondingly, the same applies to pubertal feminization of the male. Rather, the pubertal incongruity is experienced as a disfigurement (Money and Ehrhardt, 1994). Like adolescent acne and other cosmetic disfigurements that affect both boys and girls in adolescence, it is alien, and something to be corrected surgically, pharmacologically, or by whatever promising method available, as soon as possible.

Examples of incongruous pubertal hormonalization, as in female virilization and male feminization, regardless of their underlying etiology, demonstrate a major sexological principle, namely that the hormones of puberty do not, in and of themselves alone, dictate the gender of the body image, nor the gender of identity and role (G-I/R).

Another variety of incongruity at puberty is demonstrated when the G-I/R, the body image included, is discordant with both the natal sex as declared at birth and the hormonalization of the body at puberty. This is the dilemma of a child with a history of male natal sex who develops as a juvenile with a feminal G-I/R and body image. Then, with the onset of hormonal puberty, his body masculinizes. Hormonal masculinization does not, however, include masculinization of the feminal G-I/R and body image. Instead the G-I/R continues its feminal development and the boy's sexuoerotic attraction and arousal are, in the majority of instances, directed toward a partner with a male sexual morphology like his own (Money and Russo, 1979, 1981; Green, 1987).

In the female counterpart of this developmental history, the adolescent sexuoerotic attraction and arousal are directed toward a partner with a female sexual body morphology. Female hormones at puberty do not alter the masculinal G-I/R by feminizing it.

At first glance, it may appear fussy and pedantic to specify that sexuoerotic attraction and orientation is toward the partner's sexual body morphology as either male or female. Would it not be more parsimonious to specify simply that the attraction and orientation is toward either a male or a female? Yes it would, and most of the time it would suffice to do so. However, simplicity does not survive the rigor of test cases.

Morphology: The Turn-on Test

ONE TYPE OF test case is that of a person with a diagnostic history of masculinizing female hermaphroditism, of the type, already mentioned, known as congenital virilizing adrenal hyperplasia (CVAH or CAH). Such a person has the 46,XX female chromosomal karyotype and is born with two ovaries and a uterus, and with the external genitalia masculinized (see chap. 4). In this extreme case, the external genitalia are so completely masculinized that they are anatomically a penis and an empty scrotum instead of a clitoris with labia minora and majora. In the absence of clinical intervention to induce hormonal feminization, this person, brought up as a boy with a penis and an empty scrotum undergoes hormonal puberty as an infertile male. His postpubertal body morphology is indistinguishable from that of other well-virilized males, except for lack of testes (figure 9). He has a male body image and is sexuoerotically attracted to females who, reciprocally, find themselves attracted to him and sexuoerotically turned on by him. He has sexual intercourse as a male, and marries as a man. Who then would say that he is a lesbian, or that his wife is a lesbian? The answer is obvious. Neither of them is a lesbian. He is a man with a penis, and she is woman with a vulva and vagina. The complementarity of their body morphology is what we go by.

This same line of reasoning applies to another type of test case which is the counterpart of the CAH syndrome, namely the androgen insensitivity syndrome (AIS) (see chap. 4). AIS is also known as feminizing male hermaphroditism, and formerly as testicular feminizing syndrome. The AIS person has the 46,XY male chromosomal karyotype, and is born with two undescended testes, with malformed internal sexual anatomy including a cordlike structure instead of a uterus. In the complete form of AIS, the baby is sex assigned as female at birth. The external genitalia are so completely feminized that they are indistinguishable from the normal female vulva, except that the vagina lacks depth and ends blindly. Since all cells of the body are androgen resistant, at puberty they respond only to the estrogen that testicles normally secrete. Menstruation and fertility are not possible. Otherwise the postpubertal body morphology is indistinguishable from that of other well-feminized females (figure 10). The AIS girl has a female body image and is sexuoerotically attracted to males who, in return, are attracted to her and turned on sexuoerotically by her. Vaginal depth can be augmented with dilation, or surgery in some instances, if needed to facilitate sexual intercourse. The partner is always a natal male. Hence, once again the conundrum of whether both are gay or straight. The answer once again is based not on the sameness of their chromosomal or gonadal sex, but on the difference of their body morphology. Anything else would be casuistic and absurd. One is female and the other male. Together they are heterosexual.

These two special test cases highlight the principle by which we define homosexual and heterosexual. In everyday life, when we ascribe to people the status of male or female, gay or straight, we do not first order a sex

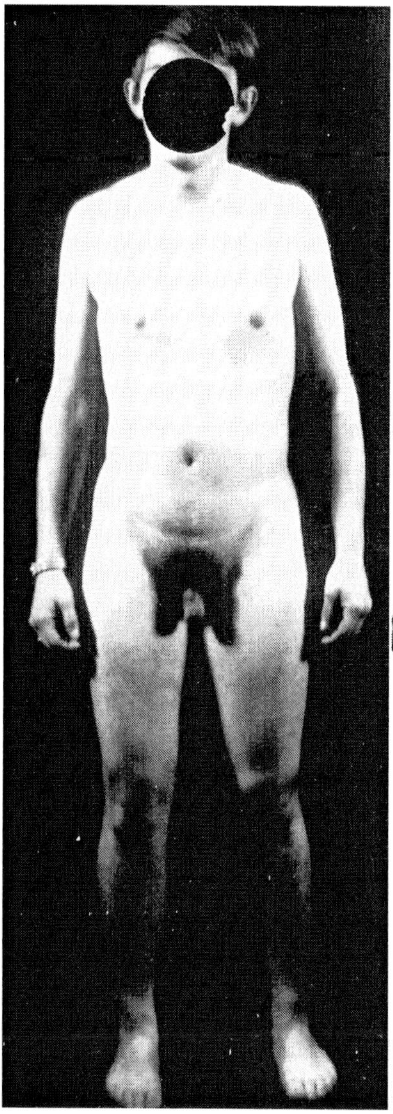

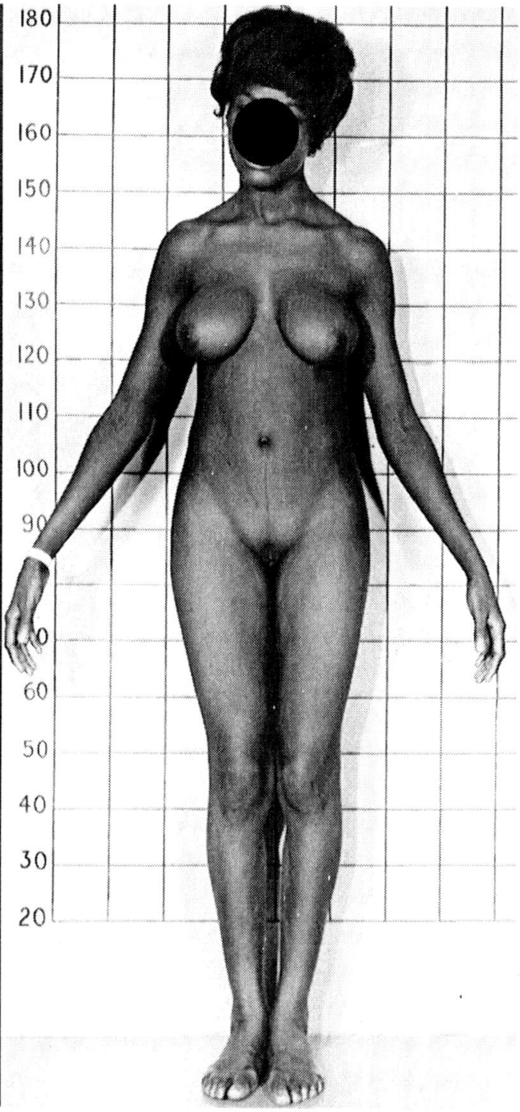

Figure 9 *Chromosomally 46, XX males with the CAH syndrome are erotosexually attractive men.*

Figure 10 *Chromosomally 46, XY females with the androgen insensitivity syndrome (AIS) are erotosexually attractive women.*

chromosome test, or a laparoscopic examination to determine whether their internal sex organs are male or female, or a biopsy to ascertain if the gonads are ovaries or testicles. Instead, we arrive at our conclusion of male or female on the evidence of a man's or, respectively, a woman's body morphology. Then we define as heterosexual the erotic orientation and conjunction of two people if each has a different body morphology and, conversely, as homosexual if each has the same body morphology. Thus the defining criterion of homosexual or heterosexual orientation is the sex of the body morphology of the person to whom one is sexuoerotically attracted and with whom one may fall in love.

Throughout the zoological kingdom of the mammals, the survival of a species from extinction is contingent on a phylism of attraction between male and female that leads to copulatory mating. It has already been said (see chap. 2) that in the human species, the eyes as the organs of sexual attraction have displaced the predominance of the nose. In addition, human females are more dependent than males on cutaneous arousal. In sexological brain research, however, virtually nothing has yet been discovered about how the sight of male or female body morphology stimulates sexuoerotic attraction and arousal in either the heterosexual or the homosexual brain.

The most parsimonious hypothesis is that, in the ultimate analysis, attraction and arousal by either heterosexual or homosexual body morphology are coded within the genome. Locating and sequencing the responsible genes will be a daunting task. Equally daunting will be the neurobiological task of deciphering, step by step, from embryogenesis to adolescence, how a brain gets imprinted with the image of either a male or a female morphology, or both, as an image that will stimulate sexuoerotic attraction and arousal. It will not be sufficient to look for a gene for so amorphous an entity as heterosexuality or homosexuality. It will be necessary to be more specific and to search for a gene that determines whether, in the brain, it will be the visual depiction of a male or a female body configuration that will trigger a response of erotic attraction and arousal. If that search ends in success, the next task will be to explain how some morphological types become more powerful turn-ons than others do, and why human morphology per se fails altogether as a turn-on for some paraphilic individuals.

Female/Male: Feminoid/Masculinoid

The Oxford English Dictionary defines feminoid as "feminine but not female; of female form and appearance," and masculinoid as "masculine but not male; of masculine form and appearance."

In the argot of folk taxonomy, gay males are classified into two categories. For those in one category, some of the terms are sissified, swishy, fruity, bitchy, limp-wristed, drag queen, Miss Thing, poofter, et cetera. For those in the other category, the terms are fewer, and the individuals less easily recognizable. The terms for them comprise faggot and queer (which are terms also used generically to mean gay), hustler, rough trade, butch queen, leather queen, and stud (also used for men who service many women). In formal writing, the two categories are effeminate and noneffeminate, and, though now outdated, passive and active homosexuals (Money, 1991d).

In today's professional terminology, it is a common practice to attribute a homosexual orientation (wrongly equated with preference) and object choice (although a person is not an object), but not a homosexual gender identity to men in the noneffeminate category. Instead, it is said that their gender identity is masculine, which is an oxymoron. Orientation and object choice both should be included as components of everyone's gender identity. It is more precise and accurate to say of homosexual men of this particular type that they are homosexuals who have a masculine body image. By contrast, effeminate homosexual males have a feminoid body image, at least in part, if not entirely.

The homosexual male with a masculine body image may pass as being straight, unless he has "come out" and openly declared himself as gay to family, fellow workers, friends, and acquaintances. Except for what he does sexuoerotically with a partner of his own sex, his gendermap is not transposed. At school, work, or sport, and in social life, comportment, dress, adornment, or body language, his gendermap is not transposed and feminoid. Even while having sex with another man, his role may be insertive only, although not invariably so. He may have a history of engaging in sexual practices only with males, or of being bisexual, or of being gay situationally only, as when living confined in a sex segregated, all male institution. Elsewhere, he would be situationally straight. Thus he would have a bisexual history. Some males are incapable of being situationally bisexual. Their penises will not erect in response to the male sexual body morphology, even after years of being deprived of females.

A macho bisexual male may belong to a cultural community, Hispanic for example, in which the male who takes the feminoid receptive role in oral or anal sex is homosexual, whereas the macho partner is not.

A macho gay male may be a sports hero, a national icon, and the very embodiment of the cultural stereotype of masculinity, except sexuoerotically. He does not have an exaggerated or theatricalized macho body image as some gay males do, namely, those of the jack-booted, chained, and leather-studded, uniformed set. With a male partner in sex, the macho gay male may be dominant (top) or submissive (bottom), or alternating back and forth.

If the terminology of the foregoing is transposed from gay male to lesbian, then its logic is parallel for both. Lesbian political philosophy adds the doctrinal proviso that lesbianism can be taken up by any female as a political statement against male patriarchal domination. This doctrine does not take account of the difference between lesbians who have a masculinoid body image and those who have a feminine one. In the argot of folk terminology, the former are called butches, butch dykes, bull dykes, and diesel dykes; and the latter fems, lezzies, and lipstick lesbians. The list is much briefer than in gay male argot.

In the juvenile years, boys who will grow up to be gay, and girls who will grow up to be lesbian may have a premonition of whether the body morphology that will attract and arouse them sexually and erotically will be, respectively, male or female. For many, however, there will be a delay until puberty before the image of attraction and arousal boldly declares itself in ideation and imagery. In boys, that declaration may occur in the first wet dream. In girls as well as boys it may first happen in waking reveries or masturbation fantasies.

As compared with the image of body morphology that will prove to be sexuoerotically attractive and arousing, the personal body image of the boy or girl who will grow up to be gay or lesbian, respectively, is not elusive, but well delineated as either concordant with the morphology of the natal sex, or in some degree discordant. The greater the discordancy, the more feminoid is the boy's body image, and the more masculinoid the girl's. The terms feminoid and masculinoid signify approximation, not being literally feminine and masculine, respectively. They mean approximating feminine and masculine as closely as possible, without becoming an exact replica. Proprioceptively, it is not possible for the cutaneous and visual body image of a natal female to be totally translocated into that of a natal male, nor vice versa.

There is no equivalent of a video camera by which to record a body image. It must be inferred from vocal and gestural language, and from the products of modeling and drawing. Some boys who grew up to become gay men (Money and Russo, 1979; Green, 1987) may show signs from as young as three or four onward of a feminoid body image which becomes progressively more fixated (Green and Money, 1960). They dress up at every opportunity in borrowed or improvised feminine attire, and like to wear jewelry and cosmetics. They become adept at assimilating and using stereotypic female mannerisms, vocalisms, and body language, which eventually they cannot shed. Until then, they are able to switch from masculine to feminine body language, walking across the room like a girl, and walking back like a boy, for example. They like doing indoor domestic chores. They play with girls and avoid male play. Boys reject them as being too sissy. They are sure that they will be able to be changed into a girl, possibly by having the penis drop off, or by other supernatural intervention. They do not get involved in juvenile sexual rehearsal play with either boys or girls. They do not have a recorded history of sexual molestation. Some are gifted at taking on the role not only of female, but of theatrical characters, too; and some become professional actors (Green and Money, 1966). Sexuoerotically, the majority have, in adulthood, a homosexual gendermap of the feminoid variety. If they cross dress, it is for specific occasions, not routinely; and they do not seek transexual reassignment surgery.

Gay men with a developmental history of the feminoid type constitute a minority of the gay male population as a whole. At the other extreme, one finds gay men with a developmental history that appears not to have differed from that of boys in general, except maybe for a disinclination to fight for position in the power hierarchy of boyhood. They may have had an awareness of being vaguely different as a juvenile, and even moreso when, early in adolescence, sexuoerotic attraction toward female morphology failed to emerge.

Their explicit recognition of sexuoerotic attraction toward, and arousal by the morphology of the male dawns later. They are more likely than nonfeminoid gay males to engage in anal-receptive sex, and thus to be a greater risk for HIV/AIDS (Weinrich et al., 1992).

There are girls who have a strongly masculinoid body image, but they are not brought to professional attention with the same frequency as are boys with a feminoid body image. Through lack of followup studies, less is known about the long term outcome. Their insistence on turning into a boy begins early in childhood and may be accompanied by domineering belligerence. They adamantly refuse to engage in stereotypically female play and academic activities, and to wear anything but boys' attire, with a male haircut. They exaggerate uncouth masculine mannerisms and behavior, and use foul language loudly in public. There is an absence of information about their history of juvenile sexual rehearsal play, and of having molested other children, or not. They are appeased only by being accorded acceptance as a boy.

These are the extreme cases of gender transposition in girls. Others are more moderate. Still others qualify only as tomboys, and tomboyism is an acceptable form of femininity in contemporary society. Tomboyism does not necessarily correlate with being sexuoerotically attracted to the female body morphology in adolescence and adulthood. Also, girl-to-girl sexuoerotic play, if it has existed between juveniles, may be a prelude not to lesbian but boy-girl attraction later. Female as compared with male sexuoerotic attraction and arousal are dependent on cutaneous in addition to visual sensation and imagery. Thus the sexual morphology of the partner's body may exercise less power visually over the female than the male. The female, lesbian or not, responds to touch, independently perhaps of the sex of the one doing the touching. Certainly a nursing mother responds to the touching and suckling of her infant, regardless of its sex. It is quite possible that the female's body image incorporates a greater cutaneous component than does that of the male.

Gynemimesis/Andromimesis

GYNEMIMESIS (FROM Greek, *gyne*, woman + *mimesis*, imitation) signifies a more complete degree of transposition of the body image and the G-I/R toward the feminine than feminoid does (Money and Lamacz, 1984). Correspondingly, andromimesis (from Greek, *andros*, man + *mimesis*) signifies a more complete degree of transposition toward the masculine.

The body image of the complete gynemimetic is that of a lady with a penis or, in the words of one such person, "a girl with a dick, or a boy with titties." The complete gynemimetic lives full time as a woman. She obtains breast enlargement by taking estrogen, with the possible addition of plastic surgery to increase the breast size by augmentation mammoplasty. Cosmetic facial plastic surgery may also be resorted to so that the appearance of the body more closely matches the ideal of the body image. Electrolysis is necessary for the removal of facial or body hair, which is a major hurdle for those who are hirsute. Cosmetics and fashion style are assiduouly attended to.

The gynemimetic's body image is confirmed if she passes in society, especially the society of men, as a woman. Thus gynemimetics gravitate toward show business and the histrionics of theatrical display. The zenith of gynemimesis is to attract and entertain a man sexually, giving him an orgasm included, using various subterfuges to conceal the gynemimetic's natal sex. In the major cities, however, there are girlie bars that cater to patrons who are gynemimetophiles, that is men who are attracted to "she males," as ladies with a penis are known in the sex entertainment industry. A gynemimetic who makes her living as a sex worker, as some do, may also have a long-term, live-in male partner.

Gynemimesis is a transcultural, not a culture bound phenomenon, and is widely distributed around the world. In the New World, gynemimetic males are known as berdache (from Persian, *bardaj*, by way of Arabic, French, and Spanish; Williams, 1986). In their own tribes, berdache functioned as shamans and healers. Some have lived as if a wife of another man. In Polynesia, gynemimetic males are named mahu (Hawaii), fakaleiti (Tonga), and faa fa'fini (Samoa), are socially recognized, not ostracized, and are integrated into the family and community.

A communal organization, part caste and part religious cult, for gynemimetic men, the hijras, is unique to Indian culture (Nanda, 1990). The hijra goddess is Bahuchara Mata. Her worship brings together Hindus, Muslims, Christians, or members of any other religion. Hijras live together in small and self-sustaining communal households under the direction of a guru. Senior gurus train their successors in the ancient technique of castration and penile amputation. Surgically they lack the technology for vaginoplasty and, until very recently, have not had access to female hormones for the induction of breast growth. Thus the transformation of the body morphology from male to female so as to be concordant with the body image has been limited to becoming a eunuch. Hijras provide sexual services, if at all, for males only, orally, anally, or digitally. They may have a regular patron, a married man, who provides a regular source of income. In Burmese culture , the equivalent of a hijra is an acault (Coleman et al., 1992), though castration is not performed.

The hijras of India and the transexuals (or transsexuals) of contemporary Western culture are the only two cultural groups of gynemimetics with a tradition of resorting to surgery to align the sex of the body morphology with the sex of the body image and with the G-I/R.

The hormonal and surgical sex reassignment of transexualism represents the apex of gynemimetic alteration of the sexual morphology of the body to be concordant with the transposed body image and G-I/R. Exact clinical descriptions of people who would today be called transexuals were given by Magnus Hirschfeld (1910/1991) under the rubric of transvestism, a term that Hirschfeld himself coined. The term transexual, was introduced by D.O. Cauldwell (1949). Spelled with a double s, it became established medically in two books, *The Transsexual Phenomenon* (Benjamin, 1966) and *Transsexualism and Sex Reassignment* (Green and Money, 1969). Although used as a diagnostic term, transexualism is more accurately used as the name for a method of rehabilitation for a psychiatric condition of gender dysphoria. Rejecting the nosological stigma of a psychiatric diagnosis, sex reassigned people themselves, in their own meetings and publications began, early in the 1990s, being self-identified as members of the transgender community. This community is comprised of pre- and postoperative transexuals, and others such as those who, in the foregoing, are categorized as gynemimetics or andromimetics. Cross dressing is what all transgenderists share in common, except for the inclusion of non-crossdressing bisexuals.

In body image syndromes requiring surgery, there are three principles of body alteration. All three are represented in sex reassignment: realignment and enhancement; obliteration and relinquishment; and augmentation and amplification.

In the case of the male-to-female transexual, the body image of the face is feminine and is discordant with that of the actual physiognomy, which in the majority of cases is bearded and has masculine features. The principle of alteration according to which congruence between the femininity of the facial body-image and the actual physiognomy is effected is realignment and enhancement. The method is electrolysis for facial hair removal, administration of female hormones for feminized skin texture, and plastic surgery for changes of the bone structure and soft tissue. Facial surgery is not invariably necessary, and in some cases there is only sparse facial hair.

The corresponding alterations for the female-to-male transexual are also of the realignment and enhancement type. In those cases with a second diagnosis of Stein-Leventhal polycystic ovary syndrome (Bosinski et al., 1997), early androgenic signs may already be in evidence. The full female-to-male transition, however, always requires treatment with a male sex hormone, testosterone enanthate by monthly injection, for example. Treatment with male sex hormone suffices to produce facial hair, body hair, masculine skin texture and, ultimately, thinning or balding head hair. By enlarging the larynx, it also realigns the voice to conform to the body image. The effortless process of vocal masculinization is unmatched in male-to-female reassignment which requires vocal retraining.

The principle of obliteration and relinquishment is of paramount importance to the male-to-female transexual with respect to the external genitals which are a reproach and an offense to the feminine body image. In a majority of cases, being rid of the offensive male genitals takes precedence over the augmenting and amplifying procedure of vaginoplasty.

In the female-to-male transexual, the offensive organs are those responsible for menstruation. Their extirpation takes precedence over the augmenting and amplifying procedure of phalloplasty (skin-grafted plastic surgical construction of a penis) or metoidioplasty (conversion of the clitoris into a micropenis) (Laub et al., 1989). For both procedures, surgical technology does not satisfy the ideal stipulations of a male body image.

In female-to-male transexuals, the obliteration and relinquishment principle applies also to surgical extirpation of the breasts. By contrast in male-to-female transexuals, it is the principle of augmentation and amplification that applies to the breasts. Hormonally induced breast enlargement (gynecomastia) may fail to match the body image of mammary hyperplasia in some patients, who may then resort to augmentation mammoplasty either by surgery, or by the very dangerous procedure of silicone injections. The latter may also be resorted to for hip enlargement.

The transexual body image is individually variable with respect to the hierarchical position of the three principles of body alteration on the agenda of sex reassignment. Thus, in a case of male-to-female transexualism in which the principle of realignment and enhancement is hierarchically above relinquishment and obliteration, even an appointment with the hairdresser may take precedence over an admissions appointment for genital reassignment surgery.

In another case, by contrast, in which the obliteration and relinquishment principle is uppermost, the patient may embark on a frantic round of clinic shopping for a surgeon who will extirpate the offending external genital organs on the basis of personal request alone, with no waiting period, and without the delay of a psychologic, psychiatric, or sexologic consultation.

In yet another case, in which the augmentation and amplification principle is uppermost, large breasts may be so high on the agenda that a patient will find a way of meeting the cost of obtaining them, despite failing to meet other medical expenses.

After male-to-female surgery, the new body morphology may be consistent with a sex life that is abstinent or, more likely, heterosexual as a female or, not too often, with being a lesbian. After female-to-male surgery, the new body morphology is seldom, if ever, consistent with abstinence and is usually heterosexual as a male, although rather rarely is homosexually gay with a natal male. Some instances are known of a postoperative male-to-female and postoperative female-to-male couple becoming married to one another, or living together, unmarried.

Ardhanari: Dual Body Image

IN HINDU MYTHOLOGY Ardhanarisvara (Basham, 1954, p. 312), one of the incarnations of Lord Shiva, is represented with his wife, Parvati, in painting and sculpture as having a right sided male body and clothing and a left sided female body and clothing (figure 11). As either he or she, Ardhanari is a symbolic representation of two body morphologies and two body images. As represented, Ardhanari's he and she are coexistent, not successive or alternating as are the he and she of people who episodically cross dress from he to she, or she to he.

Cross dressing is not possible at a nudist colony. There, the body has to declare its sex for itself, unwrapped. Cross dressing allows a person's social presentation to be concordant with the cross sexed demands of the body image. In addition, cross dressing does not require irreversible changes to the body morphology. So it may be done episodically.

Anyone can cross dress: to escape being tortured; for disguise as a spy; to play a role in a play or movie; for a masquerade party; or to play a charade. The greater the extent to which the performer's body image is feminoid (or vice versa masculinoid), the more convincing will be the impersonation. Otherwise the performance will be an awkward burlesque, belied by the body language and voice. The actor who is a drag queen, a gynemimetic, or a male-to-female transexual will turn in a more convincing performance. The same applies to female-to-male performances, except that there is no exact female equivalent of the drag queen, the new term, drag king notwithstanding. Also, andromimesis and female-to-male transexualism, although both exist, are not exact parallels of their male counterparts.

A convincing impersonation might also be expected of episodic cross dressers of the type named and classified by Magnus Hirschfeld as transvestites. Translated

Figure 11. *Ardhanarisvara. A representation in bronze of the god Shiva in union with his wife, Parvati, worshiped as respectively, the phallic and female emblems, the lingam and the yoni.*

from Latin into English, transvestite means cross dresser. The word has two meanings. Generally, it signifies anyone who cross dresses, sporadically or consistently. Specifically, it signifies an episodic cross dresser with a formal diagnosis of transvestism or, more precisely, of fetishistic transvestism.

Fetishistic transvestism, so far as is known, has been recorded only in men, not women. The fetish is women's apparel. A fetish is an object or substance prerequisite to a male's sexuoerotic arousal and attainment of orgasm. The ideal of the fetishistic transvestite male is to have sexual intercourse while wearing women's lingerie. The next best is to play a mental tape of himself engaged sexuoerotically while wearing women's apparel. If his partner is a girlfriend or wife, it is likely that, while copulating, her body will be transposed in his mental imagery into that of a male, and his own body image will be of a female. With a male partner, the fetishistic transvestite will be dressed in female attire, and will take a feminoid role.

The majority of cross dressers affiliated with the transgenderist movement have a wife or girlfriend, and not a male as an accompanying partner. The extent of sporadic bisexualism among them is not known, nor the extent of partnering only with a male.

Fetishistic transvestites have two wardrobes. Dependent on life circumstances, the woman's wardrobe may have to be kept hidden at home and worn in secret when alone, possibly with accompanying sexual arousal and masturbatory orgasm. The two wardrobes are matched by two names and two personalities (Money, 1974). The transformation from a male on one occasion to a female on another occasion can be so complete that the one obliterates an observer's recognition of the other.

The two names, two wardrobes, and two personalities phenomenon in some instances maintains itself, episodically, for years. In other instances, the episodes of being male shorten, until eventually the man lives, maybe devoid of sexual interest, full time and cross dressed as a female. In some such cases, the female personality becomes fixated on complete body transformation to agree with the feminoid body image. Especially in response to traumatic stress, this fixation may occur in mid life or later, whereas usually it occurs at a younger age, as young as during adolescence or earlier. To ensure that the body image pendulum will stay at the female position, hormonal and social reassignment come first, and then surgical sex reassignment, which is irreversible, at the end of a two-year, real-life test of rehabilitation as a female.

Ardhanari's symbolism transcends the duality of two names, two wardrobes, and two personalities. It has profound significance for the theory of body imagery, namely, that there is a duality of body image as part of the duality of G-I/R, in all of us. On one side of the duality is the body image that is mine, and the other, the body image that is thine (see chap. 6). Sex is not an undifferentiated, personalized unity. It is differentiated as male and female. In your mindbrain and mine, each must be represented, for it is by knowing what one is not that one knows what one is. The mindbrain functions in polarities.

In the male, the masculine body image is represented in the mindbrain as what mine is, and the female body image as what mine is not, which is why it is called feminoid and not feminine. Conversely, in the female, the feminine body image is represented as what mine is, and the male body image as what mine is not, which is why it is called masculinoid, and not masculine.

The variable degree to which the two body images become transposed, and change their position of priority, either episodically or for the long term, is mirrored in the variable degree of cross dressing, which itself is an observable indicator of G-I/R and its transpositions. The determinants of transposition encompass the determinants of whether sexual attraction and arousal will be triggered in response to the male or the female body morphology.

The locus in the mindbrain of the determinants of body image has not yet been seriously searched for. Research has been directed instead to the determinants of homosexuality and transexualism. Neither have yielded to more than half a century of research on hormonal determinants prenatally or pubertally (Money, 1988a; 1993a; Gooren, 1995). As entities for research, homosexuality and transexuality are too global. They comprise populations that differ individually to a high degree. They need to be subdivided into smaller, more homogenous subpopulations.

Brain research in the last quarter of the twentieth century has begun to open the door onto male/female brain dimorphisms in selected brain regions, some of them governed by hormonal differences in embryonic and early postnatal life. Within as recently as the decade of the nineties, neuroanatomical differences between human homosexual and heterosexual brains at autopsy have been found in small nuclei in the region of the hypothalamus, but the studies still await confirmation. The newest data pertain to the size of the bed nucleus of the stria terminalis (BSTc) in male-to-female transexuals as compared with control males and females. A female sized BSTc was found in male-to-female transexuals (Zhou et al., 1995). As in the case of the homosexual data (Allen and Gorski, 1992; LeVay, 1991; Swaab and Hofman, 1990; Swaab et al., 1992) the sample is small, and homogeneity of the behavioral phenomena cannot be guaranteed without additional confirmation.

In the present era of sequencing the human genome, the search has begun for what the media have dubbed the "gay gene," with preliminary evidence that there may be one, and if so that it may be on the single X chromosome of the male (Hamer et al., 1993; Hu et al., 1995). However, the first results failed subsequently to be confirmed (Rice et al., 1995).

Hypothetically, it is wise to assume that the body image is multivariately determined. There probably is a fundamental male/female pattern that is laid down in the genome, but subject to much subsequent plasticity. In prenatal life it may be under hormonal and other neurochemical control. In postnatal life the neurochemistries change to include those of social assimilation, imprinting, learning, and remembering that have a prominent influence. Also, traumatically disruptive life events within the family and community will adversely affect the plasticity of the developing body image, and with it the developing G-I/R.

Cosmetic Intervention

ALTERATION OF THE sex of the body morphology to conform to the body image is a defining characteristic of transexualism and, to a lesser extent, of gynemimesis and andromimesis. Alterations of the body not to change but to enhance the natal sex of the body are self-recognized as cosmetically necessary to align the body morphology with the body image. The predominant cosmetic criteria are youth and sexual attractiveness. The criterion standards may be set by fashion, or they may be eccentric and even bizarre.

Cosmetic plastic surgery to enhance sexual attractiveness is performed on the face, the breasts, or the genitals. More women than men get a facelift, or a resculpting of the nose, lips, and eyebrows, or the set of the ears. When the baldness pattern permits, men get realignment of scalp hair across the forehead.

On the chest, cosmetic plastic surgery is mostly for enlargement (augmentation mammoplasty) of the breasts in women to replace tissue lost in breast removal (mastectomy) in the treatment of breast cancer; and for uplifting sagging breasts. Boys with adolescent breast enlargement (gynecomastia) get breast tissue removed (reduction mammoplasty). Excess fat padding under the nipples in men may also be removed.

Males more than females undergo genital cosmetic surgery. In the early 1990s surgical lengthening of the penis by partially releasing it from its anchorage on the bone of the pubic symphysis became popularized. So also did thickening of the penis by injecting it with fat cells taken from the man's own body. Both procedures are highly dubious and may produce irreversible damage to the penis (Morain, 1994; Leithauser et al., 1995).

For those males who lose or never had two descended testes, it is possible, for cosmetic effect, to implant soft prosthetic replacements in the empty scrotum. Although an undescended testis gets too warm for sperms to be viable, surgery to bring it down is not always successful.

Foreskin restoration takes on great importance in the lives of some of the millions of American men who were circumcised in infancy. Some have undergone plastic surgery in the attempt to regain a foreskin, with dubious success or outright failure. Others have persisted for two years or longer with a difficult, daily stretching procedure and have achieved success (Money, 1991b).

The most ancient and most transculturally widespread form of cosmetic intervention that is in harmony with the sexual morphology of the body and is designed to enhance its sexual attractiveness is scarification, tattoo, and piercing. The Ice Man, frozen in the Swiss/Austrian alps for 5000 years, had tattoos on his legs and back. Beginning in the 1970s, tattooing and piercing underwent a renaissance in Western culture. Men as well as women get tattoos on covered as well as uncovered parts of their bodies, including the genitals. A few have eyebrows, cheeks, lips, or tongue that are pierced, and many more the ears or nose, for wearing jewelry in the form of gold bars, studs, chains, or rings. Nipples and navel are also pierced for jewelry, and so are the genitals—the clitoris, the labia minora, the perineum in females; and the foreskin, glans penis, shaft of the penis, the scrotum, and the perineum in males.

Some forms of intervention and alteration of the morphology of the body on behalf of the body image cross the boundary from cosmetic to self-mutilatory. The Skoptic syndrome (see chap. 14 and Appendix One) is such an example. So also is apotemnophilia, the paraphilia (see chaps. 9,16) in which there is an irrefutable, sexuoerotic fixation on becoming an amputee.

Body image cosmetic and mutilation syndromes may, to the ordinary citizen, seem crazy or bizarre, but they are not psychoses. They are more accurately classified as monomanias—intense and unyielding fixations, with resemblances to obsessions and addictions. In a few individual cases, however, the fixation is imbedded in a genuinely paranoidal, delusional system.

Fixated pathology of the sexual body image may be neither cosmetic nor mutilatory, but dysgnosic (from Greek, *dys-*, disordered + *gnosis*, knowing or recognizing). Dysgnosia means not able to recognize the evidence and know what is happening. For example, anorexia nervosa is a syndrome in which there is a body image disorder. While fasting to grow pure, even unto death, if the patient looks into a mirror, he or she does not know or recognize the figure in the mirror as one of deathly emaciation, but as one that does not yet have the ideal figure of his/her slim body image. The fasting continues, for no amount of foodless penance suffices to absolve the anorexic from impure thoughts. In the young female anorexic, the thoughts are often about impure ways of losing virginity, and in the young male about his idea of the impurity of being homosexual.

The koro or shrinking penis syndrome is another example of dysgnosic pathology of the body image (Edwards, 1984; Money and Annecillo, 1987; Ng, 1995). When the koro patient looks at his genitalia in a mirror, or in a medical photograph, he does not recognize the image of his penis there as other people do. Instead he knows that his penis is shrinking up and disappearing inside himself, where it will eventually bring about his death. Someone must assist him to pull it out and not let it go. Usually the syndrome is ultimately self-remitting. It may be transmitted by social contagion, in an epidemic spread by cognition and suggestion.

Other instances of dysgnosic pathology of the body image probably are not recognized as such. Some of them are camouflaged by a presenting symptom like impotence. For example, although the dimensions of an ostensibly impotent penis are normal, a patient may be convinced that his erect penis is too big, or too bent to be safe for sexual intercourse, without injuring a partner's vagina. Therefore, he dare not attempt to have intercourse to test whether he is actually impotent. Nonetheless he is convinced that he is impotent, and cannot be dissuaded.

16

Paraphilic Lovemaps

Love and Lust

The extent to which the adult generation censors the transmission of information on love and lust to the pubertal and adolescent generation correlates with the extent to which it would be self-incriminating for them to answer all of the younger people's questions about their elders' own sexual histories and practices.

Complete freedom of speech for members of both generations would mean no censorship of either questions or answers about personal sexual intimacies, with no holds barred. Nowadays the age taboo has been lifted for questions and answers about reproductive biology, but not about love and lust. The age taboo protects both generations from exposing personal information about love and lust in their lovemaps (see chap. 7). Exchange of sexuoerotically intimate information may be legally dangerous. It may lead to cross generational bodily intimacy.

Children assimilate when very young the virtue of evasiveness as practiced by their elders. That leaves them, as adolescents to fend for themselves unaided, except for whatever information their age mates and libraries can supply, in managing the intimacies and complexities of love and lust in their lovemaps. Their success in adolescence is contingent to a considerable degree on the extent to which their juvenile lovemap history has allowed love and lust to be reciprocally merged in the adolescent lovemap instead of dissociatively separated or vandalized (Money and Lamacz, 1989).

In the culture of Christendom, lust is a vice, satanic, and morally bad; love is a virtue, godly, and morally good. Lust is below the waist, carnal, sportive, degrading, and defiling. Love is above the waist, spiritual, limerent, uplifting, and purifying. Vandalization of the juvenile lovemap leaves love and lust divided or dissociated, instead of being unified.

Dissociation of love and lust in the lovemap is epitomized in the dichotomy of the madonna and the whore, and the provider and the playboy. The madonna is adored, and the provider respected. Both are the recipients of loving affection, but neither is defiled by carnal lust. By contrast, the whore and the playboy are providers of sportive, lustful sex—here today and gone tomorrow. However, the whore may be a kept mistress, and the playboy a kept gigolo. At its most extreme, the dissociative separation of love and lust is expressed in the paradoxical aphorism: "Never fuck the one you love." This formula frequently lurks in the background of both hypophilic and hyperphilic sexual disorders. In various permutations, its converse: "Never love the one you fuck," comes close to being a defining characteristic of paraphilic disorders. The formal definition of paraphilia is as follows.

> **paraphilia**: a condition occurring in men and women of being compulsively responsive to and obligatively and fixatedly dependent on an unusual and personally or socially unacceptable stimulus, perceived or in the ideation and imagery of fantasy, for optimal initiation and maintenance of erotosexual arousal and the facilitation or attainment of orgasm (from Greek, *para-*, altered + -philia). Paraphilic imagery may be replayed in fantasy during solo masturbation or during intercourse with a partner. In legal terminology, a paraphilia is a perversion or deviancy; and in the vernacular it is kinky or bizarre sex (Money, 1995a).

The term paraphilia was introduced into the biomedical vocabulary early in the twentieth century by Wilhelm Stekel, who broke away from Freud. He wrote in his autobiography that he had "changed perversion to paraphilia following a suggestion by I.F. Krauss." In 1980, paraphilia officially replaced perversion in American psychiatric nomenclature, but psychoanalysis and the law still use perversion (Money and Lamacz, 1989).

In dictionaries there is no entry for paralagnia (from Greek, *lagnos*, salacious or lustful) as a synonym for paraphilia. Particular paraphilias, however, like urophilia and urolagnia, or coprophilia and coprolagnia, are synonymously named. In view of the paraphilic dissociation between love and lust, lagnia has some merit. However, in usage, -philia is the winner.

There is no terminology that separates minor from major paraphilias, nor playful from pathological ones. Where the dividing line should be is arguable. There are no absolute criteria. Thus the excitement of being blindfolded, spread-eagled, and tethered to the bedposts, unable to predict what erotic stimulus your partner will apply next to increase your excitement, although technically paraphilic bondage, is playful and not pathological. If however you are tethered, masked, and gagged so that you cannot make a sound to arouse your partner from a drunken torpor, then you may suffocate and die. That also is paraphilic bondage, but decidedly across the line into being pathological. Moreover, even if you have played the bondage game many times before as a fully consenting adult, it is still pathological.

Consensual sexual games are not necessarily safe, even though "mutually consenting adults" is the platitude often used as a justification. There is a logical problem with mutual consent, namely that you can't give consent if you can't predict, at the outset, the outcome of what you are consenting to—or at least, as a gambler, what your risk is.

Unconsenting, enforced sexual bondage, or any other enforced paraphilic sexual ritual, is pathological insofar as enforcement signifies lack of situational adaptability on the part of the paraphilic person. The most extremely pathological examples of paraphilic immutability and monomaniac fixation are the paraphilia of serial violent rape (raptophilia) and of serial lust murder (erotophonophilia).

What makes a paraphilia pathological and major, instead of playful and minor, is its fixatedness. It resists vows and resolutions to be eradicated. It has its own imperative power. Its ideation and imagery exercise control over sexuoerotic arousal and orgasm, even when it is not being actually carried out in practice. It has the power, as a vivid paraphilic dream, to awaken the sleeper, and to instigate masturbation fantasies.

Paraphilia that is not obsessionally fixated and reiterative, but has the property of take it or leave it, and of being optional, is rated as minor in degree and not pathological. Even so, it may be a nuisance. To qualify as not being a nuisance, a paraphilic lovemap in one partner must have a reciprocating lovemap in the other. Thus, a partner whose own lovemap does not reciprocally match the bondage and discipline in the lovemap of his/her lover or spouse, is not sexuoerotically aroused by engaging in sexual intercourse while being tethered and blindfolded. If not aversively aroused and repelled by bondage, a partner may simulate being positively aroused. Simulated arousal is not difficult to detect, however. Coitus becomes sexuoerotically dull and disappointing to both partners. That soon leads to apathy and inertia. Sexual intercourse becomes not worth bothering about. Reciprocal matches for any particular paraphilic lovemap are not plentiful. Moreover, there is a disparity in the typology and frequency of paraphilia in males and females.

Male/Female Compared

WHEN A BOY or girl, upon reaching puberty, has a lovemap in which love and lust do not mesh, lust is more likely to have gone into hibernation, so to speak, in the girl's lovemap, and to have migrated to a place of survival in the boy's lovemap. The difference, in other words, is between hypophilia and paraphilia.

Although there is little doubt that this male/female difference exists, there is, today, voluminous argument as to whether it is a cultural and historical artifact, exclusively, or whether it is culturally and historically constructed on phyletically designed foundations.

Male/female differences exist in all three phases of human lovemap functioning: proceptive, acceptive, and conceptive (see chap. 13). There is no inconsistency, therefore, in attributing a male/female difference in the dissociation of love and lust to a phyletic origin, namely more hypophilia in females than males, and more paraphilia in males than females. There is a procreative logic behind this difference, namely that the hypophilic woman, even though unable to get sexuoerotically aroused, is not deprived of pregnancy provided that she can receive sperms, even if they are delivered perhaps through a syringe. The hypophilic male, by contrast, without an erection can deliver sperms only with the help of vibratory electrostimulation of the prostate gland. Unlike hypophilia, paraphilia preserves the capacity for sexuoerotic arousal and performance, but it does so deviously, by changing the ideation, imagery, and practices of the proceptive phase that are prerequisite to the initiation of sexuoerotic arousal and performance.

A paraphilia salvages lust from the wreckage of a derailed lovemap, but at the cost of separating it from love. Hence the aphorism that paraphilia represents the transformation of tragedy into triumph—the triumph of saving lust from extinction. The paraphilic salvage may be so triumphant that it displaces the tragedy entirely. In that case, the paraphile loses recognition of the origins of his/her paraphilia. If recognition of the tragedy is only partly displaced, or if confirmatory evidence of its history is available, then it is the logical connection between the tragedy and its paraphilic outcome that escapes recognition. When the history of a paraphilia can be traced either retrospectively or, very rarely, prospectively (Money and Lamacz, 1989), it is not uncommon to find that the tragedy over which the paraphilia triumphed traces back to the years of childhood, especially around the age of eight.

Juveniles repeatedly exposed to the tragedies and triumphs of sex, as many children are (see appendix 2), are likely to enter puberty with some sophistication concerning the paraphilic sexuoerotic imagery, ideation, and practices of their own lovemaps. Others are more naive. After they enter puberty, it may take time for the contents of their paraphilic lovemaps to unfurl, like a drama in acts and scenes written on a parchment scroll, the final scene perhaps years ahead. By contrast, others may have their paraphilic lovemap confront them fully formed, like Athena emerging from the head of Zeus, perhaps in a boy's first wet dream, or masturbation fantasy.

Paraphilia is not exclusive to males, nor hypophilia to females. However, the actual prevalence of paraphilia in females and hypophilia in males has not yet been ascertained and may not ever be, since self-disclosure of illicit paraphilias is self-incriminating. Thus a survey based on random probability sampling is always subject to a refusal rate that distorts the findings to an unspecified degree.

An epidemiological survey of the prevalence of paraphilia in males and females would include ascertainment of the types of paraphilia prevalent in females as compared with males. Contemporary statistics are biased by court and clinic cases among which males predominate. It could be that women's paraphilias are not taken so seriously as men's, or, more likely, that they are less diversified in type. Also a female's paraphilia could lurk behind a pregnancy which temporarily disguises it.

If women's paraphilias differ from men's in type, then they should parallel the male/female differences in the proceptive phase of sexuoerotic attraction and arousal, which is indeed what they do (see chap. 13). Men's paraphilic imagery and ideation are predominantly pictorial, even when narrated, whereas women's are more haptic or "touchy feely," as in being wanted, taken, swept away, or abducted into the virile arms of a warrior of sex.

Women's paraphilias also include masochism and the transformation of constraint and pain into erotic bliss. It is not difficult for a female masochist to contact a male sadist, whereas it is difficult for a paraphilic male masochist to find an authentic female sadist or dominatrix, the latter being in short supply. The void is filled by women in the role of a trained and paid counterfeit dominatrix. Noncommercial contact is more readily established between gay male than lesbian sadomasochists. They meet in clubs, bars, and by answering "personals" in periodicals and on the Internet.

Whether for noncommercial or commercial sex, straight women readily establish sexual contact with straight men. When money is involved it might possibly signify a paraphilia in either the man or the woman, namely chrematistophilia, in which maximum sexual arousal is contingent on paying or being paid, robbing or being robbed, for lust without love.

Catch-22 Dilemmas

SOME PARAPHILIAS illustrate the principal of historical and cultural constraints. For example, it was not possible to have a fixation on nylon stockings before nylon was invented. Before that, the fixation could be on silk stockings, but only after silk had been imported to the West from China and knitware manufacture had been invented.

Similarly, it was not possible to have a fetish for rubber before vulcanization of the sap of the rubber tree was patented (in the U.S. in 1844), and subsequently manufactured as waterproof sheets, coats, boots, and training pants for infants. What rubber clothing and nylon or silk stockings all share in common as paraphilic fetishes is their use to cover the human skin. As fetishes, they displace or substitute for the skin, as furry fetishes do also for human hair. They belong to the hyphephilic or touchy-feely category of the fetishes, namely, those that are derived from bodily textures. The other category is the olfactophilic or smelly-tasty one, in which fetishes are derived from bodily smells, odors, and tastes.

These two categories, the tactual and the smelly, respectively, support the proposition that fetish objects and substances are not a random or arbitrary assortment, but an assortment in which all of the items bear the phyletic imprimatur of being substitutes for bodily textures and odors. In the lovemap, they take the place that human textures and odors would otherwise have in promoting sexuoerotic arousal. By dispensing with a live partner altogether and expending the carnality of lust on the fetish instead, paraphilic fetishism allows the partner to escape the defilement of lust.

It would not be feasible to postulate a genomic locus for the smell of rubber, or the texture of a teddy bear, as a source of sexuoerotic arousal. By contrast, it would be quite feasible to postulate a genomic locus for bodily odors or textures, or both, that are associated with sexual arousal in the normophilic lovemap. It is also feasible to suspect that some individuals have a genetically programmed susceptibility to deconnect odors and textures from the body, and reconnect them with a fetish. This is an example of the paraphilic principle of dissociation.

Dissociation is the principle that enables a lovemap to be paraphilically altered so as to become, for example, a fetishistic lovemap. One may be susceptible to dissociation, however, without ever having it actually happen to onself. Susceptibility must converge with a precipitating circumstance before it materializes. In the case of paraphilia the precipitating circumstance is one that vandalizes and defaces the lovemap.

The question that then arises is: What constitutes a vandalizing circumstance? The most widely applicable answer is that it is a sex-related dilemma from which there is no escape. You're damned if you do something, and damned if you don't do anything. You are entrapped in a Catch-22 (see chap. 12), a dilemma named from the title of Joseph Heller's World War II novel (1955).

Sexuality and eroticism together constitute a minefield strewn with Catch-22s, insofar as so much that is sexual or erotic is culturally prohibited and penalized. Thus, if you don't, as a child, admit what you've said or done, sexually, then you may live in fear of the consequences of being discovered. If you do admit, the ax falls anyway. Incest is an example. A juvenile who has been conscripted into incest with a parent must collude in secret or else have the law take the parent away and break up what is left of the family; or have exactly the same reprisals taken if he/she breaks the silence by requesting help to have the practice of incest cease. There is no middle of the road along which a child may find escape.

Keeping close-mouthed in the aftermath of any form of enforced sexual abuse is prevalent not only in childhood, but in older years, also. If, however, you open your mouth and talk, then you risk being dismissed as a liar. Conversely, if you have no history of abuse to confirm, you may be subject to abusive interrogation and brainwashing to confirm a false confession—a procedure that has been much in vogue, since the 1970s, in the interrogation of children as well as in adults in child abuse cases, chiefly in English-speaking Protestant countries (Krivacska and Money, 1994).

Another minefield of Catch-22s that precipitate paraphilia in lovemap development is the minefield of abusive neglect and violence. Neglectful abuse and violent abuse may be admixed, or they may be independent of one another. The source of their power to generate paraphilic pathology in the developing lovemap is that the abuser, an ostensible protector, is also a victimizer. Whether the victimizer is an adult or another juvenile, victimization destroys the bond of trust that should otherwise exist in a pairbonded or a troopbonded relationship, respectively. The victimizer is untrustworthy. Trust is a defining quality of pairbondedness. Failure of trust in parent-child pairbondedness is particularly malignant. In the child, it vandalizes ahead of time the trust that is essential to lover-lover pairbondedness. That is to say, it vandalizes the child's lovemap by dissociating lust and love.

Abusive neglect and violence are able to disrupt the healthy development of the lovemap without themselves being specifically sexual neglect or sexual violence. The odds of paraphilically vandalizing the lovemap are greater, however, the more that neglect and violence are specifically sexual.

Abusive neglect is irrefutable in cases of birth defect of the sex organs in which the parents enwrap the defect in a shroud of silence where it is an unmentionable monster in the family's archives. Even if the child is about to undergo genital reconstructive surgery, the parents chaperone interviews lest the child ask sexual-medical questions and get them answered. To take an extreme case, a girl of eleven, born as a hermaphrodite, although already advancing into a masculinizing puberty, was withdrawn from a sexological evaluation, so as to ensure that the child would not be asked to talk explicitly about her own sexuality and eroticism as female or male, and the possibility of her own future as a boy instead of a girl. Thus, in their antisexual religious sexosophy, did the child's parents find a loophole through which to escape from consideration of a change of sex.

Neglect of children's sexological health is not officially classified as abusive neglect in Western medicine. There are no pediatric sexology courses in medical schools, and no sexology clinics in children's hospitals. Teachers receive no training in pediatric sexology. Thus, at a young age, when lovemap disorders are in the early stages of developing, and are most susceptible to intervention, they pass unrecognized. They are left to increase until they become perhaps untreatable.

Neglect of children's sex education and learning, whether in the school, church, or home is another aspect of children's sexological health that ought to be, but is not officially classified as abusive neglect. Accurate information is a prophylaxis against the disorders of lovemap formation. In the 1990s, it is also imperative as a prophylaxis against exposure to HIV/AIDS. To withhold explicit sex information should, therefore, be classified not only as abusive, but criminally abusive.

Violent abuse of children, as in brutal punishment, insofar as it desecrates a child's bond of trust in the parent or other abuser, also puts the lovemap at risk for desecration. Devastating humiliation may wreak similar havoc in the lovemap, especially if humiliation and brutal punishment go in tandem (Money, 1987a). The more explicitly sexuoerotic and brutally coercive the degree of abuse becomes, then the greater the likelihood of paraphilic defacement of the lovemap. The more threatening and dangerous the Catch-22 dilemma of whether to expose coercive abuse or not to expose it, the more greatly increased is the likelihood of the lovemap's defacement. The power of the Catch-22 is so great, that even with mild coercion, or no coercion at all, an illicit or taboo sexual activity can adversely affect the lovemap. This is a pervasive sexological penalty that society pays for its sexual taboo.

The sexual taboo is particularly pernicious when it is responsible for humiliative and punitive suppression of normal sexual rehearsal play that is actually a prerequisite of lovemap normality (normophilia) in childhood development. By way of example, a small boy, who struts around showing his erect penis to visiting girl cousins, is humiliated and beaten in their presence by his parent. He has a spunky temperament, not readily beaten down. Showing his penis becomes an act of defiance and rebellion. At puberty, the secret of his maximum erotic arousal is to exhibit his penis to a stranger, in public. His lovemap has been permanently vandalized into a paraphilic exhibitionistic one. Multiple arrests and imprisonments have not altered it, and will not alter it.

The correlation between sexual activities that are illicit and those that transform the lovemap into a paraphilic one is not total. In other words, there are some sexual violations of the law that do not harm the lovemap. Oral sex between adults is an example. Although it is a crime in some states, it is normal in the lovemap in others. First cousin marriage is another example. It is forbidden in some states and not in others. Transculturally, in some societies it fits into the lovemap as a matchmaker's ideal (see chap. 10).

Vocabulary can be manipulated to brand a particular type of lovemap as not only paraphilic but criminal. This is what happens, for example, when child molestation is used as synonym for pedophilia, and likewise child abuse. In the Oxford English Dictionary, molestation means to meddle with a person injuriously or with hostile intent. Sexually, it means to attack or abuse. Injury, hostility, and attack are not intrinsic to the meaning of pedophilia, however. An age discrepent relationship that is mutually agreeable and noncoercive may not be morally or legally acceptable, but it does not, a priori, have a universally deleterious effect on the formation of the lovemap (Money and Weinrich, 1983; Feierman, 1990), except for the possibility of a deleterious Catch-22 dilemma created by the illegality of the relationship.

In U.S. law childhood ends at the eighteenth birthday. Thus an eighteen or nineteen-year-old who has sex with a seventeen-year-old might, legally, be arrested as a pedophile. Having sex with an adolescent teenager technically is not pedophilia, however, but ephebophilia. Pedophilia applies to the prepubertal juvenile years, and is not the same as infantophilia.

Whether or not an age discrepancy will vandalize a developing lovemap is contingent in part on its magnitude, in part on whether the activity engaged in is kissing, fondling, fingering, or copulating, in part on the degree of coercion, and in part on the brutality of punishment, if discovered. When there is no age discrepancy, and in the absence of bullying and coercion, then juvenile sexual rehearsal play, not molestation or abuse is the correct terminology. Sexual rehearsal play itself does not vandalize the lovemap, but being punished and humiliated for engaging in it does.

Like all aspects of human maturation, lovemap maturation has its own orderly schedule from infancy through childhood and adolescence to young adulthood. Untimely or artifactual acceleration or deprivation of lovemap maturation puts it at risk of distortion. In a sexually dysfunctional household, too early and too vivid an introduction to sadistic or masochistic parental feuding, for example, has a damaging effect on a child's lovemap. With uncommon frequency, a juvenile with a sex-offender's lovemap has a domestic history of early exposure to lovemap pathology in other people, and entrapment in a sexual Catch-22 from which there is no escape. Lovemap pathology breeds lovemap pathology (see appendix 2). The maxim to remember is: "Sexual outcomes have sexual origins."

To illustrate: What at first appeared to be a simple case of placing the adoption of a baby whose mother was a prostitute with no place of residence, and no means of support, turned out to be not simple at all. The mother's pediatric medical chart recorded the information that in childhood she had been followed as a case of so-called psychosocial dwarfism (the Kaspar Hauser syndrome; see Money, 1992, and Money et al., 1990). In this syndrome, failure to secrete pituitary growth hormone and to grow is domicile specific, and is attributed to neglect and abuse at home.

When she was a girl of nine, her mother discovered that her husband had another woman. Intoxicated and late home one night, he fell into a drunken sleep. In jealous rage his wife poured gasoline over him and ignited it. The three children were bystanders to the crisis, with firemen, police, and paramedics, and the removal of their dying father. Subsequently, the patient "had always felt that his death was because of something I had done."

After the mother's trial and sentencing, the girl was sent to stay with friends. Their sixteen-year-old son "sexually abused me," she said. "He would come to my room. He'd grab ahold of me, and force me to have intercourse with him. . . . He would slap on my face, punch me on the arm, make me take off all my clothes."

When she was ten, there was a girl, a neighbor, who would force her to undress, and would slap her face and burn her with a cigarette while the boys she brought with her watched. The neighbor girl would kiss her lips and genitals, and require her to reciprocate. She was required also to watch the neighbor girl petting and kissing the boys. Once "she thought I had peed, and she made me lick it up."

There were twin boys, aged eleven, in the foster home where the patient was placed at age thirteen. They would "kick me, punch me, and slap me all the time." At age sixteen, when she was living with her grandmother, her older brother would slap her, to which the grandmother's response was that "men are supposed to hit on women when they do something wrong." It was at this age that the girl first realized that pain was erotically arousing to her.

She became pregnant at age twenty. Having no accommodation other than a motel room with a pimp, she took up residence in a halfway house where she gave the baby up for adoption. She was referred for a sexological evaluation and counseling and talked forthrightly except to those who responded judgmentally. Her agenda was to resume her career as a prostitute, and by the end of the year to become pregnant again by a customer who would be a heavily built black man, so that she would have a baby to love and to love her.

Paraphilic masochism was a primary feature of her lovemap. It was enhanced by the unpredictable dangers and excitements of a constant change of partners and police raids for street-corner prostitution, begun as a career at age nineteen. Her ideal customer had a big penis and was, unlike herself, black "because they are more aggressive." She disliked being paid by those who agreed to "slap on me," because it didn't seem right to receive payment for the intense pleasure (rated ten on her "Richter" orgasm scale) that she obtained from being slapped around, independently of genital contact. Sometimes while being slapped around she would be thinking back to age seven "to where my mother was standing there in a black negligee, and my father was screaming at her, calling her bitch, and getting ready to hit her, and it looked sexual, to me."

Stratagems

ALTHOUGH PARAPHILIAS bear the marks of individualized variability, they also segregate into forty-odd named types. The exact number of types depends on how many subdivisions are made, for example, in naming all the possible fetishisms, and on whether overlapping or multiplex paraphilias each are separately named. For a "Vocabulary of the Paraphilias" with definitions, see Money, 1986a, together with the Glossary of Money, 1988a.

A paraphilic person has one paraphilia, regardless of whether it is simple or compounded of multiple parts (simplex or multiplex). For example, a fetishistic transvestite has a history of no longer cross dressing in women's clothes, but of wearing adult sized baby diapers instead (autonepiophilia or infantilism). His baby name is female. So his paraphilic age has changed, but his cross-dressing, has not disappeared. He has a compound or multiplex paraphilia which does not yet have its own official name.

Despite their number and variety, paraphilic lovemaps can be classified into seven categories according to the criterion of the seven stratagems, or trickeries, by which lust has not been forfeited. Conjointly, love has not been sacrificed to lust's defilement, but has been separated or dissociated from it.

The seven are:

- Sacrifice and expiation
- Marauding and predation
- Mercantilism and venality
- Fetishism and talismanism
- Stigmatism and eligibility
- Subrogation and understudy
- Solicitation and allure

The *sacrificial/expiatory stratagem* requires sacrifice and penance as atonement or reparation for the defilement of lust. Atonement by sacrifice and expiation is a paleodigm, that is an extremely ancient paradigm, with roots far into the religious past. Sexuoerotic sadism and masochism (which is not synonymous with martyrdom) belong here. The most extreme sacrifice is lust murder (erotophonophilia) which in some instances is serial lust murder. Self-sacrifice by stage managing one's own murder is autoassassinophilia.

The *marauding/predatory stratagem* requires that only someone stolen, enslaved, abducted, or forcibly coerced is acceptable for the defilement of lust, all others being too pure. The most violent extreme of this paraphilia is brutally assaultive rape (raptophilia or biastophilia). Statutory rape is defined not on the criterion of violence but age discrepancy. Marital rape is better defined as spousal abuse, and date rape without violence as revoked consent.

The *mercantile/venal stratagem* requires that the defilement of lust can be justified only if the partner is paid, purchased, or bartered for (chrematistophilia). Only a minority of commercial sex workers and their patrons have a lovemap of this chrematistophilic type. It often passes unrecognized, but less so when couples impersonate prostitution or hustling with play money, and maybe with a third person in the role of customer. Some chrematistophiles set themselves up for blackmail or robbery as the price of lust.

The *fetishistic/talismanic stratagem* requires that the defilement of lust be displaced totally or in part from a person onto a substitute fetish object or substance which represents a smell (olfactophilia) or a textured feel (hyphephilia) of the living human body.

The *stigmatic/eligibilic stratagem* requires that the defilement of lust be directed exclusively at someone who does not belong to one's home troop by reason of religion, race, color, nationality, social class, age, or body morphology. The lovemap of acrotomophilia, a fixation of lust on the stumps of amputees, is an exceptional example of this stratagem (Riddle, 1989). It belongs in the category of morphophilia which pertains to a paraphilic fixation on the disparity of the bodily appearance of the two partners. The counterpart of morphophilia is chronophilia, in which there is a fixation on the disparity of age of the two partners. Eligibility may apply also across species to include pets, as it does in zoophilia (Matthews, 1995).

The *subrogation/understudy stratagem* requires that a victim of the defilement of lust be saved by the martyrdom of oneself as a stand-in or substitute. This stratagem applies to some cases of incest, when a son or daughter becomes the sexual partner of one of the parents and thereby rescues the other from the defilement of lust. The stratagem's applicability may be either heterosexual or homosexual, and is not restricted to parents or other family members exclusively. Rescuer's martydom may surreptitiously play a part also in adultery. Professional rescuers, namely health care providers, are vulnerable to becoming the sexual stand-ins, despite the penalty of professional censure or loss of license for having an affair with a patient or client.

The *solicitational/allurative stratagem* requires that the defilement of lust be displaced from the acceptive phase of genital union and replaced by one or more of the sexuoerotic invitations of the courtship or proceptive phase. Displaying the genitals in public as a solicitational gesture (paraphilic exhibitionism) that produces orgasm is a major example of this stratagem. In males, exhibiting the penis is named peodeiktophilia. The counterpart of exhibitionism is voyeurism, or the Peeping Tom paraphilia, which may occur also in the guise of illicitly looking at pictorial erotica. Exposure of nudity that is licit, as at a nudist resort, is ineffectual for this type of paraphilia.

Deconnected Phylisms

THE FORMATION OF a paraphilic stratagem entails the deconnection of a nonsexual, nonerotic behavioral phylism from where it usually belongs and its transfer and reconnection to the proceptive phase of sexuoerotic attraction and arousal (Money, 1983, 1986a). Phylogeny limits the repertory of paraphilic ideation, imagery, and practice that may be ontogenetically incorporated into personal lovemap development. The following are selected examples.

Paraphilic sacrifice or expiation is related to being the loser in a dispute and to the phylism of appeasement. In masochistic expiation, inflicted pain perhaps increases the brain's secretion of its own opiates, the endorphins, which in turn contribute to the metamorphosis of pain into sexuoerotic ecstasy. In this respect there is a parallel between sexuoerotic and religious ecstasy induced by flagellation. Masochism is related also to the phylism of becoming addicted to abuse (Money, 1992a).

Paraphilic marauding or predation is related to the phylism for hierarchical dominance assertion, particularly as applied to mating rivalry and partner possessiveness, and of fighting to found or join a new troop after leaving the home troop at adolescence. Predatory rape and homicidal sadism may be related also to the phylisms of stalking for food and of territorial and personal defense against attack.

Paraphilic mercantilism or venality is related to the phylism of operant training with tokens or coins as rewards. Working for tokens is not restricted to the human species. It is a basis of animal training.

Paraphilic fetishism or talismanism is related to the olfactory and tactual (haptic) phylisms of parent-infant pairbonding. The smelly or touchy stimulus becomes detached from the person onto a nonliving substance, artifact, or object.

Paraphilic eligibility or stigmatism is related to the phylism of assortative matching and mating. This phylism ensures mating between members of not only the same species or subspecies, morphologically, but in the human species also between members of the same tribe or community, at least to some degree. In the chronophilias the criterion of eligibility is age, ranging from infantophilia and pedophilia through ephebophilia (teenaged partners) to gerontophilia. The phylism related to the chronophilias is parent-child pairbonding, to which lover-lover pairbonding becomes transposed.

Paraphilic subrogation or understudy is related to the phylism of troopbonding which is augmented by lover-lover pairbonding transposed so as to be a substitute form of rescue, service, support, or advice provided to a fellow member of the troop.

Paraphilic solicitation or allure is related to the phylism of courtship display and ritual that engages the attention of a potential mate, or pays attention to a potential mate's allure. In the paraphilia, the phylism is dislocated from its appropriate time, place, and person.

Other Principles

Pairbondship Disorder. Paraphilia is not a disorder of sex overall. It does not induce irreversible pathology at the conceptive phase, and not at the acceptive phase of sexuoerotic function, though it may indicate potentially reversible functional failures at both phases. Failure at the conceptive phase, for example, may be secondary to paraphilic avoidancy of penovaginal intercourse. Incomplete genital arousal and failure to climax at the acceptive phase, as may happen in cases of rapism and exhibitionism, subsequently reverses when the paraphile replays a mental tape of the paraphilic episode while masturbating alone, or having sexual intercourse with a friend or spouse.

The primary pathology of paraphilia is at the proceptive phase of sexuoerotic function where it interferes with pairbonding by driving a dissociative wedge between the imagery and ideation of limerence, love and affection, on the one hand, and the imagery and ideation of carnal lust, on the other hand. Thus, paraphilia is a disorder of love and lust not sex. In a majority of, though not all cases of paraphilia, the recipient of affectional love is not the same person as the recipient or recipients of carnal lust.

Pedophilia may be claimed as an exception, insofar as the relationship between the older and younger partner is in many instances reciprocal, uncoerced, and affectionate as well as being genital and expressive of lust on the part of the older male or female partner. Nonetheless, the split between love and lust becomes evident when the younger partner enters puberty. Then the bodily signs and smells of puberty are incompatible with lustful attraction.

The relationship then transforms into one of fondness and friendship only, without lust.

In the human species, the proceptive sexuoerotic phase has long been recognized as the courtship phase of pairbonding. Therefore, paraphilias may also be called disorders of courtship. Courtship behavior may be paraphilically altered as it is in predatory sadism, for example; or as it is in being the recipient of an enema as part of the courtship ritual (klismaphilia). Or it may be fixated on an atypical or forbidden recipient, as in infantophilia.

There is yet a third paraphilic alteration of the proceptive or courtship phase, namely the repetition of courtship over and over again, each time with a fresh partner, so that a pairbonded relationship has no chance of materializing. In the vernacular, this alteration is known as compulsive cruising—searching for a holy grail destined never to be found.

Paraphilic alteration of the imagery and ideation of the proceptive sexuoerotic phase is predominantly by an inclusion of something different or unorthodox. An alternative possibility is a rearrangement of the proceptive sequence, as exemplified in paraphilias of solicitation and allure. For example, proceptive genital display, widespread among primates, is transposed paraphilically from the proceptive periphery to the center, where it becomes essential to the acceptive phase, and more important than genital union to the release of orgasm. Paraphilic display is genital exhibitionism which in males is peodeiktophilia. In females it has not yet been given a special name. Watching, spying, or viewing is voyeurism. In both instances, paraphilic alteration of courtship behavior is rarely, if ever conducive to a pairbonded relationship with its recipient person.

Exhibitionism and voyeurism illustrate the general paraphilic principle, namely, the principle of converse pairs. In some paraphiles the pairs alternate. In others they do not. Sadomasochism by its very name indicates that the sadist (top) may change roles with the masochist (bottom), and vice versa. The amputee paraphilia manifests itself as a fixation on amputees as partners (acrotomophilia), and simultaneously, a fixation on becoming an amputee oneself (apotemnophilia). The diaper fetishist, besides being an infantilist (autonepiophile) who impersonates a baby, may be also an infantophile who is sexuoerotically attracted to babies in diapers (nepiophilia). Similarly, a pedophile whose sexuoerotic attraction is toward juveniles is also a juvenilist with a lovemap age that is not in synchrony with the pedophile's chronological age, but is still juvenile. In the lovemap of asphyxiophilia, the adolescent who is an autoerotic self-strangulator has dreams and masturbation fantasies in which, at the approach of orgasm, the imagery is of a sexy female (or male) being strangulated or drowned. And so on.

It is difficult, but not utterly impossible for two people who are the paraphilic converse of one another to meet, even when their paraphilia is as hazardous and potentially lethal as asphyxiophilia. They do so, as aforementioned, by placing thinly disguised paraphilic personals in selected media publications, and by joining membership networks of like-minded people. No matter how well-matched a pair may recognize themselves to be, it is difficult for them to maintain a pairbonded relationship. One woman wrote that her orgasmic ecstasy with an amputee lover overwhelmed her with the guilt of wanting him only for his stump so that she had to terminate the relationship, despite his anguish and her own loss (Money, 1990a).

Opponent Process. From adolescence onward, people with a paraphilic lovemap are aware that something about them sexuoerotically is different. They know its hazards and dangers, and that in the eyes of other people they are wrong, immoral, deviant, perverted, or criminal for having it. Yet, their self-image does not confirm them as being such a person. They have no explanation of why they keep harboring their paraphilic thoughts, imaginations, and practices, instead of abominating them as other people do. Punishment is supposed to get rid of them, but they know from experience that it does not. The psychologic law of reward-and-punishment learning does not apply. One must turn instead to the principle of opponent-process learning, formulated in the 1970s (Solomon, 1980).

The most concise explanation of opponent process is by way of an example of panic transformed to euphoria. Experienced daredevils perhaps are excepted. Otherwise one's first leap in bungee jumping or in sky diving is accompanied by panicky excitement. After a few practice trials, euphoric excitement takes over, and in no time addiction replaces aversion. Addiction may not be only a metaphor. It is possible that the excitement of danger releases endorphin in brain cells, so that it literally produces the high that people say they feel.

By analogy, the opponent process of converting negative into positive can be applied to the tragedy-into-triumph formula already mentioned in this chapter. An experience that is sexuoerotically abhorent, becomes transformed in the lovemap into one that is orgasmically ecstatic.

Stoller (1975) gives an example: A three-year-old boy whose mother was dying with cancer was sent to live with her sister and his grown girl cousin. The aunt and cousin coerced him many times into being cross-dressed and made up into a frilly girl. On his fourth birthday, his mother came home from the hospital to visit, only a few weeks before she died. As a prank, his aunt and cousin dressed him up as a girl whom his mother would be unable to recognize and introduced him to her as "a new neighbor girl." They took photographs of them together before the ruse was revealed. The boy developed the paraphilia of fetishistic transvestism. From adolescence onward he was fixated on porno magazines depicting virile men being dominated and coercively cross-dressed by a group of uniformed dominatrixes. His masturbation fantasies were of himself in the same situation. Only in treatment, and through his wife's discovery of the family photo album, did he make the connection between these fantasies and his early childhood experiences.

A military or sports triumph is celebrated by a victor's parade. The neutralization of a potential lovemap tragedy by eroticizing it is a triumph to be put on parade. The paraphilic equivalent of the triumphal parade is theatricality. The paraphilias are theatrical disorders—not exhibitionistic or narcissistic—but theatrical, always on stage and before an audience, despite the risk of publicity. A paraphile under police interrogation will frequently confer self-incriminating details. Some go so far as to attribute a paraphilic crime to their own paraphilic selves, when the crime was actually committed by a fellow paraphile. Paraphilic theatricality accounts for the readiness with which paraphiles appear on television, showing and telling all.

The triumph of opponent process in reversing the polarity of negative and positive in lovemap development manifests itself not only in paraphilic theatricality, but also in paraphilic hypersexualism. In paraphilic adults, hypersexualism is manifest in the frequency of paraphilic encounters, and in the shortening of the refractory or recovery period between orgasms, which is more noticeable in males than females. Multiple orgasms, from two to six, or sometimes more, on a daily basis, although not universal are not particularly uncommon among younger male paraphiles. Since at least a few men who are not known to be paraphilic may have similar orgasmic high frequency, no definitive statement can be made about cause and effect in the relationship between orgasmic frequency and paraphilia.

Hypersexualism as a manifestation of opponent process is observed also in children. Those children are usually brought to professional attention with a complaint of sexual acting out or of sex offending, usually against other children, although they may offend against an adult also. Their past sexological history, if recoverable, is likely to be one of socially condemned, premature exposure to juvenile or older sexual practices out of synchrony with their developmental sexological age. One example is that of a nine year old girl who, despite the contempt and retaliation of boys on the school bus, persistently attempted to perform fellatio on them. The driver had no legal authority to discipline her, and no attempt was made to ascertain the sexual antecedents of her behavior.

Gender Transposition. Although homosexuality was in the early sexological literature classified as a perversion, by the time perversion was officially changed to paraphilia, homosexuality had been declassified as a disease. Paraphilias do not discriminate between homosexual and heterosexual lovemaps. They appear in both, and in bisexual lovemaps also. In this book homosexuality is classified among the gender transpositions (see chap. 6).

The gender transpositions include male tranvestophilia, also known as fetishistic transvestism. This is the syndrome that indicates a continuity between gender transposition and paraphilia. The fetishistic dependency on female attire for sexuoerotic arousal and orgasm is paraphilic. The cross dressing, per se, represents a degree of gender transposition.

Paraphilic cross dressing is a feature not only of transvestophilia, but also in the paraphilia known for its termination in autoerotic death. Usually, death is the accidental outcome of self-asphyxiation (asphyxiophilia), but it may be from electrocution or other flirtations with danger. More frequently than can be accounted for by chance alone, autoerotic self-asphyxiation by hanging goes together with cross dressing in a multiplex paraphilia. The female attire may belong to the self-strangulator's mother. Death ensues only if the safety device fails at the last moment and the person becomes unconscious. That may be the first time that the practices of self-strangulation and cross dressing become known. It is rare for an asphyxiophile while still alive to give an interview about his paraphilia.

A live example comes from the biography of a young man who, until ten years before therapeutic intervention commenced, had been an erotic self-strangulator—an asphyxiophile (Money et al., 1991). From puberty onward, his wet dreams and masturbation fantasies had been fixated on girls being drowned or strangulated, or on mental replays of his own self-strangulation. He would knot ladies' dance tights around his neck and pull on the ends to cut off his breathing. Dressed only in bikini briefs, he would be standing in front of a mirror, watching himself, his stomach heaving as he struggled for breath, his penis showing hard beneath the fabric of his bikini underwear. Seeing his body and his round little butt in the mirror was as if seeing a cute little gay boy. He was being stalked by a serial killer, like Chicago's John Gacy, who would strangulate him. No! He would release the dance tights in the nick of time and lie back on his bed until he could stop heaving and breath properly. Then the heterosexual fantasies of drowning and strangulating women, incorporating scenes from television movies, would return, as he masturbated to orgasm. There were no other occasions when he had imagery of himself as a gay boy. The very rare occasions when he felt erotically attracted to a male disturbed him. Attractions to women obsessed him as he was socially highly inept and always too inhibited to make a first move.

Another example of paraphilia and gender transposition comes from a man with the amputee paraphilia, apotemnophilia. He was fixated on having his left leg amputated and had drilled into and infected the bone in the hope of creating an absolute necessity for professional amputation—but in vain. He wrote about himself as follows.

> Since my thirteenth year, my conscious life has been absorbed, with varying intensity, in a bizarre and prepotent obsessive wish, need, desire to have my leg amputated above the knee; the image of myself as an amputee has as an erotic fantasy (each one different) accompanied EVERY sexual experience of my life: auto-, homo-, and heterosexual, since, and beginning with, puberty. . . . There are scattered occasions when I "feel like a woman," viscerally, in terms of body image, and in these situations I loathe myself—it makes me very apprehensive. Somehow this seems linked with the amputation fantasy. I would rather have this [amputation] than lose the penis which would mean that I would be like a woman. . . . My entire erotic activity now consists of trying to make "real" the fantasy that I am an amputated homosexual adolescent, for in possessing my stump I can, concurrently, possess my penis (Money et al., 1977, pp. 117-18).

Twenty years later, his paraphilia had not yielded to psychotherapy, including eight years of psychoanalytically oriented therapy. He arranged the gear necessary for a contrived hunting accident, shot his left leg, and finally had it amputated. He had climbed his Mount Everest and was satisfied with his achievement. But he did not exactly rest on his laurels. Two years later he developed a painful inflammation in the amputated stump. Instead of trying a minor surgical correction first, he obeyed the dictates of apotemnophilia and insisted on what he half seriously called a second amputation. In other words, he underwent a surgical shortening of the stump by two inches. He retrieved the remnant of the newly removed specimen from the pathology laboratory, so that he could preserve it in a specimen jar. Then followed for the second time the rehabilitation procedure of getting a new prosthesis.

Pornography. For people with the amputee paraphilia, pornography consists of stories about or pictures or videos of people showing their stumps or wearing prostheses. To be sexuoerotically alluring and arousing, the amputees do not need to be undressed, nor to have their genitalia revealed. Their stumps are the important parts of their bodies for the acrotomophilic admirer (the devotee). Amputation pornography is, therefore, legal. It is not very profitable, however. The market is too small, and it cannot be enlarged by recruiting new customers. Recruitment is ineffectual. Like all paraphilias, the amputee paraphilia is not contagious: no matter how long or extensive the exposure, it cannot be caught by looking at pictures or videos of amputees, nor by reading romantic or erotic stories about them.

For people with the cross-dressing paraphilia (transvestophilia), the principles of pornography are the same as for the amputee paraphilia. Pictures, videos, or stories of men modeling women's fashions are not illegal, though they are a sexuoerotic turn on for male transvestophiles. If, however, the depictions are of she-males, elegantly coiffured with make-up, and wearing billowy lingerie that exposes their penises, then people argue as to whether they cross the line between legal and illegal. Arguing becomes louder if the genitalia are engaged in hard core sexual activity. If the producers and distributors cannot prove that all of the she-males are eighteen years old or older, then argument ceases. Nude depiction of anyone from one day of age to the eighteenth birthday is, by U.S. federal law, prosecutable as a sex offense. Proof of being older than eighteen is required, together with signed consent.

Getting sexuoerotically aroused by depictions of males who are cross dressed, regardless of whether they are dressed to kill, or showing their penises, or carrying a birth certificate is, just like amputee pornography, not contagious. Unless you already have a transvestophilic lovemap, it will be impossible for you to get turned on by the pornography that turns on transvestophiles. In fact, you can get turned on only to pornography that matches what is already in your lovemap. The specialized pornography of all the paraphilias that do not belong will leave you cold; and it will not change your lovemap, no matter what your age.

If pornography were as virulently contagious as old wives' tales often claim it to be, then it should be possible to use heterosexual pornography to infect homosexual lovemaps with heterosexuality, and, vice versa, to infect heterosexual lovemaps with homosexuality. The pornography of the paraphilias will not infect your lovemap, no matter what your age, and convert it into a paraphilic one. People have an irrational dread of being haunted by pornography in the dark gloom of perversion and deviancy from which they will find no escape. They are in error.

17

Paraphilia: Susceptibility

Evolution and Paraphilia

Paraphilic lovemaps with their built in paraphilic stratagems have no exact parallel in the nonhuman animal kingdom. Hence, from the point of view of evolutionary sexology, the question is: What makes us human beings sexuoerotically so peculiar? Whatever the ultimate answer, at the present time it must inevitably be conjectural.

One conjecture is that the plasticity and versatility of brain function which is prerequisite to human linguistic communication evolved concurrently with, and could not have happened without, an emancipation or loosening up of evolutionarily primitive brain schemas or maps, the mating map included, that functioned with monotonous homogeneity and immutability. Their very lack of heterogeneity and diversity, however, provided predictability and reliability. The more predictably stereotyped the menu of the foodmap, for example, the less the risk of eating poisonous food. The magnitude of today's nontoxic human menu is surely an extraordinary achievement of culinary ingenuity, since there was no paleolithic FDA (Food and Drug Administration) to stage clinical trials before a new food item could be declared nontoxic and fit for human consumption.

Like primitive food maps, primitive mating maps are manifested today in subhuman species. Although predictably reliable for the procreation of the species, primitive mating maps are stereotypically monotonous in both the movements and the sounds of courtship and copulation.

As compared with other mammals, the human mating map is emancipated in four evolutionary ways. First, human beings are emancipated from quadrupedal to bipedal locomotion, thus from having the nose and the sex organs on the same plane as they are in quadrupeds that are sexually aroused by smell, and from exclusively dorsoventral to ventroventral copulatory positioning. Second, human beings are emancipated from regular hormonal and pheromonal cyclicity to sporadic periodicity in mating. Third, they are emancipated from the nose in favor of the eyes and cutaneous senses as the organs of sexuoerotic attraction and arousal. Fourth, they are emancipated from phyletically fixed communicative soundmaps to flexible and versatile speechmaps.

Whether signaling danger, welcome, food, or mating, a communicative soundmap of hoots, howls, barks, clicks, whistles, squeals, snarls, chatters, screams, grunts, and yells still today characterize the communication of subhuman primates and other mammals on land and in the ocean, and of fishes too (Lobel, 1991). Such sounds formerly held little promise for the evolution of human verbal dialogue, syntactical logic, and numerical reasoning. Perhaps, therefore, the primordial origins of human language are to be sought not in such communicative signaling, but separately, in the map for song. In the mindbrain this songmap codes for rhythmic and syllabic intonation, crooning, cooing, humming, chanting, melody, phrasing, and mimicry of audible sounds. A poetic corollary of this conjecture is that human language began as a love song. Like the mating invitation of the songbird, it would have been initially a song without words, but nonetheless a song of solicitation and allure. The songmap is the evolutionary bridge that connects the lovemap and the speechmap. Song and dance are still very intimately close to human sexuality and eroticism, as is especially evident in adolescent culture, worldwide. We may not fall in love when we sing, but we certainly sing and wax poetic when we fall in love. Music and language are, according to contemporary evidence, differently represented in the right and left hemispheres of the brain (Cohen et al., 1989; Kandel et al., 1995, A358).

Whatever its ultimate explanation, the phenomenon to be explained is the uniquely human plasticity and versatility of the mindbrain in processing, inter alia, its maps for the triad of language, music, and sexuoeroticism—the speechmap, songmap, and lovemap, respectively. This plasticity allows the lovemap to be elaborately diversified and personalized, even to the extent of being paraphilic. To a certain degree, the wide range of lovemap diversity masks the bare essentials of what is phyletically written into the human lovemap to guarantee the procreative success of the species. These bare essentials are, presumably, represented predominantly in the limbic brain, the paleocortex, whereas variations on them are represented in the neocortex. They are three in number. The names coined for them are *haptoerotic*, *morphoerotic*, and *gnomoerotic*. The age of hormonal puberty is the chronological pivot toward which the development of all three has been in rehearsal, and after which they go into full production on center stage.

Haptoerotic (from Greek, *haptikos*, to grasp or touch + *Eros*, god of love) means genitoerotic stimulation and response related to touch and the cutaneous senses. Haptoeroticism, especially in the early years of puberty, may be a sequel to frictional movement, for example of clothing, with or without accompanying erotic imagery or ideation. It may also be autoerotically induced, as in digital or some other technique of masturbation, with or without erotic ideation and imagery. Haptoeroticism has a kinship with tickling and massage in being qualitatively different when self-performed than when performed by a partner. With a partner, haptoerotic arousal typically begins with body surfaces in juxtaposition, and engaged in pressing, stroking, rubbing, licking, or sucking, and progressing to intromission. Phyletically, the bare essentials of intromission are that something is put somewhere, not only that the penis is put in the vagina, or that the vagina engulfs the penis. The fingers may take the place of the penis, and the mouth or anus may take the place of the vagina. The inserter does the mounting and thrusting, and the recipient does the presenting, (crouching, or lordosis in nonhuman mammals) and engulfing. Mounting and thrusting is predominantly a male practice, and presenting and engulfing predominantly a female practice, but they are not absolutely fixed as male or female, respectively, but are to some degree male/female interchangeable, as can be demonstrated in contrived animal experiments. Literally, therefore, they should be characterized as ambisexual.

Morphoerotic (from Greek, *morpho-*, form, + *Eros*) means genitoerotic stimulation and response related to the image, depiction, or appearance of a particular shape or form. Although morphoerotic idiosyncracies are myriad and extremely varied, what they share in common is that in the heterosexual majority of the population, males are turned on by the female morphology or some detail of it, and females by the male morphology or some detail of it. Regardless of homosexual subtyping as feminal versus virile, males in the homosexual minority of the population are turned on by the male morphology, and females by the female morphology. In the bisexual minority, males and females are turned on by both morphologies.

The equivalent of morphoeroticism in the lower mammalian species is olfactoerotism: phylogenetically they are ordained to be ruled by the nose. Thus, the male dog's nose is exquisitely sensitive to the genital odor of the bitch in heat. By contrast, morphoeroticism in the human species is ophthalmoerotic: phylogenetically it is ordained to be ruled by the eyes, more predominantly so in the male than the female. No research has yet been directed toward ascertaining how or when the developing lovemap in the mindbrain is equipped with ophthalmoerotic receptors that release sexuoerotic responsivity when activated by the matching, morphoerotic image of, in monosexuality, either male or female, and in bisexuality, both male and female.

Hypothetically, the ophthalmoerotic image could be transcribed directly into the lovemap from a male/female determining segment of the genome.

More likely, the transcription would be indirect, and modulated hormonally in fetal or neonatal life, with or without a subsequent overlay of social imprinting in infancy and childhood.

Whatever the ultimate explanation might be, the sex of the human morphoerotic image as male or female indisputably differentiates heterosexual from homosexual genitoerotic stimulation and response. What the sex of the image will be commonly declares itself contemporaneously with puberty, and with the first love-smitten infatuation or limerent attraction. It appears in erotic dreams as well as waking reveries and fantasies, and in response to cognitional stimuli.

Gnomoerotic (from Greek, *gnome*, thought, judgment, opinion, + *Eros*) means genitoerotic stimulation and response related to what one knows about sex. Under primordial conditions of troop living, like those of modern subhuman primates, human juveniles would assimilate knowledge of sex by exposure to the copulation of elders and by participating in juvenile sexual rehearsal play (see chap. 2). Contemporary children who have restricted access to explicit sexual knowledge are destined, therefore, to develop lovemaps that are susceptible to error. Then the sexuoerotic versatility of the human mindbrain may become actually a liability, insofar as it allows for the improvisation and imprinting of lovemap pathology.

Developmentally, in the human species, the lovemap and the speechmap, and also all other mindbrain maps, e.g., the foodmap, are multivariately and sequentially coded, and they have a high degree of personalized heterogeneity. In subhuman species, by contrast, mindbrain maps are phyletically ordained within each category to develop as individual replicas of one another. Their loci in the brain, are, presumably, chiefly in the limbic cortex, whereas human mindbrain maps are represented in the neocortex as well.

One pathological outcome is the multiplicity of paraphilic stratagems, each one formed when a nonsexuoerotic phylism is pried loose from its locus of origin and coopted into the service of sexuoerotic arousal (see chap. 16). Pain, for example, when pried loose from injurious hurt, may be put into the service of masochistic sexuoerotic ecstasy.

Evolutionary sexology may provide a theory to explain why the human species is, phylogenetically, a species susceptible to paraphilic and other sexuoerotic variations, but it does not provide a theory to explain the selective ontogeny of paraphilic development in some individuals though not in others. For that explanation, it may be necessary to search the genome for an alteration of the sequence of a part of the genetic code responsible for susceptibility to dissociative coding of the lovemap. That search may be like looking for a needle in a haystack, but it is not totally without feasibility. Some people are, indeed, more susceptible to dissociation than others are—for example those who are susceptible to being hypnotized.

Should genomic miscoding carry the ultimate responsibility for dissociative miscoding of the lovemap, then it might quite possibly do so by the miscoding of brain neurochemistries in the course of embryogenesis. Present evidence implicates not the sex hormones, but some other neurotransmitter substances with an as yet undiscovered role in prenatal susceptibility to subsequent dissociative, paraphilic lovemap formation. The most newly discovered potential candidates are the gases, NO (nitric oxide) and CO (carbon monoxide) (Snyder, 1992). Susceptibility might also be attributable, either prenatally or postnatally, to injury, disease, or metabolic defect affecting the brain, or to a cryptic, epileptiform type of dysfunction within the brain itself. In infancy and juvenile life, susceptibility to dissociative paraphilic lovemap formation maybe one of the sequelae within the mindbrain of traumatically abusive cruelty and neglect (see chap. 16).

Although a paraphilia is a syndrome in its own right, that does not preclude the possibility that it may overlap with another syndrome that increases the degree of susceptibility. Various syndromes that are candidates for increasing paraphilic susceptibility are as follows.

Contributory Syndromes

Supernumerary Y (47,XYY) syndrome (Money, 1994b). The extra Y chromosome carries a duplicate dose of the Y genome which affects the phenotype of both body and mind. Impulsiveness, one of the 47,XYY mental characteristics, includes impulsive paraphilic acts in some cases.

Hallucinosis. This is a syndrome of exceptionally vivid or eidetic hallucinatory imagery, but not the same as paranoia or paranoid schizophrenia. It may be induced by a toxic substance. Hallucination is not, per se, a paraphilic phenomenon, but paraphilic visual imagery, especially in dreams, is sometimes so vivid as to be, for the dreamer, indistinguishable from paraphilic practice. Although hallucinatory paraphilic imagery is chiefly visual, especially in males, it may be cutaneous (haptic) or, occasionally, olfactory; but it is rarely auditory. Paraphilic hallucinosis may take the form of attributing to oneself a paraphilic act, for example lust murder, committed by someone else, for which a false confession is made.

Asperger's syndrome (named for Hans Asperger, 1884-1954). This is a form of infantile and juvenile autism in which soliloquy and proclamation predominate over two-way dialogue. Paraphilic people are not properly called autistic, but some are loners who are inept at two-way dialogue with fellow troopbonders, as well as being inept with dialogue as pairbonders.

Bipolar Disorder. Manic-depressive bipolar disorder may coexist with a paraphilic disorder. If so, the paraphilic disorder may seem to cycle also, but not in predictable synchrony with manic-depressive cyclicity.

Head and Brain Injury. Violent compression or bruising of brain tissue in a closed head injury can induce susceptibility to paraphilia provided it damages sexual centers and pathways, notably those that cluster bilaterally in the amygdala, temporal lobe, and hypothalamus. Concealed from view, a closed head injury occurring during a difficult delivery may go unrecorded in the birth history, and be omitted, therefore, from the paraphilic sexual history at a later date. Brain trauma from open-skull wounds, or from intracranial lesions, including malignancies, may increase susceptibility to paraphilia. So also may deteriorative brain cell diseases, irrespective of age. In fact, long term follow-up studies make plausible the hypothesis that paraphilia may be a very early prodromal sign of what twenty or more years later will be diagnosed as a deteriorative brain syndrome, for example, Parkinson's disease, Huntington's disease, or Alzheimer's disease. Conversely, posttraumatic brain pathology at birth or very early in life may be responsible for susceptibility to paraphilia of delayed onset. A possible connection between early brain trauma and later onset of paraphilia is mostly not looked for and not diagnosed.

Mental Retardation. This is not a syndrome but a symptom of many different syndromes none of which is specifically associated with susceptibility to paraphilia. Paraphilias occur sporadically within a population of the mentally retarded, and quite often in response to institutionalized neglect and abuse of the expression of sexuality among the retarded.

Kaspar Hauser Syndrome (KHS). This is a type of statural dwarfism named for the retrospectively diagnosed, first known case of mental, statural, and pubertal developmental retardation as a sequel to abusive cruelty, deprivation, and neglect (Money, 1992). To thwart his claim to a princely throne, Kaspar Hauser had been confined alone in a dungeon from early childhood until his release at age seventeen, in 1828, in Nuremburg, Germany. KHS is the specific abuse and neglect variant of the type of dwarfism generically known as psychosocial dwarfism to signify that, although it resembles hypopituitary dwarfism with chronic and unremitting growth hormone deficiency, it is not chronic, but reversible by the simple expedient of a change of domicile. Following rescue, pituitary growth hormone secretion is restored, and catchup growth begins. The longer the prerescue period, the larger the permanent proportionate failure of statural (measured as Height Quotient or HQ), intellectual (IQ) and social (SQ) catchup growth. The deficit in social growth includes sexological growth and maturation of which the outcome is a susceptibility to hypophilic anhedonia in adolescence and adulthood, and also to paraphilia (Money et al., 1990).

Obsessive-Compulsive Disorder (OCD). Tourette syndrome is an example of OCD that is characterized by acts or automatisms repeated over and over, exactly replicated, without alteration. Some may involve the genitals or have sexual connotation. Those that are vocal may be sexual expletives or exclamations forbidden in polite company. Obsessive-compulsive repetition and sameness have been known to occur concurrently with paraphilia, though rarely so. It was a component of multiple pathology in one particular case of epilepsy and pedophilia. The patient would have a rage attack if he detected that household objects were out of place, for example, if an ash tray, having been emptied, was not replaced in exactly its correct position. In its unyielding fixity, this kind of ritual sameness differs from paraphilic ritualism. Paraphilic rituals are more flexible, and admit considerably more variation of detail from one episode to the next. The episodes are the entities that are obsessively repeated, over and over again in paraphilia.

OCD encompasses also obsessionally reiterative thoughts and ruminations that are unremitting. Their subject matter is widely varied in content, but is typically about something that in everyday conversation would be considered blasphemous, sinful, indecent, or immoral. That, of course, includes sexual thoughts and ruminations. For example, a woman patient with a diagnosis of OCD and also of anorexia nervosa, after much procrastination, was able to disclose that she was stricken with an obsessionally reiterative rumination of fucking Jesus Christ. The very idea was anathema to her and completely contrary to her religious upbringing. It was not related to sexuoerotic arousal, but rather the contrary, which is what distinguishes sexual obsessionalism, if it occurs in OCD, from the repetitiveness of sexual ideation and imagery that always occurs in paraphilia and always is associated with sexuoerotic arousal.

Obsessionalism of quite different type, namely obsessional hoarding, is not uncommon in paraphilia. For example, a paraphilic sadist who would hire young prostitutes for his sadistic rituals was an obsessional hoarder of huge quantities of bathroom paper and cleaning supplies, despite lack of sufficient storage space for them. They all pertained to cleaning up the mess, and maybe the blood, at the end of a sadistic session. Many paraphiles hoard vast libraries of print and electronic media material that pertain to their particular paraphilic stratagem. The hoard may be of names and addresses of fellow paraphiles and correspondents, or of photographs of every partner, systematically catalogued with biographical annotations, including name, address, and phone number, of great value to the vice police. Or the hoard may be home-made videotapes of paraphilic sessions, including those of torture and death, which are totally self-incriminating. No matter how great the risk of self-incrimination, the paraphilic hoarder cannot part with his collection.

The fact that the term *obsessionalism* can be applied to both paraphilic and obsessive-compulsive syndromes does not make the two types of syndrome identical. Their difference has significance with respect especially to pharmacologic treatment. It cannot be assumed that the same medication will be effective for both types of syndrome. A trial period of treatment is necessary.

Autonomic Instability. Knowledge of the relationship of paraphilic development to autonomic nervous system dysfunction is murky, owing largely to the logistical hurdles and costliness of prospective longitudinal follow-up studies. One example, still in need of substantiation, is that there is an increased incidence of asthmatic and other breathing problems in the infantile histories of future paraphilic self-asphyxiophiles (Money et al., 1991). The etiological connection is between early attacks of paroxysmal breathlessness and subsequent breathless orgasmic paroxysms.

Another example of paraphilically associated autonomic instability pertains to the alternation of constipation and diarrhea in the irritable bowel syndrome. The more thwarted the expression of the paraphilia, the greater the degree of constipation. An example comes from the biography of a man in his fifties with a history of compulsive cruising of men's rooms and other places of rendezvous. There he would find stand-ins, as he had done literally several thousand times, for his teenaged brothers on whom he had performed fellatio routinely in childhood, beginning at age five. Eventually, he settled down with an elderly lover who in return for financial support, required that his protegé quit cruising. Thereupon the younger man began having episodes of fecal impaction which responded to only one form of remedy: He would slip away from his downtown office to a public building where he could cruise the men's room. As soon as he was seated in a stall, and before he had the offer of another man's penis to fellate, his bowels would forcefully loosen up and empty.

It is quite possible that there are other phenomena that may have an as yet unrecognized autonomic tie-in with paraphilia. For example there is an unnamed syndrome of sneezing in response to light (Everitt, 1964), as in going from indoors into bright sunlight, and of sneezing also in response to sexuoerotic arousal. Affected individuals may also experience sleep paralysis, that is, being unable to move the limbs or the body for some time after waking from a night's sleep.

Another autonomic phenomenon that is still unrecognized in the medical literature is known in folk argot as a "piss shiver," that is a postmicturition frisson or shudder of the upper body. What relation it has to either general or paraphilic eroticism, if any, remains a complete mystery. It has been mentioned in the print and electronic media in the column, "The Straight Dope," by Cecil Adams. In the question period after Dr. Ruth Westheimer's lecture at the 1993 Milton S. Eisenhower Symposium at Johns Hopkins University a student asked for an explanation of the phenomenon. Dr. Ruth's reply was that she had never before been asked a question for which she had no answer.

Sexual Addiction. As in the sentence "Tom is addicted to alcohol," whether consuming it by mouth or as an enema, a sentence constructed with the term addicted as the predicate needs a subject and an object. He is not addicted to the physiological process of drinking fluid, but specifically to alcohol. Correspondingly, Tom cannot be addicted to the physiological process of having sex, though he might be addicted to women's clothes and wearing them while having sex, or to whips and being whipped with them while having sex, and so on. By specifying the addictive object, it is possible to construe each paraphilia as an addiction to something, though not to sex generically. The proposition that an entity named sexual addiction induces a susceptibility to paraphilia is just plain wrong. A paraphilic object is addictive when it cannot be relinquished. When it can be relinquished it is not addictive. Within the lovemap, addiction is not exclusive to paraphilia. It belongs in a normophilic lovemap also, in which case it applies to the person (who is not an object, nor an object choice!) who is one's lover or spouse, and who is the recipient of one's limerence or lovesmittenness. Being addicted to one's pairbonded lover may well be the primordial evolutionary phylism from which other addictions are derived.

Toxic Pathology. So far as is known there are no toxic substances that actually induce a susceptibility to the development of a paraphilia. Once a paraphilia exists, however, any pharmacologic substance that induces an alteration of the state of consciousness may induce also a repeat performance of the paraphilic stratagem in live action. Alcohol and marijuana have this capability, and phenobarbital and dilantin for the treatment of epilepsy may have it also. Each of these substances has been implicated as a factor in cases of paraphilic relapse during the course of follow-up while under hormonal treatment (see below) with Depo-Provera (Money et al., 1975).

Temporal Lobe Epilepsy. Some paraphilic people have epilepsy verifiable clinically and by brain wave (EEG) and brain imaging tests. It may be only by coincidence that the two conditions, epilepsy and paraphilia occur together, or it may be that epilepsy increases susceptibility to paraphilia. As yet, there is no answer one way or the other. Another possibility is that epilepsy without paraphilia, and paraphilia without epilepsy share something in common. More specifically, the shared commonality is between paraphilia and temporal lobe or limbic system epilepsy, which is also known as *psychomotor epilepsy*. There are no convulsions in temporal lobe seizures as there are in grand mal seizures, and there is no loss of consciousness. There is, however, an altered state of consciousness. Upon recovery, the person has serious difficulty in recognizing that the person who did and said things in the altered state of consciousness was not someone else other than his/her own self.

People with a sexological history in which paraphilic episodes or attacks are accompanied by an altered state of consciousness do not have a name for what happens to them. They have to find words of their own to describe it, which they do in response to open-ended, nonjudgmental inquiry, though not to forced-answer interrogation. For example, a serial rapist and lust murderer (Money, 1990c) said it was like being on automatic pilot when he raped and murdered, and only with outside intervention could automatic be switched off. Others have used expressions like, "When I realized where I was . . ." or, "After that, I wasn't in a daze any more . . ."

The most appropriate term for the paraphilic altered state of consciousness is fugue, or fugue state (from Latin, *fugue*, flight; or in music a fugue), a term borrowed from non-Freudian French psychiatry. It signifies that part of oneself breaks away and takes flight on its own. This process is also known as dissociation. The syndrome of dual or multiple personality is attributed to dissociation. One of the two or more dissociated personalities may happen to be a paraphilic one, but not invariably so. The proximity of paraphilia and dual personality is apparent when a paraphilic person has two names, like Robert and Robbie. Robert is church-going, a brilliant scholar, captain of the high school football team, and the very epitome of idealized masculinized orthodoxy. Robbie is a self-defined deviant, a cross-dressing asphyxiophile, in the closet. His paraphilia remained unknown to classmates or family until the morning when the janitor found his self-strangulated corpse, dressed in semen-stained women's lingerie, in the locker room of the school gymnasium. The coroner's verdict was autoerotic death from self-asphyxiation.

Those who live in close enough proximity to a paraphile who is subject to fugue states may become attuned to the signs of an attack. The eyes take on a glazed stare. The attention becomes fixed and arbitrarily responsive. The hands and the voice tremble. The gait is shaky. The face is flushed, the heart racing, and the lungs out of breath. The mouth is dry, the palms sweaty, and the skin goose-pimpled. Questions about what is happening do not get answered until the attack has subsided.

Antiandrogenic Treatment

THOUGH THE LOGIC is faulty, people have rationalized that, since testosterone, the male sex hormone, has a higher level of concentration in males than in females, and since males allegedly have a higher level of sexual aggression than females do, then the higher the level of aggression, the higher the level of testosterone. This line of reasoning has not been confirmed, even in the paraphilias of violent rape (raptophilia) and lust murder (erotophonophilia). On the contrary, according to the present state of empirical knowledge, there is no direct correlation between any aspect of paraphilia in the lovemap and the steroid hormones secreted from the gonads, namely testosterone from the testes and estrogen and progesterone from the ovaries. At first glance, it appears therefore, to be enigmatic that two progesterone-like, antiandrogenic steroidal hormones, known as progestins, should have been the first synthetic pharmaceutical products discovered to be successful in the treatment of paraphilic disorders (Money, 1968; 1970c; 1987). Resolution of the enigma lies in the hypothesis that, in the brain's governance of sexuoeroticism, steroidal sex hormones play a minor but important role in collaboration with other sexual neurochemistries, still to be identified. Steroidal molecules could either augment or inhibit the uptake of other molecules at cell receptor sites in the sexual brain.

One of the two antiandrogenic progestins is cyproterone acetate, trade named Androcur. It is manufactured in Germany and has not been released by the FDA (Food and Drug Administration) for use in the United States. The other is medroxyprogesterone acetate (MPA), manufactured in the U.S. as Depo-Provera, and available for treatment of paraphilia. Both of these hormones also are long-acting and reversible birth control hormones in males and females. They also suppress the secretion of estrogen and androgen, but by different pathways. Androcur does so by inhibiting an enzyme prerequisite to the synthesis of steroids in the gonads and adrenocortices. MPA does so by suppressing release of pituitary gonadotropic hormones, LH (luteinizing hormone) and FSH (follicle stimulating hormone). Without a supply of LH and FSH, the ovaries and testes cannot make their own hormones.

Both progestins, MPA and Androcur, lower the blood level of circulating testosterone to a prepubertal level, which lowers the urgency of the subjective feeling of being sexually driven. In males, so long as treatment continues, it also reduces the frequency of erection and ejaculation.

MPA also lowers the urgency and the frequency of sexuoerotic imagery and ideation in fantasies and dreams, and thus contributes to greater sexual self-governance in cases of paraphilia. The pathway of this second MPA effect bypasses the testes and begins within the brain where, in sufficient dosage, progesterone has been found to act briefly as an anesthetic. MPA reaches the brain rapidly after being intramuscularly injected. In male monkeys, in as short a time as fifteen minutes following injection, molecules of MPA were found to have been taken up by receptors attached to neurons in sexual nuclei of the preoptic area of the anterior hypothalamus (Rees et al., 1986; Michael and Zumpe, 1993). In animals, this area has been shown to be associated with governance of the behavior of mating, whereas more posteriorly lies the region associated with hypothalamic regulation of the pituitary gland and the hormones of mating and fertility.

Although MPA has seldom been offered to female paraphiles, preliminary evidence indicates that it may help them, too. The level of testosterone in the normal female is very low in comparison with the male, but sufficient to qualify it as the libido hormone, so-called, for women (Money, 1961b; Sherwin, 1988). By reducing even a low level of testosterone still lower, MPA may have the same effect as in male paraphiles, as well as having the same effect on the female as the male hypothalamus.

The history of treatment for pubertal and adolescent youths with a damaged lovemap, even a lovemap that has been severely mutilated, is that hormonal treatment has for the most part been bureaucratically withheld in psychiatry. There is no sound rationale for this practice. General practitioners have generally been more humane in not withholding treatment.

Treatment with MPA under ideal circumstances includes adjunctive sexological counseling of the patient, both alone, and in sessions with the partner. The value of group therapy is arguable. So also is the value of behavior modification therapy, cognitive-behavioral therapy, or rational-emotive therapy. Incarceration as therapy is ineffectual. By reason of being sex segregated, incarceration prevents a therapeutic excursion into a nonparaphilic heterosexual relationship.

With a combination of MPA treatment and sexological counseling together with the partner, remission is not guaranteed, although it has proved possible and has been long lasting. However, maintenance follow-up is virtually imperative to prevent a relapse, and to take advantage of new or alternative medications, as they become available, for example, Prozac or other SSRIs (selective serotonin reuptake inhibitors), lithium, or BuSpar (buspirone hydrochloride) (Federoff, 1995), and Zoladex (goserelin acetate, a synthetic decapeptide analogue and agonist of GnRH) (Reid, 1997).

The Quandary of Prevention

IT REQUIRES NO more than a fleeting moment of thought given to the HIV/AIDS epidemic to arrive at the conclusion that, whereas for those already infected, cure surpasses prevention, for those who remain uninfected, prevention surpasses cure. The way to prevent or stop the spread of an epidemic is to eliminate its source, until there are no new victims to be cured. That is how, with the technology of vaccination, small pox was eliminated from the face of the earth (Fenner, 1993).

The logic of prevention by elimination is readily recognizable when the interval between exposure to the epidemic and becoming ill from it is brief and many times multiplied in an entire population. The longer the interval, and the fewer the victims, the easier it is to overlook or deny a cause and effect connection. That is what happened at the outset of the HIV/AIDS epidemic. The easiest denial of all is when the interval between cause and effect extends from one generation to the next. Nonetheless, epidemiologists have become accustomed to waiting a whole generation for the delayed onset of the symptoms of hereditary syndromes. That is precisely what happens in, for example, Huntington's disease, and in other genealogically occurring diseases and deficiencies.

Another example of a slow-moving, transgenerational epidemic still exists in central equatorial Africa where, far from the sea, there is a deficiency in dietary iodine. Iodine is an essential element in the synthesis of thyroid hormone. Some iodine deprived babies of each generation rapidly develop the early physical and mental growth retardation of cretinism (hypothyroidism). Others succumb at a later age and develop a hypothyroid goiter. Villagers do not recognize a connection between the symptoms and iodine deficiency in the diet. So the hypothyroid epidemic continues from one generation to the next, until iodized salt in the diet brings it to an end (Thilly et al., 1977).

Yet another example of a transgenerational, slow-moving epidemic, is one that formerly affected the tribal Fore people of the Eastern Highlands of Papua New Guinea. Its mystery was solved by D. Carleton Gajdusek, for which he won a Nobel prize (Gajdusek, 1977). His genius was to discover that the Fore people were, in a quite literal sense, eating themselves to extinction. The epidemiological culprit proved to be the kuru virus, an insidiously slow acting virus that destroys the brain and is uniformly fatal. The mystery of the method of viral infection was solved when it was traced to a funerary ritual. To ensure the benevolence of the spirit of a dead villager, some of the women and children among the mourners would ceremonially eat a small portion of the corpse's kuru infected brain. After this funerary ritual was discontinued, the epidemic came to an end.

A transgenerational epidemic has such a protracted rate of diffusion that it may escape being recognized for what it is, namely, pathology transmitted successively and with an exponential increase in prevalence from generation to generation.

It is usual to think of an epidemic being spread rapidly by a microorganism accommodated in a host vector that delivers it to the victim, as when a mosquito carries the protozoan malarial parasite and delivers it to a human being while sucking his/her blood.

The host vector and the victim both may be human beings. This is the case when a person with AIDS delivers the HIV/AIDS virus alive in a body fluid, notably a sexual fluid or blood, into one of the body cavities or blood vessels of another person.

Like HIV, kuru is an example of a viral epidemic spread by direct person-to-person transfer of the pathogen. Person-to-person transfer is also involved in the example of dietetic thyroid deficiency, although in this case, the pathogen is not a microorganism but a deficiency, namely of dietary iodine. In a third example of person-to-person spread of an epidemic, the pathogen is neither a microorganism nor a deficiency, but a pathogenic doctrine or dogma.

Hitler's Holocaust doctrine was pathogenic. The Aztec doctrine of mass human sacrifice was pathogenic. The Inquisition's doctrine of witchcraft and demon possession was pathogenic. Tribal New Guinean head hunting doctrine was pathogenic. Tribal African doctrine of female genital mutilation was and still is pathogenic, and correspondingly American contemporary medical doctrine of neonatal male circumcision.

Judging by the widespread extent of its failures, contemporary American cultural ideology of sexual health in childhood is, to a significant degree, also pathogenic. Parents, teachers, preachers, politicians, and others in authority whose own sexological childhood was marred by doctrinary pathogenicity, relay the same pathogenicity to children, their own and others, generation after generation. As do all slow moving transgenerational epidemics, the epidemic of sexual pathology maintains itself and grows exponentially in the absence of public health intervention.

It could be that the persistence of doctrinary pathogenicity in matters of the sexology of childhood is a residual of the ideological pathology of the Inquisition which has left a residual imprint in the folk memory. In this imprint sex connects with danger, panic, and death. When the Inquisition was at its height, from the fourteenth to the eighteenth century, treason and/or heresy were attributed to demon possession, satanic sexual practices, and witchcraft. More women than men were victims. By the hundreds of thousands, if not millions, women were tortured to make a false confession of cohabiting while asleep with the devil or one of his demons, for which they were condemned to be burned alive at the stake as witches. Males convicted of sodomy were either burned or hanged.

For victims of the Inquisition there is still no holocaust memorial. The Church has never renounced the Inquisition and its repulsive hideosity as an epidemic of mass sadism. The evil of sex still remains entrenched, albeit equivocally, in the public mind. Moreover, as an underlying assumption, the equation of sex and evil survives in contemporary Vatican and fundamentalist antisexualism, and in secular antisexualism also.

The time has come, and is long overdue, for society to reinvestigate the extent to which it is the victim of a transgenerational epidemic of doctrinary antisexualism, and the extent to which its policies are paradoxically increasing instead of decreasing the prevalence and rate of clinical and criminal sexopathology.

Criminologically, the sexual pathologies that most terrorize society are the paraphilias of predatory abduction, assault, torture, and lust murder. In the criminal code these are augmented by the addition of exhibitionism, peeping-Tomism, obscene telephone calling, frotteurism, stalking, and pedophilia, all six of which, although predominantly nonviolent, may be resented as an invasion of privacy, and feared as projecting a threat of subsequent violence.

Reflexively, the societal response to these paraphilias is criminological: arrest, trial, imprisonment, and possibly the death penalty. The evidence of centuries is that criminalization has been singularly ineffectual in the prevention of paraphilic sexual disorders. Generation by generation they continue to proliferate. In addition, criminalization has been singularly ineffectual as a cure for individual paraphiles. In fact it is as ineffectual as putting people in prison as a cure for epilepsy.

Imprisonment combined with pharmacological treatment and/or talking treatment may be ameliorative, but it offers no permanent guarantee against the occurrence of relapse. A cure that absolutely obliterates the possibility of a paraphilic relapse would increase societal safety, but it would not halt the danger of first offenses. For society's maximum protection from paraphilias, it is absolutely essential to pursue the search for an epidemiological method of eradicating paraphilias, so that all boys and girls would be able to grow up as protected from developing a paraphilia as they are today protected from developing smallpox or poliomyelitis. In the meantime, the communities in which most children grow up will produce, in their annual pubertal crop, some dangerous preparaphilic or paraphilic offenders. Self-protection, to the extent that it is possible, entails recognition of and avoidancy of dangerous paraphilias.

Recognition and Self-Protection

FOR SOME OF the dangers and natural disasters of life on this planet, there is no protection. Likewise, there is no precaution that offers utterly safe protection against the harm and injury inflicted by some people on others. Nonetheless, forewarned is forearmed, at least to a certain extent. To minimize the risk of exposure to danger, however, one first must know explicitly and in detail what the danger is. To avoid it, one first must recognize it.

The safety and protection of children against the dangers of sex is a very touchy subject in the sexosophy and sex education of the 1990s, as it has been for all of the twentieth century, and longer. On the one hand the people want sexual safety for their young. On the other hand, they are stricken sexually mute by the social contagion doctrine that permeates folk sexology and declares of the young that whatever they hear or see sexually they inexorably put into practice. The outcome is, if not total mutism and postponement, then evasion, euphemism, and moralism. Thus, although a community perceives itself endangered by the spread of HIV/AIDS, it is immobilized and unable to lift its sanctions against and censorship of explicit and detailed description and depiction of the genital organs and sexual intercourse. Putting a condom on a banana is not a demonstration of safe sex, but of how to put a condom on a solid three-dimensional object that has none of the propensity of a penis to lose maybe some degree of its stiffness when a condom is being unrolled on it. Safe sex is not only wearing a condom, it is the entire repertory of safe sex behavior either solo or in couple interaction. In couples, it may stop short of, or culminate in penetrative genital action, with or without orgasm.

Depicting the repertory of safe sex, with live actors performing on videotape, is condemned as pornography by adults in large number who are shackled to the misconceptions of folk sexology. Without live performers, however, the pedagogy of safe sex is as ineffectually silly as the demonstration of self-examination for breast cancer using match stick figures. It transmits sexological illiteracy from one generation to the next.

Sexologically illiterate pubertal and adolescent youth cannot logically be expected to invent safe sex, each for themselves. Without explicit knowledge of the step-by-step practices of safe sex, they have no criterion standard by which to recognize and avoid unsafe sex. The penalties of not recognizing and avoiding exposure to sexually transmitted diseases (STD) are severe, as severe as the death penalty in the case of HIV/AIDS.

Sexological illiteracy in adolescence does not alone account for failure to obtain and use contraception to protect oneself against ill-timed pregnancy and parenthood. Sexologically literate adolescents may play the same roulette wheel as sexologically illiterate adolescents do, allowing chance to make the decision for pregnancy or no pregnancy. Full sexological literacy on the pros and cons of the age of first pregnancy is, however, not easy for an adolescent to obtain. Here again, as with STDs, the two generations are under societal communicational constraints to avoid detailed disclosures about eroticism, falling in love, and the practicalities of foreplay, coitus, and orgasm. Those of the older generation who disobey the constraints are themselves in danger of being accused of obscenity, child abuse, harassment, or contributing to the delinquency of a minor. The easy way out is to advocate abstinence and "just say no," and to deprive youth of the knowledge it needs to recognize what to look for and what to avoid in a sexuoerotic relationship, and when to take action self-protectively.

In matters of sexuoerotic compatibility, members of not only the adolescent generation, but also the generation of their elders, are jointly the victims of another pathogenic doctrine of folk sexology, namely, the personal choice of and responsibility for one's own behavior, sexual or otherwise. According to this doctrine, no other explanation of sexuoerotic compatibility or incompatibility is needed: voluntary choice explains everything, and the search for a scientific explanation is superfluous. The outcome of this antiscientific doctrine is that there is no satisfactory, sexologically scientific explanation of sexuoerotic compatibility and incompatibility. The adult generation lacks the scientific knowledge that the adolescent generation needs so as to predict and maintain compatibility.

The alternative is adversarialism. He blames her and she blames him for not changing. An incompatible relationship escalates to a feuding one, resisting arbitration, and subject to punitive retaliation and revenge, including murder and suicide.

The legacy of scientific sexological ignorance on how to recognize and protect oneself against sexual incompatibility is surpassed by ignorance of how to avoid becoming entangled with paraphilic sex offenders. This is a legacy of ignorance that affects juveniles and adolescents as well as adults. It is not being redressed, as would be logical, by investment in scientific sexological research. Instead it is being dealt with criminologically, by an escalation of prison sentences. Detention and punishment of the members of one generation of paraphilic sex offenders does not, however, deter the development from early childhood onward, of a new crop of sex offending paraphiles in each succeeding generation.

Children and teenagers are in double jeopardy from paraphilias. First is the jeopardy of information withheld on the premise that seeing or hearing of a paraphilia is followed by experimenting with it. Second is the jeopardy of an undersupply of specialists in the sexology of paraphilia who are able to be scientifically impartial and nonjudgmental as instructors of the teachers of the young. One outcome of this double jeopardy has been the development of a syllabus that ostensibly protects young children from pedophilia and incest by mawkishly teaching about private parts, and good touch and bad touch. Explicit mention of the sex organs by name is avoided. So also is explicit illustration or demonstration of the difference between good and bad touch. One possible consequence is that a preschooler can be maneuvered into implicating a father or grandfather for bad touch when what he did was to hug her, or dry her after a bath. He is then reported to the child advocacy police, and may be arrested.

To counteract the destructive family and personal outcome of a child's false accusation of sexual abuse, all children need explicit information of how traumatizing an investigation can be for them. They may be forcibly relocated in a foster home for months or years. With so-called anatomically correct dolls, and under the pressure of suggestion or hypnosis, they are coercively interrogated until they confirm or confabulate false testimony. In the extreme instance, children have been coerced into confabulating testimony of victimization in satanic cults. What they confabulate qualifies as pure pseudologia fantastica. As in brainwashing, the fantastic logic of confabulation becomes grafted into the child's biography. It redefines the child's identity as that of a victim. This fiction must be forever maintained with more confabulation. If its maintenance requires assistance of psychotherapy or group therapy to avert psychiatric havoc, then the victimhood of the individual is said to be iatrogenic (produced by treatment) and nosocomial (produced by procedures performed in a clinic or hospital).

In cases where testimony is not false, the trauma of the criminal court proceedings may, in the opinion of some participants and observers, exceed the trauma of the sexual experience. The sexual experience may, like statutory rape, be legally an offense but not personally offensive. The legal age of consent may be the critical issue, and it varies according to time and place. Few American adolescents realize that they are legally defined as children until the age of eighteen, and that having sex at age eighteen with a lover aged seventeen could lead to a charge of sexual child abuse.

It is commonly assumed that noncoercive pedophilia inexorably degenerates into coercive abuse, although that is not so. Nonetheless, the sporadic combination of pedophilia with capture, abduction, violence, and killing is all the more terrifying insofar as, like a terrorist ambush, there may be no protection against it. Therefore, it is obligatory to be entirely explicit in providing information to young people on the difference between coercive and noncoercive pedophilia. Knowledgeably informed, it is possible for a juvenile to recognize a noncoercive pedophile, and likewise for an adolescent to recognize a noncoercive ephebophile, and to exercise the option of engaging or not engaging in a relationship. This is an option that does not exist, legally, for minors who live in jurisdictions where the sexual activities of pedophiles or ephebophiles are classified in the criminal code as crimes, irrespective of informed consent.

Juvenile vs. Juvenile

PARAPHILIC PATHOLOGY in the lovemap has its roots in prepubertal childhood; and it may begin to manifest itself in prototypal form as pathology of sexual rehearsal play in the late juvenile or early pubertal years. In the dominance hierarchy of childhood, the older and larger dominate the younger and the smaller, either coopting or coercing them. The less dominant may have no hope of escape and self-protection without appealing to a more powerful authority for help. Hence the necessity of having help available and of being able to talk explicitly about what has happened. This requires that the younger person already has the explicit vocabulary and sexual knowledge to be able to talk explicitly. Without a common language and the requisite degree of sexual emancipation to be able to use it, the most likely outcome is elective mutism, that is, saying nothing, and therefore getting no help.

It is necessary that the young person seeking help has a guarantee ahead of time that the helper will be an ally who can be trusted and not someone who will brush off the complaint as inconsequential, nor ridicule or chastize the complainant, nor reverse the blame. When the latter happens, it may be part of a coverup which may itself signify that the principle of pathological collusionism is surreptitiously at work.

In childhood as well as adolescence and adulthood, violence and destruction are endemic in the human species, and are also intrinsic to self-protection on some occasions. They are also subject to various inherent ethological constraints that govern both when to begin and when to desist. There is no unitary explanation of what is responsible for the malfunctioning of those constraints in childhood. The possibilities range from a chromosomal error, as in the 47,XYY syndrome to abusive cruelty and neglect in infancy and childhood. They include temporal lobe epileptic rage attacks. They also include genomically coded enzymatic defects that dysregulate behavior, as in the recent discovery, already mentioned (Nelson et al., 1995), that knockout mice genetically engineered to be deprived of the gene that synthesizes nNO (neuronal nitric oxide) are deprived also of recognizing when to stop attacking and when to cease copulating.

Children who sexually violate other children too young and too small to avoid them and protect themselves have, with surprising frequency, themselves had a history of sexual violation, and of exposure to pathological relationships in the homes, foster homes, institutions or, in the case of abandoned children, the streets where they have lived. This sorry state of affairs is exemplified in the data from the public record, courtesy of Dr. L.C. Miccio-Fonseca, in the case of Lisa and Jill, as follows.

There are two protagonists in this childhood drama, Lisa aged six, and Jill aged thirteen and a half. Lisa lives with her parents. She and her older brother are dropped off at her grandparents' home for daycare while her parents work. Jill is a member of the grandparental household. One morning when Jill is scheduled to do the childcare, Lisa is in tears. She begs her mother not to leave her. She tells her mother that Jill hurts her: she puts her fingers in her private parts and a pencil up her poop hole. The brother says he doesn't know anything about it, and that Jill hasn't done anything to him. The mother calls the child sexual abuse authority which requires a medical examination. The examiner reports some redness of the genitalia, and maybe a pressure injury of the hymen. Jill maintains that she is being blamed for something she never did.

Jill has lived in the custody of her paternal grandparents since the age of eighteen months, ever since she was diagnosed as having gonorrhea in the anal region, possibly from interfemoral intercourse. Two of Jill's mother's teenaged brothers were accused. Now in their thirties, they are both serving sentences, convicted of the murder of one of their sister's female acquaintances, allegedly in retribution for cheating on her boyfriend. Their sister, Jill's mother, is also in prison, convicted as an accomplice.

Jill's father no longer lives where Jill does, at his parent's home. He too is in prison, convicted for receiving stolen jewelry. He was sixteen years old when Jill was born, and her mother was fifteen. His parents disapproved of his being the father of Jill, as Jill bore the mixed black, white, and Mexican Indian characteristics of her mother, whom they regarded disparagingly as a mulatto. Their own genealogy was white, exclusively. They bitterly disliked being investigated and interviewed.

At age thirteen and a half, Jill has begun having menstrual periods, and has begun having a sex life. She was not evasive in responding to a sentence completion test (Miccio-Fonseca, 1996). She indicated that she's had sexual intercourse with four boyfriends, that she gave one of them a "tonsil breaker" (oral sex), in a jacuzzi, and once gave a boy a "hummer" (love bite). It was very painful when she once had sex while "on my period."

The mulatto factor, together with the history of gonorrhea at age eighteen months, may be keys to Jill's biography as a sex offender. She knows that being a mulatto is a kind of impurity and that having a history of infantile gonorrhea increases the impurity. In the irrational magic of psychodynamic logic, impurity shared is impurity diluted. Lisa, Jill's cousin, is a female like herself, but unlike her has the privilege of being all white in a mulatto prejudiced family. Jill's invasion of Lisa's genitalia symbolically deprived the younger cousin of some of her purity and privilege. It may have symbolized ambiguity about lesbianism also, but that has not yet revealed itself.

Jill's fate is to be processed through the juvenile justice system and probably to be sent to a euphemistically named residential treatment facility for juvenile offenders. The prognosis is guarded, and contingent on spontaneous remission more than the efficacy of today's menu of treatments.

The line of least resistance for Lisa's parents will be to keep her and Jill permanently separated. That will mean that the two girls will not be able to arrive at a mutual reconciliation. Moreover, if Lisa is processed through a victimology center, then there is the peril of her developing the mentality of chronic victimhood.

The case of Lisa and Jill closes the circle that began in chapter 1 with ideology and history, and concludes with this example in chapter 17 of how society's faulty ideology today fails the individual. That failure in turn reinforces society's faulty ideology. Thus, this case is a bellwether of sexological illiteracy in search of sexological literacy and with it the enlightenment that may be expected from a genuinely scientific and developmental sexology in the future.

Appendix 1

The Skoptic Syndrome

Case Report

The clinical material on which this report is based comprises a typed and unsolicited biographical letter received in the mail and, as a sequel to it, by request, photographs of the genitalia and an expanded biographical statement, handwritten, part of which overlapped the contents of the letter. The letter was addressed to the present author and is here reproduced with the signed consent of its writer who elected to remain incognito.

Recently, on the advice of a friend, I obtained your book, *Man and Woman, Boy and Girl* (Money and Ehrhardt, 1972), which I read with more than passing interest. I have an unusual psychological and medical history that relates to the issue of gender identity, and I am writing this in the hope of finding out more information, if any is available, on cases like mine.

Gender-wise, I am a male and during childhood I generally accepted and identified with being masculine though I disparaged the aggressiveness of many of the other boys and sometimes found myself thinking that my personality seemed more feminine than masculine. Moreover, I was never comfortable with the anatomical characteristics that define one's gender. When at the age of six I discovered that I had testicles, I was unhappy because pinching them even lightly caused a surprising amount of pain. I disliked the penis and remember being acutely embarrassed when I had to undress and see others undress in a swimming pool dressing room. Both the male and female genital orifices were a cause of shame and revulsion. At the age of seven, I had the first erection that I can remember. When it happened I was thinking how disgustingly fat one girl in my class at school was. Generally I disliked having an erection and always associated it with some cause of disgust. When I was a little older, I found that older boys were extremely attracted by the female anatomy and liked to ogle pictures of it that I found revolting. This shocking discovery and others of similar nature made me wonder how the world of sexuality I was beginning to learn about could possibly be appropriate for me. Increasingly I turned against it as childhood ran its course.

In puberty I was horrified to discover that the lusts I found so disconcerting in others had now become my own. I was a heterosexual male, aroused by female nudity, though the old revulsions persisted. The orgasm, which I discovered through masturbation, was immensely pleasurable but utterly shattering and devastating, an annihilation of identity and after it was over, a total desecration of the self-image. I detested it and the addictive drive that erupted frequently in all-but uncontrollable behavior to bring it about. I determined to eradicate sexuality from my life. With an effort of will I was able to stop masturbating but, while essentially I remained continent through my teenage years, I despised the self-repression needed to eliminate the unwanted behavior. I considered my desires a disease and longed for a return to the much more favorable emotional climate I had enjoyed prior to puberty. I regarded the pressures of others to make me "normal" as a threat and concealed my feelings behind a facade of shyness, indifference or even humor. In particular I considered it necessary to defend myself against well-meaning adults such as parents and counselors who would have liked to see me participate in the usual social events of adolescence such as dances, parties, and dates. Generally I affected an unobtrusive but determined avoidance.

In the course of my education I studied biology and began to learn about the effects of various glands and secretions on human psychology and physiology. I read about the effects of castration, that it reduced or eliminated the sex drive I found so oppressive, and decided I wanted this operation done. But it seemed impossible to approach the medical and psychiatric professions on a matter on which I felt they would be so negative. I had never heard of emasculation being performed at the request of a patient, and thought it unlikely that I could obtain satisfaction.

By now it was the mid-1960s and I was in college. Others were astonished at my lack of the usual social and sexual concerns and at what they regard as strange, warped obsessions. They urged me to seek psychiatric help. Instead what I did was to become involved in secret acts of self-mutilation. At first these were very minor, burning the frenulum of the penis with a match or scratching it lightly with a knife, for instance. Then I became bolder. In September 1966, I removed the frenulum with a pocket knife and after this the attempts to alter the genital apparatus became more frequent and more serious. There were many blunders as the process was slowed by pain and ignorance. But by 1969 I had managed to remove both testicles. I never once sought the aid of a doctor in this because, having once committed myself, I feared the consequences of disclosure of my as yet unfinished operation more than I valued any putative benefits. (Among the fears was that I would be prevented, forcibly if necessary, from completing the operation and made to develop "normally.") I was never caught in the act of mutilation though there were near misses, and even now there are few who know about these acts even among my close friends and relatives. Generally the operations were performed in the rest rooms of the college dormitory where I lived, and without anesthesia other than sometimes ice or Alka-Seltzer. As implements I used a pocket knife and scalpels made from razor blades; I became expert at cutting razor blades into desired shapes with tools and in fashioning devices from them using epoxy and silicone glue. For an antiseptic I used Listerine or rubbing alcohol (and later, isopropyl alcohol).

With the removal of the testicles I expected and hoped for a substantial loss of the sex drive and a return to much more favorable emotional conditions. In fact there was some reduction in libido and potency but these changes were relatively minor. Underneath the seething madness of desire seemed as strong as ever. This I largely attributed to the remaining genital member and accordingly began to attack it with a scalpel in an effort to sever its nerves. Over several months I cut many of these, (very probably) including the dorsal nerve. This had a far more profound effect than castration, but unfortunately the change was devastating. Apparently my nervous system could not stand the shock of being deprived of the excitation of the penis, a stimulus on which it had come to depend heavily, even though I despised it. (That, at least, may be a possible explanation; or maybe it had to do with the uneven cutting of nerves or other trauma.) So at this point I experienced an almost total loss of ability to feel pleasure in any form, a terrifying feeling of cold and suffocation replacing all the more usual sensations of living. At this time I was in graduate school in Illinois, but being nearly incapacitated, I had to leave school and meanwhile I finally sought psychiatric help. This, however, proved a disappointing and humiliating failure.

Meanwhile the feeling of a need to alter my body persisted, and I performed operations to sever more nerves of the penis even while experiencing this severe emotional collapse. (Oddly, it seemed as if the nerves had been unevenly cut, the left side of the penis continuing to throb and irritate more than the right side. Essentially all the cutting I did from this point was on this left side.) By this time I had gone to the state where I now reside. Having given up on psychiatry, in late 1971 I found employment as a computer programmer at a research institution, a job that continued for several years. The last mutilation occurred in January, 1976. I was not entirely satisfied but the remaining problems seemed minor or not solvable in the way I had been attempting, so that I have never returned to this bizarre and dangerous behavior. (After all this, I can still urinate normally and retain a masculine genital appearance except for the absence of testicles. I retain some potency — a minor nuisance to me — but it is far less than I was once subject to.)

In late 1976 I reentered graduate school, this time in the local state university, where I eventually obtained a PhD in computer science. Now 38 years old, I am employed by the university doing computer-related work.

After the emotional collapse in 1969 my state of feeling underwent a slow recovery along less sexually biased lines. The improvement has continued over the years so that now I can say that life, while far from perfect, seems well worth living. (In fact it has so much potential, as I see it, that I have made arrangements to be frozen in the event of death, in case it becomes possible to revive frozen remains at some future date.) No longer do I feel consumed by unwanted passion, shackled by self-repression, or even prostrated by loss of feeling. With the cooling of unwanted feeling I no longer feel revolted by nudity or other expressions of sexuality. Though a nonparticipant myself, I accept and approve of all sexual behavior involving consenting adults, except when health is endangered. At the same time I feel that sexual abstinence is the best course for some of us to follow (perhaps only a few but not none), and in fact I prefer to be without the sex drive that caused so much difficulty and was a burden to me. But it hardly seems reasonable to have to go through the sort of trauma that has formed such a large part of my life. Surely there must be a better way.

Thus it was with a special poignancy that I noted, on reading your book, that drugs for suppressing sex drive like medroxprogesterone acetate and cyproterone acetate were available as early as 1965. This was before I had done any significant mutilation! One can speculate how my own history might have been different if I had had the appropriate contacts at that time. (But I have gained something from this long struggle, an appreciation of the value and meaning of life I would otherwise lack. One's identity is shaped, in large part, by the obstacles one has to overcome and the manner in which one overcomes them. Still I do not advocate the course I once followed, given the alternatives that appear to be available.)

You cite the example of the Skoptsi, a nineteenth-century Russian sect that practice emasculation and other sexual mutilations. I have read that there were thousands of them and that their numbers included several hundred women. And I hear rumors of people today who are taking cyproterone acetate, not as sex offenders but voluntarily, to reduce unwanted drives? I hope I have not burdened you too much with the details of my case. Any reply you can make will be appreciated.

The following material is extracted from the handwritten follow-up statement. It expands the foregoing biography.

I WAS PLAGUED by frequent bed-wetting up to the age of ten. All during childhood I was strongly repelled by nudity, particularly exposure of the genitals, and the aversion persisted and clashed with the sex drive that erupted with such force in puberty. At the same time I experienced some rather powerful erotic stimulation in childhood. I have already referred to the close relationship with my mother, who in fact liked to cuddle and fondle all her children (I was the oldest of four) and always seemed to have enough affection for everyone. I greatly enjoyed the attention I received, that is, as long as the genitals did not appear to be specifically involved, as they normally were not.

But there was one curious incident at about the age of five that did clearly involve the genitals and produced an ultimately negative reaction. I had a rash in the groin for which my mother administered calamine lotion with her hands. This, I noted, produced a pleasurable feeling and I even experimented with fondling the genitals myself, which was also pleasurable though the feeling was less intense. But on the last occasion that the lotion was administered, I realized my mother was overdoing it and received the distinct impression (no doubt correct) that she was aware of the pleasure and was trying to intensify it. This I found acutely embarrassing. I gave up the fondling experiments and, I believe, repressed the notion that such actions could be pleasurable. I largely forgot this experience until puberty, nor do I remember any further encounters with direct genital stimulation from others.

But I believe that the more normal cuddling and other attentions encouraged an extreme passivity since my mother served as the active partner in these encounters. All through childhood I was repelled by the aggressiveness of many other boys and sometimes found myself thinking that I was more feminine than masculine. In adolescence, too, I was repelled by the violent intensity of my own sex drive which I found loathsome and despicable.

But, to return to childhood, one important feature was a feeling of uniqueness, of being "special." I could astonish relatives with feats of memory at age three, for example, reciting stories verbatim that they had read to me. My mother was very proud and I gloried in being "different." Later I would disparage the concern with conformity shown by most other people. The thought of becoming different from others, far from inspiring fear or revulsion, was exhilarating.

But the passive enjoyment of my differences led, I believe, to a rather extreme though furtive egotism. Secretly I was very proud of my accomplishments and could not bear the thought, for example, of being outperformed in areas of expertise by anyone my own age. Besides learning and intelligence, I considered myself exceptional in such physical traits as size, strength, and swiftness. But I was generally unsuccessful in sports because of poor coordination and dislike of team participation; this, however, was no great cause of concern. I could fight when aroused but much preferred to avoid it. I cultivated friendships with boys my age but who were generally smaller and less accomplished than I was and whom I could have dominated but instead allowed to dominate me. Thus I derived a certain pleasure from being victimized, as long as there was an escape hatch.

But there were extremes of self-degradation I could not bear the thought of, that is, anything involving the loss of self-control, since self-possession was of overriding importance. Thus I was not moved to easy tears because this was degrading loss of control, and I would resist crying with every fiber of will I possessed. For the same reason I had a horror of extreme pain. I was extremely sensitive to pain but deplored this vulnerability and sought to conquer it. Thus I became strangely fascinated by pain, at times inflicting it as a test of strength. I remember at age twelve, for example, carving my initials in my arm with a broken arrowhead I had found, and what tremendous elation I felt at having been able to carry it out. (I still have a visible scar from this.) Increasingly I was able to resist pain though it always remained a threat, and I never became a masochist in the sense of seeking physical abuse as a means of gratification. . . .

So at the tender age of thirteen, when I had not yet experienced puberty, I made the fateful decision to act, so far as possible, to exclude sex from my life. This resolution produced euphoria that lasted for days. But trouble lay just around the corner. Within months puberty struck with the force of a bomb, when I first achieved orgasm through masturbation. Again I report in detail.

I had been doing a mathematical calculation when a more immediate problem presented itself. I had gotten an enormous, pulsing erection that interfered with concentration and wouldn't go away. Lately I had had indications that a mildly pleasurable feeling might result from stimulating the penis so, with the frustration of having nothing better to do, I began bumping it rapidly with my elbow. At first there was little effect. Then came the shock wave of maddening pleasure, greater than anything I had imagined or thought possible. I repeated the action and the impact of consuming gratification was so searingly intense it was actually unbearable and I had to stop — but not for long, as an incredible craving boiled up. Over and over I repeated the stimulation, stopping when the feeling grew too intense to continue, then desperately resuming to build it up again. Finally on one frantic thrashing it reached a new crescendo and collapsed in a painful, spurting orgasm. Shaken, and finding I no longer had an erection or the desires that had just been raging, it seemed that I would never want to experiment this way again.

But a few days later I had another erection and the craving returned with overpowering force. This time the masturbation was continuous. The pleasure was even greater and more maddening than before, but there was no stopping because the feeling was never unbearable, and the orgasm was not at all painful—except on a deeper level. I now had begun to notice that girls' bodies too were powerfully sexually arousing and deplored this new, loathsome lust; there was no similar effect with boys or men. Deep-seated elements of discord began to surface.

There were four more orgasms that day and three more the next. It was a terrible, shattering pleasure, as irresistible as it was unacceptable. I hated the ferocious compulsion to repeat the experience, the frantic manipulations required to bring it about, the degrading loss of control the ecstasy imposed, the aggressive pressures of the new upwelling lust. Above all I feared the implications of this habitual abandonment of self-possession and control. Orgasm was self-annihilation, temporary to be sure, but most willfully pursued, as the end of all existence. Afterward when the madness was in temporary remission there was bitterness and remorse at having betrayed one's principles. The new purpose of life, it seemed, was genital friction. That could not be. So sexuality now was no longer merely "dirty" or "insane." It had become a threat to identity.

From this point I had the strong conviction that something was wrong with my body and this needed to be changed. I remember pulling out my newly acquired pubic hair (which looked ugly) and observing unhappily that it quickly grew back. I also had the first fantasies of self-castration, though I was not yet aware of the hormonal function of the testes in affecting sexual feeling and physiology. But their primary role, I knew, was in reproduction, and thus to me they were superfluous and even insulting . . . .

Implementation of the program to get rid of the testicles and to eradicate sexuality did not begin until he was a college student.

For a typical operation I would enter a restroom stall in the school dormitory, and close the door. After undoing my clothing I would sit on the bare porcelain of the toilet bowl to make it easier to clean up the blood, which tended to drip ubiquitously around where I was sitting. (Of course I was very careful to remove the evidence after an operation.) To reduce the reaction to pain I would proceed very slowly, forcing a scalpel or knife into and through the flesh with a light but steady pressure. I discovered I had very good tolerance for a persistent dull ache but not so much resistance to sudden, sharp jolts of pain.

As an illustration I will consider one operation in detail. It was one of the more harrowing but not, in my estimation, alone in its class. It occurred in September, 1967. The previous December, in an attempt to remove the right testicle, I had succeeded in forcing an opening in the perineum through which the testicle had protruded, so that after healing, the spermatic cord was exposed within the scrotum. (This had required several hours of slow work with a pocket knife, the operation being halted prematurely due to pain, fear, and exhaustion; the wound in the scrotum was then closed with sutures of dental floss.)

For the operation in question the objective was to sever the spermatic cord. The implements were a pocket knife and a thin sliver of razor blade containing the cutting edge. A block of ice served as an anesthetic. Pressing a fold of the scrotum containing the spermatic cord down on the ice, I then pushed the knife into the skin of the scrotum and out the other side, into the ice, so the cord was now trapped between the knife blade and a length of skin. The knife was then turned so the cutting edge rested perpendicularly on the cord, though no cutting was attempted with it. By now I had realized that razor blades, being sharper and thinner, would make far more effective tools for the purpose at hand. So next I inserted the sliver down the track made by the knife so that both ends of it also protruded from the flesh, with the cutting edge likewise directed against the cord. Then, grasping the sliver between thumb and index finger I began, very slowly and lightly, to saw back and forth. This continued for some time, but I didn't seem to make much headway. I was tired and hungry, too. I removed the razor blade. I knew that if I removed the knife too the swelling would make it impossible to reinsert it and continue where I had left off. So I left it in place, packing toilet issue around it to control the bleeding.

Then I went down to the cafeteria and had dinner. After this I came back, reinserted the razor blade, and resumed cutting. Finally I gave up with the cord not fully severed. But I learned later that I had managed to cut the testicular artery (which can normally be easily felt as a strong pulse) thereby effectively destroying the testicles. I am certain this happened after I had resumed the cutting. At a certain point I felt an unusual sharp pain followed by flooding warmth and numbness which suggested a major artery being cut. Shortly after this I removed the instruments and terminated the operation. There had not been much bleeding up to then, but soon the right chamber of the scrotum became filled with fluid under high pressure which, I surmised, was surely blood. Apparently the wounds opening into the scrotum (which actually were rather small) had clotted over quickly, preventing flow from the interior. Thinking that the blood should be drained, I forced the knife into one of the wounds and was surprised at the vigorous jet that spurted up, though it quickly died down again, which I assumed again was from clotting. Then I realized that the scrotum was confining what might otherwise be major bleeding and after this left it alone. The blood eventually hardened into a large lump which slowly disappeared over a period of weeks. (Perhaps I was very lucky that there were no further complications.) But I soon noticed that the testicle had atrophied into a small, softened lump, and I was ecstatic.

After further struggles the left testicular artery was also cut (January 1968) and the atrophied testicles were finally removed (March and April 1969). I was then twenty-two, and hoped for substantial loss of sex drive that would bring about a return to more favorable emotional conditions. In fact as a eunuch I experienced some reduction in libido and potency, but these changes were relatively minor. Underneath, the seething madness of desire seemed as strong as ever.

In 1967, prior to severing the testicular arteries, there was a bizarre resurgence of the habit of masturbation after nearly seven years' abstinence. I had long despised the self-repression necessary to prevent this activity and, with the removal of the frenulum and other self-surgery, began to hope that I might have become incapable of having an orgasm, which would have been a great relief since the self-repression would no longer be necessary. So in an effort to verify this loss of capacity I experimented with self-stimulation but unfortunately it resulted in orgasm with ejaculation though I was surprised at how weak the feeling was compared to the earlier experiences. But once started, this behavior became habitual again, though with some interludes of abstinence, so that the final break did not occur until 1970. The orgasm also greatly increased in intensity of feeling though not, I thought to the level of early puberty. I despised them as before and, moreover, deplored the fact that, in spite of the lessening of feeling, the habit was not as easy to control as before.

But on occasion I used masturbation as a sort of anesthesia, finding that an orgasm before surgery not only had a calming effect but heightened the will to proceed. This occurred, in particular, in the incident of September 1967, just described. But after this I generally preferred to do without aids of this sort as well as more usual anesthetics.

The Skoptic formula of castration to get rid of orgasm inexorably gets rid of fertility and procreation also. In this case, the formula broadened to substitute reincarnation for procreation. The man who castrated himself became an advocate of commercial cryogenics, that is of deep refrigeration of one's corpse, in anticipation of a future science of resurrection. The symbolic logic of the lovemap is, indeed, something to be marveled at.

Appendix 2

Murder, Martyrdom, and Masochism

Case Report

Although the story of Debbie Brownli is actually a sexological story of a lovemap gone awry since infancy, it was first publicized as the story of an adolescent white girl accused as an accessory to a murder. Using fictitious names, the following was taken from the public record. The girl was on trial with her white boy friend, Vic, aged sixteen and his eighteen year old Asian American buddy, Sid. Other schemes to get money for drugs having failed, Vic led the other two into a robbery without telling them that the victim would be his step-grandmother, aged fifty-five. This woman was afraid of Vic and did not want him to enter her house, but she yielded to his plea to make a phone call to an auto tow truck service. While Sid waited outside, Vic and Debbie went inside. Vic grabbed his grandmother and tried to strangle her. He kept yelling at Debbie to bring him a knife from the kitchen table. Debbie obeyed. After he began stabbing, Debbie ran out to get Sid, but it was too late. Vic had inflicted sixty one stab wounds. Sid helped the other two to ransack the house, and left with them in the victim's car.

Debbie subsequently disclosed that Vic had several times spoken of stealing money and eventually killing someone. Her response had been to attempt to make him angry with her, she said, so as to distract him from the idea of killing.

Debbie's relationship with Vic was one of fatal attraction, also known as pathological limerence. It had been incipient when, in sixth grade, she first saw his picture in the school year book, and continued for a year before she actually met him face to face.

I remember, she said, the first time he said *my name*. I'll never forget it. The first time that my shoulder touched his shoulder it was such a big deal to know that I *actually* had touched him. It seemed like I had been with him my whole life. Both of my sisters and Josephine, my best friend, told me I was the luckiest person to be with him, until they found out that he hit me, and then they told me to leave him. But I had an obsession with Vic. It's weird that I had such strong feelings. I was with him only one and a half months.

About sexual intercourse Debbie's story began as follows: When I first met him, he was really different. He was perfect. He didn't want to have sex with me at first. He sat at one end of the couch and I sat at the other end. . . . The first attempt at intercourse was like it didn't fit, but after that it was okay. However, Vic liked to play fighting games, pillow fights, wrestling, holding me down, pushing me around, slapping me, slapping my butt, and squeezing my breasts and nipples. He'd get really rough, where I'd hurt. Vic was rough about sex. One time he pierced my belly button. He used a safety pin.

About three weeks before the murder, Vic had forced me to have sex. I was at his house. He was trying to take my clothes off. He ripped the buttons off my pants. He ripped my leather belt. It wasn't a plastic belt, it was *leather.* He ripped it in half, like it was nothing. He left a big bruise. He pushed me. He threw me down and penetrated me. I gave in. I was afraid of him. One time he pushed a pillow over my head. I couldn't breath. It was scary. That happened about a week and a half before the murder. He would push me around a lot. He threatened to beat me. He threatened to kill me and the guy if I cheated on him. He even threatened to kill my mother. My mother changed the locks on her door.

Sucking my own blood, Debbie reported, is something that I like to do. I like the taste of blood, like if I cut myself, or if one of my friends does. I've sucked Vic's blood. One time he wanted me to bite his neck until I drew blood. I did it. Only one time. Vic started drinking blood. Mine first. One time when Vic's friend Sid cut himself, Vic got up, ran over and like attacked Sid because he wanted to drink his blood. I couldn't believe the way he ran over there!

Vic would bite Debbie on various parts of her body: toes, fingers, back, shoulders, breasts, vagina. He carved and tattooed with an Exacto knife. On Debbie he had tattooed a mushroom two inches in height and four inches across with the word "Fuck" over it. It was at the top of her right breast toward the midline. She acquiesced to his doing it, while he made comments like "I can't believe I'm doing this," and licked up the blood when the bleeding was too profuse.

The sadomasochism in Debbie's lovemap that resonated with sadomasochism in Vic's lovemap had a long history going back to early childhood. This history had been authenticated for Debbie by her maternal grandmother. I went to stay with her for two weeks, Debbie said, in order to get away from fighting with my mother. When she returned, Debbie was still in such a seriously disturbed and depressed state of mind that her mother took her to a local mental health facility. The clinic recommended antidepressant medication and psychotherapy, and made a notation on the girl's "peculiar interest in violence" but there was no follow through.

I was having nightmares, she said, and my grandmother told me that the horrible things I was dreaming about had actually happened to me when I was young. I've had a lot of dreams about what really did happen, all my life. I thought I made it up. When I told my grandmother, this summer, she cried in the grocery store because she had hoped I would have forgotten. I never told anyone else except my cousin about the dreams. My grandmother and my cousin talked about them with me. A lot of the information was news to me. It was shocking, but it was good to finally find out.

Child Protective Services had taken me from my mother when I was four. They said she knew all about what Pete [the mother's boyfriend at that time] was doing to me. He used to starve me. So, at my grandparents' I grabbed food and hid it and ate under the table [which is a sign of the Kaspar Hauser syndrome of child abuse dwarfism (Money, 1992a)].

The maternal grandparents had initially called Child Protective Services after seeing that four year old Debbie had bruises and pinch marks on the face and around the genitalia and inner thigh. Debbie's mother disregarded the evidence, ostensibly because she wanted Pete to marry her.

As a teenager, Debbie was able to recall that Pete used to make her stand against the wall behind the door and he would close the door over my toes, she said. He made me take showers with him. He put his penis in my mouth and peed in my mouth. He hit me and pushed me back down when I stood up. He took off my shirt and diaper and left me naked. My grandmother found me in a pool of blood that day. Pete tried to do a lot of things to me, but I was too little. He tried to have sex with me. I remember he put his fingers inside my butt and my vagina. He tried to penetrate me until I bled. Blood was smeared all over my leg, stomach, and thighs, and his penis, stomach, and thighs. He licked my vagina while I was bleeding. He did that more than one time, maybe four times. He would bite me and would draw blood. He would bite me on my vagina, my butt, inner thigh, arms, cheeks, fingers, toes, ears. He drew blood when he bit me.

Pete would tell me I was a bad girl. I always felt insecure, that I didn't deserve things like food, and that I didn't deserve to live. I don't know why. All my life I feel pain in my vagina, thighs, and stomach, and I have a headache and vomit when I wake up. I have dreams of little kids being beaten until they died.

Debbie's version of her history was corroborated in her file at Child Protective Services where she had been first seen at age two as a battered child. No effective action had been implemented, however, until at age four the child was sent to a far distant state to live with her maternal grandparents. Thereafter she did not see Pete again. When the mother regained custody of her daughter a year later, Pete was gone. However, the vacancy had already been filled by one named Alf, a friend of Debbie's mother's new boyfriend, Mike. Mike had a daughter, Marjorie, aged four, who was said to have been molested by Alf.

Debbie recalled that Alf fondled her as well as Marjorie, and that he had penetrated her digitally. He required Debbie to watch him having sexual contact with Marjorie, coercing her to fellate him, and to have anal and/or vaginal sex. Marjorie bled in her vagina, Debbie said. Alf tried to convince us it was okay, and not to tell. He got forceful by holding us down and yelling to sit down. He told me I was bad when I got up.

He would dress up in women's clothes, in a flower dress, dancing around, and showing us his penis. He made us watch while he did things to us. I can't remember. I get a really bad feeling. I told myself it didn't happen. He went to jail for three years.

Almost as an afterthought, Debbie said that Alf really, really reminds me of Vic. I thought that the first time I saw Vic.

The correct time sequence should, of course, have been that Vic reminded Debbie of Alf. The chronology is significant insofar as her seven-week infatuation with Vic began in the immediate aftermath of Debbie's two week vacation with her grandmother. From her grandmother she got the biography of her early traumatic sexual experiences with Pete and Alf confirmed as history, not fantasy.

Conquering a trauma by reliving it is a basic formula in both general and sexological psychopathology. Add to this a second basic formula, namely that of opponent-process, which in its sexological application means that trauma is converted into triumph by becoming eroticized.

Now consider the following sequence: Debbie's grandmother confirms the historical authenticity of what Debbie recalls of early sexual traumatization. Shortly thereafter she recognizes Vic as a lookalike for Alf, the successor of Pete. Vic fits perfectly into her lovemap as the person with whom to relive the early traumatization, and to triumph over it by eroticizing it. This transformation takes place with a vengeance, and Debbie becomes monomaniacally limerent or lovesick for Vic. Her sexological history has prepared her lovemap as a masochist and martyr to be a perfect reciprocal match of Vic's lovemap of sadism, sacrificial violence, and murder. That which was negative becomes positive, and the paraphilic behavior of sadomasochism is reiterated, unchanged.

When trauma is transformed from negative to positive, the polarity may be accredited to two different personages, each with its own name. Debbie had experienced this phenomenon of dissociation. She spoke of her alter ego as Charlie (spelled Tcharoli). I used to think I had another personality, a guy, she said. I dressed and walked like a guy. I didn't like girls. I acted only like a guy. Charlie is about my same age. I thought I was possessed. Josephine, my best friend, had "it" too, and his name was Charlie, too. They and two other friends had a secret adolescent language, Ibik.

Charlie would appear when I was in a bad mood, Debbie said. I'd think real bad thoughts. It would tell me to burn myself, or cut myself. I don't like remembering or saying the things it says to me. It began when I was in the seventh grade. I'd dress like a guy, guy shoes, long T-shirts, baggy pants. I never wore shorts or skirts. If I did, I'd wear them down to my feet. I was ashamed of my body.

Charlie started getting better because I didn't have thoughts of death. Charlie always wanted me to hurt myself. I'd feel bad about myself. The thoughts really, really started to get bad when I was in the eighth grade. Sometimes it feels like he was thinking for me. Like I couldn't control the thoughts. Like the burning of myself.

It was almost like Vic scared him away, she said, and was the protector. However, Vic brought out the evil side of me, she added. Charlie came out in my drawings. Drawings of people being hung, and stuff. I was always scared. The last time Charlie came out was three weeks before the murder.

When Debbie was arrested, the arresting officers were not at first sure whether they were arresting a male or female. She was tried as an adult, for murder, and sentenced to a twenty-five year prison term.

Treating the long-term effects of violent and sexual traumatization in infancy by the traumatization of long-term imprisonment in adolescence is ethically the equivalent of amputating the arms of an amputee as a treatment for having lost his legs in a car wreck. Although Americans are usually a kind-hearted and generous people, when it comes to matters of sex and the criminal justice system, they are prone to become a Tcharoli, themselves.

Glossary

abortion: the premature expulsion from uterus of the products of conception, either spontaneously (a miscarriage) or artificially induced.

abstinence (adj. *abstinent*): not partaking of something, for example, sex, meat, liquor, or smoking. Sexual abstinence is more complete than celibacy which, strictly defined, means abstaining from marriage.

acceptive phase: in a sexuoerotic relationship, the phase, following proception and preceding the possibility of conception, in which the genital organs become mutually involved in body contact, typically in genital union. *See also* conceptive phase; proceptive phase.

acme: the highest level, or climax.

acrotomophilia: the paraphilia pertaining to amputation and amputees.

Adam principle: in embryological development and subsequently, the principle that something must be added to the primary Eve (female) principle to induce the differentiation of a male.

adolescent infertility: sporadic nonovulatory menstrual cycles in girls early in adolescence, and in boys a possible brief period of orgasm prior to complete spermatogenesis.

adrenocortical gland: bilaterally, the external cortex or rind part of the adrenal gland, which is functionally independent of the interior part or medulla, and which secretes steroidal hormones including weakly active androgenic sex hormone.

Age of Enlightenment: A term used to characterize the eighteenth-century philosophic period of The Enlightenment. It was characterized by lively questioning of authority and religion, much theorizing in politics, and emphasis on empirical science.

AIS (androgen-insensitivity syndrome): a genetically induced syndrome in which the embryo begins differentiation as a male for about six weeks until masculinizing hormones first appear and are rejected by all cells of the body so that the remainder of differentiation internally and externally is toward female.

alkaloid: one of a large group of organic chemical substances extracted from plants. They are usually bitter in taste and physiologically active. Examples are: caffeine, morphine, nicotine, and strychnine.

alkyl phenol: one of a group of chemicals that are the byproduct of microbial breakdown of particular ingredients in paints, detergents, cosmetics, and herbicides. Alkyl phenols get into the food chain and mimic estrogen in animals that accumulate them.

Amazon: a legendary race of warrior women believed by the Greeks to have originated in antiquity in the region of the Caucasus. The Amazon River was so named by the Portuguese explorer, Pedro de Magalhales de Guandavo, when in 1576 he encountered a tribe of warrior women living there, in Amazonian Brazil.

amniocentesis: the surgical procedure of obtaining a sample of amniotic fluid from the pregnant uterus by means of a needle punch.

amoebic dysentery: severe diarrhea with ulceration of the bowel brought on by infection with microorganisms, chiefly, the protozoan *Entamoeba histolytica*. One route of infection is by oral-anal contact.

amphetamines: a group of related synthetic compounds (amines) that influence the sympathetic nervous system and are popularly known for their stimulant effect.

amygdala: an almond shaped body, bilaterally situated in the brain's limbic system or paleocortex, and closely connected with the hypothalamus. It is popularly known as a seat of the emotions.

amyl nitrite: a synthetic chemical that produces a rush of vasodilation and intensification of feeling when sniffed, in the form popularly known as poppers, at the moment of orgasm.

anabolic steroid: synthetic testosterone or one of its derivative steroidal hormones with muscle building (anabolic) effect, used therapeutically or in sports to boost muscular size and strength. It is prohibited in all levels of sports including major league and international competitive sports.

analgesic: a medication that has a pain relieving effect.

anatomically correct dolls: dolls manufactured with a semblance of sex organs for use in early childhood sex education and in the interrogation of infants and children by prosecutors of suspected child sexual abuse.

Androcur®: the trade name for cyproterone acetate, an antiandrogenic compound.

androgynine: manifesting masculine and feminine qualities either blended or coexistent.

androgynal: synonym for androgynine

androgyny: the state in which both masculine and feminine characteristics are merged or coexistent (from Greek, *andros*, man, and *gyne*, woman).

andromimesis: in a natal female, miming or impersonating being male.

andromimetophilia: the paraphilia of being sexuoerotically fixated on an andromimetic partner such as a preoperative transexual.

androsterone: a derivative of androgen secreted in the urine of both men and women.

anhedonia: lacking a feeling of pleasure in acts usually expected to produce pleasure and well being.

anorchia: lacking testicles.

anorexia nervosa: a syndrome of fasting and being unable to eat enough nourishment to prevent self-starvation even unto death.

antiandrogen: a pharmacologic substance that counteracts the secretion or cellular use of androgen in the body.
antibiotics: one of many pharmacologic substances like penicillin produced from a fungus or mold, that is able to destroy or inhibit the growth of disease producing microorganisms, like bacteria.
anticonvulsant: a medication used to prevent or reduce the occurrence of epileptic seizures.
aphroditic: having an aphrodisiac or sexually arousing effect.
apical: at the apex or summit.
apogametic (also apogamous): reproducing, as in the manner of some ferns and other spore bearing organisms, without male and female gametes, and therefore without fertilization.
apoptosis: programmed cell death as part of the overall program of growth and development.
apostrophize: to address someone in a rhetorical, exclamatory way.
apotemnophilia: the paraphilia pertaining to becoming an amputee.
apothegmatically: in the manner of a terse saying or pithy maxim; aphoristically.
aromatize: to convert chemically to an aromatic form, i.e., to a compound characterized by the benzene ring, as in aromatizing testosterone to estrogen.
artifactual: data introduced into a scientific investigation extraneously by the investigative procedure itself.
Aryan: the parent language of the Indo-European family of languages; hence the false idea of a superior Aryan race.
ascetic: practicing severe abstinence or austerity as self-discipline.
asphyxiophilia: the paraphilia of self-strangulation or self-suffocation.
atresia: congenital absence or closure of a normal body orifice, e.g., the vagina.
atrophy: a wasting away, shrinkage or developmental failure of a cell, tissue, or bodily organ.
attractive phase: in a sexuoerotic relationship, the preliminary phase in which the two individuals notice one another.
autoassassinophilia: the paraphilia of arranging the possibility of one's own masochistic death by murder.
autoerotic: erotic self-stimulation, as in masturbation.
autoerotic death: unplanned death as the outcome of a dangerous sexual practice like paraphilic self-strangulation (asphyxiophilia).
autonepiophilia: the paraphilia pertaining to wearing diapers; infantilism.
autonomic nervous system: that part of the nervous system, distinguished from the central nervous system, that governs the internal organs of the body and their involuntary functions.
Ayurveda: the ancient Indian system of medicine preserved in written records and still in practice today.
Bacchanalian: associated with riotous and drunken revelry, connected originally with the worship of Bacchus, the Greek and Roman god of wine.

bacterium (pl. **bacteria**): a single celled, self-reproducing microorganism of which there are many species; some induce illness and are popularly known as germs.

behavior modification: a system of treatment based chiefly on reward and/or punishment, used mostly by psychologists and their followers.

bell curve: a graph of a normal or Gaussian distribution. On paper it has the shape of a bell, tall at the center, representing average, and stretched out at the bottom right and left, representing the extremes of positive and negative, respectively.

betrothal: a pledge to marry; an engagement.

biastophilia: the paraphilia pertaining to violent rape as a form of pathology as compared with nonviolent nonconsensual coitus, date rape, or statutory rape; synonym for raptophilia.

biogenetic theory: Ernst Haeckel's nineteenth-century adaptation of Darwinian evolutionary theory to individual development, saying that "ontogeny recapitulates phylogeny," a principle that Freud incorporated into his theory of the stages of infantile sexuality.

biological clock: a phylogenetic and innate brain regulator of organismic rhythmicity on a daily, monthly, or seasonal schedule.

biopsy: a surgical procedure for taking a small sample of tissue from part of the body for use in laboratory diagnosis.

bipotential: having two possible ways of development.

bisexual: sexual reciprocality as both heterosexual and homosexual in varying degrees.

body image: the mental map of one's own body as it was, is, and should ideally be.

body schema: the neural map of one's body and its moveable parts as represented in the brain.

bonobo: a species of primate, formerly misclassified as the pygmy chimpanzee.

brain imaging: electronically obtained pictures of regions of the live brain while functioning or at rest, for example the PET (positron emission tomography) scan, the CAT (computerized axial tomography) scan, and the MRI (magnetic resonance image).

brainwash: systematically, coercively, and by means of torture, to revise established ideas and replace them with divergent and often contrary ones in a person's mind.

Brazelton scale: a scale of assessing infant development constructed by the pediatrician, T. Berry Brazelton, M.D.

breast envy: in boys, a counterpart of penis envy in girls.

butt plug: a device inserted into the anus for sexual pleasure.

Caesarian section (C-section): surgical delivery of a baby through an incision in the mother's abdominal wall, instead of by the usual vaginal route.

CAH (congenital adrenal hyperplasia): a genetically induced syndrome in which the embryo begins differentiation as a female until, in the second trimester, it is flooded with masculinizing hormone of its own making which changes the differentiation of the external sex organs towards male.

call boy: a male prostitute available by appointment.

canonical: conforming to a set of established, especially ecclesiastical, rules or laws.

carnal: belonging to the body, not spiritual, but of the flesh.

castration: surgical removal of the testicles or ovaries.

casuistic: logically deceptive, e.g. a casuistic argument.

Catch-22: a dilemma of having only two choices, neither of which offers a solution to the problem. Named from the title of Joseph Heller's novel.

catecholamine: any of various catechol derivatives which have amine substituants and possess neurotransmitter and/or hormonal activity, e.g., dopamine and epinephrine (also known as adrenalin).

Catharism: the religious teaching of the medieval Cathars, a sect persecuted for Manichean heresy by the Roman Catholic Church; also known as Albigensianism.

cauterize: in surgery, to apply burning heat by means of an electrical appliance to remove tissue or prevent bleeding.

CD-ROM (compact disk-read only memory): an optical-laser disk that stores audio or visual information for retrieval and/or replay on a computer screen.

celibacy: living under a vow not to marry, as in the celibate clergy; also used as a synonym for abstention from sexual intercourse.

cervix: the neck-like part of the uterus, which joins into the vagina.

chastity: state of being pure, virginal, and free from sexual sin; abstention from sexual intercourse; celibacy.

chorionic villus sampling (CVS): a needle-punch technique used for determining fetal sex or possible genetic defect as early as eight weeks.

chrematistophilia: the paraphilia of prearranging to be forced to pay for sex or to be robbed.

chromosome: within every cell, one of the forty-six strands (46 in humans) that carry the program of an individual's entire genetic make-up.

chronophilia: the paraphilia involving a major age discrepancy between the partners.

circumcision, female: in parts of Africa, ritual mutilation of the female genitalia in girls at around the age of seven by excision of the clitoris, labia minora, and in the Pharaonic form the labia majora also, leaving only one small hole after healing; infibulation.

circumcision, male: ritual mutilation of the penis by removal of the foreskin, in either infancy or prepuberty.

Clérambault-Kandinsky syndrome: obsessive and unrequited love sickness; erotomania.

clitoral hypertrophy: enlargement of the clitoris, usually congenital as an outcome of excessive male hormone.

clitoris (pl. **clitorides;** adj. **clitoridean**): the female genital organ that is the counterpart of the penis.
clitoromegaly: synonym for clitoral hypertrophy.
cloaca: a single orifice for sexual and excretory function, and in birds for egg-laying.
cognitional: pertaining to that which is known.
coitus: sexual intercourse; copulation.
collusional pathology: psychopathology of two or more people complementing one another.
come (coming): vernacular term meaning to have an orgasm; in males come is also the name for the ejaculate.
coming out: in contemporary gay vocabulary the term that signifies recognition of oneself as homosexual and declaring it to family, fellow workers, and friends (abbreviated from coming out of the closet).
complementation: reciprocal matching; the counterpart of identification.
compressive genitalism: nonmanual genital stimulation by rubbing and pressing.
conceptive phase: in a sexuoerotic relationship, the third and final phase which, if it occurs, is characterized by conception, pregnancy, and parenthood. It follows the proceptive and acceptive phases.
conceptus: the product of conception before it becomes an embryo.
concubine: in some societies a woman recognized not as wife but with a defined position in the man's household.
concupiscence (adj. **concupiescent**): thoughts and fantasies characterized by ardent desire, especially as applied to sex and lust.
condom: a contraceptive or prophylactic sheath that can be worn on the penis during sexual intercourse.
continent: self-restraint; withholding ejaculation; complete sexual abstinence.
Coolidge effect: renewed copulation in a sexually spent male animal in response to a new receptive female.
coprolagnia: a seldom used synonym for coprophilia.
coprophilia: the paraphilia pertaining to an erotic lust for feces.
copulation (v. **copulate**): sexual intercourse; synonym for coitus.
corpora cavernosa: the two cavernous or spongy bodies of the penis that traverse the length of the shaft and erect the penis when they become engorged with blood.
cortisol: a life-sustaining adrenocortical hormone, also known pharmaceutically as hydrocortisone.
counterculture: the term used to characterize the antiestablishment social and political youth movement of the 1960s and 1970s.
courtship: the phase or activity of paying attention to a partner erotically; traditionally with a view to marriage; in animals the behavior that precedes and leads up to copulation.
couvade: in some cultures a custom by which a man impersonates his wife in pregnancy and delivery.

critical period: the period in development when nature and nurture interact and leave a permanent outcome.
cruise: a vernacular term for congregating at a location where likely sexual partners are sought and possibly found.
crush: an intense infatuation usually in early adolescence and often focused on an older person.
cultural lag: the persistence of old cultural customs amidst those more recently adopted.
culture: in anthropology the distinctive customs, achievements, products, and outlooks of a society or group, and its lifestyle.
cunnilingus: oral-genital stimulation between the mouth and the vulva.
curve of voluptuousness: the term used by Albert Moll for what Masters and Johnson called the human sexual response cycle.
cutaneous: pertaining to the skin and skin senses.
CVAH (congenital virilizing adrenal hyperplasia): same as CAH.
cyproterone acetate: generic name for Androcur®, an antiandrogenic compound.
dehydroepiandrosterone (DHA or DHEA): a weak adrenal androgen.
demographic: pertaining to population data or the study of population data.
Depo-Provera®: trade name for medroxyprogesterone acetate, an antiandrogenic compound.
detumesce: to go flaccid after having been erect or temuscent.
DHA: dehydroepiandrosterone.
DHEA: same as DHA.
diagnosis: the art and science of distinguishing one disease from another.
diaphoresis: perspiration especially if profuse.
diaphragm: a female contraceptive device, molded of latex or plastic, and fitted over the cervix of the uterus to prevent entrance of spermatozoa.
diecious: denoting species in which male and female reproductive organs occur in separate individuals; antonym of monoecious.
digametic: pertaining to or producing gametes or sex cells of two different types, female ova and male spermatozoa.
digital self-stimulation: masturbation using the fingers and hand.
dihydrotestosterone: an active masculinizing hormone, a derivative of testosterone.
dildo: an artificial penis.
Dionysian: of or pertaining Dionysus, Greek god of wine, who's cult was marked by ecstatic rites; sensual and abandoned.
diosgenin: a sapogenin extracted from the roots of the Mexican yam, *cabeza de negra*, with a plentiful yield of steroid for the manufacture of human steroidal hormones from which the contraceptive Pill was developed. Named for Dioscoredes of Anazarbos, first century A.D. pharmacologist who recommended an extract of sapogenin for contraception. *See also* sapogenin; saponin.
dissociation (adj. **dissociative**): the separation of that which is developing as a unity, or has become one, so that it becomes two or more unrelated or

partially related entities. In mental life and its expression, these entities are experienced phenomenologically in trance states, alternative states of consciousness, fugue states, or multiple personalities.

diuturnity: long duration or continuance.

doggie position: in sexual intercourse, with the partner bending over or on all fours, and the male making a rear entry in the mounting position.

dominance hierarchy: in troopbonding animals, the ladder of rank and status from most powerful to least powerful position.

dopamine: a neurotransmitter substance essential for brain functioning, in some respects the counterpart of serotonin.

dose response curve: a graph of the relationship between the magnitude of the dosage of a medication and the magnitude of the bodily response.

dynastic: pertaining to a family, usually prominent, spanning several generations, and empowered in part by arranged marriages.

dysmenorrhea: painful menstruation.

eating out: a slang term used as a synonym for cunnilingus.

ecologically viable: self-sustaining in a given ecological niche.

ectopic pregnancy: a pregnancy outside of the uterus, in the fallopian tubes or the abdominal cavity.

EEG: electroencephalogram, the electronically produced tracing of brain waves.

eidetic imagery: vividly clear and realistically recalled imagery.

ejaculation: the forceful expulsion of semen from the male sexual organ; in females the expulsion of orgasmic fluid through the urethra.

electrocautery: a surgical instrument that uses heat instead of a blade.

embryo: an unborn baby for the first eight weeks of development in the womb, after which it becomes a fetus.

endogamy: in anthropology the custom of marrying only within the limits of a local community, clan, or tribe.

engagement: a promise or contract to marry.

Enovid®: trade name of the first of the early forms of the birth control Pill.

enzyme: a specific protein in living cells which is necessary for a specific biochemical reaction.

ephebiatric: pertaining to the period of adolescence up to young adulthood.

ephebophilia: a paraphilia of the chronophilic type in which the younger partner is an adolescent and the older is an adult.

epicene: characteristic of both sexes; for or used by both sexes; effeminate.

epispadias: in a male or female, a birth defect of the sex organs in which there is failure of closure down the midline effecting the bladder and the urethra, which instead of being a closed tube appears as an open groove or cleft.

epistemology: the branch of philosophy that deals with where knowledge comes from and how we know what we know.

eponym: the person whose name is used to designate a product, an institution, or a place.

erotic anesthesia: a form of hypophilia in which the sex organs feel numb.

erotomania: a synonym for the Clérambault-Kandinsky syndrome.
erotophonophilia: the paraphilia of lust murder and serial lust murder.
essentialism: in the revived nature/nurture debate the alleged equivalent of nature; the opposite of social constructionism.
estradiol: a form of estrogen.
estrogen: a female sex hormone along with progesterone.
estrus (adj. **estrous, estrual**): in animals the period of ovulating and being in heat.
ethnography: the study of peoples, tribes, or clans, their lifestyles and their customs.
ethology: a branch of behavioral science that deals with animal life, especially in the wild.
euphoriant: a drug that induces an elevation of the feeling of well being and positive mood.
Eve principle: in embryological development and subsequently, the principle that nature's primary template is that which, without any added factor, differentiates a female.
exhibitionism: the paraphilia of explicit, uninvited sexual display of the genitalia to a stranger; in males, peodeiktophilia.
exigency: that which is demanded by a situation; a requirement or need.
exogamy: in anthropology, the custom of marrying outside the community, clan, or tribe.
exogenous sex hormone: a sex hormone ingested or injected to augment or replace a deficiency of the body's own endogenous secretion of that hormone.
experiments of nature: sources of data that become available for human observation and study only on a sporadic, unplanned and unscheduled basis, as when infant is born with a rare genetic syndrome, or a new epidemic appears. Ethical considerations prohibit the contrived production of such data, except in animal experimentation.
exponential: increasingly rapid expansion in size, number, or frequency of occurrence.
extrauterine pregnancy: ectopic pregnancy, i.e., outside of the uterus and in the fallopian tubes or abdominal cavity, where it is rare and seldom carried to term.
fall in love: to have an intense sexuoerotic attraction toward another person which is sublime when it is requited and a source of abject misery when it is not.
fallopian tube: bilaterally, the tube through which the ovum released from the ovary is propelled to the interior of the uterus.
fantasy (v. **to fantasy or to fantasize**): the mental representation in imagery and/or ideation of a narrative or drama, occurring in a state of reverie, daydreaming, or dreaming.
fellatio: oral-penial sex; in slang, cocksucking or giving head.
feminal: of or pertaining to women; womanly, feminine; antonym of masculinal.

feminization: the action or process of becoming feminized; the state of being feminized.

feminoid: appearing feminine in form and appearance, but not female, e.g., in female impersonation.

fetus: a baby in the womb from the eighth week until birth.

fidelity: faithfulness to a mate.

fixation: an intense and prolonged obsession with, and concentration on an unmodifiable idea; a monomania.

fixed action pattern: in the science of ethology, a pattern of behavior that remains the same across two or more species although serving a different function.

fluoxetine: the antidepressant medication known by its trade name as Prozac®.

folk sexology: the body of prescientific sexual knowledge and ideation shared by a community, tribe, or clan, much of which may be carried over into professional sexology.

footclasp: in monkeys, the adult coital position in which the male mounts the female by clasping her legs above the ankle with his toes and feet.

foreplay: in human beings, the period of sexual activities that lead up to positioning for orgasm.

45,X Turner syndrome: *See* Turner syndrome.

47,XXY Klinefelter syndrome: *See* Klinefelter syndrome.

47,XYY supernumerary Y syndrome: *See* supernumerary Y syndrome.

frotteurism: the paraphilia pertaining to sexually close body contact with and rubbing against a stranger in a closely packed crowd.

FSH (follicle stimulating hormone): a gonadotropin secreted by the anterior lobe of the pituitary gland that stimulates sperm formation in the testis, and the formation of the graafian follicle and the secretion of estrogen in the ovary.

fuck: x-rated vernacular synonym for copulation, formerly censored as obscene, and still considered unseemly in genteel discourse.

fugue state: an altered state of consciousness in which self-recognition and recall are in some degree deconnected from what they were before, and what they will return to subsequently.

fundamentalism: the strict maintenance of traditional orthodox beliefs or doctrines, e.g., in Christianity belief in the divine revelation and inerrancy of the Bible.

fungus: one of a large division of organisms including mushrooms, molds, yeast, and microorganisms that produce pathology in human beings.

G spot: popular name for the periurethral glands of Skene in the female, also known as the Grafenberg spot, which in some females is extremely erotically sensitive to pressure through the vaginal wall.

gamete: a mature germ cell, ovum, or sperm. When both join they form a zygote, the beginning of an embryo.

gastraea theory: Ernst Hackel's late nineteenth-century adaptation of Darwinian theory to evolutionary embryology, namely, that the primitive zygote invaginates to form a mouth and stomach, then a cloaca which finally divides to form the anus and the genital organs.

gastrointestinal: pertaining to the stomach and intestines.

gelastic epilepsy: a rare form of epilepsy in which seizures take the form of mirthless laughter or chuckling.

gender: one's social presentation as feminal or masculinal, or to some extent as androgynal. Gender is constructed by neither nature (biology) nor nurture (societal influences) alone, but by both acting together at critical periods of development; also used as a synonym for sex.

gender stereotype: seminal, masculinal, and androgynal as characterized and dictated by society.

gender transposition: change from masculine to feminine properties or characteristics, or vice versa, relative to the criterion of male or female natal sex, respectively.

gender constancy: in child development, the recognition that being a boy or girl is not arbitrarily changeable.

gender-identity/role (G-I/R): the unity of role and identity as masculine, feminine, or androgynine.

gene sequencing: decoding the molecular sequences that constitute a gene or all of the genes, i.e., the entire genome of an organism.

generic: belonging to a genus or class; general or not specific; not protected by a registered trade mark.

genital constancy: in child development, the recognition that male and female sex organs are not arbitrarily interchangeable.

genome: the complete set of genes replicated in each cell of an organism that constitute its genetic constitution.

genotype: the genetic makeup of an individual which, in interaction with the environment (envirotype), produces the phenotype.

gerontophilia: the paraphilia pertaining to having a partner of parental or grandparental age.

gestation: development during the period of being carried in the womb.

ghotul: among the Gond-speaking peoples of central southern India, the compound where children congregate and sleep.

gnomoerotic: sexuoerotic arousal induced by imagery and ideation, as in fantasies, reveries, and fictions.

Gnostic: In Greek derived, early Christian philosophy, a follower of Gnosticism.

Gnosticism: the doctrines and practices of an early Christian sect, from the first to the third century A.D., ultimately suppressed as heresy.

going steady: contemporary term applied to young couples, similar to betrothal or engagement, but without signifying permanence of the relationship.

gonadectomy: surgical removal of the gonads (ovaries or testicles); castration.

GnRH (gonadotropin releasing hormone): a hormone secreted by brain cells in the hypothalamus that seeps into the nearby pituitary gland and triggers the release of gonadotropins. FSH-RH and LH-RH are gonadotropin releasing hormones.

gonadotropin: a nonsteroidal hormone (a decapeptide glycoprotein) released by the pituitary gland into the bloodstream which carries it to the gonads where it stimulates the release of steroidal sex hormones, androgen, estrogen, and progesterone. FSH and LH are gonadotropins.

gonorrhea: an infection of the internal sex organs, historically known as the clap, transmitted by the bacterial microorganism, gonococcus (*Neisseria gonorrheae*), chiefly through sexual contact.

grooming: among primates, stroking, scratching, smoothing, combing, and cleaning the pelt or skin of an associate as a sign of parental bonding, sexual bonding, or friendly bonding. In human beings, grooming includes massage, cuddling, and hugging.

group sex parties: social gatherings where interchange of sexual partners either in pairs, privately, or in a group, together, is premised.

growth hormone (HGH, human growth hormone): a pituitary hormone that regulates statural growth.

gynecomastia: abnormal growth of glandular tissue of the breasts in males, so as to resemble those of a female. It occurs spontaneously in some boys at puberty.

gynemimesis: in a natal male miming or impersonating being female.

gynemimetophilia: the paraphilia of being sexuoerotically fixated on a gynemimetic partner, e.g., a preoperative transexual.

hallucinosis: a hallucinary attack, usually acute in onset and self-remitting, and possibly triggered by a toxic drug reaction.

halo effect: augmentation of the effect of a drug defined by the social situation in which it is taken; applied especially to recreational drugs.

hamartoma: in the brain, a benign tumor-like nodule in the hypothalamus composed of an overgrowth of otherwise normal cells.

haptic: pertaining to the sense of touch

haptoerotic: sexuoerotic arousal induced by being held, touched, or fondled.

harassment: in the workplace, reiterated annoyance, insult, solicitation, discrimination, or persecution, usually, although not invariably, of a woman by a man.

harlot: originally a vagabond or rogue; now also a rarely used synonym for a woman of easy virtue or prostitute, as in the ancient occupation of temple harlot.

heavy petting: sexual activity, especially in youth, premaritally, that goes "all the way" except for a veto on penial-vaginal insertion.

hedonic: enhancing pleasurable feeling and well being.

hepatitis-B virus: one of several viruses that severely damage the liver. It is highly contagious, e.g., sexually, and is spread by contact with infected feces or blood. There is now a vaccine that provides immunity.

heretic: a person who adheres to an unorthodox doctrine that contravenes official teaching, especially of the Christian Church.
hermaphrodite: reproductively, a person or other mammal of ambiguous or indeterminate sex; in lower species, an organism able to function reproductively as both male and female.
herpes virus: an infectious virus of the type responsible for blisters around the mouth or genitals, chicken pox, and shingles.
heterogametic: having two types of gametes, e.g., in males, sperms with either an X or a Y chromosome.
heterosexuality: sexual reciprocality between two individuals who are natally male and female, respectively.
heterozygous: having a pair of chromosomes of which one carries the gene for a given trait or syndrome, whereas the other does not.
heuristic: learning by doing and discovering principles of knowledge for oneself, not by rote.
HIV/AIDS (**human immunodeficiency virus/acquired immunodeficiency syndrome**): the virus transmitted in body fluids, predominantly blood and sexual fluids, and the syndrome which it has spread worldwide, creating a pandemic.
homosexuality: sexual reciprocality between natal males or natal females.
hormonal age: the degree of hormonally controlled developmental maturation, which may be ahead of or behind the criterion of the birthday age.
hormone: a chemical messenger secreted by specialized cells or glands to communicate with and activate other cells or glands within the body. Hormones circulate in the bloodstream.
horse rider position: in sexual intercourse, the man on his back and the partner facing him and sitting on (riding) his erect penis.
hyperbole (adj. **hyperbolized**): an exaggeration so as to emphasize and intensify the impression one gives.
hyperphilia: the category of copulatory disorders characterized by excessive or insatiable genital functioning.
hypersexual: synonym for hyperphilia.
hypertrophic: overgrown or overdeveloped; too large.
hyphephilia: the paraphilia pertaining to leather, feathers, hair, fur, rubber, and such like.
hypnosis: a trance-like state of heightened response to rhythmicity, suggestibility, and indoctrination induced in one person by another and used by some practitioners in hypnotherapy.
hypogonadism: having gonads that are too small and deficient in hormonal secretion and in fertility.
hypogonadotropic: being deficient in gonadotropic hormone and hence in gonadal size and function.
hypogyneismus: synonym for vaginism.

hypophilia: the category of copulatory disorders characterized by insufficient or incomplete functioning of the genital organs.

hypopituitary dwarfism: statural growth failure secondary to failure or deficiency of growth hormone from the pituitary gland, with or without gonadotropic failure at the expected age of puberty; treated with hormonal replacement therapy.

hyposexual: synonym for hypophilia.

hypospadias: a birth defect of the sex organs in which the urethra does not open at the tip of the penis, but further back, possibly so far back as to render the sex organs ambiguous. Mild hypospadias may be a sequel to defective circumcision.

hypothalamus: a small region of the brain deep beyond the bridge of the nose that mediates several vital functions, including those of mating and reproduction.

hysterectomy: surgical removal of the uterus, with or without preservation of the ovaries.

hysteria: colloquially, an exaggerated display of irrational behavior; psychopathologically, a neurosis, in antiquity attributed to a wandering womb, formerly diagnosed only in women, and now officially changed to histrionic personality disorder.

iatrogenic: physician or treatment induced disorders or side effects.

identification: in child development, the process by which a child absorbs and assimilates influences and examples from and models him/herself upon another person so as, in some degree, to be or do the same as that person; antonym of complementation.

ideology: a rational or irrational system of ideas, beliefs, explanations, principles and practices pertaining to various crucial social and related issues in one's life.

idiot savant: French term meaning wise or learned idiot, i.e., a person who is severely mentally retarded in some respects, for example conversing, and a prodigy in others, for example, calculating, sketching, or memorizing music. Today's politically correct term is savant.

immutable: resistant to change.

impostor or **imposter:** one who deceives by playing an impersonating role secretively, for example, a medical impostor presents self-induced symptoms as being those of a mysterious disease of unknown origin.

impregnation: sexually, making a female pregnant.

imprinted: in the science of ethology, the type of learning that is extremely durable and takes place only when and if, at a critical developmental period, an innate releasing mechanism encounters a precisely signified stimulus that releases it.

in utero: within the womb.

in vitro fertilization (IVF): fertilization outside the womb to produce a so-called test tube baby. A ripe egg is harvested from the woman's ovary and, in a glass Petri dish, fertilized with semen from the man, and soon thereafter the zygote is put into the womb where, if successful, it grows into a normal baby.

inamorata (masc. **inamorato**): a woman beloved or in love.

Incas: indigenous Indians of the pre-Columbian civilization of Peru and the high Andes.

incest: marriage or sexual intercourse between close kin, the criterion of closeness being transculturally variable, except for prohibition of parent-child incest which is widespread although not total.

infanticide: the killing of infants, especially of unwanted newborns, either violently or by neglect.

infantile autism: a syndrome of very early onset in infancy, if not at birth, characterized by extreme social aloofness, deficient pair-bonding with the mother or anyone else; virtually total lack of bonding with same-aged peers; and various manifestations of bizarre behavior, including muteness.

infantophilia: the paraphilia pertaining to infants at the diaper age.

infatuation: a state of being intensely love smitten at an age or with a partner which others in authority deem unsuitable.

infibulation: ritual excision of the entire female vulva and closing of the wound so as to leave only a small orifice for urination and, after puberty, menstruation. The custom is common in northern and eastern Africa where it predates Islam. It is usually performed on girls in mid-childhood, without anesthetic. To permit intercourse, the scar is incised by the husband. Synonym for Pharaonic circumcision.

innate recognition mechanism: in the science of ethology, innate preparedness to recognize the highly specific stimulus which releases the innate response that then becomes imprinted.

instinct: an innate propensity to manifest a fixed pattern of behavior under specific conditions of stimulation; to know or do something, by natural propensity, untaught and without thinking.

intelligence: in psychology, the mental capacity that intelligence tests are alleged to measure, but which has resisted a universally agreed upon definition, over and above being clever, smart, and high in achievement.

intercourse: habitual interaction between two or more people, as in social intercourse. Sexual intercourse includes the complete episode of sexual interaction, although the term commonly used to signify the act of penial-vaginal union only.

interfemoral: between the thighs, as applied to sexual interaction when the penis is thrust up and down between the thighs, front or back, with or without a lubricant, and without intromission.

Internet: the worldwide telecommunication system of interconnected computers. It allows virtually instantaneous access to a vast array of audio and audiovisual programs, entertainments, and exchange of information and personal mail.

intersexuality: synonym for hermaphroditism

intoxication psychosis: psychotic symptoms like hallucination precipitated by a drug or other intoxicant.

intracavernosal: within the spongy tissue of the corpora cavernosa of the shaft of the penis, as in intracavernosal injections of PGE1 for the treatment of impotence.

introitus: the opening into the canal of the vagina.

isosexual: same sexual; synonym for homosexual, equally applicable to homosexual acts and to homosexual relationships; antonym of contrasexual.

IUD (**intrauterine device**): a long-term method of contraception, whereby a specially designed device is fitted into the uterus by a trained expert.

IVF: in vitro fertilization.

jongleur: in the troubadour era (twelfth to fourteenth centuries), the French name for a juggler, poet, singer, and street entertainer.

Kallmann syndrome: a syndrome of pubertal inadequacy characterized by testicular failure and total or partial absence of the sense of smell.

Kaposi's sarcoma: a once rare form of skin cancer, external and internal, now prevalent in advanced HIV/AIDS infection.

Kaspar Hauser syndrome: a syndrome of severe all-round developmental retardation with statural dwarfism, induced by major child abuse and neglect; named for one of the earliest cases identified (1828), Kaspar Hauser.

keeping company: the old term for dating.

kinetic: pertaining to movement and motion; of children, constantly on the move.

kleptophilia: the paraphilia pertaining to sexual arousal associated with irrational stealing.

Klinefelter syndrome (47,XXY): a sporadically occurring genetic syndrome with a male phenotype except for testicular failure at puberty with ensuing sterility and sex hormonal insufficiency which is partially correctable by high dose testosterone therapy.

klismaphilia: the paraphilia pertaining to receiving enemas.

labia: the internal (labia minora) and external (labia majora) lips of the female genitalia.

lactating: secreting milk from the milk glands of the breasts, through the nipples.

lagnesis: obsolete synonym for erotomania.

laparoscopy (adj. **laparoscopic**): a surgical procedure for visual examination of intraabdominal organs, including the female organs, without cutting, by means of a specially designed instrument inserted through small puncture of the skin.

lek (part. **lekking**): a mating ritual of a few animal and bird species in which males assemble all in one place and wait for females to visit and select a mate for copulation.

lesbian: a homosexual female; named for the island of Lesbos, home of the woman poet, Sappho who in antiquity wrote love poems for women lovers.

Leydig cell: in the testis, "bunch of grapes" cells packed between the seminiferous tubules, and responsible for the secretion of the male hormone, testosterone.

LH (luteinizing hormone): a gonadotropin that stimulates the ovary to secrete progesterone in synchrony with the ovulatory cycle, and in large quantities during pregnancy. LH stimulates the Leydig cells of the testes to secrete androgen.

libertarian: an advocate of the doctrine of personal liberty, not licentiousness, and not arbitrary social and political control.

libido hormone: androgen; at very low levels, it supplements the subjective sense of sexual desire in women, especially after the menopause, without masculinizing the body. Males tolerate a higher optimal level, beyond which there is no further effect.

licentiousness: behavior that defies common conventions; applied chiefly to indiscriminate and promiscuous sexual relations.

limbic system: the "old brain" or paleocortex that includes the thalamus, amygdala, hippocampus, hypothalamus and septum, and governs the more rudimentary functions of mental life as compared with the neocortex which governs the higher mental life of speech and logical reasoning.

limerence: the personal experience of having fallen in love and of being irrationally and fixatedly love stricken or love smitten, irrespective of the degree to which one's love is requited or unrequited.

lordosis: the crouching copulatory position, with hind end elevated, assumed by quadrupedal female mammals.

love: pairbonded affection and hedonic attachment with or without erotic passion.

love smitten: intensely in love; lovesick.

loveblot: a person metaphorically likened to a Rorschach inkblot onto whom one's own romantic and erotic interpretations are projected.

lovebondship: the status or qualification of being lovebonded.

lovemap: an organizational pattern or template in the mind and brain (mindbrain) that encodes the idealized details, either normal or pathological, of one's sexuoeroticism and sex life.

lovemap age: the developmental stage of one's lovemap as compared with one's chronological age.

lovesickness: the state of languishing with romantic love, or of being lovelorn.

lubrication: sexologically, the droplets of slippery fluid exuded from the wall of the vagina in connection with sexuoerotic arousal; also water soluble or greasy preparations applied to the penis or vagina to facilitate sexual stimulation, or saliva used as a substitute.

lust: sensuous appetite, passion, or longing, especially although not exclusively genital and erotic, with or without romantic love.

lymph: transparent, yellowish fluid derived from tissue fluids and found in the lymphatic vessels and glands of the body where lymphocytes, of importance to the immune system, are formed.

making out: among adolescents, the term used to signify that on a date, especially in the era of drive-in movies, the girl permitted light petting to include the breasts, but usually nothing below the waist, and probably did not touch the boy's genitalia.

mammoplasty: a plastic surgical procedure to either enlarge or reduce the size of the breasts.

maniacal psychosis: the manic phase of bipolar (manic-depressive) psychosis; a monomania so invasive of time and logic that other people rate it is madness, which may progressively evolve into a full blown psychosis.

Manicheanism: the heretical doctrine of Manes, a Persian who in the third century A.D. taught a religious system compounding Zoroastrian dualism and Christian salvation, namely, that the human soul belongs to the Kingdom of Light and seeks escape from the body which belongs to the Kingdom of Darkness.

masculinal: of or pertaining to men; manly, masculine; antonym of feminal.

masculinization: differentiating and developing according to the criterion of male from embryonic life onward, or else switching from initial feminization to masculinizing. Also, correcting deficient masculinization by hormonal and/or surgical intervention.

masculinoid: appearing masculine in form and appearance, but not male.

masculist: an advocate of the rights of men, the counterpart of feminist.

masochism: the paraphilia of arranging to be the recipient of pain, humiliation, bondage, and discipline.

mastectomy: a surgical procedure to remove the breast or breasts, performed either for treatment of cancer, or in boys to flatten the chest in the treatment of gynecomastia.

masturbation: erotic genital self-stimulation with usually although not invariably the hand(s) and fingers; digital stimulation of the genitals of a partner, singly or mutually.

matrix: in brain mapping theory, an organizing mold or schema of interconnecting informatic pathways and destinations that code and maintain the map and its manifestation in ideation, imagery, and practice.

meatus: an opening or passage, e.g., the opening of the urethra at the tip of the penis.

medroxyprogesterone acetate (MPA): generic name for Depo-Provera®, Upjohn.

menarche: developmentally, the beginning of menstrual cyclicity.

menses: in females, the monthly period of menstrual bleeding; menstruation.

mentor: a trusted teacher and advisor; a personal tutor.

micropenis: a very small penis with dimensions no greater than those of a clitoris, or smaller. If the organ is also hypospadiac, it is generally referred to as a microphallus.

micturition: urination.

migraine: an episodic, acutely painful, throbbing headache associated with constriction of the cranial arteries and various other symptoms.

MIH (mullerian inhibiting hormone): a hormone produced by the embryonic and fetal testis that prevents differentiation of the mullerian duct into a uterus and fallopian tubes in the male.

milk ejection: under the influence of the hormone, oxytocin, release of milk when the nipple is sucked.

minnesinger: from the twelfth to fourteenth centuries in Germany, the counterpart of the troubadours who originated in Provence in the south of France.

miscegenation: crossbreeding between members of different ethnic groups, especially in the U.S. between those classified as white and black.

missionary position: sexual intercourse with the female lying on her back, and the male mounting her face-to-face; ventroventral position.

mnemonic: a device or jingle to aid in memorizing and recalling lists and rules of procedure.

mold: a growth or colony of one of many varieties of minute fungi that proliferate on damp foodstuffs, or organic textiles, paper, leather, and such like.

monoecious: denoting species in which male and female reproductive organs occur in the same individual; antonym of diecious.

monopotential: developmentally, having only one way to go; not bipotential.

monosexual: not bisexual, but either heterosexual or homosexual.

morning-after pill: for use after unprotected intercourse, a hormonal contraceptive of specially prescribed dosage to prevent, according to the phase of the menstrual cycle, ovulation, fertilization, or implantation of the fertilized ovum.

morphoerotic: sexuoerotic arousal induced by body build and appearance.

morphophilia: the paraphilia involving a major discrepancy in bodily appearance, size, or shape between the partners.

multiform: having diverse forms or kinds.

multiplex: manifold; having many interrelated elements or features.

Munchausen's syndrome by proxy: a syndrome of medical imposture, commonly by the mother of a child in whom factitious symptoms are produced; named after Baron von Munchausen, a character in German fiction.

natal sex: the sex into which one is classified at birth. The term circumvents the dilemma of defining biological sex and differentiating it from so-called nonbiological sex when the two overlap.

natural childbirth: delivery of a baby with minimal medical or technological intervention. Both parents attend childbirth rehearsal classes in relaxation, breathing, and pushing, and the father is a "coach" in the delivery room.

neocortex: the new cortex, the outermost level of the brain, most highly developed in the human species.

Neoplatonism: a philosophical and religious doctrine, originating with Plotinus in the third century A.D., derived from the fourth century B.C. writings of the Greek philosopher, Plato. It postulated mystical union with a supreme being from which all reality is ostensibly derived.

nerd: slang for a person who may be intellectually a champion, but is socially inept, e.g., a computer nerd.

neurohormone: a hormone secreted from a nerve cell that communicates with nearby cells or, transported in the bloodstream, with others at a distance.

neuromodulator: an in vivo neurochemical substance, e.g., a neurohormone, that modifies the neurotransmitting action of other substances, but does not act directly.

neurosis: a nonpsychotic form of mental pathology ostensibly originating in stress or conflict, although its complete etiology remains to be ascertained; also known as psychoneurosis.

neurotransmitter: one of a wide range of chemical substances released by brain and nerve cells that convey information from cell to cell across neuronal junctions.

19-norprogestin: one of a variety of synthetic steroidal hormones, related structurally to both progesterone and testosterone, from which the birth control Pill was manufactured.

nNO (neuronal nitric oxide): the form of NO used by neurons as a neurotransmitter.

nNOS (neuronal nitric oxide synthase): the enzyme responsible for the release of NO as a neurotransmitter.

NO (nitric oxide): the first nonfluidic, gaseous substance recognized (in the 1980s) to have the properties of a neurotransmitter. It plays an important role in penial erection.

nonagenarian: a person between the ages of 90 and 99 years.

norepinephrine: one of the naturally occurring catecholamines, a neurohormone, released from nerve cells and also secreted by the adrenal medulla. Also known as noradrenalin. Its counterpart is epinephrine (adrenalin). It influences blood pressure.

normophilia: the category of genital or copulatory function that is ideologically and possibly arbitrarily socially defined as normal.

nosocomial: hospital or clinic induced, such as symptoms or illness.

nuclear family: mother, father, and children; not the extended family or kinship.

nymphomania: in popular usage, excessive or unseemly sexuality in a female, the counterpart of satyromania in a male; a synonym for Clérambault-Kandinsky syndrome and for lagnesis.

object constancy: the psychological principle that the name or meaning of an object, e.g., a chair, remains constant despite changes in appearance by being rotated, broken, or stylistically altered. When the principle fails to apply, young children are challenged e.g., in assimilating the idea of genital constancy versus inconstancy of haircut or clothing style.

obsessional fixation: reiterative ideas, thoughts, images, and practices that can't be stopped.

obstetrics: the branch of medicine that specializes in pregnancy and delivery.

oedipus complex: the Freudian doctrine that young children have fantasies of rivalry with the parent of the same sex for the sexual attention of the parent of the other sex, which if not resolved lead to psychopathology.

olfactoerotic: sexuoerotic arousal induced by smell or odor.

olfactophilia: a paraphilia pertaining to smells or odors associated with the human body and its functions.

olfactory lobe: a specialized region of the brain, rudimentary in the human species, situated bilaterally on the under surface of the frontal cortex. It receives and transmits information pertaining to the sense of smell.

Onan: Biblical character (Genesis 38:9) from whose name Onanism became synonymous with masturbation, although his sin was coitus interruptus, thereby wasting his seed by spilling it on the ground.

ontogenesis: the development of the individual as compared with that of the species (phylogenesis).

ophthalmoerotic: sexuoerotic arousal induced by something seeable.

opioid: a naturally occurring neurochemical substance released by brain cells that resembles opium in chemical structure and function.

orgasm: the climactic peak of sexual arousal and activity, alone or with a partner, usually, though not invariably signaled by the simultaneous occurrence of ejaculation in the male and less frequently by the spasmodic expulsion of fluid in the female, and accompanied in both sexes by spasmodic muscular contractions in and around the genitalia, usually with generalized sensation of an ecstatic nature.

orgasmology: the science and study of orgasm and related pathology.

orgastic: able to experience orgasm.

ovum (pl. **ova**): the female sex cell that, in union with a sperm, begins a new life.

oxymoron: contradictory or incongruous words that in combination have a rhetorical, epigrammatic, or ridiculous effect.

oxytocin: a peptide hormone formed in neural cells of the hypothalamus and stored in the posterior lobe of the pituitary gland. It has uterine-contracting and milk-ejecting actions, and may also play a role in affectionate pairbonding.

pain agnosia: inability to feel or recognize pain, in some cases traceable to a genetic origin, and in some male cases associated with sterility; synonym for painblindness.

pairbond: a closely intimate and lasting interdependency between two people as between mother and baby, or lover and lover.

pairbondship: the status or qualification of being bonded together as a pair.

paleocortex: the old cortex, the level of the brain below the neocortex; its structures are evolutionarily old and, unlike the neocortex, are well represented in subhuman mammalian species.

pallor: paleness; of wan appearance.

paradigm: a model or pattern.

paralagnia: from Greek *para*, altered, and *lagnia*, lust; a seldom used synonym for paraphilia (altered love).

paramour: a lover, especially one whose love is illicit, secret, or forbidden.

paraphilia: the biomedical term for the category of sexual and erotic function popularly recognized as kinky and legally classified as perversion.

paraplegia: paralysis from the waist down, secondary to a spinal cord injury or lesion.

parasite: an organism that subsists by living on or in another organism.

parental investment theory: in evolutionary sociobiology, the idea that mammalian females invest more time and energy than males do in producing and rearing young and maximize the likelihood of perpetuating their genes by mating with a genetically superior male, whereas males, abundantly supplied with sperms to invest, can afford to be indiscriminate in perpetuating their genes by impregnating a maximum of partners.

paroxysm: an acute attack or occurrence, as in a paroxysmal fit of coughing or a convulsive seizure.

parthenogenesis: virgin birth; producing young from unfertilized ova.

pathogenic: producing or inducing pathology or disease.

pathognomonic: diagnostically, a sign or symptom that decisively indicates a particular syndrome or condition.

patriarchal: in feminist theory, characterized by the social, religious, and household tradition of male dominance and female submission; antonym of matriarchal.

pedigree: in genetics, a kinship in which an inherited characteristic or condition appears among the descendants of an earlier generation of forebears.

pedophilia: the paraphilia pertaining to juveniles after the age of infancy up to the age of puberty, the partner being adolescent or adult.

peodeiktophilia: exhibitionism, specifically of the male genitalia.

penetration phobia: in both sexes, but probably more prevalently in females than males, pathological aversion to penial-vaginal penetration while engaging in sexual intercourse.

penicillin: the first antibiotic medication; purified originally (in 1939) from cultures of the mold, *Penicillium chrysogenum*, and now produced synthetically.

penis (adj. **penial**): the male copulatory and urinary organ.

penis envy: in Freudian theory, the doctrine that the psychosexual development of young girls is marred by their recognition of the superiority of possessing a penis.

penovaginal: in sexual intercourse, genital union; synonym for penial-vaginal or vaginopenial.

penumbra: the area of partial illumination around a dark shadow; also used metaphorically, as in penumbra of doom and gloom.

peptide hormone: a hormone that in chemical structure is a protein; counterpart of a steroid hormone.

perineal: pertaining to the perineum, the region between the genitalia and the anus.

periodic psychosis of puberty: acute episodes of psychosis in females beginning at puberty and alternating with periods of lucidity and behavioral normalcy in synchrony with changes in the ratio of circulating estrogen and progesterone, and subject to remission under progestinic treatment.

periurethral: situated around, or encircling the urethra, e.g., Skene's glands which in the female are the counterpart of the prostate gland in the male.

perversion: legal and psychoanalytic term for sexual deviation, for which the biomedical term is paraphilia.

Petri dish: a shallow glass or plastic saucer with vertical sides and a cover, used in laboratories for tissue culture.

PGE1 (prostaglandin E1): one of several related hormone-like substances (long chain hydroxy fatty acids) produced in the body. They regulate a variety of vital functions, and were first isolated in fluid from the prostate gland in semen. Injected into the shaft of the penis, PGE1 produces an erection and is useful in the treatment of impotence.

phallus: synonym for penis; the penis as a ceremonial symbol of power or fertility.

phantom limb: following an amputation, the persistence of sensation that appears to originate in the missing extremity, possibly with unpleasant tingling or painful burning. It is likely that the phantom originates in that part of the brain where the missing part was formerly represented.

Pharaonic circumcision: synonym for infibulation.

phenomena (sing. **phenomenon**): data recorded or described literally as manifested, prior to secondary overlay of interpretation as to their significance or meaning.

phenotype: the physical makeup and behavior of an individual resulting from the interaction of the genetic endowment (the genotype) with the type of environment in which it develops.

phenylethylamine (PEA): in the brain, a neurotransmitter conjectured to be elevated at the onset of each occurrence of a new love affair in a repetitive series alternating with depressive episodes.

pheromone: an odoriferous secretion that acts as a chemical attractant or repellant between members of the same or other species. *See* hormone.

phobia: morbid fear.

phthalate: chemically, a salt of phthalic acid used in the manufacture of plastics, adhesives, paints, and inks. Phthalates are among the chemicals suspected of entering the food chain and, masquerading as estrogen, being responsible for lowering the sperm count in males.

phylism: one of the rudimentary building blocks of behavior that belong to all members of the species and are phylogenetically transmitted, not ontogenetically inculcated.

phylogenesis: the evolutionary development of the species as compared with the personal development of one member of the species (ontogenesis).

physique age: the developmental stage of bodily maturation that may or may not match the chronological age.

Pill: a combination of progestinic and estrogenic hormone effective as contraceptive and popularly named the Pill.

pituitary gland: a small gland deep beyond the bridge of the nose connected with the hypothalamus, responsible for regulating multiple sexual and other hormonal functions of the body.

placenta: the round, flat, spongy organ which grows at the site of implantation in the uterus and through which the fetus receives oxygen and nutrition from the mother's bloodstream. At delivery, it is expelled as the afterbirth.

PMS (premenstrual syndrome): in some women, major loss of well being for some days prior to the onset of menstruation, accompanied by irritably, fatigue, aches, and bodily symptoms.

Pneumocystis carinii: the highly contagious, opportunistic microorganism responsible for the prevalence of an otherwise fairly rare type of pneumonia in patients with HIV/AIDS.

pollution: a once commonly used term for masturbation (self-pollution) and for wet dreams (nocturnal pollution).

polyamory: having, sharing more lovers than one.

polyandry (adj. **polyandrous**): having more than one husband or long term partner at the same time.

polycystic ovary syndrome: Stein-Leventhal syndrome, characterized by irregularity or loss of menstruation and ovulation, ovarian cysts, and some degree of hormonal masculinization of the body.

polygamy (adj. **polygamous**): being married to more than one spouse at the same time.

polygyny (adj. **polygynous**): having more than one wife or long term partner at the same time.

pornography: the depiction in print, film, or electronic media of explicitly sexuoerotic material that does not conform to arbitrarily defined community or legal standards.

postpartum: occurring in the mother in the immediate period after giving birth, as in postpartum depression which may be mild and transient, or morbid and prolonged.

pregnancy envy: in boys, a counterpart of penis envy in girls.

prepuberty: the juvenile period of childhood between late infancy and the onset of puberty and adolescence; it is variable from approximately age 8 to age 11, 12, or 13.

priapism: prolonged erection of the penis, in some cases secondary to a blood clot requiring surgical intervention which, if unsuccessful, may result in irreversible tissue damage and impotence. Priapism may also be a sequel, usually transient, to intracavernosal injections of the shaft of the penis with, for example, prostaglandin E1, for the treatment of impotence.

proceptive phase: the preparatory sexuoerotic phase that precedes the acceptive and conceptive phases, and that includes foreplay. Also called the phase of courtship or, in animals, the mating dance.

profane: not sacred, as in profane love.

progesterone: a steroidal sex hormone named for its role in gestation. It's level in the bloodstream fluctuates with the menstrual cycle, being high after ovulation just prior to menstruation, and higher still when secreted from the placenta during pregnancy.

prognosis: forecast of the probable course and outcome of a disease or pathology, based on the diagnosis and type of treatment.

promiscuity: characterized by indiscriminate, casual, and multiple encounters, especially sexual.

prophylaxis (adj. and n. **prophylactic**): avoidance or preventive treatment of illness or infection. Also, a condom for prevention of sexually transmitted disease, and colloquially for prevention of pregnancy.

proprioceptive: pertaining to information, especially about position and motion, transmitted from within the body.

protolimerent: developmentally, an early, precursor manifestation of limerence.

protozoa (sing. **protozoan**): varieties of eukaryotic (i.e. possessing a nucleus) microorganisms, usually unicellular, e.g., amoebas, but not bacteria.

Prozac®: pharmaceutical trade name for fluoxetine, a widely used antidepressant.

pseudologia fantastica: a disposition or tendency to invent fictions with self-reference and to present them as autobiographical actualities, not phantasmagorias.

psychoanalysis: the theory of mind and of mental pathology and its treatment originated by Sigmund Freud (1856-1939) and modified by his followers.

psychomotor epilepsy: synonym for temporal lobe epilepsy.

psychopathology: a mentally and behaviorally disordered state and its symptoms.

psychosexual development: in general, the maturation of sexuality and eroticism from birth onward. In psychoanalysis, the Freudian stages of infantile sexuality, namely oral, anal, genital, oedipal, and latency, together with their fixations, repressions, and regressions.

psychosocial dwarfism: failure of statural growth and development secondary to abuse and neglect at home, and subject to catch-up growth by change of domicile. *See also* Kaspar Hauser syndrome.

puberty: the stage of development during which the secondary sexual characteristics mature, culminating in menarche in girls, and semenarche in boys.

pulsatile: functioning rhythmically with a pulse or throb.

puppy love: romantic attraction and bonding between juveniles.

quim: bawdy term, probably of Celtic origin, for the female organ of sexual intercourse; and for having sexual intercourse.

random probability sampling: in polling or survey research, using a statistical method of enrolling participants in proportion to their percentage in the general population, and without bias in favor of any one characteristic or criterion.

raptophilia: synonym for biastophilia.

receptive phase: in sexual encounter, a synonym specifically for the acceptive phase that follows the proceptive phase, when the female is receptive to mounting and thrusting by the male; applied chiefly to laboratory animals.

reconciliation fuck: slang term for sexual intercourse with an exceptionally intense orgasm in the wake of dispute and fighting.

refractory period: in the male, the period after an orgasm until the recurrence of erection and readiness to begin again.

rehearsal play: in infancy and juvenility the playful enactment of an activity that will be full fledged in maturity, e.g., hunting play, and sexual rehearsal play.

rejuvenation: becoming as if young again.

releasing stimulus: in ethological theory, the stimulus that triggers an innate response pattern, and the imprinting of the response.

retrograde ejaculation: backflow of the semen into the bladder instead of the urethra, usually after injury or genitourinary surgery.

RH **(releasing hormone):** a hormone released from a nerve cell, e.g., in the hypothalamus, that stimulates the release of another hormone from an adjacent cell or gland, e.g., the pituitary gland.

rimming: slang term for oral-anal sexuoerotic stimulation.

ritual: a customary or habitual formal procedure or observance regularly reiterated, unchanged, often with superstitious, occult, or mystical symbolism.

romantic love: an idealized and sentimentalized yearning for a pairbonded love affair untainted by lust and carnality and often doomed to be unattainable.

Rorschach inkblot: one of a standard set of ten inkblots designed by Herman Rorschach and reproduced on cards that constitute a projective test, i.e., the viewer projects meaning into the shapes and a complex scoring system ostensibly yields a personality and/or diagnostic profile.

RU-486: an antiprogestinic, antigestational steroidal hormone, generically named mifepristone. It displaces progesterone and, in conjunction with prostaglandin E1, is effective in inducing nonsurgical abortion as early as from the sixth week or earlier. It may also function as a morning-after pill.

Russian roulette: a group game or act of daring in which after loading one chamber of a six cylinder revolver, spinning the cylinder, and holding it to the head, the player pulls the trigger.

sadism: the paraphilia of violent assault, cruelty, inflicting pain and humiliation.

salt-losing crisis: in the CAH syndrome of the salt losing subtype, a life threatening crisis secondary to inadequate hormonal replacement therapy and insufficient dietary salt.

sanitary pad: a highly absorbent pad designed especially for menstrual hygiene and used with or without a tampon.

sapogenin: steroidal plant substance like saponin and diosgenin. When shaken with water, it makes a soapy froth (from Latin, *sapo*, soap).
saponin: a sterol extracted from plants and converted into progesterone-like steroidal hormones, which made possible the discovery of the birth control Pill (from Latin, *sapo*, soap). *See also* sapogenin; diosgenin.
sartorial: pertaining to tailoring; male and female style of clothing.
satyriasis: synonym for satyromania.
satyromania: in popular usage, excessive and unrelenting pursuit of sexuality in a male, the counterpart of nymphomania in a female.
sauna: a hot, dry steam bath or the steam room in which it is taken, possibly with a hot and a cold pool adjacent.
savantism: the politically correct diagnostic synonym for idiot savant.
schema: in psychology, a design or mental model or representation simultaneously in the mind and brain (mindbrain).
schizophrenia: a major mental illness or psychosis characterized by severe thought disorder, including hallucination and delusion, and often bizarre behavior.
scissors position: in sexual intercourse, lying side to side with him facing her back, except that both their legs are skewed so as to permit penovaginal penetration.
SDN/POA (sexually dimorphic nucleus of the preoptic area): a very small region of the hypothalamus in the vicinity of the left-right crossing of the optic nerves (the optic chiasma), noteworthy for being among nuclei that show a male-female difference in size, or possibly a male homosexual-heterosexual difference in size.
secret vice: synonym for solo masturbation implying condemnation.
secular: not religious. Also, occurring every hundred years.
seduction theory: the theory originated by Freud and revived in the 1980s that sexual abuse or molestation in early childhood produces subsequent symptoms of posttraumatic stress disorder (PTSD).
seizure disorder: a disorder with major or minor epileptic seizures.
self-pollution: term of disapproval for solo masturbation.
semen conservation theory: the theory that wastage of semen produces degeneracy.
semen depletion theory: synonym for semen conservation theory.
semen transfusion theory: in folk medicine, the theory that prepubertal boys require to ingest semen to become mature.
semen: the sperm bearing fluid ejaculated from the penis.
semenarche: the developmental milestone of first producing semen.
seminiferous: bearing or producing semen, in the seminiferous tubules of the testes.
sensate focus: an exercise in Masters and Johnson's sex therapy in which sensuous pleasure is evoked through the cutaneous senses without penovaginal performance anxiety.
sensorial coding: coding in the brain of information transmitted through the senses.
sensuoromantic: sensual and romantic at the same time.

sensual: responding to and enjoying the lust and carnality of the senses without excluding spiritual enjoyment.

sensuous: responding to, and enjoying the pleasures of the senses, ostensibly in a more spiritual than carnal way.

sequestration: state of being separated, secluded, or cut off from contact with others.

serendipity: a fortuitous stumbling upon a discovery or principle while on a quest for something else.

serial lust murder: the paraphilia involving multiple murders over an extended period of time.

serotonin: a substance produced in the body that acts as a neurotransmitter and counterpart of dopamine. Chemical name, 5-hydroxytryptamine.

sex: natally male, female, or in some degree hermaphroditic (intersexed). Sex is not unitary but manifold, e.g., chromosomal, gonadal, and hormonal sex, morphological internal and external sex, neuroanatomical sex, assigned sex, and sex of identity and role. These different criteria of sex are usually, though not inevitably concordant.

sex of assignment: the sex to which a baby is assigned at birth, which in cases of birth defect of the sex organs may or may not be consistent with other criteria of sex.

sex of rearing: the sex, male, female, or ambiguous, in which a child is reared.

sex worker: a person who makes a living in some branch of the commercial sexual services or entertainment trade.

sex coded: pertaining to activities and roles that are conventionally and maybe arbitrarily coded as masculine, feminine, or ambiguous.

sexology: the science of sex, including eroticism.

sexosophy: the social philosophy or ideological doctrine of sex as compared with sexology, the science.

sexual response cycle: as propounded by Masters and Johnson the four phases of excitement, plateau, orgasm, and resolution.

sexuoeroticism: the term that unifies sexuality and eroticism. It is virtually synonymous with erotosexuality except that focus of attention is on the first component of each term. Aphoristically, sex is between the legs, and eroticism between the ears.

shaman: among some ethnic and tribal peoples, a priestly healer, mentor, and spiritual mediator; among American Indian tribes, a berdache.

simplex: not complex or multiplex; having a single explanation or origin.

sissy boy: a stigmatizing term for a boy with feminine inclinations and behavior, and a greater likelihood of growing up to be homosexually effeminated than heterosexually macho.

Skene's glands: the female counterpart of the male prostate gland.

Skoptic syndrome: a pathological fixation on becoming a eunuch. Named for a former Christian sect in Russia and Romania in which males followed Scripture literally in becoming eunuchs for the kingdom of heaven.

social age: the stage of social development as compared with chronological age.

social coding: in postnatal life, social influences that take up where prenatal hormonal coding left off in shaping, in particular, one's identity as male, female, or ambiguous.

social constructionism: the ideology based on Michel Foucault's reading of history, and endorsed especially by feminists and social scientists, that bypasses genetics and biology in favor of the social and often arbitrary origins of, in particular, gender differences.

solipsism: the philosophical principle that knowledge is self-centric and that it is fortuitous whether there is or is not a match between what two people know, for example, in the case of a color blind and a color seeing pair encountering the same stimulus.

somnophilia: the paraphilia of awakening a sleeping stranger with erotic caresses, including oral sex, not involving force or violence; the sleeping princess syndrome.

sonogram: the visual depiction on a video screen or photographic film of an image electronically converted by a computer from ultrasonic waves reflected from a concealed source, for example, an unborn fetus.

sperm: the male sex cell that, in union with an ovum, begins a new life; abbreviation of spermatozoon, (plural, spermatozoa).

spermatic tubule: synonym for seminiferous tubule.

spermatogenesis: the production and development of sperm cells in the testicles.

spermatorrhea: outmoded nineteenth-century term for the nonexistent disease of loss of sperm, as in wet dreams.

sphincter: a contractile muscular ring that opens and closes a body orifice, e.g., the bladder or anus.

spoon position: in sexual intercourse, both partners lie on their sides like two spoons stacked together, her back against his belly, with rear-entry intromission.

sportscaster technique: in interviewing, a play by play account of what was said and done, without attribution of motivation or interpretation of significance.

SSRI (selective serotonin reuptake inhibitor): one of a class of antidepressant medications, e.g., Prozac®.

stalking: nefarious and stealthy pursuit and harassment of someone, e.g., a lover or spouse, by whom one has been jilted.

staphylococcus: a widely distributed bacterium, a frequent agent of localized suppurative infections, and from time to time lethal.

STD: sexually transmitted disease.

Stein-Leventhal syndrome: bilateral polycystic ovaries with menstrual irregularity or failure, infertility, and androgenic masculinization of the body in varying degree.

steroid: in biochemistry, any of a large class of organic compounds the members of which include sterols, gonadal and adrenocortical hormones, bile acids, and many other compounds with important physiological effects.

steroid hormone: a hormone that in chemical structure belongs to a class of bodily substances derived from cholesterol; counterpart of protein hormone.

stratagem: a tricky devise, ruse, or schema to outwit an opponent. As applied to paraphilia, a circuitous way of outwitting the destruction of lust.

stricture: closure of a duct or tube by the constriction of tissue, e.g., constriction of the urethra by progressively enlarging scar tissue.

sukra: in Indian Ayurvedic medicine, the Sanskrit name for semen, the most precious of the vital fluids.

supernumerary Y syndrome (47,XYY): a sporadically occuring genetic syndrome with a male phenotype, with a high prevalence of sterility but not hormonal insufficiency, and with a high prevalence of impulsive behavioral pathology.

sustentation: that which is life sustaining, e.g., food, shelter, and clothing; sustaining or being sustained.

swingers' club: a club of which the members, as couples, or as a group, exchange partners for sexual intercourse.

swive: in fourteenth century English, a term for a male's having sexual intercourse with a woman. By the seventeenth century it became bawdy.

Swyer syndrome: a syndrome occurring in phenotypic females with 46,XY chromosomal karyotype and complete agenesis of the gonads and, therefore, pubertal failure which is correctable with hormonal replacement therapy.

sympathetic nervous system: formerly a synonym for the autonomic nervous system (ANS); now the name of only the thorolumbar (chest and spinal cord) outflow of the ANS. Its counterpart is the craniosacral (brain and far end of the spinal cord) outflow, which is the parasympathetic nervous system. Also a synonym for the now outmoded term, vegetative nervous system.

syntax: the meaning of words conveyed by their order and sequence and their relationship to one another in phrases and clauses.

syphilis: a systemic infection, historically known as the pox, transmitted by the bacterial spirochete, *Treponema pallidum*, chiefly through sexual contact.

taboo: forbidden in general usage, or for a particular category or class of people; classified as prohibited, offensive, obscene, blasphemous, or too sacred to be approached or practiced.

talisman: an object supposed to have occult or mystical power.

talismanism: belief in and adherence to the superstitious practices of talismanic magic and power; fetishism.

tampon: a highly absorbant, tube-shaped device designed especially for insertion into the vagina for menstrual hygiene, and worn with or without a menstrual pad.

taxonomy: the orderly classification of organisms into an ascending order of categories or taxa (sing. taxon), namely species, genus, family, order, class, phylum, and kingdom; the classification of diseases, languages, and other phenomena.

televangelist: an evangelical preacher who appears regularly on television.

template: a mold, pattern, gauge, or guide from which multiple copies may be produced.

temporal lobe: bilaterally, a lobe of the cerebral hemisphere at ear level which is the primary auditory cortex. In right handed people, the left temporal lobe specializes in language.

temporal lobe epilepsy: a type of epilepsy in which seizures originate in one of the brain's temporal lobes deep inside the head interior to the front-upper ear. Although occurring without a loss of consciousness, seizures may induce a prolonged altered state of consciousness during which behavior may be bizarre.

temporal lobe rage attacks: irrational outbursts of rage triggered by a neuro-electrical "storm" in one of the temporal lobes, measurable by EEG.

testosterone: the major male sex hormone secreted predominantly from the Leydig cells of the testes.

tomboy: a term, nonstigmatizing, for a girl with masculine sports and activity interests; she is more likely to grow up with heterosexual than homosexual inclinations.

totemic clan: in anthropology a kinship group whose criterion of membership is not a shared genetic ancestry but a shared ancestral totem.

toxicosis: a disease or condition induced by a toxin or poisonous substance.

toxin: a poisonous substance.

transcultural: occurring in two or more cultures.

transexual: pertaining to a person who undergoes social, hormonal, and surgical sex reassignment; or to sex reassignment as a method of rehabilitation.

transfusion: transferring, e.g., blood or other fluid, from one person to another.

transvestitic: characterized by cross-dressing.

transvestophilia: the paraphilia of fetishistic cross-dressing.

trauma: shock or injury, physical or mental, and the effects thereof.

troopbond: a close, personally recognized and lasting interdependency between people (and animals that live in troops) who are members of the same kinship, tribe, or community.

troopbondship: the status or qualification of being bonded together as members of a troop, e.g., a family, tribe, or community.

troubadour: from the eleventh to thirteenth century, in Provence in the south of France, a member of a wandering group of entertainers, poets, and musicians who sang especially of chivalry and courtly love.

tubal ligation: tying of the fallopian tubes as a secure method of contraception.

tumescence: swelling, especially of the sexual organs in response to erotic stimulation.

Turner syndrome (45,X): a sporadically occurring genetic syndrome with a female phenotype except for agenesis of the ovaries and hence sterility and absence of pubertal sex hormones. The latter is correctable by hormonal replacement therapy.

ultrasound: sonic vibrations too high pitched to be detected by the human ear, used in making a sonogram image.
umbilical cord: the cord that connects a fetus with its placenta and mother. It is cut at birth, leaving the belly button.
unisex: styled for wear or use by both males and females.
urolagnia: a seldom used synonym for urophilia (meaning erotic lust for urine).
vagina: in females, the canal that connects the uterus with the external vulva.
vaginal dilation: relaxation of the walls of the vagina, e.g., in childbirth, or by stretching with a penis-shaped object in cases of congenital or postsurgical tightness.
vaginism: a constriction or dryness of the vagina which either prevents or makes sexual intromission painful; vaginismus.
vaginopenial: synonym for penovaginal, or penial-vaginal.
vaginoplasty: plastic surgery to the vagina to correct a defect.
vasectomy: in the male, a secure form of contraception by cutting each vas deferens, the tubes along which sperms travel from each testicle to the penis.
vasocongestion: swelling produced by accumulation of blood in the blood vessels, as in the swelling of the sexual organs in response to erotic stimulation; tumescence.
vasodilation: widening or relaxation of the blood vessels, e.g., in response to a drug or medication.
vasopressin: a polypeptide pituitary hormone that regulates kidney function and, by vasoconstriction, blood pressure.
virginity: the status of not having had sexual intercourse; sexual chastity.
virus: a submicroscopic organism that can multiply only by living inside and borrowing from a host cell.
vocalism: a sound signal emitted from the vocal organs.
voluntary: performed with self-consent.
vomeronasal organ: a sense organ, recently recognized in humans, situated about an inch or so inside the nostril, that may respond to sexual pheromones directly, bypassing the sense of smell.
voyeurism: the paraphilia of surreptitious sexual spying, the spy being popularly known as a peeping Tom.
vulva: all of the external genitalia of the female, including the opening or orifice of the vagina.
wet dream: in males, especially at puberty, a discharge of semen while asleep, with an accompanying erotic dream.
yin and yang: in Chinese medicine since ancient times, female (negative, dark) and male (positive, light) principles, respectively. The ideal is to have them in balance.
zenith: the highest or culminating point.
zoophilia: the paraphilia pertaining to cross-species sexual interaction.
zygote: the cell with which embryonic life begins after the fusion of male (sperm) and female (ovum) gametes.

Bibliography

AASECT. Sexuality and the law. *Contemporary Sexuality: The International Resource for Educators, Researchers, and Therapists*, 30(3):9 ff, 1996a.

AASECT. Studies in short. *Contemporary Sexuality: The International Resource for Educators, Researchers, and Therapists*, 30(3):7-8, 1996b.

Abrahamson, D. Tamarins of the Amazon. *Science 85*, 6(7):58-63, 1985.

Akers, J.S. and Conaway, C.H. Female homosexual behavior in *Macaca mulatta*. *Archives of Sexual Behavior*, 8:63-80, 1979.

Alexander, G.M. and Sherwin, B.B. Sex steroids, sexual behavior, and selective attention for erotic stimuli in women using oral contraceptives. *Psychoneuroendocrinology*, 18:91-102, 1993.

Allen, L.S. and Gorski, R.A. Sexual orientation and the size of the anterior commissure in the human brain. *Proceedings of the National Academy of Sciences USA*, 89:7199-7202, 1992.

Allen, L.S., Hines, M., Shryne, J.E. and Gorski, R. Two sexually dimorphic cell groups in the human brain. *Journal of Neuroscience*, 9:497-506, 1989.

Anderson, C.M. and Bielert, C. Adolescent/adult copulatory behavior in nonhuman primates. In *Pedophilia: Biosocial Dimensions* (J.R. Feierman, ed.). New York, Springer-Verlag, 1990.

Anon. *Onania, or the Heinous Sin of Self-Pollution and All its Frightful Consequences, in Both Sexes, Considered with Spiritual and Physical Advice to Those Who Have Already Injur'd Themselves by this Abominable Practice.* No date. [Facsimile reprint of 1724 edition, Boston, John Phillips, in *The Secret Vice Exposed! Some Arguments Against Masturbation* (C. Rosenberg and C. Smith-Rosenberg, eds.). New York, Arno Press, 1974].

Anon. *The Beginning of Life*. Teikoku Hormone Manufacturing. Distributed by Cine-Science, Tokyo, No date.

Bakwin, H. Masturbation in infants. *Journal of Pediatrics*, 40:675-78, 1952.

Bakwin, H. Erotic feelings in infants and young children. *American Journal of Diseases of Children*, 126:52-54, 1973.

Bancroft, J. (ed.). *The Pharmacology of Sexual Function and Dysfunction*. Amsterdam, Excerpta Medica, 1995.

Bancroft, J., Sherwin, B.B., Alexander, G.M., Davidson, D.W. and Walker, A. Oral contraceptives, androgens, and the sexuality of young women: II. The role of androgens. *Archives of Sexual Behavior*, 20:121-35, 1991.

Basham, A.L. *The Wonder That Was India: A Survey of the Culture of the Indian Sub-Continent before the Coming of the Muslims*. New York, Grove Press, 1959.

Baugh, R. A principal's observations. In *The Sexual and Gender Development of Young Children* (E.K. Oremland and J.D. Oremland, eds.). Cambridge, MA, Ballinger, 1977.

Baulieu, E.E. Contragestion and other clinical applications of RU 486, an antiprogesterone at the receptor. *Science*, 245:1351-57, 1989.

Baum, M.J., Everitt, B.J., Herbert, J. and Keverne, E.B. Hormonal basis of proceptivity and receptivity in female primates. *Archives of Sexual Behavior*, 6:173-92, 1977.

Baum, M.J. Neuroendocrinology of sexual behavior in the male. In *Behavioral Endocrinology* (J.B. Becker, S.M. Breedlove and D. Crews, eds.). Cambridge, MA, Massachusetts Institute of Technology Press, 1992.

Beach, F.A. Sexual attractivity, proceptivity, and receptivity in female mammals. *Hormones and Behavior*, 7:105-38, 1976.

Benjamin, H. *The Transsexual Phenomenon*. New York, Julian Press, 1966.

Berkeley, B. and Tiffenbach, J. *Foreskin: Its Past, its Present and . . . its Future?*. San Francisco, Bud Berkeley (Privately published), 1983.

Berlin, F.S., Bergey, G.K. and Money, J. Periodic psychosis of puberty: A case report. *American Journal of Psychiatry*, 139:119-20, 1982.

Bick, D., Franco, B., Sherins, R.J., Heye, B., Pike, L., Crawford, J., Maddalena, A., Incerti, B., Pragliola, A., Meitinger, T. and Ballabio, A. Intragenic deletion of the *KALIG-1* gene in Kallmann's syndrome. *New England Journal of Medicine*, 326:1752-55, 1992.

Bigelow, J. *The Joy of Uncircumcising! Restore Your Birthright and Maximize Sexual Pleasure*. Aptos, CA, Hourglass, 1992.

Bobrow, N.A., Money, J. and Lewis, V.G. Delayed puberty, eroticism, and sense of smell: A psychological study of hypogonadotropinism, osmatic and anosmatic (Kallmann's syndrome). *Archives of Sexual Behavior*, 1:329-44, 1971.

Borneman, E. *Childhood Phases of Maturity: Sexual Developmental Psychology*. Amherst, NY, Prometheus Books, 1994.

Bosinski, H.A.G., Peter, M., Bonatz, G., Arndt, R., Sippell, W.G., and Wille, R. A higher rate of hyperandrogenic disorders in female-to-male transsexuals. *Psychoneuroendocrinology*, 1997. In press.

Boswell, J. *Christianity, Social Tolerance, and Homosexuality*. Chicago, University of Chicago Press, 1980.

Bradley, S.J. Childhood female masturbation. *Canadian Medical Association Journal*, 132:1165-66, 1985.

Breuer, J. and Freud, S. *Studien über Hysterie*. Leipzig and Vienna, Franz Deuticke, 1895.

Bullough, V.L. *Sexual Variance in Society and History*. New York, John Wiley and Sons, 1976.

Bullough, V.L. *Science in the Bedroom: A History of Sex Research*. New York, Basic Books, 1994.

Bullough, V.L. and Bullough, B. (eds.). *Human Sexuality: An Encyclopedia*. New York, Garland, 1994.

Burbank, V.K. *Aboriginal Adolescence*. New Brunswick, Rutgers University Press, 1988.

Burnett, A.L., Lowenstein, C.J., Bredt, D.S., Chang, T.S.K. and Snyder, S.H. Nitric oxide: A physiologic mediator of penile erection. *Science*, 257:401-403, 1992.

Calderone, M. Fetal erection and its message to us. *SIECUS Report*, 9(5/6):9-10, 1983.

Caras, R. *The Private Lives of Animals*. New York, Grosset and Dunlop, 1974.

Carey, M.P. and Kalichman, S.C. Letter to the editor. *Archives of Sexual Behavior*, 24:655-61, 1995.

Carter, C.S., Williams, J.R., Witt, D.M. and Insel, T.R. Oxytocin and social bonding. In *Oxytocin in Maternal, Sexual, and Social Behaviors* (C.A. Pedersen, J.D. Caldwell, G.F. Jirikowski and T.R. Insel, eds.). New York, New York Academy of Sciences, 1995.

Cate, R.M. and Lloyd, S.A. *Courtship*. Newbury Park, CA, Sage, 1992.

Cauldwell, D.O. Psychopathia transexualism. *Sexology*, 16:247-80, 1949.

CDC. Kaposi's sarcoma and pneumocystis pneumonia among homosexual men New York City and California. *Morbidity and Mortality Weekly Report*, 30:305-308, July 3, 1981.

CDC. Pneumocystis pneumonia—Los Angles. *Morbidity and Mortality Weekly Report*, 30:250-52, June 5, 1981.

Christhilf, S.M., Jr. A dissertation on health care in Anne Arundel County, 1649-1976. In *Anne Arundel County, Maryland: A Bicentennial History, 1649-1977* (J.C. Bradford, ed.). Annapolis, Anne Arundel County and Annapolis Bicentennial Committee, 1977.

Cleary, T.G. and Kohl, S. Overwhelming infection with group B beta-hemolytic streptococcus associated with circumcision. *Pediatrics*, 64:301-303, 1979.

Clopper, R.R., Adelson, J.M. and Money, J. Postpubertal psychosexual function in male hypopituitarism without hypogonadotropinism after growth hormone therapy. *Journal of Sex Research*, 12:14-32, 1976.

Clopper, R.R., Mazur, T.A., MacGillivray, M.H., Peterson, R.E. and Voorhess, M.L. Data on virilization and erotosexual behavior in male hypogonadotropic hypopituitarism during gonadotropin and androgen treatment. *Journal of Andrology*, 4:303-11, 1983.

Cohen, H., Levy, J.J., and McShane, D. Hemisperic specialization for speech and nonverbal stimuli in Chinese and French Canadian subjects. *Neuropsychologia*, 27:241-5, 1989.

Cohen, H.D. and Shapiro, A. Vaginal blood flow during sleep. *Psychophysiology*, 7:338, 1970.

Coleman, E., Colgan, P., and Gooren, L. Male cross-gender behavior in Myanmar (Burma): A description of the Acault. *Archives of Sexual Behavior*, 21:313-321, 1992.

Conniff, R. When it comes to moths, nature pulls out all the stops. *Smithsonian*, 26(11):68-81, 1976.

Conn, J.H. Children's reactions to the discovery of genital differences. *American Journal of Orthopsychiatry*, 10:747-54, 1940.

Cornog, M. and Perper, T. For *Sex Education, See Librarian: A Guide to Issues and Resources*. Westport, CT, Greenwood Press, 1996.

Constantine, L.L. and Martinson, F.M. (eds.). *Children and Sex: New Findings, New Perspectives*. Boston, Little, Brown, 1981.

Crews, D. Functional associations in behavioral endocrinology. In *Masculinity/Femininity: Basic Perspectives* (J.M. Reinisch, L.A. Rosenblum, S.A. Sanders, eds.). New York, Oxford University Press, 1987.

Crews, D. Unisexual organisms in the behavioral neurosciences. In *Evolution and Ecology of Unisexual Vertebrates, Bulletin #466* (R.M. Dawley and J.P. Bogart, eds.) Albany, NY, New York State Museum, 1989.

Crews, D. and Fitzgerald, K.T. "Sexual" behavior in parthenogenic lizards. *Proceedings of the National Academy of Sciences USA*, 77:499-502, 1980.

Cullberg, J. Mood changes and menstrual symptoms with different gestagen/estrogen combinations: A double blind comparison with a placebo. *Acta Psychiatrica Scandinavica,* Supplementum 236, 1972.

Currier, R.L. Juvenile sexuality in global perspective. In *Children and Sex: New Findings and Perspectives* (L.L. Constantine and F.M. Martinson, eds.). Boston, Little, Brown, 1981.

Dekoker, B. Sex and the spinal cord: A new pathway for orgasm. *Scientific American*, 275(6):30-32, December 1996.

Demyttenaere, K. and Vanderschueren, D. Selective serotonin reuptake inhibitors and sexual function. In *The Pharmacology of Sexual Function and Dysfunction* (J. Bancroft, ed.). Amsterdam, Excerpta Medica, 1995.

Diamond, J.M. Rediscovery of the yellow-fronted gardener bowerbird. *Science*, 216:431-34, 1982.

Dittman, R.W., Kappes, M.E. and Kappes M.H. Sexual behavior in adolescent and adult females with congenital adrenal hyperplasia. *Psychoneuroendocrinology*, 17:153-70, 1992.

Djerassi, C. The making of the pill. *Science 84*, 5(11):127-29, 1984.

D'Occhio, M.J. and Ford, J.J. Contribution of studies in cattle, sheep and swine to our understanding of the role of gonadal hormones in processes of sexual differentiation and adult sexual behavior. In *Handbook of Sexology, Vol. VI: The Pharmacology and Endocrinology of Sexual Function* (J.M.A. Sitsen, volume ed., J. Money and H. Musaph, series eds.). Amsterdam, Elsevier, 1988.

Dodson, B. *Sex For One: The Joy of Self-loving*, Revised ed. New York, Harmony Books, 1996.

Early, J.T. How masturbation can improve lovemaking. *Sexology*, 41(7):44-46, 1975.

Edwards, J.W. Indigenous koro, a genital retraction syndrome of insular southeast Asia: A critical review. *Culture, Medicine and Psychiatry*, 8:1-24, 1984.

Ehrhardt, A.A., Evers, K. and Money, J. Influence of androgen and some aspects of sexually dimorphic behavior in women with the late-treated adrenogenital syndrome. *Johns Hopkins Medical Journal*, 123:115-22, 1968.

Eibl-Eibesfeldt, I. *Love and Hate: The Natural History of Behavior Patterns*. New York, Holt, Rinehart and Winston, 1972.

Eibl-Eibesfeldt, I. Patterns of parent-child interaction in a cross-cultural perspective. In *The Behavior of Human Infants* (A. Oliverio and M. Zappella, eds.). New York, Plenum, 1983.

Eibl-Eibesfeldt, I. Dominance, submission, and love: Sexual pathologies from the perspective of ethology. In *Pedophilia: Biosocial Dimensions* (J.R. Feierman, ed.). New York, Springer-Verlag, 1990.

Ellis, H. *Studies in the Psychology of Sex, Vols. I-VI* (copyrighted 1900-1910). Philadelphia, F.A. Davis, 1920.

Elwin, V. *The Muria and Their Ghotul*. Bombay, Oxford University Press, 1947.

Elwin, V. *The Kingdom of the Young*. Bombay, Oxford University Press, 1968.

Elwin, V. *Verrier Elwin, Philanthropologist: Selected Writings* (N. Rustomji, ed.). Bombay, Oxford University Press, 1989.

Everett, H.C. Sneezing in response to light. *Neurology*, 14:483-90, 1964.

Everitt, B.J. and Herbert, J. Adrenal glands and sexual receptivity in female rhesus monkeys. *Nature*, 222:1065-66, 1969.

Everitt, B.J. and Herbert, J. The maintenance of sexual receptivity by adrenal androgens in female rhesus monkeys. Abstract, Proceedings of the Society for Endocrinology. In *Journal of Endocrinology*, 48:xxxviii, 1970.

Farabollini, F., Hole, D.R. and Wilson, C.A. Behavioral effects in adulthood of serotonin depletion by p-chlorophenylalanine given neonatally to male rats. *International Journal of Neuroscience*, 41:187-99, 1988.

Federoff, J.P. Antiandrogen vs. serotonergic medications in the treatment of sex offenders: A preliminary compliance study. *Canadian Journal of Human Sexuality*, 4:111-22, 1995.

Feierman, J.R., (ed.). *Pedophilia: Biosocial Dimensions*. New York, Springer-Verlag, 1990.

Fenner, F. Smallpox: Emergence, global spread, and eradication. *Pubblicazioni della Stazione Zoologica di Napoli, Section II: History and Philosophy of the Life Sciences*, 15:397-420, 1993.

Field, T.M., Schanberg, S.M., Scafidi, F., Bauer, C.R., Vega Lahr, N., Garcia, R., Nystrom, J. and Kuhn, C.M. Effects of tactile/kinesthetic stimulation on preterm neonates. *Pediatrics*, 77:654-58, 1986.

Finkelhor, D. Sex between siblings: Sex play, incest, and aggression. In *Children and Sex: New Findings, New Perspectives* (L.L. Constantine and F.M. Martinson, eds.). Boston, Little, Brown, 1981.

Fisher, H.E. *The Anatomy of Love: The Natural History of Monogamy, Adultery, and Divorce*. New York, W.W. Norton, 1992.

Fleisher, D.R. and Morrison, A. Masturbation mimicking abdominal pain or seizures in young girls. *Journal of Pediatrics*, 116:810-14, 1990.

Foster, C.M. Adolescent menstrual abnormalities. In *Pediatric Endocrinology*, 3rd ed., (F. Lifshitz, ed.). New York, Marcel Dekker, 1996.

Foulkes, D. Dream ontogeny and dream psychophysiology. In *Sleep Disorders: Basic and Clinical Research* (M. Chase and E.D. Weitzman, eds.). New York, SP Medical and Scientific Books, 1983.

Francouer, R., ed. *The International Encyclopedia of Sexuality*. New York, Continuum, 1997. In press.

Francoeur, R.T., Cornog, M., Perper, T. and Scherzer, N.A. (eds.). *The Complete Dictionary of Sexology*. New York, Continuum, 1995.

Frank, R.T. The hormonal causes of premenstrual tension. *Archives of Neurology and Psychiatry*, 26:1053-57, 1931.

Fratta, W., Biggio, G. and Gessa, G.L. Homosexual mounting behavior induced in male rats and rabbits by a tryptophan-free diet. *Life Sciences*, 21:379-83, 1977.

Frayser, S.G. and Whitby, T.J. *Studies in Human Sexuality: A Selected Guide*. Englewood, CO, Libraries Unlimited, 1995.

Freud, S. The Etiology of Hysteria. In *The Standard Edition of the Complete Psychological Works of Sigmund Freud*, 3:189-221, 1896, (J. Strachey, ed.). London, Hogarth Press and The Institute of Psycho-Analysis, 1953.

Freud, S. Three Essays on Sexual Theory. In *The Standard Edition of the Complete Psychological Works of Sigmund Freud*, 7:125-43, 1905, (J. Strachey, ed.). London, Hogarth Press and The Institute of Psycho-Analysis, 1953.

Friberg, T.R., Braunstein, R.A. and Bressler, N.M. Sudden visual loss associated with sexual activity. *Archives of Ophthalmology*, 113:738-42, 1995.

Frydman, R., Testart, J., Parneix, I., Raymond, J-P., Fries, N. and Bouchard, P. Pregnancy in a 46,XY patient. *Fertility and Sterility*, 50:813-14, 1988.

Gaden, J.R. The church and sexuality — on not getting it together. *St. Mark's Review*, Number 106:13-23, 1981.

Gajdusek, D.C. Unconventional viruses and the origin and disappearance of kuru. *Science*, 197:943-60, 1977.

Getz, L.L. and Carter, C.S. Social organization in *Microtus ochrogaster* populations. *The Biologist*, 62:56-69, 1980.

Getz, L.L., Carter, C.S. and Gavish, L. The mating system of the prairie vole, *Microtus ochrogaster*: Field and laboratory evidence for pair-bonding. *Behavioral Ecology and Sociobiology*, 8:189-94, 1981.

Gilmartin, B.G. *Shyness and Love: Causes, Consequences, and Treatment.* Lanham, MA, University Press of America, 1987.

Goldberg, S. and Lewis, M. Play behavior in the year-old infant: Early sex differences. *Child Development*, 40:21-31, 1969.

Goldfoot, D.A. Sociosexual behaviors in nonhuman primates during development and maturity: Social and hormonal relationships. In *Behavioral Primatology: Advances in Research and Theory*, Vol. 1., (A.M. Schrier, ed.). Hillsdale, NJ, Lawrence Erlbaum Associates, 1977.

Goldfoot, D.A., Westerborg-van Loon, H., Groeneveld, W. and Slob, A.K. Behavioral and physiological evidence of sexual climax in the female stump-tailed macaque (*Macaca arctoides*). *Science*, 208:1477-79, 1980.

Golombok, S. and Fivush, R. *Gender Development.* Cambridge, Cambridge University Press, 1994.

Gooren, L.J.G. Biomedical concepts of homosexuality: Folk belief in a white coat. *Journal of Homosexuality*, 28:237-46, 1995a.

Gooren, L.J.G. Effects of androgens on the human brain. Presented at the Congenital Adrenal Hyperplasia Symposium, Baltimore, Maryland, June 11-13, 1995b.

Gorman, C. Blood, sweat and fears: A former heavyweight fighter is HIV positive. *Time*, 147(9):59, February 26, 1996.

Gorski, R.A., Gordon, J.H., Shryne, J.E. and Southam, M.A. Evidence for a morphological sex difference within the medial preoptic area of the rat brain. *Brain Research*, 148:333-46, 1978.

Gorski, R.A., Harlan, R.E., Jacobson, C.D., Shryne, J.E. and Southam, M.A. Evidence for a morphological sex difference within the medial preoptic area of the rat brain. *Journal of Comparative Neurology*, 193:529-39, 1980.

Grafenberg, E. The role of the urethra in female orgasm. *International Journal of Sexology*, 3:145-48, 1950.

Graham, S. *A Lecture to Young Men.* Providence, RI, Weeden and Cory, 1834. Facsimile reprint edition, New York, Arno Press, 1974.

Granata, A.R.M., Bancroft, J. and Del Rio, G. Effects of psychological factors on erectile response to intracavernosal prostaglandin E1. In *The Pharmacology of Sexual Function and Dysfunction* (J. Bancroft, ed.). Amsterdam, Excerpta Medica, 1995.

Green, R. *"The Sissy Boy Syndrome" and the Development of Homosexuality.* New Haven, Yale University Press, 1987.

Green, R. and Money, J. Incongruous gender role in boys: Nongenital manifestations in prepubertal boys. *Journal of Nervous and Mental Disease*, 130:160-68, 1960.

Green, R. and Money, J. Stage-acting, role-taking and effeminate impersonation during boyhood. *Archives of General Psychiatry*, 15:535-38, 1966.

Green, R. and Money, J. (eds.). *Transsexualism and Sex Reassignment.* Baltimore, Johns Hopkins Press, 1969.

Gregersen, E. *The World of Human Sexuality: Behaviors, Customs, and Beliefs.* New York, Irvington, 1994.

Hall, W.S. *Sexual Knowledge: Sexual Education for Sex Problems.* Philadelphia, International Bible House, 1913.

Halliday, T. *Sexual Strategy.* Oxford, Oxford University Press, 1980.

Hamer, D.H., Hu, S., Magnuson, V.L., Hu, N. and Pattatucci, A.M.L. A linkage between DNA markers on the X chromosome and male sexual orientation. *Science*, 261:321-27, 1993.

Hare, E.H. Masturbatory insanity: The history of an idea. *Journal of Mental Science*, 108:2-25, 1962.

Harris, W.H. and Levey, J.S. (eds.). *The New Columbia Encyclopedia*. New York, Columbia University Press, 1975.

Heller, J. *Catch-22, A Novel*. New York, Simon and Schuster, 1955.

Henican, E. Judge's ties survived her three marriages. *New York Newsday*, November 10, 1992, p. 3 ff.

Herdt, G.H. *Guardians of the Flutes: Idioms of Masculinity*. New York, McGraw-Hill, 1981.

Herdt, G.H. (ed.). *Ritualized Homosexuality in Melanesia*. Berkeley, University of California Press, 1984.

Herdt, G.H. *The Sambia: Ritual and Gender in New Guinea*. New York, Holt, Rinehart and Winston, 1987.

Herdt, G.H. and Stoller, R.J. *Intimate Communications: Erotics and the Study of Culture*. New York, Columbia University Press, 1990.

Herek, G.M. and Greene, B. (eds.). *AIDS, Identity, and Community: The HIV Epidemic and Lesbians and Gay Men*. Thousand Oaks, CA, Sage, 1995.

Hertoft, P. Nordic traditions of marriage: The betrothal system. In *Handbook of Sexology* (J. Money and H. Musaph, eds.). Amsterdam, Elsevier/Excerpta Medica, 1977.

Himes, N.E. *Medical History of Contraception*. New York, Gamut Press, 1963.

Hingsburger, D.J. *Hand Made Love: A Guide for Teaching about Male Masturbation through Understanding and Video*. Eastman, Quebec, Diverse City Press, 1995.

Hingsburger, D.J. *Under Cover Dick: Teaching Men with Disabilities about Condom Use through Understanding and Video*. Eastman, Quebec, Diverse City Press, 1996.

Hirschfeld, M. *Die Transvestiten: Eine Untersuchung uber den erotischen Verkleidungstrieb*. Berlin, Pulvermacher, 1910.

Hirschfeld, M. *Transvestites: The Erotic Drive to Cross-Dress* (M. Lombardi-Nash, trans.). Amherst, NY, Prometheus Books, 1991.

Hoglund, J. and Alatalo, R.V. *Leks*. Princeton, Princeton University Press, 1995.

Holden, C. Winning with testosterone. *Science*, 269:1341-42, 1995.

Hopkin, K. Sugar 'n spice vs. puppy-dog tails: Sex differences in the brain. *Journal of NIH Research*, 7(11):39-43, 1995.

Horton, C.E., Devine, C.J., Jr., Devine, P.C., McCraw, J.B. and Arganese, T.J. Aesthetic reconstructive genital surgery. *Clinics in Plastic Surgery*, 8:399-406, 1981.

Hrdy, S.B. *The Langurs of Abu: Female and Male Strategies of Reproduction*. Cambridge, MA, Harvard University Press, 1977.

Hu, S., Pattatucci, A.M.L., Patterson, C., Li, L., Fulker, D.W., Cherny, S.S., Kruglyak, L. and Hamer, D.H. Linkage between sexual orientation and chromosome Xq28 in males but not in females. *Nature Genetics*, 11:248-57, 1995.

Insel, T.R. and Carter, C.S. The monogamous brain: Or, what a small midwestern rodent has taught us about the chemistry of mammalian love. *Natural History*, pp. 12-13, August 1995.

Jackson, P., Barrowclough, I.W., France, J.T. and Phillips, L.I. A successful pregnancy following total hysterectomy. *British Journal of Obstetrics and Gynaecology*, 87:353-55, 1980.

Jefferis, B.G. and Nichols, J.L. *Searchlights on Health: The Science of Eugenics*. Naperville, IL, J.L. Nichols, 1919.

Johnson, E., with Novak, W. *My Life*. New York, Random House, 1992.
Jordan, H.W. and Howe, G. De Clérambault syndrome (erotomania): A review and case presentation. *Journal of the National Medical Association*, 72:979-85, 1980.
Jowett, B. *The Dialogues of Plato Translated into English with Analyses and Introductions*. New York, Macmillan, 1892.
Kagan, J. and Moss, H.A. *Birth to Maturity: A Study in Psychological Development*. New York, John Wiley and Sons, 1962.
Kallmann, F.J., Schoenfeld, W.A. and Barrera, S.E. The genetic aspects of primary eunuchoidism. *American Journal of Mental Deficiency*, 48:203-36, 1944.
Kandel, E.R., Scwartz, J.H., and Jessell, T.M. *Essentials of Neural Science and Behavior*. New York, Appleton and Lange, 1995.
Kano, Y. The bonobos' peaceable kingdom. *Natural History*, pp. 62-71, November 1990.
Kano, Y. *The Last Ape: Pygmy Chimp Behavior and Ecology*. Stanford, Stanford University Press, 1992.
Kappy, M.S., Blizzard, R.M. and Migeon, C.J. (eds.). *Wilkins, The Diagnosis and Treatment of Endocrine Disorders in Childhood and Adolescence*, 4th ed. Springfield, IL, Charles C Thomas, 1994.
Karacan, I. The developmental aspect and the effect of certain clinical conditions upon penile erection during sleep. In *Proceedings of the IV World Congress of Psychiatry*. Excerpta Medica International Congress Series No. 150. Amsterdam, Excerpta Medica, 1966.
Karacan, I., Rosenbloom, A.L. and Williams, R.L. The clitoral erection cycle during sleep. *Psychophysiology*, 7:338, 1970.
Karacan, I., Williams, R.L., Thornby, J.I. and Salis, P.J. Sleep-related penile tumescence as a function of age. *American Journal of Psychiatry*, 132:932-37, 1975.
Katchadourian, H.A. and Lunde, D.T. *Fundamentals of Human Sexuality*. New York, Holt Rinehart and Winston, 1972.
Kelch, R.P. and Beitins, I.Z. Adolescent sexual development. In *Wilkins, The Diagnosis and Treatment of Endocrine Disorders in Childhood and Adolescence*, 4th ed., (M.S. Kappy, R.M. Blizzard and C.J. Migeon, eds.). Springfield, IL, Charles C Thomas, 1994.
Kellogg, J.H. *Plain Facts for Old and Young, Embracing the Natural History and Hygiene of Organic Life*. Burlington, IA, I.F. Segner, 1888. Facsimile reprint edition, New York, Arno Press, 1974.
Kempe, C.H., Silverman, F.N., Steele, B.F., Droegemuller, W. and Silver, H.K. The battered-child syndrome. In *Traumatic Abuse and Neglect of Children at Home* (G.J. Williams and J. Money, eds.). Baltimore, Johns Hopkins University Press, 1980.
Kennedy, D.M. *Birth Control in America: The Career of Margaret Sanger*. New Haven, Yale University Press, 1970.
Keverne, E.B. and Vellucci, S.V. Social, endocrine and pharmacological influences on primate sexual behavior. In *Handbook of Sexology, Vol. VI: The Pharmacology and Endocrinology of Sexual Function* (J.M.A. Sitsen, ed., J. Money and H. Musaph, series eds.). Amsterdam, Elsevier, 1988.
Keyes, R.W. and Money, J. *The Armed Robbery Orgasm: A Lovemap Autobiography of Masochism*. Amherst, NY, Prometheus Books, 1993.
Kinsey, A.C., Pomerory, W.B. and Martin, C.E. *Sexual Behavior in the Human Male*. Philadelphia, Saunders, 1948.

Kleeman, J.A. Genital self-stimulation in infant and toddler girls. In *Masturbation from Infancy to Senesence*, (I. Marcus and J.J. Francis, eds.). New York, International Universities Press, 1975.

Kolodny, R.C., Masters, W.H. and Johnson, V.E. *Textbook of Sexual Medicine.* Boston, Little, Brown, 1979.

Komisaruk, B.R. Vaginocervical afference as a trigger for analgesic, behavioral, autonomic, and neuroendocrine processes. In *Behavioral Biology: Neuroendocrine Axis* (T. Archer and S. Hansen, eds.). Hillsdale, NJ, Lawrence Erlbaum Associates, 1991.

Krafft-Ebing, R. von. *Psychopathia Sexualis with Especial Reference to Contrary Sexual Instinct: A Medical Legal Study*, 12th ed., (F.J. Rebman, trans.). Chicago, Logan Brothers, 1931.

Krugman, S. Hepatitis virus vaccines: Present status. *Yale Journal of Biology and Medicine*, 55:375-81, 1982.

Krivacska, J.J. *Designing Child Sexual Abuse Prevention Programs: Current Approaches and a Proposal for the Prevention, Reduction, and Identification of Sexual Misuse.* Springfield, IL, Charles C Thomas, 1990.

Krivacska, J.J. and Money, J. (eds.). *The Handbook of Forensic Sexology: Biomedical and Criminological Perspectives.* Amherst, NY, Prometheus Books, 1994.

La Barre, W. *Muelos: A Stone Age Superstition About Sexuality.* New York, Columbia University Press, 1984.

Ladas, A.K. and Whipple, B. *The G Spot and Other Recent Discoveries about Human Sexuality.* New York, Holt, Rinehart and Winston, 1982.

Langfeldt, T. Childhood masturbation: Individual and social organization. In *Children and Sex: New Findings, New Perspectives* (L.L. Constantine and F.M. Martinson, eds.). Boston, Little, Brown, 1981a.

Langfeldt, T. Processes in sexual development. In *Children and Sex: New Findings, New Perspectives* (L.L. Constantine and F.M. Martinson, eds.). Boston, Little, Brown, 1981b.

Langfeldt, T. *Sexologi.* Oslo, Ad Notam Gyldendal, 1993.

Laub, D.R., Eicher, W., Laub, D.R., II and Hentz, V.R. Penis construction in female-to-male transsexuals. In *Plastic Surgery in the Sexually Handicapped* (W. Eicher, ed.). Berlin, Springer-Verlag, 1989.

Laumann, E.O., Gagnon, J.H., Michael, R.T. and Michaels, S. *The Social Organization of Sexuality: Sexual Practices in the United States.* Chicago, University of Chicago Press, 1994.

Lawrence, R.J., Jr. *The Poisoning of Eros: Sexual Values in Conflict.* New York, Augustine Moore, 1989.

Leithauser, L.G., Gilbert, E. and Barton, J. Complications of fat grafting to the penis. *Annals of Plastic Surgery*, 34:173-75, 1995.

LeVay, S. A difference in hypothalamic structure between heterosexual and homosexual men. *Science*, 253:1034-37, 1991.

Lewis, V.G., Money, J. and Bobrow, N.A. Idiopathic pubertal delay beyond age fifteen: Psychologic study of twelve boys. *Adolescence*, 12:1-11, 1977.

Liebowitz, M.R. *The Chemistry of Love.* Boston, Little, Brown, 1983.

Liebowitz, M.R. and Klein, D.F. Hysteroid dysphoria. *Psychiatric Clinics of North America*, 2:555-75, 1979.

Lifshitz, F. (ed.). *Pediatric Endocrinology*, 3rd ed. New York, Marcel Dekker, 1996.

Lightfoot-Klein, H. *Prisoners of Ritual: An Odyssey into Female Genital Circumcision in Africa*. Binghamton, NY, Haworth Press, 1989.

Lightfoot-Klein, H. Orgasm in ritually circumcised women. In *Proceedings: The First International Conference on Orgasm* (P. Kothari and R. Patel, eds.). Bombay, VRP, 1991.

Livingston, S., Berman, W. and Pauli, L.L. Masturbation simulating epilepsy. *Clinical Pediatrics*, 14:232-34, 1975.

Lobel, P.S. Mating strategies of coastal marine fishes. *Oceanus*, 34:19-26, 1991.

Lorenz, K. *King Solomon's Ring*. New York, Thomas Y. Crowell. 1952.

Louganis, G., with Marcus, E. *Breaking the Surface*. New York, Random House, 1995.

Luria, Z., Friedman, S. and Rose, M.D. *Human Sexuality*. New York, John Wiley and Sons, 1987.

Lutz, D. No conception. *The Sciences*, 36(1):12-15, 1996.

Mahood J. and Wenberg, K. *The Mosher Survey: Sexual Attitudes of Forty-Five Victorian Women*. New York, Arno Press, 1980.

Marshall, W.A. and Tanner, J.M. Variations in the pattern of pubertal changes in girls. *Archives of Disease in Childhood*, 44:291-303, 1969.

Marshall, W.A. and Tanner, J.M. Variations in the pattern of pubertal changes in boys. *Archives of Disease in Childhood*, 45:13-23, 1970.

Masson, J. 1984. *The Assault on Truth: Freud's Suppression of the Seduction Theory*. New York, Farrar, Straus and Giroux.

Masters, W.H. and Johnson, V.E. *Human Sexual Response*. Boston, Little, Brown, 1966.

Masters, W.H. and Johnson, V.E. *Human Sexual Inadequacy*. Boston, Little, Brown, 1970.

Masters, W.H., Johnson, V.E. and Kolodny, R.C. *Human Sexuality*. Boston, MA, Little, Brown, 1982.

Matthews, M. *The Horseman: Obsessions of a Zoophile*. Amherst, NY, Prometheus Books, 1995.

Mathur, A.K. and Joshi, A. Variation in the expression of sexual behaviour of rams under different rearing conditions. In *3rd Asian Conference of Sexology Abstracts* (R. Shah and V. Kulkarni, eds.). New Delhi, India, 1994.

Mathur, A.K., Joshi, A. and Khuswaha, B.P. Influence of introducing tubectomized ewes in expression of sexual behaviour of rams reared in unisexual flock. In *3rd Asian Conference of Sexology Abstracts* (R. Shah and V. Kulkarni, eds.). New Delhi, India, 1994.

McClintock, M.K. Menstrual synchrony and suppression. *Nature*, 229:244-45, 1971.

McGarry, M.C. The discovery of the contraceptive pill. *Medical Tribune*, 28(10):22-23, 1987.

McManus, J. "Miracle" in genital surgery. *Boston Globe*, July 8, 1982.

Meizner, I. Sonographic observation of in utero fetal "masturbation." *Journal of Ultrasound in Medicine*, 6:111, 1987.

Mendelsohn, H., Tirosh, E. and Berant, M. Masturbation in infancy simulating convulsive disorder [Hebrew]. *Harefuh*, 122(2):79-80, 1992.

Meo, R., Bilo, L. and Striano, S. A unique case of "masturbatory" seizures in primary generalized epilepsy. *Acta Neurologica*, 7:409-15, 1985.

Miccio-Fonseca, L.C. *Personal Sentence Completion Inventory*. San Diego, CA, Privately published, 1996.

Michael, R.P. and Zumpe, D. Medroxyprogesterone acetate decreases the sexual activity of male cynomolgus monkeys (*Macaca fascicularis*): An action on the brain? *Physiology and Behavior*, 53:783-88, 1993.

Michael, R.T., Gagnon, J.H., Laumann, E.O. and Kolata, G. *Sex in America: A Definitive Survey*. Boston, Little, Brown, 1994.

Migeon, C.J. and Forest, M.G. Androgens in biological fluids. In *Nuclear Medicine in Vitro* (B. Rothfield, ed.). Philadelphia, J.B. Lippincott, 1983.

Migeon, C.J. and Donohoue, P.A. Adrenal disorders. In *Wilkins, The Diagnosis and Treatment of Endocrine Disorders in Childhood and Adolescence*, 4th ed., (M.S. Kappy, R.M. Blizzard and C.J. Migeon, eds.). Springfield, IL, Charles C Thomas, 1994.

Migeon, C.J., Berkovitz, G. and Brown, T. Sexual differentiation and ambiguity. In *Wilkins, The Diagnosis and Treatment of Endocrine Disorders in Childhood and Adolescence*, 4th ed., (M.S. Kappy, R.M. Blizzard and C.J. Migeon, eds.). Springfield, IL, Charles C Thomas, 1994.

Moll, A. *The Sexual Life of the Child*. New York, Macmillan, 1912.

Money, J. Components of eroticism in man: I. The hormones in relation to sexual morphology and sexual desire. *Journal of Nervous and Mental Disease*, 132:239-48, 1961a.

Money, J. Sex hormones and other variables in human eroticism. In *Sex and Internal Secretions* (W.C. Young, ed.). Baltimore, Williams and Wilkins, 1961b.

Money, J. Discussion on hormonal inhibition of libido in male sex offenders. In *Endocrinology and Human Behavior* (R.P. Michael, ed.). London, Oxford University Press, 1968.

Money, J. Matched pairs of hermaphrodites: Behavioral biology of sexual differentiation from chromosomes to gender identity. *Engineering and Science*, 33:34-39, 1970a.

Money, J. Use of an androgen-depleting hormone in the treatment of sex offenders. *Journal of Sex Research*, 6:165-72, 1970b.

Money, J. Two names, two wardrobes, two personalities. *Journal of Homosexuality*, 1:65-70, 1974.

Money, J. The syndrome of abuse dwarfism (psychosocial dwarfism or reversible hyposomatotropinism). Behavioral data and case report. *American Journal of Diseases of Children*, 131:508-13, 1977.

Money, J. To quim and to swive: Linguistic and coital parity, male and female. *Journal of Sex Research*, 18:173-76, 1982.

Money, J. *Love and Love Sickness: The Science of Sex, Gender Difference, and Pairbonding*. Baltimore, Johns Hopkins University Press, 1980.

Money, J. The genealogical descent of sexual psychoneuroendocrinology from sex and health theory: The eighteenth to the twentieth centuries. *Psychoneuroendocrinology*, 8:391-400, 1983a.

Money, J. New phylism theory and autism: Pathognomonic impairment of troopbonding. *Medical Hypotheses*, 11:245-50, 1983b. [Reprinted in Money, J. 1986. *Venuses Penuses: Sexology, Sexosophy, and Exigency Theory*. Amherst, NY, Prometheus Books].

Money, J. *The Destroying Angel: Sex, Fitness and Food in the Legacy of Degeneracy Theory, Graham Crackers, Kellogg's Corn Flakes and American Health History*. Amherst, NY, Prometheus Books, 1985.

Money, J. *Lovemaps: Clinical Concepts of Sexual/Erotic Health and Pathology, Paraphilia, and Gender Transposition in Childhood, Adolescence, and Maturity*. New York, Irvington, 1986a. [Paperback, Amherst, NY, Prometheus Books, 1988.]

Money, J. *Venuses Penuses: Sexology, Sexosophy, and Exigency Theory*. Amherst, NY, Prometheus Books, 1986b.

Money, J. Masochism: On the childhood origin of paraphilia, opponent-process theory, and antiandrogen therapy. *Journal of Sex Research*, 23:273-75, 1987a.

Money, J. Treatment guidelines: Antiandrogen and counseling of paraphilic sex offenders. *Journal of Sex and Marital Therapy*, 13:219-23, 1987b.

Money, J. *Gay, Straight, and In-Between: The Sexology of Erotic Orientation*. New York, Oxford University Press, 1988a.

Money, J. The Skoptic syndrome: Castration and genital self-mutilation as an example of sexual body-image pathology. *Journal of Psychology and Human Sexuality*, 1(1):113-28, 1988b.

Money, J. Paraphilia in females: Fixation on amputation and lameness: two personal accounts. *Journal of Psychology and Human Sexuality*, 3(2):165-72, 1990a.

Money, J. Pedophilia: A specific instance of new phylism theory as applied to paraphilic lovemaps. In *Pedophilia: Biosocial Dimensions* (J. R. Feierman, ed.). New York, Springer-Verlag, 1990b

Money, J. Forensic sexology: Paraphilic rape (biastophilia) and lust murder (erotophonophilia). *American Journal of Psychotherapy*, 44:26-36, 1990c.

Money, J. *Biographies of Gender and Hermaphroditism in Paired Comparisons: Clinical Supplement to the Handbook of Sexology*. Amsterdam, Elsevier, 1991a.

Money, J. Sexology, body image, foreskin restoration, and bisexual status. *Journal of Sex Research*, 28:145-56. 1991b.

Money, J. Semen-conservation theory vs. semen-investment theory, antisexualism, and the return of Freud's seduction theory. *Journal of Psychology and Human Sexuality*, 4(4):31-45, 1991c.

Money, J. The transformation of sexual terminology: Homosexuality in sexological history. *SIECUS Report*, 19(5):10-13, 1991d.

Money, J. *The Kaspar Hauser Syndrome of "Psychosocial Dwarfism": Deficient Statural, Intellectual, and Social Growth Induced by Child Abuse*. Amherst, NY, Prometheus Books, 1992a.

Money, J. Orgasmology, the science of orgasm: Brain, genitals, phantom orgasm, clinical syndromes. In *Proceedings of the First International Conference on Orgasm* (P. Kothari and R. Patel, eds.). New Delhi, VRP, 1992b.

Money, J. *The Adam Principle: Genes, Genitals, Hormones, and Gender — Selected Readings in Sexology*. Buffalo, Prometheus Books, 1993a.

Money, J. Honk if you masturbate: How safe must safe sex be? Milton S. Eisenhower Symposium, Johns Hopkins University, November 18, 1993b.

Money, J. Aesop's lost fable: The takahe. *GEMS News*, #17:25-27, September, 1994a.

Money, J. *Sex Errors of the Body and Related Syndromes: A Guide to Counseling Children, Adolescents, and Their Families*, 2nd ed. Baltimore, Paul H. Brookes, 1994b.

Money, J. *Reinterpreting the Unspeakable: Human Sexuality 2000; The Complete Interviewer and Clinical Biographer, Exigency Theory, and Sexology for the Third Millennium*. New York, Continuum, 1994c.

Money, J. *Gendermaps: Social Constructionism, Feminism, and Sexosophical History*. New York, Continuum, 1995a.

Money, J. Safe sex in the era of AIDS. *Trends in Health Care, Law & Ethics*, 10(3):27-33, 1995b.

Money, J. Sexology of ictal masturbation in infancy. *Journal of Sex and Marital Therapy*, 22:280-83, 1996.

Money, J. and Alexander, D. Psychosexual development and absence of homosexuality in males with precocious puberty: Review of 18 cases. *Journal of Nervous and Mental Disease*, 148:111-23, 1969.

Money, J. and Annecillo, C. Body-image pathology: Koro, the shrinking-penis syndrome in transcultural sexology. *Sexual and Marital Therapy*, 2:91-100, 1987.

Money, J. and Annecillo, C. Paraphilia as a sexual disability: Outcome study in a female with a history of the Kaspar Hauser dwarfism syndrome. *Sexuality and Disability*, 9:297-309, 1991.

Money, J. and Clopper, R. Psychosocial and psychosexual aspects of error of pubertal onset and development. *Human Biology*, 46:173-81, 1974.

Money, J. and Daléry, J. Iatrogenic homosexuality: Gender identity in seven 46,XX chromosomal females with hyperadrenocortical hermaphroditism born with a penis, three reared as boys, four reared as girls. *Journal of Homosexuality*, 1:357-71, 1976.

Money, J. and Davison, J. Adult penile circumcision: Erotosexual and cosmetic sequelae. *Journal of Sex Research*, 19:289-92, 1983.

Money, J. and Ehrhardt, A.A. *Man and Woman, Boy and Girl: The Differentiation and Dimorphism of Gender Identity from Conception to Maturity*. Facsimile reprint edition. Northvale, NJ, Jason Aronson, 1994. First edition, 1972.

Money, J. and Hampson, J.G. Idiopathic sexual precocity in the male. *Psychosomatic Medicine*, 17:1-15, 1955.

Money, J. and Hirsch, S.R. After priapism: Orgasm retained, erection lost. *Journal of Urology*, 94:152-57, 1965.

Money, J. and Hosta, G.M. Laughing seizures with sexual precocity: Report of two cases. *Johns Hopkins Medical Journal*, 120:326-36, 1967.

Money, J. and Lamacz, M. Gynemimesis and gynemimetophilia: Individual and cross-cultural manifestations of a gender coping strategy hitherto unnamed. *Journal of Sex and Marital Therapy*, 10:105-16, 1984.

Money, J. and Lamacz, M. *Vandalized Lovemaps: Paraphilic Outcome of Seven Cases in Pediatric Sexology*. Amherst, NY, Prometheus Books, 1989.

Money, J. and Musaph, H. (eds.). *Handbook of Sexology*. Amsterdam, Elsevier/Excerpta Medica, 1977.

Money, J. and Russo, A.J. Homosexual outcome of discordant gender identity/role in childhood: Longitudinal follow-up. *Journal of Pediatric Psychology*, 4:29-41, 1979.

Money, J. and Russo, A.J. Homosexual vs. transvestite or transexual gender-identity/role: Outcome study in boys. *International Journal of Family Psychiatry*, 2:139-45, 1981.

Money, J. and Sollod, R. Body image, plastic surgery (prosthetic testes) and Kallmann's syndrome. *British Journal of Medical Psychology*, 51:91-94, 1978.

Money, J. and Weinrich, J.D. Juvenile, pedophile, heterophile: Hermeneutics of science, medicine and law in two outcome studies. *Medicine and Law*, 2:39-54, 1983.

Money, J. and Werlwas, J. Folie à deux in the parents of psychosocial dwarfs: Two cases. *Bulletin of the American Academy of Psychiatry and the Law*, 4:351-62, 1976.

Money, J. and Werlwas, J. Paraphilic sexuality and child abuse: The parents. *Journal of Sex and Marital Therapy*, 8:57-64, 1982

Money, J., Annecillo, C. and Hutchison, J.W. Forensic and family psychiatry in abuse dwarfism: Munchausen's syndrome by proxy, atonement, and addiction to abuse. *Journal of Sex and Marital Therapy*, 11:30-40, 1985.

Money, J., Annecillo, C., Lobato, C. Paraphilic and other sexological anomalies as a sequel to the syndrome of child-abuse (psychosocial) dwarfism. *Journal of Psychology and Human Sexuality*, 3(1):117-50, 1990.

Money, J., Cawte, J.E., Bianchi, G.N. and Nurcombe, B. Sex training and traditions in Arnhem Land. *British Journal of Medical Psychology*, 43:383-99, 1970.

Money, J., Jobaris, R. and Furth, G. Apotemnophilia: Two cases of self-demand amputation as a paraphilia. *Journal of Sex Research*, 13:115-25, 1977.

Money, J., Joshi, V.K. and Prakasam, K.S. Kama Sutra: Woman's sexology versus semen conservation theory in Sanskrit teachings. In *The Present and Future of Preventive Research: In Honor of George W. Albee, Ph.D.* (M. Kessler, S.E. Goldston and J.M. Joffe, eds.). Newbury Park, CA, Sage, 1992.

Money, J., Leal, J. and Gonzalez-Heydrich, J. Aphrodisiology: History, folklore, efficacy. In *Handbook of Sexology, Vol. VI: The Pharmacology and Endocrinology of Sexual Function* (J.M.A. Sitsen, ed., J. Money and H. Musaph, series eds.). Amsterdam, Elsevier, 1988.

Money, J., Schwartz, M. and Lewis, V.G. Adult erotosexual status and fetal hormonal masculinization and demasculinization: 46,XX congenital virilizing adrenal hyperplasia and 46,XY androgen-insensitivity syndrome compared. *Psychoneuroendocrinology*, 9:405-14, 1984.

Money, J., Wainwright, G. and Hingsburger, D. *The Breathless Orgasm: A Lovemap Biography of Asphyxiophilia*. Amherst, NY, Prometheus Books, 1991.

Money, J., Wiedeking, C., Walker, P., Migeon, C., Meyer, W. and Borgaonkar, D. 47,XYY and 46,XY males with antisocial and/or sex-offending behavior: Antiandrogen therapy plus counseling. *Psychoneuroendocrinology*, 1:165-78, 1975.

Morain, C. Men who think bigger is better. *San Francisco Chronicle*, October 3, 1994.

Morgen, K.B. *Getting Simon: Two Gay Doctors' Journey to Fatherhood*. Bearsville, NY, Bramble Books, 1995.

Moritz, C. Parthenogenesis in the endemic Australian lizard *Heteronotia binoei* (Gekkonidae). *Science*, 220:735-37, 1983.

Morris, N.M., Udry, J.R., Khan-Dawood, F. and Dawood, M.Y. Marital sex frequency and midcycle female testosterone. *Archives of Sexual Behavior*, 16:27-37, 1987.

Mosovich, A. and Tallaferro, A. Studies on EEG and sex function orgasm. *Disease of the Nervous System*, 15:218-20, 1954.

Moss, H. Sex, age, and state as determinants of mother-infant interaction. *Merrill-Palmer Quarterly*, 13:19-36, 1967.

Moy, R.J.D. Paediatric AIDS: A major challenge to child survival in Africa. *9th World Pediatric Congress: Abstracts* (A. Russell, ed.), 1995.

Mulaikal, R.M., Migeon, C.J., Rock, J.A. Fertility rates in female patients with congenital adrenal hyperplasia due to a 21-hydroxylase deficiency. *New England Journal of Medicine*, 316:178-82, 1987.

Musaph, H. and Abraham, G. Frigidity or hypogyneismus. In *Handbook of Sexology* (J. Money and H. Musaph, eds.). Amsterdam, Elsevier/Excerpta Medica, 1977.

Nadler, R.D. Laboratory research on sexual behavior and reproduction of gorillas and orang-utans. *American Journal of Primatology Supplement*, 1:57-66, 1982.

Nanda, S. *Neither Man Nor Woman: The Hijras of India*. Belmont, CA, Wadsworth, 1990.

Nelson, R.J., Demas, G.E., Huang, P.L., Fishman, M.C., Dawson, V.L. and Snyder, S.H. Behavioral abnormalities in male mice lacking neuronal nitric oxide synthase. *Nature*, 378:383-86, 1995.

Neumann, F. Permanent changes in gonadal function and sexual behaviour as a result of early feminization of male rats by treatment with an antiandrogenic steroid. *Endokrinologie*, 50:209-25, 1966.

Ng, M.L. Environmental and personal risk factors for koro in southern China. *Journal of Psychology and Human Sexuality*, 1997. In press.

Nilsson, L. *The Miracle of Life*. Filmed by Lennart Nilsson for NOVA, WGBH Public Television, Boston. Distributed by WGBH Public Television. No date.

NOCIRC. National Center for Health Statistics report. NOCIRC Newsletter, 9(1):3, 1995.

Nottebohm, F. and Arnold, A.P. Sexual dimorphism in vocal control areas of the songbird brain. *Science*, 194:211-13, 1976.

Otto, S.V. Rare condition found in Chesapeake Bay blue crab. *Commercial Fisheries News*, 12(5):1, September 1979.

Pang, S.Y., Wallace, M.A., Hofman, L., Thuline, H.C., Dorche, C., Lyon, I.C., Dobbins, R.H., Kling, S., Fujieda, K, and Suwa, S. Worldwide experience in newborn screening for classical congenital adrenal hyperplasia due to 21-hydroxylase deficiency. *Pediatrics*, 81:866-74, 1988.

Peles, U.P. and Panter, B. *Erection Magic: A Proven, Integrated Treatment Program to Immediately Overcome Sexual Problems*. Los Angeles, In press, 1996.

Pendergrast, M. *Victims of Memory: Incest Accusations and Shattered Lives*. Hinesburg, VT, Upper Access Books, 1995.

Perez, C.J. and Rubio, E., (coords.). *Antologia de la Sexualidad Humana*. Mexico City, Miguel Angel Porrua Grupo Editorial, 1994.

Perkins, A. and Fitzgerald, J.A. Luteinizing hormone, testosterone, and behavioral response of male-oriented rams to estrous ewes and rams. *Journal of Animal Science*, 70:1787-94, 1992.

Perkins, A., Fitzgerald, J.A. and Moss, G.E. A comparison of LH secretion and brain estradiol receptors in heterosexual and homosexual rams and female sheep. *Hormones and Behavior*, 29:31-41, 1995.

Perper, T. *Sex Signals: The Biology of Love*. Philadelphia, ISI Press, 1985.

Perry, M.E. (ed.). *Handbook of Sexology, Vol. VII: Childhood and Adolescent Sexology*, (J. Money and H. Musaph, series eds.). Amsterdam, Elsevier, 1990.

Persky, H., Lief, H.I., Strauss, D., Miller, W.R. and O'Brien, C.P. Plasma testosterone level and sexual behavior of couples. *Archives of Sexual Behavior*, 7:157-73, 1978.

Peterson, R.T. *Penguins*. Boston, Houghton Mifflin, 1979.

Phoenix, C.H., Goy, R.W., Gerall, A.A. and Young, W.C. Organizing action of prenatally administered testosterone propionate on the tissues mediating mating behavior in the female guinea pig. *Endocrinology*, 65:369-82, 1959.

Pranzarone, G.F. Sexuoerotic stimulation and orgasmic response in the induction and management of parturition: Clinical possibilities. In *Proceedings: The First International Conference on Orgasm* (P. Kothari and R. Patel, eds.). Bombay, VRP, 1991.

Pusey, A. Mechanisms of inbreeding avoidance in nonhuman primates. In *Pedophilia: Biosocial Dimensions* (J.R. Feierman, ed.). New York, Springer-Verlag, 1990.

Rathbun, L.L. Behind the gold. *Pacific Way* (United Airlines Magazine), p. 41, November 1993.

Rees, H.D., Bonsall, R.W. and Michael, R.P. Preoptic and hypothalamic neurons accumulate [^{3}H] medroxyprogesterone acetate in male cynomolgus monkeys. *Life Science*, 39:1353-59, 1986.

Reid, R.W. The use of goserelin in compulsive sex-offenders: A follow-up report of two cases. Presented at the 13th World Congress of Sexology, Valencia, Spain, June 25-29, 1997.

Rice, G., Anderson, C., Risch, N. and Ebers, G. Male homosexuality: Absence of linkage to micro satellite markers on the X-chromosome in a Canadian study. *Abstracts: International Academy of Sex Research, 21st Annual Meeting.* September 20-24, 1995.

Richards, M.P.M., Bernal, J.F. and Brackbill, Y. Early behavioral differences: Gender or circumcision. *Developmental Psychobiology*, 9:89-95, 1976.

Riddle, G.C. *Amputees and Devotees.* New York, Irvington, 1989.

Ridley, M. *The Red Queen: Sex and the Evolution of Human Nature.* New York, Macmillan, 1994.

Riley, A.J. Alpha adrenoreceptors and human sexual function. In *The Pharmacology of Sexual Function and Dysfunction* (J. Bancroft, ed.). Amsterdam, Excerpta Medica, 1995.

Robertson, D.R. Social control of sex reversal in coral-reef fish. *Science*, 177:1007-1009, 1972.

Rosen, R. and Rosen, L.R. *Human Sexuality.* New York, Alfred A. Knopf, 1981.

Routh, D.K. and Schroeder, C.S. Masturbation and other sexual behaviors. In *Behavioral Problems in Childhood* (S. Gabel, ed.). New York, Grune and Stratton, 1981.

Rowan, E.L. Continence and conservation: Masturbation according to the Boy Scout Handbook. Presented at the 31st Annual Meeting of the Society for the Scientific Study of Sex, San Francisco, November 12, 1988.

Sapolsky, R. Testicular function, social rank and personality among wild baboons. *Psychoneuroendocrinology*, 16:281-93, 1991.

Sauer, M.V., Lobo, R.A. and Paulson, R.J. Successful twin pregnancy after embryo donation to a patient with XY gonadal dysgenesis. *American Journal of Obstetrics and Gynecology*, 161:380-81, 1989.

Schanberg, S.M. and Kuhn, C.M. The biochemical effect of tactile deprivation in neonate rats. In *Neuroendocrine Control and Behavior: Perspectives in Behavioral Medicine,* Vol. 2, (R.B. Williams, Jr., ed.). New York, Academic Press, 1985.

Schanberg, S.M. and Field, T.M. Sensory deprivation stress and supplemental stimulation in the rat pup and preterm human neonate. *Child Development*, 58:1431-47, 1987.

Schlegel, A. and Barry, H., III. *Adolescence: An Anthropological Inquiry.* New York, The Free Press, 1991.

Schreier, H.A. and Libow, J.A. *Hurting for Love: Munchausen syndrome by proxy.* New York, Guilford, 1993.

Schuster, R.H. Lekking behavior in *Kafue lechwe. Science*, 192:1240-42, 1976.

Segraves, R.T. Antidepressant-induced orgasm disorder. *Journal of Sex and Marital Therapy*, 21:192-201, 1995.

Selfe, L. 1977. *Nadia: A Case of Extraordinary Drawing Ability in an Autistic Child.* New York, Academic Press, 1977.

Sevely, J.L. and Bennett, J.W. Concerning female ejaculation and the female prostate. *Journal of Sex Research*, 14:1-20, 1978.

Sheidlower, J. (ed.). *The F Word.* New York, Random House, 1995.

Shepher, J. Mate selection among second generation kibbutz adolescents and adults: Incest avoidance and negative imprinting. *Archives of Sexual Behavior*, 1:293-307, 1971.

Sherer, D.M., Eggers, P.C. and Woods, J.R., Jr. In-utero fetal penile erection. *Journal of Ultrasound in Medicine*, 9:371, 1990.

Sherwin, B.B. A comparative analysis of the role of androgen in human male and female sexual behavior: Behavioral specificity, critical thresholds, and sensitivity. *Psychobiology*, 16:416-25, 1988.

Sherwin, B.B. and Gelfand, M.M. The role of androgen in the maintenance of sexual functioning in oopherectomized women. *Psychosomatic Medicine*, 49:397-409, 1987.

Shilts, R. *And the Band Played On: Politics, People and the AIDS Epidemic.* New York, St. Martin's Press, 1987.

Shirozu, H., Koyanagi, T., Takashima, T., Horimoto, N., Akazawa, K. and Nakano, H. Penile tumescence in the human fetus at term — A preliminary report. *Early Human Development*, 41(3):159-66, 1995.

Silver, R. Biparental care in birds: Mechanisms controlling incubation bout duration. In *Hormones and Behaviour in Higher Vertebrates* (J. Balthazart, J. Pröve and R. Gilles, eds.). Berlin, Springer-Verlag, 1983.

Silver, R. Parental behavior of ring doves. *American Scientist*, 66:209-15, 1978.

Silverstein, C. *Man to Man: Gay Couples in America.* New York, William Morrow, 1981.

Simpson, J.L. Pregnancy and the timing of intercourse. *New England Journal of Medicine*, 333:1563-65, 1995.

Sipe, A.W.R. *A Secret World: Sexuality and the Search for Celibacy.* New York, Brunner Mazel, 1990.

Sitsen, J.M.A. (ed.). *Handbook of Sexology, Vol. VI: The Pharmacology and Endocrinology of Sexual Function* (Money, J. and Musaph, H., series eds.). Amsterdam, Elsevier, 1988.

Snyder, S.H. Nitric oxide: First in a new class of neurotransmitters? *Science*, 257:494-96, 1992.

Solomon, R.L. The opponent-process theory of acquired motivation. *American Psychologist*, 35:691-712, 1980.

Sotos, J.G. *Zebra Cards: An Aid to Obscure Diagnosis.* Philadelphia, American College of Physicians, 1989.

Spitz, R. Autoeroticism re-examined: The role of early sexual behavior patterns in personality formation. In *Sex in Childhood: Children's Medical Center, Third Annual Seminar, Tulsa, Oklahoma, 1970.* Tulsa, Okla., Children's Medical Center, 1971.

Smale, L. and Holekamp, K.E. Growing up in the clan. *Natural History*, 102(1):42-53, 1993.

Stall, S. *What A Young Boy Ought To Know.* Philadelphia, Vir, 1909.

Steinach, E. *Sex and Life: Forty Years of Biological and Medical Experiments.* New York, Viking Press, 1940.

Stevens, J.E. Sex and the spotted hyena. *Image: San Francisco Examiner*, pp. 13-17, August 8, 1993.

Stiles, H.R. *Bundling: Its Origin, Progress, and Decline in America.* Facsimile edition. Chester, CT, Applewood Books, 1871.

Still, G.F. *Common Disorders and Diseases of Childhood*, 3rd ed. London, Oxford Medical Publications, 1915.

Stoller, R.J. *Perversion: The Erotic Form of Hatred.* New York, Pantheon, 1975.

Stoller, R.J. *Observing the Erotic Imagination.* New Haven, Yale University Press, 1985.

Sulloway, F.J. *Freud, Biologist of the Mind: Beyond the Psychoanalytic Legend.* New York, Basic Books, 1979.

Swaab, D.F., Gooren, L.J.G. and Hofman, M.A. The human hypothalamus in relation to gender and sexual orientation. *Progress in Brain Research*, 93:205-17, 1992.

Swaab, D.F. and Hofman, M.A. An enlarged suprachiasmatic nucleus in homosexual men. *Brain Research*, 537:141-48, 1990.

Taddio, A., Goldbach, M., Ipp, M., Stevens, B. and Koren, G. Effects of neonatal circumcision on pain responses during vaccination in boys. *Lancet*, 345:291-92, 1995.

Tanner, J.M. *Growth at Adolescence*. Oxford, Blackwell Scientific, 1962.

Taub, D.M. The functions of primate paternalism: A cross-species review. In *Pedophilia: Biosocial Dimensions* (J.R. Feierman, ed.). New York, Springer-Verlag, 1990.

Taylor, R. Singin' in the brain: Bird song and gene expression. *Journal of NIH Research*, 4(10):49-53, 1992.

Temerlin, M.K. My daughter Lucy: Puberty of a chimpanzee. *Psychology Today*, 9(6):59-62 ff, 1975.

Tennov, D. *Love and Limerence: The Experience of Being in Love*. New York, Stein and Day, 1979.

Teresi, D. How to get a man pregnant: My (true) adventures on the frontiers of science. *The New York Times Magazine*, pp. 54-55, November 27, 1994.

Thilly, C.H., Delange, F., Ramioul, L., Lagasse, R., Luvivila, K. and Ermans, A.M. Strategy of goitre and cretinism control in Central Africa. *International Journal of Epidemiology*, 6:43-54, 1977.

Tischner, M. Patterns of stallion sexual behavior in the absence of mares. *Journal of Reproduction and Fertility - Supplement*, 32:65-70, 1982.

Tissot, S.A. *A Treatise on the Diseases Produced by Onanism*. Translated from a new edition of the French, with notes and appendix by an American physician. New York, Private, 1832. [Facsimile reprint edition in *The Secret Vice Exposed! Some Arguments Against Masturbation* (C. Rosenberg and C. Smith-Rosenberg, eds.). New York, Arno Press, 1974].

Tomkins, S. *Affect, Imagery, Consciousness. Cognition: Duplication and Transformation of Information*, Vol. IV. New York, Springer, 1992.

Treiman, K., Liskin, L., Kols, A., and Rinehart, W. *IUDs—An Update*. Population Reports, Series B, No. 6. Baltimore, Johns Hopkins School of Public Health, Population Information Program, 1995.

Trumbull, H.L. and Newton, E.B. Rubber: Production and manufacture. *Encyclopedia Britannica*, 19:605-11, 1958.

Tutin, C.E.G. Mating patterns and reproductive strategies in a community of wild chimpanzees (*Pan troglodytes schweinfurthii*). *Behavioral Ecology and Sociobiology*, 6:29-38, 1979.

Udry, J.R. and Morris, N.M. Distribution of coitus in the menstrual cycle. *Nature*, 220:593-96, 1968.

Velde, T.H, van de. *Ideal Marriage: Its Physiology and Technique*. New York, Random House, 1926.

Vernon, A. Return of the takahe. *International Wildlife*, 22(2):22-27, 1992.

Vincent, A. and Grall, G. The improbable seahorse. *National Geographic*, 186(4):126-40, 1994.

Waal, F.B.M., de. The communicative repertoire of captive bonobos (*Pan paniscus*) compared to that of chimpanzees. *Behaviour*, 106:183-251, 1988.

Waal, F.B.M., de. *Peacemaking Among Primates*. Cambridge, MA, Harvard University Press, 1989.

Waal, F.B.M., de. Sociosexual behavior used for tension regulation in all age and sex combinations among bonobos. In *Pedophilia: Biosocial Dimensions* (J.R. Feierman, ed.). New York, Springer-Verlag, 1990.

Waal, F.B.M., de. *Good Natured.* Cambridge, MA, Harvard University Press, 1996.

Wallerstein, E. *Circumcision: An American Health Fallacy.* New York, Springer, 1980.

Wallis, S.J. Sexual behavior and reproduction of *Cercocebus albligenia johnstonii* in Kibale Forest, Western Uganda. *International Journal of Primatology,* 4:153-66, 1983.

Warner, R.R., Robertson, D.R. and Leigh, E.G., Jr. Sex change and sexual selection. *Science,* 190:633-38, 1975.

Weinrich, J.D., Grant, I., Jacobson, D.L., Robinson, S.R., McCutchan, J.A. and the HNRC Group. Effects of recalled childhood gender nonconformity on adult genitoerotic role and AIDS exposure. *Archives of Sexual Behavior,* 21:559-85, 1992.

Wilcox, A.J., Weinberg, C.R. and Baird, D.D. Timing of sexual intercourse in relation to ovulation — Effects on the probability of conception, survival of the pregnancy, and sex of the baby. *New England Journal of Medicine,* 333:1517-21, 1995.

Williams, G.J. Cruelty and kindness to children: Documentary of a century, 1874-1974. In *Traumatic Abuse and Neglect of Children at Home* (G.J. Williams and J. Money, eds.). Baltimore, Johns Hopkins University Press, 1980.

Williams, W.L. *The Spirit and the Flesh: Sexual Diversity in American Indian Culture.* Boston, Beacon Press, 1986.

Wilson, C.A., Pearson, J.A., Hunter, A.J., Tuohy, P.A. and Payne, A.P. The effect of neonatal manipulation of hypothalamic serotonin levels on sexual activity in the adult rat. *Pharmacology Biochemistry and Behavior,* 24:1175-83, 1986.

Wilson, G.D. *The Coolidge Effect: An Evolutionary Account of Human Sexuality.* New York, William Morrow, 1982.

Wolff, C. How FBI closed in on top New York judge. *The New York Times,* pp.A1,B4, November 10, 1992.

Woodward, T.E. The golden era of microbiology: People and events of the 1880s. *Maryland Medical Journal,* 38:323-28, 1989.

Wright, J. Sexuality within the Old Testament. *St. Mark's Review,* Number 106:3-12, 1981.

Wright, K. The sniff of legend. *Discover,* 15(4):60-67, 1994.

Wulff, C.H., Ostergaard, J.R. and Storm, K. Epileptic fits or infantile masturbation? *Seizure,* 1:199-201, 1992.

Wyshak, G. and Frisch, R.E. Evidence for a secular trend in age of menarche. *New England Journal of Medicine,* 306:1033-35, 1982.

Yalcinkaya, T.M., Siiteri, P.K., Vigne, J-L., Licht, P., Pavgi, S., Frank, L.G. and Glickman, S.E. A mechanism for virilization of female spotted hyenas in utero. *Science,* 260:1929-31, 1993.

Yalow, R.S. Radioimmunoassay: A probe for the fine structure of biologic systems. *Science,* 200:1236-45, 1978.

Young, W.C., Goy, R.W. and Phoenix, C.H. Hormones and sexual behavior. *Science,* 143:212-18, 1964.

Zacharias, L., Wurtman, R.J. and Schatzoff, M. Sexual maturation in contemporary American girls. *American Journal of Obstetrics and Gynecology,* 108:833-46, 1970.

Zaviacic, M. and Whipple, B. Update on the female prostate and the phenomenon of female ejaculation. *Journal of Sex Research,* 30:148-51, 1993.

Zhou, J.N., Hofman, M.A., Gooren, L.J.G. and Swaab, D.F. A sex difference in the human brain and its relation to transsexuality. *Nature,* 378:68-70, 1995.

Name Index

Subject Index

Introduction

This reference work is a must read for any small business owner or individual who is considering publishing a new website, or is looking to improve on an existing website design. It caters for anyone who either wants to know how to brief a website designer or feels they have, or can learn, the necessary skills to create their own website; with a little guidance to steer them away from potential pitfalls.

Brian has been involved with technological developments for over 30 years and has worked in both project and departmental management at a senior level.

He has come to recognise over the years that many people, who have never been exposed to a technical environment, may struggle to understand what needs to be communicated to designers in order for them to complete a design task that meets their requirements.

Website design is no different to any other project in this respect. Just having a basic understanding of what is required, in layman's terms, can facilitate a means to effective communication between designer and client.

The book is split into two distinct parts.

Part one:

Gives you the knowledge you need to help you brief website designers and webmasters as they create your new website, . . . or seek to improve your existing one. It describes in layman's terms where the costs for a website come from, how to communicate the style and functionality you require, and how to both maintain and promote your website once it has been published on the Internet. Everything is here that you need to know to achieve your objectives for the website you want, and a little more.

Part two:

Builds upon the information in part one, offering detailed information to enable the computer savvy to dispense with outside help and create a new website or improve their existing one - saving even more money in the process. You will find links to many useful sources of technical support the author has used during his time as a website designer. The emphasis of the second part is to describe the optimum approaches to web design and then point readers towards online training that will allow them to develop the necessary skills needed to implement those techniques.

What are the costs of designing a website

The first thing that springs to mind for most people considering purchasing a new website is 'What is it going to cost?' This tends to be true for both individuals and businesses.

Where the costs arise

When estimating the cost of creating an average website, there are three principal considerations to take into account. These involve:

- Buying a domain name (a name that is exclusively for your use – like www.myveryownsite.com)

- Web Hosting (the internet organisation you pay annually to 'host' your website on their 'servers' so that anyone, anywhere, anytime can visit it)

- Website design and development (the fees a professional needs to be paid to create your website so that it looks good and does what you want it to do)

Buying a domain name

The first thing to understand is that you never actually own a domain name outright; you lease it by the year from a domain name provider and as a result it needs to be renewed periodically as the lease period expires. Think of it as leasehold, rather than freehold: but as long as you pay the rent, nobody can take it away from you.

That said the fees for leasing a domain name are low. For example, a standard .co.uk domain name can cost as little as **£3 ($4.50)** pounds a year and a standard .com domain name **£10 ($15)** a year. There is normally a minimum period to register and maintain the domain name but typically it will be for no more than two years and is more likely to be only one.

Renewal fees pretty much stay at the level you paid when you bought the domain name. This is a highly competitive marketplace and you can move the domain name to another domain provider if you feel you are no longer getting value for money.

More on domain name registration later.

Hosting a website

Websites need to be hosted on a server (a powerful PC) that is connected to the Internet permanently. There are many companies offering such web hosting services. They rent you space on one of their PCs at their business location and maintain your website online on your behalf. They ensure your connection to the Internet is always intact and that any additional services they offer as part of the hosting package are functioning correctly.

For small businesses just starting out on the Internet the costs for hosting can be kept to very moderate levels. Typically a starter pack (more than adequate for most small businesses) can begin for as little as **£3 ($4.50)** a month and you may only need to commit to a period of twelve months.

Website design costs

There are a number of different approaches to creating a website. The traditional approach has been to ask a web designer to produce a bespoke design to meet specific requirements. This is still a viable option and, when done correctly, means you can achieve the functionality, style and appearance you want, unique to you and catering for your needs. This approach is unlikely to be the very cheapest option but should still be affordable depending on the specifications required. And it is the route that the non-computer literate should plump for.

The cost will be affected by the design's degree of complexity. Factors to take into account include

- the number of pages required - a page is a section of a website with its own unique address made up from the domain name plus a file name for the page e.g. *www.myveryownsite.com/mypage.html*

A 'page' all appears on a single screen, but one that might, in theory, scroll downwards for ever.

- the content you can provide i.e. text, and graphics (photographs, charts, illustrations – all non-textual material)

- whether animation and/or video is required

- whether the site will be an eCommerce site, i.e. one that enables visitors to purchase goods or services instantly off your site making use of 'shopping carts' and 'Buy Now' buttons

- whether you wish to be able to personally update the content of your website on a regular basis, without outside help. If so, a content management system needs to be built into the design so that this can be achieved cheaply and easily.

Once your requirements are known a quote can be prepared by the designer to define the costs and timescale involved. But as a guide, a simple website can usually be produced for anything from **£100 to £300 ($150 to $450)** on the basis that the required text and photographs are supplied by the customer.

To keep costs down it may be worthwhile to adopt an existing design (a standard format or template) which is then populated with the text and graphics you supply. The design can usually be modified in terms of colours and font to ensure an individual look and feel. Taking this approach generally means the designer has far less work to undertake . . . and charges less.

So there you have it, for a straightforward website design your costs can be modest:

- *Domain Registration from **£3 ($4.50)** per year*

- *Domain Hosting from **£36 ($54)** per year*

- *Website Design from as little as **£100 ($150**) - a one-off cost.*

Before leaving the topic of website design costs we should discuss marketing and promotion. Anyone seeking to gain business through the Internet should be aware that their website is unlikely to be found without some form of promotion and optimisation for search engines. There are of course many ways of promoting a website, much of which is discussed later in the book, but the services, if bought, do come at a cost which can represent significant expenditures.

Often these additional costs are necessary and justified when certain expectations are to be met. But they *are* additional costs and need to be considered because there are occasions when promoting and marketing a product via a website in a highly competitive commercial arena can be, and often is, more expensive than the web design itself. This aspect of what your expectations are for a website is discussed in more detail later.

What do you want your website to do for you

An important aspect of website design is deciding *what you want your website to do for you?* This is something that needs to be considered not just for the short term, meeting the immediate requirement, but also for the longer term, anticipating the likely evolution of your business.

People have many different expectations when they decide they want a website. Some of the common ones are to:

- use it as a company catalogue

- attract customers from new or existing markets i.e. to build their business

- provide access to information that visitors to the website can download to a personal computer

- sell products directly to customers while they are online visiting your website

- help you sell products on your website on behalf of other companies

- generate advertising revenue – your website offers advertising space for sale

- communicate with your peers, friends and family

- share and disseminate information

- promote a cause, support a charity

-own and make use of a personalised email address (Jason.Trump@FamilyTrump.Com)

- start a blog (an online platform where you can publicise views, ideas, and articles to prompt debate)

The point of this dialogue is that *'what you want from a website'* will have a big impact on the design approach taken.

For example, there could be features that should be included in the website's construction which will help search engines find it (services like Google and Bing). If a site is purely there to give existing customers a point of reference, and will never be anything more than that, then such considerations need not arise.

If all you need is a personalised email address, this can be done without a website at all. You simply need to register a domain name and use a simple email service to send and receive the email via a domain provider.

Establishing the short and long term objectives for a website can mean the difference between a complex design, with associated higher costs, or a simple design at minimum cost.

Some of the costs associated with developing a website and establishing it on the Internet can go beyond the actual design of the website. This becomes more apparent as you enter the arena of measuring performance, promotion and marketing.

The way it looks – style

The look and feel of a website is determined through the choices made with respect to colour, type and size of fonts (for example, Arial or Times New Roman), the use of graphics, and where all the various elements are positioned on the page.

Your aesthetic requirements for a website need to be communicated to the website designer.

A useful question to prompt ideas is - have you seen any websites on the Internet that you found really appealing? This is not to suggest that you should steal someone else's design, but rather to get an idea of what is required for the new design that can be given a new interpretation.

Your designer can employ a couple of useful tools on your behalf:

- a sitemap

- a storyboard

A sitemap shows how many pages the website will have and how they are going to be connected to one another. This may not at first glance seem like it is anything to do with the look and feel of the website, but it does dictate how complex the page interlinking (part of navigation) is going to be. Page interlinking is a critical element that needs to be included on every web page. It's also worth noting at this point that every website starts with an 'index' page, often referred to as the 'home page'.

A Simple Sitemap

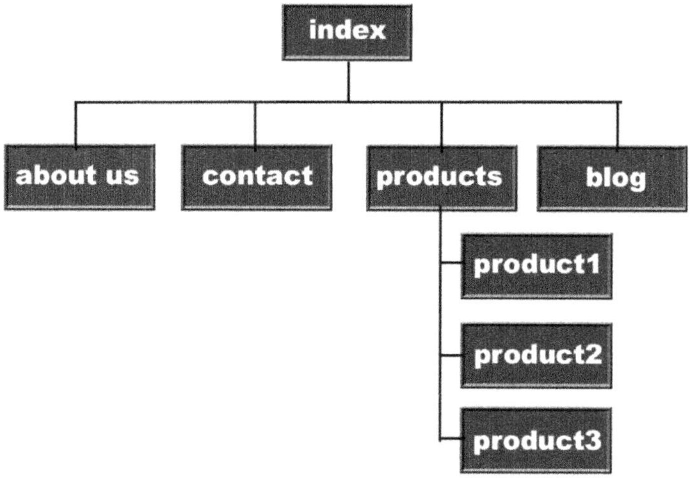

A storyboard, on the other hand, is a tool used to establish the look and feel of a website: it is a mock-up of a proposed design.

A storyboard represents graphically what the website pages will look like.

This could be a single representation or a series of representations for different pages that are going to form part of the design. They can be in digital format, hand-drawn or perhaps be even a collage of photographs put together as a representation. It doesn't really matter how the representation is created as long as it communicates to the designer what you seek.

Ideally this should be driven by your ideas rather than the designer's otherwise the designer will only ever be able to second guess what is in your mind and may misinterpret what you want. This could result in repeated attempts to try and capture the correct image and feel you seek.

There will be a technical aspect to consider as part of this exercise, in that what you ask for may not be technically feasible or potentially cost prohibitive with respect to your budget. But if that impasse is reached then compromises will need to be made.

So establishing the way a website looks, as you have probably begun to realise, is possibly one of the more difficult hurdles to overcome in the web design process because it really is subjective. It is down to artistic interpretation and I am afraid, just to throw another spanner in the works, consideration of whether it will appeal to the intended or target audience.

Some websites deliberately adopt an oldie-worldly image because that is what pleases the people it is aimed at; others are, conversely, 'leading edge', sharp and contemporary because their audience demands that of the design.

A few examples: you would be inclined to adopt an old traditional feel for a website promoting country cottages in Cornwall. But you wouldn't consider adopting that sort of style for the latest and greatest on Internet war games or perhaps a hip hop music promotion.

So yes, it is subjective, and it is very much down to personal taste and negotiation, but there are common sense elements to the equation; approaches that clearly will not work dependent on the site's subject matter. But at the end of the day the finished product must meet your expectations. You are, after all, the paymaster for the design and more often than not you will understand what you want to get from a design better than the designer.

Designing a logo

One final aspect of the way it looks concerns logos.

Designing a logo is a relatively specialist skill that requires a slightly different approach to simply optimizing graphics for use on a website.

A logo is, or can be, a first step towards establishing a brand in a graphical format. It is something that may work better through its simplicity or alternatively it may need to be complex. Discussions with a good graphic designer are typically required to establish a logo that is appealing to you as the customer and memorable for anyone visiting your website.

Some famous logos that spring to mind are Coca-Cola, Lego, Mercedes-Benz and Microsoft. You can see what they look like by visiting the Famous Logos site below.

(ref: http://www.famouslogos.org/)

What it does – functionality

People have different opinions on what a website should or shouldn't do. But what I want to illustrate, with respect to what a website does, is its functionality.

The reason I am discussing it in terms of functionality is because I want to separate '*what it does*' from '*what a website does for you*' which was discussed earlier.

Coding and scripting

Coding and scripting provides additional functionality for a website. Additional functionality may be something as simple as a message form where a visitor can send you a message, or it may be something more complex, like responding to a site search box on one of your pages to present relevant results. Another possibility is that you will want to manage what happens when someone makes an online purchase from your site.

So coding and scripting can be likened to the utility room of a website design; the part of the design that works behind the scenes and out of the public eye, quietly ensuring that when you fill in a form or make a purchase, that something actually happens - that the message gets sent or the purchase is actually progressed to the next stage.

Animation and flash

Another aspect of web design that might be considered specialist is the production of animated graphics.

One of the most common uses of animation is to create a slideshow that presents a continuous series of different images to a visitor.

Another might be a sophisticated navigation system that responds to the mouse movements of a website visitor, so that as the mouse pointer moves over the images they change in dramatic fashion adding interest to the website.

Animation adds a dynamic aspect to web designs, the purpose of which is, as stated, to add interest. Care does need to be taken when employing the use of animated graphics, however, as they can also be seen as an irritation or distraction if they are implemented inappropriately.

The program typically used for animating graphics is Adobe Flash but there are many others including the use of Java.

Graphics

Key elements of any website design are the graphics used. The Flash program discussed above draws heavily on the use of static graphics to make up the dynamic elements of its timeline (the series of images that create a dynamic effect). Like static images that are presented in the web content, the graphics need to be optimised for web pages so that an acceptable level of quality is maintained whilst allowing the graphics to load as quickly as possible. There are programs that allow your web designer to optimise graphics and you should always ensure that any graphics used on your website have in fact been optimised for web page use. More on this later.

Finding your way around website – navigation

First things first; what exactly is website navigation? Simple: it is the consistent way you decide to guide visitors around your website, using headings as signposts. The signposts are collectively known as the menu.

There are two aspects to this: the first is the need for a menu and the second is ensuring it is easy for visitors to find and use.

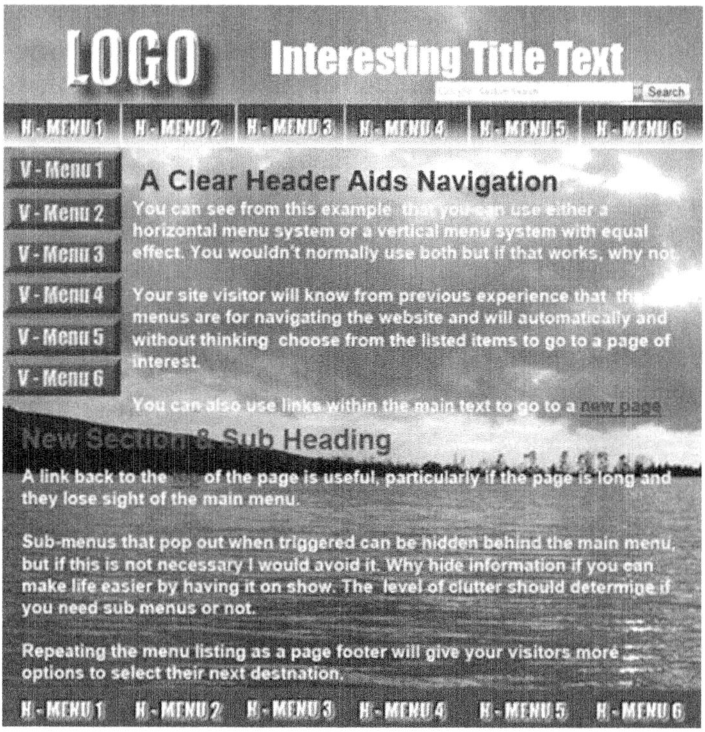

The menu enables visitors to go directly to specific parts of a website and should clearly identify to a visitor what that part is, through the name it is given.

Every good website has at least one menu and ideally a search feature for finding information if the menu is not intuitive enough for the visitor to find what they want.

Remember we are all unique; what seems obvious to one person may be an enigma to another. How many times have you visited a website page and spent endless time wondering where on earth to go next, other than to escape the place quickly?

Having a search feature is a fall back or contingency option that might keep someone on your site long enough to deliver what they are looking for. Ideally it shouldn't be needed, but the larger and more complex a website is, with lots of pages and subjects, the more necessary it becomes.

This also applies with respect to whether you decide to dedicate a page as a 'Site Map', i.e. a page that lists all the visitor pages on your website with links to those pages. This is the first of two types of site map and shouldn't be confused with a site map that gets submitted to search engines, which is an entirely different animal, to be discussed later.

The second aspect of usability is how easy is the menu to figure out and use.

Typically figuring out how to use a menu should take seconds rather than minutes. Most people visiting a website will not spend more than five to ten seconds (probably less than this, in truth) trying to figure out a menu. If they fail they will be off back to Google looking for what they consider to be a better site, on the same subject, that has a menu they can understand immediately.

There are essentially ten rules that need to be applied to make finding your way around a website easy.

The ten rules of navigation

Functionality - the menu should complement the website's content rather than dominate it. People come to a website either to get information or to buy something, and normally they want to do that as quickly as possible, then leave again as soon as they are done. The menu must not get in the way; ideally it should be barely noticeable to them that a menu is being used; it really should be that easy. If visitors have to stop and think about where to go next then the navigation is not doing its job.

Identifiable - the menu must be easy to find and identify and must stand out from the content of the website. Think about how many times you have visited a website and could not identify the menu system from the actual content of the website. The result is that you click a couple of times on what you think are links and nothing happens. You don't do that too often before you are off elsewhere, looking for an easier site.

Readable - common sense, perhaps, but I think we have all come across websites where readability has taken second place to artistic license: websites perhaps with a really fancy font or very subtle colour differentiation that ultimately results in illegibility. So text and graphics must contrast sufficiently with their backgrounds to be readable and chosen fonts must be clear and large enough to read easily off the screen.

Scanability - the menu items must jump out from the background and be obvious. This is because it's a fact that people scan when they look at website pages - they do not read to great levels of detail. For that reason and reasons already mentioned the menu items need to be short, succinct and clear as to their target.

For example a button that says 'Home' (the opening page of your website) will clearly convey its message, whereas something like '*click here for the home page*' is totally unnecessary and detracts from rather than adds to an effective navigation system

Operable - Most people use a mouse or pad which controls some sort of pointing device. The signposts, part of the menu, needs to be large enough and secondly sufficiently spaced out from other links to ensure that the visitor can select the link of choice with ease and do not end up having difficulty selecting their chosen link or, even worse, selecting the wrong link.

Expected behaviour - When people are familiar with functions, it means they have already learned how to use them. So if you follow known standards for presenting navigation systems you are half way to the system being usable. This does not mean you can't be inventive or come with new and interesting ways of doing things, but you need to be sure that the new ways are easy to learn and provide enough of a wow factor to make them worthwhile.

Load speeds – first, a definition: the load speed refers to the time it takes for a website to reveal itself to you in all its glory, from the moment you click on a link to take you there. A properly designed website will load in seconds.

And not just pages but also menus need to load quickly. People using the internet tend to get frustrated in a couple of seconds and start to think their PC has locked up if they have to wait longer than a few seconds. Little tricks like saying the page is loading may help, but ultimately if the navigation system does not load quickly enough then your visitor will again be heading for the back button or returning to the Google search page for alternative websites.

Usability versus branding - make sure that usability takes precedence over branding; if the corporate colours, graphics and logos cause a website to become unnavigable then it is the branding that must compromise. The sweetest images in the world will not keep a visitor on the site if they cannot get to the information, services or product they want.

Handicap accessibility- blind or visually impaired people may not be able to see your menu system and may have to use an electronic Braille reader or voice system to navigate your site. These types of system rely on plain text or alternative addresses to interpret menus so you need to make sure that these tools are employed.

Multiple browsers – ensure that everything created on the website will work on all browsers – the programs your computer uses to access the internet. Make sure the design is checked on a range of browsers to ensure that they function correctly, or at the very least, on the most popular browsers in use. These are Google Chrome, Internet Explorer or Mozilla Firefox. There are others but the three listed are the primary ones and will cover most of the market.

These rules are important and need to be followed without compromising artistic intent. If your designer adheres to these rules while at the same time wowing your visitors with an artistically stimulating presentation then you will have achieved the ultimate combination for retaining visitors on your website. This, of course, assumes you have put something useful and or interesting on the website in the first place.

How to make Google your best friend

Before we get too far into how you make Google, and other search engines, your best friend I ought to explain there are two ways to do this: one is called 'on page optimisation' and the other, 'off page optimisation'.

What this basically means is that, for the first, it is all about what you put on or in your website pages and, in some cases, also where you put it. The second is more about business marketing and website promotion, little to do with the website design itself but rather what you use to promote the website once it is published.

This chapter is going to consider the first aspect which is about the website design, the content of the website pages and what goes where.

It's also worth pointing out at this stage that if you don't care whether the search engines find your website or not, then this is really not a critical aspect of the design. All you need to do then is to make sure the content included, be it the text (also known as copy), the images and animations, appeals to your intended audience.

On page optimisation

You may well have read references to SEO, or search engine optimization; doesn't mean a thing to many people. But search engine optimization essentially is about making your website visible to the search engines so that they find it, for the right reasons. In other words, they can easily establish what your website is about and also what the topic of the content is.

Why do these search engines want to know that? Basically, so that they can match it to the enquiries typed into their search boxes when people look for information, products and services.

Search engines live and die on the quality of the results they return when someone uses their website to look for information. If the results don't match the enquiry and they consistently fail to deliver what people are looking for, that search engine facility will no longer be used, and it is highly likely they will go out of business. Google now has over 85% of the market because most competitors failed this very test.

This is where the term 'keywords' comes in. Keywords can be a single word or a combination of words that form the enquiry being entered into a search box. For example, someone looking for a holiday in France might put in the search box 'holidays in France'. So that phrase is considered to be the keyword and it is the keyword that the search engines focus on to deliver the right results.

But they don't just stop there. They look for verification that the keywords they find on a website are supported by relevant content on the webpage. Notice I say '*webpage*' there, not '*website*'. This is because search engines treat each web page that makes up a website as a separate entity that contains specific information in its own right. In other words, a website focused on Europe may have an individual page about France, or specific information about how to get to France, or even listings of different '*holidays in France*'.

So that you are clear, a quick word about how search engines like Google work. They all have what is known as 'spider software' that regularly visits all websites. This is to see what's new, what's changed, and what might interest the millions of people that are conducting searches by typing all sorts of things into their search boxes. These visits are automatic and regular and there is no human input. When the spider software visits the website to examine the content, this is referred to as 'crawling'.

So when a search engine programme 'crawls' a website it records which specific page matches certain enquiries best. They can then show the inquirer the page they think is the closest match to the enquiry or keywords entered in the search results.

In order to optimise a webpage – make it 'catch the eye' of the spider software – it is necessary to match the content of the webpage to the keyword (or keyword phrase) that is entered into search engines and position them where they will be found quickly and easily by the search engines.

Incidentally there is little point in trying to fool the search engines into thinking a webpage is about something it isn't because when 'human' visitors arrive on the page, they will simply leave again feeling disappointed and let down.

Where to position keywords

The first thing to do is to come up with a name for your webpage; but that's easy isn't it? You just say what the subject matter is and, hey presto, you have a title. Well that is true, but have you considered exactly what it is the search engine programs see first? Would you think perhaps that it is the page title? Well yes and no, this is certainly one of your primary, and probably most important keywords or keyword phrases, and one of the first that the search engine looks at when trying to match the enquiry that has been made.

The title of a page is a little special, because it is not a visible part of the actual web page; it is the text that you see at the top of the browser in the page tab. It is included in the page information via its own 'tag' that forms a part of the 'head' section of a web page. This is discussed in more detail later, so for now just trust me on this.

Equally, if not more important, is the URL (Uniform Resource Locator), or to mere mortals, the website address for your webpage, blog, or article which is the first thing that is found, it may not form part of the article itself i.e. your visitors don't see it as part of the content, but it is the link that the search engines see and registers first. So search engine optimisation starts as soon as you are looking to register a domain name and also when you are naming the files for the individual pages.

This is because the URL is made up of both the domain name and the file that is published on that domain e.g.

- *www.mykeyword.com/myprimarykeyword.html*

It is difficult to say whether the URL or the title is the most important, but they are both up there at the top in the importance tree, numbers one and two, I would say, whichever way around they are.

Ideally you should identify six or seven keywords or keyword phrases and prioritise them in terms of importance. Obviously the top priority keywords you select should be placed in the optimal positions, as shown below in their order of importance:

1. domain name or page file name

2. in the page title

3. in the page headers i.e. header 1, header 2, header 3 and so on. The headings are actual page elements; they form the main headings and subheadings of your pages.

4. throughout the content of the page

5. in the descriptions and file names of the graphics

To recap, if possible you should be aiming for at least two primary keywords and up to five secondary ones. These should all appear in the content of the webpage and are to be aimed directly at your target audience in terms of the content they represent. The most important ones should be located in the most important places

It is also important that the text flows naturally and appeals to your human audience. Don't sacrifice the quality of the content in order to match what you think are the best keywords. Exact matches are the optimal solution but not at the cost of overall content quality. Search engines will still see the words even if they are not in the exact order of the enquiry or if synonyms are used that are more appropriate.

For more information on keywords phrases visit *www.blogaude.com/website-search-optimization-keyword-phrases/* and if you are having problems identifying appropriate keywords then it might be worth a look at how you use a suitable *Keyword Tool.*

(ref: www.blogaude.com/using-the-google-traffic-estimator-keyword-tool/)

So keywords are an important aspect of on page optimisation, but they are not the only considerations and more recently Google have been penalising pages they consider to be over-optimised. Just make sure the content of the page looks natural and don't use exact match keywords more than once or twice on a page. Far better to support the primary keywords with related wording associated with your main topic for a page or synonyms.

Avoiding excessive use of java script and flash

Earlier the use of Java script and Flash was discussed, briefly, as tools that can provide additional functionality i.e. dynamic and interactive elements to a website. But they also represent a problem with respect to 'on-page optimisation' because search engine 'spiders' do not have the capability to understand the language they use to function. This means, for example that if a navigation menu is Flash- or Java-based the search engines will not be able to spider through the code to find the pages they link to. So there is a potential for not finding all the pages on the website. It is for this reason that certain elements of web design, such as navigation systems, should utilise alternative, more search engine-friendly options.

Load times and graphics

One of the biggest culprits for slowing down the load speed of a page is the use of high resolution graphics. But it is possible to reduce the resolution of graphics without affecting their appearance when viewed on a website.

The reason for this is that photographic images, for example, are typically viewed on the majority of computer screens at a surprisingly low resolution, even today. Therefore the high resolutions associated with printing and photography are totally unnecessary. High resolution images take an age to load, and yet the screens are incapable of displaying them to those higher resolution levels!

Proper selection of the graphic format will also help with maintaining quality at faster load speeds. There are three types of graphics that can be used on a web page:

- Graphic Interchange Format or GIF

- Joint Photographic Expert Group or JPEG

- Portable Network Graphic or PNG

Without getting too technical just think of the GIF format as generally being best for cartoon-like illustrations and line art. JPEG are generally better for photographs. PNG, on the other hand, is a format developed specifically for the web and has some unique capabilities such as variable transparency levels; great for getting some of those highly valued special effects that people look for in a website design.

Without putting too fine a point on it, load speed is a component of the page rank calculation that Google uses to assign importance to a page and is why it should be taken seriously. Anything that slows the load speed of a page needs to be sorted out.

Defining and using metatags

I can almost hear the groans when mentioning 'metatags'; what in the world does that mean? Well quite simply metatags are descriptions used 'behind the scenes' on a webpage, actually hidden in the 'head' section of the mark-up language that passes information to the search engines when they arrive on a page.

They not only convey information such as the '*title*' of the web page (although strictly speaking the title is a tag in its own right), already identified as an important optimisation feature; but also the description or summary of the webpage content; the keyword list for a webpage, and how often the search engines should visit. The language the page is written in is also an important factor defined by Meta tags.

Metatags are regarded by many as having less importance these days, in terms of search engine optimization, but they are so easy to put in place that it seems a good idea to use them. Some also relay information as to how browsers should handle the information included, in terms of the way it is presented, which is equally important as optimisation, from a human perspective.

So certainly there are some that still do hold a level of importance; the two main ones being the aforementioned title tag plus the description tag.

A description should not, ideally, be more than 160 characters in length and should convey succinctly and accurately what the web page is about or offers e.g.

For an idyllic self-catering holiday in France for up to nine people. Prices start at £600 per week including towels and linen. Exclusive pool, and rural location.

Note how much useful information the description provides, within the 160 character count, and how it could easily lead to someone clicking on the link to the webpage.

More often than not the description is included in the search engine results along with the title and the URL of the website page.

I say more often than not because the search engines decide whether to display it, or not, and if they prefer to select text from the main content, they will display that instead. The reason for that might be as simple as the content having words that match the enquiry exactly, whereas the description doesn't.

Rather than detail all the different metatags here it is probably worth pointing you in the direction of a *metatag generator* with explanations on what each does and how they should be used. This is a job best left to your designer in truth.

(ref: www.scrubtheweb.com/abs/builder.html)

But bear in mind the title and description are your responsibility and should be constructed with care; just make sure the designer is aware of your requirements.

The page copy

Page copy simply means the text - your written content. Why it is so important is twofold.

Firstly search engines are basically reliant on text and need a level of textual content in order to understand what the page is discussing. Every page should ideally contain a minimum of 450 words; you can provide less but you will be limiting how well you can convey the keywords or their synonyms and the subject of the page whilst retaining a natural flow, I would certainly not drop lower than 300 words per page. The point is that search engines need text to establish content, and with too few words it is more difficult to establish and verify the content to the search engines.

What you should be attempting to do with your copy is to include your chosen keywords, ensure your grammar and punctuation are correct, all while providing great information delivered with a natural flow in your own inimitable style. Not much to ask really!

This leads to the human element, the second aspect. Given the recent changes to Google algorithms, (a posh word to describe what Google developers ask their spider software to hunt down) a lot of emphasis has been placed on high quality, unique content. Web pages deemed not to deliver this are likely to be listed lower down the search engine results. Why the human element? Because the faster a human lands on and then departs from a page the less likely it is that they found what they were looking for, or liked what they discovered. The technical term for this is bounce rate. High bounce rate – the site is not retaining visitor interest; low bounce rate – you are getting things right.

So if visitors find the contents of the page useful, informative, and problem solving or just downright interesting they will not only stay on the page, but also bookmark it, and possibly like and share the page with others. Content, as the old adage goes, is king and nothing persuades a visitor to stay on a page more than a good and relevant video.

How to write persuasive copy for your website

These are five writing guidelines many people overlook:

Rule one: Hit your reader between the eyes in your first sentence. You are competing against hundreds, perhaps hundreds of thousands of websites. So don't hold back. Tell them straight away what you can do for them, how you can solve their problem, answer their question or entertain them. Whatever it was you promised when you selected your keywords. Research indicates that potential customers browsing through websites make up their minds whether or not the site is for them in less than ten seconds.

This should also tell you something else: don't let your website designer persuade you to fall for a graphically enchanting opening page that spends countless seconds showing a chicken laying an egg, or the dawn rising over Wapping or Wyoming. The 'landing page', the first page visitors see on your website, should open immediately, and the prime message should appear at the top, either as a heading or as the first sentence of 'the copy' – the words that communicate the message.

Rule two: Having made an opening claim on the page, don't ruin things by veering off-message and introducing other products or services you can offer, unless they directly bolster the initial claim made. If, for example, you initially claim to help people to write and publish books, for goodness' sake don't follow that powerful sentence with a second stating, '. . . but if book writing is not for you we also show you how to become a proof-reader!' They will just think, 'what on earth's going on?' The focus will be ruined, and so will your website visitor's experience.

Rule three: Don't try to be Shakespeare or Charles Dickens. Go for the shortest words possible, unadorned with adjectives and adverbs, which convey signals unambiguously: 'Contact us today. Our editors are standing by. Excellent. Not, 'as soon as we receive your enquiry one of our professional editors will email you within twenty-four hours so that you can explain precisely what your writing project is all about.' What you've written may be valid, but it's also long-winded and deflates the urgency of your appeal.

Rule four: Unless your business is set up to 'sell off the website page' and you intend to seduce visitors to make an instant online purchase of a product or service the moment they reach the end of your pitch, don't waste words on trying to sell anything. Why? because unless you are 'selling off the page', you are overlooking the one thing that has to happen first before you can do business with the visitors and potential clients: they first have to decide whether you are a worthy potential supplier of that product or service, and then they will need to contact you for further details. So make it easier for them to do just that. This takes us to,

Rule five: Keep the opening page uncluttered. Make a single powerful claim, and back it up. By all means offer links to further pages that describe complementary products and services, but don't go into selling mode about these as well because the focus of the prime message will evaporate in seconds. If your website designers know their business they will have helped you identify what your prime marketing objective should be, and then provided a website page that hits all the right buttons. And these buttons should end the page, ideally a couple of large buttons, offering a choice of actions: click here, for example, could enable them to instantly email you for further info; click there and you'll be offered further information on the product or service you seek. Words matter, as does the order in which they are introduced. Great websites have simple messages, well supported by graphics that call for simple responses.

Social sharing

You will notice on many modern websites the presence of social sharing buttons. The purpose of these buttons is to allow visitors to your site to quickly and easily share your website with their friends on different social media sites or perhaps to email them directly with the webpage address.

Services such as *www.sharethis.com* will allow you to register with them so that you can have a little bit of code placed on your web pages that provide sharing functionality. Adding this code will take your web designer literally seconds and you can benefit by visitors to your web pages promoting your site to their friends. A bit of a no-brainer really, especially when those sites consist of the likes of Facebook, Twitter and Google+.

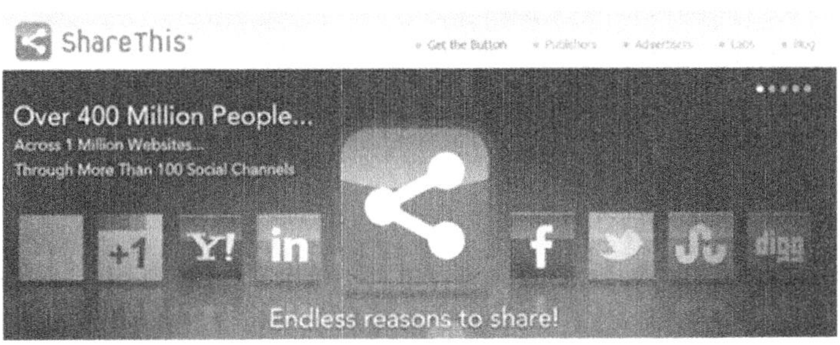

Ensuring web pages fit onto all standard computer screens

That heading sounds a bit ominous doesn't it, but as usual there is a straightforward explanation. Monitors display in a certain number of pixels, i.e. in accordance with their resolution, as was explained in a previous paragraph in relation to graphics optimisation. To clarify further, a computer monitor presents what you see on the screen in thousands of tiny dots (pixels), so for a set screen width and depth (vertical height) there will be a corresponding set number of dots. The more dots there are, the higher the resolution.

A typical example for older style monitors was a screen resolution of 800x600, meaning there were 480,000 pixels displayed on the screen.

A more modern monitor might have a screen resolution of 1024x768, meaning there are 786,432 pixels displayed on the screen.

Fixed width layout

So not so long ago a typical computer screen (monitor) could only show a web page to its full width if it was no more than 800px wide (usually restricted to 750px). Now the typical monitor can show pages up to 1024px wide due to better technology and the introduction of flat screens. Although most designers limit this back to around 980px as a standard, leaving some free space at the sides.

Just so that you know, if you do exceed this width on a webpage you've designed, it will show on a monitor smaller than the set width, but scroll bars come into operation. This is, so that the full page can be at least accessed even if it can't be viewed in its entirety (width-wise).

For the majority of websites, having to scroll sideways to find out what's fallen off the screen is a mark of disaster. Going up and down is far more common, and acceptable. You will probably notice that most websites have a vertical scrollbar at the side of the screen so you can scroll up and down. This is there because most web pages simply do not fit lengthwise onto a screen. If they do, the vertical scrollbar disappears as well. But the consequence of that is that there will hardly be room for any content on the page because length-wise there is typically only around 768px available. That really isn't a lot.

The vertical portion of the page that is visible on a computer screen when the page opens is referred to as being *above the fold*. The fold then is the point you get to at the bottom of a screen before you need to start scrolling.

It's also worth noting that websites tend to look better if they are horizontally centred, i.e. they sit in the middle of the screen with space either side - when there is space still available.

So now you know why website pages and their elements are typically measured in terms of pixels and not millimetres or inches, those units of measurement just don't work when it comes to computer screens.

Fluid width layout

There is another option to using a fixed width and that is the fluid width layout. What this means is that the web page adjusts to the size of the monitor it is being viewed on. For example you can control the size of the web page and the design elements using percentage of screen as the means of defining the width rather than a set amount of pixels.

The problem with a fluid layout is that it doesn't really suit complex designs with lots of design elements in them. The reason for this is that the elements can start to move around when viewed on different monitors and the designer loses control of how the webpage is presented. Not a desirable feature when you are trying to make a site look the same on all monitors.

The latest trend in designs standards is the introduction of responsive design layouts. These have come more to the fore as a result of having to cater for multiple mobile devices such as Smartphones and tablets. Responsive designs, if done properly, adapt to the device they are being viewed on.

But there are responsive designs and responsive designs, depending on the designer and how good he is. To be honest some responsive designs just don't work that well and for good reason, getting it right is quite tricky.

One of the easiest ways to get a responsive design that really does work well is to adopt a reliable Wordpress theme. If you try one and it doesn't work, just chose another until you get the result you are looking for.

You can then either decide to do this as your primary website or you might decide to make a mobile version that can be clicked to from your primary website using either a sub-domain or directory to house the extra mobile pages.

How you can update your own content easily and cheaply (Content management systems)

One of the biggest gripes any web designer's customers have is that once they have paid for a website, it is all up and running, and then they need to make updates and changes they find that further costs start arising. Why? Because most website designs are carefully laid out by the designers to accurately position all the design elements and accommodate the text they have been provided with. And this is usually done with web design software and associated tools that probably cost a pretty penny.

So where does that leave the poor old customers who, in truth, probably haven't thought about ongoing maintenance and changes up front? Right in the lurch!

They will usually be stuck with a complete redesign to address the problem or end up having to pay the web designer to do the updates on their behalf each time they are required. Not happy bunnies then!

So what are the options? What design features will allow you as, an ordinary Joe, to make ongoing changes or updates yourself? Enter the content management system (CMS).

CMS. Now that is a bone of contention in its own right. What is a content management system exactly?

According to Wikipedia a CMS is "*A content management system (CMS) is a system providing a collection of procedures used to manage work flow in a collaborative environment.*"

So that's clear then, enough said I think, or perhaps not!

In actual fact, content management systems mean different things to different people.

In the engineering world it may be a database or document store that holds all the engineering information that not only supports products for manufacture, but also technical information, specifications and any other reference information. All this has to be strictly controlled with any revisions being made under an appropriate engineering configuration control regime.

But that is in the engineering world, definitely not for you if all you want to do is the odd update or change to a website.

So let's get real, there are many content management systems out there that can be used as part of a web design process. Some may double up as blogging platforms but don't be fooled by that; they can be used just as effectively for CMS.

One of the best content management systems, simply because of the ease with which content can be added to, updated or changed, is once again...**Wordpress**.

So why is a blogging platform also a content management system?

In a few words, because it allows different users to access content modules for editing at different authority levels? The users range from administrators to subscribers. Each role defined has access permissions assigned to allow the users to perform the various actions associated with their role. They use a simple '*what you see is what you get*' user interface, which is accessed from an equally easy to use dashboard, as seen below There will be a learning curve to go through to use it, but compared to web design software this should be relatively simple. Plus of course, if you are the only user then you simply don't need to add other users.

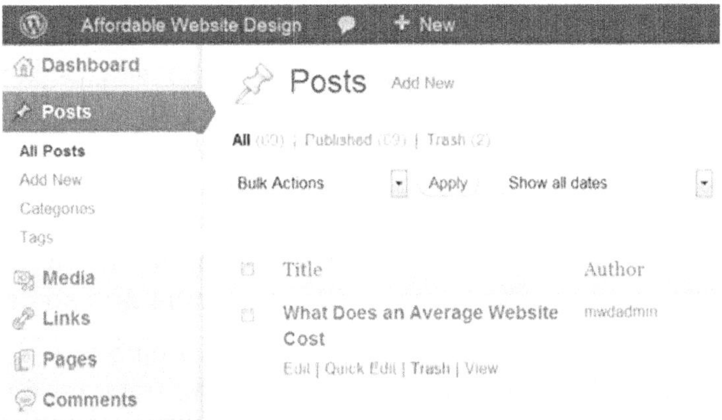

New pages can be added, existing pages can be edited and graphics or media can all be included with relative ease utilising the 'WYSIWYG' interface illustrated below.

There are many other content management systems, some of the better known ones are: Joomla, Drupal and Movable Type

They all perform a similar function and all you really need to do is make your choice for which one you prefer, and get on with best. That might be a little tricky without actually working with the program to find out.

For the paid versions, suppliers often offer a free trial period to let you use their software before buying; this can be a convenient way to test out its suitability.

Control panel

Control panel comes free with many hosting packages and provides access to the services and features that come with the hosting package. These include content management features plus access to database management, domain management and email management. You can use the latter for setting up email accounts, mail forwarding, auto-responders and so on.

Basically, it is the user interface for everything that needs to be or can be managed directly on the host server i.e. via a web browser interface.

I am a big fan of hosting services that come with CPanel because of the level of control and flexibility it offers. You as the owner of the website can have access to its features and take on the responsibility for the level of website management you are comfortable with.

You will have heard the saying give a man a fish; you feed him for a day. Teach a man to fish and you feed him for a lifetime.

Well CPanel is a bit like that, learn how to use it and there will be aspects of website management that you will never have to pay out for again and much of it is really easy to grasp, even for a complete novice.

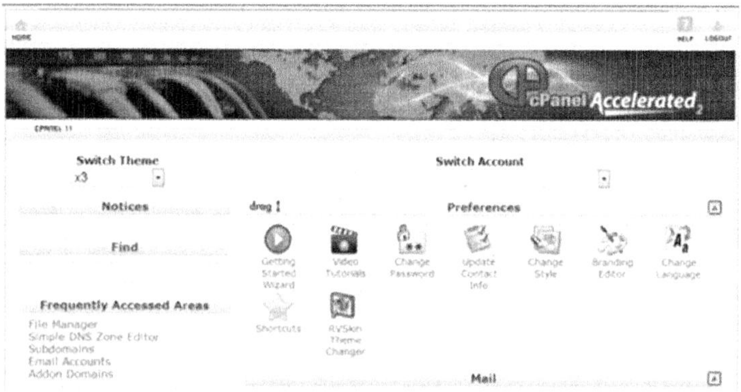

The 'File Manager' function for example gives you access to all the files published on the host server and even more importantly the ability to edit them using the built in cditors, hence the content management capability. The 'HTML Editor is in itself a WYSIWYG editor much like the one that you would find via the Wordpress dashboard.

This means that, within reason, and if your website design has been sympathetically done to provide user friendly web pages, you can make changes to the pages using CPanel as a web browser interface, because that is exactly what it is.

If you do decide to retain the services of a web designer, once the design is complete, you need to be aware that when you save the file after making the changes, your updates are immediately live and implemented on the Internet.

So you do need to be cautious when you do this and make sure that your web designer is aware of any changes you have made so that he doesn't inadvertently overwrite anything you have done. This would be very easy to do for example, if he typically makes changes to a copy on his local PC and then updates the server from there.

If this is something you are concerned about but you still like the idea of being able to edit web pages yourself, then you could also consider using Adobe Contribute,

(ref: www.adobe.com/products/contribute.html)

This is a relatively simple program that allows you to access web page files and edit them; again using a WYSIWYG editor. But Contribute also uses a checkout system to ensure no one else can edit the files while you have them checked out from the server. Of course Contribute comes at an additional cost whereas CPanel is typically included in the cost of your hosting, but you do get what you pay for and it could save you a whole lot of grief.

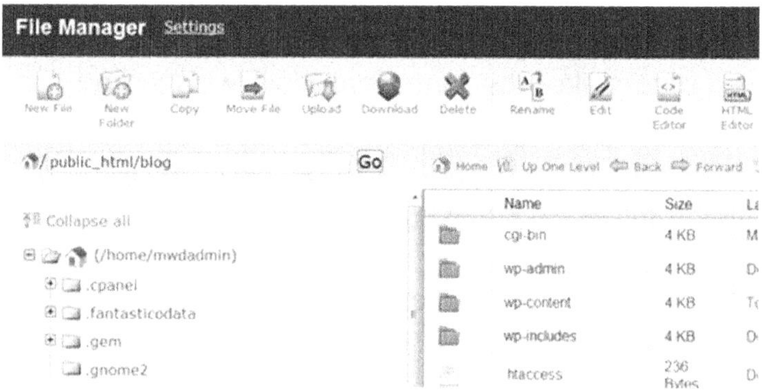

Maintaining a uniform look using cascading style sheets (CSS), server side includes (SSI) & design templates

Using Cascading Style Sheets is a method available for formatting a website page. The technicalities of using CSS can be quite complex and will be discussed in more detail later in the book. In this section however we will simply bc discussing how CSS can be used in combination with two other techniques to maintain a uniform look across a website.

Using this combined approach you will see how this is an easy way of managing all of your pages and also how the use of CSS combined with either templates or 'server side includes' (SSI) will ensure that not only can you maintain a uniform look and style across all pages, but you will also be able to apply changes to the pages easily and quickly.

Cascading style sheets

CSS comprise a set of formatting rules that control the appearance of content on a web page. The primary purpose of CSS is to separate the content from the presentation.

There are two ways in which CSS can be used to format the contents of a page:

- embedded CSS in the '*head*' section of the page i.e. the same location as the meta tags that were discussed earlier. But this time defined inside a '*style tag*' rather than a '*meta tag*'.

- in an external style sheet with the file extension (CSS)

For improved efficiency and improved load times (an element of on page search engine optimisation), the recommended method is to use an external style sheet which is linked to the page(s) where that styling is going to be applied. Ideally there will only be one external style sheet that controls all the formatting and styling of whole website by linking it to each page that makes up the website. In reality it is more common to find a combination of approaches are used to format a webpage. But putting as much as possible in the external sheet is the best approach, even if occasionally there is a need to have more than one external style sheet.

The reason an external style sheet is better than embedded CSS are twofold.

Firstly, all of the linked pages can be updated or modified at once from one location on one page. Secondly when the website loads on the PC of a visitor to the site the external sheet with code relevant to the formatting of all pages only has to be loaded once and is not repeated for every page on the website that uses common formatting.

Note: whenever you view a website on the Internet, in order to be able to see the pages, certain information is loaded on to your PC and is also placed in what is called the 'cache' as temporary Internet files. This is so that the next time you visit the website the pages will load more quickly. If you use external CSS this process is more efficient, loads more quickly and takes up less space.

Let me explain that further: if the CSS for controlling a paragraph is embedded in the head of multiple web pages then, for every page, the CSS for the paragraph has to be loaded individually. Alternatively if the CSS for a paragraph for a web page is in an external CSS page, it loads once only and is linked to every page that is subsequently loaded.

It is no more complicated than that really, with the embedded approach, the same code is loaded multiples of time, but with an external page, the same code is loaded only once. So from the perspective of communicating your requirements you should discuss with the designer your preference for using an external style sheet where possible to control the formatting.

Using templates

There are two types of template that you will be offered with respect to web design. The first is a web page design that can be taken and modified for your use. This reduces design time and consequently cost. That's not what we will be discussing here, but was mentioned earlier.

The second type is of the kind utilised by programs like Dreamweaver (a specialised software program for website creation) that aids the rapid update of a web page. This is achieved by splitting web pages into two distinct regions.

- editable regions

- non editable regions

The editable regions are where you would expect to be adding and changing the content of the page on a page-by-page basis, and with fairly regular updates after initial publication.

The non-editable regions are the regions that are typically considered to be the fixed design elements of a page which, if changed, the changes would be required on every page the template is applied to.

The editable regions then would contain the page contents in the form of text, graphics, media and so on. They would also contain the 'head section' elements that need to change on a page by page basis. Elements such as the title, the description, the keywords and so on. This is because all these things are used on an individual page by page basis.

The non-editable regions would contain elements such as the navigation system, footer information that is fixed, basically anything that is unlikely to change on a regular basis, or when it does you can update the template and apply the changes to all pages and re-publish.

This is one of the reasons that I would advocate a designer should use web design software that is in itself designed to do the job of web design, for features that can make the whole process of design and maintenance go much more smoothly.

It isn't just about the software though, sometimes it is about which techniques are employed over other techniques, which brings me nicely to the next chapter.

Server side includes

Server side includes (SSI) are an alternative to templates that do not depend on a specific program. So while I advocate the use of industry standard software to design and develop web pages, it is also appreciated that not everyone wants to.

There are a number of functions that can be performed using SSI but one of the main ones is placing a lot of common text or code on different web pages; a completely different technique to using templates, but the end result is pretty much the same.

Being able to use SSI does make you a little more dependent on the web hosting service, and they do have to support this function. But to be fair that is relatively common and all you have to do is ask to find out.

Using flexible web pages to make adding content easier

There are a number of different approaches to laying out a web page when designing a website. Some are better than others, but one thing that should be kept in the back of your mind when you are commissioning a website is how flexible the design is in respect to adding content, especially if you are intending to maintain the content yourself rather than using the services of a web designer.

The reason for making this statement is that there is nothing more frustrating than trying to update a page that will only allow you to add a fixed amount of content before the need to go back to the style formatting to create more space and then finding out that by adding more space other pages that have been created previously no longer work.

What can happen, if the design is not approached in the right way, is that essentially you end up with multiple versions of the same layout with minor adjustments to accommodate slightly different page requirements in terms of available space.

Far better to adopt a technique that grows automatically with the content i.e. as more content is added the space for it adjusts accordingly to accommodate it. This is discussed in more detail in Part 2 with recommendations for what is the best approach.

Registering a domain name

The ideal domain name you choose will communicate the nature of your business in a clear and succinct manner that is easy for visitors to remember and perhaps recommend to others.

It is a good idea to avoid unnecessary hyphens and words that are tricky to spell or are convoluted in nature.

You will need to be reasonably imaginative in coming up with a name because most obvious words and phrases such as *'holidays.com'* or *'onlineshopping.com'* have been snapped up years ago.

If you can afford to, and it is important to you from a business perspective, it would be a good idea to register your selected name (and potentially misspellings) in all the available top level domains. The following list is some of the more popular and currently available options: -

- .com

- .co.uk

- .eu

- .net

- .biz

- .org

- .mobi

The list goes on and the names displayed are only a small selection of the extensions now available, with more being added on a fairly regular basis. The new extensions are actually the ones that give you the opportunity to get a two or three word domain name. The problem of course is that there will almost definitely be competing websites with an alternative extension.

The clear favourite for most people registering a domain is the ever popular ***.com*** but as can be seen above that is by no means your only choice and you may even find that one of the other options is a more suitable alternative. For example if you are marketing to the UK it makes sense to have a .co.uk domain name.

For more information on domain names and how they are used you can visit the Nominet website (www.nominet.org.uk/). Be sure to have a look at the terms and conditions when you are on the site and visit the FAQ's list which is very good for providing the information you need.

Nominet UK is the registry for .UK registered Internet names where all UK unique domain names are registered using a numerical address that is mapped to a more memorable name. Different countries have different registries but they all operate in a similar way.

Domain name registration can be likened to a post code: the numerical address is a part of the full address and is used to point to the server where the website is physically located. It doesn't really matter where the server is actually located, more important is how reliable it is, although search engines do tend to return results for countries where an enquiry is made from sites hosted in those countries first.

The numerical part of the address is not visible to the website visitor but when a URL (uniform resource locator) is entered into the address line of a browser, the numerical address associated with that URL is used to locate the server where the website resides i.e. the Domain Name System (DNS) translates easy to recall names (domain names) such as *http://french-holidays-aude.com* into a numerical address and that address points to the server where the website resides.

It is the domain names that are used in advertising, are placed on business cards or listed by search engines in order to help people find them on the Internet. From a search engine perspective if the domain name is something that is likely to be included in a search query (keyword or keyword phrase) then the chances of the website being listed first in the results are increased.

The choice of a domain name depends on a lot of factors: it could be an existing brand name, a completely new brand starting from scratch, a company trading name, a trademark or perhaps a generic service being provided. But whatever is selected must be unique and they are always issued on a first come, first served basis.

You can use hyphens, numbers or underscores to make the name unique but generally, if you can avoid these options, it is considered better. Although I have to say if it works for you, you like it and people will remember it then I don't see a problem.

Probably the best way to find a name is by sitting down and brainstorming a list of about twenty names, which ideally would be no more than seven characters long. This will be more difficult than you think but it is a worthwhile exercise.

Hosting a website

Choosing the right web hosting service is an important decision for anyone entering the internet arena.

A poor choice will leave you with limitations on how you can develop your internet presence and what your website can deliver.

So choose with care and make sure you have the options you need available

There are four main types of hosting available:

- free Web Hosting Services

- collaborative/community Web Hosting Services

- shared Web Hosting Services

- dedicated Web Hosting Services

Free web hosting services

There are a number of free web hosting services out there; some are better than others and there may actually be one or two that could satisfy your requirements depending, of course, on what those requirements are.

Generally I would say that if you are advertising your business on the internet, even if it is in a simple way such as using the website as a company brochure, then normally it would be better if you take the time to register your own domain name, and then pay for your hosting service with a reputable company that suits your current and future needs.

My reasoning is that you don't really get anything for free; a "free" web hosting service almost invariably will require that you allow advertising on your site; it is likely to be very busy which may limit access to your web pages, and the URL address will frequently contain the name of the free hosting service before your name - which could be confusing and puzzling for your visitors.

You might also find that the technical support is lacking and that there is little if any flexibility in what you can do should your requirements change or grow. Email facilities are likely to suffer the same problems with potentially long and convoluted email addresses that are hard to remember and often have to include numbers to keep them unique.

If you are happy with what a free web hosting service provides and are prepared to overlook the possible disadvantages highlighted above then let the wind be behind you . . . and the best of luck.

Collaborative/community web hosting services

There are a number of what I call collaborative website hosting services, two of the better known ones are *squidoo.com* and *hubpages.com*.

These work by providing templates from which websites can be constructed. The modules range from simple text modules, to modules for graphics, video, RSS feeds, advertising modules and more. Let's be frank: you need to be computer savvy to adopt this route. The learning curve can be steep, and there's no guarantee you will end up with a great website.

Because these hosting services maintain a significant presence on the internet they tend to get the attention of the search engines and, providing you take the necessary steps to promote your websites (you have to do most of that work as well), you can establish a fairly high site ranking and search engine position relatively quickly. Results will still depend on you producing unique content on subjects of interest however.

Again there is no such thing as a free ride and these types of website are no exception; they do take a percentage of the advertising revenue your site raises. This comes mostly from the Google Adsense adverts that are placed strategically around on your web pages but may also come from the affiliate adverts you agree to place on your site, assuming you do, because that is an optional choice. You can see what I mean by looking at some of the Squidoo Lenses I have published from my Lensmaster Profile

(ref: www.squidoo.com/lensmasters/BrianS)

Shared web hosting services

This the cheapest option for hosting your dedicated domain name. Your designer and or webmaster will not have exclusive access to your own server but will be sharing a server with other domains. But in terms of the look and feel of the domain the address will be simple and refer only to your website URL. This also applies to the email if you select the right host.

You can of course have your own website designed for this option, although many of the hosting companies do offer templates and site-building software to supplement their service to you. Some people find this a perfectly acceptable alternative to using an independent design service, particularly if you are reasonably computer savvy.

Dedicated web hosting service

This is the most expensive option and is really only required if you have a heavy data-driven, multimedia site or possibly a comprehensive e-commerce one. You get your own server with this choice, hence the reason it is the most expensive, and of course all the same facilities of the shared server but without other domains sharing access to your server.

So what are the questions that need answering in order to make the right hosting choice?

- how much does the host package cost? Make sure there are no added extras.

- what is included in the package: space, speed of access, security features?

- how long is the contract period?

- how many email addresses are supplied and is there also a SMTP facility?

- what technical support is available, is it free, and when is it available?

- what operating systems are available?

- is there database support available?

- are traffic reports/analysis included?

- how often are the servers backed up? It should be daily.

- is there flexibility built into the system to accommodate changing needs?

- can you conduct an e-commerce business?

- clearly storage space is important. As a guide, for a properly constructed website, 25MB should be enough to store around 500 normal web pages with text and images. When you start to order flash, video and other multimedia data then the storage space will of course be used up more quickly.

Bandwidth equates directly to the number of people who visit your site each month. In other words how much traffic you get. For standard web pages with text and images 1GB would provide the facility for around 100,000 hits per month. But again start to put additional multimedia on the site and that number comes down because more bandwidth is used on these functions. A good rule of thumb for bandwidth versus storage space is a ratio of 10:1

Operating systems are important if you are having a database maintained on your site. Different databases are compatible with different operating systems, for example, you would need Windows servers for Microsoft Access database.

Upgrading is something that should be considered at the outset because you never know where the website may need to go or do as your business builds. One approach is to take a cheap option at the early stages as long as there is an upgrade path available should you need it.

For example, not all hosts support .php scripting but this is not necessarily a problem if you don't, for instance, want a feedback form that works through the host server or you don't care if RSS feeds are not search engine identifiable.

On the other hand if you do require these feature then you will need some form of scripting facility and if you want to generate traffic through the search engines the script needs to be in a format that the search engines can read (this doesn't apply to feed back forms).

Email - Most web hosting comes with free email addresses. Having POP3 (Post Office Protocol) or IMAP functionality allows mail clients such as Outlook to retrieve mail from the server.

Likewise SMTP (simple mail transfer protocol) allows you to send email via the server using your mail client. Not all hosts provide these facilities as part of their basic package, but they may offer it as part of an upgrade path. You need to decide if you want this capability from the outset and whether you are prepared to pay a little more in order to have it.

How Google ranks your website

The good news is that at the time of writing this I have a pretty good idea how Google ranks a website. The bad news is, that may change tomorrow; the reason - Google are constantly evolving their search algorithms to produce better results to match the enquiries made.

Companies offering search facilities like Google live and die on the results that are returned and placed in front of the enquirer. Fail to deliver and as mentioned previously it really won't be long before people stop asking you and go and ask someone else. Google now have over 85% of the market to themselves because their former competitors did just that: they failed to deliver.

So where does that leave you when it comes to promoting your website. We have already discussed in detail what was referred to as '*on-page optimisation*' Now we are going to discuss the other side to the coin: 'off-page optimisation'.

This means the things you can do, away from the actual website design, to ensure search engines seek out your website and put it at the top of their list when the contents of your website are enquired about.

Promotion and links

So you are sitting looking at your website and considering all the 'on-page optimisation' work that has been done. If you have followed the guidelines, described earlier in that 'on-page optimisation' section, you will have lovingly researched a subject you are passionate about, picked all your best keyword terms, and written them into your web page content according to priority and positioned the most important ones in the best keyword locations. The content should also consist of unique and refreshing information that perfectly matches your target audience in terms of complexity and detail. Well in the ideal world that would be the case.

Then your website is published on the Internet. What happens? Well at this point it's probably not much!

Now it's time to spend some of your precious time promoting and advertising your website. That's easily said, but what does it mean and how do you do it, I hear you asking?

Social Book Marking Sites

There are many, too many to count, social and book marking sites. The most famous of course is Facebook, closely followed by Twitter and LinkedIn. Many people use these sites and don't even realise that they can be used to promote businesses, websites and blogs. But of course they can.

A recent big player to enter this field is Google+ which has gone in direct competition with Facebook, but at the time of writing their campaign is lagging well behind the ever-popular Facebook, but membership is growing and growing quickly.

Sites like StumbleUpon, Digg, Reddit, and Delicious also compete in this arena. LinkedIn is worth a special mention, mainly because LinkedIn targets professionals and businesses.

Social marketing is a relatively new phenomenon which can appear bewildering to many people, but is it really that complicated?

This is very much dependent on how complicated you want it to be. You can, if you choose, be, totally overwhelmed by the multitude of social media sites there are available and what they offer. Some to be fair are a little more complicated than others, Facebook, LinkedIn and Google+ are good examples of sites that probably need their own dedicated books to explain how they can be used most effectively.

There are less complicated sites however, and good examples of these are Digg, Mixx, and StumbleUpon.

So consider this proposal: let's say the less complicated social media sites are really only about four things:

- giving an online publication a name or description

- saying whether you like it or dislike it

- sharing the information with friends

- building a trusted relationship with like-minded people

Giving an item a name or description - What you provide on the Internet, through a digital medium, is content and that content has a subject. So when that content is given a name or description it is generally so that other people can find it by searching. The name you give your content is often referred to in social media sites as a tag or if you want to get technical, it's the keyword(s) we have already talked about at great length.

So clearly then, your website or blog could be shared on a social media site and will ideally be described on that site using the keywords (tags) that you are promoting for your site.

Saying whether you like it or dislike it - So now you need to indicate what you think of the content, you can vote it up, vote it down or give it a star-rating. These are just ways to communicate whether you like the content or not. Obviously if you are the one providing the content then you are hoping people will vote for it in a positive way. Clearly the best way to ensure they do this is to make the content valuable and of a high quality.

Sharing information - When you join a social media site you are effectively joining a community and you are normally seeking like-minded people or at least people who are interested in the same things that you are.

Let's face it; people wouldn't be searching for keywords (tags) unless they were interested to some level. So when they find the stuff you are interested in and they are also interested in it, then they are likely to want to become friends with you so that you can continue to share similar content on that subject.

Building a trusted relationship with like-minded people - This is the next natural progression of this process: you will either discover that you can go on to trust this person and enjoy sharing content with them or you may find that actually you didn't have that much in common after all. The latter get dropped and the former become friends that you continue a relationship with (online relationship that is) and ultimately you will begin to trust one another.

When you have reached that point of being trusted then the other person is likely to listen to and take your recommendations seriously.

So, from a marketing perspective, which is where we started from with this, it becomes pretty obvious that until you are at the fourth stage you are unlikely to be able to convince anyone that you know what you are talking about and have something valuable to offer, whether that is products, services or simply opinions.

So there you have it; Social Media Marketing in a nutshell. You need to earn the respect and trust of your online friends before you can use social media to sell what you are offering.

This is equally as true for large organisations as it is for individuals. Take Amazon or eBay as examples. They would not be nearly as successful as they are if they were not a trusted online presence that people feel comfortable dealing with.

As a cautionary note, you will not be able to follow these rules for every social media site, there are simply too many. You can join a good proportion of them and you can post your website or blog URL's on those if you wish. At least that will be links back to your site. But to really make the most of a social media site you need to fully engage, and I would suggest that you will only be able to do that with one or two at the most. What you need to decide is which ones suit you or your business best and then use the site properly for its intended purpose.

Be careful not to fall into the trap of spending all your time on social book marking sites however. There is only so much value they can bring and you will come across a lot of people where it is all one-way traffic: they ask a lot and give nothing back. To be honest you are better off without those people even if they do help make your friend numbers look good.

Always remember, as well, that social sites really are all about engaging with the community; it shouldn't be all about you because that is a little like spamming. It should be about the community and making friends, You can only do that by engaging and helping people out, ***just like real friends***.

Networking - this is not unlike social marketing; it is a similar process that just uses different mediums. It is the network of friends we build up within the various communities we engage with, using forums, blogs, squeeze lists, and favourites (via your web browser). So yes, you should use all or as many of these resources as possible for promotion.

But again not forgetting that this is a two-way street and if you want people to help you then it is a good idea to help them, plus you never know, you could learn a thing or two in the process.

Squeeze lists - a squeeze list is your list of email addresses of everyone who has ever been in touch with you for one reason or another, e.g. by subscribing to your blog.

Squeeze lists are dangerously close to being a spam tool and what I would say is that it's fine to use them as long as you consider that the addressee has a genuine interest in what you have written and/or they contact you on a similar basis. If its 'email and hope' then I would say don't do it, you will just become an annoying little irk.

Getting links to your site - So what else is there you can do, surely that is enough. Well not really, we are back to those highly revered search engines and their aspirations of what you need to do in order to fulfil their needs.

Reciprocal linking, one way linking and triangular linking. What on earth does that mean?

OK, you probably know about reciprocal linking. It's someone with a site that has the same subject matter as you and swaps links with you so that you both benefit, grouping your own related articles and linking to other articles from a post or page does a similar thing.

Actually Google are not particularly keen on these types of links, they see it as a mutual back patting exercise, rather than the natural occurrence of one website pointing to another as a source of genuinely useful information, which is what they really want.

You can see their point really. That said as long as this is not done excessively you will probably get away with it. Something like a link farm on the other hand is really a waste of time and likely to be seriously detrimental. Link farms are sites that exist purely for one reason: to game the search engines. They do that by publishing hundreds of links to various websites indiscriminately and with no regard to relevancy or whether the links add any value to a site. They are totally disregarded by the search engines and are highly likely to result in your site being downgraded if you use their services.

One way links - You can get some one way links by posting comments on blogs and leaving your URL, by answering questions in Yahoo Answers (as long as you follow the rules) and using your URL as the reference for the information or by simply asking other website owners to link to you, not usually successful unless they really see the value, a possible solution to this is to write guest articles so they at least get some benefit. These are some ways of getting one way links into your site.

Article writing and posting your websites in directories is another. How this works is that you write an article and post that article, for public use, in an article directory. Article directories allow you to place some resource links at the end of the article; these can point back to your website. When someone visits the article directory and decide to use your article for their own website, they have to retain your links. The more popular the article is, the more links you can get to your website.

Of course the best way of getting one-way links is naturally, i.e. visitors to your website consider the content of your website to be of high quality and valuable. So they refer to your website from theirs.

The other side of this coin is who you point to for good quality reference information. Wikipedia is a fantastic resource for this sort of link, but any site that has high quality content, especially if it has been rewarded with a good search engine ranking for its contribution, is worth pointing to i.e. you link to their site but they may not necessarily point to yours.

Never forget the relevancy, relevancy, relevancy rules for this. Break these rules and there is a good chance you will do more harm than good.

As for the triangle, this where you point to a website which points to another website that points back to you. Fantastic! You tie three websites together without a direct reciprocal link; call it reciprocal linking with a twist.

Those search engines are sneaky, they like this because it is not seen as the back-patting exercise. Albeit this is a very simplistic approach and if abused, again it is likely to have the opposite effect to the desired one. This is because search engines don't like to think they are being manipulated or gamed; if they suspect they are they will take a dim view of it. So if you participate in three-way linking, make sure the sites you are engaging with are indexed, ranked and relevant to your chosen topics.

One final point, and another judgement call I am afraid. Sometimes there are times when you do not want to give too much information freely - for example, if you are going after Adsense revenue it is a good idea for the ads to be your outgoing links. In other words, to get to the information they are after, visitors need to click on an ad that offers that information. This is perfectly legitimate; you should have ads that are relevant to your content so that visitors to your site may want to explore what they have to offer, the whole point of the exercise I would say, so sometimes less is more as they say.

In summary, use every resource available to you for promoting and making people aware of the existence of your website including social networking tools, linking to high quality relevant websites for reference, use reciprocal & three-way linking responsibly, post comments and participate in forums/self-help groups etc.

Sometimes it is also enough to bring your site to the attention of another relevant site's webmaster with email outreach. Just contact them and make a genuine request for them to link to your site as a resource. Your site will have to offer some value, but if it does....why wouldn't they?

There is a lot of information here, so representing that information in graphical format was probably always going to be a good way to provide a ready reference.

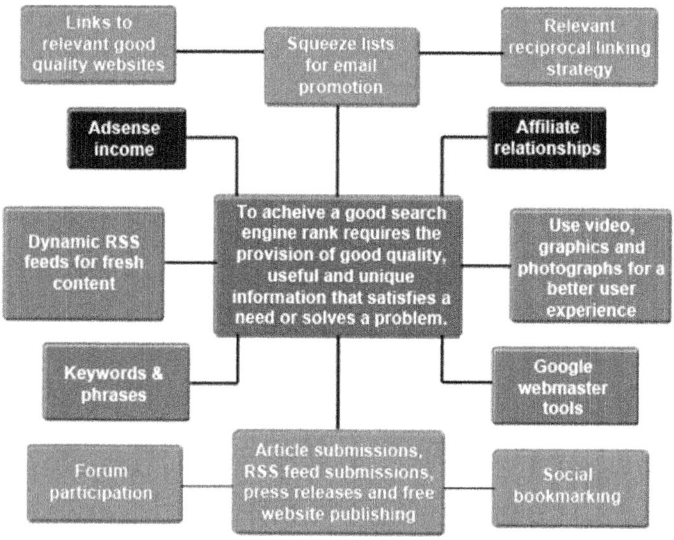

A Picture Paints a Thousand Words

Something else to bear in mind is that, in themselves, these tactics do work. But they should ideally only be necessary to get your website noticed in the first instance. Once people start to notice the existence of the website you really need natural adoption to take place and people to link to the website because it has something to offer that is useful.

This will only really happen if the website successfully does the following:

- answers peoples questions

- provides good quality information

- solves problems
- entertains

Website performance

Website performance measurement is a critical aspect of website search optimization because you can use the tools available to tell you exactly how your website is doing and perhaps more importantly how you are doing it.

The 'how you are doing' it part comes from examining where your traffic (visitors) is coming from and how they ended up on your website. The following is a list of factors you need to be aware of and how you can use them:

- referring sites - these are the sites that have links to your website that people are clicking on

- geographic sources - where in the world your visitors are coming from

- bounce rate - how long your visitors stay on your website

- number of visitors - ideally you would like to know how many unique visitors you get and how many loyal followers you have who make repeat visits to your site. This is not easy for any software to sort out and often you can only really believe the number that says how many visitors you get in a day

- which keywords were used to land on your site

Referring sites If you notice there is a site that sends a lot of traffic your way then it is worth focusing in on that site to see if you can further enhance the relationship and get even more traffic. For example, you could contact the webmaster and offer to write some articles to post there and you could also offer a reciprocal arrangement: they could write articles for your website making it a more attractive proposition.

Sometimes as an option, and if you think it is worth it, you could offer to pay for some advertising on that site. Basically you need to identify what it is about the site that encourages people (the referrals) to come to your site and see if you can give them exactly what they want.

Geographic sources You need to know where your real market is and where visitors are coming from so that you can optimise your site for their needs. For example if all your traffic is coming from international sources rather than a local market there would be no point offering products that can only be obtained locally; you need to provide international options. So if you are in the UK and your visitors are from the States you might have links to amazon.com rather than amazon.co.uk. Again the alternative to this is to change the features that are bringing the wrong type of visitors to attract the right type. Might be something as simple as adding UK or USA to the title, but you would need to establish what works.

Bounce rate As mentioned earlier, the faster a human lands on and then departs from a page the less likely it is that they found what they were looking for, or liked what they discovered. The technical term for this is bounce rate. High bounce rate – the site is not retaining visitor interest; low bounce rate – you are getting things right.

The possible reasons for a high bounce are: either you didn't have the items your keywords promised or they couldn't find what they were looking for due to poor page layout or navigation options. Either way you need to resolve those problems to deliver on the promise or make it clear where to find the information.

Number of visitors This number is an indication of whether your keywords and SEO optimization are working, i.e. this is the traffic that is arriving on your website as a result of all your efforts to optimise your site. There are two types of visitors, unique and repeat. They are both important because you want to see both varieties, although any software program will struggle to differentiate between them and there are likely to be errors in the data presented.

You should really only use the number that gives you the overall quantity in combination with page views to assess how much traffic you are getting.

A word of caution: do not mix up page views with hits, they are different. Hits are how many times images and files get viewed, so a page with multiple images and files may appear to be having a lot of traffic but really this a multiplication of the page views that is inconsistent depending on which pages have been viewed. That is why it is page views and total visitors that give you your real indication of traffic; these numbers are not skewed for any reason.

Keywords You should look at what keywords actually delivered your traffic for two reasons:

- to make sure that you provide your visitors with what they were looking for when they arrive

- to see if you should be optimising your site for different keywords

Not only should you know which keywords are delivering results (more visitors), but you should take action on what you find. You have to deliver on the promise and you do that by either changing the content or changing your keywords so that you get different traffic that seeks the content you have in place.

My recommendation is that you use *Google analytics* to extract the information you need for your websites. Everything I have discussed here and much more can be found using this tool. You will need to register with Google and put tracking code on your site (a simple task for your designer), but as you can see, the potential benefit from using these statistics and indicators are enormous. You may also want to consider signing up to Google Webmaster Tools another very useful free resource.

Other useful indicators are your page rank (and that of competitors) as awarded by Google, primarily as a result of how many links there are to your website, although there are other factors. Also your Alexa ranking, because Alexa ranks websites in accordance with how many visitors it gets, in other words, the better the Alexa ranking the more visitors the site gets.

Both these indicators can be shown in your browser by downloading the Google toolbar and the Alexa rank extensions that you can find depending on the Internet browser you use.

Benefits of well-designed websites

A well designed website is basically a website that ticks all the required boxes because it

- meets your requirements, as the owner, - at a reasonable cost.

-is aesthetically pleasing to the intended audience

- delivers on the promise to visitors to the site, i.e. they find what they were looking for when they arrive, in terms of the content

- is easy to navigate both for human visitors and search engines

- it functions as required from a technical perspective. There is nothing worse than clicking on a link that doesn't work, or filling in a form that refuses to be sent

- Search engines can easily find the topic of the content without being misled

- is easy for you to update and maintain without having to ask the designer or a webmaster to take on the task – incurring extra costs each time

- is reliable and always available; a website should function without problems as closely as possible to 24 hours a day, 365 days a year, without question

- should conform to all the necessary website design standards

So if your website is achieving the above objectives you should consider that as a job well done. On the other hand, if some of the boxes have not been ticked, it might be time to revisit the design to take corrective action or replace it from scratch. Sometimes it is easier to start from scratch than modify a poor design. Hard to swallow, but true.

Briefing a designer

Now that you have a better understanding of how a website should be assembled and specified, you need to be sure not to forget to put all this new found knowledge to good use. This simple list of discussion points will ensure you communicate your requirements effectively:

- Costs. Be sure to discuss both the initial costs and ongoing costs once the site is published on the Internet. You should always set yourself a budget, and it might be a good idea to share that information with the designer so that his and your expectations are realistic.

- Work with the designer to produce a simple sitemap that will indicate how many pages the website will have.

- Use a storyboard and a list of websites that appeal to you to communicate the style and type of website you are looking for. Pay particular attention to how you want the navigation system to look.

- Ensure, if you are building a website to attract business and/or visitors from the Internet, that the website takes into account the search engine optimisation (SEO) features that will be required, starting with a suitable domain name. You also need to think about and discuss who will be marketing and promoting the website.

- Discuss what hosting options are available to you; a reseller package may be suitable, but if you have plans for multiple sites or need 24 hours a day support, you may be better going directly with a host company.

- Have the text, images and, where required, logo details prepared for each page. Again, for the text and contents, think about the SEO needs.

- Talk about the functionality of the website: elements such as databases, feedback forms, search features, social book marking facilities and content management systems.

- Let the designer know if you want to submit a sitemap to the search engines, monitor the websites performance and provide a method for potentially offering links to other sites.

There will be other factors to consider which only you as the customer will be aware of but using these guidelines will get you off to a good start.

****

Part Two

As we enter the second part of the book it is necessary to understand that we are now moving on from the subject of what are the best and necessary features of a website to the more technical aspects of taking on a website design yourself. So now it is less about specifying the requirements and more about the technicalities of how you actually design the website. Of course you need to keep in mind the discussions from the first part of the book to ensure that you do in fact incorporate those guidelines.

Website Costs from the designer perspective

Producing a website can actually be a relatively cost effective process and need not cost a lot of money, if you know what you're doing.

Many websites being designed for small businesses or individuals really shouldn't be overly expensive. Domain registration for as little as £3 ($4.50) a year, hosting from £36 ($54) a year and a one-off cost for the design of between £100 ($150)and £300 ($450) are realistic prices for a relatively simple website.

From the perspective of anyone trying to decide whether to take the time to learn how to design their own website, especially if it is a one-off, there is a need to consider whether their time might be better spent working on other aspects of their business and just employing someone else to design or set up a website on their behalf. Time is money after all.

Moulin Website Design for example, offers a design service that offers web designs in line with the costs quoted, including bespoke static designs or the setting up of a blog-formatted website. This is relatively quick and easy to do and with a few modifications can soon be given a unique appearance. The added benefit of this is that they have a CMS (content management system) built in, making updates and modifications much simpler for the site owner and avoiding the need to pay the web designer for any ongoing changes and updates. This brings us nicely onto the next chapter where we discuss the difference between a website and a blog and how you can produce something that meets your needs.

(ref:www.moulinwebsitedesign.com)

Website or blog?

Why do some of us create blogs and why do others read them? This is an important question since its answer covers the working principle behind the entire phenomenon. First of all, it's not far from the truth to say that bloggers are like journalists, and that the material found in blogs can often be much more interesting than articles the media produces; mainly thanks to the personal touch blog writers add to their content.

Furthermore there is an interactive dimension to blogs which cannot be ignored; this is probably the greatest advantage in itself. There are comment boxes for instant responses, links to documented materials, plus videos and pictures which can all be quickly and easily added for extra interest to the visitor and to keep bounce rates low.

Blogging is trendy, without doubt. Not only is it popular with people of all ages but it also gives bloggers a feeling of being part of a community. You get an idea of what people appreciate in your writing, you get to comment on and actually experience some events of public interest, and you have the chance to have your say and speak your mind.

Everything you post on the blog, every piece of original material is recorded and now it provides easy access to the information when you need it, the information you post as an article in your blog becomes a point of reference for you and for other people who visit the site and agree with what you have written.

Many would-be writers actually take blogging seriously since they are offered the opportunity of getting published without the intermediary of another publication, or the approval of a publishing service.

The writing of eBooks is following a similar course: authors who once would have only been able to publish a printed book, with all the associated costs, can now produce their written works in digital format and publish those writings at a much reduced cost.

Of course what has made this more viable is the advance of mobile technology & ereaders. But there is still not that interactive element that a blog can deliver; a book at the end of the day still tends to be a one-way communication, whether in digital or printed format.

Many blogs offer the advantage of a debate area where you'll find all sorts of opinions. There is no point getting upset at the viewpoints of others when they have entered into the debate. Especially when the comments are not what you had hoped for.

Points of view are simply perspectives and they should not hurt feelings or be taken personally. You simply have to accept things are like that and not to worry about it. Everyone is different and they are entitled to their viewpoint.

Something that should also be mentioned is the popularity and promotion advantages that are specific to a blog; just like niches, small business blogs provide an environment for easily reaching targeted Internet users.

Many business owners have discovered that blogs are the perfect way to regularly keep in touch with customers and even employees, since these web pages function as online journals that are frequently updated.

The advantage that blogs clearly have above other sites is that they express something specific in the most active or dynamic of ways whereas "classic" style websites are definitely more static in nature; they convey reference information mostly that does not change.

Without doubt the voice or personality of the writer is the element that makes a blog unique and interesting at the same time. It conveys opinions and viewpoints which their viewers can agree with or disagree with, that's why it's fun! Of course a static website can illustrate the voice of the writer as well, but much more akin to the eBook option discussed previously.... a one-way conversation.

Taking this discussion forward a step, a significant slice of the content of this book was about using a content management system. The recommendation in fact was to utilise the blogging platform Wordpress, or other similar programs, as the basis of a content management system.

On that premise it is not unrealistic to turn that around and use a blogging platform presented as a static website or in fact to combine its use so that a blog element is included.

With the latest versions of Wordpress for example, the physics of it means that the owner can simply elect for the home page to be a static page instead of the traditional blog format that comes with chronological postings. These postings can be transferred to an alternative page and then they can be added to a menu or navigation system for easy access. Adding more pages to the equation then provides the look and feel of a static website.

If you are not interested in including a blog as a section of the website then you simply do not make any chronological postings i.e. the traditional blog format and just use the platform for static pages only.

The whole point is that firstly you need to decide on which media you prefer to present your information and then which technology you prefer to create that presentation. And of course what is being stated is that you can use a blogging platform exactly as that, as a combined static website and blog (the best of both worlds), or just to look like a static website in its entirety. The choice is yours.

So the choice in effect is about whether you are reaching out to an audience that wants to engage and join in, the blogging option, an audience that may want to engage or just be informed, the combined option, or an audience that just seeks to be informed, the static website option. You will need to decide.

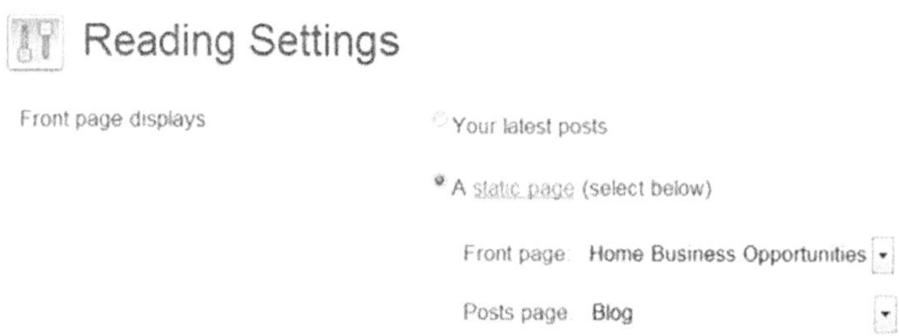

There is no doubt that there is a place for blogs in the purest interpretation of the meaning and there is a place for static or traditional websites. It really is down to the preferences of the individuals concerned, and as indicated what level of engagement with your visitors is being sought.

What has changed if anything are the mechanics behind the design process and the degree of individuality and functionality required. Where high levels of individuality and functionality are required; especially at the same time, there is also a high likelihood that most individuals or businesses are going to require the services of professional designers and or developers to get what they want. Even blog themes have to be constructed.

But if your philosophy on life is compromise and you are happy to take an existing blog theme, of which there are many thousands, take some time to learn how to operate the dashboard and implement the approaches discussed.

You can in fact get yourself a web presence quickly either entirely through your own efforts or by using services that can take care of the elements you are concerned about or don't have the time to take on.

Either way, that web presence can be secured at a much lower cost taking the blogging platform route.

That doesn't mean that the traditional approach to web design has died a death, it just means that for individuals entering into the world of the Internet on a relatively small scale, there are options.

Learning to design a static website or in fact create a blog theme from scratch is going to involve a more in-depth commitment and a steeper learning curve.

Although there are ways of creating 'blog themes', that doesn't necessarily require technical skills but would involve a financial investment in programs that facilitate this, as mentioned below.

Wordpress is one of the best known blogging platforms and is my recommendation for creating a blog-based design, probably because it is a 'state of the art' publishing program which is an amazingly popular CMS in addition to being a blogging platform.

The program has massive support through open source development. This means literally thousands of people have developed different plug-ins that can be used to extend the functionality of the website.

The plug-ins are the route to pretty much every feature anyone might ever require. Plus there is the availability of literally thousands of themes, both free and purchasable, that will take care of the look and style of the pages.

If that isn't enough then you can purchase programs that require no coding skills to create a theme of your own design, ensuring that if it is a unique and bespoke design you want, then you can have it.

As a final point on adopting a blogging platform to create your media of choice we should return to the discussion on hosting.

I have found through personal use that HostGator provides really good value for money. You can start with a basic package, host unlimited domains or if you are really serious you can take a reseller option, something I have done so I can provide hosting to clients and anyone seeking an affordable hosting option over a shorter period. You can find my review of HostGator via the reference below, but please be aware that I do have an affiliate relationship with HostGator so do earn commission from any sales made, although I do believe my review to be an honest and accurate appraisal.

(ref: http://blogaude.com/hostgator-review/)

It's worth noting that .php and email including SMTP come as standard with HostGator but as with most hosting companies the cost is related to a minimum contract period, if you ask for a shorter period the price per month increases.

For the bloggers out there, a real benefit of HostGator is that it comes with CPanel, which was discussed earlier, and there is a facility within CPanel that allows you to easily create and set up a Wordpress blog, worth its weight in gold for serious bloggers

The facility in question is called the '*Fantastico*' module; this can be used to install various additional functional programs onto the host server, including a range of free Content Management Systems. You can see these in the illustration below.

Wordpress is listed under Blogs rather than Content Management, the reason for that is that Wordpress is more generally recognised as one of the primary blogging platform which is only really rivalled by Google's Blogger platform. But don't let that distract you from the fact that it is a superb CMS as well.

There are a number of organisations that provide the facilities for writing and generating blogs out there with more scope for getting your own look and feel particularly if you opt for something like the 'WordPress' facility which is particularly flexible.

The best known ones are:

- Wordpress
- Blogger
- Posterous
- Tumblr

There are others 'b2 evolution' and 'nucleus' for example, which you can research yourself, but those listed are the four primary ones including of course, my personal recommendation, Wordpress.

Something else to bear in mind with Wordpress is that there are many themes available that now encompass a fully responsive design layout making them much more useful for mobile technology, even if you choose to have a separate mobile site to your primary site.

That is it for the blogging options, the next topic is how to best approach a static website design using traditional methods that include the use of HTML and CSS.

Taking a static web design approach

Discussed earlier in the book was the difference between what a website does versus what it does for you. This was to open up the topic of website design versus website development and whether when creating a website you need to employ the services of a website developer.

HTML & CSS

The only way to really clarify this point is by understanding the difference between mark-up language and cascading style sheets versus script writing and programming.

A standard website in its most basic form will use a combination of HTML (hypertext mark-up language) and CSS (cascading style sheets).

Put simply HTML defines what the content is and CSS defines how it is presented.

The paragraph or <p> mark up, for example, is one of the most basic elements of HTML and is represented as follows:

<p>*Text goes between the opening and closing mark-up elements and the closing element contains a forward slash to differentiate from the opening element*</p>

So the text between the 'p' command mark-up is defined as a paragraph.

Note: the actual mark-up language elements will not be visible when you view the web page, only the text in between will be visible.

Now you can control how that paragraph is presented using a cascading style sheet that is applied to the page. The styling for the 'p' command might look something like this in CSS format:

```
p{
 text-align: left;
 margin-right: 5px;
 margin-left: 5px;
}
```

It's not too hard to work out that the cascading style sheet in this example is defining the paragraph as being left aligned with 5 pixels of clear space either side of any text identified as a paragraph using the 'p' command. Of course the instructions can be much more detailed and complex but this is the basics of what it does.

So the application of CSS may be simple in practice, but the construction of CSS rules can become quite complex. There are three types of rules:

- Custom CSS rules or Class Styles
- HTML tag rules of which the 'p' tag was an example
- CSS selector rules or Advanced Styles

CSS formatting also consist of two parts, the selector and the declaration. The selector basically identifies the element the rule is going to be applied to and the declaration defines what is going to be applied to the element.

I am sure you can imagine that styling something like a multiple drop down menu using CSS could become quite complex. But once it is done, unlike Flash and or Java the elements of the menu are all individually visible to the search engines, which means it is a more search engine friendly approach, also to modify and adapt it quickly and easily is much more achievable.

If you want to know more about creating Multiple Drop Down Menus with CSS use this link.

(www.blog.moulinwebsitedesign.com/css-formatting-for-mulitple-drop-down-menu-and-relative-position-divs/)

Any web designer should be able to use these tools to define the front end visible elements of a web page and how they are presented. You can visit Formatting Web Pages with CSS for a more detailed explanation of how it works.

(www.blog.moulinwebsitedesign.com/formatting-web-pages-with-css/)

The point being made however is that this is mark-up language and formatting for presenting website content normally considered to be the front end visible elements. It is not the coding or scripting that supports additional functionally.

A web developer takes website design a step further by introducing additional functionality using programs specifically written for tasks or writing scripts to respond to user requests. In other words, what the website can do behind the scenes, sometimes referred to as the back end.

The truth is that many of the functions that can be added by a developer are often available as free resources on the Internet, certainly functions such as message forms, embedding RSS feeds and creating buy now buttons are all readily available as are many more functions. If they are not completely free then they are usually available for a modest cost.

So often there is no need to employ the services of a developer unless the customer, or you (if you are designing your own website), have exacting requirements that step beyond what would be considered standard website functionality.

Typical scripts used in web design are Javascript, PHP, ASP and ActiveX. To find tutorials on the nitty-gritty of scripting and web design in general you can visit w3schools.com .

(www.w3schools.com/)

Again there are options for using free versions of animated products on a website, slideshows for example can quickly be embedded into a web page using free Java scripts and then populated with photographs of choice. The link provided is one of many such sites that offer this facility.

(www.javascriptkit.com/)

The problems start when the effects required are specific and a free or low cost version is not available to meet the requirement. Under these circumstances the animation needs to be-developed. Often this may involve combining a few different programs and/or scripts to get to the desired result Of course these skills can be learned but they do tend to be a bit specialist when taking on complex arrangements

The reality is that many web designers have overlapping skills that cover some elements of web development and producing animated effects. But for larger more complex projects specialists in the discipline are highly likely to be required.

It is also worth knowing that there are programs available that are considered to be the industry standard in website design. For a little more information on this, you can visit:

www.squidoo.com/webdesign-tools

This will give you an introduction to the most popular website design program, graphic editing program and one of the most popular animation programs, all of which, incidentally, are Adobe products.

A lot of Adobe then but these tools do readily integrate with one another and consequently make the web design process go a little smoother.

Avoiding excessive use of java script and flash

As was discussed earlier, search engines do not have the capability to easily read through Flash, Java script and many of the other scripting codes. So using these functions for elements such as navigation menus will potentially prevent them finding all the published pages on a website. Likewise RSS feeds embedded using Java will not be able to be read and will not be considered to form the actual content of a webpage.

Using HTML and CSS effectively is a good way to overcome some of these script-related problems. It's also useful to know that not all PCs run Java and Flash and therefore will not be able to access the part of the design using it. This is even truer of mobile devices.

Using flexible web pages to make adding content easier

Another subject that was touched on earlier was utilising flexible web pages that allow you to add content easier. But exactly how do you do that and what is the preferred method?

There are two primary ways in which you can accommodate content automatically. One is bad practice, although a popular method, and the other is a recommended technique for up-to-date modern designs.

Nested tables

So let's look at the very popular, but bad, first method, using tables, sometimes with other tables nested inside them.

This is a powerful tool for presenting text and graphics on an HTML page and the use of tables as a quick and easy method for producing a layout in a tabular format. As you add more content the table cells expand to accommodate that content.

But is it the best solution? The answer to that is, no, not really; building tables in the first instance can seem relatively straightforward and while you are doing it you are familiar with what you are doing and why. Revisit the page six months later to make a change and things may be a little different. Remembering what you did and why might be a bit tricky. Also when you look at the mark-up for tables it doesn't really show in a familiar sequence e.g. left to right. This makes the probability of making an error more likely.

Tables are also not particularly screen-reader-friendly and they load less quickly than say a CSS controlled layout.

So is there a place for tables in a page layout? Yes there is, to present tabular data, but not as a primary layout tool.

CSS layout positioning

You have probably guessed from the previous section that I am not a fan of using tables for laying out web pages. So let's move on to what is considered to be the best and correct way to lay out a web page, using CSS.

Now you face a new dilemma, because when it comes to *CSS positioning*, which is what we are talking about, there are four options available and depending on what you choose your automatic accommodation of content will either be successful or will fail dismally. So here are the four different position properties:

- Static
- Relative
- Absolute
- Fixed

The 'static' position is not really positioning at all; it occurs where it normally would in a document. In other words it is where it is in the mark-up.

Relative positioning allows you to use CSS declarations for top, bottom, left and right so that you can move the element relative to where it is in a document.

Absolute positioning means the element is put in a position defined by the declaration irrespective of where the div is placed (or irrespective of where it is relative to in other words).

The fixed position is used to place an element on a page and keep it there when everything else is being scrolled. The effect is that the rest of the page moves past the fixed element when you start to scroll the page. So this positioning type is a bit specialist in terms of its purpose.

(www.w3.org/Style/Examples/007/menus.en.html)

In this written text I can just imagine it is blindingly complicated and probably making your head hurt, but there is a lovely little tutorial on using CSS positioning that describes most of the above principles in a fairly easy to follow series of block diagrams.

(www.barelyfitz.com/screencast/html-training/css/positioning/)

I say fairly easy because there isn't too much about CSS 'Div' positioning that is easy to grasp. But what I can tell you and what you can take away is this:

Absolute positioning does not provide automatic sizing of elements that can take variable amounts of text and or graphics, even when combined with relative positioning.

What you actually need to do is combine a relative positioning element that contains further elements with a float declaration and then clear the floats to allow even more elements to take a position beneath those floating elements. Simple!!

The floating elements are the ones that allow you to add text or graphics at will and will simply keep pushing anything below further down as required, provided you use the 'clear' instruction in the right place. An automatically adjusting element controlled by CSS positioning which is screen-reader- friendly and fast-loading.

But note**, you still need to work within the width constraints of the floating elements in the example shown (via the link above), otherwise things will get messy, i.e. if you size an element at 190px you cannot then put in a graphic that is more than 190px in total width. Text isn't such a problem, it will just carriage return when it hits the margin or edge of the element.

All you have to remember to do then, is to make sure all the CSS formatting is located in your external style sheet and you will be in good shape

Yes, I am sorry it can't be described in simpler terms. Coding can be confusing but if you are technical and refer to the lessons recommended and put them into practice, trust me it will start to make sense.

Optimising website pages the technical perspective

There have been a few discussions in this book about the need for optimising web pages for the Internet and search engines. These requirements are important both from a human and a search engine perspective. The human perspective is so that visitors to your website have a better user experience, and the search engine perspective is so that your website can enjoy as high a ranking level as possible.

Graphics - Being able to view and compare the various formats when saving a graphic for the web in terms of quality, transparency, size and load speed is handy when you are deciding which format to use. This is something you can do using tools such as Adobe Photoshop and it is one of the reasons the program is considered an industry standard, even though it's not the only program with this functionality.

Photoshop Elements is a lightweight version of Photoshop that comes with less functionality, but also at a much reduced price. I am sure that most web designers would find the program more than adequate however, so if you are on a budget it is worth consideration.

One thing you cannot do, whether building a website for yourself or for a third party, is ignore the need for optimising website graphics. Even more true if those graphics are going to be included in a Flash file. So it is strongly recommended that you make an investment in a suitable program, purchased or otherwise. I would recommend Photoshop Elements personally but there are also free program which may be worth investigating if you really can't afford it. I have not used them but it looks like they may do the job. Please don't consider this a recommendation however and evaluate this at your own risk.

(ref: www.squidoo.com/webdesign-tools)

Logos - Logos come under the remit of graphics as well, but they are a little more specialist in nature, as was discussed earlier in the book. Where there is an exacting requirement, there is no dishonour in suggesting to a customer that they seek the services of a specialist. Designing a logo can, and often is, done by a website designer using available tools. But more often a logo design comes under the scope of a desktop publisher or graphic designer. It is a skill that requires a slightly different approach to simply optimizing graphics for use on a website.

If as a designer you have developed, or want to develop, those skills then that is absolutely fine. But on the other hand if you don't really have the skills required and don't have the time to learn them, don't let yourself be drawn into producing a half-hearted attempt; that takes way too long and doesn't offer value for money.

Server side includes & templates

Server side includes (SSI) as discussed earlier are an alternative to templates that do not depend on a specific program. So if you don't have Dreamweaver, for example, but like the benefits that Dreamweaver templates offer, you can gain a similar result by using server side includes.

There are a number of functions that can be performed using SSI but one of the main ones is placing a lot of common text or code on different web pages (a navigation menu maybe). You can find a Tutorial for SSI via this link.

(www.thesitewizard.com/archive/ssiprimer.shtml)

I have used SSI to a limited extent, but because I have Dreamweaver, my preferred option is to use templates, an excellent lesson on using templates can be found via this link. Look for the video in the quick updates section.

(www.blog.moulinwebsitedesign.com/css-formatting-for-mulitple-drop-down-menu-and-relative-position-divs/)

The second type will clearly need to be visible on the site to visitors and will be included in the standard navigation system.

Organising information

Organising your information so that you can find it and access it, is just a matter of common sense. For the most part the system you use is entirely up to you, as long as you can find what you are looking for when you need to.

There are some aspects that need to be organised to service the website in a logical way. For example it is good practice to keep all your images in a single directory and the same for templates. Also if you have a requirement to section off some pages of your website for some reason, it is a good idea to place them in a directory of their own for consistency. One example of this might be a bilingual website, where the alternative languages are segregated into their own directory; this is a nice approach from a search engine perspective as well.

Something everyone should know is that using lower case for file naming is the preferred format in virtually all cases and essential for the '*index*' or homepage of your website, which does actually have to be called 'index' for the website to be found.

One exception to the lower case rule is the 'Sitemap.xml' file for submission to search engines; the protocol requires that the S of sitemap is actually in uppercase.

The diagram below is a good starting point for a simple website. Organising the files in this way will ensure that you can find the original source files for your website content and know intuitively where the files that make up your website are located by function. You can of course add further files, directories and/or sub-directories as required.

The essential files required for the site to operate are located directly under the site name, the 'index.html' file being an example of one such essential file.

The structure shown in the figure is deliberately simplified to illustrate the proposed organisation of the website files. It should also be noted that only the files actually used by the website need to be published on the server.

It would be quite acceptable, for example, to leave the template directory and the source files directory on a local PC. The exception to this might be if there was more than one person working on the design who needed access to those files. Then it would be a matter of convenience to place them on the server so they can be easily accessed.

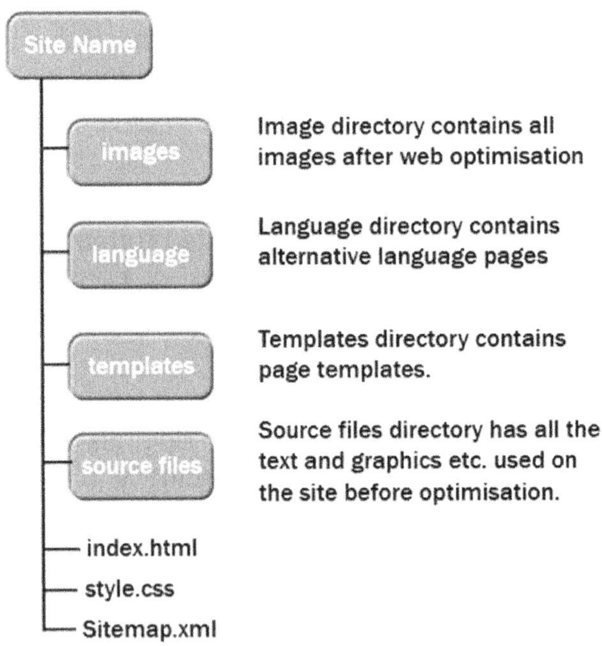

How to put your website on the internet

Clearly the way you put your website on the Internet depends entirely on what type of hosting you have selected and the related options for each type.

Free platforms provide a browser-based user interface. This means that once you have registered and provided a password all you need to do is access their design modules through their website using your Internet browser and then publish your web pages once they have been populated with content.

The design modules will be different for each type and there will be a learning curve to go through as you become familiar with the process. But typically there are plenty of places where you can find help and support to ensure you are successful. The collaborative options work in much the same way as the free hosting blog platforms.

Moving onto shared or dedicated hosting, most web designers would elect to use a FTP (file transfer protocol) interface to upload web pages. This can appear to be much more complex initially but once you understand what you are doing and what the requirements of the host service is, it really isn't much more complex.

The main difference is that for FTP what you would normally be doing is designing the web pages on your local PC and then once they are ready to be published you connect to the server and transfer the finished files and any dependent files, images or CSS files for example.

Once again with a specialist web design package such as Dreamweaver, this facility is built in. But there are also free programs available that will provide the facility to transfer files from a local PC to a server using a protocol such as FTP. One of the most popular FTP clients available for free is a program called FileZilla

(ref: www.filezilla-project.org/)

So what do you typically encounter when signing onto a server? Well that will depend entirely on the hosting company you have selected but there will be common information required by each.

First of all you need to define the type of access - select ***FTP***, and then you will need to provide the following information:

FTP Host: - this is normally a name e.g. ***ftp.mywebsite.com*** or it can be an IP address e.g. ***123.456.789.10*** If it is a different format your service provider should tell you, but the IP is a failsafe, that should work irrespectively.

Host Directory: - this is not always required, but when it is your provider will tell you, for a Hostgator account it would be ***public_html***

Login: this would be the user name you chose. e.g. ***myusername***

Password: again this would be the password you chose for the site e.g. ***mypassword1***

There may also be an option to select the 'Use Passive FTP' check the box for this and if it works use it. If it doesn't work, just uncheck it and try again.

There is also sometimes an option to check a 'Use Firewall' box. For independents working from home this is not normally used.

Reference information

W3 Web Standards - standardising website designs.

(www.w3schools.com/web/web_standards.asp)

HTML and CSS Tutorials - learning to create static websites.

(www.w3schools.com/web/web_standards.asp)

www.wordpress.org - Wordpress for own domain and hosting blogs

www.wordpress.com - free blog publishing platform

Blogger Free Blogging Platform - free blog publishing platform

(https://accounts.google.com/ServiceLogin?service=blogger&passive=1209600&continue=http://www.blogger.com/home&followup=http://www.blogger.com/home&ltmpl=start#s01) probably easier to search for this.

Posterous Spaces - free blog publishing platform

(www.posterous.com/)

www.tumblr.com/ - free blog publishing platform

www.photoxpress.com- Stock Photographs

Search Engine Results - find out where you are ranked for specific keywords

(www.searchenginereports.net/)

Page Rank Checker - find out the page rank for your website pages

(www.prchecker.info/check_page_rank.php)

Bad Neighbourhood Checker - make sure you do not inadvertently link to a bad website; this could affect your status detrimentally with search engines.

(www.bad-neighborhood.com/text-link-tool.htm)

Domain Naming - recommendations for domain naming.

(www.blog.moulinwebsitedesign.com/finding-a-domain-name/)

Nominet - official domain management site for the UK

(www.nominet.org.uk/)

Hostgator Web Hosting Review - a recommended hosting option

(www.blogaude.com/hostgator-review/)

How to Create a Wordpress Blog - free step by step eBook

(www.blogaude.com/basics-of-blogging-creating-a-blog/)

Best Web Design Tools - industry standard website design tools

(www.squidoo.com/webdesign-tools)

www.moulinwebsitedesign.com is a web design service that caters for the needs of small businesses, sole traders and individuals. If after having read this book you have decided to commission rather than design your own website. Please consider paying us a visit, we would be happy to hear from you.

If you would like an even more comprehensive look at Web Marketing & SEO visit Amazon and search for ASIN B00B3KWAKO

Or just go to www.amazon.co.uk/dp/B00B3KWAKO in the UK

and www.amazon.com/dp/B00B3KWAKO for the USA

If you have enjoyed this book and believe it provides value for money, then please go back to the site where you bought it and provide the author with an honest book review so that others can make a more informed buying decision.

CPSIA information can be obtained at www.ICGtesting.com
Printed in the USA
LVOW04s1732120615

442286LV00034B/1336/P